THE WORKS AND DAYS OF JOHN FISHER

THE WORKS AND DAYS OF JOHN FISHER

An Introduction to the Position of St. John Fisher (1469–1535), Bishop of Rochester, in the English Renaissance and the Reformation

by

EDWARD SURTZ, S.J.

HARVARD UNIVERSITY PRESS

CAMBRIDGE, MASSACHUSETTS

1967

DISTRIBUTED IN GREAT BRITAIN BY
OXFORD UNIVERSITY PRESS, LONDON
LIBRARY OF CONGRESS CATALOG CARD NUMBER 67-17319
PRINTED IN THE UNITED STATES OF AMERICA

PREFACE

READING and research in America and Europe on St. Thomas More's *Utopia* and its backgrounds led to the conviction that a major figure in the English Renaissance and the Reformation was being neglected: St. John Fisher (1469–1535), Bishop of Rochester. He is the clerical and episcopal counterpart and peer — one might almost say, the complement — of the layman Thomas More in his age.

Fisher's effect in general was deep and lasting, first, as a scholar and as a patron of scholars; then, as chancellor of the University of Cambridge, where he fostered the new learning; and, lastly, as a religious reformer and controversialist of far greater importance and reputation on the Continent than Thomas More. As More wrote chiefly in the English tongue for an English audience, so Fisher composed chiefly in Latin, the international language, for a European audience.

The purpose of this book is not to make a biographical study of Fisher but to see him against the intellectual background of the Renaissance and the Reformation. It tries to ascertain his precise position on such key points as the nature and function of a university, humanism and Scholasticism, Greek and Hebrew, corruption and reform, orthodoxy and heresy, faith and justification, grace and the sacraments, the Church and the pope, the bishops and the councils, priesthood and laity, tradition and Scripture, and so on.

The term *position* implies personal relationships to his opponents and to his allies — and there were many of both, Catholics

as well as Protestants. He had hardly ended his refutation of continental Reformers (especially Luther and Oecolampadius) when he himself became the target for English Reformers (such as Tyndale and Frith). The term *position* also involves connections with what comes before (the Schoolmen and the Fathers, now seen with new eyes) and with what comes after (the Council of Trent and theologians like Robert Bellarmine). In view of his writings he merits the title which undoubtedly will be awarded him in time: Doctor of the Church.

The designation *position* likewise includes Fisher's role in the history of ideas. Independently of his major contributions in the open conflict with Protestantism, revealing concepts appear almost as *obiter dicta* in unlikely places: the development of dogma in the controversy with Lefèvre and Clichtove, the possible errancy of general councils in that with Luther, and the character and limits of natural law in his divorce tracts.

Not least interesting are his views on such personalities as More, Erasmus, Agricola, Savonarola, Cochlaeus, Reuchlin, Luther, Oecolampadius, Campeggio, Henry VII, and Henry VIII.

Finally, this book attempts to evaluate the degree of Fisher's conservatism and liberalism in regard to the new movements in England and on the Continent and to indicate his reputation and influence in his lifetime and after his execution. To keep the focus in the text on Fisher himself, allusions and references to him have been placed as much as possible in the Notes.

The study was intended originally and principally for the student of literature in order to enable him to put Fisher's works, especially his English sermons and his ascetical treatises, into their context. But a reader of the manuscript pointed out that it would interest the church historian and the theologian almost as much (to say nothing of the historian and theologian of the ecumenical movement). There is danger in knowing and using only Fisher's English writings, particularly his controversial sermons of the 1520's, because they are brief and summary; yet the full development of their ideas is found in his Latin tomes. Excellent studies of the early English Reformation have been weakened by failure to employ the context of Fisher's entire output. Since the present work tries to supply such a context, it is exploratory rather than exhaustive, comprehensive rather than detailed, but without sacrificing, it is hoped, a relative thoroughness. The comprehensiveness is intended to disclose the great riches waiting only to be mined. Hence comes, to change the figure, the liberal sampling of quotations, usually brief, to whet the reader's appetite. Hence comes the title, for Fisher's works or writings serve to illumine his days, and his days help to throw light on his works. The word and the deed are wedded everlastingly.

The writing and the publication of this book constitute a testimonial to the encouragement and cooperation of the administration at Loyola University of Chicago. The necessary leisure, travel, and materials were made available through generous financial assistance: a summer fellowship received from the Frank L. Weil Institute for Studies in Religion and the Humanities and a summer grant and a year's fellowship awarded by the American Council of Learned Societies.

No word can express adequate gratitude for the courtesy and help of the British Museum not only through microfilm assistance over a number of years but also through personal service during three whole months. The Public Record Office, too, has been of invaluable aid. I must not pass over in grateful silence the staffs of the Institute of Historical Research and the Warburg Institute of the University of London, the Lambeth Palace Library, the Cathedral Library of Canterbury, the Bodleian Library of the University of Oxford, the St. Thomas More Project of Yale University, the Newberry Library of Chicago, the Cambridge University Library, and especially the St. John's College Library, Cambridge. I am appreciative of the privilege of examining the Episcopal Registers at the Cathedral in Rochester, the acts of the ecclesiastical courts preserved in the Archives at Maidstone, and the manuscripts preserved at Westminster Cathedral, where the Reverend Bernard Fisher, Archivist, was most kind and generous. The Very Reverend J. F. McMahon, M.S.C., and Mr. David Rogers of the Bodleian Library were kind enough to make available a preliminary draft of the bibliography of Fisher's publications to be issued by the Oxford Bibliographical Society. Assistance by the staff of the Cudahy Memorial Library, Loyola University of Chicago, was equalled only by unfailing patience and graciousness.

The kind Editors of *Studies in Philology* have granted permission to revise and employ an article on Fisher and Scholasticism which appeared in their journal. The British Museum and the Cambridge University Library generously have given leave to quote and to translate passages from their manuscripts. Transcripts and translations of Crown copyright records in the Public Record Office appear by permission of the Controller of Her Majesty's Stationery Office.

A word of thanks — and of congratulations, too — must be extended to Miss Carol Bowes and Mrs. Stephanie Lamb of London, who converted an almost indecipherable manuscript, written in pencil, into a typed copy of beauty and accuracy.

E.S.

Chicago
January 6, 1966

TABLE OF CONTENTS

PRINCIPAL ABBREVIATIONS FOR FISHER'S WRITINGS

Note. Wherever possible, references are made to the *Opera* (1597) and the *English Works* (1876) because of their greater availability. When citations are made to other editions, attention is called to the fact in the Notes. It would be useless, for example, to list below all three editions of *De veritate corporis et sanguinis Christi in Eucharistia* of early 1527 simply because of variations in the parerga of the work. Because English translations of the titles of the major Latin works are used in the text for the sake of readability, they appear below after the respective Latin works. As mentioned in the Preface, a bibliography of Fisher's works compiled by the Very Reverend J. F. McMahon, M.S.C., is to be published by the Oxford Bibliographical Society.

"Assert. Luth. confut." "Assertionis Lutheranae confutatio," *Opera,* p. 272–col. 745. Eng. tr. of title: "Confutation of Luther's Assertion."

Causa. De causa matrimonii serenissimi regis Angliae liber, Alcalá, M. Eguia, August 1530.

"Charit." "Epistola . . . ad D. Hermannum Letmatium . . . de charitate Christiana," *Opera,* cols. 1704–7.

Confut. sec. discept. Confutatio secundae disceptationis per Iacobum Fabrum Stapulensem habitae, Paris, Badius, September 1519. Eng. tr. of title: *Confutation of Lefèvre's Second Disquisition.*

"Consolation." "A spirituall consolation, written by Iohn Fyssher . . . to hys sister Elizabeth . . . ," *Eng. Works,* pp. 349–363. See "Praefatio ad Elisabetham sororem suam dilectissimam" (Ioanne Fen a Monte-acute interprete), *Opera,* pp. 1643–47.

"Convulsio." "Conuulsio calumniarum Vlrichi Veleni Minhoniensis, quibus Petrum nunquam Romae fuisse cauillatur," *Opera,* p. 1299–col. 1371. Eng. tr. of title: "Shattering of Velenus' Misrepresentations."

"Def. reg. assert." "Assertionum regis Angliae de fide catholica aduersus

Lutheri Babylonicam captiuitatem defensio," *Opera,* p. 101–col. 271. Eng. tr. of title: "Defense of the Royal Assertion."

Eng. Works. The English Works of John Fisher, Part I, ed. J. E. B. Mayor, London, Early English Text Society, 1876.

Eversio. Euersio munitionis quam Iodocus Clichtoueus erigere moliebatur aduersus vnicam Magdalenam, Louvain, Martens, [1519]. Eng. tr. of title: *Destruction of Clichtove's Bulwark.*

"Henry VII." "This sermon . . . was compyled & sayd . . . the body beynge present of . . . kynge Henry the .vij. . . . ," *Eng. Works,* pp. 268–288.

Heretickes. A sermon had at Paulis . . . vpon quinquagesom sonday / concernynge certayne heretickes / whiche than were abiured for holdynge the heresies of Martyn Luther . . . , London, Berthelet, [1526?].

"Liceity." *See* "Licitum fuisse matrimonium."

"Licitum fuisse matrimonium." "Licitum fuisse matrimonium Hen: 8: cum Catharina relicta fratris suj Arthurj," Cambridge University Library MS. 1315. Eng. tr. of title: "Liceity."

"Luther." "The sermon . . . made agayn the pernicyous doctryn of Martin luuther . . . ," *Eng. Works,* pp. 311–348. See "Concio habita in celeberrimo nobilium conuento Londini, eo die, quo Martini Lutheri scripta publico apparatu in ignem coniecta sunt, versa in Latinum per Richardum Pacaeum a serenissimi regis Angliae secretis," *Opera,* p. 1372–col. 1392.

"Magdal." "De vnica Magdalena, libri tres," *Opera,* p. 1393–col. 1462. Eng. tr. of title: "The Single Magdalene."

"Margaret." "Here after foloweth a mornynge remembraunce had at the moneth mynde of the noble prynces Margarete countesse of Rychemonde & Darbye . . . ," *Eng. Works,* pp. 289–310.

Margaret, ed. Baker-Hymers. *The Funeral Sermon of Margaret . . .* Preached by Bishop Fisher in 1509, with Baker's Preface to the Same, Containing Some Further Account of Her Charities and Foundations . . . Edited by J. Hymers . . . with Illustrative Notes, Additions, and an Appendix, Cambridge, Eng., University Press, 1840.

Opera. Opera, quae hactenus inueniri potuerunt omnia . . . , VVirceburgi, apud Georgium Fleischmannum, Anno MDXCVII.

"Or." "Tractatus de necessitate orandi," *Opera,* cols. 1708–33. Eng. tr. of title: *Prayer.* See also *Prayer.*

"Oratio coram Hen. VII." "Oratio habita coram illustrissimo Rege Henrico VII. Cantabrigiae, A.D. 1506 . . . ," in John Lewis, *The Life of Dr. John Fisher . . . ,* ed. T. H. Turner (London, Joseph Lilly, 1855), Coll. No. *VIII, II, 263–272.

"Passion." "A Sermon . . . vpon thys sentence of the Prophet Ezechiell, *Lamentationes, Carmen, et vae,* very aptely applyed vnto the passion of Christ: Preached vpon a good Friday . . . ," *Eng. Works,* pp. 388–428. See "Concio, de passione Domini; habita feria sexta in Parasceue" (Ioanne Fen a Monte-acuto interprete), *Opera,* cols. 1648–73.

"Perfect Religion." "The wayes to perfect Religion . . . ," *Eng. Works,* pp.

364–387. See "Methodus perueniendi ad summam religionis perfectionem" (Ioanne Fen a Monte-acuto interprete), *Opera,* cols. 1686–1703.

Prayer, Eng. tr. 1560. *A Godlie treatisse declaryng the benefites, fruites, and great commodities of prayer, and also the true vse therof,* London, Cawood, 1560. *Prayer,* Eng. tr. 1640, refers to the translation of R. A. B., London, Burns & Oates, 1887 (orig. Paris, Baudry, 1640). *See also* "Or."

Priesthood, tr. Hallett. *The Defence of the Priesthood,* tr. P. E. Hallett, London, Burns Oates & Washbourne, 1935. *See* "Sacerd. def."

"Psalms." "This treatyse concernynge the fruytful saynges of Dauyd the kynge & prophete in the seuen penytencyall psalmes. Deuyded in seuen sermons . . . ," *Eng. Works,* pp. 1–267. See "Commentarii in septem psalmos qui de poenitentia inscribuntur . . . lingua vernacula habiti editique, & latine redditi, Ioanne Fen a Monte-acuto interprete," *Opera,* p. 1463–col. 1642.

Psalms MS. Fisher's Latin Commentary on the Psalms, Public Record Office, S.P. 2/R, foll. 28–277.

"Responsio." "Responsio Roffensis," British Museum MS. Otho C.x, foll. 187^{v}–198.

"Responsum." "Responsum ad libellum impressum Londini 1530," British Museum MS. Arundel 151, foll. 202–339^{v}.

"Sacerd. def." "Sacri sacerdotii defensio contra Lutherum," *Opera,* p. 1232–col. 1298. Eng. tr. of title: "Defense of the Sacred Priesthood." See also *Priesthood,* tr. Hallett.

Statutes. For Christ's College: *Early Statutes of Christ's College, Cambridge . . . ,* ed. H. Rackham, Cambridge, Eng., Fabb & Tyler, 1927. For St. John's College: *Early Statutes of the College of St. John the Evangelist in the University of Cambridge,* ed. J. E. B. Mayor, Cambridge, University Press, 1859.

Two Sermons. Here after ensueth two fruytfull Sermons, made & compyled by . . . Johñ Fyssher . . . , London, W. Rastell for P. Treuerys, 1532. See "Concio . . . de iustitia Pharisaeorum et Christianorum, ex Anglico in Latinum conuersa, a Ioanne Fennio sacerdote Anglo," *Opera,* cols. 1674–87.

"Ver. corp." "De veritate corporis et sanguinis Christi in Eucharistia . . . aduersus Iohannem Oecolampadium," *Opera,* p. 746–col. 1231. Eng. tr. of title: "Christ's Body."

THE WORKS AND DAYS OF JOHN FISHER

Chapter I

WORKS AND DAYS OF THE HUMANIST AND CHURCHMAN

THE delay on the way to his death on Tower Hill allowed the deprived Bishop of Rochester to rise from his chair and lean against the wall, to pray for an appropriate text, and then to open his little New Testament — by chance or by grace at the seventeenth chapter of the Gospel according to St. John.[1]

"Now this is everlasting life, that they may know thee, the only true God, and him whom thou hast sent, Jesus Christ." The knowledge and love of God and Jesus Christ seemed to be his intention always: whether he was engaged in preaching at Rochester and London, or in the foundation of new colleges at Cambridge, or in the refutation of new heresies, or in the defense of the marriage bond and of papal jurisdiction.

"I have glorified thee on earth; I have accomplished the work that thou hast given me to do." The mute testimonials to his life's work were many: sermons printed from 1508 to 1532, voluminous controversies with reformers like Lefèvre and Luther and Oecolampadius, as well as published and unpublished tracts on the divorce, and so forth. To him, too, was dedicated the work of other men: Desiderius Erasmus, Polydore Vergil, Sebastian Muenster, John Cochlaeus, and others.

"And now do thou, Father, glorify me with thyself." Even during his earthly days as a model bishop, he had often been hailed for his sanctity and learning by men like Ammonius, Erasmus, and More. His beheading would call forth tributes from Paul III, Francis I, and Charles V — to say nothing of lesser men. His works would receive praise, as well as use, from the Spanish

Francisco de Vitoria, the Italian Robert Bellarmine, the Polish Stanislaus Hosius, and the English Thomas Stapleton. His books would frequently be consulted and quoted at the Council of Trent, and yet adversaries like Bishop Jewel would cite them against Catholic apologists. Through emissaries like Stephen Gardiner and Richard Morison, Henry VIII would try to denigrate his character, and yet Protestants as well as Catholics would vindicate his name. In brief, he could say: "I am a part of all that I have met." No historian of England could ignore his relations with the new Tudor monarchy, no student of the Renaissance his patronage of scholars and universities, and no chronicler of the Reformation his clashes with its leaders.

John Fisher shut his little book and proceeded to his execution. But characteristically his New Testament in all probability was written in Latin, not in English. Less than a decade before, he had preached at St. Paul's when Tyndale's translation might have been burnt for the first time. In *The Obedience of a Christian Man* (1528), Tyndale condemned "the malicious blindness of the bishop of Rochester, his juggling, his conveying, his foxy wiliness, his bo-peep, his wresting, renting, and shameful abusing of the scripture."[2] Referring to the events of 1526 and later, George Joye in 1544 did not hesitate to put Bishop Fisher with Cardinal Wolsey and Sir Thomas More and others dramatically in hell[3] — even if heaven be the place assigned to him at his canonization exactly four centuries after his demise.

Heaven or hell: where is Bishop Fisher? Saint or devil: which is Bishop Fisher? Reputation, he himself had written, is "the most precious of all creatures" (*famam, rem omnium preciosissimam*).[4] A snap or smart answer would be: a devil in hell to Protestants, a saint in heaven to Roman Catholics. But the esteem of both parties for Sir (or Saint) Thomas More stands as a refutation to such a facile judgment. Does the warm picture of Thomas More as a family man, that is, as husband and father, contrasted with the sharp sketch of John Fisher as an austere bishop, perhaps account for the different appeal of the two men? If so, the difference is then created by image-makers, artistic and literary, and is not based on historical reality. What is the truth? How close can one come to the truth?

The biographical facts began to receive notable attention more than a hundred years ago with T. Hudson Turner's edition (1855) of the research of John Lewis (d. 1746). J. E. B. Mayor edited *The English Works* (1876). The sixteenth-century life of Fisher was published with great care and full notes by François van Ortroy (1891–93) and was issued in a transcription from Harleian MS. 6382 by Ronald Bayne (1921). The pioneer work of T. E. Bridgett's *Blessed John Fisher* (1888) was supplemented by E. E. Reynolds' *Saint John Fisher* (1955). One must recognize also the work of historians, e.g., Pierre Janelle in *L'Angleterre catholique à la veille du schisme* (1935) and Philip Hughes in *The Reformation in England* (1950–54). Biographies and histories alike point up the importance of Fisher's neglected writings. Are these, perhaps, the key, if not to his personality, at least to his fame when alive and his influence when dead? At any rate, the present study intends to probe thought, method, and style in all his readily available works, published and unpublished, in order to reveal their significance not only for Fisher's life but also for the sixteenth century, especially in the movements commonly called the Renaissance and the Reformation.

For the study of an individual in revolutionary times, John Fisher is an ideal subject. Because most of his works can be dated, it is possible to tabulate the changes, if any, in his doctrines and attitudes. The extant writings fall roughly into three major periods, which might be labeled as those of (1) the Catholic humanist (1497–1517), (2) the ecclesiastical protagonist (1517–1527), and (3) the royal antagonist (1527–1535).

In the first period, that of chaplain and bishop, of humanist and educator, Fisher's religion is epitomized in his English sermons. Those on the Seven Penitential Psalms (Vulg. Ps. 6, 31, 37, 50, 101, 129, 142), preached in August and September 1504 before the Lady Margaret, mother of Henry VII, were published at her request in June 1508 and then reprinted at least six times before 1529.[5] These ingenious combinations of commentary and moralization have been recently praised as "very fine: with a sort of succinct strength." [6] At St. Paul's, on May 10, 1509, a year after their publication, the Bishop of Rochester preached the funeral oration, startlingly frank for modern ears, for Henry VII. In late July of the same year he praised the virtues of the Lady Margaret in a eulogy delivered at a mass thirty days after her death. Almost a score of years later, in the dedication of his work against Oecolampadius, Fisher refers to these two orations: on Henry VII, "who then guided the reins of government with the highest wisdom, a prince unquestionably worthy of admiration by all ages, and that on many counts," [7] and on the Lady Margaret: "Here I only add (what I frankly confess) that I learned more from her outstanding virtues about what conduces to a course of upright living than I ever communicated to her in reciprocity." [8] These three works are significant especially because in them Fisher, so to speak, is off his guard. He is a Catholic speaking familiarly with Catholics. There is no fear of the Protestant menace, no need for caution in statement, and no retirement from possibly extreme positions, recognized as assailable because of attacks which are realized to be justifiable.

The Catholic aspect of Fisher's mind and work cannot be divorced from his humanism. The latter is manifest especially in his devotion to the University of Cambridge as a seedplot of learned Christians and in his personal study of Greek and Hebrew for biblical purposes. The statutes of Christ's College and St. John's College can be used as indicative of Fisher's thought. Even though some for Christ's depend upon earlier Godshouse statutes and some for St. John's are adopted from Corpus Christi College, Oxford, nevertheless the fact is that Fisher at least tacitly approved them by embodying them in his own statutes.[9] While negotiations were under way in 1506 for the final conversion of Godshouse into Christ's College, Fisher delivered before Henry VII an oration, his first complete extant Latin work.[10] After extolling the virtues of ancient Cambridge and deploring its low present state, he made a direct appeal for royal support and patronage — with rich results.[11]

In his statutes Fisher attempted to make provision for lectures on Greek and Hebrew. In addition, he had only words of praise for the labors of their representatives: Erasmus and Reuchlin. Finally, he himself in his late forties heroically undertook the study of Greek and Hebrew with a view to the better knowledge of the Bible. Here, of course, his correspondence, especially with Erasmus, is of primary importance.

The dedication of St. John's College at Cambridge joined

such major events as Bishop Foxe's foundation of Corpus Christi College at Oxford and Erasmus' publication of St. Jerome's letters and the *Novum instrumentum* at Basel to make A.D. 1516 seem very much an *annus mirabilis* to the humanists. Their common cause seemed to be on the verge of universal triumph. But the very next year saw two events which were to usher in the second major period of Fisher's activity, that of the ecclesiastical protagonist (1517–1527). The term *ecclesiastical* is chosen designedly because at stake is the current conception of the *ecclesia* and of tradition and authority in the *ecclesia*. One event, of course, was the posting of Luther's ninety-five theses on the church door at Wittenberg on October 31. The other was the *Disquisition on Mary Magdalene* (*De Maria Magdalena . . . disceptatio*, Paris, 1517), in which Jacques Lefèvre d'Étaples questioned the traditional identification of Mary, "who is called the Magdalene, from whom seven devils had gone out" (Luke 8:2), with the penitent woman who anointed Jesus' feet in the Pharisee's house (Luke 7:36–50) and with Mary, the sister of Martha and Lazarus, who similarly "anointed the feet of Jesus" (John 12:1–9). Fisher had first read the discussion without alarm; but the ambassador to England, Stephen Poncher, Bishop of Paris (1503–19) and Archbishop of Sens (1519–25), like an "outstanding father and most vigilant pastor" (*egregius Pater & Pastor vigilantissimus*), had awakened him to "what great peril lay hidden, and what great confusion and disgrace could arise for the whole Church of Christ from this difference of opinions." [12]

Fisher's defense of the common position of the Latin Church, entitled *The Single Magdalene* (*De unica Magdalena*) and published in Paris under date of February 22, 1519, unwittingly constituted his training ground in the use of Scripture and tradition for far more fundamental controversy with Luther, Oecolampadius, and Henry VIII's partisans for the divorce. A prefatory epistle by *Mauricius Durand* reveals the amazement of the Parisian theologians at the extent of Fisher's learning, the acumen of his argumentation, and the elegance of his style. Persons who have no personal knowledge of Fisher, especially his integrity and charity, may object to his rather rough treatment of Lefèvre, a man of excellent name, conduct, and knowledge; but the bishop is inspired, not by hatred of Lefèvre, but by zeal for the Church, the Magdalene, and the common people. At least, so reads the epistle.[13]

In a letter to Fisher, April 2, 1519, Erasmus, admitting that he has only glanced at the book but that "everyone confesses you have the upper hand on every score" (*nemo non fatetur te tota causa superiorem*), reveals the same reaction of some to Fisher's mistreatment of the well-deserving Lefèvre. This latter has been gratifying to the extreme conservatives, but wise and cool moderation in such a conflict, Erasmus concedes, is almost impossible.[14]

Six weeks later, Erasmus wrote Wolsey about the ridiculous suspicion that Fisher's work was his own — in spite of the great difference in style and his lack of "that divine bishop's learning." [15] Even though Thomas More was not guilty of such rash confusion, he could tell the bishop: "Such is your Paternity's style that it could appear Erasmian. Certainly you have besides handled your cause so well that not ten Erasmuses could have done so more perfectly." [16]

At any rate, in *The Single Magdalene* Fisher refers to Josse Clichtove's espousal of Lefèvre's cause. He declares that Lefèvre would have been better off without Clichtove's weak and thin supporting arguments.[17] The work in question must be Clichtove's preface to subsequent editions (1518, 1519) of Lefèvre's *Disquisition*. In April 1519, however, Clichtove published a complete volume: *A Defense of the Disquisition concerning the Magdalene*, addressed to Archbishop Poncher — of all people. His strictures are specifically directed against the *Apology* of Marc de Grandval, who claims to have been urged to the task by the Bishop of Limoges and by the Archbishop of Sens (Poncher).[18] In refutation of Clichtove's position, Fisher published a special work in the middle of 1519: *Destruction of the Bulwark Which Josse Clichtove Toiled to Erect against "The Single Magdalene"* — amazingly without a word of reference to Marc de Grandval.[19] In his *Confutation of Luther's Assertion*, Fisher refers back to this work as containing many arguments for the proposition: "A custom once introduced by the consent of Christendom appears to obtain equal authority with written law." [20]

When Lefèvre undertook his own defense again with *A Second Disquisition on the Three and the Single Magdalene* (*De tribus et unica Magdalena, disceptatio secunda,* Paris, 1519), Fisher countered with *A Confutation of the Second Disquisition . . .* (Paris, September 3, 1519). It was to Lorenzo Cardinal Campeggio, whom as papal legate on behalf of a crusade he had entertained at Rochester in July 1518,[21] that he dedicated this third exertion in defense of the single Magdalene.[22] To Fisher, Lefèvre's and Clichtove's endeavors have simply made crystal clear Jerome's dictum against Pelagius: Truth can be in distress but it cannot be defeated.[23] He generously speaks of Clichtove as a "man otherwise learned and upright" (*vir alioqui doctus & probus*).[24]

In a letter of October 17, 1519, Erasmus tells Fisher that he was just about to report on his *Single Magdalene* when this *Confutation* appeared — which he has not read. He begs him to be satisfied with the victory voted him by the learned. Besides, poor Lefèvre is much harassed by the Parisian theologians, especially the Dominicans, above all for his suspected support of Reuchlin.[25] (The cunning Erasmus knows of Fisher's unbounded admiration for Reuchlin!) The sale of the book is so good that Fisher will have no trouble with a publisher in the future.[26] In a communication of February 21, 1520, Erasmus hopes that Fisher's endeavor to reconcile Erasmus with Lee, and Erasmus' effort to call off Fisher's attacks on Lefèvre, have not created a coolness between them. Erasmus declares the style of the *Confutation* to be commendably more polished and less choleric than that of *The Single Magdalene* (*vt stylus est cultior, ita minus est stomachi*), but he regrets that the matter has been made a point of the faith — much to the grief of Lefèvre, "whom I should prefer to see encouraged, especially since he both admires and reveres you" (*quem subleuari malim, praesertim cum ille te et suspiciat et veneretur*).[27]

After the publication of *The Single Magdalene* Fisher had delivered before a synod called by Wolsey as papal legate, possibly in 1519–20 (or 1523), a stern address against the faults of the clergy, which survives only in his sixteenth-century biography.[28] After the printing of his three works on the Magdalene and perhaps even before the condemnation of Lefèvre by the theological faculty of the University of Paris in late 1521, Fisher composed the *Tractatus de orando Deum,* first published in the original Latin at Douay in 1576 with Richard Hall as editor, but earlier translated into

English and printed by John Cawood in London in 1560. A clue to the date is given on the title page: "Written in Latin fourtie yeres past," a statement which must be qualified by a phrase in the Preface: "more than fourtie yeres past." [29] The latter would seem to be supported by the frank condemnation of ecclesiastical evils and by the silence about new heresies. If it be thus doubtfully assigned to 1520, the treatise becomes a pastoral document, written between the end of the controversy with Lefèvre and the beginning of that with Luther. Fisher's *Lyfe* states: "You shall not finde a stowter champion against him in all his time nor since then was this religious bishop." [30]

The first public encounter of Fisher with Luther was a brilliant affair, staged at Paul's Cross on May 12, 1521, with all the pageantry of which Wolsey was capable. This burning of heretical books need not detain us here except for Fisher's sermon, which centered about the Holy Spirit's continuing guidance of the Church. Shortly afterwards, this sermon was published by Wynkyn de Worde, who reprinted it twice (1522?, 1527).[31] It was undoubtedly Fisher's stalwart defense of the pope as *iure divino* head of the universal Church that later caused Henry VIII to issue a proclamation for the surrender of all copies.[32] It was not published again until the reign of Queen Mary — in 1554 and 1556. Richard Pace, first Wolsey's and later Henry VIII's secretary, translated Fisher's sermon almost immediately into Latin and saw it printed by John Siberch at Cambridge in early 1522.[33] Fisher received "the popes grete thanks for the sermon." [34]

To deliver this oration at Paul's Cross, Fisher undoubtedly interrupted his *opus magnum* against Luther, that is, the *Confutation of Luther's Assertion*. At this time his chaplain wrote: "My lord takith great labours agayns Luther I thynke verely that ys worke shall pass all other mens." [35] Fisher had already spent some months on the work when Cuthbert Tunstal, "distinguished no less by uprightness of life than by learning" (*non minori vitae probitate quam eruditione conspicuum*), handed him the publication of a so-named Ulrichus Velenus, "the most impudent I have ever read" (*quo nullum vnquam legerim impudentiorem*).[36] Fisher countered with his *Shattering of the Misrepresentations of Ulrichus Velenus Minhoniensis by Which He Quibbles that Peter Was Never in Rome: PETER WAS IN ROME.* In this work, as in several others, Fisher refers to a previous publication of his; and, in turn, he mentions this work in a future publication. In response to Velenus' Persuasion XVIII (for Velenus had set forth his thesis in eighteen "Persuasions"), he declares that he has no need to enlarge on the papal primacy since he has done so already in his refutation of Luther's articles — an allusion to his forthcoming *Confutation* rather than to his sermon against Luther.[37] Three years later, in *The Defense of the Priesthood,* he declares that he has already proved against Velenus "that the succession of pastors which began in Christ is not to be ended until the fulfilment of all that Christ foretold." [38]

Ulrichus Velenus' identity has not been established. Bohemia is judged to have been his native country from a reference in his work to "we Bohemians" (*nos . . . Bohemi*)[39] and from Luther's mention, in a letter to Spalatin (February 3, 1521), of "a learned young man from Bohemia" (*E Bohemia juvenis eruditus*) who handed him a copy. Luther himself concluded that Velenus "does not carry his point" (*non euincit*) and contested only the alleged twenty-five-year sojourn of Peter in Rome.[40] Nevertheless the book made its way. In October 1521 it was discussed in Brussels with some heat at a dinner attended by Erasmus, Aleander, and "a great Lutheran" (*vn grande Lutherano*).[41] In the same year it was translated into German,[42] with an Italian translation appearing as late as 1566.[43] One difficulty was that readers who would have tossed Velenus' book aside as a piece of irresponsible bravado were attracted by Fisher's distinguished name to examine an attack which he deemed worthy of his attention and rebuttal. Such a reader was the pseudonymous Simon Hessus, who in July 1523 ended his *Apology against the Bishop of Rochester* by declaring the controversy between Fisher and Velenus a draw.[44] Fisher did not make the same mistake by deigning to answer this critic, probably to be identified as a writer addicted to pseudonyms, to wit, Urban Rieger (Rhegius, Regius, 1489–1541), who by 1524 had definitely gone over to Luther.[45]

In Germany itself, John Cochlaeus took up the cudgels against Velenus in his *Peter and Rome.*[46] His offensive was made easier because, according to Veesenmeyer, he followed the lead of Fisher who "was no unimportant but a learned and acute adversary." [47] Velenus' book naturally found its place on indexes of forbidden books: beginning with those of Venice (1554) and Paul IV (1559) and ending with its omission on that of Benedict XIV (1758).[48] Robert Bellarmine considered the work to be worthy of a lengthy refutation in his *Controversies*. In his conclusion he states that he had heard of Fisher's volume, but he could never get to see the work itself.[49]

One reason for Bellarmine's failure might have been that Fisher's *Shattering* was issued only twice, once at Antwerp and once at Paris. Fisher's next work, on the contrary, was printed at least fifteen times within the next forty-one years in such centers as Antwerp, Cologne, Dresden, Paris, and Venice. This was the *Confutation of Luther's Assertion*. Sharpe, as we have seen, expected "verely that ys worke shall passe all other mens." Fisher himself thought highly of the manuscript of the articles: "The Power of the Pope" (*de potestate pape*) and "Indulgences" (*de indulgencijs*), as did "diuers other well lernyd that hath redd thes ij articles." As Sharpe informed Metcalfe: "There is no man that will say my lord hath wrytyn *frigide & jeiune*." [50]

Fisher's *Assertionis Lutheranae confutatio* was published on January 2, 1523, by M. Hillenius in Antwerp. There is no need to rehearse here the well-known background. Suffice it to recall that Leo X's bull *Exsurge Domine* on June 15, 1520, had condemned forty-one articles drawn from Luther's works. Far from submitting within sixty days, Luther had published the *Assertion of All the Articles of M. Luther Condemned through Leo X's Latest Bull* and had publicly burned the papal document (December 10, 1520).[51] That Fisher's *Confutation* filled a need for Catholic apologists appears evident from the number of editions through which it speedily went. Almost immediately in 1523, for example, Thomas More in his defense of Henry VIII under the pseudonym of William Ross praised and used part of it:

> The Reverend Father John Fisher, Bishop of Rochester, a man famous for the richness of his erudition, and most famous for the purity of his life, has so unraveled and confuted Luther's statements, that, if Luther had any shame, he would manage, even at a great price, to have his arguments burnt by his own hand. . . Certainly, as regards the primacy of the Pope, this same Reverend Bishop has made the matter clear from the Gospels, the Acts of the Apostles, the whole body of the Old Testament, and the agreement of all the holy Fathers . . . finally, from the definitions of a General Council, and from the

testimony of . . . the Armenians and Greeks. So clearly has the Bishop presented the primacy, that it seems vain for me, and as if I were to undertake a work already accomplished, to attempt to write again on the primacy of the Pope.[52]

The attention paid to the Armenians and Greeks points the reference to Article 25 of Fisher's *Confutation* rather than to his published sermon against Luther or to his still unpublished work in defense of Henry VIII.[53]

Not only in England but also in Germany advantage was taken of the work in the polemical war. John Cochlaeus translated by August and published by December 1523 most of Article 15 on preparation for the reception of the Eucharist.[54] In August 1524 his complete translation of Article 15, as well as of Article 16 on communion under both species, made its appearance.[55] The following year saw a freer reworking of the materials from the Fathers given by Fisher in Article 8 on the necessity of confession.[56] Finally, another German translation appeared at Leipzig in 1536.

In quite characteristic fashion, Fisher refers the reader to the *Confutation of Luther's Assertion* in his next two works. *The Defense of the Royal Assertion* and *The Defense of the Sacred Priesthood* were published together at Cologne in June 1525. In the former, he declares that a reading of the *Confutation* will make Luther's self-contradiction manifest in almost all the articles condemned by Leo X.[57] In the dedicatory epistle of the latter on the priesthood, he acknowledges his gratitude for the encouragement of Cuthbert Tunstal, Bishop of London, because the *Confutation,* after five printings, is expecting a sixth.[58] He also mentions his full treatment of the unwritten apostolic tradition in the *Confutation.*[59]

In like manner, both books issued simultaneously in June 1525 make reference to each other. The reason is evident. Luther had composed in the summer and fall of 1521 and had published in January 1522 the Latin treatise entitled *The Abrogation of Private Mass* (*De abroganda missa privata*).[60] Upon the appearance of Henry VIII's *Assertion of the Seven Sacraments* in 1521, followed by two German translations by Hieronymus Emser and Thomas Murner in 1522, Luther replied immediately and vigorously with his work *Against Henry, King of England* (*Contra*

Henricum regem Angliae) (1522).[61] Henry VIII did not compose a personal reply. Instead, his defense was undertaken by Sir Thomas More and Bishop Fisher. In contrast with More's abusive manner, one historian notes: "The Bishop's reply was calmly written but, seen quite objectively, lacked incisive strength in the theological argument, a defect aggravated by the diffusive length of the rejoinder" [62] — a criticism applicable to many sound but unexciting controversial works. In his dedicatory epistle to Nicholas West, Bishop of Ely, who had read and praised a good part of the rejoinder two years previously, Fisher explains that the pressure of business and some hope of Luther's return to a more wholesome frame of mind had caused him to hold publication in abeyance.[63] In the meantime, he had undertaken to reply to Luther's denial of a special and visible priesthood in *The Abrogation of Private Mass*. In the dedicatory epistle, he reveals the praise and help given by Bishop Tunstal to this work as earlier to the *Confutation*.[64] The *Defense of the Sacred Priesthood* in its Third Rejoinder alludes at least three times to the *Defense of the Royal Assertion,* Chapter 6, on the mass as a true sacrifice.[65] Chapter 6 itself, however, in referring to many ancient Hebrews' interpretation on the sacrifice of bread and wine to be offered according to the rite of Melchizedek in the age of the Messiah, speaks of the *Defense of the Sacred Priesthood* as already published.[66]

In 1525, the very year of Fisher's two publications, Luther offered to make Henry VIII an apology,[67] but the monarch declined to accept it. The reformer never took pains to answer either More's or Fisher's defense of their king's book. In the entry for 1525 in his *Commentaries on the Acts and Writings of Martin Luther,* Cochlaeus took occasion to praise the zeal of Fisher's and Clichtove's publisher, Peter Quentell of Cologne, and explained that Luther ignored the two writers because their doctrine was too sound and their life too upright for him to attack.[68]

Fisher's final work concerned with Luther was a sermon preached in St. Paul's Cathedral on February 11, 1525/6.[69] His reputation was so high that, when it was suggested to have "a notable clerk to prech . . . a sermond contra Lutherum, Lutheranos . . . et contra inducentes eadem opera in regnum . . . his Grace thinks My Lord of Rochestor to be moste meete to make that sermond . . . bothe propter auctoritatem, gravitatem, et doctrinam personae." [70] Like his first sermon against Luther in 1521, it was in English, but, what is more significant, the occasion was provided by an incident much closer home. In Fisher's own Cambridge, the Augustinian prior Robert Barnes had preached at St. Edward's on December 24, 1525, a sermon which appeared frankly Lutheran. According to the account which Barnes has given of his trial on twenty-five points of heresy, Fisher would not for a hundred pounds condemn his article that "vnto a faythfull christean man, euery day ought to bee Christmas day Easter day, and whitsonday . . . but it was folishely sayde (quod hie) to preache this afore the butchers of Cambryge, As who say, they were all butchers that were at the sermon And not the most parte of the vniversity." [71] In the matter of holydays, however, Fisher held Barnes to be "not learned" for answering that the observance of the Sabbath was a ceremonial and not a moral precept.[72] Barnes recanted but had to sustain a public ceremony of abjuration, which was attended by Wolsey and thirty-six prelates. The affair was marked not only by Fisher's sermon but by a great fire fed by baskets of books, which Tyndale writes included copies of his scriptural version and which Joye maintains numbered more than five hundred New Testaments and other publications in English.[73]

In "an Epistole vnto the reder," Fisher gives the reason for printing his sermon: "By the mocion of dyuerse persons / I haue put forth this sermon to be redde / whiche for the great noyse of the people within the churche of Paules / whan it was sayde / myght nat be herde." [74] Ironically enough, his printer, Thomas Berthelet, was arraigned in March 1526 before the Vicar-General of London, Richard Foxford, for printing, without the ecclesiastical permission required since 1524 for new books, "a certain sermon made by the Lord Bishop of Rochester in the vulgar tongue . . . not at the request or command of the said Bishop but of a certain Chaplain of his." But Berthelet's fault was "a technical one." [75] Even more ironical was the fact that in 1531 Henry VIII employed the relapsed Barnes, now a refugee in Germany, to win approval of the royal divorce from Martin Luther. The latter's verdict, however, turned out to be similar to Fisher's in support of Queen Catherine.[76] As England's reputedly most learned bishop, Fisher was involved in other cases of heresy, such as those of John Browne, Thomas Hitton, and Thomas Bilney;

but the details are meager and come to us at second hand, for example, through Thomas More and John Foxe.[77] Like Robert Barnes, Thomas Bilney belonged to the group that convened at the White Horse Tavern in Cambridge but at his trial expressed his agreement with Fisher's condemnation of Luther.[78]

Fisher closes his second major period, that of the ecclesiastical protagonist (1517–1527), not with a work against Luther, but with a work in which he stands with Luther in partial agreement against a common adversary, John Oecolampadius (1482–1531), the reformer at Basel. The point of consensus, of course, is the real presence of Christ in the Eucharist — with radical disagreement, however, on transubstantiation and the sacrificial character of the Lord's Supper.[79] In fact, in *The Reality of Christ's Body and Blood in the Eucharist,* published at Cologne in February 1527,[80] Fisher labels as "absurd" Luther's interpretation of Christ's words, "This is my body." He does so in passages in which he refers back in usual fashion to a recent work: *The Defense of the Royal Assertion.*[81]

But, as Hubert Jedin notes, the rise of a new type of Protestantism with Zwingli and Oecolampadius in Switzerland became evident not only to native Catholics (Grüt, Edlibach, and Marius) but also to great foreign Catholics (Eck, Faber, Cajetan, and Fisher), who subsequently entered the fray.[82] The Bishop of Rochester's contribution, writes Bridgett, is "the longest and most important of all his writings, and there are many beautiful passages, showing his lively faith and tender love of that great mystery." [83] Fisher was driven to write by the consideration that so many copies of Oecolampadius' book had been "scattered through all Europe that there are now very few who have not read or at least heard of the same." [84] Except for his heresy, Oecolampadius appears to Fisher a man "otherwise distinguished for learning and full of it, as they say, to a sickening degree" ("licet alioqui literis clarus, & ad nauseam vsque quod aiunt plenus").[85] In spite of his uprightness, learning, gravity, and resolution to leave all things and follow Christ in the monastic life, he has turned back like Lot's wife.[86] Fisher's lengthy book takes the form of a running commentary on Oecolampadius' short one — and for that reason it is less readable.

The dedicatory epistle of *The Reality of Christ's Body and*

Blood in the Eucharist, addressed to Richard Foxe (d. 1528), Bishop of Winchester, is interesting for its autobiographical allusions. Foxe has shown his devotion to the Eucharist by applying the name Corpus Christi to his magnificent new college at Oxford. Fisher owes no one a greater debt than Foxe, whose favor had enkindled him to a more fervent zeal not only for the liberal arts but for an upright life. It was Foxe's recommendation, not the Lady Margaret's prayers, that had induced Henry VII gratuitously to bestow upon him the bishopric of Rochester.[87]

Early in 1525, upon learning that Oecolampadius had termed him "our great Erasmus" (*magnus Erasmus noster*) in the preface to one of his works, Erasmus had become alarmed about the reaction of Bishop Fisher (as of Charles V, Clement VII, Ferdinand I, Henry VIII, and Cardinal Wolsey, a distinguished company for Fisher!).[88] To the urging of Claudius Cantiuncula that he write against Oecolampadius, he replied that he had had no time to read the book but that he had already begun something on the Eucharist.[89] In a declaration to the Town Council of Basel soon afterwards, he passed sentence on Oecolampadius' book as "learned, eloquent, and painstaking" and "also pious if anything could be pious which conflicts with the mind and consensus of the Church — disagreement with which I judge dangerous."[90] When the Swiss scholar Conrad Pellican (1478–1556) spread a rumor about Erasmus' adoption of the Eucharistic views of Carlstadt and Oecolampadius, Erasmus reacted vigorously with a letter of protest to Pellican.[91] Similarly, when his name was coupled with Luther's in the title of an anonymous publication on the Lord's Supper (April 18, 1526), he countered with his *Detectio* (June 1526), which Thomas More (December 18, [1526]) deemed an excellent refutation.[92] It is perhaps characteristic of Erasmus that his view on the Eucharist should take the form of a letter classified since 1540 among his apologies. For such it was — rather than a defense of the traditional view or an attack upon Oecolampadius' book. On October 19, 1527, he wrote the German humanist Willibald Pirckheimer (1470–1530) that he still possessed the beginning of his refutation of Oecolampadius' opinion begun a year before. He had desisted from further writing because the populace of Basel was all on Oecolampadius' side and because he had heard that Fisher and the theologians of Paris were girded for the fray.[93] The previous year (1526) Pirckheimer himself had published a reply to Oecolampadius: *Christ's True Flesh and His True Blood* (*De vera Christi carne et vero eius sanguine,* Nuremberg, 1526). A hasty reading had led Erasmus to the conclusion that Pirckheimer was closer to agreement with Luther than with the Church — from the consensus of which Erasmus never departs.[94]

The doctrine and consensus of the Church, in fact, had been expressed in the best scholarly and theological fashion by Erasmus' friend, Bishop Fisher, in 1527. It is little wonder that in 1528 Cochlaeus published a literal German translation of the most readable and lively sections of Fisher's work, to wit, the prefaces to five books.[95] These contain the central ideas in summary and concentrated form. In his prefatory letter to Hieronymus Walter, Cochlaeus acknowledges the unselfish and charitable anti-Lutheran labors of foreigners, especially the English. He singles out Henry VIII and, above all, the Bishop of Rochester, whom neither Luther nor his followers have answered — because unanswerable.[96] His translation is so literal as to contain occasional references meaningless in the context. The omissions and changes are few and slight; the rare additions give the German terminology for Latin words.[97]

Commenting on Fisher's controversial works, his sixteenth-century biography repeats Cochlaeus' judgment: "For nether to these bookes, nether yet to any other of his workes that he wrote before or since, hath any heretick to this daie yet made answere or refutacion, which I thinke can hardly be said of any other catholic wryter in his time." [98] On March 25, 1529, however, Erasmus wrote that even Fisher's works were neglected, but Erasmus was always on the defensive because of his own failure, in spite of many appeals, to write more against the Protestants.[99] Unlike the latter, Fisher published only his English works for popular consumption and directed his Latin controversies mainly to the learned world — as did Bellarmine after him. It is well to remember that Fisher had been a Doctor of Divinity[100] since July 5, 1501, and that he had become the first Lady Margaret Reader in Divinity at Cambridge in 1503. As Bishop of Rochester, he realized that he was a *doctor* in virtue not only of his degree but also of his office as a successor of the Apostles. His appointment as an English representative unfortunately never materialized into actual attendance at the Fifth Council of the Lateran (1512–1517). The success of his books therefore is actually to be measured by their theological quality as well as by the number of editions through which they passed.

In the academic world of his day, Fisher was recognized for what he was: an *avis rara* among contemporary bishops for his knowledge of the faith and for his writing against the heretics. For example, during a course of lectures at the University of Salamanca in 1534–35, the great theologian Vitoria singled out Fisher as the only bishop in the Church conscientious and capable enough to join battle against the Lutherans.[101]

Chapter II

WORKS AND DAYS OF THE FAITHFUL OPPOSITION

FISHER'S Latin book against Oecolampadius was printed separately for the last time in April 1527. It had been very much concerned with the interpretation of the relatively few passages on the Eucharist in the New Testament. This note sounds the end of the second major phase of Fisher's writings, that of the ecclesiastical protagonist (1517–1527). As if he were to have no rest from controversy, Fisher was already involved in the king's divorce by June 2, 1527. On that day Wolsey dispatched to the king Fisher's affirmative answer as to the pope's power to grant a dispensation for a man to wed his brother's widow.[1] With that response the third major period, that of the royal antagonist (1527–1535), might be said to begin. Whereas the exegesis of a handful of verses in the New Testament had been the burden of his polemic against Oecolampadius, now two or three verses in the Old Testament on marriage with one's sister-in-law (Lev. 18:16, Lev. 20:21, Deut. 25:5) would busy him for five years or longer. Previously his adversaries, like Luther and Oecolampadius, had lived across the sea among the Germans of the Empire and Switzerland, except for such relatively few followers as they found in the British Isles. Now his opponents would be English: his own king and his king's servants. In the previous period it had been foreign heresy that was the problem. From 1531 on it was to be the crucial question of domestic schism. A certain kind of victory had crowned the previous period with the sermon at Barnes's abjuration and with the three editions of *Christ's Body* inside three months. His opposition to the king on both issues, that of the divorce and that of the spiritual supremacy, was to end in temporal defeat and death.

Since our primary interest lies in Fisher's role in the divorce, especially his writings, there is no need to rehearse the well-known story here.[2] A month after Fisher's affirmative verdict (as to the pope's power to grant a dispensation for a man to marry his brother's widow) had been forwarded to the king, to be exact on July 4, 1527, Wolsey on his way to France tried to change Fisher's views — at length and without notable success.[3] In a letter to a certain Paul, usually dated about July 5, 1527, Fisher declares: "I can make a mistake, and if anyone should point out this mistake, I should concede it to him most gladly, being always ready to hear the truth." [4]

It seems that a year later Henry VIII himself consulted Fisher personally regarding the tormenting scruples about his union with Catherine — only to receive the answer that he should rest quiet in conscience, with Fisher ready to defend him against all objectors to the marriage.[5] Henry, however, proceeded with the divorce. Soon after his arrival in England as colegate with Wolsey to hear Henry's suit, Cardinal Campeggio in an interview on October 25, 1528, tried to enlist Fisher's help in inducing Catherine to take vows in a religious order, thus dissolving the marriage: "When he left me he [Fisher] seemed to be satisfied with what I had urged." [6] But the queen refused to cooperate and consent.

The legatine court opened on May 31, 1529, with the first session on June 18. At the second session, on June 21, Catherine made her famous personal appeal to Henry VIII. She was declared contumacious upon refusing to appear again. Everything was progressing in the king's favor when at the fifth session, on June 28, the Bishop of Rochester made an unexpected and dramatic declaration for the validity of the marriage. He was prepared like John the Baptist to die a martyr in the cause of marriage — a statement giving great offense to the king, who would be the modern Herod by implication. "At the end [Fisher] presented them with a book which he had written on the subject." [7]

Is this book one of Fisher's surviving tracts on the divorce? It is generally identified with the incomplete Cambridge University Library MS. 1315. The angry reply of the king was written by Gardiner.[8] The manuscript was handed to the Bishop of

Rochester, whose marginal comments are preserved.[9] Brewer conjectures that Campeggio began, "perhaps, to pluck up courage at the opposition offered by Fisher." [10] At any rate, the sittings of the court were merely occupied with evidence relative to Catherine's marriage with Arthur until July 23 (or 30) when it was prorogued to October 1.[11] It never reconvened because the cause had been cited to Rome. The end of the legatine court in England did not spell the end of Fisher's pronouncements. On the contrary, he continued to espouse Catherine's cause, certainly as late as the middle of 1532 because a dispatch dated June 21 of that year states: "About twelve days ago the bishop of Rochester preached in favor of the Queen." [12] There was rumor of another book, perhaps as late as 1533.[13]

But the number and the order of Fisher's writings on the divorce are not clear. Fortunately, however, it is possible to establish the approximate date of the three longest. When Fisher was asked in 1534 or 1535 how many books he had composed on Henry VIII's marriage and divorce, he answered: "I am not certain how many, but I can recall seven or eight that I have written. The matter was so serious, both on account of the importance of the persons it concerned, and the expressed command of the king, that I gave more labour and diligence to seeking out the truth lest I should fail him and others, than I ever gave to any other matter." [14]

The first clue to these "seven or eight" books is given in a list, July 9, 1529, of *libelli* submitted to the legatine court, apparently up to that date: eight for the king and six for the queen. Two of the latter are by Fisher: *Libellus primus Roffensis incipiens Constat inuictiss. / etc.*, and *Libellus secundus Roffensis incipiens / Reverendissimis in Christo patribus / etc.*[15] The first of these two is preserved in great part in the Cambridge University Library MS. 1315.[16] Yet this is hardly Fisher's very first writing on the divorce. Relatively early in the tract he speaks of having discussed exactly and satisfactorily elsewhere *(alibi)* whether the Levitical prohibition (on not uncovering "the nakedness of thy brother's wife," Lev. 18:16) is to be judged a moral precept or a precept of the law of nature.[17] There is no such discussion up to this point in the manuscript itself. The existence of prior writings is borne out also by the fact that on the list of July 9 the eight libels on the king's part includes "one in refutation of the bishop of Rochester." [18] In fine, the only thing about which one can be morally certain is that Cambridge Univ. Lib. MS. 1315 is a book presented to the legatine court itself before its prorogation at the end of July 1529.

Fisher's defense of Catherine had repercussions even on university life. When during Advent of 1529 Hugh Latimer delivered as St. Edward's Church, Cambridge, his "Sermons on the Card," and Buckenham countered with his Dice Sermon, the ensuing dispute finally provoked a directive from Fox, the royal almoner, to Buckmaster, the vice-chancellor, to impose silence on both parties. Certain bachelors of divinity at St. John's were especially severe on Latimer. In his letter Fox says: "It is not unlikely but that thei of St. John's . . . be anymated so to do by their master Mr. Watson and soche other my Lorde of Rochester's freendes, Which malice also peradventure cometh partly for that Mr. Latymer favoureth the kinge's cause. . ." [19]

On February 6, 1530, the imperial ambassador, Eustache Chapuys, reported to Charles V that Fisher, whose "learning and piety are well known," having finished the revision of a book previously sent to the emperor, had written another, which the queen was forwarding.[20] It is not clear which of these two books, if either, was published at Alcalá in August 1530. M. de Eguia printed the book at the instance of his patron, Alfonso de Fonseca, Archbishop of Toledo, a member of the Council of State (1527) in the absence of Charles V from Spain.[21] On November 27, 1530, Chapuys speaks of an arrangement to have Fisher's "two later books" published and distributed at the opening of Parliament because Henry VIII, in spite of all fears of his displeasure, had "shown himself quite indifferent" to the circulation of Fisher's book in Spain.[22] On December 4, 1530, Chapuys announces that Fisher "has finished a book in favor of the Queen, now sent." [23] More than four months afterward, Dr. Pedro Ortiz, the imperial proctor in Rome, saw "two works by Fisher different from that which was printed in Spain," perhaps the "two later books" mentioned earlier by Chapuys.[24] The precise character and the present location of these manuscripts seem to be unknown.

This latter statement is not true of Fisher's third major extant work on the divorce. Dated April 1530 in the colophon but undoubtedly issued later because the decision of the University of Toulouse is given as of October 1, 1530, Thomas Berthelet had published in London a Latin volume containing the opinions of Italian and French universities in favor of Henry's cause, followed by seven chapters devoted to the defense of their opinions.[25] The editor probably was Edward Fox. Clement VII had shown Ortiz a copy of this book "composed in favor of the King of England." At the pope's request, Ortiz had completed a refutation by July 19, 1531. But already "the bishop of Rochester, certainly one of the most learned men living, has sent an answer to the reasons contained in the said book." That the book in question is the *Censurae* dated April 1530 is evident from Ortiz's statement that Fisher began with "all the reasons" set forth by the universities of Orleans, Paris, Angers, Bourges, Bologna, Padua, and Toulouse — the very order followed in the *Censurae*.[26] Whether Ortiz actually saw Fisher's answer or whether he was merely repeating a description is not clear. On August 23, 1531, he mentions "the bishop of Rochester's apology, which has just been sent from England, in which he answers the two chapters of the book composed in favor of the King." [27] On October 24 he asks Chapuys for "the rest of Fisher's apology." [28] As for Chapuys, he had sent Charles V on October 1 a copy of the apology which Fisher had just completed, begging him to forward it to Rome, "for it is of great importance." [29] This appears to have been only the first part because two months later (November 25, 1531) he forwarded "the last part" of the reply, now completed by Fisher.[30] By November 28 Ortiz himself had received the second part.[31] On December 21 he recommended the publication of both his and Fisher's works unless the case should be finished soon by the pope in Rome.[32]

In the meantime, under date of November 7, 1531, Thomas Berthelet in London had printed an English translation of the Latin *Censurae*.[33] On November 25 Chapuys reports that Henry VIII has "scattered it over the kingdom to gain the people and influence Parliament." [34] The fact that Fisher makes no reference to this English translation or to its relationship with the Latin original indicates that his reply to the *Censurae* was completed by early November 1531.[35] For example, he complains about the failure of the authors of the *Censurae* to name and explain two axioms to which they refer, but he makes no comment about the endeavor of its English translator to remedy the deficiency.[36] In fact, one must conjecture that the English translator had seen Fisher's response to the *Censurae.*

The student of Fisher's writings is fortunate to have Harpsfield's detailed English summary of Fisher's Latin response in the first book of *The Pretended Divorce Between Henry VIII and Catharine of Aragon.*[37] Here are "certain reasons and arguments," Harpsfield tells his reader, "which we have compendiously gathered out of a book made by [Fisher] in Latin and never yet printed as far as we know." A little later, he declares his intention to follow Fisher's "Responsum" exactly.[38] He promises "we will insert or intermingle nothing of our own." [39] Harpsfield remains scrupulously true to his pledge. On four occasions at least, he attacks the author of the English version of *Censurae* for mistranslation.[40] As for omissions, it is difficult to speak of such in a summary, but there are slight ones at rare intervals.[41] Harpsfield inverts Fisher's order by taking the case of the Corinthian excommunicated by Paul before that of John the Baptist and Herod's wife.[42] Finally, *The Pretended Divorce,* Book I, closes with an excellent epitome of Fisher's whole treatise devised by Harpsfield himself but including a previous summary made by Fisher.[43]

Harpsfield's *Divorce,* Book I, is extremely useful in making references to Fisher's "Responsum." The latter, after all, is the most important statement of his case against the divorce, coming as it does after more than three years of thought and debate and in answer to his adversaries' most formal and formidable declaration in the *Censurae.*

How much writing about the divorce Fisher did after the "Responsum" it is difficult to discover. In the same document in which Fisher admits to writing seven or eight books, he states that he did not trouble about the number of copies made of them "except for the last two which contained the substance of the others. One of these is now in the hands of the Archbishop of Canterbury [Cranmer]." [44] As late as August 1533 Thomas Cromwell received an indirect report that a Latin book against the divorce, "intermyngled with Greke and Spanyshe," was attributed to Fisher on the Continent.[45] Robert Wakefield, too, in a letter addressed to Fisher himself and probably written in 1533, mentions having heard that Fisher had composed another book on the royal marriage. In this same letter, he states that he had been consulted by the king's present almoner on the Levitical prohibitions "almost seven years ago" (*annos ante hac fere septem*).[46] Fisher's sermon in favor of the queen which was delivered in June 1532 appears not to have been printed.[47] His battle for Catherine was lost irrevocably in 1533 with Henry's secret marriage to Anne Boleyn on January 25, with Cranmer's sentence on May 23 against Henry's first marriage, and with the coronation of Anne on June 1.

Writings by Fisher as the royal antagonist abound for his first great struggle — over the divorce. This statement cannot be applied to his second and last grand conflict — over spiritual supremacy. His sole extant treatise on the matter seems to be an unoriginal defense of the privileges of the clergy, written in English and preserved in the Public Record Office in fragmentary form.[48] Otherwise his opinions come to us at second hand, that is, through the pages of historians and biographers. But even if Fisher had not left a single written or reported word, his behavior would have been his word (in the scriptural sense). His resistance and his execution are at once his most eloquent word and his clearest comment.

In the struggle he was no grand spiritual leader as Archbishop Warham should have been as primate and actually showed himself only at the end in imitation of his predecessor, Thomas of Canterbury.[49] But he was the councilor of the clergy, as, for example, when he was apparently consulted by the Convocation in May 1532. As in the matter of the divorce, he was "faithful found; / Among the faithless, faithful only he." At the very end what a contrast there was between the prelate announcing the repentance of Henry VII like any ordinary man on his deathbed and the deprived bishop lying down on the scaffold to have his head severed by Henry VIII's orders!

Only the briefest summary of his role in the contest over the spiritual supremacy is needed here in view of our purpose. As soon as Parliament met on November 3, 1529, the Commons adopted a bill of grievances against clerical abuses. In the House of Lords Fisher delivered a strong speech, including the words: "Now with the Commons is nothing but doune with the Church, and all this me semeth is for lacke of faith only." [50] The text of the speech does not survive, but the "effect" of it appears in the sixteenth-century life of Fisher.[51] Upon the complaint of the Commons and the plea of the king for moderation, the bishop offered an apology of uncertain nature. During the same session, in a successful speech against the king's proposal to alienate minor monastic properties to a sum of two thousand florins, he used the fable of the handleless axe which, upon being granted a sapling for a handle, then felled both little trees and great.[52]

On September 12, 1529, a royal proclamation had been issued against appeals to Rome on the new law regarding plural ecclesiastical benefices. On this account, Bishop Fisher of Rochester, together with Bishop Clerk of Bath and Bishop West of Ely, were arrested in October for an indefinite period. "Fisher," explains Bridgett, "was the last man in England to encourage the abuses of pluralism; but the matter was one of ecclesiastical competence." [53] At the important Convocation in February 1531 it was reportedly the Bishop of Rochester who suggested the addition of the saving clause *quantum per Christi legem licet* to the title of "the supreme head." [54] Nevertheless, Fisher's disappointment over this *Concessio* made by the clergy, writes Chapuys, made him seriously ill at the time.[55]

Fisher, like Tunstal, was not summoned to the session of Parliament in January 1532, although he came up to London and even greeted the king.[56] Neither was he present at the Convocation which on May 15, 1532, agreed to the Submission of the Clergy which put an end to their legislative authority in spiritual matters.[57] A delegation was sent on May 10 to Fisher lying ill at his palace by Lambeth Marsh, whether to argue with him or to consult him in their perplexity is not clear.[58]

On March 26 of the following year, Fisher alone dared to oppose the Convocation's two decisions in favor of the divorce.[59] At the time of Cranmer's pronouncement of sentence and of Anne's coronation, he was a prisoner in charge of Bishop Gardiner of Winchester (April 6–June 13). On July 11 came the papal annulment of Cranmer's proceedings, and on August 8 the papal brief of censure against Henry, Anne, and Cranmer. Elizabeth was born on September 1. Through Chapuys, Fisher twice urged Charles V to an invasion of England where he said the majority were ready for rebellion.[60]

Like Thomas More, John Fisher was involved in the affair of the Holy Maid of Kent. In the Bill of Attainder passed by the Lords on March 12, and by the Commons on March 17, 1534, his name stood first on the list of six persons indicted for misprision of treason. He courageously refused Cromwell's advice to ask the royal pardon and mercy. In the letters written in his illness to the king, to Cromwell, and to the House of Lords, he pleaded that he had had no obligation to reveal what was public knowledge and what the Holy Maid had told the king himself.[61] Henry VIII approved the verdict on March 30 but remitted the penalty to a fine of a year's revenue (£300).

On March 23, 1534, Clement VII had declared the validity of Henry's marriage to Catherine. As for the Act of Succession passed on March 30, Fisher agreed to that part of the oath which fixed the succession on the heirs of Henry VIII and Anne Boleyn but rejected that part which impugned the validity of the marriage to Catherine and forbade obedience to any foreign authority, to wit, that of the pope. This refusal took place on April 13. After a short time in charge of Cranmer, who tried unsuccessfully to effect a compromise by having him swear to the succession but not to the objectionable preamble (thus deceiving the public into the belief that he had taken the whole oath),[62] he went to the Tower on April 17. The severity of his physical and spiritual privations is evident from his pathetic letter to Cromwell on December 22.[63]

The Act of Supremacy, passed by Parliament on November 18, 1534, made it high treason maliciously to deny the title of Supreme Head. Fisher was falsely informed that More had taken the oath, but he remained firm — as he did when various bishops, including Tunstal and Gardiner, tried to persuade him.[64] In consequence the see of Rochester was declared vacant on January 2, 1535. After an unusual examination by some privy councilors headed by Cromwell on May 7, a special commission was set up for Fisher's trial. The records of the interrogatories to which he was subjected in June are still extant.[65] Arguing in vain from the term *maliciously,* he was tried and condemned by a jury on June 17 and beheaded on June 22.[66] On May 20, Paul III, the successor to Clement VII who had died the previous September, had created Fisher a cardinal with a view to the reform of the Church and to Fisher's own safety. Upon hearing of Fisher's execution, the pope addressed indignant letters to Ferdinand of Hungary and to Francis I.[67]

Like Thomas More in his imprisonment, John Fisher in the Tower turned to noncontroversial writing. For his half-sister, Elizabeth White, he composed two treatises entitled *A Spirituall Consolation* and *The Wayes to Perfect Religion.* The former urges the reader to look to his own repentance betimes and to beware of reliance on others. The latter develops most ingeniously a comparison of the seeker after perfection to the hunter after game. Another comparison which often seems stretched to the limit of endurance for the contemporary reader is that of the crucifix to a printed book. This occurs in Fisher's sermon on the passion of Christ.[68] All three works were published posthumously. *Two Fruytfull Sermons,* however, had been printed on June 28, 1532.[69] Their date of delivery has been assigned to 1520 because of the references to the Field of Cloth of Gold, but time would have permitted some rewriting before publication. One wonders what particular occasion called for their printing after a dozen years. At any rate, the peculiar advantage attaching to these sermons is that he is here a Catholic speaking to Catholics, as in his earliest works, but that, unlike his discourses on the Psalms (1508), the two sermons saw publication some fifteen years after the beginnings of the Protestant Reformation. Hence any change in his popular teaching would indicate the surrender of untenable positions and a retreat to safer and more defensible lines.

It will be remembered that Richard Pace had translated and published Fisher's English sermon against Luther almost immediately. Others of his English works had to wait. It was perhaps for the *Opera omnia* (1597) that John Fen (d. 1615) translated *The Seuen Penytencyall Psalmes. A Spirituall Consolation* appears as a "Praefatio" to "Conciones duae, vna de passione domini; altera de iustitia pharisaeorum et Christianorum," the latter of which is none other than *Two Fruytfull Sermons,* naturally conceived as a single work. This section is followed by the Latin translation of *The Wayes to Perfect Religion.* A piece hitherto unpublished is Fisher's letter entitled "De charitate Christiana" and directed to Herman Lethmatius (Goudanus, Laematius, Lethmannus),

Dean of St. Mary's in Utrecht, a brilliant student and theologian according to Erasmus.[70] There has been, and will be, occasion to refer to Fisher's other correspondents, many of them distinguished: Erasmus, More, Vergil, Reuchlin, Cranmer, Cromwell, Campeggio, Stokesley, Foxe, West, Croke, Wakefield, Siberch, Cochlaeus, the Duke of Bavaria, and others.

In addition to Fisher's printed books, many works exist only in manuscript. Some of these, such as his writings on the Vulgate Psalms, the divorce, and the clergy, have been mentioned above. In addition, the Public Record Office has a gathering of miscellaneous papers, including prayers in Latin and English.[71] Besides a commonplace book, there are also fragmentary sermons, meditations, or treatises on peace, wisdom, confession, the Septuagint, the Eucharist, the passion, and the Angelic Salutation. As might be expected, not even fragments might survive of one or more writings of Fisher. One composition about which information is definite seems to be a kind of harmony of the Gospels. This endeavor, Erasmus writes Fisher under date of April 2, 1519, would have done him more credit than *The Single Magdalene*.[72] On the other side of the balance is a Latin work, attributed to the Bishop of Rochester because of his great reputation but certainly not his. No malice need be involved. It is entitled *A Brief Work on Confidence in God and His Mercy*.[73] The structure with its clear division into twelve *axiomata,* thirty-two *loci* from the Gospels, forty-one *loci* from the Pauline epistles, and sixteen *loci* from other parts of the New Testament might deceive an unwary reader, but the absence of references especially to the Church, the Fathers, and the Scholastics would seem to prove that the contents did not come from Fisher's pen. Early placed upon various Indexes, it was very soon labeled: "Falsely attributed to John Fisher." [74]

Such, then, are John Fisher's extant writings, from the academic oration delivered before Henry VII and Prince Henry (later Henry VIII) at Cambridge in 1506 to the spiritual works written in the Tower and published posthumously. To his contemporaries he was primarily the bishop *sans pareil.* All his attitudes and all his achievements took their rise, in a general but true sense, in his episcopal office. William Rastell, the nephew of Thomas More, perceived this phenomenon clearly when he came to sum up

Fisher's life and work: "[He was in holi]nes, learinyng and dylygence in his cure and in fulfylling his office of byshope such, [that of many hundred years] England had not any byshop worthie to be compared unto hyme." To his office of bishop, Rastell attributes his liberality to the poor, his study by day and by night, his bounty to scholars, his concern for the "brynging up of the youth of England in vertu and learnyng," his role as "the protector [of the university] of Cambrigge," and his diligent preaching, which was outstanding "as well for his excellent lernyng as [also for edifying] audyens, and moving the affections of his hearers to cleve to God and goodness." But, for the last and climactic position, Rastell reserves Fisher's theological writings:

> So highlie and profowndly was he lerned in dyvynytie, that he was and is at this da[y well known,] esteymed, reputed and allowyd (and no lesse worthie) not onelie for the cheiffeist dyvyne that was [many years] in England, but also for one of the chef flowers of dyvynytie that lyved in his tyme, thro[ughout all] christendome. Which haith appered ryght well by his works that he wrott in his mater[nall speech,] but moche more by his lerned and famous books wrytten in the Latten tonge.[75]

A knowledge of John Fisher's writings therefore can do justice to the man and his work — such justice as has been done recently to Thomas More. Apart from the world-wide and age-long importance of *Utopia* and More's greater personal appeal as the family man, a comparison of the two saints on theological grounds makes Fisher loom much more prominently than More on the historical horizon. Because of his vernacular controversies with Tyndale and other Englishmen, More's importance in the Reformation might justly be called national but insular. On account of his Latin works against Lefèvre, Velenus, Luther, and Oecolampadius, Fisher's significance was international and continental.

Even independently of the question of historical justice and equity, the investigation of Fisher's theology has present-day implications. In any dialogue between Christian churches, a knowledge of pre-Reformation and pre-Tridentine doctrines and attitudes can create a more fluid and a less rigid framework wherein to effect not mere coexistence and cooperation but mutual influence and adjustment. The shock of the new forces released in Christendom during Fisher's lifetime can be accurately gauged by his writings — and by his deeds and death. He always saw himself as friends and enemies saw him — as a bishop, one of the successors of the Apostles to whom Christ had entrusted His Church. This fact helps to explain even the force of his style, "for he was teaching them as one having authority" (Matt. 7:29). Yet he shied away from the charge of tyranny constantly leveled against the episcopacy: he had no intention of "lording it over [his] flock, but becoming from the heart a pattern to the flock." He cherished only the expectation of receiving "the unfading crown of glory" from the Chief Shepherd (1 Pet. 5:3–4). Consequently, when on his way to execution he opened his New Testament at the seventeenth chapter of the Johannine Gospel, he could make the words his own: "I have glorified thee on earth; I have accomplished the work that thou hast given me to do. And now do thou, Father, glorify me with thyself. . ."

Chapter III

FISHER'S CHURCH OF CHRIST

WHAT strikes the reader immediately as he begins to analyze Fisher's theology is a characteristic which he shares with his contemporaries but by which he differs from modern man, to wit, his presuppositions. He does not need to say a word on the necessity of religion and on the obligation not only of private and internal veneration of God but also of external, public, and social worship. Nor does he ever have to prove the possibility and necessity of supernatural revelation. Only once, it seems, and then in passing, does he refer to a truth which can be known only from revelation, namely, eternal happiness as man's final end.[1] In the same way, because of acceptance by his adversaries and readers, he never has to labor to establish the role of Christ as the divine messenger — prepared for by the prophets, distinguished by His exalted doctrine, approved by His sinless character, abounding in miracles and prophecies, and later witnessed to by the humanly unaccountable spread of His religion and by the constancy of the martyrs. Of all these proofs Fisher mentions one, Christ's resurrection, because, being the foundation of all else, it demanded "solid arguments." [2]

When there is question of a particular article belonging to Christ's revelation, Fisher applies such negative tests as error, contradiction, fraud, unreasonableness, baseness, and evil consequences less than the single positive criterion of miracles. In fighting for a single Magdalene against Clichtove, he narrates at length two miracles wrought through appeal to her.[3] His approach is more serious in *The Defense of the Royal Assertion.* If Luther wishes to introduce new and different doctrines into the Church, he should prove his authority by signs and miracles — as did

Christ, the Apostles, and the Fathers. In fact, says Fisher, "If we be now deceived, I dare declare that God Himself deceived us of set purpose." [4] The signs and miracles promised by Christ to His followers (Mark 16:17–18) have ceased precisely because their purpose has been fulfilled in the successful propagation of the true faith during the apostolic and patristic periods — an explanation learned not from Scripture but from the interpretation of the Fathers only.[5]

It is, however, in *The Reality of Christ's Body and Blood in the Eucharist* that Fisher gives his most considered views on miracles. He approves the behavior of Hugh of Lincoln who, refusing the invitation to gaze upon a miracle, answered that infidels found their signs in miracles but that Christians believed without them to increase the merit of their faith.[6] Visible or sensible miracles are designed to draw the weak to faith, whereas invisible miracles, as in baptism and the Eucharist, serve to enlighten the recipients.[7] When Oecolampadius attempts to discredit the value of miracles by citing wonders among the pagans, Fisher asserts that no one denies the power of demons to perform such wonders by God's permission but that they are not pertinent to the Eucharist.[8] From the circumstances of the deeds (*ex factorum circumstantiis*) it is easy to discern between the tricks of demons and the good works of angels.[9] Nevertheless, Fisher relies upon miracles (or revelations) not as the only solid proofs but as subordinate to the testimony of Scripture as confirmed by the consent of the past and the authority of the Church.[10] The miracles worked on behalf of the Eucharist advance and strengthen the same faith preached by the Church on the Eucharist.[11] The preface to Book III gives the details of eight miracles drawn from Eusebius, Cyprian, Ambrose, Augustine, Gregory, and Bede, and directs the reader to others in the history of Vincent of Beauvais. Only fear of boring the reader keeps Fisher from reciting those in the lives of the saints. He names nine saints in particular, among them Hugh of Lincoln and Edward the Confessor.[12] At the end of the fifth and last book, Fisher declares that he has no obligation to prove the teachings of the Fathers by *new* miracles, according to the unreasonable demand made on Erasmus by Luther, since they were sufficiently confirmed in the past.[13]

In passing, it is interesting to note John Bale's declaration that, like John Forest and Thomas More, John Fisher "wrought . . . no miracles." Bale expresses the Protestant attitude: "Of his own chosen martyrs Christ looketh for none other miracle but that only they persevere faithful to the end." [14]

In addition to miracles, the Bishop of Rochester makes use of another criterion of divine revelation which has practically disappeared as a tool or weapon of professional theologians, namely, private revelations. Perhaps it is no accident that in controversy he makes progressively less and less use of them. In his *Single Magdalene* he relies upon the revelations of Ubertino of Casale and Bridget of Sweden. Of the former he interestingly observes that, if the humanist Lefèvre finds his rather crude style unpleasant, Ubertino himself discovered vain learning and stylistic preoccupation to be an impediment to illumination by Christ, whose conversation is with the simple.[15]

In the *Destruction of Clichtove's Bulwark* he finds it necessary to set forth his position more clearly. Before one can put one's faith in private revelations, three requirements must be fulfilled: the sanctity of the person to whom they are made, thorough examination by learned and holy men, and papal approbation. If these conditions are satisfied, as in the case of Bridget, a reasonable person cannot refuse to believe in them without committing sin. The argument is that, in these matters as in all others believed through the Church, the reason is the same: "The faith of the whole Church rests upon this as a firm foundation, namely, that whatever has been revealed by God is most true." [16]

Besides the revelations of Bridget, Fisher appeals also to those of Elizabeth and Mechtilde; but on the authority of the historians, Enea Silvio and Flavio Biondi, he rejects, as spectral illusions, those of Amadeus, which are favored by Clichtove.[17] In his last work on the Magdalene, *A Confutation of Lefèvre's Second Disquisition,* he mentions the testimony of private revelations with the Fathers, the Church, miracles, and the Gospels in favor of Mary's fall into a sinful life.[18]

Far more sparing use of private revelations is made in Fisher's controversies with Protestants. In two articles in the *Confutation of Luther's Assertion,* he refers to Bridget's prediction of the downfall of Constantinople unless the Greeks returned to the unity of the Catholic Church.[19] In the *Defense of the Royal*

Assertion, he declares that, if Luther appeals to private revelations for his teachings, "such revelations for the most part are deceptive; for those supposed to have proceeded from God are disclosed for the most part to have issued from an evil spirit." Of this phenomenon Savonarola is a prime example, in spite of his learning, virtue, and orthodoxy. He was discredited when his prophecies remained unfulfilled after his death.[20] Yet even the pope, in a council, for example, would have to hearken to someone who received a revelation on the matter under discussion and to judge whether it came from God or not.[21] In his work against Oecolampadius, Fisher returns to the revelations of Bridget, Elizabeth, and Mechtilde, but this time adds those of Hildegard and of an anonymous priest recorded by Chrysostom.[22]

There is a more or less final statement of Fisher on private inspiration in the matter of Henry VIII's divorce. The king's book, prefaced by the favorable verdicts of continental universities, declares (in a close translation of the original Latin): "As many as beinge toucht by the holy gost, do ones playnely perceiue, that they do kepe suche mariages, as be incest: they may / yea and are bounde . . . not only to breke streichtwey suche mariages / but also . . . be bonde to withstande and resyste valiantly the Pope / all thoughe he wolde threten them by a .M. cursynges and excommunications, that they shulde do the contrary." The book cites the analogy of a secular priest, who, inspired by the Holy Spirit, flees to become a religious in another diocese against the canons. Fisher concedes that obedience is due rather to the private law of the Holy Spirit than to the canon or public law which was passed to suppress abuses, but he warns that "the spirit of God never moves anyone against Holy Scripture or God's public law": one must beware against guidance by Satan rather than by the Spirit of God (2 Cor. 11:14). He resorts to Thomas Aquinas and John Gerson as authorities. He concludes a long development with emphasis: "No one, surely, ought so to follow the guidance and instigation of his own spirit as to transgress the plain precept of Christ. Wherefore since Christ commanded a man to leave father and mother and cleave to his wife because of the sacrament of matrimony, he ought not to leave her on account of the instigation of some spirit or other."[23]

It was in the case of "the king's great matter" that Fisher's belief in private revelations had an ironic, serious consequence in his involvement with the Holy Maid of Kent. One charge against her was that "the obstinacy of the bishop of Rochester against the marriage was confirmed and strengthened by her revelations, as appears from the bishop's confession." [24] The details of the story, not pertinent here but instructive in themselves, can be found readily in Fisher's biographies.[25]

It was not only by countless miracles and numerous prophecies but by all possible criteria that Christ had established His divine mission and revelation. Since the divinity of His mission and revelation, however, was an assumption of all parties, Fisher hardly had to touch on the proofs for it. Rather, the point at issue was whether Christ had left behind any supreme and infallible authority to continue His mission and to preserve His revelation. For Fisher until almost his fiftieth year, there was no dispute — there was only the accepted fact of the Church: a society of living men united under the teaching and ruling power of their legitimate pastors, the bishops and especially the pope, united too by their profession of the same Christian faith and by their participation in the same sacraments, all with a view to the attainment of eternal life.[26] But when Luther with his scriptural conception challenged and repudiated this historical image, Fisher had to rethink and to reassess his views.[27] In fact, one theologian sees not the doctrine about justification but that about the Church as separating them: "It was for its ecclesiastical consequences that Fisher reprobated the doctrine of justification by faith." [28]

The conception of the Church which Fisher entertained before the Reformation finds confident and eloquent utterance in his sermons on the Penitential Psalms. "Ihesu cryste," he says, "made open & shewed vnto his chyrche the hyd & preuy mysteryes of his godhede. . . He promysed also at his ascencyon the holy ghost to come that sholde teche parfytely the knowlege of euery thynge, so that now no thinge may be more certayne to vs than it whiche is taught by holy chyrche. No meane may be founde so spedefull and redy to proue the certaynte of ony thynge concernynge our fayth as that the chyrche hath so affermed and ordeyned." [29] In the same series of sermons, he seizes upon the conception of the Church as "a spiritual house" built of "living stones" (1 Pet. 2:5–8, cf. Eph. 2:20–22), stones that must be "stronge & stedfast in fayth and good werkes" in order to preach the Gospel throughout the earth. He begs the Lord to "make ones an ende & fynysshe the buyldynge of thy chyrche that thou begannest a longe tyme past, that now a grete whyle hath suffred moche wronge" — the latter being a reference to the lax clergy.[30]

This metaphor of "living stones" recurs in the *Confutation of Luther's Assertion*. The Church can be only a perfectly arranged, not a confused, construction of rational stones that live by a faith that is alive, with Peter as the foundation.[31] The figure is admirably suited not only to a monarchical conception (the primacy of Peter and his successors) but also to a hierarchical conception (the power of bishops) of the Church. After marshaling the Fathers as witnesses to a special priesthood, Fisher bluntly asks: "What else was the Church, but a congregation [*coetus*] composed entirely of prelates and subjects? And clearly, all these prelates from the beginning taught this doctrine, and all the subjects accepted it." [32] In *Christ's Body* he introduces a slight change: "What else is the Catholic Church but one body [*corpus*] composed of people and Fathers wherever scattered through the world?" [33]

It is this conception of the Church as the Mystical Body of Christ that predominates in Fisher's thought and speech. He must have found a great attraction in the comparison of a society to a body. In its statutes he sees Christ's College "under the plan of one body, of which the Master or Keeper is the head; the two Deans, the arms; the Steward and the Prefect of the Common Chest, the two hands; the Fellow Scholars, the solid and principal members of the body itself; the Reader, the member deputed to the procreation of new offspring; the Pupil Scholars a most suitable seminarium; and lastly the hired servants are, as it were, the feet at the base of all." [34] In his manuscript commentary (of uncertain date) on the Psalms (Vulg. Ps. 26:4–5), he meditatively prays: "*This will I seek after:* that, incorporated into the Mystical Body of Christ which is the assembly of the faithful and the house of God, I may remain in it always — *that I may dwell in the house of the Lord,* nor be separated or fall therefrom by any heresy or perverse view as long as I live, *all the days of my life;* for, in that assembly whatever is the good pleasure of the Lord is taught most truly through the Spirit dwelling in the same, so *that I may see the delight of the Lord;* by adhering to her doctrines I shall dare to console myself more confidently by the contemplation of the heavenly temple." [35]

When he enters upon his controversies, Fisher makes various refinements of the concept of the Mystical Body. At the head of a particularly sensitive section in his *Confutation of Luther's Assertion* he declares: "So great indeed is the unity of this Mystical Body (which is the Church) that all we Christians are called, and actually are, not only one Body but also one Spirit on account of the Holy Spirit dwelling in us." In a marvelous manner its members recognize one another and the head.[36] The sinner remains joined to the Mystical Body by faith.[37] By fall from faith, however, the heretic cuts himself off from the Body and its vivifying Spirit.[38] Granted that the bond with the Mystical Body is through faith alone (*per solam fidem*), the eating of Christ's Body and Blood effects a deeper and firmer incorporation. In this respect the Jews, who before the incarnation belonged to the Mystical Body by faith, are less favored than Christians who through the Eucharist become "members of His Body, made of His flesh and of His bones" (cf. Gen. 2:21–24).[39] Here the symbol of Eve is important in regard to both the Church and its members. "As Eve had been formed from the side of Adam, so also the life of the Church came forth from the side of Christ Himself." And: "As Eve came forth from Adam, so we who are the Church and the Spouse of Christ, by eating His flesh and blood, are made one Body, and members of the Body of Christ, and so from two is made one flesh." [40] One evident consequence of this doctrine is that the Church is the Spouse of Christ (Eph. 5:24–32; Apoc. 21:1–6, 22:17; John 19:34–35) and the Mother of Christians.[41]

This lofty conception, however, does not keep the Bishop of Rochester from realistically deploring the sad condition of the historical Church. In his treatise on prayer he cries out: "O miserable estate of ours, O time most worthy bewaylyng, into the which most vnfortunately our deare and holy mother the Churche, the spouse of Christ, is fallen . . . and lyke an inchaunted woman, nothing regardeth nor reputeth of any moment, that moste excellent pryce [Christ's blood], wherewith she was so excedyng louynglye and dearely redeemed." [42] Many years before, he had called for prayers for the Church which was like a foundering ship in which Jesus slept as of old: "But & we take hede

& call to mynde how many vyces reygne now a dayes in crystes chyrche, as well in the clergy as in the comyn people . . . perchaunce we shal thynke that almyghty god slombreth not onely, but also that he hath slepte soundly a grete season. None ordre none integryte is now kepte" — and much more of the same.[43]

Nevertheless, in spite of all its imperfections, this Church is still the Spouse of Christ. To prove it to be such, Fisher makes relatively sparing use of the line of argument constantly employed by Catholic apologists in later centuries, namely, the "four notes" which Christ wished to mark His Church. The most explicit and yet compendious statement is found in his sermon against Luther:

> Neuerthelesse the chyrche of christ is but vna. sancta. catholica. et apostolica. this chirche is one hauynge one heed the pope. whiche is the vycare of christ. of whome it is called vna. And though there be in this chyrche many synners. yet for the holy sacramentes that reneweth & repareth synners dayly. & for the holy spyryte that contynually remayneth in it. it is called sancta. that is to say holy. And for bycause it is not lymyt to any certayne nacyon. but it is comen to all nacyons. therfore it is called catholica. that is to saye vnyuersall. And fynally bycause it is deryuyed from the apostles. & specyally from the prynce of the apostles saynt Peter. therfore it is called apostolica. that is to saye apostolyke. This onely chyrche is the spouse of chryst.[44]

Of these four notes the one which is dearest to Fisher and which is most important and evident in his works is that of unity, not only of head but also and much more of mind and heart, according to the exhortations of the Apostle Paul.[45] The heretics, on the other hand, have fallen out among themselves like the builders of Babel. In fact, Fisher thanks God for raising dissension among the Church's enemies — for example, the disagreement between Luther and Oecolampadius.[46] This unity of head and doctrine holds not only at present but extends back into the past, for example, to "the truth of the priesthood . . . abundantly and unanimously witnessed to by all the Fathers through the whole history of the Church": "Consider the unanimous agreement of all the churches, with no exception through so many centuries." [47] The unity of time enters even into his explanation of the note of catholicity: "The succession of Christis churche / . . . hath contynued and shall continue vnto the worldes ende / euen like a floode that passeth continually / the waters go & passe / but yet the floode continueth / and reteyneth styl the name of the floode: so the succession of Christis churche euer continueth / & is called the churche catholike / though the people yerely renewe." [48]

The unity of the Mystical Body in space and in time is effected by its soul, the Holy Spirit. Here, in regard to the object of belief, the development of Fisher's ideas (or, perhaps one should say, of his emphases) is particularly interesting. Speaking in 1519 to Clichtove and Lefèvre, as a Catholic to Catholics, as it were, he argues that there has been no change in the Church's attitude on the single Magdalene such as in the case of the Immaculate Conception, the Assumption, and the veneration of images. In fact, "there are very many points, capable of mention unless tedious to the reader, on which the Church has changed its opinion under the guidance of the Holy Spirit — as all Christians must positively believe." [49] The Church would not have rejected the contrary opinion "unless the Holy Spirit had evidently been leading it" (*nisi plane ducente eam spiritu sancto*). "Only the warped mind would attribute this change to any other than the Holy Spirit" (*alteri quam spiritui sancto*). "No one doubts that this change proceeded from the Holy Spirit" (*a spiritu sancto profecta*).[50] A practical conclusion is that the Christian who espouses an opinion opposed to that of the whole Church should declare the submission of himself and all his words to the judgment of the whole Church — something Lefèvre has neglected to do.[51]

The basis for this confidence, as Fisher tells his audience in his sermon against Luther in 1521, is that Christ, out of love for "oure mother holy chyrche," has sent her the Spirit "that sholde abyde with her for euer. to acertayne her fro tyme to tyme of euery trouthe wherunto bothe she & euery chylde of hyrs . . . sholde gyf assured fayth." [52] This "ascertainment" of truth in time of error receives special proof in the *Confutation of Luther's Assertion*.[53] Commenting on the Eucharist in Article 16 of this same work, he admits "the many and the great ways in which the Church has varied from Christ's institution" as recorded in the New Testament, e.g., the words of consecration, the mingling of a little water with the wine, and the use of leavened bread for a period. However the variations came about, "whether through the Apostles or through the Holy Spirit" (*siue per Apostolos, seu per*

Spiritum sanctum), the Church's teaching is most safe because it is "the pillar and mainstay of the truth" (1 Tim. 3:15).[54]

This last verse constitutes one of three scriptural arguments for the Church's infallibility in Fisher's *Defense of the Royal Assertion,* e.g., on the sacramental character of matrimony. The other two proofs are Christ's promise to be with His Church to the consummation of the world (Matt. 28:20) and to send the Spirit of Truth who "will teach you all the truth" (John 14:16–17, 14:26, 16:13).[55] In the *Defense of the Sacred Priesthood,* too, Fisher repeatedly finds it incredible that Christ and the Spirit of Truth should have allowed the Church, from its earliest days and through the centuries, to be involved in error and in a lie about the sacrament of orders.[56] Therefore, he tells his audience at Barnes's abjuration in 1526, "If he haue nat broke his promyse: than hath he ben with his churche all this long tyme of fyftene hundred yeres . . . and his moste holy spirite also hath bene al this tyme present in the churche." [57]

To Oecolampadius he soon explains that another of Christ's promises, "that thy faith fail not" (Luke 22:32), is directed not to the individual but to the whole Church.[58] This is another ground for disbelieving that Christ and the Holy Spirit would suffer the Church for centuries to persist in error, e.g., about the Real Presence.[59] Hence the truth of the Christian faith has come down to present time "through a continual succession of prelates after prelates, succeeding one another by turn." [60] The last time that Fisher expresses disbelief in this respect is in the cause of Henry VIII's divorce: God would not suffer His Church, through the voice of the Fathers of all centuries, to err in applying the Deuteronomical text (Deut. 25:5) to a brother-german (*de germano fratre*).[61] But Wakefield turns the argument on Fisher: If Christ had allowed marriage with a dead brother's wife and if the Catholic Church had forbidden it as incestuous, then the Paraclete had not taught the Church every truth necessary for salvation, and it is in error and heresy.[62] But Fisher would answer, as he actually did, that the degrees of consanguinity and affinity fall under disciplinary and not doctrinal decrees on matrimonial impediments and hence are alterable.

It might be well to halt here a moment for a review. To Fisher's mind, Christ had left behind an infallible and indefectible Church to safeguard His revelation and mission. This Church is the Mystical Body, animated by its soul, the Spirit of Truth. It is the Spouse of Christ and the Mother of Christians. It is indelibly marked by a jurisdictional and doctrinal unity persevering in time and space. Whoever spurns any truth believed by the one Body composed of people and prelates will perish "because salvation can be the lot of no one outside the Catholic Church." [63] But where do heretics, schismatics, and the excommunicated stand in relation to salvation and the Church? It is implicitly evident from our past treatment that the Church is conceived in hierarchical terms as consisting of teachers and taught, rulers and ruled, sanctifiers and sanctified; but Fisher's reasoning on this point will be left for later analysis. At present, let us consider the membership of people in the Church. The term *people* will here be understood in the sense of laity, that is, ordinary members as distinct from prelates, to wit, pope and bishops.

For membership Fisher plainly requires at least valid baptism, belief in the one faith, and union with the pope and the bishops. Hence the duties of reverence, obedience, love, and cooperation with the hierarchy. Hence the privilege of participation in the task of teaching, ruling, and sanctifying the Church. For example, to exhort the sinner "mekely with good & swete wordes . . . to leue his wyckednes" is deserving of reward not only for "them that haue auctoryte to rebuke synne" but also for "al crysten people, for euery persone in maner hath charge of other." [64] A decade later, when Lefèvre labels "the common opinion of the whole church" about the *single* Magdalene as "the common opinion of the whole people [*totius vulgi*]," Fisher wonders how Lefèvre would classify the prelates of the Church because pope, cardinals, archbishops, and bishops would all be "of this people" (*ex hoc vulgo*) since none of them would have held for *two* or *three* Magdalenes.[65] But Fisher had hardly to concern himself with the intricacies of membership until Luther's affirmation of the priesthood of all the faithful and his denial of a special visible priesthood.

Even in the *Confutation of Luther's Assertion* Fisher's pronouncements on the matter are few in comparison with those of the two Latin works published in June 1525. His most important statement occurs in answer to the query as to why Peter calls all

Christians "a royal priesthood" (1 Pet. 2:9): either because they are united with Christ who is king and priest or because they are to offer "spiritual sacrifices" (1 Pet. 2:5), that is, themselves. Since it is the function of priests to offer victims (as Jewish priests sacrificed irrational or brute victims), "therefore Christians who offer themselves as rational victims deservedly are called by Peter a holy priesthood by way of metaphor [*per metaphoram*]." [66] So, too, when Paul says: "We are God's helpers, you are God's tillage, God's building" (1 Cor. 3:9), the people (*plebs*) constitute the earth that is tilled or the wooden material with which to build.[67]

To this scriptural comparison and distinction, Fisher returns often, for example, in his *Defense of the Royal Assertion* published two years later.[68] In regard to the Eucharist also, "the people [*plebs*] take the role of the poor man, and the priest the role of the rich man, that is, of Christ Himself." [69] The people are deservedly imposed upon by the Lutherans and their biblical commentaries if they forsake the salutary writings of their pastors, approved by holiness of life, genuine erudition, and numerous miracles. Little need to wonder about the deception of the people (*vulgus*) whose lack of scriptural training makes them unable to distinguish right from wrong in Lutheran commentary. The "ignorant rabble [*imperita plebecula*]" can hardly pass sound judgment on matters where even experts, unless they keep their wits sharp, go astray not infrequently.[70] Such are Fisher's sentiments in his dedicatory epistle to Bishop West, but it is his eleventh chapter that is wholly devoted to the problem.

In this chapter, Fisher finds Luther completely dependent on popular favor (*plebeio . . . fauori*), which every intelligent man has always regarded as foolish according to Seneca's apposite saying: "Popular favor [*fauor popularis*] is sought by evil artifices." [71] Popular minds (*plebeiorum animos*) have always been light, inconstant, and ready for the worst. The nature of popular opinion (*iudicium populare*) is sufficiently evident from profane history (Lycurgus, Solon, Camillus, and the Scipios), sacred history (the golden calf), the New Testament (Christ's crucifixion within a week after His triumph, and Paul and Barnabas' experience at Lycaonia), and ecclesiastical history (Donatists, Arians, and Macedonians).[72] Judgment (*iudicium*) on dogma belongs to the spiritual and perfect, not to the carnal and dull multitude (*ad multi-*

tudinem), who will always be in the majority and who need milk, not solid food (1 Cor. 3:2–3, Heb. 5:12–14).[73] Yet in a sense, Fisher concedes the people (*populus*) have the right of judging, that is, the right of believing and giving assent to the Word of God; but they have not, he insists, the right of dissenting from their legitimate teachers as long as they are not suspect of heresy or heterodoxy or deviation from the teaching of the Fathers.[74] In the course of history, dogmatic matters were referred, not to the people (*plebem*), but to Moses, Aaron, Hur, and the seventy elders in the Old Testament and to the twelve Apostles and seventy-two disciples in the New Testament.[75] In the early Church, too, the canonicity of the presently accepted four Gospels and the rejection of those according to Peter, Thomas, Nicodemus, and others, were not left to the judgment of the people (*iudicium populi*). In the same way, the acceptance or rejection of St. James's epistle should be referred to the learned bishops, who are shepherds, not to the ignorant people (*populus rudis*), who are the flock.[76] In these matters, as in all others, many of Christ's sheep who have strayed from the path of truth and followed Luther will return to the Catholic faith as did some Arians — such, at any rate, is Fisher's confidence.[77]

In the *Defense of the Sacred Priesthood,* published in the same year and month as the *Defense of the Royal Assertion,* the Bishop of Rochester needs to go into great detail on the status of the people in the Church. The reasonableness and the necessity of having "some men . . . set apart to . . . bear responsibility for the whole multitude" arise from "six special dangers to which the vast majority of Christians is certainly liable": (1) "the grave danger of falling away from the faith"; (2) "the dullness of men's minds"; (3) "the facility with which men fall into every kind of sin"; (4) "men's sluggishness to good"; (5) "diabolic temptation"; and (6) "the poisonous errors of false teachers." Hence the need for special guides, monitors, pastors, and teachers.[78] Fisher naturally cannot deny the bestowal of grace upon the people (*populus*) as well as upon their rulers, but the measure or amount marks the difference between house and builder, between field and farmer.[79] If Luther insists that all Christians have been anointed, and indeed as priests, no Christians are left to serve as the people (*populus*) with lesser priests as their mediators with Christ the

High Priest. Hence the people would be priests without authority, and each Christian would be a priest for himself alone — without the requisite individual calling, ordination, and mission.[80] All Christians, Fisher explains, are anointed — "anointed, however, to fight, not to preach the Gospel." [81] For, "not all are called to the office of feeding, teaching, and ruling the flock." In comparison with these special priests, the people (*plebs*) have a priesthood which is metaphorical (*metaphoricum*). Just as each Christian is a king insofar as he rules himself, so is he a priest to himself alone. "All Christians, then, are kings and priests, but to themselves, not to others." [82]

The Holy Spirit interiorly enlightens the heart of the individual Christian because otherwise the external teaching would be useless. But, as already indicated above, the enlightenment is different for rulers and subjects: "This illumination . . . for the vast majority of men is so dim as to be totally insufficient without the help of another teacher." [83] Fisher proves this point from Paul's urgent exhortation to Timothy and Titus to watch over their flocks and from the evident need of teachers on the part of the converted Hebrews (Heb. 5:11–14), Galatians (Gal. 3:1–6, 6:1), and Jews (Acts 15:1–6). If this be true, "what shall we say of the multitude [*turba*] of present-day Christians? Do not they too need teachers?" [84] The whole New Testament witnesses to the distinction between people and priests (*inter plebem & sacerdotes*): "Constantly we read that the people [*plebs*] are spoken of under the figure of a vineyard, field, building, flock, or are called subjects, whilst those whom before we referred to as mediators between Christ and the people [*plebs*] are called vine-dressers, husbandmen, builders, shepherds, prelates and rulers." [85] As one would expect from a model bishop of the time, Fisher's favorite picture of the people (*plebs*) is that of "a flock over which the priests are placed as shepherds and rulers." After graphically describing evils of the shepherdless flock, he refers near the close of his treatise to the contemporary situation: "Men might be bold enough to deny the truth of this picture were it not that we see it daily enacted before our eyes. Where the priests feed the flock committed to them both by their word and by their example the people [*populus*] are preserved from many errors. But on the other hand when the priests are negligent in the performance of their duties the people [*populus*] fall headlong into the abyss of all evils." [86]

It was in fulfillment of his duty as shepherd that at Barnes's abjuration the following year Fisher adapted his sermon to the capacity of his audience. Consequently if any follower of Luther finds Fisher's reasons and arguments inconclusive, the preacher says: "I dyd shape them to be spoken vntyll a multitude of people / whiche were nat brought vp in the subtyll disputations of the schole." [87] As for Luther's reasons for his doctrine on faith, a whole day will be insufficient for explanation and refutation — "nor yet the people can attayne to the conceyuyng of it." [88] With respect to Luther's appeal to popular judgment, Fisher asks in *Christ's Body* a year later, what becomes of its normative and certitudinous value when Oecolampadius too has his popular adherents? [89] He sardonically tells the latter to trap with his quibbles, if he can, "the ignorant populace [*stolida plebecula*]." [90] By his manipulation of the tropes and expressions of the Fathers, Oecolampadius can more easily impose on "the minds of the populace [*vulgaribus ingeniis*]." [91] His corruption of the ancient authors leads to the eternal ruin of "the Christian people that foolishly trusts in you" ("Christianae plebis, quae stulte vobis credula est").[92] In fact, so great was popular credulity that Cochlaeus, who translated Fisher's prefaces into German and who found that no one to date had undertaken to answer Fisher's work against Oecolampadius, complained: "So great is the perversity and the stubborn adherence of the crazed folk [*dementata plebs*] that they deign neither to hear nor read anything to the contrary lest they seem to entertain any hesitation or doubt in regard to an opinion once conceived." [93]

When does a person, whether lay or clerical, such a one as adheres to the doctrines of Luther or Oecolampadius, cease to be a member of the Church? The most obvious means, namely, excommunication, in regard to both use and abuse, had been subjected to increasing attention and criticism. The first extant record of Fisher's encounter with the problem occurs in the case of Richard Gavell of Westerham. On December 5, 1507, the latter abjured various opinions, one of which was the following: "That the corse or sentence of the churche is of none effect, nor nothyng to be regarded or to be sett by. Ffor the corse of the churche is not to be sett by or dred, but only the corse of God, which the prestes have not in their poor. . ." [94] Fisher in his sermon on Vulg. Ps. 31, on the contrary, ranks with temporal death "the grete curse," i.e., major excommunication, among "the grete punysshements of this lyfe." He emphasizes not its vindictive but its corrective medicinal aspect: "It is better for a synner to suffre trybulacyon & punysshement in this lyfe wherby he maye gete profyte & be rewarded than to be eternally tourmented in hell, for all the punysshement there be it neuer so sharpe and greuous shall not profyte." [95]

His horror of excommunication is even more evident in the case of the anonymous defacer of the papal condemnation of Luther's doctrine, posted at the University of Cambridge, presumably in 1521. Fisher threatened the culprit, unless he repented and confessed, with the ecclesiastical remedy used "against those kind of malefactors, who lyke rotten members are by the censure of excommunication cut of from the body of the Church, and so deprived of all such grace and benefitts, as obedient and trew members to their great comfort doe inioy. . . For the malefactor so cut of, be he never so odde or secret in his naughtines for a time, yet can he not be hidden from God, who will not faile to lay his hand upon him, when it shall be too late for him to repent." When the malefactor failed to act by the appointed hour and when Fisher began to read the sentence, its gravity "so much pearced his hart, that even before them all he could not refraine weepinge." He had to postpone the censure until another day when "he pronounced this tirrible sentence from the beginning to the ending . . . but not without weeping and lamenting, which strooke . . . a feare into the hartes of his hearers." [96]

On such occasions, the conduct of Fisher, a man of principle, springs from and corresponds to his theory or theology. The latter is found formulated in his criticism of Luther's doctrines as stated in Leo X's bull of condemnation: "Excommunications are only external penalties, and do not deprive a man of the common spiritual prayers of the Church" (art. 23);[97] and: "Christians should be taught rather to love than to fear excommunication" (art. 24).[98] In order not to obfuscate the issues, Fisher dwells on the case of the incestuous Corinthian (1 Cor. 5:1–5), that is, of someone who is excommunicated justly. By his serious sin, he has lost charity and to that extent he is spiritually dead. "But through faith he is still a member of the Church and united with the Mystical Body . . . just as a lifeless limb is still joined to the body by sinews and skin and is somewhat warmed by the body's heat." Being helped by the prayers and other spiritual benefits of the whole Church, he has not yet come under Satan's complete domination. "But after he has been struck by the sword of anathema, he is cut off from the common benefits of the Church not otherwise than an arm, if amputated from the body, receives absolutely no warm nourishment from it." [99] Temporal death was the penalty in the Old Law, "so now also in the Church, those struck by the spiritual sword incur eternal death unless they at once recover from their obstinacy." [100] To a man, such Fathers as Gregory, Augustine, Ambrose, and Chrysostom, teach that excommunication is very much to be feared, especially the eternal torments of hell. "For if anyone happens to die in this state [of excommunication], he dies outside the Church, outside which there is no salvation." [101]

The justly excommunicated person has already lost charity through his serious sin and obstinacy in evil. The unjustly excommunicated Christian suffers no spiritual harm. Fisher agrees with Luther: "There are certain spiritual goods of which excommunication can deprive no one, namely, faith, hope, and charity." [102] The same is true of other spiritual benefits as he later concedes to Oecolampadius. If through no fault of his own a Christian is excommunicated by a perverse or invincibly ignorant judge, and if, excommunication permitting, he would want to be present at mass and give thanks to God with great affection of heart, Fisher entertains no doubt that he shares in the sacrifice then being offered in church.[103]

So much for excommunicated persons, but what about heretics who have not been excommunicated? Are they members of the Church? If so, to what extent? Fisher seems not to draw sharp distinctions on these points. Heretics who are so in secret or heretics who in spite of some external acts hold to the creed, obedience to their legitimate pastors, and participation in the liturgy of the Church would appear to continue their membership until subjection to the censure of excommunication. As for public heretics, who deny Catholic dogmas and resist the ruling and teaching authority of bishops, council, or pope, and who belong to a denomination with its own doctrine, worship, and government, such would no longer be members of the Mystical Body. This statement applies both to formal heretics, who deliberately and pertinaciously persist in their errors, and to material heretics, who belong to the sect through birth, invincible ignorance, and so on. But all heretics, as well as all schismatics, retain their obligations and duties toward the Church, especially that of returning to the fold. It is never too late. No man alive is so much subject to Satan's power as to be incapable of striving for good: "The bosom of the Church our common mother is closed to none, no matter how crime-laden, provided that they desire to return and to do appropriate penance." [104]

What constitutes a heretic? Fisher maintains that whoever opposes a truth (even the sainthood of Thomas Aquinas, for example) long believed by common consent of the Church in agreement with the pope cannot avoid the stigma of heretic, provided he acts from obstinacy (*ex pertinacia*) and with insolence (*contumaciter*).[105] For the Bishop of Rochester there are three classes of believers: "one of them that be in the way / an other of them that be nigh vnto the way / thyrde is of them that be farre out of the way." The first is the Christian who believes in God, Christ, and the Church. The third is the Turk who believes only in God, not in Christ and the Church. As for the second, the "hereticke beleueth in god and in Christe . . . but yet his faith is nat sufficient: for he doth nat assent vnto the doctryne of the churche: whiche is inspired by the holy goste." He cannot be saved "if he be nat ioyned with this multitude of christen people . . . if he hath nat gyuen his ful assent vnto the doctryne of the churche catholicke." [106] Can the heretic be compelled to return to the right way and to admit the true doctrine? Insofar as the use of violence for a person's own good results in no harm, insofar as it is beneficial to show the truth to the ignorant and the right way to the erring, compulsion is permissible and necessary. The spiritual basis, Fisher tells Luther who has espoused the freedom of belief in purgatory, is Christ's own counsel: "Go out into the highways and hedges, and make them come in" (Luke 14:23).[107]

The duty of keeping the faithful in the right way and of resisting the heretics who are in the wrong way falls upon the bishops, who, alas, are negligent and remiss. Fisher returns to this point in almost all his controversial works. In his *Confutation of Lefèvre's Second Disquisition,* he reminds Cardinal Campeggio that "the senators of the whole Christian commonwealth" are obliged to counteract perverse opinions as early as possible lest they grow stronger by delay or produce even worse harms later, incapable of extirpation.[108] The prologue to the *Defense of the Royal Assertion* declares that if those whose business it was to "catch us the little foxes that destroy the vines" (Cant. 2:15) caught heretics in their early stages, Luther would not now be a large and wily fox, impossible to restrain.[109] The reader of the sermon delivered at Barnes's abjuration hears Fisher say that, insofar as he has been consecrated a minister unto "the christen people / whiche be the spouse of Christe": "My duty is to endeuer me after my poure power / to resist these heretickes." Because of the prophecies of Christ and the Apostles, no one need wonder that "in this miserable tyme / these heretickes multiply / and theyr heresies do sprede." The diagnosis and remedy are to hand: "Nowe therfore whan so litell diligence is done about the ministrying of this true doctryne / it is necessary that all tho that haue charge of the flocke of Christe / endeuour them selfe to gaynestande these pernitious heresies." Fisher is willing to have any disciple of Luther come to him in secret for discussion — "and I trust in our lorde . . . that either he shal make me a Lutheran / or els I shal enduce hym to be a catholyke." [110] Finally, in *Christ's Body* Fisher declares that it is up to ecclesiastical superiors, to whom the care of souls has been committed, either to destroy the wolves or with a foolish pity to allow them the cruel slaughter of their sheep.[111]

In this last work, the author comments that "we are indeed by nature all wonderfully inclined to evil" but that never more than at present has the whole world been more disposed to hear and accept heresies.[112] Yet the history of the Church of Christ, according to his sermon against Luther, reveals that after a period of tranquil faith "hathe rysen many a tyme some black clowde of heresy. & stered suche a tempest & made suche a lyghtnynge and so terribly thonderyd that many a weyke soule hath myscaryed therby." [113] His list of major heretics is interesting: Arius, Macedonius, Nestorius, Eutyches, Helvidius, Donatus, Jovinianus, Pelagius,

John Wyclif, and now Luther. Six years later, a much longer list in *Christ's Body* omits Helvidius, Jovinianus, and Pelagius; but it adds others, many of whom were favorites of the people: Cerinthus, Marcion, Ebion, Montanus (with Priscilla and Maximilla), Florinus, Valentinus, Berillus, Novatus, Manes, Sabellius, Dioscorus, Apollinaris, Paul of Samosata, the Albigensians, the Waldensians, and the Beghards.[114] Against their errors the Church has always been guarded by Christ her Spouse. The most prominent defenders of the faith in the ten years since Luther's initial attack, too, are enumerated in *Christ's Body*. Among Luther's own countrymen are Erasmus, who stands at the head of the list, John Cochlaeus, John Eck, Jerome Emser, John Faber, Gasper Schatzgeyer, and John Dietenberger. In France there are Josse Clichtove and Stephen (Christopher?) Longolius. In Flanders there is James Latomus, and in Italy Ambrosius Catharinus. Among the English, Henry VIII merits first place. His example has been followed by Sir Thomas More, John (i.e., Edward) Powell, and William Melton (Chancellor of York, Fisher's former teacher at Cambridge), whose work, like that of many others, has not been printed.[115]

The heretical and excommunicated Luther and his open followers, attacked by these defenders of the faith, clearly stand outside the pale of the Church. But what must be said about the more complicated problem of the Greek Church? Fisher's first plain statement occurs in his *Destruction of Clichtove's Bulwark* where, in interpreting a passage of a letter from Jerome to Damasus, he declares that heresies have corrupted the Eastern Church but that the legacy of the Fathers is preserved incorrupt in the Western Church. Hence the appeal of his adversaries to the Eastern tradition of more than one Magdalene is suspect and vain.[116] In his *Confutation of Luther's Assertion* he specifies the doctrine on the procession of the Holy Spirit as one of the many errors of the Greeks.[117] Yet, insofar as the latter have always been opposed to the Roman Church, the testimony of their Doctors on Peter's primacy, carries much more weight.[118] What guilt is therefore involved in the separation of the Greek Church? For this Church, as for the Churches of India, Persia, Egypt, Africa, and even Bohemia, Fisher gives one answer. Their withdrawal is due either to malice or, as he would rather believe of some members, to non-culpable ignorance. Simple folk in particular have been led astray by scriptural interpreters just like Luther, or they have never heard the matter discussed. Since they implicitly believe all Christ's teachings, they would gladly believe also this truth of papal primacy, if instructed properly. As for those who have withdrawn maliciously, they belong no more to the church of the orthodox than do the churches of the Arians, Donatists, and others.[119] Later, Fisher again concedes that not all deniers of the primacy of the Roman Pontiff are sinners and heretics provided that they have no ill will and pertinacious opinion, but he refuses to excuse the Greeks and the Bohemians on the score of simplicity, inadvertence, or nonexaction of this obedience by the pope.[120] The cleavage between the Greek Church and the Roman has finally ended, in accordance with St. Bridget's prophecy, in divine vengeance with the fall of Constantinople.[121] But elsewhere Fisher draws another moral from this calamity: "Often we are conquered by our own negligence and slothfulness; for thus was even Constantinople . . . captured by Mohammed, while all other Christians would bring no help to the city." [122]

The schismatic, the heretic, and the excommunicate have cut themselves off from "the christen people / whiche be the spouse of Christe." [123] It is noteworthy that in the latter clause there is no suggestion of a distinction between people and priest, laity and clergy. The simple reason is that the Church is *one.* It is one in spite of its organization into taught and teacher, into sanctified and sanctifier, into ruled and ruler, for which Fisher's favorite and persistent metaphor is that of sheep and shepherd. His conception of the Church as hierarchical, that is, as a society in which the rulers receive authority immediately from God and not mediately through the people, is so evident and insistent as hardly to need statement.

Chapter IV

AUTHORITY IN THE CHURCH

IN Fisher's first stage, Christ Himself, having chosen twelve Apostles, promised and conferred upon them the power of teaching, sanctifying, and ruling the faithful. For the bishop, "Christ appointed these twelve pastors to watch over His flock, . . . not only to teach, but to rule and, if necessary, to correct it." [1] He makes much also of the choice and mission of the seventy-two disciples to whom "was given authority to teach, together with some responsibility for the flock, although not equal with the twelve apostles." Hence the "distinction of ranks" in the Church was, he insists, "ordained by Christ." [2]

The duty of the Apostles, under the guidance of the Holy Spirit, was to perpetuate the distinction. Hence, in the second stage, that of the Apostolic Age, Fisher sees (a) the Acts as manifesting the primitive churches, especially Jerusalem, as hierarchical, and (b) the epistles as showing the Apostles correcting, teaching, judging, legislating, and sharing their authority with others: deacons, priests, and bishops. Yet the Church as a whole remains marked by unity — like a temple with the Apostles and Prophets as its foundation, and like a body with many members but one Spirit, one God, one faith, as well as one baptism, with a hierarchy of members and ministers. Christ had promised to be with His Apostles in these relations with His faithful even to the end of the world (Matt. 28:20).[3] Since the Apostles now are dead and since the faithful still need to be instructed, guided, and made holy, Christ must have willed the Apostles to have successors in their office. Hence Fisher declares: "Now we cannot think that Christ wished this variety of orders to be a purely temporary measure, but rather that He wished it to last so long as the Church

Militant should endure on earth." [4] Even in the Apostolic Age, therefore, Fisher finds the Apostles selecting and consecrating prelates with full power over the churches in Jerusalem, Crete, Ephesus, and other cities of Asia Minor. As a result, who would be so insolent, he asks, as to maintain that "this distinction of rank was not instituted by Christ, but introduced later by the apostles"? [5]

For the next stage, that of the second and third centuries, Fisher stresses the declarations of Clement of Rome, Ignatius of Antioch, and Polycarp of Smyrna as links with the Apostolic Age: "either contemporaries of the apostles or so very close to their times that they merit the name of apostolic." [6] He then seeks his proof also in Irenaeus, Tertullian, and Origen.[7] Finally, for good measure, he steps into the fourth and later centuries. Quotations are given from the Latins (Augustine, Jerome, Hilary, and Cyprian) and from the Greeks (John Damascene, Gennadius, Chrysostom, Gregory Nazianzen, Basil, and Eusebius).[8] He says nothing of "more recent writers" for a simple reason: "No one denies that they all attest a priesthood." [9]

The Bishop of Rochester, however, does not follow the chronological sequence just outlined. For the sake of effectiveness, he reverses the historical order and adopts the method of the controversialist whose mind and candor seem so congenial to his own, to wit, Tertullian. Not only did the latter always uphold against heretics "the prescriptive right of long-accepted truth," but he also wrote *On Prescription,* "in which he adduces numerous reasons to prove . . . that Catholic truth enjoys a prescriptive right." This argument from prescription, Fisher feels, is peculiarly applicable to the defense of a special priesthood.[10] Beginning with the Latin Augustine and the Greek John Damascene, he calls the early writers to witness until he ends with Clement of Rome. Before taking up the scriptural proof proper, he cites the six special dangers, already listed above, as his First Axiom: "It is reasonable, in matters concerning the salvation of souls, that some men be set apart to act in the name of, and bear responsibility for, the whole multitude." [11] The succeeding nine Axioms continue and clinch the argument from Scripture. Finally, he takes up one by one the scriptural texts advanced by Luther in favor of a universal priesthood.

The last words of *The Defense of the Sacred Priesthood* declare that the orthodox doctrine on the sacrifice of the mass flows from that on the priesthood but now needs no special proof because of full treatment in Chapter 6 of his *Defense of the Royal Assertion*.[12] In the course of the treatment, Fisher could also have observed that he had upheld the power of pope and bishops to make new laws in Article 27 of his *Confutation of Luther's Assertion*.[13] In fact, when Alphonsus de Castro (1495–1558) in his dictionary of heresies lists the error of Johann Rucherat von Wesel and Martin Luther on the legislative power of the Apostles and their episcopal successors, he mentions this particular article of Fisher's.[14] The spread of this error by September 1532 is glimpsed also in a case brought before the Bishop of Rochester — that of Peter Durr of Gravesend. The latter, who abjured after maintaining, among other things, that "the pope and archbishops had no authority to make laws," was sentenced to carry the faggot in church and to leave the diocese at once.[15]

But in his acts and writings Fisher lays relatively little stress on this power of the individual bishop to rule the faithful and clergy — to pass regulations on matters of faith and worship, to act as judge in cases of violation, and to punish offenders with canonical censures. Instead, his usual emphasis is on the power — which is much more the duty — of the shepherd to feed his flock. This obligation consists not merely in the condemnation of error and the prohibition of noisome books but far more in preaching the Gospel of Christ. As a preacher he is not infallible, but the presumption must be that he is teaching the authentic doctrine until the contrary is proved. The second point emphasized by Fisher is the need for the good example of the clergy — for a life lived by them in accordance with the Gospel taught by them. Learning *and* virtue are indispensable.

Fisher has the intention, not of minimizing the ruling and sanctifying powers of the hierarchy, but rather of making it aware of its neglect of preaching the Word of God, its very grave responsibility. He evidently sees that the universal decline of the Church has been due to the low state of preaching. This in turn has been caused by oversight or ignorance of the Scriptures, the function of which is at once to preserve and to inspire the authenticity of the preaching.

Preaching by the English bishops in their own person, it has been claimed, was infrequent. According to Hughes, the practice was carried on only by Bishops Fisher, Fitzjames, and Longland. All three were theologians rather than the usual canonists[16] — or the king's servants. Three of More's associates on his "Utopian" embassy to Flanders in 1515, for example, later were created bishops: Tunstal, Sampson, and Knight. Hence the surprise at Henry VII's nomination of Fisher to the bishopric of Rochester in 1504, "for non other cause, but for the grete and singular virtue, that I know and se in hym, as well in conyng and natural wisdome." In this same letter to his mother, Lady Margaret, King Henry hoped that the royal appointment would encourage others to follow Fisher's example and would compensate for his past sins: "I have in my days promoted mony a man unavisedly, and I wolde now make some recompencon to promote some good and vertuose men." [17] In fact, Fisher did not scruple to announce at Henry's funeral, as one of the king's three deathbed promises, "that the promocyons of the chyrche that were of his dysposycyon sholde from hens forth be dysposed to able men suche as were vertuous & well lerned." [18] The anonymous biographer attributes Fisher's elevation to "the kinge of his owne meere motion, inspired by the holy Ghoste." [19] Fisher does the same in the statutes for St. John's with the plain words: "citra cuiusquam preces aut intercessionem aut obsequium aliquod," [20] and in the prefatory letter to *Christ's Body* with the more rhetorical phrases: "mero motu . . . citra quoduis aliud obsequium, citra cuiusquam preces." But this statement does not exclude every other influence. Fisher himself thanks Bishop Foxe of Winchester for having created Henry's high opinion by frequently impressing his merits on the king (*te toties inculcante*).[21] In the same place he explicitly excludes the intervention of the Lady Margaret. Once he was created bishop of England's smallest and poorest diocese, however, she endeavored to secure a richer bishopric for him. (Failing in this plan, near death she presented him with a large sum for his own use, which he devoted to founding four fellowships and two scholarships at St. John's.) [22] As he later told Richard Foxe, incumbent of England's richest bishopric, he had charge of fewer souls, and when he came to God's judgment seat to render an account, he would not wish his lot a farthing the richer.[23] Foxe himselfe had been transferred from Exeter to Bath and Wells to Durham to Winchester. Fisher's predecessor, Richard Fitzjames, had passed from Rochester to London. Such transfer was extraordinarily common. Decades later, when Bellarmine declared such transfer without necessity or utility to be against the canons and the examples of the saints, he cites among the latter, not only Gregory I and Malachy, but also "John of Rochester, bishop, cardinal, and martyr," who "never wished to desert his church, although of the tiniest." [24]

In his Cambridge address to Henry VII in 1506, after referring to everybody's incredulity at his episcopal nomination in spite of his youth, lack of courtly position, and want of benefices, Fisher says that it was done for the good of the students.[25] What he wanted in the foundation of his colleges, as Erasmus wrote Archbishop Fonseca in 1529, was men "well versed in true learning and in sober discussion, men who can preach the Word of God in a serious and evangelical spirit, commending it to the minds of learned men by well-nigh irresistible eloquence; men such as the Bishop himself has long made himself for the service of Christ's Church." [26] This was also the intention of the generous Lady Margaret, according to Fisher's declaration to Cambridge University in 1528: to have the graduates "spread Christ's Gospel throughout the confines of this whole Britain, not without fruit and that indeed as plentiful as possible." [27] To beget "theologians who would share the fruit of their studies with the people," the statutes of St. John's decreed that one fourth of the fellows should devote themselves to preaching to the people in English at least eight times a year anywhere in the kingdom.[28]

But even before he had been made bishop, Fisher as vice-chancellor had manifested his zeal for the preaching of the Gospel by procuring for Cambridge from Alexander VI the following privilege (1502): "That the Chancellor of the University and his successors shall have license to chuse every year xii Doctors, Masters, or Graduates, who shall be in Priests' Orders, to preach through the whole kingdom of England, Scotland, and Ireland, under the common seal of the University, without any other license from a Bishop." [29] In 1503 Fisher became the first official Lady Margaret Reader at Cambridge, who in a sense was to supply the solid scholarship necessary for the popular preachers. On October 30, 1504, the Lady Margaret endowed at Cambridge a perpetual public preacher, who was to be paid an annual ten pounds for delivering six sermons each year in specified churches in the dioceses of London, Ely, and Lincoln.[30]

There is a statement in Fisher's statutes which may be an oblique comment on the evil of episcopal nonresidence: "Since it is suitable for the head to be united and associated with the rest of the members . . . the aforesaid Master or Keeper . . . shall [not] be absent from the College . . . beyond the space of one month in each quarter, under pain of losing his Mastership." [31] Residence in his diocese was an ardent desire of the Bishop of Rochester, who, according to the Rastell Fragments, "[was in holi]nes, learnying and dylygence in his cure and in fulfylling his office of byshope such [that of many hundred yeares] England had not any byshop worthie to be compared vnto hyme." [32] At the synod of clergy called by Wolsey in 1519 or so, he complained: "When I have setled and fully bent my self to the care of my flocke committed unto me, to visit my diocesse, to governe my church and to answere the enemies of Christ straight waies, hath come a messenger for one cause or other sent from higher authoritie by whom I have benne called to other busines and so left of my former purpose. And thus by tossinge and goinge this way and that waie, time hath passed and in the meane while nothinge donne but attending after tryumphes, receiving of ambassadors, haunting of princes courtes and such lyke." [33] The clergy preach "humilitie, sobrietie and contempt of the worlde," but their flock "may evidently perceive in them hawtines in minde, pride in gesture, sumptiousness in aparell and damnable excesse in all worldly delicates." People see the misuse of "the tythes and other oblacions geven by the devotion of them and their auncestors to a good purpose." [34] As for Fisher's own revenues, "one part was bestowed upon reparacion and maintaynance of the church, the second upon the releef of poveritie and mayntaynance of schollers and the third upon his howsehold expenses and buyinge of bookes, wherof he had great plentie." [35] His biographer sums up the account of the bishop's household: "His famelie was governed with such temperance, devocion and learninge, that his pallace for continencie seemed a verie monasterie, and for learninge an universitie." [36]

After nearly four years of experience as a bishop, Fisher published his views on the episcopal office — but passingly and indirectly — in his sermons on the Penitential Psalms. In that on Psalm 37, for example, he declares: "Thoffyce of correcyon longeth fyrst vnto prelates and vnto suche as hath cure of soule, . . . but . . . they spare to saye the trouth." *Either* "bysshoppes be absent from theyr dyoceses," *or* "All we vse bypathes & circumlocucyons in rebukynge them." As a result, erring souls "must nedes come into the deuylles power." [37] In the sermon on Psalm 50, his revelation is much more personal: "To take the offyce of a doctour or techer of goddes lawes is no small charge, it is a grete Ieopardy, wherin I myselfe remembrynge the same am ofte aferde, for many tymes I thynke on saynt Poules sayenge . . . If I teche not the lawes of god vnto the people I shall be dampned." [38] In another context, in the discourse on Psalm 101, he extols the power of the spoken word by quoting St. Jerome: "The effecte of the worde spoken by a mannes owne mouth hath a meruaylous preuy and hyd effycacy or strength, so meruaylous that I can not tell what it sholde be called." [39]

In the same sermon, his reflections on the contemporary clergy constitute perhaps the most eloquent and colorful passages in all his works. He enunciates, for example, the following principle: "All fere of god, also the contempte of god cometh and is grounded of the clergy, for yf the clergy be well and ryghtfully ordred gyuynge good example to other of vertuous lyuynge, without doubte the people by that shall haue more fere of almyghty god." After developing this point, he finds that the Church's "glory & worshyp standeth not in sylke copes of dyuers colours craftely broudred, neyther in plate of golde or syluer, nor in ony other werke or ornament be it neuer so rychely garnysshed with precyous stones. . . The thynge that was sygnefyed in the olde lawe by golde is clennes of conscyence. And by precyous stones vertues of the soule. As saynt Poule wytnesseth sayenge . . . Our Ioye is the testimony of a clene conscyence, whiche Ioye without fayle shone more bryght in the poore apostles than doth now our clothes of sylke & golden cuppes."

Having compared the suffering and laboring Paul with contemporary bishops and archbishops in their rich apparel, he laments: "In that tyme were no chalyses of golde, but than was many golden prestes, now be many chalyses of golde, & almoost no golden prestes." Attila, Totila, and Theodosius feared Leo, Benedict, and Ambrose respectively, not because they wore gold, jewels, and dazzling garments, but "truly bycause they herd theyr doctryne, & sawe theyr lyues so good & honest." His petition therefore is the following: "O blyssed lord how gloryous & beautefull sholde thy chirche be yf it were garnysshed & made fayre with suche vertuous creatures, for than sholde al people fere thyn holy name, & all kynges & prynces shold drede thyn excellent glory." After reciting miracles, scriptural and apocryphal, performed by the poor Apostles Peter, Paul, John, and Bartholomew, he explains: "Our blyssed lorde gaue no hede to the goodly apparayle of theyr bodyes, for they had none suche, but he regarded onely the clenlynes & fayrenesse of the soule, that is to saye he dyde beholde theyr stedfaste & grounded fayth, both hope & charite was in them, they were shynynge in fayth, stedfast in hope, & brennynge in charyte, who soeuer had so grete fayth, all thynges sholde be possyble for hym to do." Himself full of faith, the preacher ends this particular section: "Augment and encrease the fayth of thy chirche, wherby it may be gracyously herde of the, and werke meruayles, to thentent that all people sholde fere thy blyssed and holy name, and kynges of the erth drede thy glory." [40]

The note of buoyant hope, characteristic of these sermons on the Psalms, largely disappears from his treatise on prayer, written perhaps a little more than a decade later. In the preface of 1560, the English translator remarks how this "Bishop of great learning and marueilous vertue of lyfe . . . weepeth vppon the euyll examples of Byshoppes, Priestes, and Cleargie, who shoulde moue other by the perfection of theyr life." [41] The passage in question finds "almoste none other thynge nowe lefte in the Churche of Christ, but eyther manyfest iniquitie, or counterfeit holynes," and then continues: "For now amongest the ministers of the same Churche, the great lyght of theyr example, in vertuous, and holy liuing, is almoste vtterly extinct, who were wont, and in deede ought styll, lyke lyghtes to the worlde, to shine in vertue and godlynes. . . And now there commeth no light from them, but rather an horrible mistie cloude or darke ignoraunce, and a pestilent infection therein, with the which innumerable being deadly infected, are dayly drawen to their destruction." [42]

After the treatise on prayer, Fisher understandably does not play up the corruption of the clergy. In his controversies with the Protestants, his whole effort instead is to defend them, and indeed not on the level of actual conditions but rather on that of doctrine and theory. Resistance to the Lutheran heresies is evidently part of his episcopal duty unto "the christen people / whiche be the spouse of Christe. Unto whom (though unworthy) I am ordeyned a minister for my lytell porcion." [43] An interesting epilogue to this whole matter is found in Fisher's response to the king's book, *Censurae* (1530), in favor of the divorce. When the book advances the resistance of St. Dunstan of Canterbury and Bishop Grosseteste of Lincoln (among others) to the papal command to admit certain individuals into communion again, Fisher points out that their refusal was based not on violation of the Levitical prohibition of marriage to one's sister-in-law but on the scandalous life and impenitence of the offenders. Hence Dunstan behaved thus "for breaking of the law of God" (*propter offensam legis Christi*), and Grosseteste under the circumstances "was not bound to obey the command of the pope but to oppose it even to death." [44] It was to death that Fisher opposed Henry VIII on the matter of the divorce and the spiritual supremacy. He was not successful like Leo, Benedict, and Ambrose in the face of Attila, Totila, and Theodosius, but he was himself a greater miracle — a golden priest.

At least the Bishop of Rochester was a golden priest in the eyes of his Catholic contemporaries, Erasmus for example. Eleven years before his execution, Fisher received this message from Basel: "I know death not to be dreadful to persons living piously, but it is the whole Church's concern that such a bishop as you remain alive in such a dearth of good ones." [45] In 1529 Erasmus ranks Fisher with Alfonso de Fonseca of Toledo, Christoph von Stadion of Augsburg, and Conrad of Thuengen of Würzburg as bishops who by their piety, learning, and prudent rule presage happier days for the Church.[46] Finally, the "Expositio fidelis" (1535), after cataloguing Fisher's virtues, sums it all up in the phrase that he "behaved like a true bishop" (*verum agebat Episcopum*) — whose death was hastened by his appointment as a cardinal.[47]

Before taking up Fisher's cardinalate, it might be well to sketch his relationship to Erasmus on a topic important and dear to his episcopal heart — that of preaching. In early 1523, Erasmus told Christopher of Utenheim, Bishop of Basel, that, health permitting, he intended to proceed with *Ecclesiastes; or, The Art of Preaching,* promised to "the excellent prelate, John, Bishop of Rochester," who had long and often urged it upon him in view of their old friendship and devotion.[48] Writing to Fisher himself in September 1524, he explains that a dire illness and other events had interrupted his work but that he would resume it in the winter.[49] *Ecclesiastes* did not appear until 1535, after Fisher's death, but in the prefatory epistle to Christoph von Stadion he states his former silent intention of dedicating it to Fisher because of their old and close friendship. He reviews all of Fisher's achievements at Cambridge, particularly his zeal for the training and endowment of popular preachers who were to reform the people by scattering the seed of the Gospel teaching. "He himself," he reveals, "was gifted with a singular charm of utterance" (*singulari linguae gratia praeditus*).[50] According to a long laudatory passage on Archbishop Warham in the *Ecclesiastes* itself, Warham loved and venerated Fisher as if Fisher were the metropolitan and he the suffragan "because he [Fisher] showed himself a true bishop both in all the other offices worthy of a prelate and especially in zeal for teaching the people." [51]

This "true bishop" was named a cardinal by the new pope, Paul III, on May 20, 1535. According to Casale's dispatch to Cromwell, the pope "had not the bishop of Rochester more in mind than any one else, but when he heard in what estimation his books were held in Germany and Italy, and how Campeggio and others praised him, it seemed a good thing to make him a cardinal." [52] According to the early biographer, when Cromwell, hypothetically, asked Fisher his reaction to a papal offer of the cardinal's hat, he replied: "I knowe myself farr unworthie of any such dignitie, that I thinke of nothing lesse then such matters; but yf he do send yt me, assure yourself I will worke with it by all the meanes I can to benefit the Church of Christ; and in that respect I will receive yt upon my knees." [53] Perhaps more in accordance with Fisher's character and situation is his reply to one of the interrogatories on June 12, 1535, "that *yf the Cardinall's hatt were layed at his feete he wolde not stoupe to take it up, he did set so little by it.*" [54] Yet both reports may be true: the first being his official reply to enemies of the pope like Cromwell and Audley, the second his spontaneous personal revelation, heartsick and weary, to two servants, George Gold and Richard Wilson. At any rate, in his brief of July 26, 1535, to Francis I, the pope mourned "that most holy prelate, whom we for his learning and holiness had placed in the number of Cardinals." [55] In his treatise *Pro ecclesiasticae unitatis defensione,* presented to Henry VIII in late May or early June 1536, Reginald Pole reminds the king of his former boast about having in his realm Fisher, a bishop perfect and incomparable on all counts.[56] His later *Apology* to Charles V for this treatise repeats the story more pointedly and personally.[57]

But Henry VIII ordered justices of the peace to show and declare "unto the people, at your said sessions, the treasons traitorously committed against us and our laws by the late Bp. of Rochester and Sir Thomas More, Kt. . ." [58] In his sermon of June 27, 1535, Simon Matthew accuses the Bishop of Rome of causing the king's subjects "dampnably to disobeye the ordynaunce of god, as of late you haue had experience of some . . . I meane doctour Fysshare and syre Thomas More, whom I am as sory to name as any man here is to here them named: Sory, for that they being somtyme men of worshyppe and honour, men of famous lernynge, and many excellent gracis, & so tenderly sometyme beloued of their prince, shulde thus vnkyndely, vnnaturally, and traiterously vse them selfes. . ." [59]

Outside England the most vocal apologist for his friends was Cochlaeus. In an epistle addressed to Henry VIII and prefatory to the history of a similar case, he does not hesitate to accuse him of the murder of two martyrs of Christ who spoke out for truth and justice. In defending them against Sampson, he declares that they are to be congratulated rather than commiserated because of their fame on earth, their happiness in heaven, and other blessings.[60]

In his answer to Cochlaeus, Richard Morison charges this holy Fisher with inability to distinguish sanctity from hypocrisy in the Nun of Kent, with being a fierce enemy to Christ's Gospel, with extolling the pope against God, with spending his life in fighting, with greater zeal for his own fame than care for his flock, with choosing death to preserve his glory, and with other offenses.[61] Cochlaeus' reply, containing little that is new and giving its own account of Fisher's and More's unjust slaying, lays stress upon two causes: the royal divorce and the spiritual supremacy.[62]

The real cause for the execution of Fisher and More entered very conspicuously into the controversy over the oath of allegiance under James I. In his letter to the Archpriest Blackwell, reproduced in James I's *An Apologie for the Oath of Allegiance,* Cardinal Bellarmine reminded Blackwell that "these most holy and learned men . . . for this one most weighty head of doctrine [papal primacy], led the way to Martyrdome to many others. . ." "The Answere to the Cardinals Letter" pointed out that "in K. *Henry the eights* time, was the Oath of Supremacie first made: By him were *Thomas Moore* and *Roffensis* put to death, partly for refusing of it." In comment upon "that one most weightie head of doctrine," James I enumerated other causes: the succession, the Nun of Kent, and the new marriage. Thomas More "tooke the cause of his owne deathe, to be onely for his being refractary to the King in this said matter of Marriage and Succession; whiche is but a very fleshly cause of Martyrdome, as I conceiue"; and as for Fisher, "his imprisonment was neither onely, nor principally for the cause of Supremacie." Bellarmine in his pseudonymous *Responsio Torti* replied that he had said, not that "for this only cause of the primacy they had sought death," but that "for this one cause they led the way to Martyrdome to many others," for example, to the English Martyrs under Elizabeth who died for the primacy. James I himself had admitted previously that Fisher and More had died for papal supremacy. Moreover, by dying rather than approving the second marriage, they suffered death for the legitimate dispensing power held by the pope.[63] Suarez maintained that even if the divorce and the second marriage had been the only cause of their death, it would have been sufficient for martyrdom, as in the case of John the Baptist. In answer to Suarez, Marco Antonio de Dominis, Archbishop of Spalato, admitted denial of the royal supremacy as one cause of their death, but asserted that such an additional one as the new marriage was merely human and political — and as for the imitation of John the Baptist, they should have died not against the divorce but for the divorce because of the illicit union between Catherine and Henry.[64]

It is indeed ironic that John Fisher, this exemplary bishop and ardent defender of the papacy, should never see, in spite of all his plans, the pope and the city of Rome. At least three times he made preparations, and at least as many times he had to call off his visit. The first occasion was the summoning of the Fifth Council of the Lateran, to which he was appointed as one of the English delegates in February 1512.[65] Fisher immediately invited Erasmus to accompany him but too late for his friend to settle his affairs.[66] But the commission was recalled shortly, perhaps, as Erasmus suggests, because of papal postponement of the council to November.[67] At any rate, Fisher was not included in the new embassy, named on April 1, 1512. He received reappointment three years later because on March 10, 1515, he named the priors of the cathedral church in Rochester and of Ledes in the diocese of Canterbury as proctors in his absence.[68] Again the trip never eventuated. Finally, on his own initiative, he apparently prepared for a Roman journey in 1519, but "behold, when every thing was readie and the iorney about to begin, all was sodenly disapoynted." The reason, according to his biographer, was "a sinode of bishops then called by cardinall Woolsey." [69] Wolsey also frustrated a possible trip by doing nothing about Clement VII's request of June 20, 1524, that he send two or three suitable bishops, Tunstal and Fisher perhaps, for consultation about abuses in the Church.[70] Preparation for a general council was one of the reasons for Paul III's creating Fisher a cardinal in 1535,[71] but martyrdom put an end to all that.

What is significant is Fisher's views on the bishops' exercise of the power of teaching. Evidently for him, the bishops as a college, even though dispersed throughout the world, form with the Roman Pontiff a moral body which is infallible in setting forth Christ's doctrine. Otherwise all in vain would be Christ's promise of the lasting divine assistance (Matt. 28:18–20) and the conviction of the councils and Fathers about the truth of doctrines actually held by the scattered bishops. The supposition that the faithful cannot rely on the teaching of their pastors as a body is intolerable to Fisher. Lefèvre cannot plead that the doctrine of the single Magdalene has never been the object of a decree or judgment by the Church. The Church's judgment can be twofold: either express or tacit. One must obey not only the express but also the tacit judgment of the Church.[72] Yet in his works as a whole Fisher makes remarkably little use of this argument, nor does he enter much into its theological bearings. The latter statement, however, is hardly true of his opinion on the ecumenical council, that is, the lawful gathering of the pastors of the whole Church to judge on doctrinal matters or to legislate on disciplinary points. In general, of course, Fisher cannot but hold for the infallibility of the general council, for then, if ever, the Holy Spirit keeps the teaching Church, that is, the assembled pastors, safe from error in matters of faith and morals.[73]

Fisher's first really significant statement on councils occurs in his *Destruction of Clichtove's Bulwark* (1519): "For I do not deny that sometimes even in general councils themselves a certain delusion has been allowed, no doubt that they might so know themselves to be men, yet that error has never remained long in the Church but has been soon amended by another synod." If the Church changes its opinion, as it has done, says Fisher, on the Immaculate Conception, the Assumption, the veneration of images, and very many other points, it has done so always for the better under the guidance of the Holy Spirit — and all Christians must now believe in these teachings.[74]

A similar declaration, but now couched hypothetically, appears two years later in the English sermon against Luther. The Holy Spirit had always suppressed heresies, sometimes through the Fathers and Doctors, "somtyme by generall councelles and assembles of many bysshoppes togyder" — 309 at Nice, 150 at Constantinople, 300 at Ephesus.[75] Later, with reference to the Councils of Constance (1414–1418) and Basel–Florence (1431–1449), he declares: "And the councelles also thoughe some one of the last councelles whiche perauenture was not gadred in that mekenes & charyte that was expedient though one of them (whiche thyng I wyl not afferme) in some artycle were permysed to goo amysse. Shold we therfore damne al the resydue? It were no reason." [76]

Fisher's more formal treatment of councils, however, takes up Articles 28 and 29 of his *Confutation of Luther's Assertion,* which acquired a certain fame, as is evident from later references, e.g., by Castro and by Bellarmine.[77] Before taking up Luther's *Assertion* word by word, Fisher tries to establish ten Truths (*Veritates*), of which the eighth reads: "If the Spirit has spoken for the instruction of the Church through the mouths of the individual Fathers, much more must He be presumed to have done so in the general councils of the Fathers." He concludes his disquisition by asking whether, granted the disagreement between recent councils, belief should be denied all the rest. Just as the prophets, Apostles, and holy doctors left to themselves sometimes erred, "so also the councils, especially recent ones which were summoned in time of schism, where perhaps there had not been the greatest harmony of souls nor sincere simplicity of minds," but rather factionalism, currying favor of the pope, etc. What wonder if on some minor point they had gone blind — "like those suffering something human" (*vtpote quiddam humanum passi*). Such an error can easily be detected by comparison of the conciliar decrees with the Scriptures and with patristic commentaries.[78]

Nevertheless, since disagreement is unavoidable, Fisher holds to the reasonableness of assembling bishops from all nations to decide disputed matters, e.g., communication of the laity under one species, which was settled at Constance.[79] Later he argues for the jurisdictional primacy of the Roman Pontiff from the formulas signed by the Greeks and the Armenians at the Council of Florence.[80] Still later in the *Confutation,* he brings up the proposition defended by his admired Scotus: "The Church cannot establish whatever it pleases to be true or not true" (Sent. IV, dist. 2, q. 3). Fisher remarks: "But even if the Sovereign Pontiff together with a council, that is, the Church Catholic, cannot make anything either true or false, and hence establish new articles of faith, nevertheless whatever these propose for our obligatory belief as an article of faith, all persons truly Christian ought to believe not otherwise than as an article of faith." [81] Here he calls to his side Scotus himself, who teaches that whenever the Church makes articles of faith more explicit than they are in the various creeds, they must be believed to be of the substance of the faith (*de substantia fidei*) after the Church's solemn declaration. The Church does not make something true but, taught by the Spirit of Truth, it chooses a certain understanding of a matter of faith as true and sets it forth explicitly. After further arguments in favor of this position, Fisher concludes: "If he refuse to hear even the Church, let him be to thee as the heathen and the publican (Matt. 18:17). But when are we to hear the Church more than when the council agrees with the pope and the pope with the council? For these (beyond all controversy) represent the Catholic Church." [82]

As he goes deeper into the subject, Fisher can hardly approve the handling of matters not pertaining to salvation by pope and council, but some authority must decide as to what is relevant and important, or otherwise, if opinions differ. Further on, he repeats that, according to the Scriptures, the Church cannot err on points *de substantia fidei,* but "there is no doubt that the pope with the council represents the universal Church." Of course, "it lies not in their power (as Scotus states) to make something this or that, but rather, instructed by the Spirit of Truth, they now pronounce to be of the substance of the faith that which already before was really of the substance of the faith." [83]

Fisher proceeds to describe the confusion in faith and doctrine which would follow the denial of the authority of general councils. He is far from denying the errancy of councils. He instances those assembled neither in the Holy Spirit nor by papal authority, such as those of the Donatists which boasted of many hundreds of bishops or that at Rimini with its numerous bishops, or that held at Constantinople by three hundred bishops against the veneration of images. Besides, there were councils assembled by papal authority but without the Holy Spirit, such as that of Stephen VI against his predecessor Formosus, marked by hatred rather than charity, and similar papal councils mentioned by Platina. The general councils of which he is speaking assembled at the call of the popes and gave them full assent in the Holy Spirit. "For I always view as suspect those where the pope differs from the council or where the council differs from the pope, unless the latter has happened through the very palpable fault of the pope." [84]

This suspicion of the Bishop of Rochester was destined to be singled out later. In his *Supplication* (1534) made to Henry VIII, for example, Robert Barnes comments: "Who did euer heare such a rule of a Christean man? yea and of a bishop? yea and of a doctor of Diuinitie, where hath hee learned this Diuinitie? to recken a counsell to bee trew, because the Pope and so many men doe agree in one, yea and that such men as haue so often tymes erred in their counsels, as hee doth declare hym self rekening the counsell of Constantinople thet had .300. Byshops and yet did erre, and hee knew no other cause, but beecause the Pope did not agree to them. Is not this a resonable cause? can not the Pope erre? let hym read his own [canon] lawe . . . and there shall hee fynde that the Pope hath erred. Wherefore then should the matter stande in his iudgment? Now how will hee by thys rule saue the counsels of constance, and of Basell where in both counsels, the Popes were condemned for heretykes? As the same counsels make mencion, also that the councels have erred, that graunted hee hymselfe, but peraduenture hee will saye, that they were not full Councels." [85]

In his next work, *The Defense of the Royal Assertion,* Fisher adds little to his doctrine on the general council. The Spirit of Christ, who promised not to desert His Church, must be present here as it was in the first council in Jerusalem which set a pattern for the future.[86] Subsequently he makes the more startling statement that "it is permissible for any general council to change something of Christ's institutions for urgent reasons, just as it was permissible also for the very first heads of the Church, who changed the form of baptism, far otherwise than Christ had instituted it." [87] His sermon at Barnes's abjuration merely has a reference to the condemnation of heretical errors by "many generall counsayles / had in the churche. At the whiche counsayles were present great noumbre of honorable fathers assembled to gether by the holy gost / men of singular lernying and excellent holynes / the whiche was confirmed by many great miracles." [88]

In his books on the divorce, however, Fisher must deal at greater length with the nature and activity of councils. The most germane statement occurs in "Licitum fuisse matrimonium." Even if he concedes a point (which in fact he tenaciously denies), namely, that the Levitical prohibitions are moral and still in vigor today, nevertheless nothing forbids a general council, if it thinks it for the best of Christendom, to constitute anew and restore the Deuteronomical command that a man must marry his dead brother's childless widow, since the latter marriage was never forbidden by the law of God.[89] Later his opponents on the divorce cite the decrees of Toledo II, Agde (*anc.* Agatha), Neocaesarea, Gregory the Younger, and Constance. Fisher's answers for the councils other than Constance may be summed up as follows. They were particular, not general councils, one at least with only a handful of bishops. They enacted decrees on matrimonial matters not of divine or natural law, without denying their dispensability. They also passed decrees on other points which are now dispensed with or abrogated. As for Constance, Fisher cannot find in its conciliar acts the proposition of Wyclif which they say was condemned, namely, "that all the precepts of the 18 of Levitt. were judicial only." Besides, this council had no intention of condemning Scotus and his whole school for maintaining that "among the Christians there is no degree of affinity by the law of God that stoppeth or letteth marriage." [90] Hence whatever impediments are established by the Church, whether by individual or assembled bishops, whether in particular or general councils, can be dispensed from — and by no one more than by the pope. And this last phrase brings us to Fisher's views on the status of the pope in the Church of Christ.

It has been observed more than once that, in unavoidable cases of disagreement among Christians, three positions on the power of final decision are possible: dependence on the Scriptures exclusively, appeal to the tradition, and reliance on the episcopacy. The first, according to Fisher, was that of all heretics, presently of the Protestants; the second, that of the Greek Orthodox with their emphasis on the first ecumenical councils; the third, that of Roman Catholicism, with its later culmination in the formal definition of papal infallibility and the proposed definition of collegial infallibility of the bishops, whether in separate dioceses or in general councils. This very last point is especially pertinent in the labors and lives — and deaths, too — of John Fisher and Thomas More.

On More's own admission of March 5, 1534, "I was my selfe some tyme not of the mynd that the prymatie of that [Roman] see shold be bygone by thinstitution of God, vntill that I redd in that mater those thingis that the Kyngis Highnes had written in his moost famouse booke agaynst the heresyes of Marten Luther." [91] Fisher gives absolutely no hint of such a change of opinion in any work of his. Contemporaries might have been quite aware of the difference between the bishop and the layman. Richard Morison, a partisan of Henry VIII, for example, writes in 1537: "It is quite possible that the Bishop of Rochester who had spent by far the greatest part of his life in the study of those authors whose sole object was to establish the authority of the Roman Pontiff, it is quite possible, I say, that *he* may have believed the Pope to be the Vicar of Christ. But there are many reasons why I cannot persuade myself that More always entertained this opinion." [92] Nevertheless, both More and Fisher rose to the defense of Henry VIII's declaration on this doctrine — and ironically both were to die for this doctrine a dozen years later. It might be significant, however, that in 1523 More is content with Fisher's treatment without undertaking his own — although on other occasions he never hesitates to set forth his own views in spite of full and adequate treatment by other writers. He states: "As regards the Primacy of the Roman Pontiff, the same Bishop of Rochester has made the matter so clear from the Gospels, the Acts of the Apostles, and from the whole of the Old Testament, and from the consent of all the holy fathers, not of the Latins only, but of the Greeks also (of whose opposition Luther is wont to boast), and from the definition of a General Council, in which the Armenians and Greeks, who at that time had been most obstinately resisting, were overcome, and acknowledged themselves overcome, that it would be utterly superfluous for me to write again on the subject." [93]

The adequacy and the importance of Fisher's doctrine on the papal primacy were recognized not only by Thomas More but by later authorities so that Fisher's name always appears in the bibliography, as it were, on the subject. Castro, for example, praises Fisher's excellent handling of the matter in Article 25 of his *Confutation of Luther's Assertion* as on a par with the work of John Eck, John Faber, and James Latomus.[94] The redoubtable Bellarmine lists Fisher and his Article 25 in giving the names and works of the six outstanding Englishmen from Thomas Netter (*Waldensis*) to Thomas Stapleton who defended papal authority. Later, his chapter on the Roman primacy which is devoted particularly to the refutation of Calvin ends as follows: "Luther's arguments are altogether trivial and can be refuted by anybody quite easily from what has been said; and besides they have been carefully refuted by Eck, Faber, Rochester, and Cajetan, whose books are well known to all, and therefore I pass them over." [95]

To turn now to Fisher's own writings. The need for a head seems to be ingrained in Fisher's personality and mind. The statutes both for Christ's (1505) and for St. John's (1516, 1524, 1530) open the chapter on the Master or Keeper by announcing that "it is proper to begin with the head, by which it is fitting that the other members should be ruled and controlled." [96] Yet Fisher is only too aware of the abuses arising from indiscriminate bestowal of dispensations. Consequently the Master must give a bond for £200, and the Fellows for £100 each, to be forfeited "if the aboue bounden N. in his owne parson or by any other parsons obteyne or impetrate, or cause to be pursued, obteyned or impetrate, priuely or opynly, directly or indirectly, from the pope, the courte of Rome, or from any other parson or place eny dispensacion or license" that is contrary to the statutes.[97]

As for controversy, the argument from papal authority is used by Fisher first against Clichtove. He declares that in important matters, especially in those relating to Scripture, "the authority of the Sovereign Pontiff is great, but it is still greater if the custom of the Roman see is added to it, and it is greatest if the consent of the whole Church accrues to it." To prove his point, he stresses and magnifies the letter to Damasus written by Jerome, who defers to the pope's judgment even though he himself is an incomparable biblical scholar. Hence there can be but a single Magdalene.[98]

Fisher's next pronouncement occurs in his popular sermon against Luther, which is important especially because it was taken up later by English Reformers. Here, as the second of four "Instructions," he proves at great length that "the pope iure diuino is the heed of the vnyuersall chyrche of christ." In the recapitulation of his three proofs, he says: "Consyder now how eche of these testymonyes conferme & strengthe one another. Fyrste the fygure & shadow of the olde lawe [according to which Moses and Aaron represent Christ and Peter]. Secondly the testymony of the gospels answerynge vnto the same [for, according to Matthew 17:23–26, only Christ and Peter paid the didrachma because they were the heads of the household]. Thirdly the declaracyon of saynt Austyn vpon the same [for Augustine in *Quaest.* 75 confirms this interpretation of the didrachma]." At this point Fisher produces also the testimony of other Fathers: Ambrose, Gregory, and Cyprian among the Latins and Chrysostom and Origen among the Greeks.[99]

In his *Obedience of a Christian Man* (1528), Tyndale refers to

Fisher's "fygure & shadow of the olde lawe." He blames pope and bishops for wishing to lord it over others and then continues: "Such philosophy, and so to abuse the scriptures, and to mock with God's word, is after the manner of the bishop of Rochester's divinity. . . Moses, saith he, signifieth Christ, and Aaron the pope. And yet the epistle unto the Hebrews, proveth, that the high priest of the old law signifieth Christ. . . Nevertheless, Rochester proveth the contrary by a shadow; by a shadow, verily: for in shadows they walk without all shame. . ." [100] Later, Tyndale distinguishes Aaron as he was before and after reception of the high priesthood. Before, Aaron "represented not Peter only or his successor, as my lord of Rochester would have it . . . but signifieth every disciple of Christ, and every true preacher of God's word." After, he "representeth Christ, which purgeth us from all sin in the sight of God." [101]

Just as Tyndale picks up Fisher's "fygure & shadow of the olde lawe" in Moses and Aaron, so also he criticizes his "testimony of the gospels" from Matt. 17:23–26. "Mark here," he writes, "how past all shame our school-doctors are, (as Rochester is in his sermon against Martin Luther,) which of this text of Matthew dispute that Peter, because he paid tribute, is greater than the other apostles . . . and was head unto them all: contrary unto so many clear texts, where Christ rebuketh them, saying, That it is a heathenish thing that one should . . . desire to be greater. To be great in the kingdom of heaven is to be a servant. . ." [102] Later, Bishop Gardiner and Bishop Jewel refer to Fisher's use of the argument from the payment of the tribute.

The spirit of humility and submission is stressed also in Tyndale's rebuttal of the patristic argument used by the Bishop of Rochester, who "allegeth, for the pope's authority, St Cyprian, St Augustine, Ambrose, Jerome, and Origen; of which never one knew of any authority that one bishop should have above another. And St Gregory allegeth he, which would receive no such authority above his brethren, when it was proffered him." [103] In addition, he challenges Fisher to produce the interpretation of the rock and the keys (Matt. 16:18–19) by "Jerome, Augustine, Bede, Origen, and other doctors." As for John 21:15–17, "*Pasce, pasce, pasce,* which Rochester leaveth without any English, signifieth not poll, sheer, and shave." [104] Tyndale objects especially to the appeal to

Origen: "Consider also, how studiously Rochester allegeth Origen . . . which Origen of all heretics is condemned to be the greatest. 'He is an ancient doctor,' saith he; yea, 'and to whom in this point great faith is to be given.' Yea, verily, Aristotle and Plato, and even very Robin Hood, is to be believed in such a point, that so greatly maintaineth our holy father's authority. . ." [105]

After calling the Latin and Greek Fathers to his aid, Fisher voices Luther's possible objection "that he can not conceyue duos summos." Reverting to Moses and Aaron, he declares that Aaron "was summus sacerdos & Moyses was no whit benethe hym." Arguing from 1 Cor. 11:3, he says: "Se here be thre heedes vnto a woman. god, chryst, & hyr husbande. & yet besyde al these she hath an heed of hyr owne. . . How moche rather our mother holy churche which is the spouse of christ. hath an heed of her owne. that is to saye the pope. and yet neuerthelesse chryst Iesu hyr housbande is her heed. & almyghty god is hyr heed also." [106]

Another proposition of Fisher's that did not go unchallenged was his theory on the source of unity: "This chirche [of christ] is one hauynge one heed the pope. whiche is the vycare of christ. of whome it is called vna." [107] Tyndale, for example, questions the need for an immediate head other than Christ since the pope never visits or preaches to us. He continues: "How cometh it also that Rochester will not let us be called one congregation by the reason of one God, one Christ, one Spirit, one gospel, one faith, one hope, and one baptism, as well as because of one pope?" [108] In the sermon delivered in St. Paul's Cathedral five days after Fisher's execution, Simon Matthew discounted the same view: "For this feythe, were they made one in Christ, and of his churche. So that it was of no necessytie for them to knowe Peter, as many haue rekened in the byshoppe of Rome, that excepte we knewe hym and his holy college, we coulde not be of Christis churche." [109]

When Fisher in 1521 was exalting the pope in his sermon against Luther, he was perhaps still at work upon the papal defense in his *Confutation of Luther's Assertion*. Shortly afterward, Cuthbert Tunstal, between his nomination as bishop of London in January and his consecration in October 1522, handed him Ulrichus Velenus' book which discounted Peter's residence in Rome. Fisher recognized at once that if Velenus' arguments were true they would for the most part undermine what he had already written against Luther on the papal primacy, especially in Article 25 of his *Confutation.* He had had trouble in getting the manuscript printed on the continent because of the current war with France (begun officially at the end of May 1522),[110] but he was now glad of the delay because the readers of the *Confutation* might have been less receptive unless they had first seen his refutation of Velenus — which he had made as brief as possible.[111] His method is simple. In Part I, he first quotes each of Velenus' eighteen arguments (called *Persuasiones,* which Fisher christens *Calumniae*), then summarizes it in a few words, and lastly answers it. In Part II, he first quotes each of seven arguments for Peter's residence as stated by Velenus (who calls them *Cavilli*), then gives Velenus' reply (*Responsio*), and finally refutes Velenus' reply.

It is hardly necessary to examine in detail the way in which Fisher shows that Velenus' contention is in most evident conflict with all historians who have written up to that time, whether Greek or Latin, sacred or profane. In accordance with contemporary custom, he conveniently heads his work with a list of authors whose testimonies are cited. Most pertinent here are the Renaissance historians. In his very first *Persuasio,* Velenus himself points to the suspicious variation in dates for Peter's arrival and martyrdom in such works as the *Enneades* of Antonius Sabellicus (Marcantonio Coccio, 1436–1506) and the *History of the Popes* by Platina (Bartolomeo de Sacchi di Piadena, 1421–81). Fisher answers simply that, in spite of disagreement on the time, all agree on the fact — just as in regard to Christ's death.[112] After quoting the older authorities in the answer to *Persuasio* 18, Fisher feels no need to cite those "most scholarly men" — Platina, Sabellicus, Volaterranus, and Joannes Baptista — who have testified to the same fact in their writings. Joannes Baptista is perhaps Mantuan (J. B. Spagnolo or Spagnuoli, 1448–1516); Volaterranus is Raffaele Maffei (1451–1522). Fisher refers also to Volaterranus' bibliography of Greek and Latin historians of the popes — "and all of these unanimously assert that Peter was the first bishop of the city of Rome." [113] Two interesting historical sidelights are (1) Fisher's defense of the possibility of Christ's apparition to Peter in the "Quo vadis" story (as related in the "Passio Lini" and confirmed by Eusebius, Hegesippus, and Ambrose) [114] and (2) his rejection of the spurious Pauline-Senecan correspondence on the authority of Erasmus, whose single judgment in this matter is enough for him against a thousand other people.[115]

Toward the conclusion of his work Fisher points out that such former apostolic centers as Antioch, Jerusalem, Achaea, and Asia Minor, have all come into the hands of the infidel, and that the faith has survived indefectibly only at Rome. He is acutely aware, however, of the clash between ideal and practice. He writes:

> Perhaps someone will say, "Nowhere else is the life of Christians more contrary to Christ than in Rome, and that indeed among the very prelates of the Church, whose manner of living rather is diametrically at variance with the life of Christ. For Christ was the lover of poverty; they fly poverty so much that they are zealous for nothing more than the accumulation of riches. Christ spurned the glory of this world; there is nothing they do not suffer or do for the attainment of glory. Finally Christ afflicted Himself with frequent fasts and ceaseless prayers; they neither fast nor pray but are wholly given over to luxury and lusts. These same persons, moreover, are to all who lead a sincere and Christian life a very great scandal, namely, as men whose morals are so divorced from the teaching of Christ that through them Christ's name is blasphemed in the whole world." These things perhaps are an adversary's objections against our stand. But these very things confirm our argument. For since we behold the sees of all other Apostles now to be occupied everywhere by infidels and this see alone which was Peter's continue under Christian rule yet which has deserved destruction with all the others because of its unspeakable crimes and vices, what else can we think but that Christ is most true to His word, who in spite of being aroused by their many and great injuries still keeps His promises even to His fiercest enemies? The faith preached by Peter in Rome has not failed heretofore, and there still remains the true succession in the Church whose rise comes from Peter and whose rock and steadfast foundation, as it were, Christ made Peter.[116]

As one might expect, no conscientious critic could fail to challenge Fisher's last statement. Thus Simon Hessus in his *Apology* tells him: "You boast that the faith preached by Peter in Rome has not failed heretofore. Who does not join with you in this boast if it is as you preach?" Theirs can hardly be true faith whose life is much contrary to their belief: "One has no little fear that those persons do not believe in the immortality of human souls who grow so brutish with beastly passions and lusts." As for the argument on the survival of only Peter's see, Fisher is ridiculously confusing outer place with inner spirit against the testimony of Scripture: "The kingdom of God is within you" (Luke 17:21). Hessus then asks: "But what has this to do with the papacy . . . with the Romans . . . with the Liberiuses, Bonifaces, and Juliuses whom we know to be not very Christian in their lives?" The result of the Petrine claim has been "that sea of decretals" with its source in ambition and tyranny. To shake off the heavy yoke from mortal shoulders, it was necessary to deny Peter's primacy.[117]

Hessus ridicules as "empty . . . womanish . . . and foolish" Fisher's fear that the denial of Christ's passion could follow on that of Peter's residence in Rome: the former is based on the clearest testimonies and prophecies of Scripture, the latter on uncertain Scripture and on human opinions. In answering Fisher's parallel between the disagreement about the time of Christ's death and that about Peter's residence in Rome, Hessus holds that neither salvation nor faith is involved in the time of Christ's death or in the place of Peter's martyrdom.[118] Telling Fisher also that the undue acceptance of Jerome's authority on Peter's Roman residence has resulted in "that desolation, standing in the holy place" (Matt. 24:15), he proceeds to quote Fisher's own long indictment of Rome's immorality, as given above, and to ask why he does not also believe Jerome's prophecy about Antichrist reigning in the city of Rome and in the very Church.[119] After commenting on the first two of Fisher's refutations he deliberately passes over all the others because they are idle issues, based on human conjectures and reasons and not on Scripture.[120]

Just as Hessus took exception to Fisher's animadversions on Velenus, so others disputed his claims for the papacy in the *Confutation of Luther's Assertion*. John Frith in *An Aunswere to my Lord of Rochester,* for example, observes "that notwithstanding the Bishop is not content to give the Pope this power [of indulgences] only, but he has granted him full authoritie to deliver all men from hell, if they be not damned already. *For,* saith he, *whosoever hath committed a capital crime, hath thereby deserved damnation: and yet may the Pope deliver him both from the crime, and also from the paine due unto it.*" The reference is to Article 21 where Fisher concedes that the pope can snatch no one from hell after his death and condemnation, "but before his death (as long as one lives here), just as the pope can absolve him from the guilt, so he can free him also from the punishments of hell." Frith taunts Fisher with a dilemma: "If he [the pope] *can* do it, then let him deliver every man that is at the point of death, both from the crime and from the pain, and so shall never man more neither enter into hell, nor yet into purgatory: which were the best deed and most charitable that ever he did. Now if he *can* do it, and *will* not, then is he the most wretched and cruell tirant that ever lived." [121]

It is in Article 25 that Fisher undertakes to prove, according to his frequent previous promises, that "the Sovereign Pontiff is the head of the whole Church." Article 25 is divided in Fisher's typical fashion into three parts: (1) the proof from Scripture, which gives Peter ten prerogatives in the Gospels and shows him exercising them in ten places in the Acts; (2) the testimony of the Fathers, both Latin and Greek, concluding with the Council of Florence; and (3) the word-for-word refutation of Luther's reassertion of the twenty-fifth article, with special and full attention, as is to be expected, to Luther's interpretation of the texts on the Rock (Matt. 16:18) and the feeding of the lambs and sheep (John 21:15–17).[122] In proving Christ's bestowal of a direct and immediate primacy of honor and jurisdiction over the whole Church upon Peter and his successors, the Bishop of Rochester is at his best and strongest in handling the scriptural texts. The patristic argument is comparatively weaker because of reliance upon the Fathers of the fourth and fifth century instead of concentration upon the events and writings of the first three centuries.[123]

Several points that are new or interesting, either theologically or historically, might be indicated. Luther claims that Rome has never been over all the Churches of the world, as witnessed by those of Greece, India, Persia, Egypt, and Africa. Those Churches, replies Fisher, stand apart because of forgivable ignorance or of malice. If the latter, they belong no more to the orthodox Church than did the Arians or Donatists. The successor of Peter is the vicar of Christ over all churches that are joined to the one Catholic Church as members. In addition, the pope likewise has charge (*cura*) of all other men, even Jews and Turks, even though they refuse to acknowledge this power of his. Even if a rebellious and contumacious subject rejects the jurisdiction of his bishop, the latter does not cease to have charge of him. According to Christ's words, "other sheep I have that are not of this fold" (John 10:16), Christ's vicar, that is, Peter and his successor, has charge of all men good as well as bad and must strive to bring them to the fold of Christ, the bosom and unity of the Church — "nor can rebellion exempt anyone from all charge and zeal of the shepherd." [124] Now this primacy has a twofold meaning: its plenitude can be understood either in regard to the possession of the power or in regard to the exercise of the power. Thus, the pope's fullness of power is like Christ's, to whom "all power in heaven and on earth has been given" (Matt. 28:18): each possesses it but chooses not to exercise it.[125]

For having such a single head, Fisher furnishes many reasons. How can a head be wanting in a Church which stands midway between the shadow — the synagogue with its one high priest — and the pattern — the Church Triumphant with the one God as head over nine choirs of angels? In nature itself, the many branches of a tree have but the one root, every animal has many members but one controlling head, the bees have one king, the flock has one leader, the herd one master, and the state one governor. The Church, too, has need of one head for three reasons above all: the settlement of controversies in faith and in Scripture, the convocation of general councils in time of peril, and the suppression of the contumacious especially when bishops disagree.[126] In this same article Fisher relies much upon the principle that everything that happened to the Jews was a shadow of future events: *cuncta (quae Iudaeis contigerunt) futurorum vmbrae fuerant.* This principle serves as a springboard for an analogy between Moses and Christ and between Aaron and Peter, far more extended than the treatment in the sermon against Luther and now established on the basis of four points in particular. Again he insists that nothing prohibits two supreme heads (*duos summos*), the one (Moses or Christ) being so absolutely and simply, the other (Aaron or Peter) being so comparatively but truly.[127]

Apart from such purely theological matters, Fisher's judgments on historical events are worthy of attention. He declares that the condemnation of John Hus (1415) can hardly be blamed on the pope because the judges were hardly friendly to him and the deed was done neither at his instigation nor with a view to his favor.[128]

So much for the Council of Constance. As for the Council of Florence, his authorities for the subscription of the Greek ambassadors to its decrees (1439) are Eugene IV's secretary, *Blondus* (Flavio Biondi, 1388–1463), the greatest historian among Italian humanists, and *Franciscus Comes Mirandulanus* (Giovanni Francesco Pico della Mirandola, 1470–1533), who personally saw the document signed by the Emperor.[129] There is also an interesting reference to Pius II in answer to the objection that the dispatch of Peter and John to Samaria by the other Apostles (Acts 8:14) disproves any superiority of Peter. According to Fisher, the business in hand was so serious that it required the presence of the head — just as in the case of Pius II who on the advice of all the cardinals personally appeared with the crusade organized by himself.[130]

Fisher realizes that an impressive argument against his splendid theory of papal power to rule, teach, and sanctify the universal Church was the actual practice of the pope and the Roman curia. His statements on corruption understandably become less emphatic and definite than in previous writings. He declares, for example, that his intention is to investigate Christ's bestowal of power on Peter and his successors, not to inquire whether the pope is behaving truly like a head and shepherd and not to defend "the crimes (if any are rife in the Roman curia)." [131] Later, he does not deny that the devil's wiles have prevailed against individual popes, as against Peter himself in his denial, but not against the true succession from Peter, who remains the foundation of the Church.[132]

Fisher refers a number of times to the pressure of business which keeps recent popes especially, from personally engaging in the office of teaching, but that does not make them cease to be head. Fisher cannot excuse them from feeding the Church unless occupied with urgent business: their failure, however, should be credited to their slothfulness, not to their exalted apostolic position.[133] The scriptural texts alleged by Luther all exhort to humility so that if the Roman Pontiffs set aside all pomp and pride there would be nothing against which he could open his mouth. "Would that at last," exclaims Fisher, "they would reform the morals of their court and put to flight ambition, avarice, and luxury: otherwise they will never impose silence on abusive attacks."[134] Toward the end of Article 25, Fisher tries to assign a reason for Luther's attacks on the papacy in the many troubles brought by the Romans on "your Germans"; but if country is dear, God and Scripture should be dearer.[135]

When Luther flaunts the case of Savonarola, Fisher expresses the opinion that he was burned, "not because he publicly taught anything against the faith, but for his contumacy and his contempt for excommunication." On every other point his doctrine was correct, including papal supremacy over the whole Church.[136] To Luther's animadversion on the pope's involvement in the wars of kings, Fisher replies that he personally wishes neither to be a warmonger nor to praise popes who get mixed up in warlike enterprises unless driven by the greatest necessity (*nisi maxima fuerint adacti necessitate*).[137]

The Bishop of Rochester certainly sees the greatest necessity in the crusade against the Turks. No matter what Luther may say because of the drain on German finances, life under the Turks is worse than life under the Romans. Many learned and pious persons in Rome find as vexing as Luther whatever waywardness exists in the curia (*quicquid erroris in curia fuerit*), but the culprits share at least in the same faith and sacraments even if not in the same morals — unlike the infidel Turks. If "your Germans" do not contribute financial help, they will lose not only their money but their country and their lives to the Turks — as is evident from Thrace, Macedonia, Achaea, Mysia, and other lands. Fisher then proceeds to give a history, based on Platina and Sabellicus, of the crusades as fostered by holy popes looking to the salvation of Christendom.[138] Granted that the one or other pope has led a detestable existence, there have been many who were distinguished for learning, sanctity, and humility, whose behavior in the crusades was far superior to such dastardly conduct as that of the emperors, Frederick II for example.[139] At the end of his treatment of Article 34, Fisher declares that his defense is not intended to offset any reformation of the pope and his court — "if anything in their life has been at variance with Christ's teaching." He does not know the truth or falsity of the many charges of the people (*vulgus*) against them, but the report is persistent. "Would that (if anything of this kind exists) they would personally reform themselves and remove the scandals from the souls of the little ones; for it is to be feared that unless they do that as soon as possible, the divine vengeance is not far off. But it would hardly be fitting for the emperor or secular princes to undertake the business and force them to a more worthy standard of living." [140] In a later article Fisher reiterates his uncertainty about Rome's quest for riches, pleasures, and glory (that is, the world and the flesh) since he has never been to Rome: his concern is for the truth of its doctrine and faith — which is indisputable and obligatory on all Christians.[141]

Chapter V

FISHER'S CHURCH AND HENRY'S STATE

THE previous chapter has already touched upon two points involving the relationship between Church and state, namely, the conduct of war and the reformation of the clergy. It is difficult to determine Fisher's precise thinking on the latter point. On the one hand, he is clearly opposed to state control over such matters as ecclesiastical property and clerical discipline. On the other, there is no indication that he would subordinate the state to the Church in its temporal affairs. The civil power looks to the temporal welfare of its citizens directly but to morality and religion only indirectly, i.e., insofar as they impinge on public order and prosperity. Note Fisher's remark in his speech in Parliament on the close tie between true faith and temporal well-being in Bohemia.[1] On its side, a state like Catholic England should promote morality, render public worship to God, safeguard ecclesiastical laws and privileges, and defend the Catholic religion. For its part, the Church must foster public morals, advance the cause of peace and order, and furnish aid in special cases, for example, in that of a just war. The disagreement on the respective roles of state and Church, of king and pope, assumed a rapid crescendo in Fisher's life, to be climaxed in his death. It is possible to treat this matter quite briefly here because most, if not all, of it is the burden of ecclesiastical historians and Fisher's biographers. What is important for us is to see the way in which theory and practice, thought and action, supplement one another throughout his life but especially at the disputed frontier where king and bishop, state and Church, confront one another.

It is easy to forget that earlier in his life Fisher was almost as intimately connected with the royal court as Thomas More was to be later. Consequently Fisher was not ignorant of the mood or the power of his adversary. His introduction, to be sure, was made under most favorable circumstances. The Lady Margaret was a worthy representative of her class with a strong Christian sense of *noblesse oblige.* She was, as Fisher declares in his funeral sermon, a mother to university students, a patroness to the learned, a sister to virtuous individuals, an example to the nobility, and a "true defenderesse" to "all good preestes and clerkes." Her death is to be mourned also by "all the comyn people of this realme for whom she was in theyr causes a comyn mediatryce, and toke ryght grete dyspleasure for them." [2] He was executor not only for the Lady Margaret but also for her son, Henry VII.[3] He witnessed the treaty with Scotland on August 29, 1509.[4] In Henry VIII's early years, according to Brewer, Fisher was a member of the Privy Council, on which were also the Archbishop of Canterbury (Warham) and the Bishops of Winchester (Foxe), London (Fitzjames), and Durham (Ruthall).[5] But in the Convocation held in 1523, simultaneously with the Parliament, Bishops Foxe and Fisher, together with Rowland Phillips, Vicar of Croydon, opposed Wolsey's proposal for a higher tax on clerical incomes to support the unpopular war with France — the same one which had earlier interfered with the publication of Fisher's *Confutation of Luther's Assertion.* After Wolsey had frightened Phillips, the heart of the opposition, into withdrawal from the Convocation, he was able to secure a substantial subsidy from the clergy.[6] If Phillips' failure to reappear in the Convocation resulted, as Vergil reports, in "very gravely impairing his integrity [*innocentia*]," the enemies of Fisher, if the early biographer is to be believed, could resort later to more violent methods, as in the case of the poisoned pottage and that of the gun shot through his housetop,[7] but in no way could they touch his uprightness. The inevitable way out was the scaffold for the Bishop of Rochester, "a man of great learning and the highest honour and piety [*innocentia*]." Vergil continues: John Fisher and Thomas More "finally preferred to abandon their lives rather than their convictions." [8]

It is unfortunate that Fisher has left no personal portrait of the younger Henry VIII, such as he read in More's letter to himself in 1517–1518: "The King has virtue and learning and makes great progress in both, with almost daily renewed zeal, so that the more I see His Majesty increase in all the good and really kingly qualities, the less burdensome do I feel this life of the Court." [9] There is no reason, of course, to question the sincerity of Fisher's admiration for Henry's learning and orthodoxy as expressed in his *Defense of the Royal Assertion* and other controversial works. It need not have been, and most probably was not, only vanity which led Henry to write in support of the sacramental system. The closest thing to a revelation of Fisher's views toward his king is found in a commentary on Vulg. Ps. 20, which is extant only in manuscript. Of the two entirely different commentaries on this psalm, the one applies to Christ, the other quite evidently to Henry. To the scribe's manuscript of the latter, several additions are made in Fisher's own hand (which will be indicated in italics). Early in the commentary there seems to be almost an explicit doubt as to whether a truly Christian king could be found ("regi christiano, si quis eiusmodi repertus fuerit"). Fisher shortly continues: "Make our king confidently rejoice in Thee and in Thy strength; and not in himself nor in human powers *let him glory ever,*" and here Fisher adds the marginal gloss: "*let him not glory in his own* [strength]." In verse 5 ("He asked life of Thee: and Thou hast given him length of days for ever and ever") he comments: "What had happened to his brother [Arthur] could have happened to him [Henry], namely, to be carried away either by illness or by some other danger, unless Thou hadst given him the life he asked." The whole crisis of a royal male heir seems to furnish the background for the notes on verse 11: " 'Their fruit shalt Thou destroy from the earth' — *They shall perish without all fruit.* And even their offspring on whom they congratulated themselves and in whom as their successor they gloried will be without honor in the future — 'and their seed from among the children of man.' " [10] This document is so enigmatic and so noncommittal that it is difficult to determine its precise tone. A note of sadness is certainly present. There might also be the fear that the lion has discovered his own strength — which is not God's or His Church's. There might be also the threat that pride and violence would receive divine vengeance in the lack or the loss of a royal heir.

The concept of divine punishment being visited upon sinners even in this life and this world is recurrent in Fisher. Almost as much as Luther he sees the Turks as the instrument of God for punishing the sins of Christians. As early as 1504 he surveys the situation as follows:

> Our relygyon of crysten fayth is gretely dymynysshed, we be very fewe, & where as somtyme we were spredde almoost thrugh the worlde, now we be thraste downe in to a very streyght angyll or corner. Our enemyes holde awaye from vs Asye and Affryke, two the gretest partes of the worlde. Also they holde from vs a grete porcyon of this parte called Europe whiche we now inhabyte, soo that scante the syxth parte of that we had in possessyon before is lefte vnto vs. Besyde this our enemyes dayly lay awayte to haue this lytell porcion. Therfore good lorde without thou helpe the name of crysten men shall vtterly be destroyed and fordone. But trouth it is we haue deserued more greuous punysshement for our synnes than euer dyde Sodome and Gomorre.

Fisher concludes this section with a prayer: "If there be many ryghtwyse people in thy chyrche mylytaunt, here vs wretched synners for the loue of them. . . If in thy chyrche be but a fewe ryghtwyse persones, so moche the more is our wretchednes & the more nede we haue of thy mercy. Therfore mercyful lorde excercyse thy mercy." [11] Hence arises Fisher's praise for the Lady Margaret: "whom I haue many tymes herde saye that yf the crysten prynces wolde haue warred vpon the enmyes of his faith, she wold be glad yet to go folowe the hoost & helpe to wasshe theyr clothes for the loue of Ihesu." [12]

In the light of Margaret's attitude, Luther's contention was novel and shocking: "To fight against the Turks is nothing but to strive against God who is punishing our sins by means of the Turks." Fisher's defense of the liceity of such a war merits later mention in works like Castro's *Heresies* and Suarez's *War*.[13] The reference, of course, is to Article 34 in the *Confutation of Luther's Assertion*. Fisher's proofs are traditional: (1) from Scripture, for example: "Be content with your pay" (Luke 3:14) — advice which John the Baptist could not have given if military service were forbidden; and (2) from patrology, especially Augustine's counsel to Count Boniface on a just war.[14]

To refute Luther's appeal to Christian failures against the Mohammedans as proof of divine displeasure and divine disapproval of Christian resistance, Fisher produces historical evidence

— the victories of Baldwin, Bohemund, Godfrey, Ladislas, John Hunyadi, and *Cassanus*. The reasons for the lack of success of the Christians, as of the Hebrews in the Old Testament, are three: "our negligence and idleness," as when other Christians abandoned Constantinople before it fell; "the luxury and lust" of the soldiers, as in the many disasters of the First Crusade under Urban II; and the boastful attribution of success to our own strength, not God's, as in the case of John Hunyadi. Complaints about financial collections are unreasonable since money is the sinews of war. Misuse of the funds does not destroy the merit earned by the donors. The popes cannot be blamed because their aim is "partly to protect, partly to regain, the common possession of Christians [*communem Christianorum rem*]." It is from Platina, except for a single comment of Sabellicus on the sanctity of Celestine III, that Fisher gets his account of papal relations with the Crusades, from Urban II (1088–99) to Urban V (1362–70), with a later reference to Calixtus III (1455–58).[15] What irony that, exactly one decade from the publication of this article in the *Confutation*, the Bishop of Rochester should approve Chapuys' suggestion for armed intervention by Charles V in behalf of Queen Catherine (*and* the beleaguered Church): an attack on Henry VIII would be "a work as agreeable to God as going against the Turk." [16]

The recommendation had been caused by a series of events which had begun formally with Fisher's consultation on the divorce in 1527 and was to end with his execution in 1535. Throughout these years he stands forth as a bishop who is a champion of Catholic unity, including its implications as to such matters as papal supremacy, episcopal collegiality, and clerical privilege. The English Reformation which he withstood has been described as "the classic example of a religious revolution carried out by the temporal power almost wholly according to the dictates of political exigency." [17] His recognition of Henry's power is revealed early and almost in passing in a letter (1527) to an unknown correspondent (Paul ——), in which for his "soul's health" (i.e., for "the salvation of his soul"), he defends his opinion on the royal marriage: the king should lay his troubles before the pope, "especially as kings, from the fulness of their power, are apt to think that right which suits their pleasure." [18]

The first essay of strength came after the fall of Wolsey and at the beginning of the "Long Parliament" when the Commons usurped ecclesiastical rights by bills aimed at abuses, e.g., "the probat of testaments and wills . . . mortuaries . . . pluralities of benefices and takinge of farmes by spirituall men." In defense of the liberty and authority of the Christian clergy, Fisher delivered his frank speech, with its famous reference to the downfall of Bohemia and with its ambiguous designation of cause as "lacke of faith." When accused of disparaging the Commons, Fisher defended himself before Henry VIII by declaring the remark was intended for the Bohemians.[19] But at a joint conference in the Star Chamber to end the deadlock, the spiritual lords were outvoted by the Commoners and temporal lords so that the bill was passed.

Fisher, however, like the Bishops of Bath and Ely, bestowed benefices contrary to the law, appealed to the Holy See, and was arrested (but the outcome is unknown).[20] It is likely that Hugh Latimer was referring also to Fisher's words and actions when he wrote to Henry VIII a year later (December 1, 1530): "Your grace may see what means and craft the spiritualty (as they will be called) imagine, to break and withstand the acts which were made in your grace's last parliament against their superfluities. Wherefore they that thus do, your grace may know them not to be true followers of Christ." [21]

In this first test of power Fisher had failed. In the second test (which is second in the sense that the anonymous biographer places it after the conflict over probate, mortuaries, and pluralities, but which cannot be dated with any certainty), he won the field. His speech defeated the proposal to "recompence him [Henry VIII] in their convocacion by graunting unto him all the small abbaies and monasteries within this realme of the valew of two hundred pounds landes and under." Fisher warned that the great monasteries would soon follow the small and reinforced his point by telling the fable of the handleless axe, which, upon being granted a small tree, felled the whole wood: "Wherof cannot but ensewe the displeasure of Almightie God in that ye take upon you to geve the thinge, that is none of your owne." [22]

The irony lies in the fact that among the charges laid against Wolsey in the House of Lords (December 1, 1529) was one for "shamefully slandering many good religious houses, by which means he suppressed thirty," and that Fisher had cooperated with him in 1526 by investigating the wealth of Lesnes Abbey, intended for Wolsey's colleges at Oxford and Ipswich.[23] Earlier, Fisher had helped to establish St. John's at Cambridge with the revenue of the suppressed nunneries of Bromhall in the diocese of Salisbury and of Lillechurch in his own diocese of Rochester, as well as the Maison Dieu of Ospringe.[24] Nevertheless, all this had been done with the proper ecclesiastical and especially papal permission (however deviously secured) and not without considerable precedent in the previous centuries. Nevertheless, the action served as ready ammunition for later controversialists, for instance, for Bishop Jewel against T. Harding: "The first suppressors of monasteries within this realm in our memory were two of your dearest friends, cardinal Wolsey, and Doctor Fisher, the bishop of Rochester; either of them well warranted thereto by the authority of the pope." [25]

The third great struggle (1531) was climaxed by a resounding victory for the royal forces, yet Fisher and the episcopal body retired from the field with at least the semblance of honor. The prelates yielded to Henry's demand for the title of Protector and Supreme Head of the English Church and Clergy but insisted upon Fisher's proviso: *quantum per legem dei licet.*[26] Yet the gravity and the ambiguity of the concession were not lost on Fisher. On February 21, 1531, Chapuys wrote from London to Charles V: "The Bishop of Rochester is very ill with disappointment at it. He opposes it as much as he can; but, being threatened that he and his adherents should be thrown in the river, he was forced to consent to the King's will." [27]

The Bishop of Rochester was not summoned to the next session of Parliament which met in January 1532, but he went up to London just the same and even met the king.[28] He lay ill in his house at Lambeth Marsh in May when the king demanded of Convocation that royal consent be required for promulgation of all future canons, that a royal commission revise canon law, and finally that royal permission be necessary for summoning Convocation. Bishop Longland of Lincoln and Bishop Stokesley of London were part of a commission sent to consult Bishop Fisher, but no record of his reaction exists. The submission was voted in Convocation on May 15, 1532, delivered to Henry on May 16, and embodied in a statute a year and a half later. There were vain protests from the clergy of York, Durham, and Canterbury. Among the protesting signers from the archdiocese of Canterbury were associates of Fisher: Nicholas Metcalfe, Archdeacon of Rochester and Master of St. John's College of Cambridge; Robert Johnson, for the Chapter of Rochester; and John Willo (?), for the clergy of Rochester.[29]

In the submission of the clergy, Fisher had been rendered, as it were, *hors de combat.* He was still free enough as late as June 1532 to preach a sermon on behalf of Queen Catherine. But he was put under restraint from April 6 to June 13, 1533, during the final proceedings for the marriage and coronation of Anne Boleyn. His enemies were now determined upon his complete submission or his final destruction. Their principal means were, first, the case of the Nun of Kent, from which he escaped with only a fine of one year's revenue, and, secondly, the oath required by the Act of Succession and later the Act of Supremacy, the refusal of which resulted in his imprisonment and ended with his execution on June 22, 1535. The issue at stake and the course of events are so familiar from the earliest lives and from modern biographies of both Fisher and More, not to mention histories of the period, that it is otiose to repeat the details here.

What is to the present purpose is Fisher's reputed answer to six or seven bishops sent to his prison to persuade him to take the oath. In part he said: "Me thinketh it had rather bene all our parts to sticke together in repressinge these violent and unlawfull intrusions and iniuries, daily offred to our common mother the holy Church of Christ, then by any manner of perswasions to helpe or sett forward the same. . . The fort is betraid even of them that shoulde have defended yt."[30] The bill of indictment listed as Fisher's statement: "The Kyng owre soveraign lord is not supreme hed yn erthe of the Cherche of England." After the sentence of condemnation, he told the judges: "I thinke indeed and alwaies have thought and do now lastly affirme that his grace cannot iustly claime any such supremacie over the Church of God, as he nowe taketh upon him, neither hath it ever bene seene or heard of, that any temporall prince, before his daies, hath presumed to that dignitie."[31]

The pope (currently Paul III) for whom Fisher had claimed

the supremacy recognized the fundamental and ultimate issue for which he had died: "What shall we first mourn in such a wound of the universal church? . . . the cause of his death is most to be lamented, since this most holy man laid down his life for God, for the Catholic religion, for justice, for truth, while he was defending not merely the particular rights of one only man [*leg.* church], as Thomas of Canterbury formerly did, but the truth of the universal church [*vt . . . vniuersalis ecclesiae veritatem tueretur*]." [32] In his reply, the tract on Fisher's execution, Bishop Gardiner picks up this assertion: "The churche is heylyd, and nott woundyd, by the deth of a trayter . . . as though it war for god, to contrary his prince beyng the vicar of god [*principi dei vicario*], for the catholike relligion, nott to geve suche obedience as thatt same relligion requiryth, and asthough it war for Justice to breke the lawes lawfully promulgat, and finally asthough it war for the troth, to repugne agaynst the troth." [33] Rome paid no attention to Fisher when he wrote against its Lutheran adversaries and when he lived "miserably att home, like a man onknowen and litle spoken of." Gardiner continues: "But now in the last ende of his lif, when he agaynst all lawes as well of god, as of man, resistyd his prince, and the ordinance of god, and beyng also a traiter, was imprisoned therfor, he was then incontinently estemyd of thatt holy see worthye to bee a cardinall." The title harmed rather than benefited Fisher.[34]

A twentieth-century historian has written: "Fisher and More, *par nobile fratrum,* stand for the passive resistance of an oppressed conscience." [35] It is the word *conscience* that is sounded ominously, persistently, and dolorously by Fisher, as by More, throughout the suspenseful months in the struggle over the supremacy. In the seventh session of Parliament (November–December 1534), the statute of treason was broadened to include not only action and word but also thought. Henceforth it was estimated high treason "maliciously to wish, to will, or desire by words or writing, or by craft imagine, invent, practise, or attempt any bodily harm to be done or committed to the king's most royal person . . . or slanderously and maliciously publish and pronounce, by express writing or words, that the king our sovereign lord should be heretic, schismatic, tyrant, infidel, etc." [36] The Commons had insisted on the word *maliciously,* but, as predictable and predicted, it was to prove worthless. Robert Fisher's comment to John Fisher is apropos: "For now . . . speaking is made high treason, which was never heard of before, that words should be high treason." [37] Actually the act went beyond speaking to thinking and was repealed in the next reign.

Fisher had touched on this matter of thinking, or conscience, in his concern with the divorce. The king's book had maintained: "For in tho [*sic*] thinges / that be forbidden by the lawe of god / we must obey our conscience: and in other thinges the churche." Fisher, of course, could not but assert that every action against conscience is a sin. But perplexity on the law of God can easily (*facile*) be resolved by recourse to Scripture properly understood: "For on the law of God no man is left perplexed provided he desires to free himself." [38] After study Fisher did not feel perplexed as to the king's "great matter," as is only too evident from his divorce tracts. Touching this point he wrote to Cromwell, January 31, 1534, that "it was his purpose to decline being obliged to offend the King, 'for then I must needs declare my conscience, the which, as then I wrote, I would be loth to do any more largely than I have done; not that I condemn any other men's conscience: their conscience may save them, and mine must save me.' " [39] He told the commissioners that he was willing to swear to part of the oath in his own way, "So both mine owne conscience shall be therby satisfied and his Majesties doings the better iustified and warranted by lawe." When forced to take the oath as it stood, he answered plainly: "For asmuch as mine owne conscience cannot be satisfyed, I doe absolutely refuse the oath." This occurred in April 1534. On December 22, he wrote Cromwell that he agreed to the law of succession: "Albeitt I refused to swear to sum other parcels, bycause that my conscience wold not serve me so to doo." Later, too, he told Cromwell the reason for his fear of God's displeasure: "Bycause I know how mine owne conscience it standeth, and so do I not an other mans." [40]

This note of conscience has a curious echo in More's case, which should be cited insofar as it directly involves Fisher's. In Margaret Roper's revealing letter to Alice Alington, the great, learned, and friendly lord who had called More's refusal "a right simple scruple" goes on to say: "Where you say your conscience moueth you to this . . . almost all other men . . . sticke not therat, saue only your self and one other man [Fisher]: whom though he be right good and very well learned too, yet wolde I wene, fewe that loue you, geue you the counsaile against all other men to lene to his [Fisher's] minde alone." Even though all these other men believed what they swore, More replied, "That wolde not make much to me, not though I shoulde see my Lorde of Rochester . . . swere the oth hymselfe before me too." He later continued:

> For albeit, that of very trouth, I haue hym [Fisher] in that reuerent estimacion, that I reken in this realme no one man, in wisdome, learning and long approued vertue together, mete to be matched and compared with hym, yet that in this matter I was not led by hym, very well and plainly appereth, both in that I refused the othe before it was offered him, and in that also that his Lordship was content to haue sworne of that othe . . . either somwhat more, or in some other maner than euer I minded to doe. Verely, Daughter, I neuer entend . . . to pynne my soule at a nother mans backe, not euen the best man that I know this day liuing; for I knowe not whither he may happe to cary it. Ther is no man liuing, of whom while he liueth, I may make myself sure.

More of the same tenor follows.[41]

According to Harpsfield, "after the statute passed he [More] never opened his mind what he thought in that matter [or what he would do in that matter] to any man living, no not to . . . the Bishop of Rochester, craving it at his hands." The letters which passed between them in the Tower were burned. Fisher told his interrogators on June 12, 1535, that they contained "nothing else but exhortacion either of other to take patience in their adversite, and to call God for grace, and praying for their enemies. . ." On July 6, Thomas More confessed of the letters: "Some were about private matters connected with our old friendship." If they independently compared the statute to a two-edged sword, "it must have been from the agreement between us in opinion, not because we had ever arranged it between us." Yet the bishop had asked More about the content and the manner of his answer to the statute: "Wherevnto," More later said, "I aunswered nothing els but that I had informed and settled my conscience, and that he should informe and settle his." [42]

Conscience is the point at which God, Church, state, and individual meet. If the Bishop of Rochester was so scrupulous about the following of his conscience, why was he so insistent upon the extirpation of heresy? Among Protestants of the sixteenth century, both the living and the dead Fisher had an unsavory reputation. John Foxe records the lurid testimony of the wife of the heretic John Browne who reported "how by the two bishops, Warham and Fisher, his feet were heated upon the hot coals, and burned to the bones." [43] With his fame for learning, it was hardly possible for him not to be involved as examiner or judge with famous heretics — Robert Barnes, Thomas Bilney, Hugh Latimer, Thomas Hitton, and doubtless many others, with whom his relations often survive just by chance reference.[44] "Everywhere," he laments from personal experience, "nothing is now talked about but the vain dogmas of Luther and the false liberties and licenses which he labors to proclaim." [45]

Actually the reason for Fisher's fear and hatred of heretics is extremely simple: they destroy human souls and therefore are a worse enemy than the Jews or the Roman emperors were to the early Church. In his sermon against Luther, he declares: "For the persecucyon of the Iewes was soone at a syde. and the persecucyons of the tyrauntes had his course for a season. but the herytykes hath persecuted the chirche from the ascencyon of christ. & shal do vnto the comynge of antichryst. . . The Iewes & the tyrauntes whan they had slayn the bodyes of christen men. yet they sent theyr soules to euerlastyng glorye. but the heretykes . . . doth slee the soules of chrysten people. & send them to euerlastyng damnacyon." [46]

At first this conception of heretics as persecuting the Church rather than of the Church as persecuting heretics may seem like an odd inversion of the reality in the sixteenth century. Fisher, however, has in view the Church as the Spouse of Christ and the whole course of its history to his day. Five years later, at Barnes's abjuration, he gives the full list of persecutors: "Great malice and persecution hath ben vsed agaynst this generation [that is to say / the generation of christen people] / bothe by the Jewes and by the gentiles / by the tyrantes / by the philosophers / and the heretickes: but all they myght nat preuaile agaynst this generation / according as our sauiour Christe hath promised." [47] The same five classes appear several times in his manuscript commentary on the Psalms. There are only minor variations, e.g., the substitution of Turks for tyrants or of idolaters for gentiles, or the addition of schismatics, demons, or even bad Christians.[48]

Hence the timeliness of Henry VIII's able vindication of the sacraments, "wherin al englond maye take grete comforte and specyally al those that loue lernynge." [49] As for Luther as "a man of grete lernynge . . . grete redynes in scryptures . . . vertuous lyuynge," many heretics before him had the same reputation. Fisher asks, for example, about Arius: "Was not he a man of grete lernynge. of synguler eloquence. of vertuous lyfe in outwarde apparence. & all his opynyons he grounded vpon scrypture. and so dysceyued many a soule. Saynt Hierome saythe . . . In the cyte of Alexandre Arrius was but one sparkle. but bycause this sparkle was not soon quenched the flam that rose of it raged thorugh all the world." Besides, heretics resorted to physical violence against their opponents, as is evident in the case of the Arians, Donatists, and Wyclifites.[50] The reasonable course is to forestall all this harm: to quench the spark and to catch the little fox still young.

As one might expect, Fisher's most explicit statement on the relation between Church and state in regard to heresy is found in his refutation of Luther's thesis: "The burning of heretics is contrary to the will of the Holy Spirit." [51] As wolves, heretics are not merely to be kept at a distance. Fisher goes much further: "For my part, I hold that they are to be done away with when you cannot otherwise save the flock. This course even Christ Himself, it seems to me, designated openly enough when He called them ravening wolves. For who, fearing for his flock, would not kill the ravening wolf before allowing the sheep to be butchered by him? . . . Now, the speech of heretics is more destructive to men than wolves to sheep. For 'their speech' (as Paul says [2 Tim. 2:17]) 'spreads like a cancer.'" All means other than death have proved ineffective: censures, confiscation, exile, or prison. This, too, has been the verdict of the history of heresy.[52]

As for Luther's appeal to Paul's exhortation to avoid, and not with fire or sword to kill, an *haereticus homo* (Tit. 3:10, really, "a factious man"), Fisher retorts that neither did Paul command the hanging of thieves on gibbets and yet the security of cities and citizens requires laws against theft — "so too the public safety of souls demands the condemnation of heretics to the punishment of fire." He counters the accusation of inclemency with the charge of cruelty in suffering numberless souls to perish. As for burning as improper for "the sons of the good spirit," Fisher cites the parallel of public officials. For using the gibbet to maintain the peace of a city or even a kingdom at the price of a few men's lives, they cannot be accused of an evil spirit but rather of manifest love and charity toward their country. The analogy of a rotten member on the body politic follows.[53]

Particularly interesting is Fisher's solution to Luther's serious objection: "Christ did not wish to force men to the faith by violence and fire." He answers: "Neither was that fitting at the beginning of the infant Church when He wished the wise to be converted through the foolish, and the strong to be drawn through the weak, to the faith. But now, in regard to those converted to the faith, these must be forced to persevere in the faith." It is meet that, after being admonished once or twice, heretics be handed over to the secular power. It is more permissible for the government to execute disturbers of spiritual salvation than those of temporal safety. Hence heretics, who are the chief enemies of eternal salvation, must be suppressed and put out of the way by fire and sword through the might of the secular power. Fines, confiscation, prison, exile, all are useless; only the extreme penalty of death remains.[54]

But how are heretics to be detected? The Bishop of Rochester in the sermon delivered in 1526 professes to find in St. Peter (2 Pet. 2:10–11) three signs for their recognition: "The fyrst is this . . . they . . . walke in the vnclene desires of the same [flesh] . . . The seconde condition is . . . they dispise al gouernours / and them that be in auctorite. . . The thyrde condition is this . . . they drede not . . . to skoffe . . . and rente the fames and lyues of noble men." The most dangerous of these is the demand to "haue euery man lefte vnto theyr libertie." The reason is that "the nature of man is more prone to all noughtynes / rather than to any goodnes. And therfore many muste be compelled / according as the gospel sayth in an other place: Compellite eos intrare [cf. Luke 14:23]." Otherwise heretics would be everywhere. It is better to follow St. Paul on their avoidance or their excommunication: "Wherfore it is not lefull that any man shall haue libertie to speke in these matters concernyng our fayth / what so euer that he liste: but he must be compelled to conforme hym vnto the holsome doctryne of the churche." Naturally Fisher makes reference to both Henry VIII and Wolsey. His prefatory letter to the reader concedes that "litell diligence is done about the ministryng of this true doctryne" and advises pastors "to gaynestande these pernitious heresies. Wherin doutles . . . my lorde legate hath nowe meritoriously traueiled / and so entendeth to perseuer and to continue / to the full extirpation of the same [pernitious heresies]." And, of course, "the kynges boke," mentioned in the sermon itself, both opposes Luther and sets forth true doctrines.[55]

Toward the close of his sermon, Fisher gives a long litany of Luther's blasphemies and reproaches, ending with these two against Luther and Germany:

> Agaynst hym selfe and his herers and folowers / intrikynge & snarlyng bothe hym and them in so pestilent errours and heresies / to the high displeasure of god / that he hath suffred them to tomble *in mentem improbam* / that is to say / into a peruersed iudgement / approuyng this wretched carnalitie / wherin they nowe lyue. Agaynst his owne countrey / gyuyng occasion by his moste mischeuous doctryne to the subuersion of that contrey (whiche was the floure of the empire) by insurrections amonge them selfe: Wherby . . . suche a murdre of men / as in our dayes hath nat ben herde of in so shorte a tyme: Doutles it is the hande and stroke of god vpon them / for the fauoryng & subportyng of his most mischeuous doctrines: Suche a murdre of men / as credebly and faithfully is reported aboue an .C. thousande. This is the frute / which is spronge of this moste wicked sede.[56]

It is these two points, but now in reverse order, that Fisher repeats in the preface to Book I of *Christ's Body,* published just about a year after the sermon at Barnes's abjuration. First of all, Providence is evidently at work against those Germans who have rebelled against the Church and followed Luther's doctrines by having many thousands of them engage in mutual self-slaughter (as in the Peasants' War, 1524–25). The second and worse act of divine vengeance is that, according to Paul's words, "God has given them up to a reprobate sense [*in reprobam mentem*] so that they do what is not fitting" — by marrying despite their vow of celibacy and by citing Scripture in support of their action.

If the Germans had only listened to the warnings of John Cochlaeus, "a man of the greatest learning, a most ardent protagonist of the Catholic faith, a person of immense zeal and no less love for his country." This note of pity, coupled with the hope of the Germans realizing their sorry predicament, sounds a number of times in *Christ's Body*.[57] This same preface expresses Fisher's pleasure at Eck's visit to England in 1525 ("Eckius, quem in Anglia vidisse pergratum fuit") and names, among others, the same Catholic apologists given in the sermon of 1526 (Henry VIII, Catharinus, Emser, Cochlaeus, and Eck). One suspects either that Fisher had both works in hand at the same time or that he borrowed for one from the other, more probably for *Heretickes* from *Christ's Body*. As for Eck, he declares that "when last summer I passed over to England to visit the king and the Bishop of Rochester, though tumults and seditions were raging in Germany, I never once heard the name of Luther mentioned except in malediction." [58] Fisher and others undoubtedly knew otherwise. Only the previous year, on October 12, 1524, Bishop Tunstal had had to warn several booksellers not to import heretical books from Germany nor henceforth to sell foreign books "so far as the books were newly composed and made," without the approval of Cardinal Wolsey, Archbishop Warham, Bishop Tunstal, or Bishop Fisher.[59]

At this stage it is possible to summarize Fisher's view on freedom in thought, speech, and conscience insofar as it is related to himself and to heretics. Quite clearly, as in the case of Henry's divorce, he holds for a legitimate freedom of thought, since man has a right to embrace the truth, to weigh the evidence for it, and to choose freely among divergent opinions. But he does not envision this right as absolute because in his eyes no one has a right to error. A heretic, for example, can err in good faith but he has no right to reject the truth which is clear to him from intrinsic evidence or from extrinsic evidence, that is, from the pronouncement of the Church. As long as there is no external expression of opinion on his part, only God can be his judge. One should note Fisher's willingness at one juncture to take the oath yet without openly denying the king's supremacy. In fact, he would maintain that man has a strict right to free speech, provided that the matter is truthful and harmful to no one. But since there is no such just claim to teach error, the civil or ecclesiastical government has the right and the duty to suppress error to the extent required by the good of society.

Society for the Bishop of Rochester is a Catholic society, having Catholic citizens in the vast majority and enjoying a government to be run on Catholic principles. Even a society overwhelmingly Catholic in number and in spirit cannot deny a true liberty of conscience in embracing and professing the true religion, while observing only the limits set by God or by the authority established by Him. One such limit is that a man choose the religion approved by God and not the one which pleases his reason or his fancy; another is that external acts and worship do not work against the good of society. On the one hand, Fisher agrees with Luther (and every thinking Christian of his day) that the Church cannot force a person to profess a religion which he has never recognized as true. On the other hand, because Holy Mother Church has the duty and right of leading her children to their eternal goal, she has the right and duty to the necessary means of protecting them, e.g., by expelling individuals who spread moral corruption or errors of faith — even to the extent of seeking help from the civil power. Fisher would gainsay that the exposition and defense of the true doctrine is the only legitimate means at the Church's disposal — because of the perversity and corruption of human nature, which is "more prone to all noughtynes / rather than to any goodnes." [60] But he would also vehemently deny to the state any competence in suppressing every moral or religious error: its competence here is restricted to religious matters which would harm the good of society, that is, temporal prosperity, peace, order, and happiness. Hence his objection to the interference of king and Parliament in ecclesiastical affairs.

To conclude. Many of Fisher's statements which seem odd or contrary become explicable in the light of his conception of the Church. For him the Church is not primarily an historical and juridical body, a society monarchical and hierarchical in its structure, consisting of rulers and subjects. This aspect, although external and secondary, unfortunately has to be defended and elaborated because of what Fisher deems to be the too highly spiritualized conception of the Protestants. Rather, personally — and officially, too, so to speak — he favors what might be termed the mystical vision — without neglecting either visible body or invisible soul. His basis is deeply and strongly scriptural, and not predominantly traditional and canonical.

The Church in its essence is the Mystical Body of Christ, of which believers, whether high or low, whether clerical or lay, whether king or serf, are members or parts. Christ is the Head who unites all members with Himself and with the other faithful. It is He that governs them and that gives them the life and activity of the Spirit. For the soul of this Mystical Body is the Holy Spirit always enlivening, always renewing, always filling, the hearts of the faithful with individual inspirations, by the preaching of pastors, and through the administration of the sacraments.

The Church is also the Spouse of Christ, who unites Himself with her and begets spiritual sons. In consequence, the Church is likewise the Mother of Christians and is worthy of filial love and protection. Divine in origin, international in scope, lasting to the end of time, fruitful in justice and holiness, and marvelously balancing hierarchy and obedience, authority and freedom — she has always been defended by her free and loyal sons against her five great persecutors: Jew, gentile, philosopher, tyrant, and heretic. The Bishop of Rochester undoubtedly feels it to be his personal destiny and duty to shield her to the death against two particular classes of contemporary persecutors: against the tyrannical government of Henry VIII, Cromwell, and Parliament, and against the heretical horde of Luther, Oecolampadius, and Protestants.

Fisher cannot and does not ignore the many failings and abuses existing in the contemporary Church, but he tries to put on "the mind of Christ" (1 Cor. 2:16) and to maintain Christ's view of His Spouse — "just as Christ also loved the Church, and delivered himself up for her, that he might sanctify her . . . in order that he might present to himself the Church in all her glory, not having spot or wrinkle or any such thing, but that she might be holy and without blemish" (Eph. 5:25–27).

Chapter VI

TRADITION AND TRADITIONS

FISHER evidently views the contemporary Church as the living, authoritative, and infallible interpreter of Christ's revelation. The voice of this Church for him is the ever-present voice of Christ. But where does Christ's Church find the revelation which it is to preserve and to propagate? Indisputably it is at hand in the written word which under the inspiration of the Holy Spirit has God for its author and which properly interpreted yields the truths of faith. There exists also tradition, that is, the divine word on faith and morals transmitted from generation to generation by lawful pastors. But there are all kinds of traditions: those divine, those human, those proceeding from the mouth of Christ, those coming from the lips of the Apostles, those proposed by the Apostles as Christ's, those enunciated by them as their own, those merely ecclesiastical, to say nothing of those set forth by ordinary episcopal and papal teaching, public rites and prayers, the councils, the creeds, the Fathers, the theologians, and the consensus of the faithful. Tradition — or traditions — can set forth truths already clearly revealed in Scripture. It can give an accepted and plain explanation of points rather obscurely expressed in Scripture. But can it legitimately — that is, according to Christ's will and plan — transmit doctrines in absolutely no way found in Scripture?

To be fair to Fisher's thinking and to discover any change or development in his opinion, it might be best to study his works in the order of their publication.

It is significant that in the very first work in which he makes extensive use of the Fathers, that is, in his controversy with his fellow Catholic, Lefèvre, over the single Magdalene, the Bishop of Rochester does not hesitate to stress the limitations of individual Fathers. When the Fathers write, not as witnesses to the faith of the Church, but as private teachers who are expressing their own mind, they are to be treated respectfully, yet the value of their opinion depends upon the degree of their scholarship and the force of their arguments. When Lefèvre cites St. Ambrose in his favor, Fisher declares: "I certainly respect Ambrose's authority everywhere — where it does not differ from the common opinion of the Catholic Church." He himself prefers to trust Augustine in his corrections of Ambrose. Actually Ambrose says different things on the Magdalene in different works; "but whatever Ambrose has said in this place, when he has not produced satisfactory proofs for his assumptions, everyone is free to accept them or not, and especially when the Roman Church holds the contrary view." It is common knowledge that Origen, Chrysostom, and Ambrose (Lefèvre's authorities) were careless, not to say wrong, about certain points in Scripture and that Augustine caught up their slips. Hence Fisher prefers to defer a little bit more to Augustine than to his predecessors. His supposition is that it is only natural for later scholars to correct the inaccuracies of earlier ones.[1]

Early in his next work, *Destruction of Clichtove's Bulwark,* the Bishop of Rochester interestingly touches on contemporary popular preaching as the vehicle of faith. Lefèvre should not contemn such preachers, because who but they are to keep alive the memory of the anointing at Bethany (Matt. 26:13, Mark 14:9)? Consequently they are to be believed on any point on which they agree unanimously.[2] Fisher challenges also the universality of Clichtove's assumption that the earlier the ecclesiastical writers the greater their authority. This opinion cannot stand up, especially against the common custom of the whole Church. He offers two historical examples: Mary's virginity as contrary to an earlier theory about her being the mother of other children besides Jesus, and the celebration of Easter on Sunday as opposed to an earlier observance of the fourteenth of Nisan which might fall on any day of the week.[3]

To test the validity of Clichtove's eight Suppositions, Fisher applies them at great length to the disagreement between Jerome and Augustine on Paul's reprehension of Peter (Gal. 2:11–14). Jerome holds that it was pretended, Augustine that it was real.

Although Lefèvre should logically follow Jerome, he prefers Augustine on this point. To be consistent, he should also follow Augustine, not the older writers, on the single Magdalene.[4] Even though Lefèvre cites Origen, Chrysostom, Ambrose, and Jerome as authorities, Fisher undertakes to show that they do not hold absolutely the same view as Lefèvre. (At one point, Fisher observes that the Catholic Church has preferred the opinion of Jerome by himself to that of older writers.) In an absorbing section, Fisher rises to the defense of Gregory the Great but lists the errors of Lefèvre's authorities: Jerome, who attributes no more power of forgiving sins to a priest of the New Law than to one of the Old Law; Ambrose, who for adultery allows divorce with remarriage; Chrysostom, who forbids Christians to swear even justly; and Origen, charged with the many heresies listed by Jerome in his apology against Ruffinus.[5]

Toward the end of the *Destruction,* Fisher enumerates various customs not found in writing: the baptism of infants, their designation as members of the faithful, the rites of baptism, the sign of the cross, the words of consecration, and others. Consequently one must have faith not only in Holy Scripture and apostolic traditions, but also in ecclesiastical custom. Fisher holds Augustine's threefold division of ecclesiastical institutions, namely, "into those which are contained in Scripture, and into apostolic traditions which are not written, and lastly into those which custom has confirmed by approved practice." [6] Finally, Fisher comes to "the consensus of the whole Catholic Church," which is twofold: express, as in the definition of a general council, and tacit, as in the private and public opinion of all the faithful, scattered through the world but united in one Spirit. The prime example of the latter is the Assumption of the Blessed Virgin Mary, which Fisher cautiously but characteristically asserts has never been confirmed heretofore by "the express decree of the whole Church (as far as I know)." The opinion on the unicity of Magdalene is close to this instance.[7] In the *Confutation of Lefèvre's Second Disquisition,* the Bishop of Rochester insists that only an incontrovertible proof from Scripture or an irrefutable argument from reason should make one abandon faith in the accepted and confirmed custom of the Church and follow one's own bent of mind.[8]

Two years later, Fisher's views on tradition receive clearer and fuller statement in his sermon against Luther. After quoting Ambrose, Gregory, Jerome, and Cyprian in favor of Peter's primacy, he adds: "All these be of the latyn chyrche. holy fathers. all men of grete lernynge. all men of synguler holynes. whose vertuous lyuynges be confirmed by myracles." The last clause is noteworthy: not their learning but their virtue is singled out for miraculous approbation. Then citing two Greek writers, Chrysostom and Origen, he concludes: "I trust there is no true crysten man but that he wyll be moued with the testimonye of all these [grekes and latyns]. specyally whan they be grounded of so playne & euydent a fygure of the olde lawe: and of so clere a lyght of the holy gospels." The last clause is significant: the Fathers can and do have a foundation in the Scriptures.[9]

But should the witness of the Fathers be admitted for truths not in Scripture? In the following section of his sermon, Fisher would seem to give and defend an affirmative answer: "More testimony must be admytted for sufficyent authoryte. than only that that is wryten in the byble." This assertion he proceeds to prove at great length. God the Father taught the Jews by the prophets, whose prophecies are preserved in Holy Scripture: "yet was there many moo thynges which they spoke vnwritten that was of as grete authoryte," to wit, the Cabala. God the Son then instructed men by His Apostles, who "left vnto vs also many thynges by mouth. which is not written in the byble." The evidence lies in Paul's statement (in Fisher's translation): "Be ye constaunt & kepe those instruccions & erudicyons [*traditiones*] that ye haue lerned of vs. other by mouth, or els by wrytyng" (2 Thess. 2:15). This interpretation is confirmed by Origen, "which is an auncyent doctor & to whome in this poynt grete fayth is to be gyuen."[10] Origen's examples of unwritten tradition are like those already listed by Fisher in his *Destruction of Clichtove's Bulwark*: praying on one's knees, facing east, Eucharistic observances, and baptismal rites. Lastly, the Holy Spirit was sent by Father and Son to teach and to abide with Christ's Church forever: "But by whome I pray you speketh he vnto vs? by whome techeth he vs any trouth? by whome elles but by the fathers & doctours of the chyrche." Their status has been confirmed by miracles, as by the wonderful light seen about Basil at his baptism and about Ambrose when commenting on Psalm 43. Their inspiration has been especially marked in "generall councelles & assembles of many bysshoppes togyder."

In summary, the teachings of the Church, whatever they be, find irrefragable support in these three foundations: "Fyrst the prophetes that were instructed by the father almyghty god. and also theyr Cabala. that is too saye theyr secrete erudycyons not wryten in the byble. Secondly the apostles. whiche were instructed by oure sauyoure chryst Iesu. and also theyr tradycyons not wryten in the byble. Thyrdely the holy fathers and doctours of the chyrche. that were enformed by the holy spyryte of trouthe. aswell in theyr exposycyons of scrypture. as also by theyr general assembles and counceyles had here to fore." [11]

Very soon Fisher brings forth Luther's objection that since the Fathers often disagree, now on one point now on another, he need believe none of them. Fisher responds that even the prophets and the Apostles sometimes deviated from the truth. He furnishes examples in Nathan in his encouragement of David to build the temple (Vulg. 1 Par. 17:2, cf. 2 Reg. 7:3) and Peter in his dissuasion of Christ from His passion (Matt. 16:22). "Almighty god suffred the prophetes and the apostles also somtyme to erre to thentent that we myght knowe they were but men. And whan they sayd trouthe that that they had of god. & whan they sayd otherwyse than trouth that that came of themself. And so lykewyse I saye of the doctours. though they somtyme erred. bycause we myght knowe that they were men. & that than they were left to themselfe. we shal not therfore denye them generally." [12] The examples of erring Nathan and Peter are to be used again by Fisher, who, however, must have come to see that his view on the inerrancy of the Fathers needed to be refined and fortified.

Typical early Protestant opposition to patristic authority thus understood occurs in Simon Hessus' apology for Ulrichus Velenus. According to Hessus, Fisher should not complain about Jerome's inconsistency on the length of Peter's sojourn in Rome because human words are but uncertain and misleading. Fisher, too, should cease to employ the sayings of Jerome and other Fathers as Delphic oracles, and he would gain even Jerome's favor if he did not put "too much faith in his sayings in matters of faith." Experience has shown how human dogmas once admitted increasingly taint the pure light of the Gospel teaching and how human tradition "spreads like a cancer" (2 Tim. 2:17) and takes the place of faith until it brings destruction. Nor should Fisher wonder any more at Velenus' sagacity in uncovering an error in the Pauline epistles undiscovered by the acute and devoted ancient Doctors than at the stupidity of the Apostles in the face of Christ's predictions of His passion and resurrection.[13]

Fisher's most extended treatment of the Fathers is to be found in his *Confutation of Luther's Assertion*. Bellarmine later singles out its introduction as one of the standard discussions of tradition.[14] Fisher's letter to the reader praises the Fathers as "always the more distinguished part of the Church," who have shone like stars because of their learning and holiness.[15] Beginning his introduction by denying to Luther the choice of weapons, he is following in this respect Tertullian who "plainly teaches that they [heretics] are to be prevented from disputing about the Scriptures." After a long quotation from Tertullian, he characteristically sets up, as the arms to conquer Luther, ten Truths (*veritates*). Of these the last five deal with tradition. Some of the arguments previously reviewed reappear. Truth 6 declares: "The Holy Spirit hitherto has used, and always will use, the tongues of the orthodox Fathers for the extirpation of heresies and for the full instruction of the Church in doubtful matters." Here Fisher refers again to the symbolic but visible descent of the Holy Spirit upon Basil, Eubolus, Ambrose, and Gregory.[16]

Truth 7 reads: "It is manifest that whoever does not accept the orthodox Fathers contemns the teaching of the Holy Spirit, nor does he possess that Spirit." The proof stresses the doctrine of the Mystical Body with its one Spirit, who teaches through the early Fathers. To Luther's objection from the errancy of the Fathers, he answers as he did in his sermon: they were allowed to err that we might know their humanness, and they erred as did also the prophets and Apostles, e.g., Nathan and Peter. But Fisher goes beyond his position in the sermon by stating that the truth of the interpretation of any Father can be established "by the mutual comparison of the Scriptures with him, or of all the other interpreters, or of the apostolic traditions, or of the general councils, or of the customs of the Catholic Church, or finally of all these things together. For these so support one another mutually that the truth or the falsity of even whatsoever has been written by a particular interpreter (provided that we be wide awake in comparing all these things with one another mutually) can be easily detected so that it is not at all necessary, because of some errors found in them, to contemn all the other traditions which they have otherwise transmitted in a true and Catholic way." [17]

After establishing in Truth 8 the general councils of the Fathers as the mouthpiece of the Holy Spirit, Fisher argues from Paul's letter to the Thessalonians (2 Thess. 2:15), from the failure of some Apostles to write anything at all, from Pseudo-Areopagite's *Ecclesiastical Hierarchy* in Ambrogio Traversari's Latin translation ("hi multa, partim scriptis, partim non scriptis institutionibus suis . . . nobis tradiderunt"), and from several Fathers (especially Origen's quotation already given in the sermon against Luther) to prove Truth 9: "The apostolic traditions, although they have been set forth in no way in Holy Scripture, are nevertheless to be observed by persons truly Christian." He uses Paul and the Fathers to support Truth 10 also: "But even besides the [apostolic] traditions, likewise the customs which are observed by the universal Church are to be spurned by no Christian." As an example, Fisher gives the headdress for women in church and Paul's own appeal to the authority of ecclesiastical custom (1 Cor. 11:4–5, 11:16). Here he also makes reference to his fuller treatment of the point in the *Destruction of Clichtove's Bulwark*.[18]

In the body of the *Confutation,* the Bishop of Rochester repeats statements previously made. For example, he concedes that the Fathers erred sometimes because they were men, but therefrom he draws a lesson of humility for those far inferior to such pillars. He again praises Origen, "acknowledged to be most brilliant no less for erudition than for subtlety in pondering the Scriptures." Returning to Tertullian's argument from prescription, he denies the appeal of heretics to the Scriptures in controversy. He repeats that Christ and His Apostles handed down many doctrines only by word of mouth without committing them to writing — and then surprisingly continues: "Nevertheless I have no doubt that each one of these doctrines could be founded on Holy Scripture." His most evident and startling declaration occurs in Article 37 (on purgatory): "And because Sacred Scripture is a certain receptacle [*conclaue*] for all truths which are necessary for Christians to know, it can be ambiguous to no one that the truth of purgatory also is contained in it and that it can be proved therefrom." Luther, therefore, who himself still professes belief in purgatory goes too far in declaring that everything to be believed is fully set forth in the Scriptures. If so, whence, asks Fisher, this disagreement of Luther's with the Fathers; or how does he see in Scripture what they could never perceive? Where in Scripture, Fisher begs, will he find the authority for observing Sunday, for venerating images of the saints, for calling the Father unbegotten, for terming the Son homoousian, for the procession of the Holy Spirit from the Father *and* the Son, for celebrating Easter on no day of the week except Sunday, and for not rebaptizing a person baptized by a heretic? [19]

In the *Confutation,* the Bishop of Rochester defends not only the Fathers and Doctors but also Schoolmen like Thomas Aquinas. Luther should not belittle the latter since many scriptural scholars have called him "The Flower of Theology." Here Fisher's comment on the times is interesting: "Many of us today are more intent on scholarship (*doctrina*) than on a good life (*bona vita*) with the result that we care not a straw for even the best writers, although no writer has been found so bad that we may not learn from him very many good things." To later disparagement by Luther, Fisher points out that the pope's approbation of Aquinas does not force one to believe his every teaching to be true, no more than the Church has subscribed to the doctrine of Augustine or Jerome or any other Father or Doctor so as to allow no dissent: "for they in many places have openly declared themselves to be men, and many times to have erred." In the third book of his work on purgatory, John Frith quotes this passage, "my lordes owne words," and then continues: "Now sith the doctours somtime erre, and in certayne places are not to be admitted (as he [Fisher] graunteth himselfe) how should we know when to approue them and when to deny them? If we should hang on the Doctoures authority, then should we as well alow the vntruth, as the truth, sith he affirmeth both. Therfore we must haue a iudge to discerne betweene truth and falsehode. And who shoulde that be? the pope? Nay verely: for he being a man (as well as the Doctours were) may erre as they did. . . Who must that be? Verely the scripture and woord of God. . ." [20]

The *Confutation of Luther's Assertion* furnishes the solid foundation for the *Defense of the Royal Assertion*, published two years later. Fisher again admits the occasional slip on the part of one or the other Father (*homines enim sunt*) but, in view of Christ's promise, denies the possibility of their simultaneous and unanimous error in a matter of faith. The closer they come to apostolic times, the more pure, exact, and solid is their judgment in points of Scripture. He refers to the story of Polycarp who used to shut his ears against heretical teaching. The touchstone for orthodoxy of both prelate and people is conformity with the scriptural and dogmatic teachings of the Fathers. Here the tradition which receives special treatment is that of ecclesiastical usage and custom, which Fisher has to explain and defend in order to justify communion of the people under one species only. According to the Scriptures themselves, he argues, even the Apostles handed down many things, as is evident from the acts of the Council of Jerusalem (Acts 15:28–29) and from the veiling of women in church (1 Cor. 11:3–16). If it is not found in Scripture, a custom must be holy, salutary, and generally approved by all Christians; if so, it was inspired by the Holy Spirit. Lay communion under one species, for example, gradually crept in by the tacit consent of both the clergy and the people — "that people which is governed by the Holy Spirit." Fisher objects to Luther's silence on the king's argument that this custom grew up without lay protests. The sacrificial character of the mass, too, is clear from ancient custom stretching back to apostolic tradition, as is established by Tertullian who in his book *De corona militis* gathers together many things which rest on no Scripture but on custom. But a person would be quite unfair to demand the testimonies of the Apostles themselves, since whatever they might have written on the mass as a sacrifice could quite credibly have perished through injurious time (*iniuria temporum*).[21]

It is Tertullian's "prescriptive right of long-accepted truth," reaching back from Augustine to the Apostles, that Fisher uses in defense of the priesthood. In opposition, Luther can produce no orthodox writer and no scriptural text. "Therefore," Fisher says at the end of his First Rejoinder, "the obviously safer way is to follow these Fathers; nor can anyone, without manifest peril to his soul, desert them and follow Luther." His Second Rejoinder declares that there are necessary truths not expressly set forth in Scripture, e.g., the imposition of hands in baptism, practiced by the Apostles, who nowhere in Scripture are instructed to do so by Christ or the Holy Spirit. There are many such teachings never committed to writing, as Eusebius of Caesarea testifies when referring to Ignatius of Antioch's book on these traditions: "If only that book were still extant . . . it would supply much that is now lacking." Here Fisher objects to Luther's argumentation: "If Luther wishes to adduce any testimony that is not in the Scriptures he is acting unfairly, for when it tells against him he will not admit any such evidence." The issue concerns Timothy, whose circumcision by St. Paul Scripture states clearly (Acts 16:3), but not his baptism — something to be proved by Luther.[22]

The Third Rejoinder declares that Luther should direct his attacks not against the contemporary clergy for usurping the name of priests but against the Fathers quoted by Fisher, all of whom "were inspired by the Holy Ghost. If, then, Luther is inspired by the same spirit he would hold no other opinion than theirs, especially as they are so unanimous." Luther's only arguments are negative and therefore worthless with learned men. As for texts on adding nothing to Scripture or to Christ's testament, why did Christ say that He had many things yet to tell His Apostles who could not bear to hear them until the coming of the Spirit of Truth after His ascension (John 16:12–13): "Who can deny that Christ left many other things to be afterwards added?" Why did Paul make additions of his own (1 Cor. 7:12, 11:34, 2 Thess. 2:14), some of which evidently were never written down? Fisher concludes with a statement which is at once extremely comprehensive and yet cautiously limited: "The Scriptures, then, are not to be understood in the perverse way in which Luther understands them, as if nothing whatever was to be allowed beyond what they contain, nor anything added to them, for many things besides the Scriptures have been handed down from the apostles by tradition, and many things added wisely by their successors. But rather we are to understand that nothing can be accepted which is contrary to the Scriptures, nor must anything be added which in any manner conflicts with them."[23]

This last quotation from Fisher's *Defense of the Sacred Priesthood* is so surprising in its breadth that it would seem to leave the door open for countless abuses. It would tend, moreover, to reduce Scripture to a negative norm rather than a positive force. To this difficulty Fisher would counter that his statement refers to certain specific traditions and immemorial customs. Some are outward observances, like the headdress of women in church, the sign of the cross, the veneration of saints' images, the sanctification of Sunday by Christians, and the celebration of the Resurrection on Sunday only. Others have to do with the sacraments: the imposition of hands in baptism, the baptism of infants, the denial of rebaptism to persons baptized by heretics, the words of Eucharistic consecration, and the communication of the laity under only one species. Still others concern Mary: her virginity and her assumption. Finally, some reach the dogmatic level and even touch the Trinity: the Father as unbegotten, the Son as homoousian, and the Holy Spirit as proceeding from both Father and Son. Fisher points to the Council of Jerusalem (Acts 15:1–35) as illustrating the genesis of a tradition nowhere found in the Gospel: abstention "from things sacrificed to idols and from blood and from what is strangled and from immorality" (Acts 15:29).

A notable contribution made by Fisher's next work, the sermon at Barnes's abjuration, is the metaphor used to describe the role of the Fathers in the salvific scheme. It is Christ that sows the seed or word of truth: "The preachers of this word be nothyng els / but as the cophyns and the hoppers / wherin this sede is couched." Just as Christ spoke in St. Paul (2 Cor. 13:3), so also He spoke in the Fathers: "And nat only Christ dyd sowe this sede by their mouthes: but also the spirite of god gaue his gratious influence vnto this sede by theyr mouthes / in lyke maner" (cf. Matt. 10:20). In the course of his development, Fisher makes the following most significant analysis:

> This is than the ordre and the holle cheane: the blyndenes of our hertes can nat be put away / but by true faith: true faith can nat be gotten / but by herynge of this worde. The heryng of this worde shal nat be had / but by the meanes of preachynge: prechynge can nat be ministred without the preacher: the preacher can nat profitte / onles Christe Iesu (whiche is the veray sower) speke within hym: and also the spirite of Christe gyue his influence vnto the same.

If the Fathers preached error and if their people believed error, then Christ defaulted on His promise to be present in the Church forever in His own person and through the Holy Spirit. On the other hand, "if the doctryne of the fathers be true (as it must be / if our sauiour spake by their mouthes) Luthers doctryne / whiche is contrary / muste nedis be false." By cutting himself off from the Fathers, "men of singular lernynge and excellent holynes," with whom he had formerly agreed, Luther has cut himself off from the Church. As Fisher in his prefatory letter had impressed upon Luther's follower: "Though his maister Luther dyd lyue neuer so well and perfetly / yet for as moche as his doctryne is dyuerse from the doctryne of the churche he is to be fled." [24]

In his refutation of Oecolampadius, the Bishop of Rochester naturally makes extensive use of the Fathers but without adding materially to his theory on their role in Christianity. The method of prescription is resorted to in the preface to Book IV to prove the reality of Christ's Body and Blood from the common consent of the Fathers. The same method is used also in the preface to Book V to show that John's sixth chapter pertains to the sacrament of the Eucharist. The Fathers were hardly lacking in erudition, skill in languages, experience in Scripture, holiness of life, or the miracles necessary to prove the truth of their doctrine. Individual Fathers went astray at times because they were men, but neither the promise of Christ nor the perpetual presence of the Holy Spirit would suffer them to err collectively in difficult matters of faith. Fisher shows that the Fathers cited by Oecolampadius, such as Tertullian, Cyprian, and Origen, actually do not support his interpretation. Reference is made again to St. Ignatius of Antioch's lost book on traditions.[25]

In the books on the divorce, composed within the next few years, Fisher had to appeal to the Fathers on many points, especially scriptural. In his response to the king's book, *Censurae* (1530), for example, he comments almost sardonically: "Of course, no orthodox person denies that Christians are obliged to many as it were divine commands of laws concerning which not even a word is read in the New Testament." The basis for these unwritten ecclesiastical traditions is John 21:25: "There are, however, many other things that Jesus did. . ." Fisher naturally denies that this fact has anything to do with the case in hand, marriage to a dead brother's childless widow. What is noteworthy is that all parties agree on the existence and validity of unwritten apostolic traditions.[26]

In passing, one might note that at the end of 1530, with its feverish writing and publication on Henry's divorce, we have another glimpse of Fisher's continuing absorption in the Fathers: Erasmus' gift to him of his Latin edition of Chrysostom's *Opera,* published by Froben at Basel that same year.[27] After his execution, even Henry VIII's apologist, Richard Morison, admitted his biblical and patristic knowledge (although he might give a twist to prove such a point as papal authority): "For a long time he occupied himself with the Holy Scripture. There was nothing he did not read. He perused the tomes of all the Doctors." [28]

It is now possible to comment on Fisher's attitude toward traditions of the tradition. Nowhere does he assert that tradition should be esteemed as much as Scripture. Men, although helped by the Holy Spirit, are authors of the former (tradition) but God is the author of the latter (Scripture), which fundamentally is sufficient in itself without need for extrabiblical tradition. The latter (tradition) is operative above all in the area of ecclesiastical, liturgical, and ritualistic forms. Hence heretics have no call to oppose the authority of Scripture to the authority of tradition when properly defined and delimited according to the whole history of the Church and not that of a particular age, which might have abused the original tradition. When both the heretical and the orthodox quote Scripture, Fisher resorts to tradition as expressed in the Fathers for the true meaning, but he does not stop here in the case of the most important texts. As will be seen later, he examines and tests the exegetical methods used by himself and by his opponents. Consequently the Fathers are primarily interpreters of Scripture, not its complement or fulfillment or final formulation. They explain but do not fix or determine the meaning of the text. They evidently have no intention of making their interpretations articles of faith, except insofar as they are witnesses to apostolic authority on these articles.

For Fisher, therefore, the ecclesiastical tradition of the Fathers, the creeds, the councils, and so forth is distinguished but not distinct from Scripture and the teaching episcopacy and papacy. The Holy Spirit makes all these things parts of a single whole or system of authority. One modern scholar has noted a change in Luther's attitude on this point: "In his earlier days . . . he had felt able to defy the tradition of the church or even to ignore it altogether, almost as though there had been no church between Patmos and Wittenberg. But in his mature thought . . . he came to realize the importance of what had intervened between the New Testament and Luther. What helped him to realize this importance was the construction other Protestants were putting on the right of private exegesis," especially in regard to baptism and the Lord's Supper.[29] If this view is true, Fisher is defending tradition against the works of a Luther who has not come to terms with tradition as a valuable and necessary asset to both the Church and Scripture. It is to Scripture that we now turn. Its study is bound to clarify and develop, perhaps also modify, what has already been said about Fisher's Church and Fisher's tradition.

Chapter VII

SCRIPTURE: ITS NATURE AND USE

THE Bishop of Rochester's death is permeated by irony. This great defender of the Church, its episcopacy and its papacy, did not die officially a bishop because he was deprived as of January 2, 1535. This ardent advocate of the sacraments was long kept back from their consolation so that he had to beg Cromwell for a confessor at Christmastide. This pious apologist for traditional ceremonies had to meet death and burial without the last rites and ceremonies of the Church. This convinced champion of the Fathers and Doctors saw no wonder worked on his behalf. All this is bitterly — and gloriously — ironic. What is not ironic but in strict consonance with his whole character and life is that this man of learning carried to execution no other book than a copy of the New Testament and opened it randomly at John 17:3–5: "Now this is everlasting life, that they may know thee, the only true God, and him whom thou hast sent, Jesus Christ. . ." As he mounted the scaffold itself, the sun shining into his face inspired him to recite from memory Vulg. Ps. 33:6: "Come ye to him and be enlightened: and your faces shall not be confounded." He closed his life with the hymn *Te deum* and with the psalm *In te Domine speravi* (Vulg. Ps. 30 or 70).[1]

These prayers were fitting because he had labored to preserve and spread the Gospel and because he had held the Psalms in special esteem, as evidenced by his first major publication, the popular English sermons on the Penitential Psalms, and by his voluminous Latin commentary on the Psalms still in manuscript. In both works he describes the Scripture as the spiritual food of the soul. In the unpublished commentary on Vulg. Ps. 22, he enumerates four consolations, of which the very first is "the food of the soul, namely, the Sacred Scriptures, by which the soul is to be just as attentively nourished as the body with material bread; nor does the mind truly Christian taste less pleasure in the exposition of the Scriptures than the bodily palate in a banquet prepared by the art of cooks." The first English sermon on Vulg. Ps. 101 reads: "This spirituall brede the worde of god maketh the soule to be ful of Iuse [juice], full of the lycour of good deuocyon, & also it maketh the soule stronge & hardy to withstande all trybulacions." It is necessary not merely to receive the word, that is, to hear it, but also to chew and swallow it, that is, to practice it: "Many there be that receyue this spirituall brede the worde of god by heryinge it spoken of the precher, but they neyther chewe it nor swalowe it downe, that is to saye they do not therafter, for it sauoureth not in theyr mouthes." A remarkable comparison with "the bread of the devil," worked out at length, follows. For example, the bread of the devil "maketh that the concupyscence of the flesshe hath dominacyon and reason is set aparte & layde vnder, where contrary wyse the very brede of the worde of god maketh reason lady and ruler & the flesshe to be thrall and as a seruaunt. The worde of god causeth all goodnes in the soule, it maketh it moyste and redy to sprynge in good werkes. The worde of the deuyll maketh drynesse, dull & sluggysshe to do ony thynge that is good." [2]

The final end of man's every spiritual activity is union of soul with God. In his treatise on prayer Fisher declares: "We may be brought vnto this vnion by some comfortable text or exposition of the scriptures." The delight of the Scriptures alone, however, is less strong and plentiful than that of direct union with the divinity itself. Fisher proceeds to explain: "For the scripture albeit it did proceade from God, yet is it a creature. And what creature so euer possesse our mindes, be it neuer so excellent, so as it be not God hymselfe, that same standeth betwene God and vs, insomuch that it is an impediment vnto our mindes, that we be not ioyned euen face to face, and perfectly coupled with God him selfe." [3] Fisher, of course, has no intention of depressing the dignity of the Scriptures. But the difference between God and His written word is that between fountain and stream, Creator and creature, end and means.

The Bishop of Rochester plainly holds that the Scriptures are inspired, that is, that under the inspiration of the Holy Spirit they have God as their author. This inspiration is so evident to him and his readers that he refers to this fact (or to the precise way in which God uses His free and reasoning instrument) only in passing. For example, in the quotation just given, he says that "the scripture . . . did proceade from God." In *Christ's Body,* he approves Erasmus' statement: God's Scriptures have certain secret and dark recesses into which man must not and cannot penetrate too deeply without growing more and more blind and which stand as witnesses to the inscrutable majesty of God's wisdom and the feebleness of man's mind. But God leaves clues, as it were, for the diligent exegete or reader. The Holy Spirit speaks in the Scriptures with the greatest caution and foresight; for example, Luke reads, "This cup is the new covenant in my blood," not "This is the cup. . ." (Luke 22:20), which could have been subject to misinterpretation.[4]

A most explicit statement on inspiration occurs in a divorce tract of Fisher's (Camb. Univ. Lib. MS. 1315). The Holy Spirit cannot err in His legislation as do men whose lack of vision demands later emendation of their laws. "The Holy Spirit who inspired the Scriptures could not be ignorant of the future." Hence the Deuteronomical command to marry one's dead brother's childless widow (Deut. 25:5) in no way changed, added to, or derogated from the Levitical prohibition not to marry one's brother's wife (Lev. 20:21), especially under the Mosaic dispensation.[5]

It is interesting to note that for Fisher inspiration does not extend to the preservation of books having the Holy Spirit as their author. For example, if the Apostles had written anything about the mass as a sacrifice, it is not incredible for it to have perished "because of the injury of time." [6] As for the writings that have survived, inspiration means that whatever God as author either expressly or tacitly sets forth as His own is free from error and its very possibility. The difficulty lies in determining the sense or meaning or truth intended by the divine author. Fisher evidently adopts the "senses" current at the time.[7] The two main categories are the literal, when the words retain their natural meaning, and the metaphorical, when the words involve a figure of speech. The mystical sense, called also the spiritual or the typical, is not suggested immediately by the letter, or words, but by persons or things ordained by Providence to signify other persons or things. This sense is used especially to explain the Old Testament in relation to the New. Its subdivisions are usually three: the allegorical, when it relates to truths about Christ and the Church Militant; the tropological, when it refers to the moral virtues and vices; and the anagogical, when it prefigures heaven and glory. It is above all the literal sense which reveals the truths of faith. The spiritual sense also can be the source of revelation provided it can be proved to be God's intention. This sense can be used even in controversy provided it is admitted by both parties.

Fortunately Fisher's sermons on the Penitential Psalms, being noncontroversial, furnish good examples which foreshadow future use. When a Jew was rendered unclean by acts like touching a dead body, he was purified "with ysope dypped in the blode of certayne beestes and sprencled vpon hym." At the time, "it was vncertayne, it was hyd, what the wysdome of god wolde to be vnderstande by this aspercyon or sprenklynge of blode." Fisher then explains that the hyssop signified Christ and that the sprinkling with the blood of animals "sygnefyed and represented the effusyon of the blode of Cryst for our redempcyon." So, too, in the sacrifices offered by the Jews for their sins, the "sleynge of those bruyte beestes after Moyses entent fygured the deth of our sauyour cryste Ihesu. . ." [8]

Later, the Bishop of Rochester declares that the second part of Vulg. Ps. 101 is "more derke & harde to vnderstande than is the fyrst parte of it." He explains that "thre noble places . . . sygnefye thre dyuers kyndes of people in thre dyuerse tymes": (1) Mount Sinai "betokeneth the people of Iewes, in the tyme of Moyses lawe"; (2) Mount Sion signifies "the crysten people, in the tyme of grace"; and (3) "the hygh celestyall Iherusalem . . . representeth the blyssed people in the tyme of glory." At the end of a long development, he sums up his points as follows:

Fyrst in the tyme of Iewes whiche is done and paste was grete fere and drede of the greuous punysshement of god. In the tyme of crysten people whiche is now, is grete hope & truste of forgyuenes, for the excellent treasure of grace & mercy of god. But in the tyme of those that shall be blyssed euerlastyngly which is yet to come shall be the surete of the rewarde by confyrmacyon of eternall and incessaunt Ioye.[9]

In these sermons, Fisher quite naturally uses not only the mystical sense but also the so-called accommodated sense; that is, he applies the words of Scripture to a situation not at all intended by the Holy Spirit as author. In a notable example in the sermon on Vulg. Ps. 129, he "figuratyuely" compares the stages in the fall of a sinner to the seven "degrees & ordres of his dyscencyons" in the fall of Jonah. As he begins to work out the parallel in great detail, he has to face the difficulty that according to Matthew 12:39–41 Jonah signifies Christ. He explains: "One & the same thynge by a dyuers consyderacyon may be taken fyguratyuely for two contraryes. Somtyme in holy scrypture the lyon sygnefyeth Cryst [Apoc. 5:5] and somtyme by the lyon is sygnefyed the deuyll [1 Pet. 5:8]. . . why may not Ionas somtyme sygnefy Cryst and somtyme the synner." [10] A briefer instance of the accommodated sense is found in the sermon on Vulg. Ps. 142: "Blyssed lorde, lyke as the wylde harte after he hath dronken poyson desyreth to come vnto the fresshe spryngynge fountayne for his synguler remedy & comforte, euen so dooth my soule after the remembraunce of my synne, desyre for to come vnto the by the fountayne of penaunce." [11]

In his English sermon against Luther, Fisher attempts to use the mystical sense for controversial purposes. After detailing the resemblances between a tree and its shadow, he proclaims in general: "The lawe of Moyses. & the gouernaunce of the synagoge of the Iewes. was but a shadowe of the gouernaunce of the vniuersall chirche of christ." It follows in particular that Moses and Aaron must be "the shadowe of chryste & of his vycare saynt Peter whiche vnder christ was also the heed of chrysten people." The proof lies in three points of resemblance: (1) Moses and Aaron were both priests, and so also Christ and Peter; (2) Moses was intermediary between God and Aaron as Christ between God and Peter, and Aaron was intermediary between Moses and the people as Peter between Christ and his brethren; and (3) just as Moses ascended the mount and Aaron stayed behind, so Christ ascended to heaven to intercede for us and Peter remained behind to teach the people. We have already seen how Tyndale objected to this interpretation in the face of the assertion in the epistle to the Hebrews (chap. 9) that, whether Moses or Aaron, "the priest of the old law signifieth Christ." [12]

Actually Fisher had anticipated such an objection in his *Confutation of Luther's Assertion.* Here, too, he maintains that "all things of the Old Law were nothing else than certain figures of the New Law and certain foreshadowings of those things that are contained in the Gospel." He again works out the comparison between a tree and its shadow and at even greater length the prefiguration of Christ and Peter by Moses and Aaron respectively. Denying that Aaron can represent Christ alone, he declares: "But what prevents the same thing from being the figure of different things?" Just as the lion signifies both Christ and the devil, just as leaven represents now faith now sin, so Aaron can be a figure of both Christ and Peter.[13]

In this whole matter Fisher should probably have heeded St. Jerome's advice which he had earlier given to Luther: "Never can dubious understanding of parable and allegories contribute to the authority of dogmas." When one tries to establish dogmas, especially against the common sentiment of the Church, one should produce evident and irrefragable texts or reasons, "not parables, which can be twisted to different and manifold meanings." Yet Fisher himself has to resort to a parable, that of the rich man and Lazarus (Luke 16:19–31), for confirmation of the doctrine of purgatory. John Frith exposes the weakness of this procedure. He gives the rules for expounding parables and maintains that this particular parable was spoken to the Pharisees, "playnly concludyng that they should haue no such apparitions of the dead . . . but that they had Moses & the Prophetes." [14] "My Lord" was to pay much more attention to the proper use of Scripture in his controversy with Oecolampadius.

With the delivery of the sermon at Barnes's abjuration, the Bishop of Rochester began to define more carefully the relations between the Old and the New Testaments. As for the Fathers and peoples of the two covenants, "Both these make but one people: for they be al of one faythe." The main difference is that those who preceded Christ "were vnder the lawe of Moyses / whiche was a lawe of drede / and of rygour . . . But tho that folowed Christ were and be vnder the lawe of grace and marcy." [15] Later, he concedes to Oecolampadius that both Christians and Jews eat and drink Christ by faith, but Christians do so more fully because they eat His Body and drink His Blood in the Eucharist. Hence there is a tremendous difference between "our truth and their shadows." Melchizedek, the paschal lamb, and the manna — all were foreshadowings of the Eucharist; that is, "the species, the substance, and the efficacy of this sacrament were prefigured through those three shadows." In addition to differences in the commandments and in the sacraments for the two peoples, there is the disparity between the promise and the fulfillment of the promise: Christians eat corporally and really what Jews ate figuratively and typically.[16]

When Oecolampadius quotes Origen to his purpose, Fisher insists that no argument can be established from allegories. Origen's contention that all things in Scripture are figures and to be accepted mystically does not win the favor of Augustine, Jerome, and the other scholars. "For the letter, too, has its own truth which is also much more certain than allegory, since innumerable allegorical and mystical senses swarm from the same letter. Only the literal sense, for all that, has a strength and firmness of its own, which cannot be contradicted. As for allegories, each reader approves of them insofar as they please his inclination and opinion." [17] But Fisher hastens to explain that the truly literal sense is not, for example, that crude and cannibalistic sense in which the people of Capharnaum erroneously understood Christ's words in His promise of the Eucharist (John 6:22–70). "But there is also for these words another letter and another literal sense which is true . . . and that letter is so far from killing that it assuredly vivifies believers." [18] Fisher is referring, of course, to that subdivision of the literal sense which is not proper but metaphorical. The literal sense does not altogether exclude the other senses. Later, Fisher explains that, according to the true literal sense, Christ's true Flesh and true Blood are in the Eucharist but that, "according to the anagogical sense, Christ's Flesh and Blood are eaten likewise spiritually in the reading of the Scriptures." [19]

In the last book of *Christ's Body*, Fisher returns to the relationship between the Christian and the Jewish religion. If "religion" (*religio*) is restricted to the sense of "faith" (*fides*), Christians and Jews share the same religion because they have in common but one faith, hope, and charity. But the differences in worship (*cultus*) are tremendous both exteriorly and interiorly. Christians have the fullness of the grace of the Holy Spirit, the abiding presence of Christ in His Church till the end of time, new commandments promulgated in the Sermon on the Mount, and new sacraments of which the old sacraments were but figures and shadows.[20]

No matter what senses he may employ in his sermons or in his controversies, the Bishop of Rochester in his scriptural interpretation always follows the rule which is called the analogy of faith. He rejects every sense which would make the various human authors, even though inspired, seem to conflict with one another — or, for him, with the doctrine of the Church. From his first to his last work he observes this norm. In the second sermon on Vulg. Ps. 50, for example, he wonders why David applies three names to the Holy Spirit: *spiritum rectum, spiritum sanctum,* and *spiritum principalem.* He says: "But for as moche as it is lawfull for euery clerke in ony suche doubtes to shewe theyr myndes *not contraryenge other places of scripture.* I shal in fewe wordes declare (as me semeth) what he meneth." He then proceeds to give his explanation with many more than a "fewe wordes." [21]

The Bishop of Rochester's sermon against Luther in 1521 brings up a far more serious point: the relationship between faith and works. He states the apparent contradiction between Paul and James as follows: "The same example that saynt Paule vseth vnto the Romaynes to proue that faythe iustyfyed a synner withouten workes. the same vseth saynt Iames to the contrary. the example I meane of Abraham." St. Paul writes: "For if Abraham was justified by works, he has reason to boast, but not before God" (Rom. 4:2), whereas St. James writes: "Was not Abraham our father justified by works . . . ?" The easy way out is to admit: "Syr be these apostles one contrary to another." Fisher himself resorts to Augustine's solution: "For saynt Paule meaneth of the workes that gothe before faythe. & saynt Iames meaneth of the workes that folowe after the faythe." The same objection and the same answer occur in the *Confutation of Luther's Assertion.*[22]

The foundation for the analogy of faith as an exegetical principle is spelled out in the sermon at Barnes's abjuration. The seed of the word of God is one for three reasons: (1) "it is sortable and agreable / and lyke vnto it selfe in euery parte," i.e., it is all wheat without admixture of cockle; (2) "ther is in it no discord / no repugnancy / no contradiction / of one parte of it with an other" — like an harmonious song in which the Apostles and Evangelists sing the plain song and the Fathers furnish the discant — "at the leest in any poynt concernyng the substance of our faithe"; and, for the plainest declaration of the analogy of faith, (3) "Though there be many bokes of scripture / bothe in the olde testament and in the newe also / yet all these bokes be so fully agreed by the expositions and interpretations of the holy doctours / that they make but one boke / and one body of scripture: and haue in them all but one spirite of lyfe: that is to saye / the spirite of Christe Iesu." In a remarkable metaphor based on Ezekiel (chaps. 1, 10), Fisher voices his faith in the unity and harmony of all the Scriptures:

> The psalter of Dauid is a roundell of trouthe / and eche of the gospels is a roundell of trouthe: The gospelles be in the psalter: and the psalter is in the gospelles: and the spirite of Christe maketh one roundell of them all. The newe testament is a roundell / and the olde testament is a roundell / and either of them is in the other: but there is but one spirite of lyfe in them bothe: and so in euery roundell of scripture: and this spirite maketh one roundell of all. And with these also the expositions of the fathers / whiche were inspired by the same spirite / make one roundell with the same.[23]

Consequently, in the light of the analogy of faith, an extremely damaging charge by Fisher against Luther is that "Luther by his intricate expositions maketh one parte of scripture to be repugnant agaynst an other / as he confesseth hym selfe / that he can nat frame his other expositions with the Epistole of saynt Iames / and with the gospell of Luke." In his peroration Fisher labels this inability a blasphemy and reproach "agaynst certeyn bokes of scripture / namely the gospel of Luke / and the Epistole of saint Iames."[24] In *Christ's Body,* too, the Bishop of Rochester takes pains to show that although Luke's words for the Eucharistic consecration are different, his meaning in no way departs from Matthew's and Mark's.[25] Finally in his book on the divorce (Camb. Univ. Lib. MS. 1315), he twice demands the reconciliation of Lev. 20:21 and Deut. 25:5 because "there is nothing which is more abhorrent to all authors than someone's assertion that the Scriptures are mutually inconsistent."[26]

From the start of his controversies, Fisher undoubtedly began to see the necessity of treating the Scriptures not only as divinely inspired writings but also as human documents. As the latter, they betrayed the characteristic traits of their authors, they belonged to a certain period in history, and they reflected the linguistic and literary peculiarities of medium, writer, and time. In these respects they had to be analyzed and judged like purely secular documents. In *The Single Magdalene* Fisher remarks, for example, that each Evangelist has his own habit, with Luke observing one order of narration and John another. Luke anticipates future events by speaking early of "Judas Iscariot, who turned traitor" (Luke 6:16), whereas John treats time exactly by describing Judas Iscariot as "he who was about to betray him" (John 12:4). In the *Destruction of Clichtove's Bulwark,* too, Fisher uses Judas to exemplify John's references to future events as in the future and to past events as in the past. In fact, in the *Confutation of Lefèvre's Second Disquisition,* Fisher's first Supposition is that, unlike Matthew who uses temporal expressions like "then," the other Evangelists, especially Luke, do not observe the chronological order or give distinctive circumstances. His eighth Supposition declares that failure to interpret the Evangelists considerately (*civiliter*) involves the exegete in many contradictions or in unnecessary multiplication of persons and events, as in the stories of the centurion's servant, the robbers crucified with Christ, the indignation of Judas or the disciples at Christ's anointing, the time of the women's coming to the sepulcher, and finally the number of Magdalenes. The reason is that the Evangelists "not only narrate events but endeavor much more so to narrate them as to express them as pregnant with many mysteries; whence it follows that one Evangelist relates the same event in one way, another in a different way, and very often, unless they are interpreted rather liberally, they seem to assert contradictory things." [27]

One might note other views of Fisher on the Evangelists. When Velenus rejects even Platina's acceptance of the story that Peter, at the urging of the Romans, had had Mark write his Gospel, and when he claims that not John Mark but Mark Aristarchus had written this Gospel, Fisher defends the traditional report and proves that Mark and Aristarchus are two different persons. In the *Defense of the Royal Assertion,* however, he mentions the universally received opinion that "Mark was, as it were, the abbreviator of Matthew." Finally, in *Christ's Body,* he observes that John silently passes over events sufficiently related by the other Evangelists and concentrates on those omitted by them.[28]

The Bishop of Rochester is far from denying that heretics "were redy in scryptures. & coude brynge the scryptures merueylously to theyr purpose." But, he continues, "for lacke of the spiryte of trouthe they misconstrued these scriptures. & as saynt peter saythe. Deprauabant. or as saynt Paule saythe. Inuertebant, they tourned the wronge syde of the scryptures outwarde." [29] In particular, he has difficulty with their demand that controversies be settled by Scripture alone. Private scrutiny more often than not never reaches certitude on the true meaning of the disputed text, and the multiplying sects stand as evidence of failure to agree on the authentic interpretation.

Hence in the introduction to the *Confutation of Luther's Assertion,* one of his ten Truths is that "every controversy which arises cannot always be refuted and disposed of by only the help of the Sacred Scriptures." Two truths admitted by Luther, the existence of purgatory and the perpetual virginity of Mary, can hardly be proved by scriptural texts alone against the heretics. Helvidius, who maintained that Mary bore children after Jesus, based his argument on obvious grammatical sense: Joseph "did not know her till she brought forth her firstborn son" (Matt. 1:25). Tertullian is cited again on the uselessness of scriptural argument with confirmed heretics.[30]

Fisher objects to the isolation of scriptural texts with subsequent criticism and rejection of them one by one. Instead he espouses the gathering of texts which mutually support one another. "For, the greater the agreement of any scriptural text with many others, the greater the support it receives from its connection — greater than if it were severed from all the others." He uses two homely examples: it is easy to pluck out a horse's tail by taking one hair at a time and to break one stick but not a bundle of sticks (Plutarch). For a froward opponent no single argument is telling even though all taken together prove the case in the clearest manner possible. The context here is that of the Petrine and papal claims.[31]

In his *Defense of the Sacred Priesthood,* the Bishop of Rochester has to face a different problem: the failure of the New Testament to apply the term *priest* (*sacerdos*) to those Christians who are called priests (*sacerdotes*) at present. He resorts to history: "The apostles avoided the term . . . because the ancient priesthood was still in existence and daily sacrifice was offered in the Temple." In this way no confusion could result. Instead, "there is constant mention of them [Christian priests] under the name of presbyters and bishops." To make clear that the Apostles were not scrupulous in their use of terms, he gives three examples: (1) *ministry* and *minister,* as applied to all Christians and yet to a special group (Acts 1:25, 13:2, Col. 4:17, 2 Tim. 4:5); (2) *presbyter,* as common to all elderly men and yet given to young men of ecclesiastical rank, as well as to bishops (Acts 20:28, 1 Tim. 4:12, 5:1–2, Titus 1:5); and (3) *apostle,* as shared with the seventy-two disciples and yet restricted to the Twelve (Luke 10:1, John 13:16). The exact distinction between these terms can be found only in oral tradition. If one still insists upon the term *priests,* Fisher "could as easily prove that St. John the Evangelist [John 13:16] thought that there was no distinction between the apostles and the disciples." Hence in his epilogue he asserts: "Even if in the Scriptures priests were never mentioned by name, there is so much about the substance of their office that it would be more than foolish to assail it."[32]

To settle Luther's difficulties in regard to these terms, Fisher puts scriptural verses in their context. When Luther appeals to Paul's statement: "He [God] also it is who has made us fit ministers of the new covenant" (2 Cor. 3:6), Fisher answers: "Anyone who will attentively read the chapter . . . will see that St. Paul speaks here not of all Christians, but in his own person." In like manner, Christ said, "He that heareth you heareth Me, and he that despiseth you despiseth Me," not to all Christians but to the seventy-two disciples only. From the context (Luke 10:1–20), Fisher argues as follows: "Now, if these words were said to all Christians, so must all the preceding words have been. Therefore this, too, was said to all, viz., 'Carry neither purse, nor scrip, nor shoes, and salute no man by the way' — which is obviously false." So, too, when Luther maintains that women *may* prophesy and teach in church but have surrendered the right for good reasons, Fisher shows that the prohibition comes not from St. Paul but from God. Moreover, prophecy has three senses: announcement and praise of the wonderful works of God (Acts 2:11, 10:46, 19:6), "the foretelling of the future" (Acts 11:28, 21:10–11), and "the interpretation of Scripture and of tongues, as it is more frequently used by St. Paul." Whenever women in the Bible "prophesy," they do so in a private capacity, not as public and official teachers.[33]

In *Christ's Body* the Bishop of Rochester declares that, far from distorting Christ's words, he has openmindedly followed "Hilary's canon": the ideal reader expects rather than imposes a meaning on scriptural dicta. A word like "eat," for example, can have a double significance: a real eating of the Body of Christ or an eating of the word of God — but Oecolampadius more than once excludes the former through the latter. Another norm of interpretation is given later with a rare autobiographical reference. Fisher's erstwhile teacher of geometry, William Melton, now "Chancellor of York, a man distinguished for upright life and every kind of learning," had often admonished him "that if I thought the least letter in any geometrical figure to be superfluous, I had not yet grasped Euclid's true and total mind." Like a student (*discipulus*) of Euclid, "certainly a student [*discipulus*] of Christ ought so to weigh the single words of Christ as to persuade himself that nothing in them is superfluous."[34]

Hence, in his reply to the *Censurae* of 1530, Fisher marvels that the universities so concentrate on the text in Leviticus (20:21) as to ignore the other books: "for they ought . . . to have weighed the single words of Moses which he gives not only here but elsewhere too." They should have realized the practice of Scripture to set down a general prohibition with very many exceptions being taken for granted. As examples, Fisher offers the prohibitions against work on the Sabbath (with its obvious exceptions), against slaying (but criminals are slain justly), against image-making (yet God gave command to sculpture two cherubim), against marriage of blood-relatives (with explicit exceptions), and against deformity in priests (but only against the blemishes specified elsewhere).[35]

Except for Fisher's critical use of the original languages, which will be treated later, all the rules for interpretation given thus far, have been internal or intrinsic to the text, such as the context, which ranges from the particular passage to the historical occasion, and the parallel texts, which modify or illuminate the text in question. Additionally, is there any legitimacy or validity to norms which might be termed external or extrinsic to the text, such as the living voice of an infallible Church or the consent of the Fathers? Calvin would say that the same Holy Spirit that inspires the text gives people sufficient grace to understand and accept the truth imparted by the text without the necessity for further authority.[36] Luther would recognize the right of private interpretation "with the proviso that such interpretation be carried on in the midst of, for the benefit of, and subject to examination by, the church." [37] Where does the Bishop of Rochester stand on this problem? This query might seem idle in face of his opinions, reviewed above, on the living infallible magisterium of Holy Mother the Church, on the unanimous consent of the Fathers, and on the deplorable rebellion of heretics. Yet details and reasons, especially when given over a period of years and under differing circumstances, are bound to modify the position of any intelligent man no matter how fixed his basic principles. Moreover, the special topic of reference here will be the Scriptures.

At the very beginning of his controversial period, Fisher tries to impale the Dominican Lefèvre on the horns of a dilemma. Are the pronouncements of Holy Scripture everywhere so clear and open to every mind that no need exists for any expositor or interpreter? If the answer is affirmative, whence the variety of opinions and meanings? If negative, whom should the Christian people (*plebs*) trust for an explanation? Fisher's response is most definite: first, the Sovereign Pontiffs; then, the orthodox Fathers and authors; and finally the preachers who faithfully and assiduously minister the word of God to the people. If the entire last class be discovered to have set forth even a single untruth, the people need not trust them in anything else. Of course, it is extremely perilous to assert that they have conspired even in a single untruth. When Lefèvre confesses his search for those who know the inner force (*energia*) of the Gospels, he is resorting to a diversionary tactic, for a Latin Father like St. Augustine has all the gifts necessary to reach that inner force: native perspicacity, holy life, scriptural expertness, talent for harmonizing the Gospels, and knowledge of the Greek commentators.[38]

In the *Destruction of Clichtove's Bulwark,* Fisher again defends the Latins: they are not all dull and stupid since they have the same Gospels in both Latin and Greek and know the Greek commentators and their dissensions. Every exponent of an opinion different from the Church's has produced texts from Scripture and often has deceived simple souls more easily by the appearance of holiness. How much better to adhere to the consensus of the churches scattered throughout the world — as did Augustine, who testifies that "in no other way than by the authority of the Catholic Church had he been induced to believe the Gospel," and who shortly adds that, "if the authority of the Catholics be weakened, I shall not believe even the Gospel because through them I had come to believe in it." [39]

This same Augustine, according to the Bishop of Rochester's sermon against Luther, had catalogued fifty-seven important heresies. Their originators had counterfeited the qualities found in the Fathers of the Church. "And euery of these herytykes grounded his heresye vpon scrypture. and many of theym were men of fell wyttes. of depe lernynge. of myghty reason. & of pretensed vertue. . . Fynally theyr lyfe lernynge. & handlyng of scryptures. were suche that they had many grete adherentes & fautours. as wel of the bysshoppes. as of the emperours. & of other chrysten prynces also. which were abused by them." Christ had warned His followers about these scandals (John 16:1) but had given them "another Advocate to dwell with you forever, the Spirit of truth" (John 14:16–17). When heresies darken the skies, Fisher's admonition is this: "Be ye than constant in your faythe. byleue as dothe your mother holy chirche. lyfely & put your trust in the spyryte of trouthe. whiche shall be your comforter vnto the worldes ende." [40]

Florentius Volusenus, in his dialogue *Tranquillity of Mind* (1543), reports that during a visit to the Bishop of Rochester, Fisher had confessed his great wonder at the design of divine providence in permitting a number of Lutherans to expound the Holy Scriptures most happily in spite of being heretics. Volusenus cautiously declares that the answer surpasses his powers and that "we ought always esteem very highly the authority of the Church." [41]

So, too, at Barnes's abjuration Fisher says: "The fayre speche / the eloquence / the knowlege of languages / these be but the veray hulle of the scriptures. This hulle these heretickes haue. . ." In his manuscript commentary on Vulg. Ps. 16, Fisher seems almost to assume the person of the Church when he allows heretics to boast of their linguistic knowledge and their eloquence, but as for himself he is content with God's grace, the dogmas of the ancients, and the justice not only of faith but also of charity and works: "But as for me, I will appear before thy sight in justice." [42]

After the hassle with Ulrichus Velenus, Simon Hessus feels that he ought to admonish Fisher not to use the opinions of popes and men more than the pronouncements of God's word as his weapons in theological dispute.[43] Fisher's reply would undoubtedly be that since Velenus' difficulty was basically historical and not scriptural, he had to employ the testimonies of the past as for any other temporal fact. More significantly, he subsequently does not assume but proceeds to prove the need for recourse to the Fathers and other means. He accomplishes this step at greatest length in his introduction to the *Confutation of Luther's Assertion* where he designates ten Truths as his weapons. The history of heresies and texts from Peter, Paul, and John establish his first Truth: "In the interpretation of Holy Scripture it is most evident that very many, trusting in their own abilities, have gone foully astray." An appeal to Tertullian bolsters the second Truth: that today, too, anyone that relies on his own spirit will easily fall into error. Statements of the Fathers establish the third Truth: "When controversy arises about Holy Scripture . . . it is fitting that the dispute be capable of being settled by some judge," the judge being the Roman Pontiff.[44] Fisher's other Truths have been touched on in previous chapters.

As for the Fathers as commentators on Scripture, Fisher denies Luther's assertion that all their words are "conclusions." (A "conclusion," theologically speaking, is a truth which one's own investigation surely and clearly deduces from two premises, of which one is formally revealed, usually in Scripture, and of which the other is known naturally.) More often than not, their commentaries are expositions and representations of the Scriptures: "for they are better known to us, and by them we are led into the knowledge of the Scriptures, although, on the other hand, Scripture is better known in itself but not in us." They light up the obscure places of Scripture. The latter's obscurity, of course, in no way detracts from its certitude, "for the Scriptures have from God their solid power, concerning which no man may doubt." To sum up, the Scriptures are surer and stronger in themselves, the commentaries the better known and clearer in our regard, for the Fathers throw light on obscure places in the Scriptures.[45]

But the Fathers have not exhausted the understanding of the Scriptures: they have left many places incompletely explained, or unsatisfactorily discussed, or simply untouched. Hence "the Christen Reader" is later told by John Frith: "My Lord of Rochester doth testifie him selfe writyng vpon the xviij. Article, that there are many pointes both of the Gospels and other Scriptures which are now discussed more diligently, and more clearely vnderstand, then they haue bene in tymes past. And addeth furthermore that there are diuerse places in Scripture yet some deale darke which he doubteth not, but that they shalbe more open and light vnto our posteritie, for why shal we dispaire of that (saith he) sith that the Scripture is for that entent left with vs, that it may be vnderstand of vs exactly, and to the vttermost point." Frith proceeds on his own: "Of this may you euidently perceaue that the old fathers and holy Doctours haue not sene all the truth. But somewhat is also left, through the high prouision of God, to be discussed of their successours." [46]

In the *Defense of the Royal Assertion,* as elsewhere, Fisher repeats that "the Church, always taught adequately by Christ's Spirit, has kept rejecting the interpretations of the heretics and consistently clinging to the opinions of the Fathers." The whole of Chapter 10 is aimed at proving that faith must be placed in that interpretation of the Scriptures on which the Fathers have uniformly agreed. Their interpretation and usage can give a surer understanding than the bare words of the Gospel itself. The chapter closes with the confession: "As for me, I indeed cry boldly with Augustine that I would not believe even the Gospel, were it not that I believe the Church and the Fathers." [47] One such point is the acceptance of St. James's epistle as apostolic, authentic, and canonical because of the approval of all the Fathers and all the Church. Fisher shows that Luther's reason for its rejection, namely, its silence on Christ's resurrection, is a mere cavil since other canonical books also are silent thereon. The decision on such a point is not up to the people but to the succession of legitimate pastors in the Church.[48]

As Fisher tells Oecolampadius, penetration into the meaning of Scripture demands humility, and such humility is shown in proper respect for the unanimous opinion of the Fathers. In another passage he accuses Oecolampadius of putting the cart before the horse in saying that from Paul's mind we grasp that of Irenaeus, "for Irenaeus and his like, full of the Holy Spirit, give a longer and clearer interpretation of matters which Paul wrote obscurely and briefly." Where the Fathers disagree, of course, freedom is allowed; whence, for example, Fisher prefers Chrysostom's interpretation of Paul's words, "the rock was Christ" (1 Cor. 10:4), to those of Origen and Augustine.[49]

The whole question of authority in scriptural interpretation ceases to be scholarly and theoretical and becomes urgent and practical in the case of Henry's divorce. The Bishop of Rochester's stand is unequivocal: it is permissible for the Sovereign Pontiff to remove the ambiguity by declaring the Levitical prohibition (Lev. 20:21) to be only judicial and not a part of the natural law.[50] Unless men had to abide by the papal decision, their lot would be worse than that under Moses. Freedom of interpretation had recently begotten countless new heresies, of which there would be no end unless there were a supreme arbiter and judge. Consequently, in cases of doubt and dispute, the right of interpreting Scripture belongs to the pope as it did formerly to the Jewish priests. As for the respected authorities cited by the advocates of the divorce, they not infrequently twisted the Scriptures to make a good point and hence are forgivable.[51]

Before launching into the next important topic, it might be well to take our bearings. According to the Bishop of Rochester, the Holy Spirit had inspired the Holy Scriptures, which He intended to have not only a literal meaning but often a spiritual or mystical sense, usually allegorical, that is, relative to Christ and His Church. As a source of revelation and as a weapon in theological controversy, the mystical, and even the allegorical, sense is not to be rejected when it depends upon the literal and enjoys the favor of exegetes. Predominantly, however, the literal sense must be used. It may be abandoned only for necessary or serious reasons. In the determination of the literal sense, no hermeneutical principle may be ignored. In particular, one must scrutinize the context, examine the parallel places, and study the commentaries. It belongs to the hierarchical Church to interpret and set forth the true sense of scriptural texts. Because the Church has made her own any unanimous testimony of the Fathers, the faithful Christian must accept and follow their interpretation. Under no circumstance may a person develop a meaning which sets the inspired authors at odds with one another or with the teaching of the Church.

Chapter VIII

THE THREE LANGUAGES

WE have left until now one norm of biblical interpretation for independent discussion because of its special importance to Fisher and the religious Renaissance. The presumption underlying the norms treated in the previous chapter is that it is the living author and the original version that are inspired by the Holy Spirit and that are immune from error. A most serious problem of the exegete, then, is to get at the original text — in a word, to prepare and to use critical editions. This involves knowledge of at least Latin, Greek, and Hebrew — the famous three languages of the Renaissance. Where does Fisher stand in their regard? His attitude can furnish a yardstick to measure his humanism, at least on its religious side. The term *attitude* rather than *achievement* is used here deliberately because what a man thinks and wants determines his party. His is not the accomplishment of Erasmus, or even Reuchlin, but he is their admirer, their helper, their defender, their user.

In spite of early but feeble preliminary negotiations, the Council of Trent was a quarter of a century away from Fisher's initial controversies and actually convened only a decade after his death. Consequently no general council had told Fisher that the Vulgate was to be read in public lectures, disputations, sermons, and exegesis (Session IV). For the Old Testament, Fisher continued to use the Vulgate because no recent translation was at hand. For the New Testament he could and did use Erasmus' Latin version, sometimes without acknowledgment, sometimes with specific mention of Erasmus. In the *Defense of the Sacred Priesthood,* for example, he names Erasmus only once: "The old translation has: 'As they were ministering to the Lord and fasting'

['Ministrantibus autem illis Domino & ieiunantibus']; but Erasmus renders it: 'As they were sacrificing to the Lord and fasting' ['Quum autem sacrificarent Domino, ieiunarentque']." But he silently uses Erasmus' version elsewhere at least three times: for Acts 1:1–2, 1 Cor. 3:4–5, and 1 Pet. 5:1–2.[1]

The Bishop of Rochester might well have been interested in Erasmus' version from the beginning. It was during his second visit to England (1505–1506) that Erasmus seems to have undertaken the task of a new Latin translation, and it was during his extended stay at Cambridge (1511–14) that he revised and completed it. At the end of October 1513, much concerned about the possible loss of his only copy of the translation of Matthew's Gospel, he had written to Colet: "If my *Matthew* is not in your possession, it must be at the Bishop of Rochester's (this is what I rather guessed anyway); but he failed to add it to the others because I'd given them to him separately." [2]

After the publication of the New Testament in early 1516, it is not altogether surprising to learn that Erasmus had originally intended its dedication for Fisher but had changed his plan in favor of Leo X. His reasons, he writes to Fisher on June 5, 1516, have been set forth in previous letters. These unfortunately have not survived. The best conjecture probably is that, considering the furor over *The Praise of Folly,* Erasmus felt the need for the most powerful protector in Christendom. He even had his friend Paolo Bombasio secure an approbatory papal brief for the second edition. In character with the *humanitas* and *prudentia* which Erasmus had praised in him, Fisher gave no sign of disappointment or resentment in his letter of thanks for a copy of the first edition. Instead, he marked the places where Erasmus had praised the patronage of Archbishop Warham of Canterbury, who, upon being shown them by Fisher, urged Erasmus' return to England with a promise of even greater liberality.[3]

In June a year later the Bishop of Rochester declares that no sensible man could reasonably find fault with Erasmus' Latin translation but that he had noted the printer's omission of Greek phrases and entire sentences. He then continues: "This too I owe to you, Erasmus, that I can to some extent guess where the Greek does not exactly correspond with the Latin text. I should like to have been permitted to have you as my teacher for a few months." [4]

In March 1518 Erasmus thought highly enough of Fisher's scholarship to beg him for suggestions and emendations for the second edition. From this letter Fisher would seem to be much interested in the reconciliation of the two forms of Christ's genealogy as given by Matthew and Luke. In the quarrel between Erasmus and Edward Lee (*ca.* 1482–1544), future Archbishop of York, over the annotations to the New Testament, the Bishop of Rochester, who was cited as a court of appeal by both sides, tried to play the role of a conciliator without departing from his approval of Erasmus' work. There survives a letter of Erasmus, dated April 2, 1519, in which he betrays unusually strong emotion: "Again and again I have fondly kissed that hand of yours, well-known and friendly to me. My pleasure has been increased by the fact that not only have you written but that you have written also copiously, for your habit is always to write affectionately." [5]

In a communication to Lee, May 1, 1519, Thomas More alludes twice to Lee's proposal to have Fisher act as mediator in the quarrel with Erasmus. More's celebrated Letter to a Monk (1519–20), referring to continental and English scholars who praise and thank Erasmus for his New Testament, reads: "In my list the place of honor goes to the Reverend Father in Christ, John, Bishop of Rochester, distinguished for virtue as well as for learning, qualities in which he has no superior among living men." [6]

Of Fisher's attitude he has no doubt, writes Erasmus to Tunstal on October 16, 1519; but he is anxious to get a copy of Lee's annotations before the appearance of the third edition of the New Testament. The next day he begs Fisher himself to send him a complete or at least a partial transcription of Lee's manuscript — or, if he is too busy, to assign the task to Thomas More. Erasmus asks this favor of Fisher with unusual fervor: "by your love of sacred studies, and by your piety becoming a bishop, and by our friendship, and by any influence at all that Erasmus might have with you." [7]

The next year, on February 1, 1520, Lee himself told Erasmus that Fisher had been given a copy of Lee's annotations with

Erasmus' own consent. Fisher apparently had not sent Erasmus a list of Lee's criticisms, perhaps because he had been too busy with his controversy with Lefèvre and Clichtove, perhaps because he had promised Lee not to show them to Erasmus, perhaps because he had hoped not to exacerbate Erasmus further before effecting a reconciliation with Lee. At any rate, on February 21, 1520, Erasmus began a letter to Fisher: "If Your Reverend Lordship suspects me to be offended in the least, either because you have answered Lefèvre or because you have not sent me Lee's manuscript, you do not yet know Erasmus. Nevertheless, I do not catch the significance of your three letters to date on this affair; and yet, believe me, I do not care. I no more doubt your attitude towards me than mine towards myself." Erasmus concluded by begging Fisher to allay any suspicion because he would always be mindful of his relationship as a poor client to a well-deserving patron. By August 2, 1520, Erasmus was able to report to Fisher that Germany was showing its rage against Lee in a deluge of publications.[8]

A message of the early 1520's from Richard Sharpe, chaplain of the Bishop of Rochester, to Nicholas Metcalfe, Archdeacon of Rochester and Master of St. John's College, reveals Fisher's persevering interest in Erasmus' scriptural labors. Sharpe writes: "Also my lorde desyreth yow to send *annotationes Erasmi* left with Arnold to mende the byndyng of them." [9] Evidently, too, Fisher continues to make suggestions to Erasmus. For example, in a letter (November 29, 1522) to Ferdinand, brother of Charles V, Erasmus declares that, among the many urging him to write the paraphrase of John, were especially the Cardinal of Mainz and "the distinguished prelate, John, Bishop of Rochester in England, a man of incomparable sanctity and learning." [10]

Just as Fisher had been connected with the first three editions of the New Testament, so also the fourth involved the mention of his name. Writing to Natalis Beda (Noel Bédier) on April 28, 1525, Erasmus discloses how for the second edition he had begged many scholars, including the Bishop of Rochester, to admonish him about offensive passages: their only reply was praise. His work had won the approval of Leo X, Adrian VI, Bishop Tunstal of London, and Bishop Fisher of Rochester. The last-named "has thanked me more than once, testifying that he had gathered very much fruit from this work of mine." The following June he declares his readiness to learn from anyone, even the half-educated: "You will say the decision rests with the theologians. I ask, does not John, Bishop of Rochester, appear to you a theologian?" In fact, on September 12, 1525, Beda suggested to Erasmus that he send the annotations criticized by Beda to "my Lord of Rochester, whom I consider to be a most pre-eminent theologian" and to ask humbly for an objective evaluation.[11]

Whether Fisher ever received the questionable annotations from Erasmus is unknown. At any rate, Beda's letter apparently contains the last extant reference to Fisher's connections with Erasmus' New Testament. What is vastly more important is what Fisher accomplished for himself and his colleges with respect to the languages that served as the indispensable tools for biblical studies: Latin, Greek, and Hebrew. There is no need here to review his educational achievements, which have been adequately treated by his biographers and by historians of education. Discussion will be restricted to subjects related to languages, theology, and Scripture. It is by no means unreasonable to believe that the excitement engendered by the publication of Erasmus' New Testament and of St. Jerome's letters in the same year (1516) exerted great influence on the Bishop of Rochester.

Fisher's statutes for Christ's College in the first decade of the sixteenth century had stringent regulations on the constant use of Latin by fellows and scholars except on clearly specified occasions. This rule, however, was not unusual and had been required, for example, in Godshouse, the predecessor of Christ's College.[12] The statutes for St. John's (1516), however, specify languages not mentioned in the statutes for Christ's drawn up scarcely a decade earlier: "Let them use no other language than Latin, Greek, or Hebrew as long as they are within the precincts of the college, except in their rooms. . ." This regulation is repeated in the statutes for 1524; and by 1530 Chaldaic and Arabic are added to the list of permissible languages. These statutes of St. John's (1516), unlike the statutes of Christ's, require also that, besides theology and philosophy and the liberal arts, "some direct their endeavor also to Hebrew and Greek literature as soon as possible." [13]

The statutes for 1524 lament that Hebrew and Greek literature is known by a very few to the no small loss of St. John's students; they consequently decree that henceforth two lecturers are to be deputed perpetually to the task: the one to teach Greek to the younger students, the other to teach Hebrew to the older, for a full hour every day. Alternate days are to be devoted to the study of grammar and to the study of the classics: in Greek any reputable author, in Hebrew the Psalms or some other part of the Bible. The statutes for 1530, however, introduce a modification and concession: if the Master and Fellows discover little fruit being derived from the course in Hebrew, they may change it into a more profitable one, for example, on Duns Scotus; then, with a humanist's love for good Latin, Fisher characteristically adds: "If anyone perchance render him in better Latin style, I shall have no objection." But it is Fisher's resolute wish that "the Greek lecturer give some attention to Hebrew literature so that all the members of the college may not be left entirely ignorant of that language." [14]

It was Fisher who in 1511 had induced Erasmus to teach Greek at Cambridge, but little is known about his lectures, either on Greek or on St. Jerome. The credit for putting Greek on a firm practical basis is due to Richard Croke (1489?–1558), who became lecturer in Greek for the university in the autumn of 1517 and for St. John's in 1523. John Cheke (1514–57), who was to become the greatest of the Cambridge Greek scholars, was educated at St. John's. The whole story, however, of the classics at Cambridge has been told well elsewhere.[15] Suffice it to say that on October 16, 1511, Erasmus had told Ammonio: "I've been lecturing on Chrysoloras' Grammar, but the audience is small." Only five years later, Henry Bullock was writing from Cambridge to Erasmus: "Here at Cambridge, men are devoting themselves ardently to Greek literature. They profoundly wish you would come; such persons hold in great favour this newly published work of yours upon the New Testament." In 1519 Erasmus told Peter Mosellanus about England's two famous universities, in both of which Greek was taught, but at Cambridge without resistance (*tranquille*) "because the head of that university is the Reverend Father John Fisher, Bishop of Rochester, marked not by theological learning only but also by a theological manner of life." This praise is followed by a brief account of Oxonian Trojans, who provoked More's Letter to the University of Oxford (1518).[16]

So much for Greek at Fisher's University of Cambridge: what about its chancellor's own knowledge of the language? Fisher had attended the opening ceremonies of St. John's College at the close of July 1516. Erasmus, arriving in England probably in early August and planning to visit Cambridge, had already mounted his horse to go there when he heard an unexpected rumor of Fisher's return to London that same day. After awaiting him for several days, he accompanied Fisher to Rochester for ten days, but he repented of his promise to visit him more than ten times (a play on *decem dies* and *plus decies*). During that time he undertook the metamorphosis of Fisher from a Latin into a Greek. On September 29, 1516, he wrote to Reuchlin that Colet was studying Greek in spite of his advanced age and that the Bishop of Rochester too was making happy progress.[17]

In reality, one consequence of Erasmus' sojourn with Fisher in August was apparently the promise to get him a Greek tutor, a project for which he enlisted the aid of Thomas More. Both Erasmus and More wrote to William Latimer (1460?–1545), former tutor to Reginald Pole (A. B. Oxon. 1515). By September 22, 1516, More had heard from neither Latimer nor Fisher. On October 31 More informed Erasmus that Latimer, determined to return to Oxford, would not postpone his departure. In a letter to Erasmus of January 30, 1517, Latimer at Oxford refused to stay with Fisher for a month or two because he had been away from Greek for many years and because Greek took years to learn. Here he cited the experience of Grocyn, Linacre, Tunstal, Pace, and More. To Latimer's suggestion that a scholar be summoned from Italy, Erasmus in February answered that this procedure was unnecessary and impracticable. Besides, a month of tutoring would be enough in the case of Fisher "who seeks to master Greek letters only so that he can occupy himself in the Sacred Books with greater profit and with surer judgment." In fact, "the matchless Bishop longs to put Greek letters as a crown [*ceu colophonem quendam*] to his perfect erudition." [18]

Meanwhile Fisher, nothing daunted, continued on his own to study Greek. By June 1517, using the methods prescribed by

Erasmus the previous August (*me exercitans . . . iuxta praeceptiones tuas*), he could point out in his tutor's New Testament the printer's omissions in the Greek text of St. Paul and could "to some extent guess where the Greek does not exactly correspond with the Latin text." Erasmus told him on September 8, 1517, of his great joy that he had no regrets for the toil spent on Greek. In view of the fact that Latimer had given no sign of yielding, he was sending him instead the Latin translation of the second book of Theodore of Gaza's grammar. This was in manuscript. The printed version was originally intended for Fisher but, because of publishing problems, was finally dedicated to John Caesarius. Erasmus sent Fisher a copy upon its publication in February 1518.[19]

This word is the last we hear about Fisher's instruction in Greek. More likely than not, he continued the private study of Greek with such aids as Theodore of Gaza's grammar and Erasmus of Rotterdam's New Testament. At any rate, when he began his first major controversy the next year (1519) with Lefèvre and Clichtove, he felt that he had acquired a sufficient mastery to use Greek for polemical purposes.

The investigator would be left in similar ignorance or doubt in regard to Fisher's Hebrew, were it not for a revelation made by his former teacher during the controversy over the royal divorce. It is not startling to learn that, as his study of Greek is associated with the achievements of the great Erasmus, so his study of Hebrew is connected with the fame of the German humanist, Johann Reuchlin. He undertook the study of both Greek and Hebrew in his forties, but he followed good humanist precedent. Rudolf Agricola had been in his mid-thirties when he started his study of Hebrew with a view to devoting his life and labor to the Scriptures. Reuchlin had been "almost forty before he began seriously to study the language." [20]

The first extant association of the name of Fisher with Reuchlin occurs in a letter of August 1514, in which Erasmus tells Reuchlin that among his learned English friends who admire his talent and desire eagerly to see his *Augenspiegel* (*Speculum oculare*), the very first is "the Bishop of Rochester, a man of exceptional moral uprightness and a most accomplished theologian," and the second is John Colet, Dean of St. Paul's, London. Reuchlin is advised to send a copy either to Fisher or to Colet. Erasmus' next communication with Reuchlin (March 1, 1515) quotes Fisher *verbatim*. First, Fisher thanks Erasmus for keeping him informed on Reuchlin, "towards whom, although personally unknown to me, I am exceedingly well-disposed." Then he requests Erasmus to forward any of Reuchlin's works not yet brought to England, "for I am extremely pleased with the erudition of the man since I believe that no other person alive comes closer to Giovanni Pico than he." Next he wishes Erasmus to ask Reuchlin two biblical questions: the source for the genealogy of the Blessed Virgin Mary given in his *Rudimenta Hebraica* (1506) and the reason she can be said to be descended from Solomon despite the complete extinction of his line according to Philo's *Breviarium de temporibus*. Finally, he wishes to be commended to Reuchlin, "whom I should certainly visit in person, if I were not clothed in these sacred vestments." Seconding the requests of "this most brilliant man," Erasmus urges Reuchlin to gratify him out of his *humanitas,* above all because of Fisher's ardent love for him. Fisher's reference to Reuchlin's *Rudimenta Hebraica* does not necessarily mean that he was studying or had studied Hebrew seriously. Reuchlin employs the genealogy "merely as a convenient instrument for teaching Hebrew letters and syllables." [21]

In a letter to be dated about June 30, 1516, Fisher tells Erasmus that to his very great pleasure he has received rather long letters from Reuchlin. The latter holds the palm "especially in the knowledge of occult matters pertaining either to theology or to philosophy." This phrase may refer, not only to Reuchlin's current controversial writings but also to his *De verbo mirifico* (1494). Fisher's familiarity with this work is attested by his manuscript commentary on Psalm 8 in which he declares: "The name *ihvh* becomes utterable through the consonant *s*," i.e., the ineffable or unutterable name *ihvh* (*Yahveh*) becomes utterable through the addition of the consonant *s* to form *ihsvh* (*Yeshuah,* i.e., *Jesus*). In *De verbo mirifico,* it is Capnio (Reuchlin) who declares that at the Annunciation the archangel Gabriel pronounced the name of the Word as *Ihsvh,* which is the "wonder-working word" (*verbum mirificum*). The letter *Shin* added to make the tetragrammaton pronounceable symbolizes "holy fire and holy name." [22]

Erasmus' letter of August 27, 1516, directed to Reuchlin, reveals that Reuchlin has very nearly displaced Erasmus in Fisher's affections. Fisher, having almost crossed the sea to visit Reuchlin, now longs to know what gift he can get him and wishes to receive in exchange some reed pens. Reuchlin is urged to write Fisher and Colet, both of whom are talented and influential. A letter at the end of September uses even stronger language: "The Bishop of Rochester almost adores you." Under date of March 1, 1517, Erasmus tells More that he is sending Fisher in one volume all the publications centering about the Reuchlin affair, that is, the controversy over John Pfefferkorn's proposal to destroy all Hebrew books in order to effect sooner the conversion of the Jews. Fisher is to read and return these works as soon as possible because some are unobtainable anywhere. A letter of March 8 discloses that Fisher had wanted them desperately and that a copy of another work of Reuchlin's, presumably *Speculum oculare* (Latin translation of *Augenspiegel*), had been dispatched to him earlier.[23]

In his letter to Erasmus, March 27, 1517, Reuchlin confesses not only veneration but love for Fisher (*sancto sacrorum praesule ac optimarum litterarum antistite*). He fears, however, that a face-to-face encounter will only diminish Fisher's esteem for him. He is sending Erasmus two copies of *De arte cabalistica* (1517), one for himself, another for Fisher. But by June the book had not yet reached Fisher. Thomas More had forwarded Erasmus' letter but not Reuchlin's book—just as in the case of the *Speculum oculare!* At any rate, Erasmus should thank Reuchlin in Fisher's behalf: "I embrace him with my whole soul." The letter is signed: "Your pupil, John of Rochester" (*Discipulus tuus Io. Roffensis*).[24]

About the same time, Colet scolds Erasmus for sending a copy of *De arte cabalistica* to Fisher and not to him also. But he perused the book on its way from More to Fisher. He dares not pronounce judgment, but it contains greater wonders of words than of things: it is best to lead a holy and pure life in the ardent love and imitation of Jesus. On September 8, 1517, Erasmus reports Colet's disappointment to Fisher and requests the return of the books on the Reuchlin affair. Reuchlin's situation is excellent. On November 7 More acknowledges the receipt of Erasmus' letters for him, Colet, and Fisher, together with a book, probably Pfefferkorn's *Streydt puechlyn vor dy warheit,* which depicts Erasmus as an escaped monk and which Erasmus has arranged to have translated into Latin for Fisher. About March 5, 1518, Erasmus is still asking Fisher for a return of the Reuchlin materials, and offering at the same time to forward to Reuchlin any letters of Fisher's. On April 23, 1518, Erasmus charitably surmises that more serious matters are keeping Fisher from expressing his opinion on *De arte cabalistica.*[25] Fisher's judgment of the volume has not survived in writing.

In spite of his extensive activities, Fisher evidently never lost interest in Reuchlin. In May 1519 a second book of letters from distinguished men to Reuchlin contains a message from Fisher, who laments the miscarriage and loss of Reuchlin's letters, urges him to further correspondence, sympathizes with him in his persecution by the friars over the Hebrew books, and professes his unsurpassed devotion to him.[26] On August 2, 1520, Erasmus gave Fisher the details of Reuchlin's transfer to Ingolstadt: "I did not wish you to be ignorant of these events." In November of the same year, he wrote Reuchlin that this English bishop, "the most learned man and the most holy prelate in that country," could not endure having Reuchlin praised sparingly by anyone: "He has in mind to visit you this coming summer." But Fisher was kept from making the trip, and Reuchlin died on June 20, 1522, celebrated by Hutten's famous tribute: "Who lives thus never dies." [27]

There has been some confusion on the date for Fisher's study of Hebrew. At least a mastery of the fundamentals of the language could be acquired from Reuchlin's *Rudimenta Hebraica* and would be requisite for an intelligent perusal of Reuchlin's publications, especially *De verbo mirifico* and *De arte cabalistica* — and Fisher was nothing if not intelligent. One would therefore expect him to be studying Hebrew sometime in the 1510's. A marginal note in Lewis' life of Fisher gives A.D. 1510; Reynolds suggests 1520 as "the most likely time." There is no doubt about the name of his teacher, to wit, Robert Wakefield (d. 1537). After receiving an A.B. degree from Cambridge in 1513–14, Wakefield went to the continent to study oriental languages. He began to lecture on Hebrew at Louvain in 1519, Tübingen in 1520, Cambridge in 1524, and Oxford in 1530. Upon his return to England in 1523, he was appointed a royal chaplain by the influence of Richard Pace, who also recommended him as an authority on the divorce in 1527. The disagreement on the time of his tuition of Fisher is caused by the difficulty of dating two printed books of his: *Kotser* (= *Fragmentum*) *codicis R. VVakfeldi* (London, Thomas Berthelet) and *Roberti VVakfeldi . . . syntagma de hebraeorum codicum incorruptione* (London, Wynkyn de Worde).[28]

Kotser codicis contains several passages which help to date it. Throughout, there are references not only to John Fisher but also to Thomas Abell and an anonymous author who is identified as possibly Luis Vives or Cornelius Agrippa. Now, Abell's *Invicta veritas* was published *Luneberge* (Antwerp?) in May 1532. After Wakefield's treatise proper occurs a letter expressing his thanks for a favor to Thomas Boleyn, Earl of Wiltshire. Boleyn had been created Earl on December 8, 1529; but, more important, Wakefield speaks of Boleyn's "daughter, our queen Anne in whose good fortune I rejoice exceedingly."

This message is followed by an interesting letter to Fisher himself, which challenges him to submit to criticism another book which he is reported to have written. At the universities of Tübingen and Paris (probably at the time that Wakefield had been sent to secure their opinions on the divorce), he had praised Fisher as being "among all mortals of this age, in almost every kind of knowledge, most learned," and as having no peer in Christendom — except for his deception in this matter: *quandoque bonus dormitat Homerus.* It was Edward Fox, royal almoner, who had approached Wakefield with three propositions on the royal marriage "almost seven years ago" (*annos ante hac fere septem*). As a result, he lost the good will of the public and of Queen Catherine herself, whom he had helped by aiding Pace with a book in her favor, but then he had learned that she had been known carnally by Arthur. Nevertheless "almost seven years ago" (*annos abhinc fere septem*), on his knees he had begged the king to stay with Catherine if at all possible. He complains that he has been ill repaid by this "noble woman," the aunt of the emperor Charles V and of Ferdinand. At the request of the University of Tübingen, Ferdinand had sent letters to Henry VIII and Fisher begging them to allow Wakefield to continue teaching

Greek, Hebrew, Chaldaic, and Arabic in Germany instead of returning to England.

Wakefield's address to Fisher is followed by a copy of Pace's letter to Henry VIII, dated 1527. He acknowledges the learned Wakefield's assistance on the book sent to Henry the previous day. Wakefield himself, without the king's express permission, will not "medle therwith" because his only aim is truth. Pace is enclosing a Hebrew alphabet for Edward Fox, who, if he masters it, "shall within the space of one monythe haue sufficient knowledge of the hebrewe tongue, for to Iudge therby the lattyn translation .lxx. interpreters in greke, and the trouth comprysed in the hebrewe bookes, wherby ye [Henry] shall haue a great auantage" when Wakefield sets the truth before the king. Evidently a little Hebrew will go a long way.

In his own letter to Henry, Wakefield pledges defense of the royal cause in "all the vniuersities in christendom" by means of Scripture, Hebrew exegetes, and Greek and Latin Fathers. He begs the king to keep this offer secret because the people would stone him to death if he, who had defended Catherine until the discovery of her carnal intercourse with Arthur, were shown to be furthering Henry's cause. His book will be an *ingens uolumen. Kotser codicis,* therefore, would seem to be only a part (*Fragmentum, Kotser*) of this volume, undoubtedly brought up to date after the answers of Fisher, Abell, and an anonymous writer to the king's book (*Censurae* in Latin, *Determinations* in English translation).[29]

Wakefield begins his *Syntagma* by declaring that the royal affair depends upon the authority of God's Scripture alone, with the papal dispensation exerting no effect on the royal marriage. His intention is to prove that the certain and infallible truth is to be found in the Hebrew codices as the source from which flow the Septuagint and other Greek versions, as well as translations by Jerome and other Latins. He will start by repeating Fisher's question on the binding force of a papal dispensation and by producing "the response which I gave to it in my book almost seven years ago" (*in codice meo . . . annos antehac fere septem*). Wakefield denies the papal power and concludes his answer by pointing to the Latin translation of Leviticus which expressly says: "Let none take his brother's wife" (*Vxorem fratris nullus accipiat*) (cf. Vulg. Lev. 18:16: *Turpitudinem uxoris fratris tui non revelabis*). Fisher replies by saying that this verse is not found in the Hebrew original nor the Chaldaic translation nor the Septuagint and consequently ought not to be received as Sacred Scripture. Most probably the verse, once a marginal gloss, was inserted in the text by an inept copyist.

Highly significant for our purpose is Wakefield's retort: "Because, reverend father, you have here called me off from the streams i.e. the translations to the fountains of the Hebrew veritie, in which you fancy yourself skilled, and would willingly be thought so by others, I very gladly and freely accept the condition. Do you therfore take care how you hereafter oppose the Hebrew verity, and object the lakes and corrupted marshes to me, who about eighteen years since [*annos antehac circiter octodecim*] taught you, and our common friend Thomas Hurskey [venerable head of the whole Gilbertine order and, after you, the splendor and glory of our country] Hebrew." [30]

Wakefield's answer in brief is that the sentence is in the original in sense and hence is acceptable exegetically on Jerome's authority. Greek and Latin translators also had the not entirely blameworthy habit of inserting explanations based on other texts. He continues with a reflection on Fisher's Greek: "If you had pondered this fact, or rather had known it (for you are hardly highly versed in their translation [Septuagint], which is Greek, on account on your little knowledge of Greek [*propter tuam in graeco non magnam notitiam*]), or if you had read more attentively St. Jerome in his preface to Solomon, saying that 'some things from the Greek have been either inserted in the Hebrew translation or added from without for the explanation of the sense or the edification of the reader,' you would never so imprudently have pronounced or said that this verse, namely, 'Let none take his brother's wife,' is not in the Septuagint because you have not found it in most corrupt Spanish, German, and Italian editions." Wakefield then turns the tables by maintaining that Fisher's text, namely, *Sororem uxoris tuae . . .* (Lev. 18:18) is not found in the Hebrew, Chaldaic, Septuagint, or Arabic texts and therefore ought not to be admitted. His proof extends to the end of the treatise.

Wakefield's very last lunge at his opponent is very illuminating insofar as it reveals the attitude of the new breed of humanist toward what might be called the hybrid Scholastic-humanist type. Even though due allowance be made for the fact that this final thrust occurs during a controversy, it nevertheless discloses the widening gap between the older scholarship and the newest learning: "In fact, Reverend Father, if by your good leave I may frankly confess the real situation, not a few things in your book are cited by you as Sacred Scripture, which ought not at all to be received as such because they have been translated not rightly but wrongly either by Jerome or by the Seventy Translators and exist only as their fancies. In your book, in addition, certain things seem to me to do violence to Scripture and to be superfluous. Many things also seem too Scholastic and not sufficiently strong and valid, seeing that they are supported by the authority of no Scripture but by most obscure interpreters, and these same are recent and sophistical men, ignorant of languages. Either to bring these into the discussion or ever to cite these would make a scholar feel ashamed. Kets or Telos [The End]."

According to Reynolds and others, "it does not seem that the bishop replied to him [Wakefield]." Fisher's "Responsio," however, in the British Museum (B.M. Otho C.x) names "R. Wakfeldus" and, because of the mutilated condition of the manuscript, gives only a fragment of a Greek scriptural quotation peculiarly applicable to the relationship between Fisher and Wakefield: Οὐκ ἔστιν μαθητὴς ὑπὲρ τὸν διδάσκαλον ("No disciple is above his teacher": Matt. 10:24, Luke 6:40).

Wakefield's *Syntagma* refers at least twice by name to his *Kotser codicis,* which therefore was at least written earlier, if not printed earlier. They were probably both written and printed quite close together because both date the same events as occurring "almost seven years ago." It is not impossible for them to have been published simultaneously because they had two different printers, Thomas Berthelet for *Kotser codicis* and Wynkyn de Worde for *Syntagma.* Fisher was one of the first to be consulted about the royal marriage but not until mid-1527, when the proceedings began to be conducted in the open. It is not unlikely that Pace and Wakefield became involved at the same time or shortly afterward. "Almost seven years" would bring the date to late 1533 or, more probably, to early 1534. On the first page of the *Syntagma,* the slur on the pope's power of dispensation as "more truly dispersion" (*dispensatio vel verius dissipatio*) may point to the First Act of Succession, proclaimed throughout England on May 1, 1534, with its preamble on the rejection of papal authority in general and papal dispensation on marriages like Henry's in particular.[31]

If "almost seven years" refers to 1527, "about eighteen years since" should make 1516 as the approximate year when Wakefield tutored Fisher in Hebrew. The time is not unlikely because at this period Fisher, as has been seen, was intensely interested in Reuchlin. His admiration for the Hebrew scholar, as well as a desire to understand everything that he wrote, would drive him to study Hebrew, at first privately perhaps with the aid of Reuchlin's *Rudimenta* (to which he indirectly refers in 1515) and then with the help of a tutor, namely, the young Wakefield. This was the course that he pursued also with Greek, except that he could not obtain the services of Latimer as tutor.

What use does the Bishop of Rochester make of his Greek and Hebrew? Beginning with his three works on Mary Magdalene, let us take them as one, without entering into the intricacies of the problem. He explains the Latin word *castellum* (John 11:1) by appealing to the Greek original, κώμη, which means, not "strong fortress or castle," as it does popularly now, but "small town or village" (*oppidulum siue vicus*), as Erasmus points out in his annotations on Luke 10:38. The word is also to be distinguished from πόλις (*civitas* "town or city"). Philip, Andrew, and Peter came from "the town"; Mary and Martha, from "the village." [32] At another time, he uses the position of the words in the Greek original to argue that the sinful woman (Luke 7:36–50) did not have to be known as such to the whole city but could have committed her sin elsewhere and long ago. The Vulgate (Luke 7:37) reads: "Et ecce mulier quae erat in ciuitate peccatrix," but the Greek original thus: καὶ ἰδοὺ γυνὴ ἐν τῇ πόλει ἥτις ἦν ἁμαρτωλός (that is, "Et ecce mulier in ciuitate, quae fuerat peccatrix").[33]

In commenting on the sentence, "Amen dico vobis, vbicumque praedicatum fuerit hoc Euangelium in toto mundo dicetur [et] quod haec fecit in memoriam eius" (Matt. 26:13), he explains that *eius* refers not to Christ but to the woman because the

Greek αὐτῆς is feminine in gender. Moreover, "quod haec fecit" is not so much the anointing as her past sin (*facinus*). Finally, on the authority of "our Erasmus," the Greek μνημόσυνον means not mere *memoria* (memory) but what moderns call *memoriale* (reminder or memorial). On another occasion, Fisher supplies from the Greek what is missing in the Latin, as at the beginning of Matthew 28:9: ὡς δὲ ἐπορεύοντο ἀπαγγεῖλαι τοῖς μαθηταῖς αὐτοῦ (that is, "Quum autem iissent ad renunciandum discipulis eius"). When Fisher has occasion to use Greek commentators on the Scriptures, he would seem not to be using the Greek text itself but rather quoting them indirectly through a Latin Father, especially Jerome, or directly in a standard Latin version. Of the latter he sometimes gives the name of the translator, for example, of *Trapezuntius* (George of Trebizond) for Chrysostom's eighty-first homily on Matthew.[34]

In the *Destruction of Clichtove's Bulwark,* Fisher discusses at length whether Paul's reprehension of Peter (Gal. 2:11) was real or simulated, with Augustine defending the former view and Jerome the latter. In one place he observes: "Where we have in the said epistle, 'Restiti ei in faciem,' the Greeks have κατὰ πρόσωπον, that is, 'iuxta vel secundum faciem' or 'in facie,' not 'in faciem.' Our Erasmus has not only annotated this phrase, but he has also explained learnedly and appropriately, just as he does everything else, the meaning of Jerome." [35]

The sermon against Luther contains only a single reference to Greek or Hebrew, namely, to the unwritten prophecies "which the mayster of Iewes calleth cabala. which is deriued fro man to man. by mouthe onely & not by wrytynge." Naturally the *Confutation of Luther's Assertion* contains many more allusions. Thus, *Berith,* it is pointed out, means *pactum, foedus, testamentum, seu lex* among the Hebrews (cf. Jer. 31:31–34, Heb. 8:8–12, 10:16–17). Against Luther's Article 31, "A just man sins in his every good work," Fisher claims that, since the Hebrew original of Ecclesiastes 7:21 has not the present tense *peccat* but the future *peccabit,* the verse should be handled as if it said: "Non est iustus, qui nunquam peccabit" ("There is no just man that will not sin"). In Article 36 on free will, the Hebrew *Ietzer* in Genesis 6:5, according to Fisher, means not *cupiditas & desiderium* but *figmentum seu plasmatio* (production or fashioning) or *machinatio* (contrivance); hence the literal Latin translation is the following: "Et vidit Deus quod multa malitia hominum in terra (supple fuit) & omnis machinatio cogitationum cordis eorum mala duntaxat omni die." Here Fisher relies upon Jerome and Nicholas of Lyra. He also corrects Luther's translation of Exodus 9:16: "in hoc ipsum excitaui te . . . ," which, according to the Hebrew, should read: "Propterea feci stare te . . ."[36]

As is to be expected, the use of Greek in the *Confutation* is more frequent than that of Hebrew. Fisher may refer to the addition of a Latin word to the Greek original (e.g., *Domini,* in 1 Cor. 3:13) or to the lack of a Latin word which is present in the Greek (e.g., *mea,* in 2 Cor. 12:9). The Greek word may be used to clarify the meaning of the Latin term, e.g., βέβαιος "firmus & stabilis" to explain *certa* in regard to vocation (2 Pet. 1:10); ἐπιούσιον "qui animae nostrae substantiam fulcit" to interpret *supersubstantialem* in the Lord's Prayer (Matt. 6:11); βόσκε "pasce" and ποίμαινε "rege vel pasce" to give the nature of Peter's primacy (John 21:15–17); and αὐτοκατάκριτος "per se damnatus" to show the heretic self-condemned. To bolster his argument, Fisher may call attention to the tense in the original Greek, e.g., the past tense εἶπον "dixi," not the future perfect *dixero* (John 14:26.); and the present tense, not the future, in John 15:6, with reference to the Day of Judgment (cf. Matt. 13:48). On one occasion he accuses Luther of willful deceit in adding "& de uno calice," which is not in the Greek text of 1 Cor. 10:17, "omnes ex eodem pane participamus." Although not generally adopted, Luther's addition is given in some Greek codices. Fisher appears to have such confidence in his friend Erasmus as to consider his Greek text infallible. The *Confutation* again quotes Chrysostom (Homily 69 to the People of Antioch) in Latin translation but this time in that of Lucas Bernardus Brixianus.[37]

Fisher's *Defense of the Royal Assertion* has two interesting Hebrew allusions: (1) a literal translation of Job 3:8, in which *Leviathan* is interpreted to refer to the society of female mourners, and (2) an appeal to *amicus noster Ioannes Capnion* ("our friend Johann Reuchlin") for the derivation of the Latin *missa* (mass) from the Hebrew *missah,* meaning *oblatio* (offering). In this same work occurs one of the rare occasions on which Fisher prefers the Latin version to the Greek original. He holds the Latin reading, "every spirit that severs Jesus is not of God," to be truer than the Greek, namely, "every spirit that does not confess Jesus is not of God" (1 John 4:3). He applies the verse to the Mystical Body.[38] In the *Defense of the Sacred Priesthood,* to prove that "both Melchisedech and Christ offered sacrifice in bread and wine," the Bishop of Rochester cites the Jewish Rabbis: Moses Hadarsan, Johai, Kimchi, Pinchas, Selomon, and Semuel, as well as the Chaldaic translation of Vulg. Psalm 71:16. He also explains the Greek term χειροτονήσαντες as used in Acts 14:23, not for the raising of hands in the election of magistrates, but for the laying-on of hands in the ordination of priests.[39]

Even in his English sermon at Barnes's abjuration, the Bishop of Rochester resorts to Greek and Hebrew. In one place he apologetically appeals to the Greek original as against the Vulgate: "Pardon me / though I reherse the wordes after the greke boke: for they make better agaynst our ennemies / he sayth: *In corde honesto / et bono*" (Vulg. Luke 8:15: *in corde bono et optimo,* ἐν καρδίᾳ καλῇ καὶ ἀγαθῇ). When he uses *honesto,* he correctly explains that it means "honeste and fayre: For the greke worde [καλῇ] is indifferent to bothe." Fisher also alludes to the Hebrew etymology of *manna:* "It is certayne that the people of the Iewes / whan the Manhu was sent vnto them from aboue / . . . they made this same question / whiche this blynde man nowe dothe aske: *Quid hoc?* What is that. And of this question that sede toke this name / and was called Manhu."[40]

Fisher's next audience was not the populace but the learned world, for his adversary was Oecolampadius, who had aided Erasmus with the Hebrew of Jerome's letters. Before this master of languages, Fisher is cautious about his linguistic skill: "Even if I should have a slight knowledge of Hebrew letters, nevertheless I clearly perceive how much you are trying to impose upon us here." He therefore shows that the Hebrews do have a substantive verb in the present tense. In fact, Fisher declares, one cause of Oecolampadius' madness is the pride rising from his proficiency in languages and letters. Misinterpretations of the Old Testament which occur in Augustine ought to be blamed on the translators from the Hebrew. Jerome was dissatisfied with his predecessors in translation, but now Oecolampadius and others skilled in language laugh at Jerome's effort, and in time their successors with equal readiness will deride Oecolampadius and his group. The Bishop of Rochester, far from being obscurantist, would seem here to have a true scholar's sense of the advance of knowledge. This confidence makes him praise Bishop Foxe in his dedicatory epistle for establishing Corpus Christi College, in which high-salaried professors teach Hebrew, Greek, Latin, and everything contributing to true theological learning. At any rate, when Oecolampadius cites the original Hebrew for Job 31:31 (*non saturabimur*), Fisher defends Jerome for giving the sense (*vt satiemur*), not a slavishly literal translation — but both translations add up to the same thing. Later, however, Fisher is forced to give the Hebrew original and a word-for-word Latin version of this very same passage.[41]

In this work against Oecolampadius on the Eucharist, the Bishop of Rochester inevitably has to use the Greek text more than the Hebrew. The verse which he emphasizes most, in five passages at least, is John 6:51/52: "panis, quem ego dabo, caro mea est pro mundi vita" ("the bread that I will give is my flesh for the life of the world"). The Greek codices, he declares, "consistently" (*constanter*) give *dabo* twice; i.e., "quem dabo" appears a second time between "caro mea" and "pro mundi vita." He bases an argument for the Real Presence on this repetition, e.g., "The Heavenly Father gave His Incarnate Word as true bread. Then Christ gave His flesh under the appearance of bread. Finally the same Christ gave His flesh to death for the life of the world." It is in connection with this verse that he praises his tutor in Euclid, William Melton, who taught him to neglect no single letter in Euclid — a principle he has carried over into his study of Scripture.[42]

In addition to the Greek New Testament, Fisher mentions on some five occasions the Mass of St. Basil which Bishop Tunstal of London has given him to read. This time the work is stated explicitly to be in Greek. The Mass of St. John Chrysostom is contained in the same volume. For Chrysostom's scriptural interpretations, names of the Latin translators are given: Lucas Bernardus Brixianus, Franciscus Aretinus, and Hieronymus Donatus. No source, however, is given for a quotation from St. Cyril. As for Chrysostom's Mass, a version, "translated very many years ago by

Erasmus of Rotterdam as a favor for the Bishop of Rochester," was not printed until 1537, but an *Officium Chrysostomi,* which Allen conjectures to be the Mass, had been presented by Erasmus to Colet on September 13, 1511.[43]

In his appeals to the original Hebrew and Greek texts, Fisher is following sound hermeneutical principles implicitly — without making an explicit statement on their authority and use. Fortunately, his only printed book on the divorce, namely, *De causa matrimonii* (Alcalá, 1530), contains a most definite declaration on the Hebrew original, the Septuagint, and the Vulgate. After showing the agreement of all these versions on the leviratic marriage, he continues:

> We think therefore that none of these versions [*codices*] ought to be rejected, unless where there is an error through the fault of copyists. For the Latin version, which has been accepted throughout the Church, is to be considered of less authority than either the Hebrew or the Greek. For the Greek version (I am speaking of the Septuagint) has proceeded from the Holy Spirit just as the Hebrew. But deference must be paid also to the Latin version, which in the course of so many years has now been approved throughout the Church, no less deference than to either of the other two, because Christ who can neither deceive nor be deceived promised to give to the Church the Spirit who would lead it into all the truth [John 16:13].[44]

Fisher would here seem to be admitting degrees, not of inspiration, but of divine assistance. It is the Hebrew text alone, as it left the hands of its human writers, which is inspired, that is, which has God as principal author. But the Holy Spirit guarded the Septuagint from containing errors in revealed truth, as He did also the Vulgate because of Christ's promise to His Church. The Bishop of Rochester, however, feels that this inerrancy of the Vulgate need in no way keep him from elucidating or correcting ambiguous or inexact Latin passages by use of the original Hebrew and Greek versions or of ancient translations. In a word, like a skilled theologian, Fisher circumspectly wishes to extol the *authority* of the original text without diminishing the *deference* to be paid to translations currently accepted by an infallible Church.

It would be interesting to have Fisher's views on a new English translation. Like Tyndale and More, he shows considerable stylistic liveliness and force in the passages translated into the vernacular in his English sermons throughout his life. Many copies of Tyndale's version, as we have seen, were burned in 1526. Fisher, as well as Henry VIII and Wolsey, was warned about the impending importation of Tyndale's New Testament. In his *Commentaries,* Cochlaeus has the following entry for A.D. 1526: "Rinche and Cochlaeus, however, immediately sent advice by letter to the king, the cardinal, and the bishop of Rochester, that they might make provision with the greater diligence, lest that most pernicious article of merchandise should be conveyed into all the ports of England." [45] In 1528, it is claimed, by Fisher's direction "a persecution was carried on against William Mafelde, the praecentor of this church [of St. Andrew], for not delivering up to his diocesan, in obedience to the orders of cardinal Wolsey . . . a copy of the gospel translated into English; and the only method he had of escaping a severe sentence . . . was by informing the bishop of the name of his friend who had purchased for him, this inestimable book." [46]

Chapter IX

PHILOSOPHY AND HISTORY: THEIR RELATION TO FAITH AND DOGMA

THE increased emphasis of humanists and Protestants on the Scriptures created a special problem for men in Fisher's situation, particularly when they had been educated in the Scholastic tradition in their universities. Luther's position was unequivocal: the liberation of Scripture and the Christian from the enslaving authority of the Fathers and from the domination of Aristotle in philosophy and theology. Against Latomus, he cries: "The sophists have imposed tyranny and bondage upon our freedom to such a point that we must not resist that twice accursed Aristotle, but are compelled to submit." On the other hand, Reuchlin, like other German humanists, was critical of modern Scholastics because of their uncouth style, over-refined dialectic, and petty questions: he was not inimical to their basically Christian premises, their pious intentions, frequently apologetic, or their religious conclusions. Fisher was so much in tune with the Northern humanists that, after reading Agricola's *Dialectica,* he wrote Erasmus in 1515: "Let me say briefly that we have never read anything pertaining to that art more pleasant and learned. . . Would that as a young man I had had him [Agricola] as a teacher!" Yet Fisher's training in Scholasticism stood him in good stead. In Philip Hughes's judgment, it made him a well-equipped theologian, whereas Cranmer, who lacked it, remained mainly "an enthusiastic student," chiefly of the Fathers.[1]

Fisher clearly holds to the principal Scholastic views on the usefulness of philosophy to theology. The Fathers, and even St. Paul before them, had used philosophy in setting forth the dogmas of faith. There was no call for Fisher to employ it in demonstrating the existence of God or the truth of Christianity, since both were accepted by his antagonists; but he did use philosophy to defend the Catholic Church as the true Church of Christ, to explain Catholic teaching, e.g., on the special priesthood and the reality of Christ's Body and Blood in the Eucharist, and to prove, not merely to state, arguments in favor of difficult dogmatic points, as, for example, the role of supernatural faith or the primacy of the Roman Pontiff. He is unlike the most conservative Schoolmen of his age in making what might be called humanistic use of Scholastic principles. According to the recommendation of Erasmus, the Scholastic method is to be treated *modice, sobrie casteque,* etc.[2] Thus, Fisher often calls his opponents back to the rules of simple logic and common sense and to the principles of faith and the Scriptures. He feels that there are some truths, especially in the Scriptures, which human reason cannot fathom. Hence he does not make man's mind the measure of articles of faith. Usually he successfully avoids taking unknown truths for known, or probabilities and possibilities for certainties. His main temptation, well resisted ordinarily, is to declare things to be of faith which really are not of faith. He devotes no time to petty, obscure, difficult, and unnecessary problems. Each of his controversial works is called forth by an immediate burning question: the unicity or plurality of the Magdalene (except as a symbol and as a training ground, perhaps the least significant of his works), the forty-one condemned articles of Luther, the defense of his king, the institution and prestige of the priesthood, the Real Presence in the Eucharist, and the dispensing power of the pope, epitomized in the dispute over the validity of a Christian's marriage with a dead brother's wife.

It is worth while having Fisher's concept of philosophy expressed independently of any controversy. His work on Christ's passion declares: "Meruayling was the cause, why the Philosophers came to so greate knowledge, as they had. They behelde and sawe many wonderfull thynges, and effectes in thys worlde, as the marueylous earthquakes, Thunders, lightnings, Snow, Rayne, & Frostes, blasinng Starres, the Eclipses of the Sunne and of the Moone, and suche other effectes. And those marueylous wonders moued them to search for the causes of the same. And so by dyligent searche and inquisition, they came to great knowledge and cunning, which cunnyng men call Philosophie naturall." This same spirit of wonder and search should obtain also in the Christian religion, which is the *philosophia Christi.* Hence Fisher proceeds: "But there is another higher Philosophie which is aboue nature, which is also gotten with marueyling. And this is the verye Philosophie of Christian people." The apex of the *philosophia Christi* is the *theologia crucis:* "And doubtlesse amongest all other things concerning a Christian man, it is a thyng muche marueylous, and most wonderfull, that the sonne of God, for the loue that he had vnto the soule of man, woulde suffer hym selfe to bee crucified, and so to take vpon him that most vyllanous death vpon the Crosse." [3]

The dominant philosophy in Fisher's lifetime was Scholasticism, and contemporary Scholasticism was under attack by Christian humanists. What was Fisher's attitude: one of rebellion and condemnation? One of approbation and admiration? One of qualification and compromise?

The first statement of his position appears in his controversy with Lefèvre on the question as to whether or not the penitent woman (Luke 7:36–50), Mary the Magdalene (Luke 8:2, Mark 16:9, John 19:25, 20:1–2, 20:11–18), and Mary of Bethany, the sister of Martha and Lazarus (Luke 10:38–42, John 11:1–45), are one or more in number. The Bishop of Rochester knows that the Greeks in general have taught that there were more than one Mary, whereas the Latins traditionally have espoused the cause of the one Mary, the Magdalene. To the view of the Latin West, of course, Fisher holds fast. His principle for the use of the Fathers is enlightening. Members of the Latin Church rightly ought in all things to esteem, after the very Apostles of Christ, the four Latin Doctors (Augustine, Ambrose, Jerome, and Gregory) as progenitors and fathers. Nevertheless, Latin Catholics readily embrace and revere the Greek Doctors in all their correct teachings. The reasons which Fisher gives for this deference are the same as those of More and Erasmus: (1) the antiquity of the Greek Doctors and their closeness to apostolic times, (2) their extraordinary erudition and their unique eloquence, and (3) their language, namely Greek, since the New Testament and the earliest commentaries are written in Greek. For the last reason it is necessary to know their language and to have recourse to them in many things. Fisher attaches a cautious proviso to this statement: one may have recourse to them as long as one remains free to disagree with them when they themselves disagree with the common opinion of the Church. But he advises the same circumspection in regard to the Latin Fathers. For example, he respects the authority of Ambrose on all points on which he does not stand opposed to the common opinion of the Church.

The Bishop of Rochester is grieved to see Lefèvre by implication disdain and scout all writers beyond the age of Ambrose (d. 397), no matter how great their sanctity or their erudition — even those gravest Fathers: Augustine (d. 430), Gregory the Great (d. 604), Bede (d. 735), and Bernard (d. 1153). He proceeds to marshal on his side the weight of authority through the ages. A little later, in addition to the four just mentioned, he cites Cassian (d. *ca.* 435), Leo the Great (d. 461), Rabanus Maurus (d. 856), Remi of Auxerre (d. 908), and Anselm (d. 1109).

When he comes to the central Schoolmen whom he names "Disputators" (*Disputatores* or *Disceptatores*) on account of their use of the formal disputation or debate, he declares that the entire group has constantly upheld the opinion of one Mary. He feels the need to cite only two of them as representative of all the rest. The University of Paris had seen both: Albert, who on account of the comprehensiveness of his doctrine is surnamed "the Great," and Thomas, who is termed the "Flower of Theology." After quoting these sane and brilliant figures of the thirteenth century, he concludes: "For myself, I see no reason why credence ought not be given them in this matter, since they were not ignorant about the statements of their forerunners and since they were both most versed in the Scriptures. But the reason they displease Lefèvre is that they were Schoolmen [*disceptatores*]."

Nevertheless, Fisher proceeds to name two writers who are "more devoted to the study of the Scriptures than to Scholastic questions," namely, Ubertino of Casale (d. *ca.* 1340), author of *The Tree of the Crucified Life of Jesus* (*Arbor vitae crucifixae Jesu,* a work variously titled, and Simon of Cascia or Cassia (d. 1348), author of *The Acts of Christ* (*De gestis Christi*). If Lefèvre finds their style crude, he should heed the confession of Ubertino that the quest of vain knowledge and finicalness of style constituted a great obstacle to his enlightenment by Christ, "whose conversation, as he said, is with the simple." Suppose that Lefèvre is left unmoved by their achievement and still insists upon literary brilliance? Fisher advises him to listen to Bede and Druthmarus (Christian Druthmar de Stavelot, fl. 850–900), both of whom are learned in Latin and Greek literature and expert in Holy Scripture. At this point he appeals also to Alcuin (d. 804) and Rabanus. And if Lefèvre prefers the saints, Fisher could produce for him a great many, but two would suffice: St. Anselm and St. Bernard.[4]

To his list, Fisher declares that he could add many others who, diligently devoting their talents to the Gospels, composed harmonies and then explained them with voluminous commentaries. Such are *Zacharias Chrysopolitanus* (Zachary of Besançon, a Premonstratensian, d. *ca.* 1157) and *Clemens Lathomiensis ecclesiae presbyter* (Clement of Gloucester, canon regular of Llanthony, d. *ca.* 1170). Fisher does not hesitate to add the testimony of Vincent of Beauvais (d. *ca.* 1264) and even of St. Bridget of Sweden (d. 1373).[5]

To offset any accusation of prejudice in favor of the Fathers and the Schoolmen, the Bishop of Rochester then calls outstanding humanists as witnesses. In chronological order they are briefly the following. First of all there is Petrarch (d. 1374), "who was not a careless investigator of such matters," e.g., in his *Life of Solitude* (*De vita solitaria*). Then comes Nicholas of Cusa (d. 1464), whom Lefèvre himself calls "both a most eminent doctor and indisputably a most distinguished scholar in every branch of knowledge." Next there is Marco Vigerio Cardinal della Rovere (d. 1516), author of the *Christian Decachord* (*Decachordum Christianum*), formerly Bishop of Senigallia and later Bishop of Palestrina, "a man of both the greatest learning and the greatest eloquence." In addition, verses of the celebrated Mantuan (d. 1516) are quoted at considerable length. Finally, Giovanni Francesco Pico (d. 1533), biographer and nephew of the "darling" of the Italian Renaissance, appears as witness to the traditional identification of the three Marys.[6]

In his next work on the Magdalene, the *Destruction of Clichtove's Bulwark,* Fisher enunciates the principle of self-consistency. The latter is most important for both philosopher and theologian. Inconsistency, of course, serves as a fruitful source for arguments in controversy. An author's opinion should be the same, whether expressed in direct treatment of the issues or mentioned in passing while handling another subject. If it is shameful for a pagan philosopher to hold different views in different places, it is far more shameful for the theologian to do so: "For, since theology is the discourse of truth [*veritatis sermo*], it becomes him who is a theologian to speak the truth everywhere so that . . . he must be presumed always to have said what appeared to him as true." [7]

Consistency is very much the virtue of Thomas Aquinas, with whose reputation and authority Fisher's first major anti-Lutheran work, the *Confutation,* is much concerned. Luther ought not to set such slight value on this learned saint, Fisher declares, since the majority of the great scriptural scholars are wont to call him the Flower of Theology. The pope, he later declares, has naturally not set the seal of approbation upon the whole doctrine of Aquinas to the extent that each and every opinion expressed in his writings must be believed as true. The Church has never approved the teaching of Augustine or Jerome or any other writer to the extent that one might not disagree with him on some points. Fisher does not hesitate to mention Aquinas in the same breath with Augustine. He has no doubt that, even if a man made progress in theology without assistance from Augustine or from Thomas, he would still reach the same conclusions on matters pertaining to faith as did Augustine or Aquinas. In case of disagreement, such a man should realize his lack of the Holy Spirit's guidance, since the Holy Spirit is the Author, not of schism but of unity, and the Teacher, not of contradictory but of concordant doctrines. Fisher challenges Luther to point out any person who has ever become a heretic from the study of St. Thomas, or who has ever taken the taint of heresy from St. Augustine alone (without his own perverse reasoning or obstinate will).

There is no proof, Fisher declares, for a command to trust only in the popes and the doctors and not to examine the scriptural bases for their teachings or the apostolic traditions found in the Fathers. "Moreover," he continues, "if there be some who abandon the Scripture and its interpreters [presumably the Fathers] and wish to trust in the Scholastics only, such would undoubtedly err on the other side, but not as much as you, Luther, who abandon and utterly scorn both [Fathers and Scholastics] and command trust in the Scriptures only, and these same falsely understood." Luther's first mistake was the repudiation of Aquinas, Scotus, and the Scholastics. The reason is that the Scholastics find his reasoning intolerable, "for take away dialectics, and you immediately take away the power either of demolishing the false or of establishing the true." It would be better for Luther to refute the Scholastics than to insult them.[8]

It is remarkable how Fisher usually relates the Scholastics and their doctrines to the Scriptures. For example, on the much agitated issue of attrition as sufficient for the sacrament of penance, he sees them as refusing to break a bruised reed and to quench a smoking wick (Matt. 12:20) and therefore as devising an easier and surer way to lure sinners into the straight path. The way of contrition being hard and uncertain for them, sinners need only restrain from placing the obstacle either of infidelity or of mortal sin. Luther himself cruelly fails to reveal how much faith is necessary for the justification of the sinner.

Fisher, however, does not hesitate to disagree with the Scholastics according to his own principles. To cite an instance, he believes that God does not ordinarily abandon sinners. On the contrary, although they are in mortal sin and not in the state of grace, nevertheless God gives them a special help by which He knocks at their hearts for entrance (Rev. 3:20). He declares that on this point he is following the opinion of the Fathers rather than that of the Scholastics, who are divided into warring camps. The Fathers, according to Fisher, claim that no one can will any good without a special help from God (Phil. 2:13) and that the general influence which some postulate is not enough. In opposition to the Fathers, some Scholastics contend that the general influence is sufficient so that, without a special help, a person can act well morally and do good.[9]

Skill in the Scholastic disputation is evidently admirable to Fisher. His dedicatory letter to the *Defense of the Royal Assertion* praises Bishop West of Ely, among other reasons for having maintained a reputation as an unbeatable opponent in dialectical and philosophical contests. In the *Defense* proper, Fisher again objects strenuously to the insults hurled by Luther against the Thomists. By this opprobrious attack, Luther is really striving to denigrate the glory of their saintly founder, whom men of outstanding learning and erudition have always held in great veneration and universally called the Flower of Theology. Although he could speak about other Schoolmen also, Fisher chooses to defend in particular that "most learned and at the same time most holy man St. Thomas Aquinas." As a controversialist, he singles him out the more willingly because "Luther's impiety cannot endure the sanctity of the man but everywhere blasphemes with polluted lips him whom all Christians venerate." In fact, Fisher says he could name a host of others who, although not recognized as saints, incomparably surpass Luther in both erudition and piety and who think the opposite from Luther. Among them are the Master of the Sentences, Peter Lombard (d. *ca.* 1160), and the biblical scholar, Nicholas of Lyra (d. 1349), and very many others capable of being mentioned. Christians ought to believe any one of these learned and saintly men before believing Luther.[10]

It is in *Christ's Body,* however, that Fisher undertakes his fullest evaluation of the Schoolmen, and precisely as scriptural scholars. Early in this work, he declares that he cannot deny that the Scholastics are lacking in elegance of style (*eloquentia*), but affirms that they are not lacking in skill in the Scriptures. He challenges Oecolampadius: "Does Thomas seem to you to be ignorant of the Scriptures?" Even the figures who acknowledgedly take first rank as stylists have admired his commentaries. Fisher cites two humanists in particular: Desiderius Erasmus and Giovanni Pico della Mirandola. In Fisher's eyes, Erasmus is a man of admirable judgment, as is clear from his annotations to the New Testament. Yet Erasmus extols St. Thomas with the following words of praise: "As far as my opinion is concerned, there is none of the recent theologians who has equal diligence, who has a saner intellect, who has more solid learning." Pico judges that Thomas is deservedly called the Flower of Theology. Nor is this all. He speaks in much the same way of all the other schools of Disputators and writes as follows: "There is something vigorous and nice in John [Duns] Scotus, something firm and steady in Thomas [Aquinas], something neat and exact in Giles [of Rome], something sharp and keen in Francis [of Meyronnes], something pristine, spacious, and grand in Albert [the Great], something always sublime and commanding respect, as seems to me, in Henry [of Ghent]." Fisher upbraids the pride of mind in Oecolampadius which makes him set at less than nought the very intellects upon which Pico lavishes such praise. It must be observed that all the Schoolmen named by Pico lived more or less in the golden age of Scholasticism; Francis of Meyronnes, the last to die, went to his grave sometime after 1328.[11]

The Bishop of Rochester's own list of approved Scholastics is more comprehensive than that of Pico and extends from William of Paris to Gregory of Rimini. Again it may be noteworthy that Fisher mentions no figure from the second half of the fourteenth century, none from the fifteenth century, and none of the contemporary Schoolmen. It is true that he speaks of the Disputators as being innumerable and that therefore he can touch only on the most distinguished or the leaders (*principes*). But his failure to name a single Scholastic who died after 1358 (the year of Gregory of Rimini's death) could have its basis in his disapprobation of the thought, expression, or spirit of later Schoolmen — or simply in his assumption of their complete agreement with his view and that of the contemporary Church.

Fisher begins his list with the name of Alexander of Hales (d. 1245), who "without doubt was endowed with an excellent intellect and great sanctity of life and was most versed in the Scriptures, as is given to understand from the huge summary which he produced." St. Bonaventure (d. 1274) also was "a man with special intellectual endowments and knowledge of the Scriptures." He "burned with a wonderful piety and breathed a spirit of holiness everywhere in his works," with the result that he earned the title of the Seraphic Doctor. St. Albert (d. 1280), surnamed the Great, had most brilliant gifts of the intellect and expertness in the Scriptures. St. Thomas Aquinas (d. 1274) deservedly is called the Flower of Theology, "both on account of his knowledge of the Scriptures in which he was marvelously versed and on account of the countless knots in sacred theology which he cut."

The Bishop of Rochester finds William of Paris or Auvergne (d. 1249) to be "a man of no less holiness of life than knowledge of the Sacred Scriptures," who wrote much reflecting the brilliant sharpness of his intellect. He approves also of William of Ware (d. after 1300), whom he calls the teacher of Duns Scotus, a nomination which modern scholarship views doubtfully. Giles of Rome (d. 1316) is outstanding, not only in life and talent, but also in knowledge of the Bible. In addition, "Henry of Ghent, mighty in intellectual acuteness and expert in the Scriptures, treated of theological questions with wonderful dignity." Richard of Middleton, too, who had extraordinary learning and a subtle mind, threw much light on many biblical difficulties. Henry of Ghent died in A.D. 1293 and Richard of Middleton about A.D. 1307.

In Fisher's view, "John Duns, whom they call also Scotus, most acutely solved very many problems by means of his perspicacious and vigorous intellect." Duns Scotus died in A.D. 1308, but his pupil (*illius auditor*), Francis of Meyronnes (d. after 1328), also enjoyed a reputation for great talent and investigative skill. Fisher looks upon William Ockham (d. *ca.* 1350) as another pupil of Scotus (*et ipse similiter auditor Scoti*), in spite of his constant attacks on Scotus' system. He was gifted with singular acuteness of intellectual inquiry, which is evident from his books, including his treatment of the Eucharist (*De sacramento altaris et de corpore Christi*). Ockham's contemporary, Durand de St. Pourçain (d. 1334), likewise was "most expert in solving theological difficulties as well as preeminently learned in the Scriptures."

Fisher's list ends with the names of Peter de la Palu (d. 1342), John Baconthorp (d. 1348), and Gregory of Rimini (d. 1358). Peter de la Palu, he finds, was "not unskilled in Sacred Scripture" and was "adroit in disputations." As for John Baconthorp, he "not only was a most keen disputator but also produced commentaries on the whole New Testament." Gregory of Rimini, "a man exceedingly versed in the Scriptures, wrote also many authoritative treatises."

The Bishop of Rochester declares that he is passing over in silence countless other Schoolmen. His contemporaries view those whom he mentions as the most distinguished names among the Disputators. One cannot help observing that, in general, the figures whom he praises, except Ockham, belong to the Old Way (*via antiqua*), that of the Realists. Why, then, does Fisher include Ockham, a founder of the New Way (*via moderna*), that of the so-called Nominalists? Perhaps because in this controversy on the Eucharist he is anxious to marshal as many authorities as possible on his side, even a philosopher-theologian whose doctrine on some points he might reject, but whose acute mind he could admire and whose faith in the Real Presence he could approve. His silence on almost two whole centuries preceding his own period might possibly be significant of his silent disapprobation of the later development of Scholasticism. Fisher therefore commends the Disputators who flourished in the golden age of Scholasticism (*die Hochscholastik*), from William of Auvergne to William of Ockham.[12]

Is Fisher's acclaim of these Scholastics uttered without reservation? One would hardly expect an exponent of humanism to give the Schoolmen unqualified approval. Fisher's criticism is one common among humanists: even these great Schoolmen are lacking in elegance of style (*eloquentia*). Here Fisher agrees with Erasmus, who had published in 1516 a statement which sums up his attitude toward the expression of all the great writers of antiquity, pagan and Christian: "Jerome never sinks so low as not to be more elegant than St. Thomas, even when the latter is at his rhetorical best." [13] But Fisher insists that, even if the Schoolmen lack style, they do not lack knowledge. Cicero himself, he declares, had not expected writing of distinction from "philosophers, i.e., strivers after wisdom" (*a philosophis, hoc est, sapientiae studiosis*). For Fisher, knowledge of truth and elegance of expression are two distinct things: a man can possess one without the other. He continues: "I do not deny, however, that the person who has attained equal proficiency in both is more blessed — and especially if he has also joined piety to the same." In Fisher's eyes, the philosopher lacking in piety, even though he knows all truth and can express it with Ciceronian eloquence, is not worth a pin's head in Christ's estimation.

The ideal philosopher should therefore possess three gifts: knowledge, style, and piety. Fisher insists that people far more readily tolerate lack of elegant expression in a man than lack of piety or of knowledge of truth. Consequently, since the Schoolmen whom he has mentioned are wanting neither in zeal for holiness nor in knowledge of truth, Christians ought not altogether to reject their testimonies. After all, St. Paul does not attribute much to style, for he says: "I . . . did not come with pretentious speech or wisdom," and: "My speech and my preaching were not in the persuasive words of wisdom" (1 Cor. 2:1, 4). Fisher recalls that he has read a similar statement in Origen. But at once he hastens to add that he has not used the authoritative declarations of men like Paul and Origen to turn the minds of students from the cultivation of style: his only purpose is to safeguard the prestige of their forefathers in case the latter have knowledge and piety but chance to be poor in the refinements of expression.[14]

It is not only the wisdom and knowledge of the Schoolmen which is important for the Chancellor of Cambridge University: their method is also of great value and necessity. This holds true even for theology. If to the uninitiated every science and art seem to contain absurdities or even impossibilities, this is even truer of theological matters since they transcend the grasp of human reason. This difficulty can best be overcome by the knowledge of Semitic languages, constant scanning of the Scriptures, and assiduous perusal of the best authorities. To these three must be added keenness of solid reasoning (*solidae ratiocinationis acumen*), conferred by God or gained by practice in the university. Speaking of ordinary theological students in particular, Fisher declares: "Even though they are equipped with the three languages [Latin, Greek, and Hebrew], nevertheless if they lack practice in the Scholastic method, they may expound the opinion which they have conceived, but when they have expounded it, that is an end to it. For they then lack the power either to establish their own views firmly or to assail the errors of others strongly."

In support of his contention that the Scholastic method is invaluable in the battle against erroneous and heterodox doctrines, Fisher points to the annals of the Church, which saw few heresies spring up after the rise of the Schools but which before had always been harassed by heresies. He would not deny that certain heresies had sprung up after the Schools, but this happened through the help of the man who had contemned the Schools in the extreme pride of his heart, namely, John Wyclif.[15]

For purposes of argumentation, the Bishop of Rochester had divided the fifteen hundred years since Christ into five periods of three centuries each, that is, five "trecenaries" (*trecenarii*). His plan is gradually to trace the doctrine of the Real Presence of Christ in the Eucharist back through the centuries to the New Testament itself. The Schoolmen just mentioned belong to the fifth trecenary, A.D. 1200–1500. The main objection which could be launched against them, as has been seen, is poverty of style. In the eyes of Fisher, this charge cannot be leveled against the principal figures of the fourth trecenary (A.D. 900–1200), which modern scholars have designated in its later phase as the renascence of the twelfth century. Here, declares Fisher, "very many appear who are not as unskilled in style" as the representatives of the fifth trecenary. He does not wish to delay the reader by enumerating them. Nevertheless he mentions twenty-eight by name — a noteworthy example of preterition. He does not marshal the names in chronological order but if one were to do so they would appear as follows: *Herigerus Abbas* (Heriger or Hariger, Abbot of the Benedictine monastery at Lobbes, France, fl. 1007), *Adelmannus episcopus Brixiensis* (Adelmann, Bishop of Brescia, d. *ca.* 1061), *Petrus Damiani* (Peter Damian, d. 1072), *Lanfrancus Cantuariensis archiepiscopus* (Lanfranc, Archbishop of Canterbury, d. 1089), *Guimundus Auersanus archiepiscopus, auditor Lanfranci* (Cardinal Guitmund, Archbishop of Aversa in Apulia, pupil of Lanfranc, d. after 1090), *Gratianus* (Gratian the canonist, fl. 12th cent.), *Honorius Augustinensis ecclesiae presbyter* (Honorius [of Autun?], fl. 12th cent.), *Anselmus Cantuariensis archiepiscopus* (Anselm, Archbishop of Canterbury, d. 1109), *Ivo Carnotensis* (Ives, Bishop of Chartres, d. 1116), *Guido abbas sancti Lenfredi* (*sic*) (Guido, Abbot of the Benedictine monastery Croix Saint-Leufroy, near Evreux, fl. 1120), *Hildebertus Thurinensis* (Hildebert de Lavardin, Archbishop of Tours, d. 1133), *Rupertus abbas Tuitiensis* (Rupert von Deutz, d. 1129), *Hugo Victorinus* (Hugh of St. Victor, d. 1141), *Guiellmus abbas sancti Theodorici* (William, Abbot of the Benedictine monastery of St. Theodoric, Reims, later a Cistercian, d. 1149), *Bernardus Clareuallensis* (Bernard of Clairvaux, d. 1153), *Gilbertus Poretanus* [*sic*] (Gilbert de la Porrée, d. 1154), *Petrus Lombardus* (Peter Lombard, d. *ca.* 1160), *Gilbertus Cisterciensis* (either Gilbert the Great, d. *ca.* 1167, or Gilbert of Hoyland, d. 1172, both Cistercians, both Englishmen, much confused), *Richardus Victorinus* (Richard of St. Victor, d. 1173), *Petrus Comestor* (Peter Comestor, d. 1179?), *Iohannes Carnotensis* (John of Salisbury, Bishop of Chartres, d. 1180), *Ecbertus Abbas* (Ekbert, Abbot of the monastery at Schönau, d. 1184), *Petrus quem Cantorem uocant* (Peter Cantor, d. 1197), *Petrus Blesensis* (Peter of Blois, d. *ca.* 1212), *Petrus de Riga* (Peter of Riga, d. *ca.* 1209), *Alueredus abbas* (perhaps Aelfric,

Abbot of Eynsham, called Grammaticus, fl. 1006, whose name appears in a great variety of forms and whose sermon on the Eucharist later caused much controversy), *Lotharius, postea dictus Innocentius tertius* (Giovanni Lotario de' Conti, later Innocent III, d. 1216), and *Robertus Lincolniensis* (Robert Grosseteste, Bishop of Lincoln, d. 1253). Every one of these men is learned in both secular and sacred letters. Fisher is content with this blanket praise, except to label Peter Cantor as "a man erudite in the Scriptures" and Aelfric the Abbot as "a holy man and a great scholar in sacred letters." [16]

To the defense of Peter Lombard, who belongs to this fourth trecenary, Fisher had come very early in *Christ's Body.* Oecolampadius had denied any intention of traducing Aquinas, Albert, Scotus, or other recent theologians, but had attacked Peter Lombard as "that infamous patcher-together [*consarcinator*] of sentences whom people call the Master, and who could communicate his own error to another miscellaneous collector [*rapsodo alii*] such as Damascene or Gratian." Fisher answers that Oecolampadius had wrongly summoned to judgment Peter Lombard, who as a matter of fact had followed the defined teaching of the Fathers and of the whole Church. As for the commentators on the *Sentences,* whom Oecolampadius later contemptuously calls "Sententiarians" (*sententiarii*), does he think that they were all asses and had no judgment? These very commentators had been praised by Erasmus and Pico for their skill in the Scriptures.[17]

For the third trecenary, A.D. 600–900, the Bishop of Rochester quotes or mentions thirteen writers. Placed in chronological order, they are: *Theodorus Cantuariensis archiepiscopus natione Graecus* (Theodore, Archbishop of Canterbury, a native of Tarsus in Cilicia, d. 690), *Beda* (Venerable Bede, d. 735), *Alcuinus* (Alcuin of York, d. 804), *Smaragdus* (Smaragdus de Saint-Mihiel, d. *ca.* 830), *Haimo Halberstatensis* (Haimo, Bishop of Halberstadt, d. 853), *Angelomus* (Angelome de Luxeuil, d. 855), *Rabanus* (Rabanus Maurus, Archbishop of Mainz, d. 856), *Paschasius abbas Corbiensis* (Paschase Ratbert, Abbot of Corbie, France, d. *ca.* 865), *Bartramus Strabus* (Ratramnus, monk at Corbie, d. after 868), *Druthmarus* (Christian Druthmar de Stavelot, d. *ca.* 870), *Remigius Antisiodorensis* (Remi of Auxerre, d. 908), *Ratherius* (Bishop of Verona, d. 974), and *Radulphus Flamacensis* (Radulphus Flaviacensis, i.e., Rodolphe or Raoul, Benedictine Abbot of St.-Germer de Flaix in the diocese of Beauvais, fl. 1157, but formerly thought to flourish *ca.* 910, a fact which would explain his place in Fisher's third trecenary). Because the commentary of Angelome is rather rare, Fisher takes special pains to cite his words.[18]

Since our concern just now is the Middle Ages, the figures of Fisher's first two trecenaries need not be discussed. From the patristic period, for example, he cites such writers as C. Vettius Aquilinus Juvencus (fl. 4th cent.), Ambrose (d. 397), Theophilus of Alexandria (d. 412), Jerome (d. 420), Augustine (d. 430), Cassian (d. *ca.* 435), Cyril of Alexandria (d. 444), Eucherius (Archbishop of Lyons, d. *ca.* 450), Leo I (d. 461), Caelius Sedulius (fl. 5th cent.), Cassiodorus (d. 583), Gregory I (d. 604), and John Damascene (d. *ca.* 749).[19]

For Fisher the only persons who denied the Real Presence of Christ in the Eucharist were heretics who were immediately refuted and condemned: the Messalians (fl. 4th and 5th cent.), Nestorius (d. *ca.* 451), Berengarius (d. 1088), Peter Abelard (d. 1142), and John Wyclif (d. 1384).[20]

Without some such systematization as that used in *Christ's Body,* the names mentioned can be meaningless to the modern reader and float about in timeless space without being fixed in date and place. Fisher's trecenaries naturally need to be supplemented because the divorce tracts contain names which do not appear in *Christ's Body.* Dates will be supplied for authors hitherto unmentioned.

Fisher's only printed work on the divorce, *De causa matrimonii,* cites a host of Schoolmen precisely for their scriptural comments. From his second trecenary (A.D. 300–600), in addition to such Fathers as Augustine and Chrysostom, he quotes Eucherius of Lyons. The third trecenary (A.D. 600–900) provides Bede, Rabanus, Druthmar, and Raoul de Flaix. The fourth trecenary (A.D. 900–1200) furnishes Hugh of St. Victor, Peter Comestor, Peter of Blois, Robert Grosseteste of Lincoln, Clement of Llanthony, and Zachary of Besançon. The fifth trecenary (A.D. 1200–1500) naturally is the source of most authorities, some not named in *Christ's Body:* Alexander of Hales, Bonaventure, Albert the Great, Thomas Aquinas, Richard of Middleton, Duns Scotus, Francis of Meyronnes, Peter de la Palu, Vincent of Beauvais, Hugo the Cardinal (Hugh de S. Cher, d. 1263), Peter of Tarantasia (Pope Innocent V, d. 1276), Robert Kilwardby (d. 1279), James of Lausanne (d. 1322), Nicholas of Lyra (d. 1349), Thomas of Strasbourg (d. 1357), Paul of Burgos (d. 1435), Alphonsus (Alonso Tostado, d. 1455), Antoninus of Florence (d. 1459), Antonius de Rosellis (d. 1466), Juan de Torquemada (d. 1468), Angelus Carletus de Clavasio (d. 1493), Wendelin Steinbach (d. 1519), and Cajetan (d. 1534).[21] From the latter names it is quite evident that Fisher consulted the latest authorities.

One must not forget, however, that Henry VIII on his side had some of the sharpest minds and most learned talents of his realm working for the divorce. The *Censurae* of 1530, for example, can quote Fisher's authorities — and others, too. One might point to *Walterus quidam de Constantia Oxfordiae Archidiaconus,* whom Fisher confesses he has never read, and *Bernardus de Trilla,* of whom he admits he has not even heard. A scholar (like Fisher) needs to be brave and sure of his learning before making such public acknowledgment of his ignorance. *Walter* is none other than Walter of Coutances (d. 1207), Bishop of Lincoln and later Archbishop of Rouen, who as Archdeacon of Oxford had written to Bartholomew, Bishop of Exeter, about illegitimate marriages. *Bernardus* is one of the first followers of Thomas Aquinas, to wit, Bernard de la Treille (d. 1292). Fisher has to answer also arguments from the writings of Hervé de Nedellec (d. 1323), Astexanus (d. *ca.* 1330), Joannes Andreae (d. 1348), Joannes de Imola (d. 1436), Panormitanus (Nicolaus de Tudeschis, d. 1445), James Almainus (d. 1515?), and Joannes de Tabiena (Cagnazzo, d. 1521). Joannes de Tabiena and James of Lausanne, Fisher claims, are authors of no consequence and have been dragged in just to swell the number of favorable authorities — although he himself had just used James of Lausanne in his *Causa*! [22]

From Fisher's method of parading authors, it is clear that, like his English contemporaries, he has no strong historical sense. The most effective use he makes of history, as has been seen, is the argument from prescription — for example, in regard to the special priesthood against Luther and in favor of the Real Presence against Oecolampadius. His theory in respect to a history of dogma is fragmentary and embryonic. He does recognize progress in dogma but as essentially a clearer and fuller explication of revealed doctrine. The most obvious instances are the major conciliar definitions on the Trinity, on the twofold nature of Christ, and on the divine maternity of the Virgin Mary. There is also patent development for Fisher in what might be termed the lesser doctrines of the sacraments, veneration of the saints, purgatory, and indulgences. God in His wisdom has revealed certain matters obscurely or implicitly in order to have Christians exercise their powers on them and in order to have their reason, enlightened by faith, discover new depth and wealth in divine revelation. Fisher considers the occasions for the development of dogma as being furnished usually but not necessarily by heretics, who force the orthodox to examine the truths of faith more closely, to understand them more clearly, and to teach them more emphatically. The Fathers and the Schoolmen furnish substantial help; yet, in Fisher's conception, the principal assistance comes from the Holy Spirit, who causes the legitimate teachers of the Church to exercise their role infallibly, whether gathered in a general council or scattered throughout the world.

Hence, in Fisher's view, the particular Catholic dogmas assailed by Protestants are not corruptions of or additions to the teachings of Christ and the Apostles. Such dogmas rather mark the progress and advance of the whole Church in understanding, knowledge, and wisdom. The content and the meaning of the dogmas are the same as in the apostolic and succeeding ages; but what before was explicit but vague is now made clear and precise (as in the dogma of the consubstantiality of the Son with the Father), or what before was implicit is now made explicit (as in the definition of the twofold will in Christ), or what before was practice is now made doctrinal (as in the validity of baptism conferred by heretics). It is natural for Fisher to make extensive use of the history of heresies in a double way. If heretics impugned a certain doctrine and were expelled from the Church for doing so, he finds therein a proof for the Church's acceptance of that doctrine at that time. If heretics still hold a certain doctrine after expulsion, he sees therein an argument for the antiquity of that doctrine.

Heresies, however, are not the only occasion for the explication of dogmas. As Fisher realizes, the impact of a particular philosophy on the science of theology also has led to the more explicit and detailed declaration of articles of faith, as in the case of the sacraments, particularly the Eucharist. Hence the Schoolmen under the influence of Aristotle have not vitiated and contaminated the pure doctrines of Christ and the Scriptures but rather have thrown a new brilliant light upon dark, obscure, and hidden elements in them — all to the glory of God and the sanctification of souls.

To reconcile the identity of meaning with the development of understanding in the field of dogma under the negative influence of heresy and the positive contribution of philosophy, it is necessary to have a grasp of the theory and content of scientific history. In his theological controversies, however, the Bishop of Rochester turns to history, not so much for an explanation of the causes of events, but rather as to a storehouse of significant facts which can serve as examples or as arguments. For instance, from the *Single Magdalene* to *Christ's Body* he accepts the apocryphal acts of the Apostles and the legends of the saints at least as testimonies to the faith of the Church, if not as literally true. This credulity is evident especially in his three works concerned with Mary Magdalene. Thus, Bethany was the patrimony of Martha; Magdala, of Mary; and a good part of Jerusalem, of Lazarus. All hagiographers agree on the Magdalene's retirement to the desert near Marseilles and to her levitation by angels seven times a day. Such facts, Fisher insists, are to be accepted if they have been adopted by the common consent of the Church, if they have been contradicted by no statements of the Fathers, and if not a word against them can be found in Scripture. He declares that, with Jerome and Bede, "we view the verdict of the people as a true law of history" (*vulgi opinionem, veram historiae legem esse putamus*). He argues also from the Roman martyrology for the identity of Mary Magdalene.[23]

Fisher's answer to Ulrichus Velenus argues that nothing is more difficult in history than the exact computation of dates. Any denial based upon differences in dating is self-defeating. In this way, even the fact of Christ's death could be rejected. So, too, in regard to Peter's sojourn in Rome, an interesting historical sidelight is Fisher's defense of Christ's apparition to Peter near Rome, that is, the story of *Quo vadis,* as related in the *Passio Lini* and confirmed by Eusebius, Hegesippus, and Ambrose. Such lives of the saints were written "for the great utility of the whole Church." [24]

The *Confutation of Luther's Assertion* contains the significant statement: "But as far as histories are concerned, since the particular items which you draw from them are questions of fact and not of right [*facti sunt, non iuris*], they mean nothing to us." The context is that of Pope Gregory's rejection of the title of *Universal* — to set an example of humility, not to deny universal jurisdiction. Even in his later works, the *Defense of the Royal Assertion* and *Christ's Body,* Fisher still appeals to the lives of Andrew and Matthew. He maintains that the orthodox biographers of the Apostles deserve no less credence than pagan writers. Among other things, he refers to the curious and persistent tradition that "Peter had celebrated the first mass at Antioch." [25]

The Bishop of Rochester is far from restricting himself to apocrypha and legends. He makes use of chronicles and histories that range from Josephus in the past to Volaterranus in his own day. In *Velenus' Misrepresentations* he quotes Josephus (d. *ca.* 105) on the martyrdom of James (but not Peter) in Jerusalem and explains his silence on Peter's residence and martyrdom in Rome by the fact that he came to Rome after Peter's death. In the response to the *Censurae* (1530), one of his witnesses to the circumstance that Philip was still alive at the time of Herodias' marriage to Herod Antipas is Josephus, whom he labels as "a most faithful narrator of Jewish events" (*rerum Judaicarum fidelissimus relator*).[26]

The next historian of whom Fisher makes extensive use is Eusebius of Caesarea (d. *ca.* 340). Because Lefèvre esteems Greek authors much more than Latin, Fisher quotes Eusebius, among other Greeks, as espousing one Mary. Against Velenus, Eusebius and Jerome are described as "hardly unimportant authors" (*haud leves autores*), who constantly assert Peter's sojourn in Rome. In the *Defense of the Royal Assertion,* Eusebius is twice held up as the example of a man who, though called by Jerome "the key of the Scriptures and the custodian of the New Testament," could nevertheless err on the consubstantiality of the Son from hearing Arius' interpretation: what, then, about the danger to ordinary people? The *Defense of the Sacred Priesthood* has two references to Eusebius: the one on John's appointment of "priests and ministers" in the provinces adjoining Ephesus, the other on Ignatius of Antioch's lost book on the traditions of the Apostles. Finally, Fisher in his *Causa* uses Africanus (d. *ca.* 250) as cited and approved by Eusebius in regard to Christ's genealogy.[27]

It is inevitable that Fisher should quote the secular history of Augustine's associate, Paulus Orosius (d. *ca.* 420), particularly on Peter's residence and martyrdom in Rome. It is just as inevitable for him to use the sacred history found in the *Historia tripartita* (based on Eusebius, Socrates, Sozomen, and Theodoret), produced under the supervision of Cassiodorus (d. 583). *Christ's Body* uses the latter work for comments on the Arians and on the Euchites or Messalians.[28]

The medieval historians, too, are well known to the Bishop of Rochester. Bede (d. 735) is mentioned and quoted many times, for example, in favor of the single Magdalene, on the time of Peter's arrival and residence in Rome, and on Herodias' remarriage despite Philip's being alive. The popular *Chronographia* of Sigebert of Gembloux (d. 1112) is cited on the removal of Magdalene's body to a safer place because of the Saracens. When the proponents of Henry VIII's divorce use William of Malmesbury for the fact that Archbishop Lawrence of Canterbury, in spite of the pope's command, refused to lift the excommunication of Eadbald, King of Kent, for marrying his stepmother, Fisher challenges the reader to find the circumstances of Lawrence's resistance to papal authority in the same William of Malmesbury (d. 1143) — or even in Henry of Huntingdon (d. 1155).[29]

Two later medieval historians used by Fisher are Peter Comestor (d. 1179?), and Vincent of Beauvais (d. *ca.* 1264). Peter Comestor, who is known to Fisher as "the Master of Histories" (*Magister historiarum*) is called upon for testimony on the Magdalene, on the Real Presence, and on the divorce. Vincent of Beauvais, "who wrote a copious history and diligently recounted very many events" (an understatement for his *Speculum historiale* with its 31 books and 3793 chapters, from the Creation to St. Louis), witnesses to the Magdalene's prostitution and to her personal apparitions to himself.[30]

Renaissance historians are by no means neglected by Fisher in favor of medieval writers. Flavio Biondi (d. 1463), often termed the most scholarly historian produced by Italian humanism, and Pius II (d. 1464), destined to have considerable influence on German historians, testify to the deluded character of Amadeus of Savoy, the antipope Felix V. In his role of secretary to Eugene IV, Biondi is witness to the Greek ambassadors' subscription to the Florentine decrees on the primacy of the Roman Church and Pontiff. In the work against Clichtove, Fisher repeats the observation of Pius II in his *History of Europe* that distant reports of marvelous events are discovered to be mere trifles and lies when investigated on the spot.[31]

Finally, the Bishop of Rochester, in answering Velenus, summons up as witnesses to Peter's sojourn in Rome four "more recent historians . . . most scholarly men": Platina (Bartolomeo de Sacchi di Piadena, d. 1481), Sabellicus (Marcantonio Coccio, d. 1506), Volaterranus (Raffaele Maffei, d. 1522), and John Baptist (perhaps J. B. Spagnuoli, d. 1516). Platina is seen by Fisher as an "historian not undistinguished" (*non ignobilis . . . historicus*) but as anticlerical (*parum Sacerdotibus fauens*). Sabellicus, the author of the *Enneades,* a humanistic world history, is described as "a man most assiduous in the compilation of history," than whom "none scarcely can be found either more trustworthy or more accurate or, if you choose, more scholarly in writing history." Volaterranus and John Baptist seem not to be characterized in any special manner.[32]

History, therefore, like philosophy, has a definite and legitimate place in the theology of John Fisher. Both subjects, of course, are unquestionably subsidiary to the twofold primary source of Scripture and tradition. Because of the level of historical scholarship in his day and the predominance of Scholasticism, philosophy understandably assumes far greater prominence than history in Fisher's work. Comparison of the views of Fisher with those of Erasmus and More on the controversial Schoolmen should prove useful and enlightening.

To Fisher, Thomas More is a man "most brilliant in his character and his intellect and not less outstanding because of his erudition," while the definitive judgment of Erasmus alone is sufficient for him against a thousand other authorities, as, for example, on the authenticity of the Pauline-Senecan epistles. All three agree in their reverence for St. Thomas Aquinas, Erasmus' admiration being less than that of More and Fisher. The three do not share Colet's antipathy to Aquinas on account of what Colet calls his supercilious omniscience and his Aristotelization of Christ's doctrine. As far as specific Schoolmen are concerned, Erasmus seems to restrict his approbation, though qualified, to the Angelic Doctor. As has been seen, Fisher has modified praise for all the leading Scholastic philosophers and theologians from the patristic period to William Ockham.[33]

In view of Fisher's simple purpose in *Christ's Body,* his list of great Schoolmen is understandably more comprehensive than that of More, whose references are more casual. More agrees with Fisher in his commendation of St. Bonaventure, whose life of Christ in English translation is one of the books which "moste may noryshe and encreace deuocion"; St. Thomas Aquinas, "that most learned and likewise most holy man" and "the very floure of theology"; and Nicholas of Lyra, "that good vertuouse and wel learned manne." Additional figures from these centuries of whom More speaks well are the "holye S. Bernard" and William Durandus (d. 1296), "that good man that made the booke of *Rationale diuinorum,*" which deals with liturgical rites and symbolism. In another passage, he refers to "a good freres booke called *Rationale diuinorum.*" Peter Lombard and Duns Scotus are mentioned without special comment. More refers to several figures before Peter Lombard. St. Anselm is spoken of as one of the saintly Schoolmen agreeing in doctrine with St. Augustine. The earliest figure cited by More seems to be "that very vertuous manne," John Cassian. Of the writers transitional to the Middle Ages, More quotes Boethius (d. 525) and the Pseudo-Dionysius (wr. *ca.* 500), the latter's *Ecclesiastical Hierarchy* to the effect that "the leaders and maisters of the christen fayth . . . deliuered vs many thynges to bee kepte, partly by writyng and partly by theyr institucions vnwritten." Of figures after Ockham, More singles out Walter Hilton (d. 1396) and John Gerson (d. 1429). Hilton is the author of the "deuoute contemplatiue booke of *scala perfectionis.*" More's treatise on the passion refers three times to Gerson: as "that worshipful father maister," as "an excellent lerned man, and a gentle handeler of a trowbled conscience," and as "a man of profound learning and excellent uertue." The

Dialogue of Comfort praises "dyuers goodly treatices of that good godly doctour. master John Gerson, intitled *De probatione spirituum.*" In his controversy with Tyndale, More erroneously regards Gerson as the author of *The Following of Christ,* another book translated into English, which "moste may noryshe and encreace deuocion." [34]

Erasmus attacks strenuously what he terms the Aristotelization of Christian truth, which is to be found in a pure state in the New Testament. He has no objection, however, if "the mixture is made with prudence and moderation." [35] On the other hand, in answering Tyndale's charge that the pope and clergy "medle philosophye with the thynges of God," Thomas More unreservedly declares that the use of philosophy in matters of faith is "a thyng that maye in place bee verye well done, sythe the wysedome of philosophy all that we fynde true therein, is the wysdome geuen of God." As a matter of fact, the Scholastic "doctours of these eight hundred yeres last passed . . . do consent and agre with the old holy [doctours] of the tother .vii. hundred yeare afore." [36] As for Fisher, he appears to have no direct and explicit statement on this point of the Aristotelization and adulteration of Christian truth. His silence would seem to signify a lack of any feeling of disapproval. Moreover, his praise for the biblical knowledge of the leading Schoolmen as late as Ockham would seem to indicate his approbation, or at least his toleration, of Scholastic doctrine and method even in scriptural study.

If one were now to attempt a generalization, the attitude toward Scholasticism of all three, Erasmus, More, and Fisher, is one of qualified approval and varying compromise. Their judgments on the Schoolmen, one must remember, usually occur in controversies, sometimes heated, on the genuine nature and true content of the Christian religion and morality, especially in relation to the Scriptures. Of the three, Erasmus seems furthest removed from and least sympathetic to the Schools. More undertakes the active defense of the most holy and learned of the Scholastics, especially St. Thomas Aquinas. Like a true humanist, Fisher objects to the apparent crudeness of the Scholastic style, but he gives his approval to far more Schoolmen than either Erasmus or More. Today many of them appear of relatively small stature, but this is due to our scholarly ignorance and not to their lack of intellectual acumen and influence. Fisher nevertheless appears to be the most conservative of the three in his stand on Scholasticism. As we know, his statutes for St. John's College provided for regular lectures in Greek and Hebrew. But they also laid down that the questions for the academic disputations were to be taken from the Subtle Doctor, Duns Scotus, whose followers were a favorite target of humanist attack. In sum, Fisher does not abandon the old Scholasticism or reject the new humanism: he wants the best of both.

This desire for the retention of perennial elements in Scholasticism does not make him a Schoolman in humanist's clothing — a judgment passed upon Ortwin Gratius and Wimpina. Like the best contemporary theologians, Fisher stands not only for a new theological method but also for a new theological content, based upon study of the Bible and the Fathers in their original languages and carried on within the compass of the Church. He initiated and advanced the movement strongly in his discussion with Luther and Oecolampadius, but the political circumstances of the royal divorce and spiritual supremacy kept him from definitive achievement and perfection.[37] Fisher's humanism helps to explain Vives' resentment at the claim of better scholarship on the part of the Protestants. He labels Luther as being more Scholastic than humanist and places Fisher solidly with those men of superior humanistic learning and eloquence who have written against the new doctrines.[38]

This present chapter, in a sense, is pivotal in assessing Fisher's place in the Renaissance and the Reformation. It shows his approach toward a medieval phenomenon which humanists in general either rejected in its entirety or accepted only with reservations. His attitude toward Scholasticism, as we have seen, is one of approval for its doctrines and its authors but one of regret for its neglect of Latin style and its ignorance of languages like Greek and Hebrew. Moreover, his training in Scholastic disputation helps to explain his orientation, his tone, and his methods — less in his sermons than in his controversies. Additionally, his mastery of Scholastic writings manifests the immense range of his reading and his learning. An unconscionable amount of time and research is required to identify and date many lesser-known Scholastics cited by him. Finally, Fisher's views on church history and especially on the development of dogma provide a new understanding of the role of history for men of the Renaissance and the Reformation.

Chapter X

EDUCATION

NOWHERE is the adjustment — or the compromise — in Fisher's attitudes more evident than in his relations with the two new colleges at Cambridge, namely, Christ's and St. John's. Their statutes reveal what historical hindsight is inclined to interpret as the ultimately transitional nature of his thought and action. At any rate, comparison with statutes previous to his disclose that his own were not revolutionary but rather reinforced and accelerated excellent but dormant programs. Despite their desirable character, these programs were incapable of immediate implementation or were desultory in execution, not because of unreasonable conservative opposition but because of lack of lecturers or auditors. To say nothing of Erasmus' experience at Cambridge, the difficulties of Fisher himself with Greek and Hebrew at his colleges verify this judgment.

The marvel is the incredibly brief time within which Christ's College and St. John's College produced "a great number of learned men well instructed in all sciences" and, as the English but not the Latin version of the sixteenth-century life of Fisher reads, in "knowledge of the three learned tongues, to the singuler benefit of the Church of God and common welth of this realme." The life then proceeds to enumerate the Catholic martyrs, bishops, and scholars who had come from the two colleges. The ferment could not help but affect the whole university. In regard to bishops, for example, A. B. Emden remarks: "In 1425 there were no Cambridge men on the bench, while there were 12 from Oxford. During the reign of Henry VIII, on the other hand, every English see was held for some period of the reign by a Cambridge man." [1]

The character and personality of Fisher himself has been recognized as a major reason for the transformation. One writer has made the following analysis: "With his soundness of judgment and his prudent reforming zeal, he combined a devotion to duty and an awareness of contemporary movements of thought that are the qualities that go to make a successful university administrator and reformer. . . he had a solidity of intellect and sureness of understanding that won for him, even, it would seem, as a young man, the affectionate confidence and respect of others." J. B. Mullinger rightly gives credit to the perspicacity of the Lady Margaret who quickly discovered his unusual business ability.[2]

Of Fisher's own education as a youth, the early biography says only that a priest of the collegiate church in Beverley instructed him and his brother Robert in "their first letters and rudiments of grammer." At Cambridge, where he went about 1483, he was deeply influenced, according to the preface to the first book of *Christ's Body,* by the Master of Michaelhouse, William Melton. His subsequent connections with the university were briefly the following: bachelor's degree (1488), master's degree (1491), fellowship at Michaelhouse (1491–96), senior proctor of the university (1494–95), master of Michaelhouse (1496–98), doctorate in divinity (1501), vice-chancellorship (1501–1504), chancellorship (1504–35), and presidency of Queens' College (1505–1508).[3]

With his intimate knowledge of the needs and potentialities of the university, Fisher was able to influence in its favor the Lady Margaret, whom he met perhaps for the first time in 1494. He became her confessor *ca.* 1498, approximately seven years after his sacerdotal ordination by papal dispensation because of his youth (1491). What he was able to effect through Margaret is attributed, in his funeral sermon for her (1509), to her great faith:

> What is that that this gentylwoman wolde not byleue? she that ordeyned .ij. contynual reders in bothe the vnyuersytes to teche the holy dyuynyte of Ihesu, she that ordeyned prechers perpetuall to publysshe the doctryne & fayth of cryste Ihesu, she that buylded a college royall to the honour of the name of crist Ihesu, & lefte tyll her executours another to be buylded to mayntayn his fayth & doctryne.

The reference is to those benefactions already mentioned: the Lady Margaret Readership in Divinity at both Oxford and Cambridge (1502), Fisher himself being the first reader at Cambridge;

the provision for a Cambridge man to give a fixed number of sermons at designated times and places (1504); the refoundation of Godshouse as Christ's College (1505); and the bequest for the refoundation of St. John's Hospital as St. John's College (chartered 1511, consecrated 1516).[4]

In regard to Fisher's chancellorship, the early biographer comments: "Knowinge in deed what a pretious thinge learninge is in all regimente, and what they were over whom this his authoritie was to be used, he did not so much esteeme the dignitie . . . as he well wayed the care therunto annexed." This is not mere hagiographical eulogy. How hard he worked for the university is evident not only from the benefactions of the Lady Margaret and the provision of lecturers like Erasmus, Croke, and Wakefield, but from even a casual reading of his addresses, letters, and publications. As we have seen, his oration before Henry VII (1506) brought very important financial results. Before the king began to show his generosity, the university, according to Fisher, had been on the decline for at least three reasons: difficulties with the townsmen, the loss of many students and ten professors from the ravages of the plague, and the paucity of patrons of the liberal arts. But the recent benevolence of Henry VII had restored to honor the neglected muses, as was evident even from the totally unexpected elevation of Fisher to the episcopacy — a measure designed to incite all others to virtue and learning. In the course of his oration, Fisher alludes — how seriously is a question — to the foundation of the university by Cantaber, king of the East Angles, who had been educated in the liberal arts at Athens, and to that of the University of Paris by two Cambridge alumni, Alcuin and Rabanus, an event to which he refers also in *The Single Magdalene*.[5]

For its part, the university did not allow Fisher to remain idle. Upon hearing of his impending departure for Rome, it wrote him to be mindful of its needs — "as one who very well knows what our needs are" (*quippe qui optime nosti quibus nobis opus est*) (February 12, 1515). Its vice-chancellor, John Eccleston, would explain the needs to him at length. But the Roman trip never materialized. The extant records of the university also testify to the many appeals made to the chancellor in its business affairs.[6] The Bishop of Rochester, however, interested himself also in individuals. A letter from John Brandisby to Nicholas Metcalfe discloses that Fisher had given him twenty shillings on his way to Paris and had promised to prefer his brothers first into St. John's College. In a revealing letter to Thomas More after the latter's reception of knighthood, he begs him, in view of his intimacy with Henry VIII, to secure a favor for an anonymous young theologian and preacher. In his gracious reply, More declares that his little influence with the king is available to Fisher and his charges. He concludes: "I owe your students constant gratitude for the heartfelt affection of which their letters to me are the token. Farewell, best and most learned of Bishops, and continue your affection for me." Their "affection" was cemented by the appointment of Thomas More as High Steward of the University of Cambridge in 1525.[7]

The program and ideal which Fisher hoped to achieve for his university and his individual scholars must be presumed to be embodied in the statutes for Christ's and St. John's Colleges. Almost two hundred years later, Thomas Baker concluded that Fisher's statutes, "though now antiquated, yet bating the Popery, were very wisely drawn." Even P. S. Allen agrees with Mullinger's conjecture on Erasmus' influence in regard to their "markedly humanistic bias," for example, the lectures on the classical poets and orators. Yet such lectures had been prescribed in William Byngham's earlier requirement for Godshouse. At any rate, it has already been seen how strongly Fisher's "corporateness," his sense of a mystical body, is found expressed even in statutes, first for Christ's and later for St. John's. A practical consequence is that fellow or scholar, if lawfully convicted and incapable of reformation, is to be cut off as a harmful limb for the following offenses, presumably named in the order of seriousness: heresy, treason, simony, usury, perjury, homicide, incest, adultery, or any similar charge. On the other hand, the good who strive more assiduously after learning and virtue are treated "more kindly and gently" (*humanius . . . et mollius*).[8]

The concern of the Bishop of Rochester for the humanities, as distinct from the more lucrative studies of medicine and law, appears from the oath required of master and fellows not "to turn aside to any Faculty other than Philosophy and Theology" (philosophy being understood to embrace the arts). Yet even this restriction appears as early as 1475 in the statutes of St. Catharine's. The two deans of these faculties have the duty, therefore, "each week of every term to hear in the College Chapel two disputations, each of two hours' length, one in Philosophy on Wednesday, the other on Friday in Theology." [9]

The fellows are to have a threefold aim: "the worship of God, the increase of the faith, and probity of morals" (*dei . . . cultus, fidei incrementum et morum probitas*). This same statement appears in the statutes for St. John's in 1516; but in 1524 and 1530, undoubtedly because of the Lutheran menace, there is a change in order and phrasing: "the worship of God, probity of morals, and the strengthening of the Christian faith [*Christianae fidei corroboratio*]." A little later, Fisher states: "After the worship of God, we will that they shall all devote themselves to the study of learning [*doctrine studio*]." What follows, however, is even more important because it sets the ultimate and proximate educational goals and the hierarchy of means by which these goals are to be achieved: "And since the increase of the Faith (which we desire above all things) takes its start from Theology, we specially commend Theology to all of them, that they may set it before them as the goal of their studies. Nevertheless we wish each of them to be initiated and instructed according to the custom of the University in Philosophy and the liberal Arts [*bonis artibus*], by which Theology is approached and without which it cannot be acquired. Every week therefore we wish them to hold two disputations in the College Chapel, one in Philosophy, the other in Theology. . ."

The above declaration appears also in the statutes for St. John's ten years later with the following highly significant sign of progress: "Some are to give attention to Hebrew and Greek literature as soon as possible." The statutes for the same college, moreover, require not two but three disputations: one in philosophy and two in theology.[10]

Apart from the disputations, lectures naturally come in for regulation, for example, at Christ's College: "On every day not a feast day . . . the Reader shall publicly deliver . . . for the space of two hours, four lectures, one in Sophistry, the second in Logic, the third in Philosophy, and the fourth from the works of either the poets or the orators." With respect to the last lecture, there is a change here from the corresponding statute for Godshouse: "the fourth in some work dealing with the modes of signification, or some other grammatical, poetical or rhetorical work." The interpretation has been given that the alteration is not the result of "the claims of the new learning" because Christ's College like Godshouse was still committed to providing schoolmasters. Nevertheless what is meaningful is revealed by what is eliminated: (1) "the modes of signification," perhaps Peter of Spain's *Summulae logicales* or *Parva logicalia* (*Small Logicals*), derided in More's *Utopia,* and (2) "some other grammatical . . . work," perhaps the grammar of John Garland or Eberhard of Bethune. The restriction to "either the poets or the orators," therefore, might well speak by its silence.[11]

With the heavy emphasis on learning, a glance at recreation at Christ's College is not without interest. Dogs and birds of prey are forbidden. Dice and cards are permitted only during Christmastide, only in the hall, and only "for the sake of relaxation" (*remittendi animi gracia*). The statutes for St. John's for 1524 and 1530 allow dice and cards to fellows but forbid them to the pupils even at Christmas and during its octave: there is no call to grant the pupils all the privileges of the fellows. In 1530 Fisher expressly declares that he has no intention of forbidding "honest and moderate hunting or hawking, when engaged in with permission outside the university." That Fisher himself indulged in hunting is evident from a letter from George Neville, Lord Bergavenny: "If it shall please you to see your greyhounds run at any time either within or without, I have commanded my keeper to give you attendance and make you such disport as if I were there present." [12]

The statutes of 1516 for St. John's lean so heavily upon those for Christ's that they constitute a clear sign of Fisher's approval. The precise nature and extent of Fisher's influence upon the code for Christ's College remain unknown. It is certainly his insofar as the Lady Margaret would be reasonable enough not to contradict or oppose the advice of the experienced and respected chancellor of the university. It is not surprising, therefore, to read the following: "We appoint therefore that John, by Divine permission Bishop of Rochester, and now Chancellor of the University of Cambridge, shall, as long as he lives, even if he happen to have resigned the Chancellorship, be visitor of the said College." [13]

Christ's College offered no problems after the Lady Margaret's death in 1509 because it was "cleane furnished in her lyfe time." St. John's College was another matter: it "was in manner nowe to be builte wholy after her death cheefly at her costes and charges." As the most active executor, Fisher did "not only beare a portion of the buyldinge upon his owne charge, but also much augmented yt in possessions, foundinge there four fellowships, a reader of an hebrewe lectur, a reader of a greeke lecture, four examiner readers, and four underreaders to helpe the principall reader." But our concern is with his statutes rather than with his difficulties and his benefactions.[14]

Fisher's statutes of 1516 for St. John's are much like those of Christ's with some differences already noted above. For his statutes of 1524 he turned to those of his friend, Bishop Foxe of Winchester, for Corpus Christi at Oxford, just as Wolsey did for Cardinal College in 1525. Fisher's statutes of 1530 depend upon those for both Cardinal and Corpus Christi Colleges. It will also be recalled how in his dedicatory epistle to *Christ's Body* the Bishop of Rochester praised Richard Foxe for his emphasis on Hebrew, Greek, Latin, and whatever learning was conducive to true theology.[15]

What Fisher deems conducive to true theology becomes more sharply defined in his new codes. For the three weekly disputations, one in philosophy and two in theology, required in 1516 and 1524, he makes a clarification in 1530. The disputations are to follow "the doctrine of John Scotus so that in each disputation two questions are to be discussed according to the order of the two distinct volumes of the said John Scotus, starting from the beginning of the first book and proceeding to the end of the quodlibets of the same, always starting anew when the end of the whole work is reached." [16] Could Fisher possibly have discovered that his humanistic program failed to give his students the intellectual discipline, strength, and acumen imparted by rigorous Scholastic training?

On the other hand, the later statutes prove to be slightly less exacting, perhaps because Fisher sees a greater need for depth rather than for breadth. Yet even this concession would be in accord with classic humanistic pedagogy: *non multa sed multum.* In 1516, the candidate for the master's degree had to treat publicly either the three books of Aristotle's *On the Soul,* or *On the Heavens,* or the *Generation of Animals,* or one of the four books of *Meteorologica,* or one of the books of the mathematicians, according to the assignment of master and fellows. In 1524, however, the choice is carefully limited to the two last books of *On the Soul,* or two from the *Generation of Animals,* or two from the four of *On the Heavens,* or two from the four of *Meteorologica,* or one of the books of the mathematicians. This form remains unchanged in 1530.[17]

Experimentation evidently caused Fisher to make his requirements more reasonable elsewhere too. In 1516, for example, he had demanded that candidates for the doctorate in theology, either inside or outside the college, publicly explain to all comers forty questions in turn, chosen from some part of Scotus by the master and fellows. This regulation had not been laid down for Christ's College. In 1524 he reduces the requirement to twenty questions on some section of either Scotus or Francis of Meyronnes. No alteration is made in 1530. Another statute of 1516, not found at Christ's, had been that candidates for the doctorate in theology had to interpret for all comers forty chapters of the New Testament in turn. The code for 1524 and for 1530, however, reduces the number of chapters to twenty.[18]

Other statutes of special interest might be pointed out. All three recensions of the statutes provide for four fellows, the first to lecture on arithmetic, the second on geometry, the third on perspective, and the fourth on the sphere and cosmography. A statute for 1516 provides for a lecturer to deliver four public discourses in St. John's hall for two hours or more: one on sophistry, one on logic, and two on philosophy, text and time being left to the choice of master and fellows. In 1524, however, a change is made to secure greater activity on the part of the students. The lecturer is now required to spend the two hours "in hearing the recitations of the students, and in examining as well as teaching the same." In 1530 two assistants are provided to help the principal lecturer in his assignment.[19]

The code of 1524 introduces a regulation which is indicative of Fisher's humanism. On every Saturday, for half an hour during term and a full hour outside term, the more gifted students are to exercise themselves in declamations by arguing in turn both sides of a case according to the manner of Seneca or Quintilian. This rule is made applicable also to those fellows who have only the bachelor's degree. The statute remained unchanged in 1530.[20] But that same year saw the introduction of a new statute which clearly shows Fisher's awareness of Protestantism and his alarm at its appeal and success. In part it reads:

> As far as the heresies of the Lutherans, Oecolampadians, Anabaptists, Wycliffites, Hussites, and all the others who do not think in a Catholic way are concerned, because that plague is rampant everywhere in so perilous a manner, we establish and ordain that, if anyone shall have been marked by the slightest suspicion whatsoever of favoring them or anyone of them or if that fact appears through deed, word, or sign . . . [after the proper inquiry and proof or confession] . . . he is immediately to be excluded from the said college and deprived *ipso facto* by force of the present statute with no other preceding warning. . .

If this regulation was necessary even at his own College of St. John's, it is indicative of the situation in the whole of the university. His sixteenth-century life records the following: "My lord speedes himself to Cambrige, and there, by vertue of his office of high chancellor, looked verie straitly to the orders and rules of the universitie: . . . which began even then to growe out of frame." [21] The most famous heterodox group convened at the White Horse Tavern and walked on Heretic's Hill. It included Thomas Cranmer, Matthew Parker, Nicholas Ridley, Hugh Latimer, Thomas Bilney, and John Frith.[22]

Fisher's concern for orthodoxy is evident also in his letter — presumably to be dated 1529 — to Richard Croke, who had retailed certain calumnies to him: If he lays down the chancellorship, as he is only too willing to do, "another will accept it perhaps who welcomes the Lutheran teachings. But I should not wish them ever to expect me to favor persons decreed by the Church to be enemies of the orthodox." After a denial that he had accused the university of heresy, he proceeds: "Doubtlessly the fathers and seniors of the university find that heresy quite displeasing — although many of you are under suspicion and some pointed out with the finger. Woe to the degenerate sons who blacken their hitherto inviolate mother, as I hear, even in public speeches . . . and bespatter her with foul disgrace. It would have been better for them if they had not been born." [23]

The statutes of 1530 were the last published by Fisher, who seems to have been working on another code before his final imprisonment. Toward the end of his life, a deputation from St. John's called upon him to ratify certain changes in the statutes but there was not time for him to read and study them. His final words were: "Then let Gods will be done; for I will never alowe under my seale that thinge, which I have not well and substantially viewed and considered." The changes requested are not known but have been said variously to be the amendments of Cranmer or Cromwell, or of both. As the new chancellor, Cromwell in the latter part of 1535 imposed on the university certain injunctions, approved by Parliament the next spring. These forbade lectures on canon law and Scholastic philosophy, including the *Sentences* of Peter Lombard, and prescribed the new Aristotle with commentaries by humanists like Melanchthon. Theological lectures and studies were made to focus on the Bible. Latin, Greek, and Hebrew naturally were emphasized. Cromwell thus destroyed the delicate balance between the new humanism and the old Scholasticism which Fisher had tried to establish and maintain at St. John's above all and which might have served to make Cambridge as famous and faithful as Alcalá or Salamanca in the revival of Scholasticism. The Schoolmen, of course, continued to be read in private at Cambridge and elsewhere.[24]

In addition to the annulment of much of its medieval legacy, St. John's and Cambridge sustained a more concrete loss in Fisher's library at his imprisonment and death. "Lykewise his librarie of bookes (which was thought to be such as no one bishop in Europe had the lyke) . . . he gave longe before his death to the said college of St. John." The royal commissioners "trussed up XXXII great pypes [i.e., casks], besides a number that were stollen away." Under Edward VI and under Mary, St. John's, in the person of men like Ascham, was still acutely aware of its loss.[25]

In his love and amassment of books, the Bishop of Rochester belongs very much to the Renaissance. As for the education which he provided and espoused, judgment on its nature can best be passed by the greatest humanist of Fisher's day, Desiderius Erasmus. The same discipline, e.g., the disputation, could be conducted either in an intellectually stultifying manner or in a way which opened up new vistas for the mind and spirit. The same classical Latin or Greek work could be reduced to grammatical and rhetorical formalities or viewed as an imaginative, creative, and fructifying masterpiece. Consequently not only the matter of study but also the spirit of learning needs to be considered.

Little is known about Erasmus' sojourn in Cambridge (1511–14), especially about his lectures on the New Testament and St. Jerome. During his stay Christ's College was operating fully, and St. John's was abuilding. Erasmus' auditors in 1511 were few, but, to judge from the many later pronouncements of his pupils, were not inconsiderable by 1514. What Erasmus sees as new at Cambridge appears to be not a drastic measure like the elimination of the Schoolmen but rather the expansion of the curriculum to allow for the new humanism. Only a few days after the formal opening of St. John's College at the end of July 1516, he writes to Henry Bullock:

> Are they [the objectors to his New Testament at Cambridge] afraid their own schools will be deserted if the youth are enticed away to these studies? Why don't they rather consider how at Cambridge, about thirty years ago, nothing was taught but Alexander [de Ville-Dieu] and the so-called "Small Logicals" (*Parva Logicalia*) and those ancient Aristotelian rules, with the *Questions* derived from Duns Scotus; how, subsequently, good letters were added, and a knowledge of mathematics, and a new, or at least refurbished, Aristotle; and how the command of Greek was added, with a host of authors whose very names were once unknown even to those lofty pundits themselves. Now tell me, what has been the effect of all this upon your university? Why, it has blossomed forth so as to rival the leading modern schools. . . Or does this class of men *grieve* that more people are henceforward to read the Gospels and the apostolic Letters. . . I have discovered that hitherto there have been some theologians whose previous neglect of the very reading of Holy Writ was such that they scarce could turn the pages, even of the *Books of Sentences,* and in fact never touched anything but the riddles of the *Questions.*[26]

The date mentioned, "about thirty years ago," carries the reader back exactly to Fisher's undergraduate years at Cambridge. How well Christ's College and St. John's College fulfilled the Erasmian ideal here set forth is evident from the points in their statutes mentioned above. Three months later, Erasmus wrote to Louis Ber, theologian at the University of Basel: "Cambridge is a changed place. This university now abominates those vain quibbles, which conduce rather to quarrelling than to piety." On the same day, December 6, 1517, he told Wolfgang Koepfel (Capito), the Dean of the Faculty of Theology at Basel: "In this place [Louvain], these subtleties already are earning condemnation; while at Cambridge they are quite banished." The following April he mentions to Marcus Laurinus an invitation from the Bishop of Rochester in the same breath with those from kings and dukes, archbishops and bishops. In May 1519, after referring to Foxe's and Wolsey's contributions to Oxford for "the study of good literature, . . . languages and studies of every kind, . . . moral training suitable to the highest studies," he continues: "As for Cambridge University, it has long been flourishing with extreme distinction under the presidency of the Very Reverend the Lord Bishop of Rochester, who in no single respect omits to play the part of a distinguished prelate." This letter is addressed to his former pupil and present patron, Lord Mountjoy.[27]

The Erasmian program for universities is again given in general terms in his letter of June 1520 to Vives: on the positive side "the better sort of literature," on the negative the elimination of the "sophistical variety of learning." He repeats Fisher's judgment: "At Cambridge . . . instead of sophistical refinements, sober and sound discussions [*disputationes*] are held nowadays among the theologians; and from these they depart not only more learned, but better men." The emphasis here is clearly on the spirit with which the disputations are conducted. Content, of course, is by no means excluded, for in his letter of October 1521 to Nicholas Everard, the stress is on the "better literature." Everard explains why "the school at Louvain is cold and deserted" and why "both in Paris and at Cambridge the study of theology is flourishing as it never flourished before." Erasmus repeats his view eight years later in his letter to Alfonso de Fonseca. Fisher's colleges at Cambridge do not prepare youth for sophistical encounters while rendering them unfit for life's serious tasks. On the contrary, exercised in true learning and sober discussions (*disputationes*), they go forth to preach God's word in a deeply evangelical spirit and to commend it to the souls of the educated with effective eloquence.[28]

At the beginning of 1529, the same year in which Erasmus sent his letter to Fonseca, his university showed Fisher its gratitude for his services and sacrifices. Its senate declared him a founder, with an annual requiem mass. In his reply Fisher declared that he was merely the Lady Margaret's servant (*minister*) in the business, that he was only doing his bounden duty, and that he would be more than satisfied with but a share in their prayers for her. He again reverts to her (and surely his) intention: the education of a multitude of youths who, when they had grown into men of learning and virtue, would spread the Gospel of Christ throughout the land of Britain with superabundant fruit.[29] Moreover, in the shadow of the scaffold, the fellows of St. John's College proved their loyalty by offering all possible help. Their letter in part reads: "You are our father, teacher, instructor, legislator, in fine, our model of all virtue and holiness. We confess that we owe to you our sustenance, to you our learning, to you whatever good we either have or know. . . You are our glory and guardian. You are our head so that whatever evils touch you necessarily bring anguish to us as your subordinate members." [30] Perhaps it gave the desolate Fisher some comfort to hear from the members of St. John's College the very comparison of the mystical body which he had used in his statutes for St. John's College twenty years before and for Christ's College thirty years before. "The wheel is come full circle."

The establishment and the regulation of the colleges at Cambridge, like all Fisher's works and labors, are directed quite explicitly to "the worship of God, probity of morals, and the strengthening of the Christian faith." Whether he is preaching before the Lady Margaret or at Paul's Cross, or disputing about the Magdalene with Lefèvre and Clichtove, or refuting the doctrines of Luther and Oecolampadius, or defending the validity of the royal marriage, he is endeavoring to know, and to make his fellow Christians know, "thee, the only true God, and him whom thou hast sent, Jesus Christ." This knowledge of God and His relationships to His creatures is to be not an ignorant but a learned knowledge, using to the full both revelation and reason. He intends the "science of faith" to find its basic principles and assumptions in the truths revealed in Scripture and tradition, to use the "scientific" methods of analysis and synthesis, and to set up a "system" of truths. It is to this end that he stresses the three languages of Latin, Greek, and Hebrew so as to get at the true meaning of Scripture. The true meaning is to be found best in the original language and text, and the genuine or "Catholic" interpretation is to be sought in the pronouncements of the Roman Church and in the Greek and Latin Fathers. Philosophy, and Scholasticism in particular, is not to be spurned but to be employed soberly and properly. It helps to give a clearer and deeper understanding of Christian mysteries, to explain dogmas with full vigor, and to defend the divinely revealed truths against infidels and heretics. History, too, has its place for Fisher, especially for the refutation of heresy and as the springboard for the argument from prescription.

In spite of the understandable stress on the Church and on tradition, practically all of Fisher's thought and writing is Bible-centered and Bible-based, as is fitting, one might venture, for a bibliophile of the Renaissance. Because the divinely inspired Bible has God as its principal author, it must be held in greater honor than tradition, which finds its voice in the human words of the Fathers and preachers, even though given divine aid. Nevertheless, Fisher would not deny that, insofar as Scripture and tradition are the source in which the word of God is preserved and from which the Church draws all its doctrines, they constitute a more or less remote rule of faith. The proximate and immediate rule of faith is the living magisterium of pope and bishops, who authoritatively teach the word of God to be believed by every Christian. It is through personal faith that the individual Christian assents to the truths revealed by God, contained in Scripture and tradition, and preached by the Church. It is logical, therefore, to seek Fisher's views on the subject of faith and the allied subject of grace. The treatment can serve also as an example of the way in which Fisher handles a problem that is overwhelmingly scriptural.

Chapter XI

FAITH AND JUSTIFICATION

IT is difficult for Fisher to conceive the individual Christian as engaging in any activity exclusive and independent of the Church. Envisioning the Church as the Mystical Body of Christ, vivified and moved by the Holy Spirit, he cannot realize how any Christian can function except as a member of the Church. This conviction is stated quite explicitly in his sermon at Barnes's abjuration. How does the heretic recover the true faith? "Thus must the heretike do that wyl haue his spirituall sight: he muste fully assent vnto the doctrine of Christis churche. . . The faith of the churche is nat made our faith / but by our assent: whiche assent cometh of vs / and is the wombe [*leg.* worke] of our soule. And therfore it is nat absolutely saide / *fides* but *fides tua:* That is to say / thy faith. The faith of the churche (whiche by thyne assent is made thy faith) doth make the safe."

Fisher shortly refines this notion in giving Luther's reason for denial of justification by works: "bycause they be our workes: and what so euer reyseth from vs / it is but synne." He comments: "Our sauiour saith / nat only *Fides* / but *Fides tua.* Thy faith (a trouth it is) is the gyfte of god: but it is nat made my faith / nor thy faith / nor his faith . . . but by our assent. By our assent faith (whiche cometh from aboue) is made ours. But our assent is playnly our worke. Wherfore at the least one worke of ours joyneth with faith to our iustifienge." It is important to point out that this brief statement stresses divine agency twice: faith is a divine gift and it comes from heaven. But man actively cooperates by giving his assent. Assent, like every other salutary act, of course, cannot be performed without divine grace: "No creature of himselfe hath power to do good werkes without the grace and helpe of God." [1]

For Fisher the term *belief* embraces "a firm inclination of the mind to accept all things which pertain to the true faith" ("firma quaedam animi propensitas, ad omnia quae ad veram fidem pertinent recipienda"). Heretics, however, always select what they wish to believe. Fisher is careful to add that this readiness to believe is not unqualified: the believer believes "according to the manner in which the things necessary of belief and practice are delivered to everyone" ("iuxta modum, quo cuique credenda faciendaque traduntur"). The believer must assume the mind of the Church, which is "the pillar and mainstay of the truth" (1 Tim. 3:15).[2] The Church may set forth the truth as explicitly revealed in the Scriptures (e.g., the divinity of the Word: "the Word was God") or as implicitly contained therein (e.g., Christ's possession of body and soul: "the Word was made flesh"). Fisher seems to hold also that the Church may propose as an object of belief a theological conclusion (that is, a truth derived from a revealed major proposition and a naturally known minor proposition, as, for instance, Christ's impeccability); but he does not designate whether the belief is divine (based on the authority of the all-knowing and all-true God who reveals the truth) or ecclesiastical (based on the authority of the divinely infallible Church). He evidently would have the believer eschew every doctrine labeled by the Church as heretical, as close to heresy, as erroneous, as temerarious, as suspect, as scandalous, as schismatic, or as seditious.

Perhaps Fisher's most definite declaration on the object of faith occurs in his refutation of Clichtove: "Whatever either is contained in the principal words in the Holy Gospels or can be deduced from the same principal words by the application of any other truths whatsoever, pertains to the faith." Insofar as the truths capable of application are not limited to truths revealed by God but embrace truths known from nature and reason, Fisher would appear to have the faith cover theological conclusions. Almost as if he had this proposition in mind, Simon Hessus four years later declares: "It is certain that only that which is set forth as established by the Word of God concerns the true faith and pertains as necessary to our justification." In consequence, Hessus concludes, Velenus cannot be labeled heretical because the Roman primacy and Roman crucifixion of Peter are not to be found in the prophets or the Gospels and therefore are necessary neither for faith nor for salvation. In support, Hessus quotes Adrian VI, "a man of blameless life," to the effect that the Church can no more change or institute a new form for any sacrament than "abolish some divine law or constitute some new article of faith which is not otherwise of faith [*qui aliter, non est de fide*]." This statement means that the article must be found in the sources of revelation: Scripture and tradition.[3]

Fisher wrote no reply to Hessus' *Apologia,* but his *Confutation of Luther's Assertion* contains his answer: "But even if the Sovereign Pontiff together with a council, that is, the Church Catholic, cannot make anything either true or false and hence establish new articles of faith, nevertheless whatever these propose for our obligatory belief as an article of faith, all persons truly Christian ought to believe no otherwise than as an article of faith." Consequently whoever contumaciously denies the sainthood of the canonized Thomas Aquinas is a heretic. In his *Defense of the Royal Assertion,* Fisher approves and defends Henry VIII's teaching that the Church can change Christ's institution for just causes, as it has done in the legislation on fasting before communion, on the mingling of a little water with the wine during the offertory, and on the laity's reception of the Eucharist under one species. As for the last, Christ left the matter to the ordination of the Church, guided by His Spirit.[4]

In *Christ's Body,* Fisher agrees with Oecolampadius on the error of those who say they can believe anything, for certain things are altogether impossible, e.g., that what is done is undone. It is evident from such a statement as this that Fisher relates the act of faith to the intellect or reason, "whiche sercheth the knowlege of many causes." Faith is no more perceptible to the human mind than grace. The text: "Put your own selves to test, whether you are in the faith" (2 Cor. 13:5), means not that faith can be felt but that anyone can experience its power and efficacy through its exterior effect and anyone can know its presence in himself "through the assent of his mind to those things which must be believed." [5]

Yet the difficulty Fisher finds with Oecolampadius is that he seeks to understand, not to believe, and tries to learn by argument, not by faith. Oecolampadius is acting in reverse order: "for you will never understand unless you first believe." He must first humble his mind and make every thought captive in obedience to Christ's words, and only then will he attain to understanding of the mystery. No one is forbidden to inquire into the sacraments — as is done daily in the Schools — provided he does so with faith and with desire of learning. As Augustine in the *True Innocence* says: "Belief opens the way to the intellect, disbelief closes it." Everything proposed by God for belief is quite removed from the senses and becomes known to the intellect through faith alone.[6]

Faith, as the first of the theological virtues, demands certitude, that is, that a person believe, explicitly or implicitly, in every sacrament and every article of faith with constancy and without any doubting. Knowledge of the sacraments, for example, comes through faith, which is a much more certain knowledge than that acquired through argument. Just as sense is often deceived in its judgments, so reason is frequently rushed into error by its own argumentation: "but the word of God, upon which faith depends, is always most certain." Pastors teach the faithful what is to be believed, e.g., concerning the sacraments, by faith; but the people's faith depends upon "infallible principles, to wit, the very words of God who neither can Himself be deceived nor can deceive anyone else." What is noteworthy about the last statement is that the Church's teaching of a revealed truth does not enter as a partial motive of divine faith and that the sole motive is the authority of God, infallible in His knowledge and truthful in His revelations.[7]

For the Bishop of Rochester, faith is a theological virtue which disposes the mind to assent, on this authority of God, to all the truths revealed by Him. To answer many difficulties of the Protestants he often uses the terms *formed* and *unformed* in regard to faith. That faith is formed or living which is joined with charity, the life of the soul, and, as it were, the form of the virtues; it is unformed or formless or dead when it exists apart from charity. He agrees with Luther that no one can be justified without faith, not even infants unless they are baptized. But if this is true, the faith infused into them must be a habit and not an act since they are incapable of an intellectual or volitional act. Consequently Fisher holds to the common opinion of theologians that "this gift of faith, infused by God into the minds of infants through the sacrament of baptism, is a certain quality and habit implanted in their minds." [8]

The habit of faith indubitably exists in the just, even infants, because "without faith it is impossible to please God" (Heb. 11:6). It evidently does not exist in infidels. But the problem revolves about sinners and heretics. Fisher holds that the habit of faith remains in sinners even after the loss of charity and sanctifying grace. For example, against Oecolampadius he cites Luther who maintains that Peter sinned mortally in withdrawing himself from the gentiles (Gal. 2:11–14) but did not lose his faith (because of Christ's words: "I have prayed for thee, that thy faith may not fail" [Luke 22:32]), but that his faith was not a living faith. The existence of faith without charity is proved also from Paul's words: "If I have all faith so as to remove mountains, yet do not have charity, I am nothing" (1 Cor. 13:2). Nor is the faith of the sinner inoperative. It puts before his eyes the multitude, seriousness, and foulness of his sins; the eternal pains of hell which he cannot escape; and the heavenly rewards which he has lost.[9]

As for the heretic, a single sin of formal heresy destroys the habit of faith. The dedicatory letter to Tunstal in *The Defense of the Sacred Priesthood* declares: "Neither is it sufficient to affirm all the other articles after denying one, but it is necessary to profess one and all articles or at least not dissent from any entirely; for the person who disbelieves even in one is not without justice to be held guilty of the whole of the faith." Even more explicitly at Barnes's abjuration the next year, the Bishop of Rochester proclaims: "One errour suffiseth to spill and to distroye any mannes faithe." [10]

As for the devils, they must have some sort of faith according to James's words: "The devils also believe, and tremble" (2:19).[11] Their faith is dead because it lacks works, but it cannot be even the sinner's dead faith with its possibility of his conversion to God. Consequently it must be faith called forth by some evident credibility of divine mysteries. It should be called "acquired" rather than "infused."

Infidels, heretics, sinners — how do they attain or regain justification? In particular, what is the relationship of their faith to their justification? Together with the recognition of Holy Scripture as sole authority and with the universal priesthood of all Christians, the doctrine of justification by faith alone has been viewed as one of the three fundamental principles of Protestantism. The Bishop of Rochester often has to touch on the point. Decades after his death, Bellarmine refers to his *Confutation of Luther's Assertion* as one of the standard treatises on justification. At the Council of Trent in December 1546 Fisher is claimed to have been the only controversialist, besides John Driedo, to be cited at the crucial meeting of prelates and theologians on the role of faith in justification.[12] Perhaps the most interesting way to set forth Fisher's views is to follow his writings in more or less chronological order.

All of Fisher's sermons on the Penitential Psalms, in a sense, deal with justification since they deal with God's mercy and man's penitence. But his discourse on Vulg. Ps. 31 is particularly significant as a pre-Reformation document because of its various emphases and omissions. He declares: "We all haue offended in many causes [Jas. 3:2], he that hath offended hath erred and gone out of the ryght waye. And the comynge agayne into the ryght waye is onely made open & shewed to hym by penaunce." The three parts of penance are contrition, confession, and satisfaction: "By those thre lyke as by soo many instrumentes, we make a perfyte rasynge & clensynge of the soule from synnes . . . By the vertue of contrycyon our synnes be forgyuen, by confessyon they be forgoten, but by satisfaccyon they be so clene done away that no sygne or token remayneth in ony condycyon of them, but as clene as euer we were." But what starts the process of returning to the right path? "There be two thynges therfore whiche be the very cause that we turne our selfe vnto almyghty god, one is whan we call to mynde his ferefull and greuouse punysshement. The other is the sorowe in our herte whan we remembre the multytude of our synnes, wherby our best and moost meke lorde god is gretely dyscontent with vs."

The process of the justification of the sinner is summarized at the end of the sermon thus: "They may be called ryghtwyse whiche haue very contrycyon with a full purpose to be confessed, or elles they be called ryghtwyse that after very contricyon had & hole confessyon made, be assoyled clene from synne of theyr ghostly fader, for they be Iustyfyed by the sacrament of penaunce whiche toke effycacy & strength by the blode and passyon of cryste. They be called *Recti corde* that haue made satysfaccyon so plentefully that god can aske no more of them." [13]

This sermon has been criticized for its heavy emphasis on man's work and for its omission of Christ's work except for a sudden and unexpected reference at the very end to His blood and passion.[14] In extenuation, one might observe that the sermon is a running commentary on a psalm concerned with the relief and joy coming from the confession of guilt and that its presuppositions are the necessity of grace and the merits of Christ. This is made explicit, though almost in passing, in the first sermon on Vulg. Ps. 50. After again mentioning the rasing by contrition, the washing by confession, and the wiping and cleaning by the satisfaction of good works, Fisher announces: "No creature of himselfe hath power to do good werkes without the grace and helpe of god. For as sayth saynt Poule [2 Cor. 3:5] . . . We be not suffycyent and able of our selfe, as of our selfe, to thynke ony maner thynge, but our suffycyency and habylyte dependeth and cometh of god onely, therfore this thynge is to be asked of god that he vouchesaue to moue our soules perfytely by his grace vnto the exercysynge & doynge of many good werkes." Here, too, the end result is the complete destruction of sin: "To do awaye synne . . . is to rase it that no spotte be seen in our soule, in lyke maner as lettres be done awaye whan they be rased, so that no thynge whiche was there wryten may be redde or knowen." [15]

The second sermon on Vulg. Ps. 37 stresses hope and trust as more basic than contrition, confession, and satisfaction. Among the many things which move God to forgiveness, "good hope is the fyrst, without the whiche euery thynge that we do is of no valure, for let vs neuer so moche wayle & sorowe our synnes, confesse them to neuer so many preestes and laste study to purge them by as moche satysfaccyon as we can, all these profyte no thynge without hope." The classic example is Judas, whose penitence, confession, and satisfaction were unprofitable without hope. Lest hope be exalted to presumption, it must be tempered with dread or fear of God. The second sermon on Vulg. Ps. 50 employs St. Gregory's comparison of hope and dread to two millstones which must fit each other perfectly.[16]

The Bishop of Rochester by no means neglects the virtue of *fiducia,* or trust. His manuscript commentary on Vulg. Ps. 26 is a lengthy development in five sections of the five ways for animating one's soul with *fiducia:* frequent renewal of our assent to confidence, assiduous cultivation of the Christian religion, ardent zeal for devout prayer, putting away of despair, and patient expectation of the divine mercy.[17]

The third point just mentioned is treated at length in Fisher's essay on prayer, where he appears uninhibited by any preoccupation with Protestantism. Whose prayer merits the "essentiall rewarde (as they call it) in heauen"? Only his "whose prayer springeth from the roote of perfect charitie, that is to say, he that is alredy by charitie in the grace and fauour of almightie God." Is this charity difficult of attainment? Fisher answers:

> Great as it is, yet may it be moste easyly of euery man obteyned, be he neuer so greeuous a synner, as Saint Chrisostome doth at large affirme, wrytyng vpon the Gospel of Saint John, saying thus: That man whiche desireth to be in that state, let him but repent and retourne from synnes, purpose assuredly with himselfe to leade a newe lyfe in folowing of Jesus Christ, and he is euen than of a synner made ryghteous, and hath this charitie so acceptable to God, and consequently (beyng thus iustified) prayeth in the fauour of God and state of grace.

After quoting Ezekiel (18:21–22), Fisher continues:

> Wherefore, forasmuche as repentaunce and amendement of our former euyls, and the mutation and chaunge of our olde lyfe, dependeth partly of our owne wyll, whiche is free to euery man, and partly of the helpe of the grace of God, whiche is denyed to no man, but hym that hath not that good wyll and desire aforesayde, to crave the same: it shalbe very easy for euery sinner, by those meanes, euen in a moment, to be made of a sinner, iust and ryghteous, so as he effectually wyll and intende the same, and therewith repose a stedfast hope in the mercy and goodnes of God.

His final summary characteristically includes faith, a new life, and the precepts of the Church:

Therefore, whosoeuer . . . eftsones renueth and refresheth his fayth in Christ Jesus, and . . . purposeth with hym selfe from thencefoorth to abstayne from synne, and to do all other thynges according to the wyll and commaundement of God and his Church, he maye vndoubtedly be accompted in the state of charitie and the grace of God.[18]

To turn now to Fisher's controversial works. In his English sermon against Luther, he develops at great length the figure of the sun, its beams, and its life-giving power. "This example," he explains, "maye enduce vs to conceyue how wonderfully the spyrytuall sonne almyghty god worketh by his spyrytuall and inuysyple bemes of his lyght spred vpon the soule of man or vpon the chyrche. . . The bemes of almyghty god spred vpon our soules quyckeneth them & causeth this lyfe in vs and the fruyte of good workes." How is this figure to be applied to the doctrine of justification by faith alone? "Fyrst they [God's beams] cause the lyght of faythe but this is a veray sklender lyght withouten the reboundynge of hope and the hete of charyte. faythe withouten hope is a sklender beme & of a lytle power. But Ioyne vnto hym hope . . . & than is he moche stronger than he whas byfore." Peter walking on the waters had faith but not "the stronge faythe that hath a confydence & hope adioyned" — not "the myghty faythe" that can move a great mountain. "Neuerthelesse yf a man had suche a faythe yet yf he wanted the hete of charyte he were but as a deed tree." After quoting 1 Cor. 13:2, Jas. 2:26, and Rom. 5:5, Fisher explains: "The hete of the charyte of god is spred in our hertes by the holy spyryte the whiche is gyuen vnto vs. hete of charyte gyueth euydence that that lyght is lyfely. Haue a man neuer so moche lyght of faythe onlesse he haue also this hete of charyte sterynge his soule and bryngyng forthe lyfely workes he is but a deed stock & as a tree withouten lyfe." Toward the end of the sermon Fisher summarizes his stand as follows: "I shewed that the hete of charyte spred in our hertes by the holy spyryte of god gyueth euydence of the lyfely lyght of faythe. shynynge vpon our soules from our sauyour christ."[19]

Without much ado, the Bishop of Rochester announces that his argument "subuerteth one grete grounde of Martyn luther which is this that faythe alone withouten workes dothe Iustifye a synner." He singles out one pernicious consequence. Luther's doctrine is an attack upon the sacraments and their custodian: "that the sacramentes of christes chirche dothe not Iustyfye but onely faythe. A perylous artycle able to subuerte all the order of the chirche." It is at this point that reference is made to Henry VIII's book on the sacraments.

Fisher attempts to explain the Pauline texts produced by Luther by using Augustine's solution: from the beginning they have been misinterpreted and in consequence had to be offset by the other Apostles who emphasize works, e.g., "A man is iustyfyed by his dedes and not by his faythe alone" (Jas. 2:24). One proof that James offers is: "the devils also believe, and tremble" (Jas. 2:19); and "yet no man maye saye that the deuylles be iustyfyed by theyr faythe." Great sinners, too, "haue the faythe of chryst Iesu & wolde rather dye or they shold renye theyr faythe. but for all that they be not iustyfyed." Fisher concludes inexorably: "But yf onely faythe dyd iustify bothe they [sinners] and the deuylles also shold be iustifyed." Tyndale, seizing on the last point, later declares: Rochester's "argument is not worth a straw. For neither the devils, nor yet sinners, that continue in sin of purpose and delectation, have any such faith as Paul speaketh of. For Paul's faith is to believe God's promises." [20]

To effect a reconciliation between the texts of Paul and James, Fisher resorts to the principle of the analogy of faith in answer to the man who says: "Syr be these apostles one contrary to another." He adopts, as has been said, Augustine's interpretation: "Saynt Iames onely contrareth that that may be construed & mystaken in saynt Paule. For saynt Paule meaneth of the workes that gothe before faythe. & saynt Iames meaneth of the workes that folowe after the faythe."

To answer Luther's claim that only James's text (Jas. 2:24) testifies against him, Fisher produces "many moo" (in this order: Luke 11:41, Matt. 6:14–15, Matt. 7:21, Matt. 5:20, Matt. 7:26, Rom. 2:13, Jas. 1:22, Rom. 8:13, Gal. 5:6, and Jas. 2:22). He concludes his second "instruccyon":

And fynally saynt Paule sayth resoluyng his owne sentence. *fides que per dilectionem operatur.* that is to saye. Faythe whiche is wrought by loue [Gal. 5:6]. accordynge to the whiche saynt Iames sayth . . . Thou seest how that faythe helped his workes and how of the workes his faythe was made perfyt. By all the whiche testimonyes ye may playnely se that not onely faythe suffyseth but also loue and workes be requyred to the iustyfyenge of our soules.[21]

As a controversialist, Tyndale naturally attacks the English translation of the Pauline text (Gal. 5:6) in a passage well worth quoting as an example of early English Protestant polemic and as a contemporary opinion of Fisher:

Rochester, both abominable and shameless, yea, and stark mad with pure malice, and so adased [dazzled, confounded] in the brains with spite, that he cannot overcome the truth that he seeth not, or rather careth not what he saith; in the end of his first [*leg.* second] destruction, I would say *instruction,* as he calleth it, intending to prove that we are justified through holy works, allegeth half a text of Paul . . . (as his manner is to juggle and convey craftily,) *Fides per dilectionem operans.* Which text he thiswise Englisheth: 'Faith, which is wrought by love;' and maketh a verb passive of a verb deponent. Rochester will have love to go before, and faith to spring out of love. Thus antichrist turneth the roots of the tree upward. . . So therefore, though Rochester be a beast faithless, yet ought natural reason to have taught him, that love springeth out of faith and knowledge; and not faith and knowledge out of love. . .

What induced Fisher to this particular English translation is not clear. In the *Confutation of Lefèvre's Second Disquisition,* he had stated explicitly: "Faith is born from hearing, and love from faith" (*fides ex auditu . . . & amor ex fide*). In his sermon at Barnes's abjuration, he uses the same text with a different translation: "What faith doth iustifie a man. *Fides* (he [Paul] sayth) *que per dilectionem operatur:* that is to say / faith whiche worketh by loue / and that is by loue pregnant with good workes." [22]

The *Confutation of Luther's Assertion,* having no limit of time unlike the sermon against Luther, has many more detailed things to say about faith and works, charity and justification. Early in the refutation of Luther's first article, Fisher sets out to establish four points: no justification by faith without works, no justification by faith without charity, justification attained by faith pregnant with good works, and justification attained in the highest degree by works. He explains the last element: "And because by a certain power it [faith] contains within itself works which have not yet been brought to light, therefore the just man is said only to be initiated through that [faith] but not made perfect. For justice made perfect cannot be acquired in any other way than by works produced and brought to light." [23] In support of the distinction, Fisher quotes St. James on Abraham's faith: "Faith worked along with his works, and by the works the faith was made perfect" (Jas. 2:22).

Robert Barnes in his "Supplication to King Henry VIII" recognizes the position taken by "my Lord of Rochester": "Fayth doth begyn a iustification in vs, but workes doe performe it, and make it perfite." He recites in Latin Rochester's own words as given above and comments: "What Christened man would thinke, that a Byshop would thus trifle, and play with Gods holy word? Gods worde is so playne, that no man can auoyde it, how that fayth iustifieth alonely, and now commeth my Lord of Rochester, with a litle, & a vayne distinction, inuented of his owne brayne, without authoritie of Scripture, and will clearely, auoyde all Scriptures, and all the whole disputation of S. Paule. . ." He then begins to upbraid Fisher as follows: "Wherefore my Lord, for Christes sake remember, that you bee aged, and shall not long tary here, and these vayne distinctions that you haue inuented to the pleasure of men . . . shall bee to your euerlasting damnation." If Fisher read Barnes, he might have shied at the charge of a distinction invented "without authoritie of Scripture." His prolix style rises from his desire to prove his points in all possible ways — in this case by scriptural texts, including 2 Pet. 1:10, which he gives in Erasmus' Latin version as being better than the Vulgate: "Strive even more by good works to make your calling and election sure." [24]

Fisher denies Luther's contention in Article 35 that "the most hidden vice of pride" vitiates all men's good works. For true purity of intention there are three requirements: no expectation of temporal gain, no seeking after human praise, and no vainglorious self-complacency. Positively there must be a desire only for God's good pleasure.[25]

The Bishop of Rochester holds to a twofold understanding of justification: justification from the guilt of sin is effected through grace, whereas justification from the remains of sin is wrought through expiation (either by indulgences or good works). The first gives life to sinners, the second justifies them to glory, for which absolute purgation from the remains of sin is necessary.[26]

The major problem revolves about the justification of the sinner. "You will never persuade me," Fisher tells Luther, "that alms, prayer, forgiveness of injuries, and other works of that kind help the sinner not at all in being able to attain grace sooner." He instances Cornelius the Centurion (Acts 10:4) and Simon Magus (Acts 8:22–24). Because the sinner is not in charity, however, he merits no reward from desert (*ex condigno*). A little later, Fisher repeats that no one can possess true contrition without grace, but that fear, trembling, and attrite sorrow commonly precede grace. He doubts not that the penitence which preceded grace at the preaching of John the Baptist (Luke 3:7–14) was true and salutary although not yet meritorious from desert (*ex condigno*).[27] On the surface these statements sound as if the sinner could merit justification, or the graces leading thereto, without the help of grace, but any such opinion is far from Fisher's intention. "Grace" as used above refers to justifying or sanctifying grace. Only in the state of sanctifying grace can a man merit from desert (*ex condigno*). The sinner, however, acting under the influence of actual grace, can merit from congruity (*ex congruo*) other actual graces which dispose him proximately for justification. The latter, of course, can never be merited from desert (*ex condigno*): "They are justified freely by his grace through the redemption which is in Christ Jesus" (Rom. 3:24).

Other declarations make it clear that the sinner at every step must be helped by grace. In the treatment of Luther's Article 36, "After sin free will exists only in name, and when it does what it can [*dum facit quod in se est*] it sins mortally," Fisher suggests three stages for the sinner's return to (justifying) grace: (1) stimulation of his mind by the help of divine grace to the detestation of his sins; (2) sorrow for having committed them; and (3) infusion of (justifying) grace by God into the repentant sinner either through the continued movement of repentance or through the virtue of the sacraments. "Even if the sinner cannot without the help of God prepare himself for [justifying] grace, nevertheless he can, before he admits the same, prepare himself for receiving it. By this preparation who can think that God becomes more hostile to him and not more inclined to grant him what he asks?" Fisher later distinguishes the same "three moments": "the first, when the sinner is stricken with a certain horror of himself, an occurrence outside grace, although the help of grace is not wanting; the second, when the sinner turns and prepares himself for grace; the third, the infusion of grace itself."

In the same article, Fisher requests the reader not to wonder at the frequent distinction between grace and the help of grace. Augustine makes the same in many passages, for example, in commenting on the centurion Cornelius (Acts 10:4). Augustine teaches clearly that "Cornelius and catechumens had the grace of faith, by which they were helped to good works, but not that great grace sufficient for obtaining the kingdom of heaven, something achieved only by grace making its possessor pleasing to God [*gratia gratum faciens*], which incorporates the sinner into Christ, and makes the same a temple of God, and renders him worthy of eternal life." [28] At least here the difference resolves itself into the more common distinction between actual grace and habitual grace.

For the just man both faith and works are necessary. The Bishop of Rochester cannot decide whether the extoller of faith alone or the magnifier of works alone does greater harm to the Christian people. He voices an oft-repeated sentiment: "Many do not doubt their possession of faith but are discovered for the most part to be sluggish toward works." The safest course is to praise works without derogating from faith and in turn to exalt faith without detracting from works.[29]

In the *Defense of the Royal Assertion,* Fisher refers several times to the ease with which the people persuade themselves that they have faith in Christ's promises — even if they do no good work. But, to protect himself from scholars, Luther exposes another view: "Faith can in no wise exist unless it be a vigorous and undoubted opinion by which a man is certain above all certitude that he is pleasing to God." Not even Fisher would keep such a man from unlimited reception of the Eucharist — but what about the wretched people self-deceived in regard to their faith?

Later in his *Defense* Fisher would not deny that the first grace of justification can be acquired by faith alone where faith is strong, but he also would not doubt that upon those whose faith is still feeble, grace is conferred by the sacraments and, once conferred, can be increased by good works.[30]

In *Christ's Body,* Fisher must repeat many ideas he has expressed earlier on faith, works, and sacraments. For example, very often the person to be baptized has only a weak and feeble faith, not the faith sufficient for salvation. This stronger faith is achieved in baptism when it is joined with charity and becomes a living faith (cf. Jas. 2:17–26). Even if a certain faith suffices for initiation, unless the same is helped by the efficacy of the sacraments and pious works, it will gradually disappear; for they are means instituted by Christ for communicating the fruits of His passion and death on the cross. This is especially true of participation in the sacrifice of the altar and the eating of Christ's Body. The man justified by the faith which works through love (Gal. 5:6) is made more just by works, and "the man who, when he can do so [*quum licuisset*], does not devote his labor to pious works, will be condemned as not just enough." [31]

Fisher repeats this sentiment in his sermon on justice. Nothing can escape the eyes of the vigilant cherubim in front of heaven: "They wyll anon perceyue yf we want our apparell (that is to say) the ryghtwysenes of good workes." Fisher explains: "Whan thou art clensyd from dedly synne, and purged from venyall synne / yet yf there be founde in the no good workes, thou shalt nat be suffryd to entre there. Thou must brynge with the a clene garment of iustyce / whiche was betokenyd by that whyte garment that was taken vnto the at the Sacrament of baptysme." Fisher would hardly deny that newly baptized infants go immediately to heaven. He is addressing himself to the individual adult who has sinned: "This garment yf thou haue lost, or torne, or solde, thou must study bytymes to repayre it agayne by som good workes." [32]

In his sermon at Barnes's abjuration, the Bishop of Rochester repeats the charge that Luther "hath blynded many a christen soule . . . sayeng / that onely faythe doth iustifie vs / and suffiseth to our saluation. wherby many one litell regardeth any good workes / but onely resteth vnto fayth." He later declares again that Luther is deceiving the people: "For doutles he maketh them in his common sermons to thynke it an easy matter to beleue / and to haue fayth / and thereby to be saued: and so they care for no good workes at all. But where he boulteth and discusseth this matter vnto the very triall / there he maketh it an harde matter." After quoting from Luther's Latin commentary on Psalm 6, Fisher asks: "Who hath this faith? who commeth to this hygh pricke of faythe / to desyre as ernestly the presence of god / as an harte / whan he is chased / preaseth and coueteth to come vnto the soile? Here ye maye se the commen people be disceyued / whiche be farre fro this poynt." In a word, it is hard for the ordinary Christian to be "certain above all certitude that he is pleasing to God." [33]

For the practically universal teaching of theologians that "men in this life cannot have the certitude of faith about their own justice, with the exception of those to whom God deigns to indicate this by a special revelation," Bellarmine lists Bishop Fisher of Rochester as one of the recent authorities.[34] It is perhaps fitting that Fisher should make his first pronouncement on this problem of certainty of salvation in regard to the Lady Margaret. To his auditors' observation that they would be glad and joyful if they were sure of Margaret's being in heaven, Fisher responds: "As for suerte veray suerte can not be had but only by the reuelacyon of god almighty." He continues: "Neuertheles as farre as by scrypture this thynge can be assured," Christ has left "a stronge argument almost demonstratyue." In essence, the argument rests on putting "full truste in cryst Ihesu." The proof for Margaret's "full fayth in Ihesu cryste" lies in her divinity readerships at both universities, her two colleges at Cambridge, her deathbed confession of the Real Presence of "cryst Ihesu the sone of god that dyed for wretched synners vpon the crosse, in whom holly she put her truste & confydence. . ." Fisher finally asks: "Who may not nowe take euydent lyklyhode & coniecture vpon this that the soule of this noble woman, whiche so studyously in her lyf was occupyed in good werkes, & with a faste fayth of cryst, & the sacramentes of his chirche . . . was borne vp in to the countre aboue with the blessyd aungelles. . ." [35]

The same views on the uncertainty of justification and salvation are expressed in the treatise on prayer. Fisher writes: "There is no man that knoweth hym selfe to haue sinned, which is assured and certayne, that he hath as yet recouered the fauoure of God, except the same be by some meanes reueled to hym by GOD." Nevertheless, "by certayne coniectures, he may assuredly beleue it": freedom from unrepented and unconfessed mortal sins, zeal for the advancement of God's honor, delight in scriptural readings and sermons, frequent attendance of divine service, and firm resolution to avoid all sin.[36]

A passage in *The Defense of the Royal Assertion,* as has been seen, tries to show that Luther contradicts himself in maintaining now that all Christians have faith because it is easy, and now that hardly a single Christian has it because it is hard to be "certain above all certitude that he is pleasing to God." No Christian has such faith, Fisher insists, unless it has been revealed to him that he has grace, is free from sin, and is pleasing to God.[37] Luther himself in his commentary on Peter's first epistle, Fisher later tells Oecolampadius, complains about the self-deception of very many on the score of faith. Fisher, moreover, repeats in *Christ's Body* the charge of self-contradiction against Luther.

But in *Christ's Body* Fisher modifies his position about the uncertainty of justification: the reception of the sacraments makes one certain that one has the living faith informed by charity which justifies and saves. "No one," he says, "can be certain without the reception of the sacraments [*citra sacramentorum susceptionem*] that his own faith is living and informed, unless he has learned this fact from revelation." He repeats this point later and gives the reason: "The sacraments have therefore been instituted for this reason, namely, that by their proper and devout reception we may become more certain about the vivification of our faith through grace. For God infallibly assists these sacraments, being prepared to grant grace to all as soon as they have received some sacrament. Thus through this grace, faith, where before it was perhaps unformed, is made living; and the same faith, if before it was informed, is made stronger and greater." In *Christ's Body,* therefore, he has a new element: "It can be certain to no one, unless through revelation or through the reception of the sacraments [*vel per sacramentorum susceptionem*], that he has achieved faith informed by charity." In fact, he does not hesitate to declare that the main reason for the institution of the sacraments is our trust, beyond all doubt, that through their frequentation we have attained the state of grace. Without their use, faith gradually vanishes. With their use, we can be certain that our faith is such as to incorporate us in Christ. His Body and Blood especially incorporates us more fully and intimately, "namely, in nature and substance [*naturaliter & substantialiter*]," something faith alone does not do. Nevertheless, references to uncertainty continue, e.g., "We are uncertain about our salvation since no one can know whether his faith is true and efficacious." Fisher, however, might well be simply maintaining that by faith alone we cannot be certain of salvation.[38]

In addition to the relative uncertainty of faith and justification, passages cited above make clear that Fisher conceives these graces as possessing degrees and as being capable of increase. Such is the declaration that "the man justified by faith is made more just by works." The point is handled especially in *Christ's Body*. Thus there are grades "in eating Christ" (*in edendo Christo*) as there are in receiving the Holy Spirit. The Apostles received the Holy Spirit (1) initially by faith through their belief in Christ's resurrection, (2) more fully by Christ's breathing on them and saying, "Receive the Holy Spirit" (John 20:22), and (3) still more fully by His descent upon them in the form of fire (Acts 2:3–4). In like manner "Christ is eaten variously" (*Christus multifariam editur*) by the Christian: (1) initially by faith in receiving baptism, which incorporates him in Christ but in a tenuous manner, (2) more fully by believing and receiving Christ's flesh under the appearance of bread, which reception results in deeper incorporation into Christ, and (3) most fully by finding himself so confirmed in Christ's love that he would rather die a thousand deaths than once be separated from His Mystical Body. A variation, or rather a combination, of these degrees appears later in regard to sanctification: (1) sanctification through baptism, (2) sanctification through the priest's absolution from sin according to Christ's words, "Receive the Holy Spirit," and (3) sanctification through "eating Christ's flesh which Spirit and Word use as an instrument."[39]

Besides being uncertain and unequal, faith and justification in Fisher's eye is losable or amissible. This concept of amissibility is imbedded in Fisher's teaching. Thus, in his sermon on Vulg. Ps. 101, he compares God's elevation of man to the state of grace to a craftsman's raising of a great stone to the top of a high building.

If the stone slips from his hand, the craftsman's strength and good intention are not to be blamed:

> In lyke maner almyghty god is not to be accused yf he at ony tyme do his good wyl to lyfte vs vp in to the hygh state of grace, & we in the meane season by the weyght of our frowarde and peruerse wyll fall downe from his handes, veryly we ourselfe are to be accused and reproued for it and not almyghty god, and our fall is the more bytterly to be wayled, that syth he wolde lyfte vs vp, we by our owne neclygence & euyll wyll be caste downe.[40]

This peril of falling is given as one of the four reasons for prayer in Fisher's treatise. He writes: "There liueth no man of the substaunce of our commune frayle fleshe, that hath not sinned and is assured he shall sinne agayne. The which beyng true, it shalbe very necessary vnto vs . . . to inuocate and call vppon our . . . Lord God, with continuall prayers . . . that by his omnipotent ayde, & almightie assistance, we fall not againe. . ." We need both "reuerent feare" and "importune prayer." After appealing to Scripture (Ecclus. 5:5, Rom. 11:20, 1 Cor. 10:12), he exhorts his readers: "Wherefore it shalbe necessary for vs to . . . demaunde of God by incessaunt prayer, that it woulde please hym to graunt vnto vs, the grace of perseueraunce, to continue in the exercise and obseruation of his wyll and pleasure. . ." [41]

In the *Defense of the Sacred Priesthood,* Fisher again refers to the capability of justice being lost. In commenting on Luther's citation of Isaiah: "I will make all thy children to be taught of the Lord" (Is. 54:13), he concludes: "For though there may be some who are taught by the Lord, who enjoy a great peace and who are confirmed in justice, yet obviously not all are in this condition. For very many who have faith, and thus even in Luther's opinion are members of the Church, do not enjoy a great peace nor are established in justice, for they frequently fall away from both." Oecolampadius, too, once had great faith, as is evident from his work on the Blessed Sacrament, but now, because of his rashness in scrutinizing Scripture, has been blinded and has lost faith altogether.[42]

Finally, Fisher in his *Two Sermons* declares that the inheritance of the kingdom can be lost. His auditors might object: "Syr we were borne and ordeyned for to haue the Ioyes and pleasures of heuyn for our inherytaunce / and it was derely bought for vs by the bytter passyon of our sauyour Chryste Iesu, and by the same it was assuredly promysed vnto vs." But the preacher replies: "No mannes inherytaunce is so sure vnto hym, but he may lese it by his foly." He then develops the point by a lengthy comparison between great noblemen guilty of treason toward their prince and sinners guilty of treason toward Christ: both rightfully lose their inheritance.[43]

Chapter XII

GRACE AND SALVATION

MUCH has been made of the emphasis laid upon man's good works and free will rather than upon the absolute dominion of God and grace in Catholic theology and preaching when the hour of the Reformation struck. One should not separate theologians and preachers, however, from their historical environment. Provided this be true, one can only conclude that the stress might have been needed, if not at that particular time, at least in the decades immediately preceding. Reactions are inevitable. In addition, one should not forget that particularly in a sermon, rarely longer than an hour or two, every aspect of a subject cannot be treated. Usually a preacher has to restrict himself to one theme, artificially excluding other aspects which are also important and, objectively, perhaps far more important. Though it might be conceded that man's part in justification and salvation is strongly emphasized in Fisher's writings, nevertheless one is surprised by the discovery that the balancing references to the necessity of grace and to the gratuity of salvation are numerous even in his English works.

Just above, the loss of faith, justice, and heaven was set forth as possible and inevitable unless God granted the reverent and suppliant Christian a special grace — "the grace of perseueraunce, to continue in the exercise and obseruation of his wyll and pleasure." The need for a very special grace for *final* perseverance is enunciated in the sermon delivered at Henry VII's funeral. In a free, interpretative translation of Ezekiel 33:12, Fisher says:

Yf the ryghtwyse man haue lyued neuer soo vertuously, & in the end of his lyf commytte one deedly synne & so departe, all his ryghtwyse delynge before shal not defende hym from euerlastynge dampnacyon, & in contrary wyse, yf the synfull man haue lyued neuer soo wretchedly in tymes paste, yet in the ende of his lyfe yf he retourne from his wyckednes vnto god, all his wyckednes before shall not let [prevent] hym to be saued. . . Let noo man also murmure ayenst this, for this is the grete treasour of the mercy of almyghty god.[1]

God's grace is absolutely necessary not only for final perseverance but for every salutary act of the just man. In the first sermon on Vulg. Ps. 50, for example, Fisher asserts that alms and other good works purify the soul (Luke 11:41).

And no creature of himselfe hath power to do good werkes without the grace and helpe of god. For as sayth saynt Poule . . . We be not suffycyent and able of our selfe, as of our selfe, to thynke ony maner thynge, but our suffycyency and habylyte dependeth and cometh of god onely [2 Cor. 3:5], therfore this thynge is to be asked of god that he vouchesaue to moue our soules perfytely by his grace vnto the exercysynge & doynge of many good werkes. . .[2]

Grace for Fisher is necessary also as medicinal, that is, as aiding man's fallen nature with its perpetual strife between spirit and flesh, reason and passion. His first sermon on Vulg. Ps. 101 reads:

We also be so feble & weyke that the stronge partes of our soules vnderstandynge and reason be wedred awaye. Our soules made drye and smyten with the hete of carnal affecyon. Our hertes voyde & barayne of al vertue & deuocyon, in so moche that we haue admytted and done after the worde of the deuyl rather than of god, wherby our flesshe is made as lorde and ruler. Syth we are in all these wretchednesses, the more nedefull & necessary for vs is the spedefull helpe of almyghty god.[3]

The helplessness of fallen man without grace is made even more vivid in the sermon on Vulg. Ps. 142. Fisher says: "Our freylte is so grete that without the mercy of god we all sholde declyne from the ryght way. Saynt Poule sayth . . . Man hath no power of hymselfe, it lyeth not in his wyll to contynue or do ony goodnes, but onely by the mercy of god" (Rom. 9:16). Fisher then turns to human experience: "A certayne wyse man sayd . . . Lorde I haue alway knowen for a surety that I can not contynue by ony meanes in my good purpose without the helpe of the. Saynt Austin sayd vnto almyghty god. *Iubes domine: & iube quod vis.* Lorde graunte me to fulfyll thy commaundement, & commaunde me what thou wylte, as who sayth the wyll of god can not be kepte without his helpe." [4]

Man, of course, must resort to prayer for God's help and grace, but prayer itself is dependent upon grace. In His mercy and love, God "condescendeth to our peticions, yea and also (which much more is) doth preuent our request with his grace, insomuch that before we begyn to pray, he moueth & stireth vs vp vnto the same." The end of man is "eternall felicitie," to which the principal means are "prayer and good workes" (cf. Acts 10:4). Like prayer, good works cannot be performed without grace: "For God his wyll is, that we should humiliate and deiect our selues in the sight of his maiestie, vtterly confessyng and acknowledgyng, that of our owne power and strength it is vnpossible that we should do well, but that a good lyfe (whiche is continued in the practise of good workes) is to be craued at his hande by continuall prayer."

Both salvation and the means thereto are dependent on God: "The health [i.e., salvation] of euery Christian dependeth principally of God, of whom of necessitie . . . euery man must require the same. And because this our health may be euery moment in daunger . . . It foloweth necessarylye, that euery moment we haue present neede to pray and call to God. For inasmuch as our health can neyther be obteyned nor continued, at any other hand than by GOD hym selfe, it appeareth what neede we haue continuallye to exalte our eyes to heauen, and alwayes our hartes to God." Fisher undoubtedly uses the word *principally* (*praecipue*) to safeguard some degree of cooperation with grace on man's part.[5]

When he comes to explain man's cooperation with God in a good work, the most apt comparison he can find is that of a hammer in the hand of a smith. All the work and all the good wrought must be attributed to the smith. The passage is so meaningful that it must be quoted in spite of its length:

> Yf any thyng be well done, [the humble man must] attribute no prayse or commendation therfore vnto hym selfe, but render the whole laude and thankes geuyng to God for all that is well, and the blame and rebuke to hym selfe for all that is euyll. And we maye truely confesse of our selues, that of our selues we neuer brought foorth peece of any good worke or deede: But that euery thing that we haue done, as farre foorth as it hath proceaded onlye of our selues, is more worthy to be called synne and vnryghteousnes, than any acte of vertue and godlynes. For we be alwayes (whansoeuer we do well) placed and set in the hande of God, lyke as the hammer is in the

hande of the Smyth. And lyke as the Smyth in his workyng vseth the hammer as a certayne toole or instrument towardes the finisshyng of his worke: euen so be we vnto God as instrumenttes to worke his wyll, whansoeuer any thyng is well done by vs. For all that euer seemeth to be well done by vs, it is not we of our selues that do the same, but god that worketh it in vs [2 Cor. 3:5]. And therfore as the hammer that worketh the iron to frame, hath no cause to boast and exalt it selfe agaynst the workeman that vseth it [cf. Rom. 9], neyther yet to ascribe vnto it selfe, that by it selfe eyther this key, or this nayle was made and fashioned, but only by the Smyth, vsyng the hammer as his toole and instrument. Euen so is it not lawfull for vs to dispute blasphemously agaynst God, that of our selues, or of our owne power we haue done these workes, but only by the ayde, helpe and workmanship of his grace, by the which he rayseth and lyfteth vs vp to do any good deede, lyke as the Smyth doth his hammer to frame his worke, and by vs as his instrumentes he bryngeth to passe this his worke in vs.[6]

The absolute and complete dependence of man upon God for every salutary and meritorious work could not be expressed with greater vigor and clarity.

Another work of the Bishop of Rochester which deals with the problem of grace, as is to be expected, is the *Confutation of Luther's Assertion*. Here he repeats many of his basic notions, as, for example, the need of being in the state of grace for any meritorious work and the necessity of good works to make justification perfect.[7] What is more interesting is his position with regard to the doctrine of the Scholastics (*disputatores*). For example, he declares that Luther is not so ignorant as not to know their opinion about contrition. According to the Scholastics, a sinner by his natural powers and with God's general influence and help can consider his sin as an offense against God punishable by the loss of heaven and the pain of hell with the result that he can now detest it, and increasingly so, until the infusion of (justifying) grace from congruity (*ex congruo*). The movement of detestation (termed attrition), when thus informed by charity, becomes contrition. Nevertheless, Fisher hastens to add, they hold that attrition springs from faith and other free gifts of God which are above nature but without charity. "There is no doubt," he concludes, "that both faith and hope and other gifts of that kind exist in many sinners without charity." (Later he explains that bad Christians who are not in the state of justice need the help of grace even to assent to articles of faith.) In this whole passage, Fisher seems to be standing aloof. His only concern is the just exposition of Scholastic doctrine.[8]

Fisher's noncommittal statement occurs in his discussion of Luther's sixth article. In his comment on the thirty-sixth, however, he sets forth his own position definitely. An adulterer cannot commit adultery without God's general influence (that is, the divine concurrence or cooperation necessary for every action or movement of all creatures), nor rise again without God's special help. Neither is lacking to a sinner unless he be hardened like Pharaoh (Exod. 7:22) or given up to a reprobate sense (Rom. 1:28). Fisher prefers to follow the opinion of the Fathers rather than the Scholastics, who disagree among themselves.[9] The Fathers maintain that no one can will anything good without God's special help. Some Scholastics contend that God's general influence is enough to perform a morally good action or deed, not only as good in general but as complete in all the requisite circumstances. If this be true, argues Fisher, then the heart-hardened Pharaoh and those given up to a reprobate sense could perform a morally good action, whereas Fisher judges them wanting in sanctifying grace and in God's special help. Consequently there are three classes of men: the just, who enjoy God's general influence, His special help, and sanctifying grace; ordinary sinners, who lack sanctifying grace but possess His general influence and His special help, by which God knocks at their heart for entrance and by which they are incited to return in marvelous ways; and the reprobate and the hardened in heart, who have only His general influence. Later in the same article Fisher again declares that he cannot subscribe to the views of these Scholastics; their error, "if it be an error," cannot excuse Luther, however, who terms every exercise of the sinner's free will a mortal sin.

If Luther is correct, according to Fisher's argument, mortal sin would have to be ascribed to the publican who "went up to the temple to pray" (Luke 18:10–14); Zachaeus the publican, who climbed a tree to see Jesus (Luke 19:1–4); the prodigal son when he came to himself (Luke 15:17–20); Paul the Apostle, who urged the incestuous Corinthian to penance before he was in the state of grace (1 Cor. 5:1–13); John the Baptist, who exhorted to repentance people not yet endowed with justifying grace (Matt.

3:1–2); and Christ Himself, who proposed repentance to his auditors, very many of whom could not yet have received sanctifying grace (Luke 13:1–5). This striving of the sinner after the state of grace can hardly be a mortal sin since it is done with God's help. God must be given all the praise according to Paul's words: "What hast thou that thou hast not received?" (1 Cor. 4:7); and "It is God who of his good pleasure works in you both the will and the performance" (Phil. 2:13).[10]

Consequently it simply is not true that everything performed without charity is "nothing, vain, and false." Prophecy, the knowledge of mysteries, and the faith that can remove mountains, can be true and profitable (1 Cor. 13:1–7) — *but* they are nothing in the sense that they are not worthy of reward in God's eyes and therefore are not meritorious. So, too, the sorrow of the sinner stirred by the fear of hell is not hypocritical, as Luther claims, but is genuine, although not yet meritorious. In fact, the faith and the hope uninformed by charity not only are not sins but can arouse the sinner by making him consider the drawbacks of sin and thus prepare him for justifying grace.[11]

Even Gregory of Rimini, favored by Luther, maintains that, without the grace which makes works acceptable to God for eternal life, a sinner can perform good and moral actions. Examples given are the usual ones: the prodigal son returning to himself, the prayers and alms of Cornelius the centurion, the good deeds of catechumens, and the sermons that make sinners repent daily. Fisher adverts to the constant conflict between flesh and spirit (Gal. 5:17), with the flesh sending evil thoughts and the spirit good thoughts into the human heart. Upon hearing the word of God, the spirit through faith but without charity can detest its sins, beg pardon, seek (sanctifying) grace, consider the loss of time and merits, and inflict punishment on the flesh for its role. This is all far from the heresy of the Pelagians, who maintained pertinaciously that such thoughts of a man not in the state of grace were *meritoriously* good.

The Bishop of Rochester offers further light in commenting on Luther's interpretation of Jeremiah 10:23: "I know, O Lord, that the way of a man is not his: neither is it in a man to walk, and to direct his steps." This verse does not reduce free will to a mere word. After making a twofold historical application to the Babylonians and the Jews, Fisher gives a triple explanation of "the way of a man." The first is to follow the lusts of the flesh against the admonitions of the spirit, something not done without God's general influence. The second is to strive to follow the suggestions of the spirit in spite of the protests of the flesh, something not performed without God's special help. The third is to progress meritoriously in the way of justice of God's commandments, something no one does or can do without the grace which makes him pleasing to God. Each of these three ways is, in some manner, within the power and will of man. Even the third, about which there might be doubt, is in man's power not in the sense that he can achieve it by his own capabilities, but through God's grace, "which is wanting to no one, as Augustine says, except to the man who is wanting to himself." God is prepared to give (justifying) grace to every man who properly asks, seeks, and knocks (Matt. 7:7, Luke 11:9). "Otherwise," Fisher concludes, "John would hardly have said that God gave men the power to become the sons of God." Fisher declares that he is walking the middle of the path with orthodox Christians. He maintains against the Pelagians that no one can merit grace and against the Lutherans that no one will be cast off from grace who seeks it with all his powers.[12]

If the good works of the sinner are not sinful, still less so are those of the just man. Consequently Fisher is at pains to prove, within relatively brief compass in his refutation of Luther's Articles 31 and 32, that the righteous man does not sin in all his good works, not even venially. It is in explanation and defense of his stand here that Fisher wrote his letter on Christian charity to Herman Lethmatius, theologian and dean, which is printed in the *Opera* of 1597. Alfonso de Castro describes him as writing "brilliantly" (*egregie*) against this error of Luther's.[13] According to Fisher's manuscript commentary on Vulg. Ps. 17:21, Catholics hold that no man can merit the first grace from desert (*de condigno*) but whatever gain he makes afterward from its use and exercise is imputed to him as merit. This is evident from the parable of the talents (Matt. 25:14–30) and from the plentiful reward given the sufferings of Job (Job 42:10–16).[14]

The English works which appeared after the *Confutation of Luther's Assertion* presuppose Fisher's basic doctrine and contain interesting sidelights on nature, grace, and merit. In his sermon at Barnes's abjuration, for example, Fisher declares that someone might criticize Christ's parable of the sower for omitting "som thyng that is chiefly necessary for the plenteous encreace of frute." This principal thing, of course, is God's grace, "the fauorable disposition & influence of the heuens." (This charge of bypassing grace is only too much like that launched against Fisher's own sermons.) Fisher's answer is that, although there is no special mention, heavenly influence is nonetheless understood: the sower is "very god" and "the very spirituall sonne of this worlde," who has "all the influence of the heuyns in his owne hande." It will be recalled that the treatise on prayer had said "that of our selues we neuer brought foorth peece of any good worke or deede: But that euery thing that we haue done, as farre forth as it hath proceaded onlye of our selues, is more worthy to be called synne and vnryghteousnes." In this sermon, Fisher's view is the same:

> An harte that is nat sowen with the worde of god / but lefte vntyll his own nature / bryngeth nothyng forthe but the weedes of carnalitie / carnall thoughtes / carnall affections / and carnal workes. But whan the worde of god is sowen / and the spirite of god gyueth the influence of his grace: than that sede of the worde of god / by his supernaturall vertue / and by the gratious influence of the holy spirite of god / worketh in that harte / and chaungeth the carnalitie therof in to a spiritualnes / accordynge as the harte is better or worse disposed. . .[15]

Resistance to flesh and nature, far from being sinful, is the source of merit, provided that the Christian be in the state of grace. "Many a good man, & many a good woman," Fisher says in *Two Sermons,* "felyth in them selfe great temptacyons, great mocions, & styringes / now to lechery, now to pryde, now to couetise. But if they . . . wrastyll against them . . . This is no synne in them / but it shall be gretly to theyr meryt." Merit is possible, of course, only during life: "Therfore our sauyour sayth (*Veniet autem nox quando nemo potest operari*). whan deth is comen ones, farewell the tyme of merytoryouse workynge" (John 9:4).[16]

Consequently one must use one's precious time in heaping up spiritual riches, advises *A Spirituall Consolation.* This activity is far from being difficult. "For assuredly no deede that is be it neuer so little, but it shall be rewarded of almightie God. One draught of water giuen for the love of God, shal not be vnrewarded: And what is more easie to be giuen then water. But not onely deedes, but also the least wordes and thoughtes shall be in likewise. O how many good thoughtes, deeds, and workes might one thinke, speak, and doe, in one day?" Such is the theory: what is the reality? As for his own good deeds, Fisher laments: "(Alas) they bee fewe or none that I can thynke to bee auayleable, they must bee donne pryncipallye and purely for his loue. But my deedes when of their kynde they were good, yet did I linger them by my folly. For eyther I did them for the pleasure of men, or to auoyde the shame of the world, or els for my owne affection, or els for dreade of punishment. So that seldome I dyd any good deed in that puritie and streaightnesse that it ought of ryght to haue bene done." [17] The reader cannot help thinking of Luther's proposition that the righteous man sins in his every good work. Fisher's view, however, would be rather that his works were indeed good but performed from imperfect or mixed motives: they were not sinful in any way.

Thus far, our treatment has centered about the necessity of grace for morally good acts and particularly for meritorious acts. But to whom and when does God distribute this necessary grace? That Fisher holds to the absolute gratuity of grace is evident from his frequent quotations from St. Paul, especially the Epistle to the Romans, and from the care taken to distinguish his position from that of the Pelagians and Semipelagians. It is also clear that the just who are solicitous about working out their salvation by prayer and good works receive the necessary grace to persevere in the state of grace and the observance of the commandments. About the salvation of infidels Fisher has little or nothing to say in particular terms, for the simple reason that no occasion offers itself for doing so. The situation, however, is altogether different in regard to sinners. His opinions have already been touched on in passing, but it is well to concentrate on them also.

We might use Bellarmine to see Fisher's views in their historical context. In discussing the question whether sufficient help is given to all men, Bellarmine finds almost all the Catholic theologians teaching that "sufficient help is not lacking to all men according to place and time, and nevertheless without prevenient grace no man can desire, seek, or receive grace." For this view the Bishop of Rochester is listed among the twelve authorities extending from Alexander of Hales to Andrew Vega. On another occasion, Bellarmine asks whether, to every man having the use of free will, there is always present sufficient help by which he can rise from sin, do good, and avoid sin. Of the three answers, the first, which denies the bestowal of sufficient help on all men, is attributed to Gregory of Rimini, Luther, and Calvin. The second is that of the Pelagians, who maintain that "free will itself is sufficient help for attaining to grace." The third is the doctrine of very many Catholics that "man without special help cannot wish to believe or to be healed, but nevertheless that such help is present to all men, either always or at least sometimes, so that on the day of judgment there will be none who can say he could not have been saved." Fisher is again cited among the twelve theologians.

Bellarmine later asks the question whether sufficient help to rise from sin, do good, and avoid sin is always present. At least as far as rising from sin is concerned, his own opinion is that sufficient help is not always present. The Bishop of Rochester's name appears among the six nominated from among the many theologians who favor the same view.[18]

Fisher's principal declarations on the distribution of grace are to be found in the *Confutation of Luther's Assertion*, but it might be well to give beforehand the few comments made in his other works, mainly English. His sermon on Vulg. Ps. 31 declares: "Truly our mercyfull lorde oftentymes entyseth by his benefytes many synners to penaunce." The examples given are the Apostles Matthew and Peter, Mary Magdalene, Anthony the Hermit, a priest described by William of Auvergne, and "many moo without nombre." Fisher asks: "And whiche one of vs may saye but that he hath ben called to penaunce by the benefytes of our lorde god." God uses either "fayre meanes . . . grete & manyfolde gyftes," or "grete & many greuous punysshementes" in this life. God will be merciful and forgiving to the greatest sinner — "were he neuer so grete a synner before (yf he despayre not of forgyuenesse)." Despair, according to the discourse on Vulg. Ps. 129, is the lowest degree to which a sinner can fall: "The seuenth degre is to despayre of the grete mercy of god whiche is moost depe, moost peryllous of all other, & nexte to the horryble pyt of hell."

On Chrysostom's authority, "Despayre wyl not suffre a man whan he is fallen downe to ryse agayne." The only remedy lies in the "stronge & stedfast hope in the grete mercy of almighty god," which is "neuer voyde but alway spoken of in scripture in euery corner." If like Jonah the sinner asks this mercy, "almyghty god without doubte shall shewe his mercy & clene delyuer hym from all peryll of dampnacyon." [19]

The treatise on prayer contains at least two references to the distribution of grace. First, God gives grace to pagans: in prayer and good works "Cornelius the Centurian was moste commonly exercysed, by the which he so pleased God, that albeit he was an ethnycke and infidell, yet was it sayde vnto hym by the Angell of God: . . . Thy prayers and almesdeedes haue ascended into the sight of god, and are remembred of him." Secondly, God gives grace to the sinner, who can easily attain justification (something possible only if His grace is always at hand): "Forasmuche as . . . the helpe of the grace of God . . . is denyed to no man, but hym that hath not that good wyll and desire . . . to craue the same: it shalbe very easy for euery sinner . . . euen in a moment, to be made of a sinner, iust and ryghteous. . ." [20] As for the Christian, Fisher writes his half-sister, Elizabeth, from the Tower that she is "partaker of all those graces and benifites that belong vnto the Christian people, which bee so many and so great, that it passeth the wittes of men, not onely to number, but also to think." [21]

In turning to the *Confutation of Luther's Assertion,* it is difficult to see how Bellarmine can claim Fisher's support for his view that sufficient grace is not always at hand for the sinner to rise from his sin. It is the refutation of Luther's Article 36 which refers several times to the presence of God's grace. Thus, "the sinner after his sin can prepare himself for grace by means of the most ready help of God [*per praesentissimum auxilium Dei*] (which . . . is wanting to no one). . . Neither does God's help, which also is at hand for everyone [*auxilium . . . praesens*], diminish the freedom of the will but rather increases it. . . For, just as that [general] influence is always present for the will, so also the help of divine grace is right at hand for all [*auxilium . . . cunctis ad manum est praesens*]. . . Consequently this power [to become the sons of God] has been offered to sinners, no matter how great, so that if they do what they can for attaining this grace, God's help will be at hand [*praesto aderit auxilium Dei*]." Fisher then gives a succession of scriptural texts, urging or inviting the sinner to conversion, to show the sinner's freedom, preparation for, and cooperation with God's ever available help: Rom. 2:4, Apoc. 2:21, Isa. 31:6, Ezek. 18:30, Joel 2:12, Zach. 1:3, Jas. 4:8, 1 Cor. 4:16, 1 Cor. 6:18, and Matt. 11:28.[22]

Is "this special help by which God knocks at their hearts for entrance" (Apoc. 3:20) available for all sinners? Even though there is room for some slight ambiguity and a more lenient interpretation, Fisher opines that the hardened in heart and the reprobate in sense are "deprived of God's special help. It is indeed plain that these are more deprived [*magis destitui*] of this help than all other sinners. . . The reprobate and the hardened have only the general influence so that they lack all the others [i.e., sanctifying grace and special helps]." The heart-hardened Pharaoh was preserved as a lesson to men and as an example of divine power. Fisher explains the process of dereliction as follows. The sinner's soul, abandoning the instinctive drive of the spirit, follows the concupiscences of the flesh, and perseveringly and increasingly so, until it no longer wishes to return because of any admonitions. By reason of his own ingratitude, therefore, the sinner is deserted by God, for he has inexcusably not glorified God as God, nor given thanks (Rom. 1:21). Therefore God has deservedly abandoned him and given him up to a reprobate sense (Rom. 1:28).[23]

Fisher does not insist, however, upon this divine dereliction of the hardened and the reprobate. "No one, as long as he is alive," he tells Luther, "comes so into the power of Satan that he cannot try for good. To none, no matter how crime-laden, is the bosom of our common mother the Church closed, provided they wish to return and to do condign penance." The same article later mentions "God's help which is wont never to be lacking even to sinners" (*auxilium Dei, quod & peccatoribus deesse nunquam solet*), and "God's help which is lacking to no sinner" (*auxilio Dei quod nulli peccatori deest*). This availability of grace is true particularly of the new dispensation: "This special assistance of God is wanting to no one who is not wanting to himself, and especially in this time of grace." It is God's grace, of course, that must be given the credit: "God's help is most ready [*praesentissimum*] for them provided they do not hope to achieve heaven by their own strength but by His help and provided they attribute to His munificence whatever they do." When Fisher does refer to those whom he views as abandoned by God, he does so briefly. For example, "God's help . . . is at hand [*ad manum*] for all who have not been utterly abandoned by him." Again: "God helps everyone except the utterly abandoned so that he [the sinner] can repent and detest his sins and also implore pardon for those committed, provided he wishes to turn himself to His clemency."[24]

Most intimately connected with the distribution and the necessity of grace is the freedom of the human will under the influence of divine grace. In fact, it is the refutation of Luther's Article 36 ("After sin, free will is a reality only in name, and when it does what it can, it commits mortal sin") which contains Fisher's most pertinent propositions on grace and which is viewed as a classical treatment by later Catholic theologians like Alfonso de Castro, Ambrose Catharinus, and Robert Bellarmine.[25] Before undertaking the study of Article 36, we might resume Fisher's doctrine as it appears in his other works.

With their heavy emphasis upon God's mercy, upon man's response, and upon good works, the sermons on the Penitential Psalms naturally presuppose the liberty of the human will and the free cooperation of man with God. The manuscript commentary on Vulg. Ps. 35 begins with the explicit declaration that "the liberty of our will is taught by this psalm." The treatise on prayer unabashedly asserts the contribution of free will to justification and the ease of its achievement:

> Forasmuche as repentaunce and amendement of our former euyls, and the mutation and chaunge of our olde lyfe, dependeth partly of our owne wyll, whiche is free to euery man, and partly of the helpe of the grace of God, whiche is denyed to no man, but hym that hath not that good wyll and desire aforesayde, to craue the same: it shalbe very easy for euery sinner, by those meanes, euen in a moment, to be made of a sinner, iust and ryghteous, so as he effectually wyll and intende the same, and therewith repose a stedfast hope in the mercy and goodnes of God.[26]

A brief passage in the *Defense of the Royal Assertion* charges Luther with denying the liberty of the will and with making God the author of the good and the evil in man. If this be true, how can God fail to be "a respecter of persons," and how can He judge "according to each one's works" (Acts 10:34–35, 1 Pet. 1:17)? *Christ's Body* declares that the orthodox neither attribute too much to free will nor detract from it unjustly. What should be ascribed to free will is taught at sufficient length by Erasmus in his victories over Luther. Fisher is often careful to distinguish the orthodox position from the Pelagian. In Article 31 of the *Confutation of Luther's Assertion,* for example, the Pelagians "think that free will without grace can avoid every sin; we, however, presume that no one can avoid sin without grace," and so forth.[27]

In Article 36 of the *Confutation,* the Bishop of Rochester realizes that Pelagianism is the easiest charge that can be leveled against his view of the role of free will in regard to salvation and grace. Nevertheless, he has no fear of making concessions to the Pelagian heresy: "We do not say that man without the grace which makes him pleasing to God has a thought meritoriously good — something which they pertinaciously maintained was possible." Later he declares: "As for us, we assert against the Pelagians that no man can merit grace." The simple test for distinguishing the orthodox Christian from the Pelagian is to discover whether he deems grace necessary or unnecessary for attaining heaven and whether he views man's own powers as able or helpless to merit beatitude. Resenting Luther's aspersions, Fisher denies absolutely any fellowship with the Pelagians. There is a world of difference between saying that man can be saved without grace and placing grace so within the power (*arbitrium*) of man that, with God's help, which is ever ready for all, he is confident it can be obtained. Whatever be the situation of the Scholastics — they can take care of themselves against Luther — all the holy Fathers fought strenuously for the cause of grace against the Pelagians.[28]

The Pelagians are not the only heretics to have suffered shipwreck, as Fisher picturesquely puts it, upon the rock of free will. The Manicheans and the Wycliffites go too far to the left, the Jovinianists and the Pelagians too far to the right. Orthodox Christians keep the middle of the road: "They confess that free will does certain things by its own strength only and certain things by the help of divine grace." All the Fathers strongly and unanimously attribute freedom to the will: Augustine, Jerome, Ambrose, Leo, Tertullian, Chrysostom, Athanasius, Damascene, Origen, and "all the other orthodox, who . . . cast the blame for sinning, not on God, not on the devil, but on the very freedom of the will." [29]

Like a good philosopher, Fisher is careful to define his terms: like a good theologian, he turns to Scripture for the threefold acceptation of liberty. "The first liberty can be termed that of nature, which is also called 'power' [*potestas*] in Paul, that of doing this or that." Augustine gives examples of the exercise of this kind of liberty on good things (working in the field, eating and drinking, having friends, possessing clothes, building a home, and marrying a wife) and on evil things (idolatry, homicide, adultery, theft, blasphemy, turpitude, sorcery, drunkenness, and riotous living). According to this liberty, Paul had "a right [*potestas*] to take about with us a woman, a sister" (1 Cor. 9:5) and a right to the necessities of life, "but we have not used this right [*potestas*]" (1 Cor. 9:12). Besides, Paul speaks about sinning "willfully [*voluntarie*] after receiving the knowledge of the truth" (Heb. 10:26).

The second freedom can be called that of grace, for Paul says: "Where the Spirit of the Lord is, there is freedom" (2 Cor. 3:17). This freedom belongs only to devout men in the state of grace. However, they do not possess it in its fullness since no one is so perfect as to be for long without all sin (cf. 1 John 1:8). The third is the freedom of glory when "creation itself also will be delivered from its slavery to corruption into the freedom of the glory of the sons of God" (Rom. 8:21). This is the only true freedom, bestowed on no one in this life. In summary, therefore, the first freedom is the power to wish or not to wish what is proposed; the second, to wish meritoriously; and the third, to execute effectively whatever one wishes.[30]

The absence of grace evidently does not destroy freedom, at least of nature. Moreover, the sinner, who with God's ever-available help can prepare himself for justifying grace, does not behold his freedom of will diminished but rather increased under the influence of that divine help. As for the latter half of Luther's Article 36 (namely, free will, when it does what it can, commits mortal sin), Fisher asks: "If free will, doing what it can, sins mortally, why does God so many times in Scripture incite sinners to try to return to Him? For, if so trying they sin mortally, God indeed is inviting them to mortal sin." He then provides the series of scriptural texts already given above. Even Luther's authority, Augustine, declares that whoever denies free will is not a Catholic.[31]

What, then, about the key pronouncement of Christ: "Without me you can do *nothing* [*nihil*]" (John 15:5)? Fisher's reply is that the New Testament quite frequently uses *nothing* for what is of no merit toward eternal life. To this effect he cites 1 Cor. 7:19, 1 Cor. 13:2–3, Gal. 5:6, and Gal. 6:3. Without sanctifying grace, free will can do many things: (1) the good and the evil things cited from Augustine above, and (2) certain preparatory good works, like those of Simon Magus (Acts 8:22–24) and Cornelius the centurion (Acts 10:4), performed with God's special help but nonmeritorious (i.e., nothing) toward eternal life.

When Luther asserts that the sinner, like a branch cut off, "withers" (John 15:6), that is, that he daily grows worse when left to himself, Fisher wishes to know the meaning of "left to himself." The only sensible interpretation is that the sinner, being now deprived of sanctifying grace, can do nothing meritorious but that he can try to prepare himself for reinsertion in Christ the vine — not, of course, without the special help of God's grace. In other words, "left to himself" does not mean being deprived of God's special help for the free will to repent. Fisher cites the Scriptural account of the prodigal son, as well as the daily experience of Christians, who can listen to sermons readily.

It might well be that Barnes is referring to this section of Article 36 when he writes in his *Supplication to Henry VIII:*

> So that all the might of freewil, when hee is left alone, is nothyng els, but firste to bee cast out: and seconde to wyther, so decayeth hee: thyrdly, to be cast into the fire. All this wors, and wors. Finally, hee burneth, this is worst of all, for here is hee past helpe, so that this is the strength, that freewill hath, to bryng him selfe to vtter destruction.
>
> Now, where will our Duns men, bryng in their *Bonum conatum?* they are so longe in bryngyng of it in, that freewill is brought to the fire, & there can hee neither saue him selfe from burning, nor yet helpe him selfe out. But to this my Lord of Rochester aunswereth in a certaine place, that freewill can doe no good meritorious, *sed tamen non omnino facit nihil.* What is this to say, but *nihil?* If he doe no good, that is meritorious, nor worthy of thanke before God, I pray

you, what doth hee, but *nihil?* Our disputation is, what goodnes that hee can doe, without grace, and you graunt, that hee can doe no goodnes, and yet you say, that hee can doe something. But let vs see how *S. Augustine* vnderstandeth this text of S. John [*Super Ioannem tract. lxxi*]. . .

My Lord, where will you bryng in here, your somethyng, that free-will doth? *Saint Augustine* sayth, without grace, can freewil doe neither litle, nor much: for if shee be not in Christ, shee burneth in the fire. Call you that somewhat? Where bee nowe M. Dunsis men, with their *bonum conatum, bonum studium, & applicationem ad bonum.* Here must they nedes lye in the fire, with all their good intentes, with their good preparations, and their holy dispositions.[32]

As for the verse in Genesis, "the imagination and thought of man's heart are prone to evil" (8:21, cf. 6:5), Fisher puts it into the historical context of the Deluge. Moreover, this proneness to evil is concupiscence, which becomes sin only by the consent of the will. In fact, "the freedom of the will can moderate this proneness so that it does not always issue in evil."

The will, Fisher insists, can be led but not forced. It is true: "The heart of the king is in the hand of the Lord: whithersoever he will he shall turn it" (Prov. 21:1). Nevertheless, everyone follows the drawing (*tractus*) of God not perforce but of his own accord. (On drawing, see John 6:44.) God attracts the king's mind by showing the reason for change of plan. Such a change does not argue that free will is a mere word. Consider Peter. First he freely denied Christ because he was afraid to die; later he freely suffered death rather than deny Him because he was prepared to die. In the first instance the will failed of itself, in the second it was helped by grace, but in both instances it acted freely, without force or necessity.

For this operation of the will, of course, God's general influence is necessary (Acts 17:28) but is presupposed always present. By this influence, as often as it chooses, the will can exercise its act of willing or not willing. Every man finds within himself a certain power of reason which passes judgment on his own (as well as other creatures') natural motions and approves some as admissible and reproves some as inadmissible. Fisher offers the frequent experience of a man who is vehemently moved to lust by the presence of a woman but who keeps this motion from going further. Unless he were free, he could not restrain himself.

A little later, Fisher insists that freedom of choice is to be reposed, not in the execution of the work, but in the consent or refusal of the will. Nothing is more perilous or ruinous than really to think that all things happen by necessity. To say nothing of the Fathers' unanimous condemnation, reason, too, sees that this doctrine puts an end to the confidence of the patient in his physician, the industry of the farmer in working in fields, and the counsels of the wise in public administration.[33]

If the just resist evil and do good by necessity, they cannot be termed just or deserving. For Paul writes: "Let each one give . . . not grudgingly or from compulsion, for 'God loves a cheerful giver' " (2 Cor. 9:7). Moreover, the same Apostle declares: "It is not what I wish that I do, but what I hate, that I do" (Rom. 7:15). But wishing and hating belong to no other power than free will; therefore with his free will Paul fought with the spirit against the flesh. Luther cannot square his doctrine with these words because he seems to identify free will with the wisdom of the flesh (Rom. 8:6) and thus makes it lust against the spirit. Fisher sees this identification as the principal cause of Luther's error. Actually man has three parts: spirit, soul, and flesh. Soul, standing between spirit and flesh, has the choice of following the inclination of the spirit or the inclination of the flesh. Free will is not given up to evil only, but is of a nature capable of turning (*vertibilis*) to good or to evil: now it consents to the flesh for evil, now to the spirit for good. Consequently, free will, although not in the state of grace, can with God's help (lacking to no sinner) prepare itself by its convertibility (*sua vertibilitate*) to the spirit. This preparation by free will does not derogate from the gratuity of justifying grace, which still depends upon the gift of God. This fact, however, does not destroy freedom of will. "For what if it is not placed in my power to become Supreme Pontiff, which depends upon election by my Lord Cardinals? On that account, am I wanting in free will?" Free will lies not in execution but in choice.[34]

The respective roles of God and man in grace and salvation are summed up by Fisher toward the end of his refutation of Article 36 by reducing Augustine's analysis to five stages: (1) the beginning of salvation, that is, the first grace, by which man is incited to good action, and this comes from God's mercy; (2) the consent of man's will to follow that incitement, and this lies in man's power; (3) the salvation of grace, by which man is made pleasing to God, and this is the gift of God only; (4) the safeguarding of this same salvation, and this is achieved by man's own care as well as God's help; and (5) the fall from this salvation which can happen only by man's own choosing and by himself.[35] From Augustine's declarations it is clear to Fisher: (1) that freedom of will remains in the sinner; (2) that when he does what lies in his power he does not commit mortal sin; and (3) that before the restoration to grace, he can do, through the help of the first grace, many good works by which he can merit forgiveness.

At the close of his response to Article 36, in commenting on Luther's hope for a restored Bible as the result of flourishing Hebrew and Greek studies, Fisher characteristically praises their advantages to student and society but warns against their misuse. Paul "did not come with pretentious speech or wisdom, announcing . . . the witness to Christ," nor "in the persuasive words of wisdom" (1 Cor. 2:1, 4), for "the wisdom of this world is foolishness with God" (1 Cor. 3:19). Besides, "knowledge puffs up" (1 Cor. 8:2). Paul exhorts rather to "being of the same mind" (Rom. 15:5, 1 Cor. 13:11, Phil. 2:2, 3:16, 4:2) and to "aiming at charity" (1 Cor. 14:1). Fisher concludes: "Neither do I say these things because I do not wish the liberal arts [*bonae literae*] to flourish, for that I desire with all my heart, but because I do not wish anyone to misuse them to the madness and ruin of many." [36]

An interpreter of Fisher's views can now see that for him faith is primarily an intellectual act of assent to revealed truth, although he has no intention of minimizing or excluding concomitant hope, trust, and confidence. He finds the motive of faith in the authority of the all-knowing and all-truthful God. His Church is the established channel for setting forth revealed truths infallibly. Miracles and prophecies, however, confirm their credibility, especially for infidels and heathens. For Fisher the content of revelation and the objects of belief are properly truths formally revealed by God in an explicit or implicit manner. Truths arrived at by the use of natural means like philosophy, science, or history are to be believed with what might be called ecclesiastical faith. Fisher insists that all doctrinal declarations and moral censures of the Church are to be respected. Nevertheless, even this Church, which has been promised and given the Holy Spirit, cannot establish a new article of faith or institute a new sacrament. Fisher sees the Spouse of Christ, however, as coming to an ever clearer, ever richer, and ever deeper understanding of God's revelation, especially when dogmas, hitherto explicitly but popularly and perhaps obscurely believed, are challenged by heretics and accorded precise formulation by pope or council.

As for the individual, only the grace which enlightens his intellect and inspires his will can incline him to belief, give him the beginning of faith, and enable him to make an act of faith. The Bishop of Rochester will have nothing to do with the Pelagians or the Semipelagians. Against the Protestants, however, he defends the freedom of the human will under the movement of divine grace. As for the virtue of faith, he considers it infused into the soul with charity, hope, and other virtues at the moment of justification. This habit is lost only by the formal sin of heresy. All other sins cause the loss of charity and justifying grace, but faith truly remains in the sinner's soul.

Justification for Fisher is something positive: the infusion of sanctifying grace, which inheres in the soul and destroys sin. In other words, justification does not consist in the mere concealment of sins and the sole imputation of Christ's merits. Justification makes the just the partakers of the divine nature, the adopted sons and heirs of the Father, the friends of God, and the temple of the Holy Spirit. Unlike the Protestants, who require only faith for justification and whose faith is the confidence in the forgiveness of their sins through Christ's merits, Fisher demands preparation for justification not only through faith but also through acts of fear, hope, repentance, detestation of sin, and incipient love — all with the special help of grace. Here his favorite texts are taken from the epistles, for example, "By works a man is justified, and not by faith only" (Jas. 2:24); or, "In Christ Jesus neither circumcision is of any avail, nor uncircumcision, but faith which works through charity" (Gal. 5:6). Justifying grace can be increased by good works, and it can be lost through mortal sin. Fisher insists that no one can be certain, without a special revelation, of his justification and salvation. Nevertheless, through the reception of the sacraments, the Christian can achieve a strong assurance.

In his controversial works, the Bishop of Rochester never slights or neglects the necessity of grace. Divine help is imperative for all the acts of faith, hope, love, repentance, and so forth, leading to and necessary for justification, including the very beginning of faith. The first grace is unconditionally gratuitous. Once a man has been justified, moreover, he needs special help to remain in the state of grace and especially to persevere to the end. On the other hand, Fisher holds that man without the help of grace retains his natural liberty and can perform naturally good deeds, which, however, are not salutary or meritorious, but at the same time they are not sinful. The first grace is so absolutely gratuitous that no naturally good work or prayer can merit it for a man, nor prepare him for it, nor obtain it for him. Nevertheless, God denies to no man, whether infidel or sinner, sufficient grace to be converted or to repent. For Fisher, the single exception is the hardened and the reprobate, given no special help in punishment for past rejection of grace.

Fisher insists, however, that efficacious grace never forces the human will but leaves it free to accept or to refuse. Hence the human will cooperates with grace. Good works are indeed the gift of God but they are also meritorious for the just man toward the increase of grace and the reward of eternal life. The sinner cannot merit from desert (*ex condigno*) the grace of justification even if he believes or does good works under the influence of God's special help. From congruity, however, he can merit further actual graces which prepare and dispose him for justification. God, Fisher holds with the Fathers against the Scholastics, is ever ready with His grace, but this grace consists not in general assistance but in special help. At every stage in the salvific process, the Bishop of Rochester safeguards at once the gratuity and the necessity of God's help and grace.

Chapter XIII

METHOD AND STYLE OF THE PREACHER

THE preceding pages have examined the response of the Bishop of Rochester to the burning issues of his day: the mission of Christ, the nature of the Church, the supremacy of the pope, the power of the bishops, the infallibility of general councils, the role of the laity, the authority of tradition, the exaltation of the Scriptures, the interpretation of the Bible, the study of Hebrew and Greek, the attitude toward Scholasticism, the new humanism at the university, the notion and object of belief, the necessity and sufficiency of faith, the essence and properties of justification, the absolute need of divine grace, the place of good works and merit, and the freedom of the will. These constitute the very foundation of the Christian religion and profoundly affect other doctrines such as man's creation and fall and the sacraments in general and in particular (especially penance, orders, and the Eucharist as sacrament and sacrifice).

With this wealth of basic material, it is now possible and advisable to discuss Fisher's theological methods: the manner in which he undertakes the exposition, proof, and defense of Catholic dogmas, such as a special priesthood; the way in which he deduces from revealed truths certain conclusions, such as the authority of the Fathers; and the fashion in which he devises a system to answer vexing questions, such as the role of faith in the process of justification. Intimately connected with method is the more complex problem of style. Precisely speaking, it is possible to treat style apart from method and content, but the whole consequence of modern criticism has been to establish that content, method, and diction all modify one another and contribute to one another. Thought, feeling, imagery, structure, allusions, sentences, and words result in a unique production, which reveals the peculiar cast of mind and spirit of its author and suffers if a single element is changed. Certainly this statement is true in Fisher's case. It is applicable not only to his sermons and treatises in English, but also to his controversial works in Latin. In the latter, the usually clear and strong structure, the demand for proof, the careful check on his adversaries' authorities, the objection to abuse, the use of dilemma, and the very prolixity of his expression, confessed by the author but excused on the score of need, distinguish Fisher's writings from those of his associates. It is beneficial, therefore, not to separate style in the narrow sense from his method.

Still another choice remains to be made. In regard to such an element as imagery, it is possible — and certainly enlightening — to treat the point synthetically, as it were. The comparisons derived from warfare, for example, could be gathered from all of Fisher's works in order to discover such factors as their frequency, their variations, and their adaptation to special circumstances. The alternative is to take up each work in turn to see its imagery in association with its other elements. In view of what has already been said about the organic uniqueness of the individual production, it will be better to consider each work by itself and, if merited, in relation to other works. It will not be necessary to touch upon all the component parts of each work, but only to point out the more striking features. After all, the present study is intended to be exploratory and by no means exhaustive.

Finally, it is necessary to decide whether Fisher's works should be studied according to language: first, English, and then, Latin; or according to type — sermons, ascetical treatises, polemical writings, and so forth; or according to chronological order of composition and publication. In view of our concern to relate Fisher to his times, the chronological procedure might well be best of the three. Unfortunately, the occasion and date of composition are uncertain for such works as the treatise on prayer, the sermon on the passion, and the Latin commentary on the Psalms. Caution with respect to these relatively few writings, however, will prevent rash judgments about Fisher's development and need be no deterrent to the study of his works in chronological order as far as reasonably possible. The English works perhaps need less treatment than the Latin since they have gradually been receiving more attention in literary histories, anthologies, and dissertations.

Fisher's first two extant works, to wit, the statutes for Christ's College and the address to Henry VII, are both in Latin, as befitting academic pieces, and date from 1505–1506. The editor of the statutes for Christ's College, of which Fisher is "the framer," declares: "In point of style the God's House Statutes have the bald precision of a legal document; whereas the Latinity of Lady Margaret's Statutes is more copious, graceful and varied, showing in a marked degree the influence of the wider classical studies of the Renaissance." [1]

It is therefore ironic that these stylistic qualities of elegance and variety should not be prominent in the oration delivered by Fisher before Henry VII in 1506. Making more than due allowance for Latin grandiloquence, one objects not so much to the flattery (excused by the ulterior motive of fund-raising and by zeal for the university) as to a certain heavy-handedness. For example, to illustrate the truth that no great man is born without some notable sign nor passes his life without many perils, Fisher deliberately slights pagan histories and applies the story of Moses to Henry VII's birth and career. Fortunately, as if realizing that this parallel were more than enough, he chooses only one other comparison, that of the king to the sun. In a catalogue of royal qualities, Henry is declared to excel all others in prudence and wisdom as the sun the stars. Toward the end the beneficent king is compared to the spring sun which revives and fecundates all herbs and trees. In varied form the figure of the sun and the miracle of spring will reappear in Fisher's later works.

Yet for all that it seems the least typical of his literary products, it shares with them a strong, coherent, unified structure. After a brief introduction which poses the dilemma involved in inadequate expression of necessary thanks and which sets forth the three points to be treated, the body of the address develops these points at length. In the first, Henry's greatness is measured by the wonder of his birth, by the magnitude of the dangers from which he has been preserved by divine providence, and by the excellence of his person, wealth, power, and popularity. The second point, the predicament from which Henry has rescued the university, sets forth its past glory and his ancestors' benefactions but describes the decline into which it has unfortunately fallen because of feuds with the town or frequent visitations of the plague or lack of advocates and patrons of the liberal arts. (This last description, undoubtedly exaggerated for effect, has been much quoted to show the low state of the university in the early sixteenth century.) The third point, arguing from Cicero's *honos artes alit,* enumerates Henry's services to learning: his elevation of Fisher to the episcopacy in order to encourage virtue and learning, his prolonged attendance at the academic disputations, and his munificence in completing Henry VI's foundation. In conclusion Fisher asks what return the university can make, and answers his own question: they can give the king their hearts in the daily remembrance of his name and benefactions and in all good wishes, temporal and eternal.[2]

Even if this oration were less successful than it actually is, it would survive for its invaluable references to Fisher himself, to his University of Cambridge, and to the members of the royal family.

Fisher's next composition, his most popular and brilliant, is undoubtedly his literary masterpiece. It is the series of ten sermons on the seven Penitential Psalms, preached in August and September 1504 and printed in June 1508. Each sermon is a running commentary on the whole psalm or on half of it, interwoven with exhortations to his audience. There can be little doubt that after each sermon every attentive hearer could give its theme in a nutshell. This happy effect is due especially to structural clarity and strength.

The first sermon does not enter immediately upon the exposition of Vulg. Ps. 6 but gives the biographical setting, namely, David's life up to and including the affair with Bathsheba, the murder of Uriah, and the numbering of the people. This account, which actually serves as background for the whole series of sermons, is prelude to the division of the psalm into three parts: "In the fyrst the mercy of god is asked. In the seconde reasons be made wherby the goodness of god sholde be moued to mercy. And in the thyrde is grete gladnes shewed for the vndoubtefull obteynynge of forgyuenesse." The petition for mercy is developed by declaring the doctrine on hell and purgatory, by exposing the sickness of sin, and by describing the sinner's return to peace as similar to Christ's stilling of the storm. The reasons which move God to pardon are given as four: His mercy, His wisdom, His justice, and His power. In the third and briefest part, David's confidence and joy in God's forgiveness express themselves in defiance of the devils and in escape from the slavery of sin. Noteworthy is the praise of grace: "The vertue & strength of the grace of god is meruaylous, that where it ones perseth & entreth in to the soule of ony creature it makyth hym bolde & to hope well. . ." The ending is abrupt but affective: the sermon and the psalm close together: "*Conuertantur & erubescant.* Blyssed lorde gyue synners that grace they may be tourned to the grete shame & confusyon of the deuylles. *Valde velociter.* And graunte that it may be done shortly."

The discourse is written with great emotional and imaginative power. David's encounter with Goliath, for example, is recounted with considerable vividness. Abstract truths are made concrete by homely comparisons. To explain how emotions like wrath can be ascribed to the immutable God, Fisher writes:

> God is without mutabylyte or chaunge, he is alway one, for as we se the beme that cometh from the sonne alway one in it selfe hurteth and greueth the eye that is not clene and perfyte, and comforteth the eye whiche is pure without ony chaunge of his operacyon. . . Truly as longe as a creature contynueth in the wretchednes of synne, so longe shall he thynke that god is wroth with hym, lyke as the eye whyles it is sore, so longe shall the sonne beme be greuous and noysome to it, and neuer comfortable tyll the sekenes & dysease be done away.

Fisher later returns to this simile to explain that the blame for punishment must be laid on the sinner and not on the all-good God:

> For where as the sonne beme is comfortable to the eye that is clene and hole, and greuous to the eye whiche is sore and watry, there is no blame in the sonne but onely in the sekenes that is in the eye. So where that almyghty god rewardeth some with Ioy & some with payne, no blame is in god, but onely in the synner whiche is so sore infecte with synne that almyghty god can do no lesse but punysshe hym as longe as he contynueth in that synne, all though almyghty god in hymselfe cannot be but all good.

The comparisons used to describe the effect of contrite weeping are more homely. First, "The yren with rubbynge anon wyll shyne full bryght. So the soule with wepynge is made fayre and whyte." Later, "In lyke wyse as we se by rusty and cankred pottes whan they shall be made clene, fyrst they rubbe away the ruste and after that wasshe it with water. So dyde this holy prophete, fyrste by his wepynge scoured and made full clene his soule from the rustynesse and cankrynge of his foule synne, and after wasshed it with his wepynge teres." [3]

The brief introduction to the next sermon, that on the second Penitential Psalm (Vulg. Ps. 31), also gives divisions and subdivisions, but the outline is so complicated that no hearer could possibly bear it in mind. Instead, in the body, unity of impression is achieved by relating practically everything to the three parts of penance: contrition, confession, and satisfaction, to which Fisher returns again and again. In fact, the very last sentences exultingly sound the same note: "Ye that be made ryghtwyse by very contrycyon and true confessyon Ioye in our lorde. And ye that be made perfyte by due satysfaccyon Ioye ye eternally in our lorde."

Early in the sermon contrition is called the bud, confession the flower, and satisfaction the fruit. Failure to bring forth the fruit of good works casts doubt upon the sincerity of the sinner's contrition and confession. Much later, this metaphor is expanded to show the special necessity of God's grace: "From the eyen of almyghty god whiche may be called his grace shyneth forth a meruaylous bryghtnes lyke as the beme that cometh from the sonne. And that lyght of grace stereth and setteth forthwarde the soules to brynge forth the fruyte of good werkes. Euen as the lyght of the sonne causeth herbes to growe & trees to brynge forth fruyte." As in the previous sermon, the sun in the physical world is thus associated with God in the spiritual world.

Fisher approvingly cites Augustine's comparison of the sins of the world to the mercy of God: "they be in comparyson no more to it than is a sparke of fyre in the grete see." For sin itself, however, he can use far less dignified similes. Sin, continually indulged in and not revealed in confession, is likened to "vryne or ony other stynkynge lycour put in a vessell, the longer it be kepte in the same, so moche more it maketh foule the vessel"; and to "a byle or botche full of matter and fylth the more & the lenger it be hyd, the more groweth the corrupcyon." The figure is different for cleansing from sin, which is likened to three successive and ever deeper erasures or scrapings of writing on paper: "By the vertue of contrycyon our synnes be forgyuen, by confessyon they be forgoten, but by satisfaccyon they be so clene done away that no sygne or token remayneth in ony condycyon of them, but as clene as euer we were."

For the first time, but briefly, allegory is used — to describe worldly pleasures as the principal hindrance to true contrition. Just as God had created paradise as a place of virtuous pleasure with its four rivers of the four cardinal virtues — "ryghtwysnes, temperaunce, prudence, and strengthe" — so the devil had made a paradise of sensual pleasure with its four rivers of covetousness, gluttony, pride, and lechery. God, the *only* refuge from drowning in these waters, saved Abraham and Job, St. Edward the Confessor and St. Louis of France. By His benefits, He also enticed to penance the Apostles Matthew and Peter, Mary Magdalene, St. Anthony the founder of monasticism, and an anonymous priest, whose conversion is narrated by William of Paris. Such allusions help to give the sermon a soaring sweep which lifts the auditors above the narrow confines of personal preoccupation and of local habitation and time.[4]

The next sermon is a remarkable *tour de force:* the simultaneous treatment of the Nativity of the Blessed Virgin Mary (September 8) and of the first eleven verses of the third Penitential Psalm (Vulg. Ps. 37). To effect the union, Fisher employs the favorite symbol of the sun for God. If Christ is the sun that shone on man engulfed in the night of sin after Adam's fall, then our Lady must be the morning. Consequently his text for the first section is taken from the Canticle of Canticles (6:9): "Who is she that cometh forth as the morning rising?" The fittingness of having a morning between night and day is proved from "nature, scrypture, and reason." The symbolism is developed with great ingenuity and at great length until Mary's three virtues as morning (mildness without storms, ascension over tyranny of night, and brightness above clouds of ignorance) are contrasted with man's three kinds of misery: fear, slavery, and ignorance. These are then treated fully according to the verses in the first half of the psalm. In verse 11 ("My heart is sore troubled, my strength hath forsaken me, and the syght [*lumen*] of myn eyen hath fayled me"), Fisher finds a useful summary of his whole discourse:

> My hert is sore troubled. Take hede & marke here the fyrst kynde of wretchednes, that is to saye the tempestous trybulacyons wherwith the herte of synners is troubled & vexed, fyrst for fere of the eternal punysshement of god in hell, for drede of his punysshement in purgatory, also by fere of deth hangynge alway in our neckes, for drede of goddes punysshement in this lyf, & last for the vgsomnes of our synnes. . . It foloweth. . . My strength hath forsaken me. Here is noted the seconde kynde of mysery wherby we be put downe myserably vnder the thraldome of synne, by whiche thraldome we be ouercomen, subdued, our old tokens of synne waxe roten agayne, we be made vnhappy, croked & sorowful, we be scourged sore & made lowe as subgectes. . . The prophete added. . . The syght of myn eyen hath fayled me. Here is the thyrde kynde of wretchednes expressed, that is to say of our cloudy blyndnes wherby we be so moche blynded that neyther for thabomynacyon of synne whiche is a foule and ferefull monstre nor for the reuerence of god beynge present we wyll refrayne but synne styl & that greuously, from whiche myseryes the moost blyssed virgyn delyuer vs, whose natyuyte we halowe this daye by her sone our lorde Ihesu cryst whome she as a fayer mornynge brought forth the moost bryght sonne to gyue lyght vnto all synners.

The difficulty of his task undoubtedly forced the Bishop of Rochester to exercise more than usual care upon this sermon. Structurally it is a magnificent piece of craftsmanship. The audience could easily get its gist in spite of its apparent complexity and richness. Like the previous sermons it contains some notable figures of speech. The allegorical representation of sin as a serpent is not uncommon: its head is "the fyrst instygacyon," its body is consent, and its "venemous tayle" is the deed itself. More unusual is the graphic picture of the serpent as the haughty tyrant in man's soul. For the sinner who does not feel that burden of sin, Fisher devises a homely comparison: "Yf a dogge hauynge a grete stone bounde aboute his necke be cast downe from an hygh toure, he feleth no weyght of that stone as longe as he is fallynge downe, but whan he is ones fallen to the grounde he is brasten all to peces by the reason of that weyght. So the synner goynge downe towarde the pyt of hell feleth not the grete burden of synne, but whan he shall come in to the depnes of hell he shall fele more payne than he wolde." Sin is "abhomynable in the syght of god, and ferre more abhomynable than is the stynkynge caryon of a dogge or ony other venemous worme in the syght of men."

There are more classical allusions in this sermon than in the first two. About light coming out of darkness, "The clerke Orpheus meruayled gretely of it sayenge . . . O derke nyght I meruayle sore that thou bryngest forth lyght." The consciousness of sin can be so painful as to drive sinners to suicide: "Example we haue of a Romayne woman called Lucrece & many other." Reference is made to the discussion between Socrates and Polus in Plato's *Gorgias* on the happiness or otherwise of the usurper Archelaus of Macedon: happiness depends upon the condition of one's soul, not on power and wealth. Fisher gives also Demosthenes' answer to the evil woman who asked a huge sum for her favors: "Hys lernynge was not to bye penaunce so dere" (*tanti paenitentiam non emo*).[5]

The heights achieved by this first sermon on Vulg. Ps. 37 are not attained by the second, which opens, not so much with an introduction, as with a prelude: a paean of praise and thanks to David for the Psalms for three reasons:

Fyrste that by these holy psalmes the myndes of synners myght be reysed vp and excyted as by a swete melody to receyue and take the study and lernynge of vertues. Secondaryly that yf ony man or woman hath fallen to grete and abomynable synnes, yet they sholde not despayre, but put theyr hole and stedfast hope of forgyuenes in god. Thyrdly that they myght vse these holy psalmes as lettres of supplycacyon and spedefull prayers for remyssyon and forgyuenes to be purchased of almyghty god.

This last comparison in particular is expanded effectively.

After developing this triple prelude, Fisher immediately divides the latter half of the psalm into three sections: (1) David's wretchedness, (2) the bases for trust in God's forgiveness, and (3) the necessity of grace for perseverance in good intention. It is the first section that is most remarkable. Friends are shown to be often a major obstacle to conversion and salvation. For example, *Amici fures temporis*, "they be theues and stele awaye our tyme of well doynge in this worlde." Moreover, when "prelates and . . . suche as hath cure of soule" neglect their duty of correction, souls fall prey to sins and devils, who, when they fail in using the crasser temptations of riches and pleasures, propose impossible ideals of perfection. Here Fisher devises two interesting similes. The devils behave: (1) "lyke as fysshers do whan they be aboute to cause fysshe to come in to theyr nettes or other engyns, they trouble the waters to make them auoyde & flee from theyr wonte places"; and (2) "lyke as men saye apes be taken of the hunters by doynge on shoos, for the properte of an ape is to do as he seeth a man do. The hunter therfore wyll laye a payre of shone in his waye, & whan he perceyueth the hunter doynge on his shoos he wyll doo the same, and so after that it is to harde for hym to lepe & clymbe from tree to tree as he was wonte, but falleth downe, & anone is taken."

The second part, concerned with the grounds for confidence in obtaining God's pardon, does not enumerate them at the start but summarizes them at the close as five: "He that asketh of almyghty god ony thynge for his soules helth & doo it [1] with good hope, [2] redy to correccyon, [3] sorowynge his offences done, [4] shewynge truly the same by confessyon, and [5] last purposynge euer after to abstayne from all occasyons of synne, without doubte that persone shall be herde & obteyne his petycyon." Of these five grounds, the most important is hope: "Good hope is the fyrst, without the whiche euery thynge that we do is of no valure," as is evident from Judas with his repentance, confession, and satisfaction, but without all-necessary hope.

The third part insists that God's help is necessary for continuance in good. Against all enemies, "Truly he that is almighty may socour vs & none other." For this reason prayer is always imperative. Toward the end Fisher recounts the anecdote of St. Anthony, beaten by devils and seemingly abandoned by God. To Anthony's complaint, Jesus replies: "Anthony I was here with the." Fisher also refers to Cassian's commendation of the last verse of the psalm: "*Intende in adiutorium meum domine deus salutis mee.* My lorde and god of myne helth gyue hede to myn helpe." (Fisher praises these words and repeats Cassian's observation also in his treatise on prayer.) The whole sermon closes very quickly with a petition for triple "helth," that is, triple salvation: "He is god and lorde of our helth, gyuyinge temporall helth to our bodyes, and to our soules the helth of grace in this lyfe, and in the generall resurrecyon to come whiche we veryly truste, euerlastynge helth bothe to body and soule, to the whiche our lorde by his ineffable mercy brynge vs. Amen." [6]

To express fallen man's absolute dependence on God for salvation of body and soul, Fisher begins his first sermon on the fourth Penitential Psalm (Vulg. Ps. 50) with the finest product of his imagination. It is an extraordinary Christian parable of the human situation, carefully but unaffectedly worked out in all its details. Only length prevents full citation here. Man is depicted as hanging over "a very depe pyt holden vp by a weyke and sclender corde or lyne, in whose botome sholde be moost woode and cruell beestes of euery kynde." He clings to "a broken boket or payle," with the rope "holden vp and stayed onely by the handes of that man, to whome by his manyfolde vngentylnes he hath ordred and made hymselfe as a very enemy." As for the bucket or pail, "what vessell may be more bruckle and frayle than is our body that dayly nedeth reparacyon," like "an hous made of claye." The silver cord is "the lyfe of man knytte togyder by foure humours." The cord is held up "by the hande & power of god," whom man has made his enemy by sin. This, then, is our "ferefull condycyon": heaven and God above us, hell and devils below us, our wickedness before us, neglected opportunities behind us, God's benefits on our right, misfortunes escaped by divine goodness on our left; and: "Within vs is the moost stynkynge abhomynacyon of our synne, wherby the ymage of almyghty god in vs is very foule defourmed and by that we be made vnto hym very enemyes." Is there no way out? "Truly the best remedy is to be swyfte in doynge penaunce for our synnes. He onely may helpe them that be penytent. . . Therfore let vs now aske his mercy with the penytent prophete Dauyd."

With these last words, Fisher begins his sermon proper with a brief statement of the three parts into which the first half of Vulg. Ps. 50 is divided: (1) David's petition, (2) reasons for God's granting his petition, and (3) the sure hope of having his petition granted. This same division is repeated quite baldly at the close of the sermon.

As for the body of the discourse, the first part, after extolling the greatness of God's mercy, shows that God is not only *misericors,* merciful inwardly, but also *miserator,* merciful outwardly, in actually performing works of mercy — unlike a human physician who might feel pity for a poor sore-covered man lying in the street but who does nothing for him. To make clear the countless acts of divine mercy, Fisher uses a variation of his favorite symbol for God: "For lyke as from the grete lyght of the sonne cometh and sheweth forth innumerable bemes, so from the grete mercy of almyghty god gooth forth innumerable mercyes, nombre the sonne bemes yf it be possyble, and the mercyes of almyghty god be more without ende." As for man, his sinful soul is like a soiled "table" which needs to be "rased" by contrition (a figure used earlier in the sermon on Vulg. Ps. 31), washed by tears in confession, and wiped by satisfaction, that is, by good works. To be salutary, all three must be the gift of God; otherwise they are merely worldly and completely unavailing.

The reasons for granting the petition are not set forth with the sharp clarity that is characteristic of Fisher, who here seems handicapped by the text of the psalm. They reduce themselves to the consideration that sorrow, confession, and satisfaction are pleasing to God. Two additional reasons are particularly interesting: original sin and Christ's promise. The first is embodied in a comparison of humanity to a weak-bodied man who, in spite of his good will, cannot fulfill the command to roll a heavy millstone to the top of a high hill. Man's body, too, "is thrast downe by the heuy burden of synne that oftentymes it boweth & slyppeth downe backwarde, for that same synne that by our fyrst fader & moder Adam & Eue was brought amonge al men is heuy & greuous on vs lyke as an heuy burden, & . . . maketh vs also prone & redy to all other vyces, therfore and for this cause haue mercy on vs." The second additional reason is Christ's promise (Matt. 9:13, 11:28, Mark 2:17, Luke 5:32, John 6:37): "Thou arte true and louest trouth aboue all thynge. Haue in mynde the promyse thou made to euery penytent synner comynge vnto the, whiche is, thou shalte not caste them awaye, & also thou shalte refresshe them."

After advancing these reasons for God's granting the petition of David and every sinner, Fisher gives the bases of David's (and every sinner's) hope and confidence for obtaining mercy. In brief, they are the penance and salvation of the Ninevites; "the secrete mysteryes of the fayth & the sacramentes of helth" for the Christian people; the enlightenment and presence of the Holy Spirit in the Church "so that now no thinge may be more certayne to vs than it whiche is taught by holy chyrche"; the merits of the passion of Christ, "whiche by the effusyon of his holy blode hath gyuen so grete effycacy and strength to the holy sacramentes of his chirche, that whan we receyue ony of them we shall be sprencled and made clene by the vertue of his precyous blode lyke as with ysope, whiche aspersyon anone foloweth the water of grace that is infused in our soules, wherby we be made more whyter than snowe"; and, finally, the joy experienced by the sinner, who now knows himself delivered from the burden and perils of sin, perceives "the clerenes of his soule," remembers "the tranquyllyte and peas of his conscyence," and glimpses "euerlastynge peas" in heaven.

Of these five grounds for confidence, the blood of Jesus Christ receives the greatest stress and the most space, particularly as the source of sacramental efficacy. It is here that Fisher employs the charming allegory of the hyssop (cf. Vulg. Ps. 50:9). The defiled Jew was cleansed "with ysope dypped in the blode of certayne beestes and sprencled vpon hym." The significance of this rite became clear after Christ had washed us from sin in His blood (cf. 1 Pet. 1:2, 1:19): "Ysope is an herbe of the grounde that of his nature is hote, and hath a swete smell, sygnefyenge Cryst whiche meked himselfe to suffre deth on the crosse." [7]

The second sermon on Vulg. Ps. 50 (verses 11–21) is remarkable not only for its architectonics, but also for minor rhetorical successes. More than the previous sermons, it is replete with instances and examples: Peter, Paul, Magdalene, Ahab, and Manasseh. It reconstructs graphically a number of scriptural passages, e.g., the career of Ahab and the parable of the Pharisee and the Publican. Comparisons may reappear in altered form. For example, instead of the painted table, a painted wall is used to represent the sinful soul. New similes are introduced: the soul being likened to a defective clock and to a new clock, and to a garden irrigated by a stinking stream. In fact, Fisher borrows a simile from St. Gregory the Great to open his discourse. The hope and confidence, which, extolled at the end of the previous sermon, might terminate in presumption, must be offset by the fear of God. Hope and dread are like two millstones which grind sins away between them.

Fisher then divides the remainder of Vulg. Ps. 50 (vv. 11–21) into three parts: a new petition, an intention of pleasing God in voicing the petition, and "desire [as] the chefe thynge wherby euery man may please god and make recompence for synne." Without more ado he states that the petition is for "the holy ghoost whiche is neuer but in clene hertes." The heinousness of sin is evident from the fall of the angels, the expulsion of Adam and Eve from paradise, the punishment of Dathan and Abiram, the drowning by the Deluge, and the shedding of Christ's blood. Consequently sins must be destroyed in the soul, for sins are like pictures painted on a wall. But the source of sins, the heart (Matt. 15:18–20), is like a pond or pit, from which flows "stynkynge fylthy water . . . in to a goodly and delectable garden." This heart, which must be made clean, is also like a clock: it is more difficult to repair it than to create it anew. In an intricate exposition, Fisher humbly volunteers an interpretation of the three epithets applied to the Spirit: *rectus, sanctus,* and *principalis.* The *spiritus rectus,* under the likeness of a dove at the baptism of Christ, is appropriate to baptized infants and symbolizes innocence. The *spiritus sanctus,* under the likeness of breath (John 20:22–23) at Christ's apparition after the resurrection, belongs to penitents and symbolizes penance. The *spiritus principalis,* under the likeness of fire on Pentecost, characterizes the perfect and symbolizes steadfastness and perseverance in virtue.

The second part, which discloses the intention for asking the Holy Spirit, is subtly and elaborately built upon the first part. The "use" of *spiritus rectus* is the good of one's neighbors: the admonition and conversion of sinners. It is here that Fisher expresses fears for his own failure or neglect in teaching God's laws. The "use" of *spiritus sanctus,* the spirit of penance, is directed toward personal deliverance from sin, achievable only by the blood of Christ (through the sacrament of penance). The "use" of *spiritus principalis* is to make men fearless in "the laude and prayse of almighty god," like Isaiah in the Old Law and the Apostles on Pentecost and afterward.

Although the third part does not come as sharply into focus as the previous two sections, it does make its point clear: "Thacceptable sacrefyce to god dependeth not by the valure of the gyfte but by the good mynde & entent of the doer," as in the account of the widow's two mites. Hence better than sacrifices and holocausts is "a sorowfull & contryte herte for synne," as is shown by the Publican in Christ's parable and by the repentance of Ahab. The living stones for the heavenly palace must be prepared here on earth, for example, by God's chastisement in the case of Manasseh and by Christ's love in the case of Mary Magdalene.

An excellent summary concludes the sermon, which closes with a vision of the heavenly Jerusalem where "we shall without ende gyue thankynges immortall vnto the in eternall glory, where vnto thou brynge vs by the merytes of thy sone Ihesu cryst that suffred passyon for all synners vpon a crosse. Amen." [8]

The next sermon, based on Vulg. Ps. 101:1–13, opens with a rather matter-of-fact division into three parts: the petition, the misery of man, and the course to be taken. The whole first part takes the remarkable form of a meditative prayer addressed to God the Father. His Son had come as a teacher who, among other truths, had extolled the efficacy of prayer and died on the cross out of love. It is here that Fisher enunciates the absolute dependence of grace and salvation on God's will:

> Therfore thou mayst take thy pleasure, it is thy choyse whether thy goodnes wyll punysshe & vtterly cast awaye synners for theyr offences & trespasses, or elles here theyr prayers & petycion for the reuerence of thy sone, whiche promysed them to be herde and obteyne theyr askynge. It is lytell force to the, it skylles the no thynge, it is no poynt of thy charge whether we be saued or dampned, thou madest vs of nought, and mayst dele with vs as it pleaseth the.

Christ's promise, however, favors their being heard and saved.

Fisher wishes his prayer to go to God, not mediately through angels, but immediately and directly: "The lyuely voyce or the voyce spoken by the mouth of the persone that is so greued or dyseased moueth moche more effectually the herer than it sholde be tolde by ony other man." This declaration is proved by four examples: Aeschines, who told his pupils that Demosthenes' speech against him was far more effective when delivered than when merely read; the sight and sounds of beggars in the street; the Good Samaritan, moved by the victim of the robbers (who, in a quasi-digression, find their counterpart in devils); and the woman of Canaan (Matt. 15:21–28). All these episodes are recreated with great on-the-scene liveliness.

The wretchedness of man's estate, which is exposed in the

second part, is evident in the shortness of his life, dramatically set forth with the *ubi-sunt* motif: "Where is now the innumerable company & puyssaunce of Xerxes & Cesar, where are the grete victoryes of Alexander and Pompey, where is now the grete rychesse of Cresus & Crassus. But what shall we say of them whiche somtyme were kynges & gouernours of this realme. . . But where be they now, be they not gone and wasted lyke vnto smoke. . ." Man's misery lies also in the fact that "vnderstandynge wyll and reason whiche muste be vnto the soule as bones and senewes to socour it be so vtterly wedred and dryed vp, that no maner of moysture of deuocyon is in them." The cause is that many eat, not the spiritual bread of the word of God, but the word of the devil, which subjects reason to concupiscence, makes the soul dry, kindles carnal desire, and renders the soul weak.

As for the allegorical threads in the third part, no summary can possibly convey their rich and complex weaving and interweaving. Briefly, the pelican, which dwells in the desert, symbolizes contrition and brings about the restoration, or reviviscence, of good works destroyed by mortal sin. The owl, abiding in ruined walls by night, symbolizes confession and causes the sun of justice to rise and shine again. The sparrow, taking refuge in house eaves, symbolizes satisfaction and makes former sinners set their minds on heavenly things. These former sinners have many enemies, not least of all their erstwhile friends, who resort to slander and backbiting. They themselves remember their former sins which now are but ashes: hence they eat ashes. They also drink tears at the memory of their sins and thereby also quench any new sparks of concupiscence. Two motives for such behavior are God's indignation with sin and the greatness of the sinner's fall. No fall could be greater than that of a Christian, for he is the Father's son and heir and Christ's purchase and brother, washed by His blood in baptism, often cleansed by it again in penance, and nourished by His Body and Blood in the Eucharist.

In a variation of the figure of the living stones used toward the end of the previous sermon, a great stone which a craftsman is earnestly attempting to raise to the top of a stately edifice falls through its own fault. "In lyke maner almyghty god is not to be accused yf he at ony tyme do his good wyl to lyfte vs vp in to the hygh state of grace, & we in the meane season by the weyght of our frowarde and peruerse wyll fall downe from his handes, veryly we ourselfe are to be accused and reproued for it and not almyghty god, and our fall is the more bytterly to be wayled, that syth he wolde lyfte vs vp, we by our owne neclygence & euyll wyll be caste downe."

A prayerful colloquy, addressed to the Lord, comprises a summary, more than usually subtle, of the third part.

The conclusion of the whole sermon, too, is more elaborate than that of any preceding it. It turns upon the manifestation of mercy. The more noble the being, the greater the disposition to pity — like the magnanimous lion that spares its prostrate and pleading foe and unlike the vengeful wolf and bear (Ovid, *Tristia* 3.5.33–36). "Syth almighty god therfore is moost noble, moost constaunt, & so myghty aboue all other without fere, he fereth no creature, it can not be other wyse but nedes he must be mercyfull & mekely forgyue vs wretched & of no strength, fallynge downe at his fete knowlegynge our owne mysery & aske of hym forgyuenes." All this mercy, of course, terminates in "the euerlastynge memoryall of thy blyssed name."

As literary art this present sermon is distinguished for its allegory and figures, its graphic representation of Gospel parables, and its classical references. They have been sufficiently indicated above, but another instance might be added to each category. In regard to the first, especially well executed is the escape of the sparrow to the eaves: "There she wypeth and feteth her byl, there she proyneth & setteth her feders in ordre, there also she bryngeth forth byrdes, & there restynge maketh mery as she can after her maner." As for the second, after a picture of diligent suitors at a king's or prince's court, the parable of the unjust judge and the importunate widow comes alive to show the need for unremitting petition. Immediately afterward occurs an instance of the third — a quotation from Vergil's *Georgics* (1.146): *Labor improbus omnia vincit,* which the English half translates and half accommodates: "Incessaunt laboure by the waye of intercessyon ouercometh all thynges." All in all, though some might complain that Fisher is gilding the simple lily of the psalm, he nevertheless succeeds in controlling unpromising materials and, by the introduction of examples from the New Testament and the classics, makes his whole address living, engrossing, and profitable for his audience — not a mean achievement for any sermonizer. The listener is aware of ingenuity and richness — but of both used always as means to the end of conveying the truth and the lesson.[9]

The next sermon is highly important for Fisher's views on the Church, not only of his own day, but also the Church of early times and of the future. He is fully aware of the evils of the day in both clergy and laity. He can be objective and severe about them, but he does not descend to particulars. For this reason, perhaps, his generalized picture is so much more poignant and depressing: the decline and the decay are universal and with hardly any exception. What a contrast he finds between the existing Church and that of the Apostles and martyrs! As he looks to the future, however, he is full of hope and confidence for God's help and mercy on His Church, His Sion, and has glorious visions of the New Jerusalem.

The allegorical structure at first seems too varied for satisfactory exposition; furthermore, it is rendered even more complex by three key symbols. These latter, however, far from obscuring the basic allegory, rather reinforce it and provide the groundwork for further symbolism. The fundamental allegory is the simple one of the three high and noble places: Mount Sinai (for Jews), Mount Sion (for Christians), and the New Jerusalem (for the blessed in heaven). The three symbols are those of gold (for the Jewish priests and the contemporary Catholic clergy, whose behavior is contrasted to homespun Apostolic virtue), the ship (for the Church, with attendant details about the slumbering pilot, the voyage, the storms, and the port), and the New Jerusalem (for heaven, constructed of living stones, which need to be prepared perfectly here on earth).

Except for a brief statement about the difficulty and obscurity of his subject, Fisher's introduction is concerned with allegory. Sinai represents the Jews under the Mosaic law, written on tables of stone and observed in the spirit of fear. Sion signifies the Church under the law of grace and mercy, written on the heart and kept in "grete hope & truste of forgyuenes." Jerusalem betokens the blessed in heaven, whose law is "wryten in the mynde of god" and whose mood is that of "eternall and incessaunt Ioye." A passage transitional to the body of the sermon explains that the first part of the psalm embodies prayer for self, the second part prayer for neighbor and the Church. The law of prayer is: "The more that ony prayer is grounded in charyte, the sooner it shall be herde of hym whose commaundemente is all charyte."

The need of the Church is desperate. Vices reign everywhere in the ship of the Church, yet Christ slumbers as He did fifteen centuries before on the Sea of Galilee. Now, as then, Christ needs to be awakened. At this juncture Fisher launches into intensive petition for the Church, couched significantly in the first person plural number, which continues for pages. The prayer, which at first seems haphazard and aimless, is found upon analysis to pivot upon the preservation and extension of Christ's kingdom upon earth.

Christendom has been reduced to one sixth of its former territory, while the number of good Christians has greatly diminished. Yet even one just man is sufficient to save Christ's Church and to fulfill the promise of everlasting sojourn with His Church. Since this is the time of grace and not of fear, the gates of mercy stand open for all, especially the frail and needy, blown about like dust. But the dust can first be rendered "moyst with the due of thy grace"; it can then be made earth which is "stronge more & more by compunccyon & wepynge for our synnes"; and it can finally become, by the heat of God's charity, as "harde as stones, that is to saye more stronge & stedfast in fayth and good werkes." In a curious deployment of the basic figure, Fisher declares that such strength and constancy must characterize those who are to preach Christ's Gospel until the whole world has heard it and comes to an end. The preachers of the past having been placed as living stones in the heavenly Jerusalem, God must prepare new stones on earth to continue the evangelization of the world. Even so had He converted the cowardly Apostles into fearless missionaries.

In fact, fear of God or contempt for God on the part of the laity, both people and princes, depends upon the example set by the clergy, whose glory does not consist in gold and silver, gems and silk, as for the Jewish priesthood, but in what is signified by these things: "clennes of conscyence" by gold, and "vertues of the soule" by gems. What a contrast between St. Paul and contemporary bishops! "In that tyme were no chalyses of golde, but than was many golden prestes, now be many chalyses of golde, & almoost no golden prestes." Why was Attila intimidated by Leo,

Totila by Benedict, and Theodosius by Ambrose? "Truly bycause they herd theyr doctryne, & sawe theyr lyues so good & honest." The virtues of faith, hope, and charity enabled Peter to heal a lame man and raise a dead woman; Paul, to make a cripple walk and free a possessed person; John the Evangelist, to turn branches into gold, to drink poison, and to raise the dead; and Bartholomew, to expel a devil from an idol. Above all, their faith accomplished these wonders. The trouble with the contemporary Church is that "our fayth begynneth to fayle & waxe scante." The remedy is the answer to the petition: "Augment and encrease the fayth of thy chirche." Upon this note ends the great prayer which constitutes the first part.

What moves God to grant such a prayer is man's "euerlastynge remembraunce of his benefeytes." This principle is the burden of the second part. Human ingratitude forestalls divine bestowal of favors. God's greatest benefaction has been the "mercyfull ereccion & buyldynge of crystes chirche," with all its channels of grace. The surest way to guarantee remembrance is to put it in writing — as Moses did for God's wonders among the Jews and as the Evangelists did for Christ's miracles. The sermon here begins to lose some of Fisher's usual clarity, undoubtedly because of the psalm's own sequence. The present generation, which is evil, cannot produce a new generation which is good — but God must create it anew. For, looking down from heaven, He saw the Jews forgetful of His wonders and the Christians unmindful even of Christ's redemption. Yet at least their children will be rescued and saved. They will be also twice honored: on earth by preaching His name to the whole world, in heaven by taking the places of their bitterest enemies, the fallen angels. At the end of the second part, Fisher holds a brief summarizing colloquy with God on the spread of His kingdom, "whan our lorde of his goodnes shall chaunge and tourne the softe and slypper duste sygnefyenge wretched synners in to tough erthe by wepynge and true penaunce for theyr synnes, and after that make them harde as stones by brennynge charyte, apte and able for to suffre grete laboures in shewynge boldly thy gloryous name thrughe out all the worlde. . ."

The theme of the third part is announced as "our petycyon vnto our blyssed lorde that he vouchesaue of his goodnes to susteyne & holde vp his chyrche mylytaunt in the same ordre & course . . . to thentent after the Iourney perfourmed in this lyfe it may the sooner ascende & come to the yeres whiche euer shall endure in heuen." Before that time the Church, symbolized by Mount Sion, must endure "many anguysshes & tribulacyons," especially in the time of Antichrist. These sufferings are like tempests and storms which hinder the ship of the Church on its way to the eagerly desired port. Generation after generation passes, and earth and heaven too will have an end. There will be a new earth, a new heaven, and a new body for man — and all will be better than the old. All things were created good, beautiful, useful, and pleasurable — and common to just and unjust, friends and foes. How far superior must be the heaven which God has created for His friends alone.

The swift and short conclusion to the whole sermon is an exhortation to a threefold petition to God: (1) "to loke vpon the mysery of his chyrche mylytaunt with the eye of his mercy"; (2) to "set in it worthy & able mynystres that may turne all the worlde vnto the fayth of Cryste"; and (3) that "the chyrche ones set stably in the course of vertue be not letted nor caste abacke in her Iourney, but shortly may ascende to the eternall pleasures of almyghty god in heuen. . ." [10]

The rich and complex metaphorical patterns in this sermon serve to reflect and express a vast and intricate subject — the contemporary Church, which reaches back to the Creation and strives forward toward its goal of eternity, but which suffers unspeakably by the comparison with the age of golden Apostles and martyrs. By the same adaptation of style and theme, a relative simplicity marks the sermon on Vulg. Ps. 129, *De Profundis,* because of its concern with the individual members of the Church. An allegorical interpretation of the story of Jonah, highly elaborated in the introduction and later referred to in the body, helps to unify the sermon and keep it from banal preachiness. In addition, details of Jonah's experiences are made very vivid on three different occasions.

In showing forth God's power to achieve His every purpose and promise, Fisher effectively uses "a comyn prouerbe. *Homo proponit & deus disponit.* Man purposeth & god dysposeth." Comparisons, however, are few. Certain words of Scripture are described as "more sweter than hony & suger." The habitual sinner is depicted as a bemired horse: "By lytel and lytel he synketh in to the fylthy pleasure of it, euen as a hors the softer myre or claye he waltreth hymselfe in the more easely he lyeth . . . but whan he is about to ryse agayne the softnes of the cley wyll not suffre to take holde wherby he myght be assysted." Far more original is the comparison of God to a wall and of the sinner to a post: "Yf at ony season . . . we do a trepasse ayenst his goodnes, let vs . . . stycke fast, lene to hym, and holde vp our selfe in truste of hys mercyfull forgyuenes lyke a poste set to a walle all though it seme to holde vp that walle, yet the poste hath more socoure from fallynge downe by the walle than the walle hath by it, for yf the walle were not, that poste sholde soone slyppe to the erth."

The lengthy introduction to the sermon declares that a sinner is like Jonah. The latter's fall had seven degrees or "descensions." To make a sinner's corresponding descensions more graphic, Fisher applies them to a chaste young man thinking of a beautiful woman. Briefly the descensions are (1) consent "to haue ado with her," (2) search for means and opportunity, (3) the act itself, (4) habit of sin, (5) boasting of sin, (6) defense of sin, and (7) despair of divine mercy, and "desperacyon is the thynge that moost maketh us deuyllysshe." Like Jonah, the sinner should cry to the Lord: *De profundis clamavi ad te, Domine.* The just man should do the same lest he fall into sin. Finally, this psalm should often be said for the souls in purgatory according to the Church's special recommendation.

The structure of the body of the discourse is somewhat different from that of previous sermons. It is divided into two parts: one short and one long. The first part relates to contrition, confession, and satisfaction. The second part, concerned with the degree of certainty about God's forgiveness, is subdivided into three sections: (1) a refutation of arguments against forgiveness, (2) the ability and the readiness of God to keep His promise of forgiveness, and (3) the infiniteness of God's mercy.

The first part opens with the mystical significance of the number three, as in the three-day wandering of the Jews in the wilderness (here Fisher appeals to "the grete doctour origine") and in the three-day sojourn of Jonah in the whale. So, too, David's petition expresses the three aspects of penance: contrition, in *de profundis clamavi ad te, Domine;* confession, in *Domine, exaudi vocem meam;* and satisfaction, in *fiant aures tuae intendentes in vocem deprecationis meae.* Most notable in the ensuing explanation is the emphasis on the depth of the human heart so that the first verse can be translated picturesquely: "*De profundis clamaui ad te domine.* Lorde I haue cryed to the from my very herte rote." As for satisfaction, it consists of almsgiving, fasting, and, above all, prayer. Significantly prayer includes both almsgiving (as in petition for sinners) and fasting (by making the body weak and subject to the soul). Prayer is also nobler because it sacrifices one's own mind, not one's worldly substance (as in almsgiving) nor one's bodily substance (as in fasting). Prayer finally is easiest of the three, because some persons are too poor to give alms and some are too feeble to fast, but all can pray. All can ask God to accept their penance and to grant forgiveness.

Yet will God carry out His promise to forgive? Fisher first answers the three negative arguments arising from the greatness of a man's sins, from God's justice, and from His law. In orderly but lengthy fashion Fisher appeals to the multitude already forgiven, to Jonah rescued after his great offense, to the redemption and reparation wrought by Christ's blood, and to the power given priests to forgive sins.

The first positive argument springs from God's persistent command to the sinner to turn from his sinful way. Unlike man, God is always true and powerful enough to keep His promise. Nor should anyone argue that the promise holds only for a single time, because God has greater goodness than man, who is exhorted to forgive seven times a day. Early or late in the day, that is, in life, God is ready to forgive, as is evident from the experience of the thief on the cross, Jonah, Hezekiah, Nebuchadnezzar, and David.

The infinitude of God's mercy constitutes the second positive argument. In fact, "alway euery houre, euery moment whan the synner is apte to receyue it [mercy], almighty god shal be redy to graunte his desyre." God is most rich in mercy because the coin is "the very innocent & precious blode of the incontamynate lambe Ihesu cryst." This blood was shed at the circumcision, the agony in the garden, the scourging, the crowning with thorns, the stripping of the clothes, the nailing to the cross, and the transfixion with the spear — in a word, seven times, "whiche sygnefyeth al tyme to thentent our synnes be they neuer so grete and many shal in euery houre, euery moment by the vertue of this precyous blode be clensed, done away. . ." Indeed God suffers the loss of His credence rather than show Himself unmerciful, as in the case of Jonah and the Ninevites. This point is confirmed by the story about Jonah and the withered yew tree. Hence God is always ready to forgive repentant sinners and "make them parte takers of that noble redempcyon which was perfourmed with the treasure of the precyous blode of his sone Ihesu cryste."

The Bishop of Rochester then proceeds to "conclude this sermon with a shorte rehersall of the same." [11]

The last sermon, on Vulg. Ps. 142, is labeled: *Domine exaudi posteri* (leg. *posterioris*). This term "second" is used here not to designate a second sermon on Ps. 142 but a second psalm which begins *Domine, exaudi*. The two sermons on Vulg. Ps. 101 had been headed: *Domine exaudi. prioris.*[12] Both Ps. 101 and Ps. 142 begin: *Domine, exaudi orationem meam*. The present sermon on Ps. 142, like the preceding one on Ps. 129, is rendered more complex and rich by amalgamation with another section of Holy Writ. The sermon before had used a tale of the Old Testament, that of Jonah, and had paid particular attention to the sinner's fall. The present sermon employs a parable of the New Testament, that of the Prodigal Son, and highlights and analyzes the sinner's return. It is the parable that furnishes the figurative language almost exclusively. The only notable exceptions are the comparison of the pleading sinner before God to a poor man appearing before a great prince or to the Queen of Sheba overwhelmed by Solomon's glory. The only classical allusion is attributed to Cicero: *Summum ius summa iniuria erit,* which is translated: "The lawe is [*leg.* if] vsed extremely after the wordes as they be wryten shall be many tymes grete wronge." It is illustrated by the example of a citizen who, against the law, climbs over the wall by night but who does so with the intention of warning the town of an impending enemy attack.

The structure is simplicity itself. The introduction narrates and allegorizes the parable of the Prodigal Son; the body develops four plainly stated points; and the conclusion summarizes the whole sermon.

There is little need to go into all the details of Fisher's allegorization of the parable. The citizens of the far country, for example, are devils. The "village," or farm, to which the son is sent represents evil company. The "pesen and oke cornes" which he longs to devour are "vnclene pleasures of the body, whiche can not satysfy hym." He then remembers the felicity of "the true seruauntes of god." Upon his return the merciful father "clotheth hym with the garmentes of grace." The slain calf is "our sauyour Iesu cryst." The introduction concludes with the four considerations to be treated: (1) "the ferre goynge awaye from his fader"; (2) "the maner of his comynge agayne"; (3) "what he shall aske of his fader"; and (4) "what rewarde he shall receyue in conclusyon."

In spite of the declaration that his first point would be "the ferre goynge awaye from his fader," Fisher proceeds to say: "Fyrst let vs call to remembraunce by what maner, & in what maner wyse this prodygall chylde came to his fader." Naturally the son and the sinner are overwhelmed with shame and repentance. Fisher then disposes of the two obstacles to forgiveness, namely, God's truth and God's justice. He next enumerates the many gifts of body and of soul, that is, the "portion" of inheritance, which many have spent unprofitably and for which they must render account. The best policy is to forestall judgment by "true confessyon and penaunce." After all, every man is a sinner — even "saynt Iohan the electe virgyn & pertyculerly beloued chylde of our blyssed lorde" and "the good lyuer Iob" — for "no creature lyuynge of his owne merytes shall be able to come afore thy syght." In fact, we should confess our servitude to the devil in the far country. The devil has put us to keeping swine ("worldly pleasures and the fylthy desyres of the flesshe"); he has taken away "the lyght of doynge good werkes"; and he has "made vs as deed without grace." Consequently it is only in the latter section that Fisher shows "the synners ferre goynge awaye from god."

The second part, on the manner of the sinner's return to God, should be particularly interesting insofar as it might reveal Fisher's views before the controversy on grace and justification. No matter how much the devil has deceived and blinded the sinner, "some sparke remayneth in the soule that can not lyghtly be extyncte and quenched, as moche to saye, the superyoure porcyon of the soule whiche alway stryueth agaynst synne." Like the Prodigal Son, "wolde god euery one of vs were in wyll to remembre the trouble of his owne soule, the whiche the inwarde conscyence dooth suffre." Fisher continues: "This remembraunce doubtles is begynnynge of the synners true conuersacyon [*leg.* conuercyon?] to almyghty god." What does he remember? (1) His "myserable errours"; (2) his abandonment of God, who is "moost myghty, moost lyberall, best, & moost fayre," and who is "our fader," sparing not His own Son; (3) his following of "the deuyl moost cruell enemy to all mankynde, also moost ferefull, moost enuyous"; and (4) his loss of "eternall lyfe & Ioyes euerlastynge."

The second step in conversion, in order to avoid despair, is undoubtedly "the remembraunce of good hope and truste of forgyuenes." Here the mercy of God is extolled, particularly as shown toward the Israelites, the Ninevites, and the kings David, Nebuchadnezzar, Ahab, and Hezekiah in the Old Testament and toward Peter, Paul, Mary Magdalene, the woman taken in adultery, the publican, and the thief on the cross in the New Law, and "other innumerable." The sinner remembers God's providence toward His servants: the lilies of the field, the sparrows, and all creatures, unreasonable and reasonable. The world's pleasures do not satisfy, but "there is an other maner lycour, & yf a man drynke no more but ones of it he shall be satisfyed and replenysshed haboundauntly, and neuer after be thyrsty." The fountain of this "moost delycate lycour" is Almighty God. The first explicit mention of grace then occurs at the end: "Lyke as the erth of his nature without moysture is drye & barayne, so is my soule of it selfe voyde from all goodnes, wherfore blyssed lorde vouchesaue to water it with the lycour of thy grace, to the entent it may fynally come vnto thyn euerlastynge blysse." The almost casual nature of the reference would seem to indicate not that grace is being slighted or neglected but rather presupposed in the whole process.

The third part of the sermon proper embodies three aspects of the sinner's conversion: to be heard, to be looked upon with an eye of mercy, and to be defended from his enemies. It is here that Fisher gives the vivid picture of a poor man in audience with a great king. Here, too, he develops the idea that God is more merciful and affectionate toward man than a husband toward his wife, a mother toward her child, or a father toward his son. Finally, the sinner must beg to be protected against relapse. Backsliding can come about through ignorance of the rule for persevering in the right way (God's readiness to help being shown by Peter's mission to Cornelius the centurion and Philip the Apostle's to Philip, "a chefe ruler of a towne called Gaza"), or it can occur through the guiles of the powerful devils (against whom "god is as a stronge toure for our defence"), or it can come about through frailty (against which only God's mercy and grace can be of avail).

Finally, the rewards listed in the fourth part are many: (1) admission into the kingdom of his Father, (2) consolation arising from his Father's words about returning to life and from the principle of equity or *epicheia,* (3) bestowal of an incorruptible body with its glorious properties, and (4) everlasting rest, without the envy of good persons like the elder brother ("whiche be occupyed incessauntly in doynge good werkes and operacions without intermyssyon of ony deedly synne, and by that presume of theyr deseruynge") and without the envy of devils (who "at all tymes laye wayte with as many subtyl craftes as they can to catche good people in to theyr daungers"). God will grant all these rewards or "commodytees" because man is His, and indeed His by three titles: creation from nothing, formation according to His own image, and "a Iuster tytle in so moche as he bought hym with so grete a pryce, that is to saye, with the precyous blode of his onely begoten sone."

The whole sermon ends with a brief matter-of-fact restatement of the four points: the sinner's fall, his rise, his petition, and his "many grete commodytees . . . whiche our blyssed lorde fader of mercy graunt vnto vs all. Amen." [13]

At the conclusion of this analysis of Fisher's sermons on the Penitential Psalms, it is worth while to view them as a whole. One must bear in mind that they are not systematic treatises or scriptural commentaries but popular sermons. Although the term "treatyse" begins the title, it is most likely used in the broad sense of "treatment." The treatment, however, takes the form of sermons, and it is the term "sermons" that is repeated in Fisher's Prologue. As sermons, they would have to be adapted to the needs and tastes of the audience. Fisher's success in his task can be gauged by the Lady Margaret's "hygh commaundement & gracyous exhortacyon" to have them printed and preserved. Unfortunately there is almost no clue to the nature of the audience and its religious, moral, and intellectual status. Presumably the audience is the household of the Lady Margaret. If so, it would be far from being a dissolute court. A year after the publication of these sermons, Fisher describes her household as being governed by "reasonable statutes & ordynaunces" read four times a year. Margaret herself would discreetly settle any strife or dispute therein and tactfully dispose of any factions among her chief officers. Through herself or by others, she would "louyngly courage euery of them to doo well." On the assumption that her household was an ordinary one, neither unusually saintly nor inordinately bad, what religious truths needed to be stressed for their good?

The choice of the Penitential Psalms is in itself revealing.[14] Fisher interprets these as the cries, not of the hardened sinner, but of the repentant offender, either one who detests his vice and is trying to extricate himself, or one who has escaped and is attempting to persevere in good. Consequently the preacher and his audience are preoccupied with the most vital questions of the Reformation and the Counter-Reformation only a few years ahead: sin and salvation, grace and justification. Fisher's solutions must be presumed to be found within the general framework of the theology of his time.

Today's reader is perplexed by the almost disproportionate effort expended upon the proof for God's mercy and upon the refutation of objections against it. Was "desperation" or despair a peculiar temptation of the time? If so, not as a theologian but as a pastor and physician, Fisher does not extinguish the smoldering flax nor break the bruised reed. In spite of a continual awareness of ultimates like the devil and hell, judgment and heaven, his theme is the relative ease of receiving the mercy of God, who is moved especially by man's likeness to Himself and by the blood of His Son. It is not without significance that the last sermon should seem to epitomize God's ways with the sinner in the parable of the Father and the Prodigal Son. The sinner need only bewail his trespasses and fix his trust and hope on the Father. Grace is absolutely necessary but it is ever at hand for the repentant.

The way to heaven is made even more secure, particularly against despair, by the Church: its preaching and its sacraments. Hence the three parts of penance, to wit, contrition, confession, and satisfaction, are treated or mentioned again and again. Why? Is relapse into sin too easy and common, and therefore must the purpose of amendment or satisfaction be stressed? This reasoning is plausible, but an even deeper reason might be the sinner's need of certainty about his justification and salvation. In less than a decade, Luther is to find the solution in fiducial faith. In these sermons, however, Fisher assures the sinner that by the threefold process of contrition, confession, and satisfaction, his sins are utterly done away with and forgotten by God. In spite of his exaltation of the Church, as the normal channel of redemption, however, Fisher is blunt about the necessity of its reformation. Once purified, the Church can resume its task of evangelization and of spreading the kingdom of God until consummated in heaven.

Just at present, however, our concern is less the content of these sermons than their style and expression. As stated previously, they are not biblical commentaries or doctrinal expositions. The strong sense of structure which manifests itself in every sermon needs no further elaboration. Fisher's architecture is no small achievement when one considers that he must simultaneously follow his text verse by verse. The emotional impact, of course, is thereby heightened and strengthened, combining as it does the voice of the mortal preacher and that of the divine Author. The main effect of the human voice, however, is probably created by Fisher's metaphors and images. The latter can hardly be reduced to a system, but they might be conveniently clustered around the parable which appears at the beginning of the sermon on Vulg. Ps. 50.[15]

This parable of the pit, it will be recalled, represents man as perilously suspended between heaven and hell. Below him is the dark dungeon filled with fallen angels that are like wild beasts. As they seek to ensnare men, these insatiate enemies roam about the world like ravening lions, tigers, and bears. They also undergo metamorphosis into human beings, sometimes taking the form of fishermen or hunters.

Far above the black hell over which man is suspended is the heaven where God resides. For Him the only fitting physical symbol can be the sun, with its beams as divine benefits and graces. The proper moral relationship of God to man can be found in paternity alone. The Father makes His grandest gesture in the sacrifice of His Son, the shedding and sprinkling of whose blood Fisher repeatedly mentions. Examples would be not only the more usual scriptural conception of redemption with blood and not with gold and silver (1 Pet. 1:18–19) but also the elaborate allegorization of the hyssop. Minor comparisons are numerous: God as a wall of support and protection, God as a noble lion sparing its suppliant foe, and others. In view of the charge of Mariolatry frequently leveled against pre-Reformation Catholic doctrine on redemption, the role of the Blessed Virgin receives treatment, albeit strong treatment, only in the sermon delivered on her Nativity.

Above man's head is heaven, which is conceived in biblical terms as the New Jerusalem. Its denizens, again in biblical terms, are viewed as living stones used in its construction. It is this metaphor that Fisher seems to favor throughout his ten sermons. Perhaps because of his literary principles, his intellectual discipline, and his pervading sense of order and hierarchy, he finds particularly appealing an imagery based on architectural rather than organic forms.

On man's right hand in the parable of the pit are God's benefits, which are not only personal graces but also tremendous mysteries, like the work of redemption and the guidance of the Holy Spirit. In particular there is the Church, envisioned not alone as Mount Sion but as a ship dramatically passing through tempests and tribulations to eternity. Just now this ship is delayed and foundering, as if Christ, its pilot, were asleep. On man's left hand are the countless misfortunes and dangers from which God has saved him as an individual and as a member of His Church. Behind him are lost opportunities for conversion and merit. Before him are his sin and wickedness.

And what does Fisher put within man dangling over the abyss of hell? There is "the moost stynkynge abhomynacyon of our synne, wherby the ymage of almighty god in vs is very foule defourmed. . ." This statement furnishes the groundwork for a favorite image for sin, predominantly olfactory: urine left standing in a pot, or malodorous water running through the fair garden of man's soul. In an allied metaphor, habitual sin is compared to pleasant mire from which, however, a horse cannot extricate himself easily. The reference to the deformed image of God points to another preference: that of colors or pictures on a canvas or a wall which must be done away with. A clock running askew likewise furnishes the basis of a comparison for the sinner. He is seen also as a stone which slips from the hands of the mason who is trying to put it in an honored place on a tall building — an evident variation of the living-stone motif. Finally the image of a serpent is used for sin.

The "broken boket or payle" which holds man up, of course, is his feeble and frail body, his house of clay. His soul is compared to a garden, through which a stinking stream flows. Understanding, will, and reason are conceived as the bones of the soul, with devotion as their marrow. The food for the soul must be the word of God.

As for the conversion and justification of the sinner, the three parts of penance (contrition, confession, and satisfaction) are compared to three successive and deeper erasures or scrapings of the paintings of sin; to the bud, flower, and fruit of a plant; to the pelican, owl, and sparrow; and to the dust, earth, and baking which prepare the living stone for placement in the building of the New Jerusalem. Jonah and the Prodigal Son furnish the best types for the conversion of the sinner. Lastly, the need for fear to temper the feeling of hope and confidence is illustrated through the simile of the twin millstones borrowed from St. Gregory.

In review, one might say that virtually all of Fisher's imagery and figurative language is oriented toward Holy Scripture. Either an explicitly biblical metaphor is extended, or the suggestion of a comparison is seized and expanded. Fisher's recent biographer finds that, independently of the Psalms themselves, there are approximately 160 quotations from Scripture. Of these, the Old Testament furnishes 40; the Gospels, 60; and the Epistles, 55. Besides, there are retellings of scriptural stories (David and Goliath, David and Bathsheba, the conversion of Hezekiah, the adventures of Jonah, and others) and of Christ's parables (such as the Good Samaritan, and the Prodigal Son). The Fathers and early writers are quoted relatively infrequently, e.g., Augustine, ten times; Jerome, four times; Chrysostom, three times; Gregory, twice; and Origen, twice. From the Middle Ages, Anselm is cited twice; William of Paris, twice; Bernard, once; and Aquinas, once. In addition to the apocryphal acts of the Apostles, e.g., John and Bartholomew, Fisher refers to the historical encounters between Ambrose and Theodosius, Leo and Attila, Benedict and Totila. There is surprisingly little use made of the lives and legends of the saints. Anthony, the reputed founder of monasticism, is mentioned twice; and Edward the Confessor and Louis IX of France, once.

As is to be expected from sermons explicatory of the Psalms and addressed to a popular audience, the classical references are few and obvious. There is an interesting pairing to illustrate vanished greatness: Xerxes and Caesar, Alexander and Pompey, Croesus and Crassus. The Greek references to Orpheus, Plato, Demosthenes, and Aeschines are evidently taken from Latin translations or secondary sources. The Latin passages from Vergil, Ovid, and Cicero, being familiar quotations, are hardly indicative of a profound mastery of the literature and spirit of Rome.[16]

These same comments are applicable to the funeral oration on Henry VII, delivered in May 1509. Fisher refers to Solon's remark to Croesus about the necessity of seeing the end and to Hannibal's pity for his fallen Roman enemies. Aristotle is quoted on the supreme terror of death, Seneca on the need for a good conclusion to life, and Cicero on the deceitfulness of human hope, fortune, and plans. The Greek Chrysostom is the authority for the view that separation from Christ is worse than ten thousand hells. The Latin Augustine is cited twice: once to prove that "the prayer of many can not be but herde," and again to confirm that absolutely nothing can exclude a truly repentant sinner from pardon. The only reference to the saints is to a revelation made to St. Anthony that "Onely humblenes and lowlynesse" enables one to pass through a world full of snares. As in the sermons on the Psalms, Ahab and Manasseh are held up as examples of repentant kings, peculiarly apt in the case of the first Tudor monarch.

Comparisons are few, actually three only, in this sermon on Henry VII. The hearse of the dead king probably spoke with more eloquence than any figurative language. To show the vanity of human hustle and bustle, Fisher uses the spider: "The spyder craftely spynneth her thredes and curyously weueth and Ioyneth her webbe, but cometh a lytell blast of wynde & dysapoynteth all togyder." The perils of hell, if grown familiar beforehand, will be less terrible at the hour of death — "euen as ye se these wood dogges these grete mastyues that be tyed in chaynes, vnto suche as often vysyte theym they be more gentyll & easy, but to the straungers whiche haue none acqueyntaunce of theym they ragyously & furyously gape and ryse ayenst them as they wolde deuoure them." As for the slave of sin: "Yf he wolde be at lyberte he must do as those prysoners doo that somtyme vndermyne the walles and crepe vnder them out at a strayte and narowe hole." This undermining is achieved spiritually "by true humblynge and lowynge of himselfe."

But it is not only in the use of sources and comparisons that this funeral oration is similar to the sermons on the Penitential Psalms. Actually it is a complete commentary on the whole of Vulg. Ps. 114, which Fisher labels as "the fyrst psalme of the dirige," that is, the first psalm recited at vespers in the Office of the Dead. As in the first sermon on Vulg. Ps. 37, which was skillfully adapted to the Nativity of the Blessed Virgin Mary, Fisher again displays his genius for uniting a preconceived plan with a special occasion. Finally, the construction is perhaps even more tight than in any of the sermons on the Penitential Psalms. It is a masterful manipulation of threes and fours.

First of all, there is the characteristic tripartite division into (1) the swift introduction, which states the occasion, the confession of personal unworthiness, the choice of "the first psalm of the dirge," and the overt following of classical orations in construction; (2) the body with its three points: the commendation of the dead person, the arousing of compassion, and the consolation of the bereaved; (3) the brief conclusion, which constitutes an excellent recapitulation of the whole oration.

To turn at once to the first point in the body. Fisher begins with an outstanding use of the device of preterition: "Let no man thynke that myn entent is for to prayse hym for any vayne transytory thynges of this lyfe," but he then proceeds to enumerate Henry's great virtues and successes at some length. After having shown final perseverance to be a special grace of God, he undertakes to prove that the king made a "vertuous ende and conclusyon" according to four points: (1) "a true tournynge of his soule from this wretched worlde vnto the loue of almighty god" — a conversion evident from regret for his ingratitude toward God and from a threefold promise: to reform his civil servants, to promote virtuous clerics, and to grant a general amnesty; (2) "a fast hope & confydence that he had in prayer" — a trust manifested in the daily collect *pro rege,* in thousands of masses offered during various Lents, in generous stipends to all devout men, and in alms to prisoners and needy; (3) "a stedfast byleue of god and of the sacramentes of the chyrche" — a faith made clear in the pious reception of the three sacraments of penance, the Eucharist, and anointing, as well as in his devotion to the Mother of Christ and to the crucifix; and (4) "a dylygent askynge of mercy in the tyme of mercy" — expressed externally in sighs, tears, and cries for mercy; for "there is no parte of his lyfe but a synner yf he truly call for mercy he may haue it."

What Fisher, perhaps unconsciously, is voicing in this first point is his view of the justificatory process. He is, as it were, off his guard. In addition to the ever-present grace of God for the repentant sinner, what is particularly interesting here is the reverse order of justification: love of God, which springs from hope, which in turn is born of faith, which finally issues in a confident cry for mercy and salvation. In the case of the sinner Henry VII, Fisher reveals that the "cause of this hope was the true beleue that he had in god, in his chirche & in the sacramentes therof," and that "by this maner of delynge he faythfully beleued . . . that the eere of almighty god was open vnto hym & redy to here hym crye for mercy." The process of justification for the sinner, therefore, would be the following: faith in God and His Church, confidence in prayer and almsgiving, turning to God in love with purpose of amendment, and finally, being in charity, trust in God's mercy. In consequence, what is most notable, because placed in the final and most emphatic position, is that, in spite of Church, sacraments, prayers, and alms, the sinner must throw himself ultimately on the mercy of God alone for his salvation.

The second point, a call "to haue compassyon & pyte vpon this moost noble kynge," likewise has four elements: "the sorowes of deth in his body," because sundering the natural union of body and soul is painful, and was so even to Christ; "the dredes of his Iugement in his soule," aroused by fear of separation of body and soul, arraignment before the Judge, and final sentence; "the miseryes of this worlde," despite Henry's houses, gardens, orchards, treasures, and meals; and "his sorowfull crye to god for helpe and socour," which should cause Fisher's hearers to have pity on Henry, as Hannibal did on the dead Romans, as David at the death of Saul, Absalom, and Abner, and as Christ at the tomb of Lazarus. Pity induced Ethai to cleave to the fleeing David and the "squire" to kill himself at Saul's death. A paternoster said for Henry's soul ends this section.

In the third part of his oration Fisher "comforts" his hearers: (1) "almyghty god is mercyfull," as is evident from Christ's promise of pardon to the penitent and from His role as mediator and advocate; (2) God "hath taken hym [Henry] into his custody," as He did the repentant Ahab, because Henry humbled himself before God, the sacraments, the crucifix, and his illness; (3) God "hath delyuered hym from al euylles," particularly three: everlasting death, everlasting weeping, and relapse into sin; and (4) "hens forwarde he shall contynue in the gracious fauoure of almyghty god" in the vision of the Lord face to face.

Without ever losing sight of the all-important personal relationship between Henry and God, Fisher attains pleasing variety by a shifting point of view. The sermon begins and ends, quite naturally, with the spotlight briefly on the preacher. In the body, however, attention is centered on Henry in the first part, on the hearers in the second, and upon God in the third. In a word, the movement is from earth to heaven — from the king's painful deathbed, through the crowd of compassionate subjects in St. Paul's, to "the presence of that moost blessyd countenaunce." [17]

There is the same upward movement in the funeral sermon delivered on the thirtieth day after the departure of the Lady Margaret, whose soul "was borne vp in to the countre aboue with the blessyd aungelles deputed & ordeyned to that holy mystery [*leg.* mynystery]." But there are many differences between the two sermons. The one for the Lady Margaret is less patterned than that for King Henry VII. It creates an impression of possible haste in writing, but this impression might be attributed likewise to the lesser solemnity of the occasion, as well as to the greater informality of the setting and the audience. Rather than a funeral oration united with commentary on a psalm, the Gospel (John 11:21–27) read in the requiem mass (*in die trigesimo depositionis defuncti*) furnishes the basis for a homily with application to the dead Margaret. Fisher is much more emotionally involved with her than he ever was with Henry. Her character and personality come through with greater clarity and intimacy.

It would not be true to say that the sermon for Margaret is more sincere than that for Henry. Fisher tactfully avoids hypocrisy and falsification by focusing on Henry's death rather than on his life. The opposite is true in Margaret's case. There is genuine and deep appreciation of her life, faith, and good works. Talking undoubtedly to persons who knew her well, Fisher finds the simple truth, expressed in a catalogue of her virtues and achievements, more effective than a display of learning and rhetoric. There are only one or two comparisons. The soul and the body "maye be thought to be as broder and syster." The risen body "shall be more nymble & more redy to be conuayed to ony place where the soule wolde haue it then is ony swalowe." Apocryphal hagiography furnishes two bits of information: that "the castel of bethany" belonged to the noble Martha and that the risen Lazarus, "after that he was restored to the myseryes of this lyfe agayne . . . neuer lough but was in contynuall heuynes and pensyfnesse." An apparition of St. Nicholas to Margaret is recounted. Quotations are very few. Augustine is cited on the inevitability of sorrow, fear, and peril in the world; Boethius, on the necessity of virtue as well as noble birth for true nobility; and Bonaventure, on greater merit in burying dead poor persons than in entombing Christ Himself.

As though grief and admiration could not brook bonds, the first half of the homily is as rigid as the oration for Henry VII, but the second half is much less restrained. The introduction possesses the usual clarity and trenchancy. After announcing the application of the Gospel of the mass to Margaret, it names the "thre thynges" to be shown: Margaret's likeness to Martha; Margaret's complaint to Jesus about her death; and Jesus' consoling answer. These "thynges" constitute the basis for the same tripartite division as in the oration for her son: "her prayse & commendacyon"; "our mornyng for the losse of her"; and "our conforte agayne."

Characteristically the first part — the comparison of Lady Margaret with Martha — is divided into four points: "noblenes of persone," "dyscyplyne of theyr bodyes," "orderyng of theyr soules to god," and "hospytalites kepynge & charitable dealing to their neybours." It is the first point that is most interesting in view of the controversy during the Renaissance about the nature of nobility. For the Bishop of Rochester there are four kinds or degrees of nobility: nobility of blood, which depends upon noble lineage; nobility of manners, that is, of virtue, which makes the nobly born ashamed to depart from "the vertuous maners of theyr auncetrye before"; nobility of nature, by which those humbly born "haue grete abletees of nature, to noble dedes"; and nobility of "increase," when "by maryage and affynyte of more noble persones suche as were of lesse condycyon maye encrease in hyer degre of noblenes." Margaret, of course, had all four, but Fisher expatiates particularly on her virtues and her native abilities. Here he incidentally throws light on the education of women in the late fifteenth century: Margaret had many English and French books, she translated books of devotion from French into English, and she complained about her failure to study Latin in her youth.

The other three points of the first part are developed largely by details. Margaret's "crysten dyscyplyne" was exercised in four practices: abstinence, fasting, hairshirts, and chastity. The "orderynge of her soule to god" was manifest also in four ways: frequent kneeling, sorrowful weeping, continual prayer, and constant meditation. Her "godly hospytalyte and charytable delynge to her neyghbours" embraced four classes: household servants, strangers as guests, suitors for justice, and the poor and needy.

When Fisher undertakes the second part, "the complaynynge & lamentacyon that the soule of this noble prynces myghte make for the dethe of her only body," he naturally must explain why a similar practice by David, Jeremiah, and Habakkuk in Scripture is not objectionable. The reason is that the prosperity of the wicked and the adversity of the good seem to violate God's mercy and God's justice. So, too, Sister Soul could complain about

Brother Body's death, since the service of God had occupied every part of Margaret's body: eyes, ears, tongue, legs, and hands. Her death was bemoaned by her ladies, kinswomen, gentlewomen, chambermaids, chaplains, priests, and "her other true & faythfull seruauntes." In fact, "All Englonde for her dethe had cause of wepynge" — the poor, students at Oxford and Cambridge, scholars, religious, priests, clerics, noblemen, and commons. If Christ prayed for His enemies and sinners, much more would He have mercy on "his faythfull & true seruaunt." This part ends with a paternoster that her soul be "parteyner of the euerlastynge lyfe with hym & with his blessyd saynts aboue in heuen."

The third part is concerned with consolation for Margaret's death. First of all, Sister Soul, which has "a natural desyre and appetyte to be knytte & ioyned" again with Brother Body, rejoices in the future resurrection of the body, which will then possess the gifts of impassibility, clarity, agility, and penetrability. In the meantime, what will the separated soul have? "A lyfe full of comfort, a lyfe full of ioye & pleasure, a lyfe voyde of all sorow & encombraunce." Margaret has been rescued from the ills of old age, the fear of adversity, and other evils. It would be unreasonable to bring her back from a joyous life to this miserable world. If his listener objects that "yf we were sure of this we wolde not be sory," Fisher's answer is that absolute certitude can arise only from private revelation but that "a stronge argument almost demonstratyue" can come from the fact that "this noble prynces she put her ful truste in cryste Ihesu, verayly byleuynge that he was the sone of god & came in to this worlde for the redempcyon of synners." The proof of her "full fayth in Ihesu cryste" lies in her two lectureships in divinity at Oxford and Cambridge, her preachers established at Cambridge, her Christ's College, her provision for St. John's College, her three priests at Westminster, her zeal for a crusade against Christ's enemies, her belief in the Real Presence, and her confession that "in the sacrament was conteyned cryst Ihesu the sone of god . . . in whom holly she put her truste & confydence." These and other signs beget "grete lyklyhode & almoost certayne coniecture" that she is in heaven.

Instead of his usual type of conclusion, in which he recapitulates the parts, and the points of each part, Fisher closes on a highly emotional note which is a fitting end to the third part:

"Therfore put we asyde all wepynge & teeres, & be not sad ne heuy as men withouten hope, but rather be we gladde & ioyous, & eche of us herin confort other. Alwaye praysynge & magnyfyenge the name of oure lorde, to whome be laude and honoure endlesly. Amen." [18]

In reference to this sermon, Mayor feels that Fisher's prose "has been unduly slighted. Contrast with the chaste and manly pathos of this 'honest chronicler' Bossuet's stilted panegyrics, or the fawning addresses with which Laud and Williams approached kings and their minions. Undazzled by the glare of majesty and right divine, Fisher portrays the woman, bowed down by the burden of greatness, keenly alive, as Ecclesiastes or Herodotus, to the vanity of human wishes." [19] The Lady Margaret never ceases in life and in death to be "the woman." Henry VII becomes "the man" only on his deathbed. In Fisher's sermon, as in Shakespeare's *Lear,* we have the redemption of the man Henry.

Chapter XIV

CONTROVERSIAL MANEUVERS OF THE TYRO

IN 1508–1509 the Bishop of Rochester had issued three different works: the sermons on the Penitential Psalms, the oration at Henry's funeral, and the address at the mass held a month after the Lady Margaret's death. Not until a decade later did he begin to publish again, and the same year, 1519, saw three works, all on the question of the single Magdalene (especially Mark 16:9, Luke 7:36–50, 8:2, 10:38–42, John 11:1–45, 19:25, 20:1–2, 20:11–18).[1] The delay is entirely explicable. He was very much involved in the difficulties connected with the foundation of St. John's College, at least until July 1516, not to mention his proposed trips to the Lateran Council. Then, too, he was busy with such private pursuits as the study of Greek and Hebrew and in such public affairs as the reception of Cardinal Campeggio, the synods of the clergy, and other matters. Possibly he worked desultorily at his Latin commentary on the Psalms, which remains in manuscript.

At any rate, under date of February 22, 1519, the printer Josse Bade in Paris issued *The Single Magdalene* in two forms, both in quarto, with only trifling differences between them. The two prefatory epistles are not uninteresting. The first, from *Didymus Lycoucarus,* a Paris student, to Nicholas Metcalfe, Archdeacon of Rochester and Master of St. John's College, praises Fisher's erudition, thoroughness, and chaste style. It then defends him against the indictment of carping criticism and envy by declaring that his is a pious and Christian zeal for truth, not for victory. The second letter, from the Englishman *Mauricius Durand* to the bishop and chancellor himself, refers to Fisher's lifelong devotion to virtue and learning, to his exemplary conduct and teaching, and finally to the admiration of the Parisian theologians for three qualities of his: comprehensive learning, manifest in the many sacred writers cited within a short compass; subtlety of wit, clear from the demolition of Lefèvre's arguments; and elegance of style, the greater in attainment because without the appearance of the least effort. The charge of excessively harsh treatment of the excellent Lefèvre is grounded not in hatred of Lefèvre but in a zeal for the Catholic Church, Mary Magdalene, and the Christian people committed in a special way to Fisher's wisdom.

The Single Magdalene is divided into three books. The introduction to the whole treatise is given at the beginning of Book I; the conclusion, which takes the novel form of a refutation of Clichtove's preface to the second edition of Lefèvre's disquisition, is found at the end of Book III.

The introduction shows Fisher at his best. First, all the circumstances are given: the presentation to Fisher by Bishop Poncher of Paris of a copy of the second edition of Lefèvre's *Disquisition on Mary Magdalene;* his previous reading of the book with misgivings allayed by Lefèvre's reputation; and a reexamination of the arguments, together with an exhaustive study of the scriptural texts. Secondly, Fisher voices his objection to Lefèvre's contempt for recent commentators, popular preachers, and all post-Ambrosian Fathers, even Gregory, Augustine, Bede, and Bernard. Thirdly, he lists the dire consequences of the opinion: the recantation of preachers, the scruples of many, the distrust of histories, and the suspicion cast upon Mother Church which had thought and had sung the opposite for centuries. Finally, he announces his purpose: to prove the weakness of Lefèvre's arguments and the inconsistency of his authorities (Book I), to use the Gospels to establish the common opinion of the whole Church (Book II), and to confirm this opinion by citing many and far from contemptible authorities (Book III).

Without a transitional word except "furthermore" (*porro*), Fisher then launches into Book I with a statement of his procedure: he will quote Lefèvre verbatim and follow each quotation with a refutation, letting the reader decide for himself whether Lefèvre's proof is more solid or Fisher's demolition more effective. His own arguments may be more prolix but will never be obscure: the reader wants clarity above all else. Thus, at the very beginning of his controversial period, Fisher reveals his main weakness, prolixity, and his principal virtue, clarity. Actually, for good reasons, there is verbatim citation of less than one half of Lefèvre.[2] Since our primary concern is with method, there is little reason for going into specific and hence multiple details. Many of them have already been discussed in previous chapters, but, at the risk of some repetition, they will be touched on now so that they can be seen in their proper context.

Fisher begins his discussion with a dilemma: either the Scriptures are so clear that they need no commentator or interpreter, or they are not. If they are clear, why the clash of opinions? If they are not, to whom should one turn for authentic interpretation but to the authorities contemned by Lefèvre: first, Sovereign Pontiffs; then, orthodox Fathers and writers; and, last, popular preachers. As for the Fathers, Augustine is to be preferred over Ambrose because the former corrected the latter's errors and was supremely assiduous in reconciling apparent contradictions in the Evangelists. In the same way, the four Latin Fathers are to be followed more than the Greek in spite of their antiquity, their proximity to apostolic times, their erudition and eloquence, and their knowledge of scriptural languages, because the Greeks had erred on such points as the fire of purgatory, leavened bread, and the procession of the Holy Spirit. Nevertheless, the Bishop of Rochester vindicates Chrysostom by quoting the whole passage on Mary from which Lefèvre has taken only a fragment. Fisher does not hesitate to use the Greek κώμη to explain the Latin *castellum* (e.g., Luke 10:38) as meaning a village or hamlet, not a fortified place.

Nor does Fisher scruple to use irony, as when he declares that the *energia,* or force, of the Gospel was hidden from Augustine, Gregory, Leo, Bede, Rabanus, Bernard, Anselm, Remi, and all the other famous theologians and was understood only by Lefèvre with a few associates. He appeals to Cassian on the whole matter of diabolic possession. In summary fashion, at the very end of Book I, after declaring that Lefèvre's arguments are ineffective, his authorities inconsistent, and his conjectures about the Gospel invalid, Fisher announces that he will now proceed to establish the common opinion of the whole Church.

At the beginning of Book II, Fisher enunciates the principle that whoever espouses a new view or revives an old one must prove it to the hilt; otherwise the prevailing common opinion must be accepted. Moreover, Mary Magdalene is an inspiration to sinners like Fisher himself, who, like Albert the Great, here indulges in a bit of allegory: Of the two great luminaries placed by Moses in the sky, the greater over the day is the Blessed Virgin Mary, and the lesser over the night is Mary Magdalene. On Easter, too, the Church compares the Magdalene with Christ's Mother (in the sequence *Mane prima sabbati*). In an *Epilogus* Lefèvre had enumerated, cited, and argued from all the pertinent scriptural texts. The verbatim repetition of Lefèvre's text, Fisher realizes, would be otiose. Instead, for ready reference, he quotes in order the five relevant passages from Matthew, the five from Mark, the six from Luke, and the five from John. After each passage he names the person — Martha's sister for example — to whom Lefèvre applies the passage. Fisher then launches into an elaborately yet closely reasoned exegesis, which takes up several pages. At the end of Book II, he confidently asserts that the four Gospels, properly reconciled, testify to a single Magdalene and that the only authorities he has employed are Lefèvre's own, and these he has succeeded in turning against Lefèvre. Of course, there are many other authorities, Fisher adds, but he has transferred them to Book III on purpose (*consulto*).

A statement at the beginning of Book III confirms the view that Fisher's construction is not haphazard but deliberate. He has postponed citations from other sources to prevent Book II from becoming too bulky. To keep Book III within bounds, he opts for great selectivity. At first the reader suspects that Fisher is going to use the argument from prescription, which he is to favor later. Rather, his argument is, as it were, from the classes of men, represented most often by pairs. No matter what class Lefèvre objects to, some other class can be found to confirm the unicity of the Magdalene.

In view of our concern with cultural attitudes at this time, what is particularly engrossing here is the nature of the general objection against each class. If Lefèvre should object to Albert, surnamed the Great on account of the breadth of his knowledge, and to Thomas, labeled the Flower of Theology, because they are two Schoolmen (*disputatores, disceptatores*), Fisher names two writers given more directly to Scripture than to questions (*quaestiones*): Simon of Cascia or Cassia (d. 1348), author of *De gestis Christi,* and Ubertino of Casale (d. *ca.* 1340), author of *Arbor vitae crucifixae Iesu.* If their style is rather crude (*incultior*), let Lefèvre listen to Druthmarus (Christian de Stavelot, fl. 850–900) and to Bede (d. 735), both of whom were learned in Latin and Greek literature. If Lefèvre gives them no credence, let him not contemn the two beginners of the University of Paris: Alcuin (d. 804) and Rabanus (d. 856). If Lefèvre prefers the saints, Fisher could produce a great many, of which let two suffice: St. Anselm and St. Bernard.

But Lefèvre insists upon exegetes who know the force (*energia*) of the Gospels — and who, Fisher ironically adds, therefore favor Lefèvre's opinion. The Bishop of Rochester then launches into a magnificent eulogy of the Bishop of Hippo as a scriptural commentator. Yet Augustine's interpretation is different from Lefèvre's. Augustine's view is held by the many who composed harmonies and then explained them with voluminous commentaries — to name only two: Zachary of Besançon (d. *ca.* 1157) and Clement of Gloucester, canon regular of Llanthony (d. *ca.* 1170). As for Lefèvre's authorities (Origen, Chrysostom, and Ambrose), their slips, not to call them mistakes, were detected and corrected by Augustine.

After re-establishing the credit of Augustine, Fisher proceeds to cite some of the Greeks whom Lefèvre extols over the Latins. Fisher appeals to Eusebius, Ammonius, Gregory of Nazianzus, Theophilus, and Severianus. The Christian poets, Juvencus and Proba, also testify to the one Magdalene. If Lefèvre is still unmoved, let the cardinals come forth as witnesses: Nicholas of Cusa (d. 1464), whom Lefèvre himself calls "both a most eminent doctor and indisputably a most distinguished scholar in every branch of knowledge"; and Marco Vigerio Cardinal della Rovere (d. 1516), formerly Bishop of Senigallia and later Bishop of Palestrina, author of *Decachordum christianum,* "a man of both the greatest learning and the greatest eloquence." Fisher quotes him at great length (*prolixius*) because he confirms the popular lives of Mary, Martha, and Lazarus — as does another humanist who is "not a careless investigator of such matters." This is Petrarch, who alludes to Mary's flight to Marseilles in his *Solitary Life* (Bk. II, Tract. V, Chap. I) and who hung verses at her tomb, of which thirty-six are quoted here.

If cardinals will not satisfy Lefèvre, there are the Supreme Pontiffs. At this point no stronger words could possibly be used about the power of the pope to settle questions concerning the Gospel. Otherwise the lot of Christians would be worse than that of the Jews, who were commanded to resort to their priests and to accept their decisions under penalty of death. "For whoever refuses to obey the decisions of these [Sovereign Pontiffs] deserves to suffer death with greater justice than he who disobeyed the pontiffs of the synagogue." He quotes in particular Leo the Great and Gregory the Great. It is the latter whom he defends at great length against Lefèvre's slurs. If Lefèvre will not accept papal authority, Fisher will turn to private revelations: the disclosures made by Christ to Bridget of Sweden (d. 1373) and the apparition of Magdalene to Vincent of Beauvais (d. *ca.* 1264), who recorded her life and miracles. If neither miracles nor revelations nor popes can sway Lefèvre, he is stiff-necked indeed.

And he is even more stiff-necked if he refuses to believe the Church. The unicity of the Magdalene is the common opinion, not only of the masses, as Lefèvre claims, but also of all popes and cardinals, archbishops and bishops, that is, of the whole Church. If the Church called Universal is narrowed down to Christians who learn the truth from Lefèvre, it will be a small Church indeed, consisting of only Lefèvre and a few others. Neither does Origen nor Chrysostom nor Jerome nor Ambrose hold exactly the same as Lefèvre, and consequently they would be excluded from his Church. If Fisher wished to be frivolous in drawing inferences according to Lefèvre's method, he could show Origen to hold four Magdalenes! It was this jesting ("too repetitious and, as seemed to many, too stinging") about Lefèvre's church which drew Erasmus' criticism in a letter to Fisher almost a year later.

It would be better for Lefèvre to think with the Church, whose mind is known not only through explicit or formal pronouncement but also through implicit or tacit opinion, as the married layman, John Francis Pico della Mirandola, points out. In case of dispute in regard to interpretation of the Gospels, who can be judge other than the Church or the Supreme Pontiff? But the Gospels are clear and consistent on the single Magdalene.

The conclusion to Fisher's work takes mainly the form of a refutation of Josse Clichtove's introductory epistle to the second edition of Lefèvre's disquisition. Clichtove brings Lefèvre no support, claims Fisher. He disposes of Clichtove's arguments from Irenaeus and Origen, defends Gregory the Great's use of *rationale animal* for angel, and censures Clichtove for falsifying the position of the great Carmelite poet Mantuan (1448–1516) on the question. To put Mantuan's words in context, he quotes the whole relatively long poem on Mary Magdalene because "learned and elegant and pertinent to our matter." The last brief paragraph does not summarize the three books but stresses that as a result there need be no uneasiness as to who is being venerated under the name of the Magdalene — to whom the author dedicates himself and his work.[3]

The *Single Magdalene* seems heavy-handed in its treatment of Lefèvre and his disquisition. Perhaps too impressed by his adversary's great reputation, or too anxious to produce an overwhelming case in his first publishing venture on the Continent, or perhaps lacking perspective because of the fury of the fray, the Bishop of Rochester had loosed a grand barrage of artillery in a minor skirmish. His writing, in a sense, exemplifies what he terms a result of the Scholastic discipline: the ability not only to state a position but to prove and defend it to the limit. He shows better control of both content and style in his second work on the Magdalene, published certainly within six months of *The Single Magdalene,* that is, *The Destruction of Clichtove's Bulwark.* This writing is not included in Fisher's *Opera omnia* of 1597.

At the end of *The Single Magdalene,* Fisher had discounted the attempt of Clichtove's prefatory letter to bolster Lefèvre's position. But Clichtove did much more to support his former teacher. He entered full-panoplied into the battle with his *Defense of the Disquisition on the Magdalene,* an answer not to Fisher's relatively late criticism (February 22, 1519) but to Marc de Grandval, one of Lefèvre's French opponents. As often happens, the controversy moves from concentration on a particular question to a discussion of the principles and assumptions of the disputing parties. Not unexpectedly Clichtove as a theologian states his in the form of eight "Suppositions" (*Suppositiones*). The debate becomes less scriptural and more theological, with much talk about theological method by the Cambridge theologian, Fisher, and the Paris theologian, Clichtove. For example, the issue of academic freedom — really theological freedom — comes in for its share of discussion. Even though the present-day reader discounts the heavy argument about a disputable and disputed scriptural question, *The Destruction of Clichtove's Bulwark* is not without interest because of these contributions, as well as indirect disclosures on more important matters, treated in previous chapters.

In a one-page prefatory epistle, the Bishop of Rochester exhorts the devotees of the single Magdalene not to waver in the least. He summarizes his arguments here, although not in the order pursued in the work proper. But, *if* he has placed them climactically, the alignment is not without significance in regard to Fisher's hierarchy of values: the paucity and dissension of their opponents, the multitude and unanimity of their advocates, the authority of the Chair of Peter, the consent of the whole Church, the witness of the four Evangelists, the patronage of the Magdalene, and Christ's own fight for His beloved Magdalene by miracles and revelations. This bit of epistolary rhetoric contains, interestingly enough, the only outstanding metaphor in the work. Our adversaries are in peril: "We ride in the harbor, and our ship, as the saying goes, is fastened by two anchors." In fact, the clause, "as the saying goes," furnishes the major device in the *Destruction,* that is, the use of the Latin adage or proverb. Examples are: "extra omnem (quod aiunt) telorum iactum, perinde acsi intra moenia Semiramidis essent constituti," "quam si de lana caprina" (Hor. *Ep.* 1.18.15), "(quod aiunt) nodum in sirpo quaerens" (Plaut. *Men.* 2.1.22, Ter. *And.* 5.4.38), "testudo leporem, quod in prouerbio dicitur, ante preuerterit, quam id efficient," and "omne verum, omni vero conuenit." The major classical reference is to Xenocrates' conversion of the dissolute Phaedo and Polemo, the first of whom was to figure as the narrator of Socrates' death, the second to succeed Xenocrates as head of the Old Academy.[4]

The *Destruction* as a whole displays Fisher's usual structural skill. A lengthy introduction is succeeded by a body consisting of three parts: (1) the theoretical evaluation of Clichtove's eight

Suppositions, (2) the practical application of the Suppositions to a special scriptural problem, and (3) the establishment of eight Truths in favor of the single Magdalene. The summary of the third part serves also as the conclusion to the whole work except for a final ten-word doxology.

Fisher's relatively full introduction begins bluntly with the avowal that Lefèvre's theory had seemed to be put forth not as exploratory but as positive. This view had been strengthened by three factors: Poncher's letters and messages,[5] Lefèvre's opening and forthright proposition in his *Disquisition,* and the absence of the customary statement that the writer was submitting his opinion to the judgment of the Apostolic See or the whole Church. For his part, Clichtove had set up eight unassailable Suppositions, as he thought, as a wall of defense for the view of Lefèvre and his followers. Accordingly, Fisher will essay three things: (1) to overthrow Clichtove's foundations; (2) to show that, even if granted, they do not issue in Clichtove's conclusions; and (3) to state and prove the single Magdalene's case positively.

In the first, the overthrow of Clichtove's foundations, the eight Suppositions are not so much destroyed as subjected to distinctions which water away all their strength and application to the case of Mary Magdalene. The Suppositions, pared to the bone, need only be enumerated here: (1) the problem of one or more Magdalenes is one of history, not of faith — a Supposition which leads Fisher to state his view on the object of faith; (2) contemporaries are the best historians; (3) succeeding writers closer to the event in time are next to be trusted; (4) of the most recent writers, those who give their reasons, especially scriptural, are superior to mere narrators of the events; (5) passages dealing expressly with the subject are to be preferred to passing comments — a Supposition for which Fisher asks Clichtove's meaning; (6) if an author gives varied or contradictory opinions, that opinion is the stronger which accords best with reason and the ancients; (7) apocrypha and anonyma that are contrary to reason and the older writers have no weight, and neither has a custom introduced through them; and (8) "the Church does not prohibit in doubtful matters inquiry into the truth through discussion, nor is the usage of the Church hurt by those who in such discussion do not wish to extirpate it but who wish to keep it, and openly declare so, as long as the Church persists in that usage." [6]

The eighth Supposition, in which Fisher sees three parts, is given full treatment and will serve, therefore, as an illustration of Fisher's similar handling of the other Suppositions. First, the Church never forbids free investigation and discussion of the truth as long as the truth shines brighter and not darker as a result. The case is different if the writer tries to establish an opinion contrary to the usage of the entire Church, especially by ignoring unfavorable statements and by manipulating sources. Secondly, the usage of the Church *de facto* is hurt. A very great part of the Church, which is weak and inconstant in faith and too inclined to novelties, will believe that the Church has long erred; hence scandals, diminution of papal authority, and complete loss of faith. Thirdly, Lefèvre's protest against extirpation of the Church's usage is meaningless: why does he instruct the common people to venerate three Marys instead of one Magdalene? His doctrine is the more insidious because seemingly proved through scriptural texts by an author of apparently upright life.

The second part of the *Destruction* takes the form of a logical *tour de force:* Fisher will grant Clichtove his eight Suppositions and still prove that his conclusion on the Magdalene is *non sequitur.* With a true artist's instinct, Fisher the polemicist realizes that his reader is now full to the ears with the Magdalene, and therefore decides upon variety through an oblique or flanking tactic. He will use as a specimen a closely parallel case, Paul's reproof of Peter (Gal. 2:11). The older Jerome regards it as simulated reprehension, the younger Augustine as real upbraiding. If Lefèvre had consistently and logically followed Clichtove's Suppositions, he should have favored Jerome's view and not Augustine's, as he actually did. What was his reason, asks Fisher? It could not have been the agreement of the ancients, or the usage of the Church, or miracles and revelations — because all these favor the single Magdalene whom he rejects! It could have been nothing else than Augustine's greater insight and better reasoning. If Augustine could succeed in winning Lefèvre's assent in the case of Peter's real reprehension by Paul, why not in the problem of the single Magdalene?

The second part stands in attitude midway between the negative first part and the positive third part. The latter, constituting more than two thirds of the *Destruction,* again reveals Fisher's usual emphasis on the positive and constructive. Without ulterior motive he terms his principles Truths to distinguish them from Clichtove's Suppositions. The Truths are eight in number.

According to Truth 1, none of Lefèvre's ancients (Theophilus, Origen, Chrysostom, Ambrose, Jerome) agrees with him *in toto,* very few in part. According to Truth 2, Lefèvre's authorities, even if they avoid violent clashing, disagree among themselves in detail. Truth 3 asserts that all but a few Fathers attribute to the one Magdalene what Lefèvre and Clichtove distribute among three. Here Thomas Aquinas, Albert the Great, and Nicholas of Lyra are cited. And, Fisher continues, whereas Jerome and Ambrose say contrary things, Augustine is always consistent — in spite of Clichtove's ignoble attempt to show otherwise. Here Fisher allows himself a rare personal reference: "As for me, assuredly I call God as witness that I have never read in Augustine a single word relating to this matter, by which he should be judged self-contradictory." After a strong defense of Gregory the Great, in the course of which he mentions the errors of Ambrose, Chrysostom, and Origen, the section closes with the declaration that Catholics for more than a thousand years after Augustine had been all but unanimous on the single Magdalene.

Truth 4, the testimony of history, interestingly relies also upon works of art, "sculptured and painted . . . in metal and stone . . . in windows and on walls." Such is the Mausoleum, erected by St. Maximinus *apud Aquensem ecclesiam* and described by *Gislebertus* and *Sigibertus.* The Magdalene's cave, too, was visited by Petrarch. Historical writers mentioned by name are Marcus Antonius Sabellicus, Jacobus Bergomensis, Vincent of Beauvais, Rodulphus Marrhensis, Jacobus de Voragine, Antoninus of Florence, and, heavy blow! Lefèvre himself.

The evidence of miracles is offered in Truth 5. If the adversaries exclaim that no miracles can make them believe against the word of the Gospel, Fisher's answer is that hitherto they have offered nothing but trivial conjectures and negative arguments — and nothing is weaker than the latter. Yet Fisher spends an unconscionable amount of time, space, and effort in refuting them. Truth 6 depends upon private revelations, for whose credibility are required the holy life of the narrator, examination by learned and holy men, and approbation by the Supreme Pontiff. Fisher therefore rejects the revelations of the Amadeus brought forth by Clichtove and turns to his own advantage those of Elizabeth, also appealed to by Clichtove. He himself stresses the revelations of the mystics Bridget of Sweden and Mechtilde. At the end he disposes of six additional scriptural conjectures by Clichtove.

Truth 7 proves at great length that the holy Gospel itself in many passages imparts the greatest strength to the common opinion of the Church. For example, only the existence of a single Magdalene actually verifies Christ's prophecy that His anointer's deed, "wherever in the whole world this gospel is preached . . . shall be told in memory of her" (Matt. 26:13).

Finally, Truth 8 establishes the unicity of the Magdalene from the general consent of the whole Church. Of the three phases of this general consent, the first is the authority of the Supreme Pontiff, attested to by Jerome and Bernard. The second phase is Roman usage, evident in the office of July 22 for St. Mary Magdalene, and in the washing of feet held in her memory on the Saturday before Palm Sunday, described by Ludolph the Carthusian, *Almarius,* and *Episcopus Minatensis.* The case produced by Clichtove, that of the three husbands and three daughters of Anne, the mother of the Blessed Virgin Mary, is different from that of the single Magdalene in every respect. As for the third phase, the general consent of the Church can be either explicit or tacit. For example, it is not allowable or safe to go now against the general but tacit agreement of the whole Church on the Assumption of the Blessed Virgin. The Church has changed its opinion on the Immaculate Conception, the Assumption, and the veneration of images; but the adversaries can never prove such a change on the single Magdalene.

The brief conclusion satisfies for this third part as well as for the whole. Truth always jibes with truth. The truth of the Fathers, the truth of history, the truth of miracles, the truth of revelations, the truth of the Gospels, the testimonies of the popes, the usage of the Roman Church, and the consent of the whole Catholic Church conspire in favor of the single Magdalene. Its adversaries agree completely neither with themselves nor with their authorities.[7]

To show just how complete is the disagreement of the adversaries appears to be the main point of Fisher's next book, *The Confutation of Lefèvre's Second Disquisition,* published in Paris on September 3, 1519. *De tribus et unica Magdalena disceptatio secunda,* addressed by Lefèvre to Bishop Briçonnet, had just appeared. Bishop Fisher dedicated his own work to Cardinal Campeggio. According to the prefatory letter, the Cardinal, having asked Fisher about the Magdalene, had received the answer that there were two — that is, Lefèvre's opinion, adopted because of his singular learning and uprightness. But after Bishop Poncher had warned him, Fisher had studied both Scripture and authorities only to discover that Lefèvre had gone entirely contrary to both the Church's usage and Christ's prophecy. The dedication to Campeggio is intended to answer his original question and to arouse him and other prelates to action against Lefèvre's view lest it grow stronger and breed new troubles. Meanwhile, Fisher declares, let the adversaries repent lest they involve themselves in inextricable straits. This warning gives the impression of a veiled threat and, perhaps for the first time in Fisher's work, seems to hint at means other than peaceful persuasion — not physical means like the prison or the stake, but authoritative, such as condemnation by a theological faculty or censure by the Church.

The introduction to the *Confutation* is long and is closely linked to the *Destruction.* After quoting Jerome's dictum that truth can get into trouble but cannot be vanquished, he first repeats, from the *Destruction,* the axiom that the truth always jibes with truth and then proceeds to detail thirteen places where Lefèvre's *Second Disquisition* disagrees with his first *Disquisition* and Clichtove's *Defense.* He expresses great indignation at their distortion of Scripture. Both men were formerly most dear to him for their scholarship and virtue, and there is still hope for their repentance. Fisher reveals his decision to combat only those propositions in Lefèvre's *Second Disquisition* markedly contrary to the unicity of the Magdalene. But he will first prefix twelve Suppositions — Clichtove's term! — of which the first seven will solve Lefèvre's arguments from the Gospels; the eighth will provide for future interpretation; the ninth to eleventh will prove a single Magdalene; and the twelfth will totally demolish Lefèvre's opinion.

The statement and the proof of the twelve Suppositions actually constitute the first part of the body of the *Confutation.* The Suppositions are briefly these: (1) no Evangelist always follows the chronological order; (2) the domicile of the three women (who, for brevity's sake, will be called the Prostitute, the Demoniac, and Martha's sister) is not evident; (3) the time of the Magdalene's exorcism is not clear; (4) probably the Prostitute was forgiven before her entrance into Simon's house; (5) all three loved Christ without rival; (6) that these women had always accompanied Christ is more probable than the contrary; (7) that Martha's sister had once been a Prostitute and a Demoniac is not repugnant to the Gospels in any way; (8) failure to interpret the Gospels tactfully (*ciuiliter*) involves one in many contradictions and in the multiplication of persons and events; (9) it is reasonable to expect in the Gospels an example of a converted lecher rising to the highest virtue; (10) many details agree in pointing toward the oneness of the woman; (11) numerous passages conspire to prove most overtly her oneness, whereas none opposes it; and (12) "no one must be given credence against the long accepted as well as deeply confirmed usage of the Church unless he produces invincible testimony from the Scriptures or an absolutely unanswerable reason." The last is the surest protection against the procedure of heretics, as is evident from the past.

Fisher passes from these twelve Suppositions to the second part of the body of his *Confutation,* which is liberally sprinkled with quotations from Lefèvre's work. It is a closely reasoned refutation of six of the fifty-five Propositions set forth by Lefèvre. Since there is little to lend relief or novelty, it is necessary only to list them: (18) "It is more likely that Mary Magdalene was absent than present when the women held the Lord's feet"; (19) "This Mary Magdalene is not Mary, the sister of Martha," in the refutation of which Fisher refers to various martyrologies; (20) "Mary Magdalene of the Gospels is one"; (23) "Mary Magdalene of the Gospels was not that sinner in the city," in the discussion of which Fisher finds Lèfevre's attitude less that of a discussant than of a propagandist; (24) "Mary, the sister of Martha, was not that public sinner in the city" — where Fisher engages in an insinuation of heresy; and (25) "There are three women, as rightly proposes Theophilus, sixth Bishop of Antioch after Peter, a contemporary in time with the disciples: Mary Magdalene, Mary the sister of Martha, and the sinner described by Luke." As for the last Proposition, after claiming that Lefèvre quotes Theophilus — but in a mutilated fashion — from Aquinas' *Catena aurea,* Fisher demolishes both Lefèvre and his Theophilus. In concluding this part, he states that only six from that collection of Lefèvre's Propositions have seemed important enough to merit special refutation, all the others depending on them or being offensive to the doctrine of the Church.

The brief ending to the whole *Confutation* acts as a coda to Fisher's three works on the Magdalene. In Fisher's view, *The Single Magdalene* disposed of the patristic authorities on whom Lefèvre heavily relied in his first *Disquisition;* the *Confutation* demonstrated the weakness of the scriptural arguments to which he resorted in his *Second Disquisition;* and the *Destruction of Clichtove's Bulwark* offered manifold proofs for the Church's opinion of only one Magdalene. There is no concluding prayer of praise in the *Confutation* as in the two previous works.

In general, the *Confutation* seems more hurriedly and less carefully written than either of his earlier productions. The controversy has now descended to hand-to-hand fighting on particular points. The Bishop of Rochester is being impelled by a sense of duty, from which joy of performance has departed. He creates the impression of weariness — and of relief that this is the last battle. The feeling for structure has not left him, but it is not sharply and explicitly defined as in the previous works. The style, as always, is at least adequate and clear, but it lacks variety and power. From the *Destruction of Clichtove's Bulwark,* Fisher repeats the instance of Xenocrates and his two converts, Phaedo and Polemo. He quotes Pliny's famous witticism on physicians: "nostris videlicet periculis discunt, & per experimenta mortes agunt." His sole striking comparison centers about the following of Christ by the public sinner after her forgiveness: "If a starving dog, shown a crust of bread, is not driven off from following, how could this most hungry woman, having tasted the bread of the word of God, be driven off? If iron, when it feels the power of the magnet, is not torn away from it, how could this woman, having received grace of such power from Christ, be torn away?" Fisher's principal rhetorical device, however, remains the Latin adage, exemplified in such phrases as "tota . . . aberrasse via" (twice), "Satius est initiis mederi, quam fini," "conniuentibus oculis," "vela retrorsum vertit," "Talpa . . . caecior," "nodum . . . Herculanum," and "Mendacem oportet bene memorem esse." [8]

In view of this analysis, it is surprising to hear Erasmus appraising the style of the *Confutation* as more polished (and less peevish) than that of *The Single Magdalene.* The latter work, it will be recalled, was suspected to be that of Erasmus, who disclaimed any marked similarity in style — or even in erudition, in which Fisher was vastly superior. Thomas More's statement about Fisher's Erasmian style and argumentative skill is usually applied to these works on the Magdalene.[9]

By the autumn of 1519, therefore, the Bishop of Rochester had not only undergone his ordeal by fire and won his spurs. His was no single battle but a whole campaign. He had entered the war on the Magdalene as a tyro, excessively eager and anxious, if one is to judge from content and style of *The Single Magdalene.* He left it as a seasoned veteran, fully aware of the hazard, difficulty, and fatigue of conflict.

Chapter XV

PEACE BETWEEN WARS: PRAYER, HEAVEN, AND JUSTICE

AFTER the publication of the *Confutation of Lefèvre's Second Disquisition* in September 1519, Fisher entered upon a short period of relative peace, in which *Two Sermons* (pub. 1532) and the *Treatise on Prayer* (Lat. pub. 1576) might have been written. But the peace was as deceptive as that of the magnificent Field of Cloth of Gold (1520) at which he was in attendance on Queen Catherine and of which he left a description in the first of the *Two Sermons*. The debate with Lefèvre and Clichtove might be said to be a parliamentary struggle since both adversaries were Catholic in their assumptions, whereas the conflict with Luther and Oecolampadius was to be more of a bitter civil war between Christians under the two standards of Catholicism and Protestantism.

Yet it is a pleasure to turn even for a while from the controversialist and apologist to the bishop and pastor of souls. Fisher, of course, remains loyal to the principles espoused in the works on the Magdalene, particularly respect for ecclesiastical authority. At least three times during his exaltation of mental and affective prayer, he cautions the reader against mistaking his remarks as reflecting on the vocal prayers, e.g., the breviary, approved by the Church. Fortunately, however, he does not have to manipulate his materials with an eye to the argumentation or criticism of opponents. He can treat his topic according to the logic of its own thought and the demands of its own style. The *Confutation of Lefèvre's Second Disquisition* was poorly organized in comparison with earlier works, undoubtedly because of speed for one reason; but the *Treatise on Prayer* has a certain utilitarian artistry of its own, like that of a vase or a chalice — it is carefully yet unobtrusively wrought.

One might note another connection, but by way of contrast, with the Magdalenian writings. About the veneration or the intercession of the saints, even of Mary Magdalene, there is not a word in *Prayer*. Instead, Fisher concentrates upon the relationship between only two persons: God and the individual Christian. To their union all else, even the Scripture and even Christ's humanity, is either an obstacle or a means.

What is of particular theological interest is the absoluteness of the Christian's dependence upon God and His grace — a truth expressed through striking figures, some of which Fisher had already used in different form. The first sermon on Vulg. Ps. 50, for example, had portrayed man as suspended above a pit of cruel beasts in "a broken boket or payle whiche sholde hange by a small corde, stayed and holden vp onely by the handes of hym, to whome I haue behaued myselfe as an enemye and aduersarye." Without any mention of an inimical relationship, *Prayer* now declares: "Euery one of vs remayneth in no better estate, then as yf he dyd hange in a basket ouer a great deepe pit, borne vp and sustayned by a corde in the hande of an other man. . ." A variation of this theme based upon Pseudo-Dionysius sees the cord as prayer: "Our prayer is lyke vnto a certaine corde or chayne of golde, let down from Heauen, with the which we labour to drawe almightie God vnto vs, when in deede we be therewith drawen by hym." [1] The longing of the Christian to escape from sin and temptation into the freedom of grace as from a prison is found both in the funeral sermon for Henry VII and in the treatise on prayer.[2]

In the second sermon on Vulg. Ps. 101, the Church had been symbolized as a ship sailing through tempests to its ardently desired haven. In the tract on prayer, vocal prayer is described as a ship which is abandoned after bringing the praying Christian to the inward prayer of the heart.[3] The favorite comparison of God and His grace to the sun and its influence, which was first seen in the sermon on Vulg. Ps. 6, occurs also toward the end of *Prayer:* "For lyke as the sonne doth euery way disperse and sprede abrode the beames of his lyght, euen so is God redye on euery syde, to powre forth vpon vs the sweetenes of his grace and goodnes. . ." [4]

Naturally there are new comparisons. In the performance of any good work, man is no more in his cooperation with God than "the hammer is in the hande of the Smyth." To illustrate the persistence or virtuality of attention at prayer, Fisher uses a stone cast through the air which continues even though the throwing hand no longer accompanies it. The spiritual exercise of prayer is compared to the physical exercise of walking: both finally result in warmth and pleasure.[5]

The dominant metaphor, however, is medical. To the objection that prayer is useless because of God's foreknowledge, Fisher answers that this fact does not keep us from availing ourselves of the physician's counsels and prescriptions. Such an argument, asserts Fisher, would mean also the ruin of farming and all other human occupations and activities. Like a good physician, moreover, God may postpone the gift of spiritual sweetness until a more opportune time. Finally, prayer is like medicine with respect to dosage and length of treatment: "For lyke as no medicine is ministred to the sicke man, in any greater quantitie than is thought sufficient to the ease and recouery of the pacient, which is thende of phisicke: euen so ought our prayer to be of so great length, as may suffise for the obteynyng the nexte end therof . . . the feruencie of christian charitie, which is vndoubtedlye the health of our soules." [6]

The treatise is relatively sparing in its use of examples. Cornelius the centurion is held up to show the efficacy of prayers and alms; and Anna, the mother of Samuel, to illustrate the power of wordless prayer from the heart. As Chrysostom explains, prayer may be said anywhere — "as Saint Paul prayed in prison, Esayas in the myre or durt, Ezechias turnyng him selfe in his bedde towardes the wall, Daniell in the denne of the Lions, Jonas in the bellye of the Whale, the thiefe on the crosse, and yet were they harde in few wordes, of God." [7]

As usual when Fisher has time to spend on composition, the *Treatise on Prayer* is neatly structured. It is well to remember that he gives us, not the process, but the product, of his profound analysis, which he aims to present in its most readily acceptable form. Hence his introduction, for example, announces that his intention of revealing the sweetness of prayer will be accomplished by showing its necessity, its profitableness, and its method. Since no man can carry out the precept of praying always by continually engaging in actual prayer, the precept must be conceived as being fulfilled in a threefold extension of prayer: the performance of charitable works like almsgiving; the intention of doing all things for the divine glory; and the constant desire for God's grace, presence, and vision.[8]

The necessity for prayer is proved in the first part by four Reasons (*Rationes*): the dependence of helpless, wretched man on the benign God's constant, indispensable assistance; the function of prayer, with good works, as one of the two principal means to man's beatitude (prayer securing the good life which leads to eternal glory); Christ's exhortation to pray always and His promise to grant every petition; and the need for perseverance in justice by making amends for past sins and by taking precautions against every future fall from grace. Under the third Reason, Fisher utters a long lament over the condition of contemporary Christians and Church — "almoste none other thyng nowe lefte in the Churche of Christ, but eyther manyfest iniquitie, or counterfeit holynes."

The second section, on the three fruits of prayer, is prefaced by a piece of advice: let the man who claims that if he tasted its sweetness he could pray oftener keep on exercising himself in prayer until he warms up to it. The first fruit is merit, for which man must be in the state of grace, or charity, but this is easy to attain. The second is the answer to one's request, which is dependent upon three conditions: absolute humility, furtherance of salvation, and relevance to oneself.[9] The third is spiritual sweetness, to obtain which a Christian needs not only charity and humility but also attentiveness and perseverance.[10] To get into the spirit, the exercitant might try the expedients used by the Fathers: genuflection, prostration, holding their arms in the form of a cross, raising their hands to heaven, sitting solitary, or singing a psalm or hymn. At any rate, it is God Himself who constitutes the sweetness of prayer. The conclusion enumerates six means: humility of soul, silence of tongue, seeing God present, remembrance of Christ's incarnation and death, thought of heavenly glory, and flight from vain thoughts.

The third and last section asks three questions on the method of prayer. The first is answered by declaring that attention to the mere words can often work against the contemplation and love of God which is the purpose for which canonical hours were originally instituted; that attention to the meaning can help as a temporary means; and that the ideal remains immediate union with the Creator Himself. To that ideal, Scripture can help but it cannot constitute the end because it too is merely a creature. The same is true of Christ's incarnation, suffering, death, and glory; but since Christ is also true God, the exercitant can rise from a corporeal remembrance of His humanity to a spiritual contemplation of His divinity. On the other hand, the sweetness tasted in God alone overflows into man's flesh, which too feels delight.

The response to the second question is that one should remain at prayer just long enough to secure its goal — "the feruencie of christian charitie." As soon as the fervor begins to cool, one should leave off and turn instead to ejaculatory prayer, which, being an elevation of the mind, can be engaged in anywhere and anytime.[11]

The third question finds its answer in the superiority of prayer of the heart alone to prayer of both heart and lips. Here the classic example is the prayer of Anna, the mother of Samuel (1 Kings 1:13).[12] Vocal prayer is like a ship which brings one to port, where abandonment to the leadership and direction of the Holy Spirit is absolutely necessary. The reason is that God is spirit and must be adored in spirit. God is like the sun shining everywhere, but He cannot shine through the heavy clouds of unreasonably numerous and anxious vocal prayers, even the Psalms. "God is muche more delyghted with our godly affection, then with our bare praier, and specially whan that affection being accompanyed with feruent sighes & aboundaunt teares, do pearse the heauens."

The conclusion to the whole treatise is a compendious exhortation which lifts the reader to heaven and its angels: for the sweetness of prayer is "the pledge and assuraunce of the felicitie to come, whiche the Angelles nowe alredy do enioye."[13]

In spite of the attention to form, the treatise is by no means a formal academic exercise. It is a pity that there is no clue to the nature of Fisher's readers or listeners. They were hardly a clerical or religious group because his ideas would be too familiar to them. On the other hand, they seem not to have been the usual congregation or household. What remains is perhaps a company of educated laymen striving for a better life. If so, Fisher has adapted his address admirably to his audience. As always, he gives his hearers or readers what he thinks they need most. The sermons on the Penitential Psalms, for example, had laid a certain stress upon God's ever-ready mercy and divine grace and upon man's cooperation and human effort. The *Treatise on Prayer,* however, emphasizes God's free gift and necessary help because Fisher's audience can understand, appreciate, and use the doctrine. Even the objection arising from God's foreknowledge is academic and is answered in an academic way. Everything is subordinated to the one necessary thing: union with God. One means — and perhaps the most important, humanly speaking — is affective prayer under the complete guidance of the Holy Spirit. Fisher has managed to suffuse his treatment with a warm emotional glow — and the ecstasy with which he describes the sweetness of affective prayer makes one suspect that it was not a strange or unfamiliar experience for him and that therefore his readers would be drawn to follow his advice and taste that sweetness themselves.

The correctness of this interpretation of the *Treatise on Prayer* can be tested by its contrast with the first of the *Two Sermons,* delivered on All Saints' Day, where the audience is evidently general or mixed in character. Great emphasis is again laid upon man's role in the drama of salvation: the considerations offered are to stir the listeners into praying and working hard in this life in order to avoid or shorten purgatorial pains and to attain heavenly joys. Doctrinally the sermon, in spite of its relative moderation and humanity, gives a picture of the purgatory which the Reformers rejected. Fisher evidently holds with St. Augustine that "the fyre of Purgatory is more greuouse than any maner of payne that can be sene in this world, or felte, or yet thought." He also repeats St. Bernard's declaration that "yf after this lyfe he myght be delyuered fro the pryson of Purgatory at any tyme before the dredfull day of Iugement: he wolde reken that he were well and mercyfully delt withall." [14]

The language is less formal and abstract, more concrete and

colorful, than in *Prayer*. The preacher catches and holds the attention of his hearers for the first third of the sermon by description and narration of the latest and greatest events of the year just four months before: the visit of Charles V to England, the Field of Cloth of Gold, and the meeting between Charles and Henry afterward at Gravelines. Details are given with unusually graphic vividness. The punishment of Herod in the Acts (12:21–23), too, is re-created briefly but brilliantly.

Familiar objects serve to drive lessons home. Earthly pleasures are passing — like shadows cast by a flying cloud. They are counterfeit — like "mydsomer games, Chrystmas games & playes." Living Christians should run to help their brethren like hogs at the cry of a suffering fellow or like sparrows at the plight of a captured comrade; they should not be friends in time of prosperity only — "lyke vnto the Swalowes / which all the tyme of Somer abyde with men / but as sone as any blast of wynter or of colde wedder doth appere, they shrynke away. . ." The pains of purgatory are described as worse than headache, toothache, gout, calculus, colic, or strangury.

The text for the first sermon — "Oneles your ryghtwyse lyfe be more habundaunt than was the lyuynge of the Scribes and Pharisees, ye shall nat entre into the kyngdome of heuyn" (Matt. 5:20) — actually occurs in the Gospel for the Fifth Sunday after Pentecost and is so strange for All Saints' Day that Fisher must explain his concentration on the kingdom of heaven by declaring his intention of discussing the justice of Pharisees and of Christians on another occasion. He will speak about souls: those enjoying heaven, those in purgatory, and those on earth, who should try to get to heaven with little or no time in purgatory.

After this introduction and a paternoster, Fisher speaks first of the pleasures and joys of heaven. They are inconceivable and inexpressible, and consequently Fisher must resort to the *via negativa,* that is, to their contrast with the magnificent meetings between Henry and Francis and Charles — "many goodly syghtes whiche were shewed of late beyonde the see, with moche Ioy and pleasure worldly." To be brief, there are five differences. The joys of earth have "a werynesse and a fastydyousenes," "many dredes" (death, sickness, poverty, greed, pride, and envy), "many interrupcyons" (dust, wind, rain, and darkness), a transitoriness "lyke shadowes," and an unnatural counterfeiting (cloth from sheep, furs from beasts, colors from dyes, gold — "what is it els but erthe?" — and precious stones from beasts, fishes, sea, and earth). In contrast, the pleasures of heaven "be pure, clene, and parfyte withouten any admyxture of dyspleasure or werynesse"; they consist in "charyte, concorde, peace, tranquylyte, and perfyte rest"; they exist in "a contynuall day, a contynuall temperaunce, a clere ayre without mystes and cloudes"; they "contynually abyde . . . they neuer lesse, but rather encrease"; and man's apparel is "the garment of gloryous immortalytye, more bryght than the sonne." In addition, men shall see the angels and saints, former friends and acquaintances, "the gloryouse vyrgyn Mary, the mother of Chryste, and the Quene of that moost gloryouse kyngedome," and, above all, the "father, which is the father of all mercyes, and his most blessed son our sauyour Chryst Iesu, and the holy spyryte, whiche is the fountayne of all graces." In an interesting contemporary comment, Fisher observes that, unlike the Three Persons, "perfytely knyt to gyder in a perfyte amytye, in one loue, in one wyll, in one wysdom, in one power insepe-rably," the three earthly princes (Henry, Francis, and Charles) had "dyuers wylles, dyuers councels, & no perdurable amyty, as after that dyd well appere."

The second part of the sermon is devoted to five "Considerations" to foster remembrance of the souls who are kept from heavenly joys in the prison of purgatory: (1) their similarity in sharing with us the same Father, Savior, faith, hope, charity, and sacraments; (2) their former friendship or kinship; (3) their helplessness in being deprived of friendly visits and celestial joys, in yearning for heaven, and in suffering sensual pain which is the same as that in hell; (4) their pitiable cries — of father to children, husband to wife, and so on; and (5) our own profit and salvation because pity will later be shown us in purgatory by the God who repays in kind, by the souls delivered through our efforts, and by the guardian angels of these souls.

The third part is not so sharply organized as the preceding two. The thought of heaven and its joys (which are skillfully repeated in summary at this point) should make us "withdraw our appetytes from this worlde, wherby we dayly gather the dust at the leest of venyall synnes"; but "myserable dulnesse of our hartes" and "cursed blyndenes" cause us to forget. The remembrance of purgatory should make us resolve to pay our debts here on earth for three reasons: the good of our own soul; the greater effectiveness of doing so ourselves and not through others (for our negligence will hardly be supplied by the diligence of others who have enough to do to take care of their own souls — like the five Prudent Virgins); and the limitation of the time of meriting to the present life. Fisher ends his first sermon with a fervent exhortation of his listeners to all spiritual activities that will enable them to shorten their delay in purgatory and that will cause them to be made partakers of heaven's "moost excellent Ioyes and pleasures . . . to the which he brynge vs that for vs all dyed vppon the crosse, our sauyour Chryste Ihesu. Amen." [15]

The second sermon on justice begins with an excellent summary of the joys of heaven described in the first sermon. This device serves to bring the hearers down to earth again. Just as in the first sermon earth had been the vantage point from which Fisher had projected them into the future and up into heaven, so earth is used in the second sermon as the point of departure into the past and Adam's paradise and down into hell. Adam's loss of paradise becomes symbolic of every sinner's loss of heaven. Recent Miltonic criticism has made such allegory seem far less farfetched than formerly.

In the introduction, the summary of the previous sermon contains an interesting deviation. Instead of referring to the three princes, Henry, Francis, and Charles, Fisher laments: "The Courte of kynge Edwarde, the Courte of kynge Rycharde, & the courte of the kynge that now is ded / where be they now? all they were . . . but a playe for a tyme." In fact, "the Ioyes of this lyfe be but as dremes and fantasyes" — like the dream of a poor man about a beautiful wife and great possessions, or of Petrarch about "a great heuy hurde full of golde," or of rich men who after sleep "have found nothing in their hands" (Vulg. Ps. 75:6). It is death that "shaketh them out of theyr dremes, and maketh theym to awake." If men thus awakened have not "the ryghtwysnes of good lyuyng," they will be excluded from the joys of the kingdom of heaven — as Adam was from those of paradise. At this point, Fisher announces his three basic likenesses: Adam represents every sinner; Adam's loss of paradise, the sinner's loss of heaven; and the cherubim's flaming sword before paradise, the obstacles to heaven for the sinner.

A preliminary note to the discussion of the first analogy declares that every person has in himself an Adam and an Eve. Adam symbolizes the soul, the ruler, and reason; Eve symbolizes the body, the ruled, and folly. The three points here are the meaning of the fruit, the tasting of the fruit, and the folly of tasting. The fruit of the tree of life, which is Christ, is pleasure in His words, doctrine, birth, death, and resurrection, and man's alms, forgiveness, prayer, and fasting. The fruit of the tree of knowledge, which is death, is pleasure taken in the breaking of the ten commandments. The fruit of natural trees is indifferent pleasure, experienced in necessary eating, drinking, walking, talking, and recreation. As for the tasting of the fruit, Eve eats the apple when the body feels unlawful pleasure, and Adam eats the apple when the soul consents to it. Mere feeling is no sin; full consent constitutes sin; and external act makes the sin more heinous. Adam's transgression is less than the sinner's because Adam saw no precedent. The folly of both consists in preferring personal pleasure to God's pleasure, the fruit of death to the fruit of life, and grievous punishment to joyous reward.

At this juncture the first major section dovetails almost imperceptibly with the second, that is, the similarity between Adam's loss of paradise and sinners' loss of heaven:

> And therfore as Adam lost the Ioyes of Paradyse: so they lese the Ioyes of a clere conscyence. As Adam was cast into mysery: so they euer after indure mysery, and suffre the frettynge and gnawynges of theyr troubled conscyence. . . Adam suffred temporall dethe / and they shall suffre euerlastynge dethe. Adam was kept in darke pryson [*limbus patrum*] fro the face of god, and fro the Ioyes of heuyn by thre .M. yeres / and they shall be kept in the pryson of hell from the face of god and all the gloryouse court of heuyn, by innumerable thousandes & thousandes of yeres / that is to say, for euer.

To the objection that the inheritance of heavenly joys has been purchased and promised by the Savior, Fisher makes a twofold answer. First, any inheritance can be lost by foolish treason, as is proved in the case of many great earls and dukes who have betrayed their prince. The sinner betrays his heart, which is Christ's stronghold, into the hands of His enemy, the devil. Second, any promise or lease is valueless if its condition is broken. In the sinner's case, the condition for eternal life is the observance of God's commandments. Fisher here indulges in a passionate outburst against what might be the greatest sinners of his day: lechers, bawds, blasphemers, perjurers, and holyday-violators.

The third and last section allegorizes the bars to the kingdom of heaven. The two-edged sword slays both body and soul but does not take away the ability to feel hell's grievous and everlasting pains. The burning flame betokens the fire of purgatory which must burn away all venial sins, that is, "these synnes that we dayly commyt / without the whiche the fraylty can nat contynue in this lyfe." Among the examples Fisher gives are excessive eating and drinking, idle words, failure to admonish others, negligence in prayer, waste of time, roughness in speech, and unnecessary flattery.

The cherubim symbolize the strict judgment to be undergone. The most startling (and perhaps the most misinterpreted) statement here is the following: "They [the cherubim] wyll anon perceyue yf we want our apparell (that is to say) the ryghtwysenes of good workes. For it suffysyth nat to them that shall entre there, yf they be scoured of theyr euyll workes / but they must haue also many good workes. . ." In the light of his doctrine on penance as set forth in the sermons on the Psalms, Fisher would seem to be referring here to amendment or satisfaction by the good works of the sinner: "This garment [taken vnto the at the Sacrament of baptysme] yf thou haue lost, or torne, or solde, thou must study bytymes to repayre it agayne by som good workes." Later he adds: "We must therfore study to recouer this clene white garment agayne by ryghtwyse lyuynge, and kepyng of the commaundementes of almyghty god." Finally, the condition for entrance into heaven is declared to be that "we begyn ones to enfourme our lyfe by the true kepynge of the commaundementes of god, to recouer agayn this ryghtwysnes, that we haue lost." He would not deny that the baptized infant without good works immediately enters heaven. Admission is denied to the sinner who has not made satisfaction or who has neglected to care for the hungry, the thirsty, the stranger, the naked, and the imprisoned (Matt. 25:31–46). Fisher closes with a summary of the whole discourse and with an exhortation to "euery true chrysten man and woman to lerne to know the commaundementes . . . to the entente that . . . by the kepynge of them, he may recouer agayne the possybylytye to entre into that ioyfull and gloryous place."

The detailed allegory of Adam and paradise, the likeness of worldly joys to Midsummer and Christmas games and plays, the awakening of men by death, the heart as Christ's stronghold betrayed to the devil, the labeling of hell twice as a dunghill, and other devices, make this sermon literarily outstanding. Fisher is also successful in using a number of comparisons to show the importance of venial sins: corns (grains) of gravel finally overloading and sinking a boat, little blains and scabs, and scaly rust upon a knife. Doctrinally, it is interesting to hear Fisher say that Adam was "perfytely created & made by the handes of god nat many houres before" his sin and that his sin was literally "the tastynge of an apple." The reference to the forbidden fruit is repeated in the second section almost like the refrain in a medieval carol: "And al was for an appil, an appil that he tok." Another noteworthy theoretical point is that certain necessary but pleasurable acts, like eating, drinking, sleeping, walking, talking, and recreation in the concrete seem to be considered morally indifferent, that is, neither good nor bad, and therefore deserving of neither reward nor punishment. In this regard, Fisher holds with Scotus against Thomas Aquinas (*S.T.* 1–2, q. 18, a. 9).[16]

The scriptural text for both sermons had been the same: "Onelesse your ryghtwysnes be more large than was the ryghtwisenes of the scrybes and the pharyseys, ye shall not enter in to the kyngdom of heuyn" (Matt. 5:20). The title of the Latin version of the second sermon is "The Justice of Pharisees and Christians." It was with "rightwiseness," or justice, in all its aspects that Fisher was concerned in his works against Luther. He was relatively well prepared. His three publications on the Magdalene had forced him to revaluate his attitudes toward interpretation of the Scriptures, authority in the Church, and the roles of the Fathers and the Roman See. His tract on prayer, destined for the individual Christian, had led him to stress the necessity of grace, the personal guidance of the Spirit, and the sweetness of charity. His two sermons made him consider heaven and purgatory, Adam's fall and man's sin, justification and merit. With the phenomenon of Luther all these topics had now to be reorientated — toward faith and toward salvation by faith alone.

Chapter XVI

THE OFFENSIVE AGAINST LUTHER

THE sermon delivered against Luther before the highly distinguished gathering at Paul's Cross in May 1521 is undoubtedly the most famous, even if not the best, of Fisher's works. One reason might be wholly extrinsic. Perhaps because of its ready accessibility to both writer and reader, it is the work most often and most vehemently assailed by Tyndale and Barnes, as well as by other contemporary or later Reformers. In addition, being a more or less popular sermon, it is more susceptible to attack than a doctrinal disquisition. Bridgett characterizes it as "rather a theological treatise than a discourse to the people"; but it is its lack of theological strength and depth, impossible to achieve under the circumstances of a sermon, that exposes it to inimical assaults. Reynolds is most probably correct in declaring that the preacher directed his address to the "chief part of the congregation . . . made up of leaders of the church and state." [1] The atmosphere of the gala occasion staged by Wolsey, moreover, could hardly give the impression of serious conflict and deep fear that was soon to come. Instead, there prevail quiet confidence, assured victory, and buoyant optimism: this cloud would pass away like all other clouds. This mood is communicated even in the attempts at humor. For example, after observing that a woman has three heads in God, Christ, and husband, Fisher adds: "Besyde al these she hath an heed of hyr owne. It were a monstrous syght to se a woman withouten an heed. what comforte sholde hyr housbande haue vpon hyr." Again, after explaining the role of Father, Son, and Holy Spirit in the instruction of mankind, the preacher declares: "Yf there were a fourthe persone in the trynyte. or another spyryte to be sent vnto vs from almighty god we myght yet be in some doute wheder Martyn luther had met with this spyryte by the waye and conueyed hym from vs."

This sermon against Luther has already been cited many times in the present work for Fisher's views on the Church, the hierarchy, the councils, the papacy, Scripture, tradition, faith, grace, justification, and salvation. Consequently it would be redundant to repeat the details here. Our purpose is rather to give the totality, or the context, into which those details fit. Bridgett, at any rate, finds the whole unsatisfactory, for "it consists of four parts with little unity of arrangement." [2] His criticism boils down to that of incoherence in the over-all pattern — an extraordinary charge to level against Fisher with his strong architectural sense. Yet "even the worthy Homer sometimes nods." To discover the truth, it is necessary to analyze the sermon ourselves. Its "popular" nature is most evident perhaps in its similes, metaphors, and symbols, which predominate in the first third of the sermon. They will be pointed out as our analysis progresses.

After citing the text ("whan the comforter shall come. whom I shall sende vnto you the spyryte of trouthe that yssueth from my father. he shall bere wytnesse of me," John 15:26), the exordium graphically describes the cloud of heresy which interferes with the light of faith issuing from the spiritual sun, Almighty God. Such clouds were the heretics from Donatus to Wyclif, with now a new cloud, Martin Luther. Four "Instructions," offered by the day's Gospel, will undermine Luther and his adherents. Fisher does not tell his audience what these Instructions are — an unusual procedure for him — but, after a prayer for faith in the Church's doctrine, he launches into the sermon proper.

The first Instruction, in which Christ promises the Holy Spirit will act as the perpetual comforter of the Church in all storms, contains three points. The first is conceded even by Luther, namely, that "the instruccyons of this holy gospell perteyneth to the vniuersal chirche of chryst." [3] The second point, that "the pope *iure diuino* is the heed of the vnyuersall chyrche of christ," is initiated by an elaborate allegory between a tree and its shadow, that is, between the Church of the New Law and the synagogue of the Old Law, according to Paul's text: "The lawe had but a shadowe of thynges for to come" (Heb. 10:1).[4] The basic truth is that both Moses and Aaron were heads of the Jews. The basic proportion is that Moses was to Aaron as Christ was to Peter. The three resultant likenesses are expressed in terms of (1) sacerdotal consecration, (2) mediatory function, and (3) earthly rule, too detailed to be repeated here. This analogy is confirmed by the Gospel narrative of paying the temple tax (Matt. 17:23–26) and by patristic authorities (the Latin Augustine, Ambrose, Gregory, Jerome, and Cyprian, and the Greek Chrysostom and Origen). If Luther says that "he can not conceyue duos summos," let him remember that both Moses and Aaron were *summi* and that, just as a woman has three heads (husband, Christ, and God, together with "an heed of hyr owne"), so the Church has three heads (the pope, Christ her husband, and Almighty God). In the third point, which is much shorter than the second, Fisher argues that Luther, by separating himself from the head, has separated himself from the Mystical Body of the Church and therefore from the spirit of that Body, the Spirit of Truth.

In this first Instruction, the line of argumentation seems to be that the Scripture is intended for the whole Church (not for individuals or for parties), that the pope is by divine right the head of this whole Church, and that by severing himself from the head Luther has severed himself from the whole Church and its Spirit of Truth. The structure of the first Instruction, therefore, resolves itself into a brief assumption about the universal Church, a lengthy proof for the pope as head of this universal Church, and a brief consequence that severance from the head means severance from the universal Church whose soul is the Spirit of Truth.[5]

The second Instruction revolves about the truth that "the hete of charyte spred in our hertes by the holy spyryte of god gyueth euydence of the lyfely lyght of faythe. shynynge vpon our soules from our sauyour." Here Fisher uses some unusual, and to us far-fetched, comparisons. God is the spiritual sun, whose beams cause life and good works. A single beam represents the light of faith. This same beam, reflected or doubled, typifies faith strengthened by hope. In the same way, a bowl must be thrown vigorously against a wall in order to return to the thrower. A double thread, too, is stronger than a single. Faith without hope and charity is like a dead tree; faith without works is like a tree without buds and leaves. This Instruction is intended to undermine Luther's doctrine on justification by faith alone, without works and the sacraments. The sacraments will be defended from Luther's attack by the forthcoming book of Henry VIII, who is like Plato's philosopher-king. The texts taken from Paul by Luther are corrected by texts taken from the other Apostles, especially St. James. Luther's claim that the only text against him is from St. James ("By works a man is justified, and not by faith alone," Jas. 2:24) is contradicted by additional texts from Luke, Matthew, James, and Paul himself—"By all the whiche testimonyes ye may playnely se that not onely faythe suffyseth but also loue and workes be requyred to the iustyfyenge of our soules. And thus moche for the seconde instruccyon."

The third Instruction aims to show that "more testimony must be admytted for sufficyent authoryte. than only that that is wryten in the byble." Each of the divine Persons has a special age for revelation. First the Father taught through the prophets, who consigned their utterances to the written Scripture and to the unwritten Cabala. Then the Son taught through Himself and the Apostles, who left their doctrines in written form and in unwritten traditions, as is confirmed by Origen, Damascene, Dionysius, Augustine, Jerome, and many others. Finally, the Holy Spirit teaches the Church through the Fathers and Doctors and through ecumenical councils. Luther has not this Spirit of Truth because "he cutteth awaye the tradycyons of the apostles. and refuseth the general councelles. and contemneth the doctryne of the holy fathers and doctours of the chyrche. and laboureth to subuerte . . . the .vij. sacramentes. and taketh awaye the fredome of mans wyll." To his purpose Fisher quotes brief texts about deceitful teachers (1 Tim. 4:1) and the great apostasy (2 Thess. 2:3).[6]

The first three Instructions, being positive and direct in nature, serve only obliquely to undermine Luther's doctrines. The fourth and last Instruction, however, refutes three points produced by Luther's adherents: (1) "Martyn luther is a man depely lerned in scryptures . . . a man of relygyous lyfe"; (2) "he hathe a faste mynde in god, and spareth for no mans authoryty to speke the trouthe. in so moche that he hath excomunicate the pope"; and (3) "he hath a merueylous feruent zeale to god for the whiche he dothe labour to conuert all the world to his opinyon." Fisher answers each of these points in turn.[7] The gist of his total response is that these same things were true of past heretics from the

Donatists to the Wycliffites, all of whom persecuted Christ's Church according to His prophecy: "These things I have spoken to you that you may not be scandalized. They will expel you from the synagogues. Yes, the hour is coming for everyone who kills you to think that he is offering worship to God" (John 16:1–2). It is at such times that the Spirit of Truth is comforter to Christ's Church, which is one, holy, catholic, and apostolic. As for the learned, virtuous, and zealous heretics, "Yf they had had the spiryt of trouth they should not haue erred in misconceyuing the scriptures."

The lengthy conclusion is the best possible summary of the whole sermon and includes even subdivisions for the four Instructions. Fisher finally exhorts his audience to heed Christ and the Spirit of Truth in His Church, and not Luther who "gothe fer wyde from the streyght waye. & is neuer lyke to entre in to the port of euerlastynge rest. whiche we all desyre & couet to come vnto." [8]

The ease with which Fisher is able to review his entire complicated sermon emphasizes its unified structure, which is at the same time less rigid than in his other works. It is certainly to Fisher's credit that he perceives Luther's three major doctrines and handles them not negatively but affirmatively. He endeavors to establish and clarify the Catholic teachings on the pope's headship over the Mystical Body; on the need of hope, love, and works in addition to faith for justification; and on the authority of traditions, the Fathers, and the councils, as well as of the Scriptures. Even in the fourth Instruction, he tries to be positive by stressing Christ's prophecy of persecution and the comfort given by the Spirit of Truth to His Church, which is distinguished by the four positive notes of unity, holiness, catholicity, and apostolicity.

In this optimistic approach Fisher seems almost to have taken inspiration from the May day on which he delivered his sermon. The first third of the sermon is filled with allusions to nature in the English spring: the sun, the clouds, the light, the stronger sunbeams, the burning glass using sunbeams to set fire to tinder or cloth, the greater warmth, the difference between the tree in winter and in spring, the stock of a dead tree, the live tree with its buds and leaves, the tree and its shadow, and so forth. Even the reference to the bowl thrown against a wall is a reminder of spring activity. Perhaps only the allusion to "the port of euer-lastynge rest" is not specifically vernal, but it keeps us in the great outdoors where sun and storm, cloud and light, alternate.[9]

This sermon against Luther has its most elaborate comparison, that of the tree and its shadow, in the section on papal supremacy. Here, too, more time is given to the various arguments — from the Old Testament, from the Gospels, and from the Fathers and Doctors. Fisher evidently realizes that the point is most important — and that at the same time it perhaps might be, for historical reasons, the weakest and the most vulnerable. But he could hardly have anticipated an assault that totally undermined his position: the denial even of Peter's presence and death in Rome and thereby the demolition of the Bishop of Rome's claim of succession to Peter's supremacy and power. Yet this is precisely what the youthful Bohemian, Ulrichus Velenus, asserted: Peter had never come to Rome. When Bishop Tunstal called his attention to the thesis, Fisher realized the seriousness of the charge and was downright glad to have the opportunity to refute Velenus before the publication, delayed by the French war, of the *Confutation of Luther's Assertion* with its long Article 25 on the primacy of Peter and the pope.

Velenus had divided his book into two parts. The first consisted of eighteen "Persuasions" (*persuasiones*) to demonstrate that Peter had never been to Rome and had died in Jerusalem, not in Rome. The second was composed of seven "Cavils" (*cavilli*), usually brought by the Roman curia against such Persuasions, but here answered by Velenus' seven "Responses" (*responsiones*). Fisher repeats Velenus' every word, including the title and excepting only Juvenal's couplet at the beginning, a distich at the end, and Velenus' letter to the reader. It is a pity that Fisher does not reprint and refute this letter of Velenus because of the glimpse it affords of an early Protestant attitude. After finding the Antichrist in the pope, Velenus names victims of papal tyranny: in the past, Wyclif, Hus, Jerome of Prague, and Girolamo Savonarola ("a man unquestionably most learned in everyone's judgment and a most active promoter of Christian piety"), and at present, John Reuchlin, John Pico della Mirandola (both being "pillars of letters"), as well as Martin Luther and Ulrich Hutten. The three-headed Cerberus with the three crowns had had one head lopped off by Valla, that "Hercules" who had proved the forgery of Constantine's Donation, and another head severed by Luther, that "Theseus" who had denounced the decretals. Velenus will dare what none have dared before — to cut off the third head, namely, the papal boast of being Peter's successor.[10]

As stated above, Fisher reprints Velenus' entire treatise verbatim. After his own letter to the reader, he uses no introduction but immediately begins to quote Velenus' title, partition, and first Persuasion. For the first part, his method is to give each of Velenus' eighteen Persuasions (e.g., *Persuasio I*), then to sum it up in a brief statement which he labels "Substance of the . . . Misrepresentation" (e.g., *Calumniae primae summa*), and finally to furnish his "Response" (*Responsio*).[11] Wonderful to report of the prolix bishop, none of his Responses (with his *summae*), except the last, is appreciably longer than his adversary's Persuasion. In fact, two are slightly shorter. In the second part, Fisher repeats each of the seven Cavils ascribed by Velenus to the Roman curia (e.g., *Cavillus I*) and Velenus' Response (*Responsio*) to that Cavil. Velenus' Response is then matched by Fisher's rejoinder, also labeled Response (*Responsio*). Here again, provided that the curial Cavil and Velenus' Response are considered a unit, as they actually are, two of Fisher's Responses are slightly shorter than Velenus', and only two, the first and the last, are much longer.

Fisher closes with what he calls the "Conclusion of the Whole Work" (*Totius operis conclusio*). Its beginning recalls Christ's words on three things: Peter's primacy among the Apostles, Peter as the rock for the edifice of the Church, and Peter's faith as unfailing. Its end repeats Augustine's words on Rome as Peter's see, on Roman bishops in unbroken succession from Peter, and on the Roman Church's perpetual immunity from heresy. Hence Peter had resided in Rome. In this conclusion occurs Fisher's declaration that Rome's continued freedom from infidel domination, in spite of the discrepancy between Christ's moral doctrine and Rome's immorality, constitutes a proof for the divine institution of the papacy.

As for method, Fisher objects to Velenus' frequent argumentation *ex negatiuis,* which he claims is lacking in all force. One instance is Paul's failure in his epistle to the Romans to salute

Peter — hence Peter simply was not in Rome. Nevertheless, Fisher says that he will not attack Velenus on this front but merely show other reasons for Paul's omission of Peter's name. In regard to interesting opinions expressed in this work, many have already been used above in the discussion of the papacy, historical method, and other topics. It is perhaps ironic to note that Fisher does not hesitate to refer to Lefèvre's Latin translation of Linus' apocryphal lives of Peter and Paul — and to disagree with a point in Lefèvre's preface.[12]

The final reaction of the reader to the *Shattering of Velenus' Misrepresentations* is that Fisher's work would hardly have suffered from the omission of Velenus' complete text. On the contrary, it would have been much more readable and attractive as a literary piece. As a controversial work directed against what Fisher considered mere cavil, it fails by spreading a preposterous opinion and causing readers to take Velenus more seriously than intended by Fisher. This was true, as has been seen, in the case of Simon Hessus, who wrote the *Apology* against the Bishop of Rochester.

Fisher's next publication, *The Confutation of Luther's Assertion,* has a number of connections with the work against Velenus. The letter to the reader in the earlier work, it will be recalled, records Fisher's pleasure at being able to refute Velenus before the appearance of the *Confutation.* In addition, according to his Response to Persuasion 18, the treatment in the *Confutation* (Article 25) had so enervated Luther's objections to papal primacy that nothing further can or need be said.[13] The general method, too, is the same: verbatim citation of the *Assertion of All the Articles of Martin Luther Condemned by the Latest Bull of Leo X.* The employment of the method, however, is far more justifiable here because the *Assertion* is a major work of a major opponent, in fact, the heresiarch of heresiarchs. The forty-one articles involve real clashes on real issues: Rome's condemnation, Luther's defense against the condemnation, and Fisher's rebuttal of the defense. Fisher, following the method of the preceding work, quotes Luther's *Assertion* from beginning to end, except for the dedicatory epistle as in the case of Velenus' treatise.[14]

As for the preliminary material, Henry VIII's letter patent to John Addison, Fisher's chaplain, for exclusive rights to the *Con-*

futation for three years, is interesting for its superlative praise of the Bishop of Rochester and of his anti-Lutheran works, for its tribute to Addison's own labor and expense in looking to their publication, and for its disclosure that certain men of ill will were plotting to bring them out in smaller type and on poorer paper, with attention to speed rather than accuracy. This letter, unusually personal and warm, is followed by two Latin poems by George Day, later Master of St. John's and Bishop of Chichester. The first, in elegiac couplets, lauds Fisher as *pugil Christi* ("Christ's boxer"); the title of the second, in Sapphic stanzas, refers to the century's clear skies as overcast by the clouds of the Lutheran heresy, a metaphor suggested perhaps by the opening of Fisher's English sermon against Luther. These poems are then succeeded by a very detailed Index and a short list of the articles to be refuted.[15] None of the items just mentioned appears in the *Opera omnia* (1597), which reprints faithfully the rest of the *Confutation.*

Fisher's letter to the reader reveals that he has no hope of effecting Luther's recovery because he is perverted and self-condemned (Tit. 3:11). As a bishop, however, placed "to rule the Church of God, which he has purchased with his own blood" (Acts 20:28), he wants to help weaker souls whose faith, poised as it were upon a razor's edge, has long been in doubt which way to turn, whether to the Church and the Fathers or to Luther, rumored to have throngs of adherents and praised to the nth degree. According to the Preface, the two works which betrayed Luther as a manifest heretic were *The Babylonian Captivity* and *The Assertion of All the Articles.* The former has been triumphantly confuted by Henry VIII, who receives the highest and warmest commendation from Fisher. The *Assertion* will be answered by Fisher, who as a bishop could hardly turn a deaf ear to Luther's attacks on everything in the Church from pope to sacraments and who would be ashamed to enjoy the delights of scholarly leisure when even his illustrious king has entered the fray.[16]

Just before quoting the first words of the *Assertion,* Fisher states that Luther insists upon the choice of weapon, to wit, the Holy Scripture only. The injustice of this demand, comments Fisher, is evident to all veterans in academic as well as military contests. Against the enemy of the commonwealth — in this case, of all Christendom — one must use any and every weapon to hand. By establishing ten Truths (*veritates*), Fisher will show the arms by which, willy-nilly, Luther must be vanquished and which neither he nor any other person bearing the name of Christian can refute. Fisher had marshaled eight Truths (*veritates*) against Clichtove and twelve Suppositions (*suppositiones*) against Lefèvre. Against Luther, too, he aligns ten Truths, but because his methods and means are always adapted to the matter in hand, these are not the same in number or formulation as the Truths and Suppositions used as bases for the refutations of Clichtove and Lefèvre. In fact, the only norms in common are consent of the Fathers, agreement of the whole Church, and respect for ecclesiastical custom. Instead, the things that receive new emphasis in the battle against Luther are the principles of biblical interpretation and the continuing guidance of the Church by the Holy Spirit. In fact, Fisher's letter to the Dutch theologian Herman Lethmatius on charity makes an interesting revelation of his secret stratagem: since Luther defers not at all to Thomas Aquinas and Aegidius Romanus but insists upon clear biblical texts, he determined to debate with him not according to the opinions of the Schoolmen "but rather by reason relying upon the Scriptures themselves" (*sed ratione potius ipsis innixa scripturis*).[17]

In brief the ten anti-Lutheran Truths are these: (1) patent lapse into error by persons relying on their own abilities in scriptural interpretation; (2) fall into error by those following their own inspirations; (3) need for some authority to decide controversies in Scripture or in dogma; (4) impossibility of solving all controversies by Scripture alone; (5) the sending and the presence of the Holy Spirit to teach the truth vis-à-vis such errors; (6) the use of the Fathers by the Holy Spirit to extirpate heresy and to instruct the Church fully; (7) the rejection of the Fathers as indicating the absence of the Holy Spirit; (8) the use by the Holy Spirit of ecumenical councils as even more important mouthpieces than the individual Fathers; (9) the obligatory observance of apostolic traditions although unrecorded in Scripture; and (10) the similar acceptance of customs of the universal Church.

"These, O Luther," cries Fisher, "are the weapons of Christians which we will use against the public enemies of the Church. You can reject none of these if you suffer yourself to be called Christian. . . With them [ecclesiastical custom, apostolic tradition, general council, or approved interpreter] you will be struck down whenever the Scriptures are lacking." Fisher at once apologizes for his prolixity in establishing the ten Truths but he has been forced to it by Luther's demand for scriptural proofs only. This apology for long-windedness occurs frequently throughout the *Confutation* — and the excuse remains the same. In the first article, for instance, to offset Luther's claim that only James's verse, "Faith without works is dead" (Jas. 2:26), stands against him, Fisher produces sixteen other texts to prove that no one, at least no adult, will be justified without works. This refutation of Luther's proem is interesting also for showing Fisher's careful planning; he deliberately passes over one statement of Luther's on the pope because Article 25 will treat the papacy.[18]

After the establishment of his ten Truths, the Bishop of Rochester begins the verbatim citation of Luther's words, more frequently than not by single sentences, and follows each quotation immediately with criticism or refutation. He pursues this method to the very end. The *Confutation* as a whole, properly speaking, has no conclusion. It simply stops with the comment on the forty-first or last article and with the word FINIS. Because of length and complexity, it is impossible here to outline the contents of the whole *Confutation,* whose order and procedure, after all, are determined by an extrinsic factor, namely, Luther's order and procedure. Besides, our main interest at present is method and style. The general impression of Fisher's work is an almost uninterrupted succession of brief quotations taken from Luther, answered by rebuttals perhaps four or five times as long — or longer — made by Fisher. The bishop's most original and independent contributions, although not very frequent, occur usually at the beginning of the refutation of each article. This procedure is understandable because immediately after the statement of Luther's thesis it is perhaps advisable or even necessary to distinguish its component parts, to outline the plan of the answer, to draw various distinctions, to lay down fundamental assumptions, to give the positive doctrine, and so forth.

The refutation of Article 25 on the papacy, of which the Bishop of Rochester himself and many others thought highly, might serve as an example.[19] Getting down to business immediately, Fisher announces that before engaging Luther he will try to establish papal supremacy, and indeed in two ways. The first is through Scripture, which attributes many prerogatives to Peter, and the second is through the most esteemed Fathers and their testimonies. Fisher gives ten prerogatives from the Gospels and ten confirmations from the Acts. The Latin Fathers quoted in detail are Hilary, Ambrose, Leo, Gregory, Cyprian, Augustine, and Jerome; those merely mentioned by name are Bede, Bernard, Rabanus, Remi, Hugh, and Richard, although innumerable others could be listed. The Greek authors from whom quotations are selected are Chrysostom, Eusebius, Cyril, Origen, Athanasius, Theophilus, Basil, Dionysius, and the Greeks and Armenians at the Council of Florence. This long positive statement makes up roughly the first third of Article 25 before the verbatim quotation of Luther's text begins. Even afterward, however, there are four relatively long comments, of which two have to do with Peter as the rock, one with his feeding of the lambs and sheep, and one with a summary refutation of all Luther's reasons. A favorite device is the use of brief enumerations: four reasons to show the fittingness of having one person as head of the whole Church, three reasons to prove its necessity for right order, four similarities between Moses and Christ and between Aaron and Peter, six outstanding arguments advanced by Luther, and so on.[20]

In fact, enumeration is employed frequently throughout the *Confutation.* Random instances are the sixteen texts, already mentioned above, to prove the need for good works (art. 1); the three meanings of *peccatum,* "sin," in Paul and the three points in Augustine on the guilt of sin (art. 2); the three ways of calling, or vocation, and the three reasons for desisting from sin (art. 5); the three arguments for Eucharistic reception under one species (art. 16); Luther's confusion of three distinct texts (art. 19); the six kinds of punishment (art. 21); Tertullian's ten identifying marks for a heretic (art. 33); the three meanings of liberty in the Bible (art. 36); the four observations preliminary to giving the scriptural proof for purgatory, and brief answers to six views of Luther on purgatorial sufferings (art. 37); and so forth. Article 38 has enumerations of three, five, and six points. The advantage of this method is not only a desirable clarity but, more important, the arrangement and unification of material that might otherwise fall apart into a thousand chaotic fragments. The expedient is probably one that Fisher had learned both as a lecturer in theology and as a popular preacher.[21]

To turn now to general characteristics of the *Confutation,* one might note Fisher's attitude toward Luther's vituperation, to which he often objects. His first comment on Luther's proem finds the *Assertion* full of flowers of this kind, which easily outnumber effective arguments; and his refutation of the last article blames Luther for hurling insults, especially against the pope, at the slightest opportunity, so that he needs only an occasion for his malice, according to the proverb in Aristotle's *Rhetoric.* And from the beginning to the end, Fisher says that he will not answer Luther's reviling. This pose does not prevent him from using very strong language. At least by way of comparison, however, Erasmus, in a letter to Ulrich von Hutten in 1523, puts Fisher among those of his friends "who with devout zeal and with discretion have censured Luther within bounds." Does Hutten expect him to cast off Fisher "this good while his singular friend and most steady patron"? [22]

In addition to Luther's abusive style, Fisher objects to his frequent argumentation from the merely negative. For example, in commentary on Luther's insistence that the just man lives by faith (Hab. 2:4, Rom. 1:17, Gal. 3:11), he does not see how it follows that charity and the sacraments also do not render a man just (art. 1). In a similar manner, the silence of Christ and the Apostles on different penalties for different sins does not disprove that satisfaction is the third part of penance (art. 5). The fact that Peter did not choose, make, confirm, and send the other Apostles does not mean that Christ could not make him greater than them (art. 25). And what if Christ did not command the burning of heretics? Must a vigilant pastor allow them to devour Christ's flock with impunity? Let Luther rather point out where Christ forbade the practice (art. 33). These and many other specimens of Luther's logic are spurned because a mere negative proves nothing.[23]

At times, Fisher simply expresses his perplexity at Luther's meaning, as when he says that, although sin is in them, it does not harm them (art. 2). According to Fisher's dilemma, either the sin remains after God's pardon or is destroyed. If it remains, what kind of pardon is that? If it is destroyed, how can it still remain? At other times, he blames Luther for confusing matters by failing to draw distinctions, e.g., between regeneration (wrought through baptism) and regeneration (effected through the sacrament of penance after a fall from grace), between concupiscence and sin, between venial sin and mortal (art. 2). He has also noticed more than once that when there are two or more ways of acquiring something, Luther will declare for one and damn the others, e.g., in Article 6 in regard to grace (by faith only, not by sacraments also), justice (by grace only, not by works also), and contrition (by love only, not by fear also).[24]

Not only Luther's logic but his use of authorities comes in for its share of criticism. When Luther claims Cassian as an advocate of his sixth article, Fisher begs him to point out the passage. He himself had diligently scanned Cassian's two volumes and, far from finding substantiation, he had discovered numerous statements largely opposed to Luther's view (art. 6). Fisher defends the Isidorian decretals (e.g., that of Anacletus on the correspondence between Moses and Christ, Aaron and Peter, attributed by Luther to Gregory IX, Boniface VIII, or Clement V) by appeal to the antiquity of the manuscripts to be found in various English monasteries and to be dated from Bede's time (art. 25). When one passage in Jerome does seem to support Luther, Fisher explains that Jerome is here behaving like a man who, wanting to straighten a crooked rod, bends it back as far in the opposite direction. Against a pushy deacon, Jerome here extols priests. Elsewhere, however, Jerome's declarations for papal supremacy are many and strong (art. 25). This same article expresses Fisher's suspicion of Luther whenever, in citing Augustine, he fails to indicate the place. He objects likewise to Luther's truncation of Augustine because such lopping of undesirable parts can make authorities confirm anything desired (art. 36).[25] Many such remarks on sources had already appeared in his works on the Magdalene, but Fisher has now learned not to belabor obvious principles but to apply them adroitly and swiftly.

As for the flowers of rhetoric, the Bishop of Rochester makes extensive use of the metaphor and the adage (in the Erasmian sense). Since the former is frequently incorporated in the latter, it would be otiose to attempt their artificial separation. They might be made to form various groups for the sake of illustration. There are many classical allusions. Not everybody can venture the passage into Corinth without a guide; nor is everybody suited to interpret Scripture without the aid of commentators (proem). Luther's retraction of his declaration on indulgences in order to make it even worse is described as being according to the manner of Mandrabulus (art. 18). This same adage is used also in regard to milder measures against heretics, which only made conditions worse (art. 33). It would be easier to wrest the thunderbolt from Jove and the club from Hercules than to disprove the truth of papal primacy (art. 25). Luther's genius is altogether like that of Anaxagoras since he can find anywhere whatever he wishes and can adapt any scriptural text to any person. The heresiarch, moreover, has more forms and shapes than Proteus (art. 27). To answer also Hus's articles defended in Luther's Article 30 would make what was supposed to be a small supplementary bag bigger than a meal sack (*Thylaco maior erit accessoria sarcinula*): let their condemnation by the learned and virtuous delegates at the Council of Constance suffice. Luther's attitude is so hopeless that an Ethiopian can change the color of his skin before Luther gives up his calumnious invective against the pope and his Church (art. 40). These adages reveal either an extensive knowledge of the classics or, as is more likely for a busy bishop, a running acquaintance with his friend Erasmus' *Adagia*.[26]

Luther's errancy calls forth many figures. He is labeled as being out of tune with the song and being out of step with the dance (art. 2). As he goes from one error to another, he is like a man who, having gotten off to the wrong start, has to break down hedge after hedge and finally has to make a fresh and better beginning (art. 23). Free will is the rock on which Luther and other heretics suffer shipwreck. His dogma on the point deviates from the Gospel *plusquam bis diapason*. Moreover, he has gone astray *toto coelo* in maintaining that the sinner has so come into the power of Satan as to be incapable of trying for good (art. 36). Fisher himself, however, wishes not to depart a finger's breadth from the steps of the Fathers (art. 1). Concupiscence is improperly called sin by Augustine in the same way that writing is labeled a hand and speech a tongue. With the help of grace, man, even without possession of the highest degree of love and perfection, can abstain from mortal faults in the same way that the eye, even though it cannot bear glaring light, can manage not to be overwhelmed by darkness (art. 2).[27]

But Fisher can avail himself of far homelier figures. Luther's ascription of a lie as well as an error to Augustine is like having the lid fit the pot (art. 2). When Luther utters a correct statement on papal authority, he is told: "You have touched the thing with the needle," i.e., you have hit the nail on the head (art. 25). At the end of this same article Fisher claims that whoever has followed his arguments and joined thread to thread can no longer doubt the papal primacy. In failing to prove that the just man sins mortally in every good work, Luther has lost "both oil and labor," i.e., both time and trouble (art. 36). In discoursing about faith, Luther is twice termed more slippery than an eel (art. 1). In regard to scriptural proofs for purgatory, the fact that a pearl cannot be found in one or another gulf does not mean that no pearl can be discovered in the whole sea (art. 37). Attention has already been called to the comparison between the tree of the New Testament and its shadow in the Old Testament (art. 25). In the reference at the end of Article 36 to the flourishing state of Greek and Hebrew at the time, Fisher comments that nothing is so good as to be incapable of being turned by someone to the ruin of others.[28]

Rhetorical resources such as the adage and the metaphor help to lighten and to brighten the dead earnestness of the *Confutation*. On the defensive, its tone is confident and assured; on the offensive, it is courageous and optimistic. It shows surprisingly little sign of weariness and fatigue. Among his works it is not the greatest: it lacks the epic stature, simplicity, and unity of *Christ's Body* — and necessarily so, because of the nature of Luther's *Assertion*. For the same reason it lacks also the relative oneness and brevity of the *Defense of the Sacred Priesthood:* it is rather a succession or compilation of little *Defenses,* now up now down, now long now short, now bright now dull. Nevertheless, for better or for worse, it is the best known of Fisher's Latin writings — and the most important. Independently of the solid excellence of select articles, the *Confutation* is a great storehouse of theology because there is hardly a dogma, except for the Trinity and the Incarnation, on which it does not touch. In content, therefore, it is like a great theological *summa* — and many a reader wishes it were so also in form. Verbatim citation of an adversary may be used with the intention of keeping him from leveling the charge of misrepresentation, but fragmentation of his work is itself a species of distortion. What often counts is the total effect rather than the individual parts. In addition, perhaps no other method militates more against readability and interest and, in general, against effective writing than that of quoting and refuting an opponent passage by passage.

Be that as it may, the *Confutation* is a good place to get Fisher's reasoned and seasoned view on a point. Here he is not hurried, as he must be in a sermon, but he can take all the time needed to make himself clear and to refute the opposite opinion. Here, too, there is no need to simplify and summarize matters for an audience or congregation, but rather he is speaking as *Dr.* Fisher — to *Dr.* Luther and for the same educated reader as Luther. Consequently, even if the *Confutation* is a controversial work for a wide audience — as wide as Luther's — it remains on a high theological level always.

The sterling qualities of Fisher's *Confutation* have brought recognition from Catholic and Protestant scholars. Veit Ludwig von Seckendorf, referring to the year 1523, declares that Fisher "must be held to be without doubt the most learned" of Luther's adversaries.[29] Jeremy Collier finds the *Confutation* "his most considerable performance." [30] In a significant study, now more than a century old, Hugo Laemmer views the work as one of the most worthwhile polemical writings of the first half of the sixteenth century because of Fisher's knowledge, erudition, and logic.[31] Hubert Jedin, who considers Fisher "the most significant personality among the humanist theologians" on the side of the Church and his refutation of Luther on free will as the most penetrating and meaningful one to appear, feels that his whole theology has failed to receive the attention it deserves. He surmises that Hochstraten, Cochlaeus, and Wimpina refrained from composition or publication of their own work against Luther's *Assertion* because of Fisher's able *Confutation*. In spite of his sharp condemnation of Luther vis-à-vis the Church, Jedin places Fisher with Erasmus, Latomus, Giese, and Schatzgeyer, who tried to see and stress the positive in Luther's teaching, rather than with Catharinus, Cochlaeus, and Campester, who had little sympathy.[32] Under this aspect, it is interesting to find the eirenic Gerhard producing Fisher (with Erasmus) as a witness to Luther's worthy life.[33]

The early reputation and influence of the *Confutation* become evident only by accident and at random. In regard to Article 18 on purgatory, for example, Frith declares: "How be it the chefest of his scryptures hath master More perused & hath in a maner nothinge but that was before wryten by my lord of Rochestre . . . My lorde of Rochestre is the fyrst patrone & defender of this phantasye." This is a repetition of what he said before: "Master More . . . hath in a maner nothynge but that he toke out of my lorde of Rochestre / althoughe he handle it more suttellye." Frith delights in manifesting the disagreements between Fisher and More about the nature of purgatorial punishments.[34]

The *Confutation* naturally was used by Catholics in preparation for the Council of Trent. In 1537, Cochlaeus refers to Fisher's extensive refutation of Luther's and other heretics' claim that sin remains in infants after baptism.[35] In 1538, or thereabout, Bartholomew Guidiccionus, in his report to Paul III on the Church and the reformation of its ministers and their abuses, cites twenty-six of Fisher's forty-one articles.[36]

Chapter XVII

ON THE DEFENSIVE AGAINST LUTHER

UNLIKE the *Confutation of Luther's Assertion,* the *Defense of the Royal Assertion,* written in 1522–23 and published in 1525, is more controversial than theological — and understandably so because Fisher has to keep himself to the task in hand: the defense of Henry's *Assertion* against Luther's strictures, printed in mid-1522.[1] The most interesting contribution made by this work to Fisher's thought is the clarification of the role of the people (*plebs*), or laity, in the Church, a topic which has already been treated in Chapter III. As for method, Fisher as a loyal subject can hardly reproduce verbatim Luther's text, which is full of insults to his king. He must therefore raise the controversy to a more polite if less vigorous plane. At the very end of his *Defense,* in fact, he claims to have omitted no important point in Luther's work except his insults, which in their violation of all restraint he has permitted to descend on their author's head of their own accord. Nevertheless, even the critical Cochlaeus, who usually praises Fisher's "marvelous moderation," as well as his profound learning, must confess that Fisher's "beginning in his defense of the king's book, on account of the extraordinary malignity of his adversary, is somewhat more acrimonious, because of just grief, than the superlative mildness and meekness of the man in his customary speech." [2] In a short time, Erasmus, who considers his own *Diatribe* relatively moderate and mild, will wonder why Luther should choose to attack him rather than Emser, Cochlaeus, Clichtove, Longolius, Zwingli, Capito, Oecolampadius, and, "in England, besides Roseus [More] and others, John, Bishop of Rochester, who challenges you with his just tomes." [3]

Rhetorical devices are less frequent in the *Defense of the Royal Assertion* than in the preceding publication. The dilemma is used. For example, did the ancient Fathers have the true faith or not? If Luther answers negatively, he will be justly jeered by everyone; if affirmatively, he, like everyone else, ought to cling to the patristic opinion as true and solid. Moreover, in regard to the man who claims to have his every doctrine from heaven, proof of a single lie completely negates all his other teachings. Furthermore, if the Scriptures are most clear and to be understood according to simple grammar, then Peter can bind and loose as he wishes. On this point Luther is guilty of the very fault charged against his adversaries: mere assertion without scriptural proof. It is simple grammar, too, that should be applied to the demonstrative pronoun in the clause: "*this* is my body" (*hoc est corpus meum,* not: *hic* [*panis*] *est corpus meum*). In the denial of a centuries-old ecclesiastical custom, for example, the conception of the mass as a sacrifice, the burden of overwhelming proof is on the innovator. The fear of prolixity, expressed at the end of the refutation of the third of Luther's nine reasons, forces from Fisher the promise to answer the remaining six more succinctly. If Luther asks why Matthias was not ordained by the imposition of hands, Fisher wants to know the source of Luther's knowledge; for Luther frequently employs a useless argument from the negative.[4]

Metaphorical expressions, too, are relatively infrequent. Taking the sacrifice of the mass from the Church is like snatching the sun from the world. The function of the priest is not single but multiple: like a pharmacist, who grinds substances, mixes liquids, and heats compounds, so the priest now consecrates, now offers, now prays, and now commends living and dead to God through the virtue of the sacrifice. Paul addresses his words, "Test all things, but hold fast what is good" (1 Thess. 5:21), not to individual Christians but to the spiritualty, who perform the same function for the Mystical Body that the sense of taste does for the physical body. But the figure that dominates the whole work is that of Luther as the fox. This theme is sounded in the prologue, or introduction, and is repeated like a *leitmotiv* in the course of the *Defense.*[5] Even more important is the use of enumeration, for it helps to impose order on Fisher's response to a relatively free attack. In fact, comparison and enumeration meet in the prologue and set the tone of the whole work. But it might be best first to glance at the preliminary material.

A prefatory letter from the Dominican, John Host (or Horst) von Romberch, reveals that Fisher's two works, whose preparation for publication has been assigned to him, seem inspired by the Holy Spirit and in turn have encouraged him to publish his own lucubrations against Carlstadt, Justus Jonas, and others. As editor he has added the marginal glosses, especially the scriptural citations, and the Index, which is detailed and full.[6] Romberch's address does not appear in the *Opera omnia* (1597), as does Fisher's dedication to Bishop West of Ely, who had read a good part of the book two years before. Publication of the whole work had been postponed, however, because of false rumors of Luther's repentance. Actually, in the meanwhile, the Lutherans, hard at work upon their Scriptures, have been leading astray simple folk — who deserve their lot because they have spurned the salutary teachings of countless learned and virtuous shepherds of the Catholic Church, as will be seen at length in Chapter 11 of Fisher's present work. Bishop West is dear because he is a resident bishop assiduously teaching his flock the word of God, because he has encouraged Fisher in polemics, and because from his early years he had been Fisher's associate in academic exercises in which he continues unsurpassed. The present work will be an everlasting memorial to their mutual love.[7]

The prologue opens with Christ's admonition in the Canticles to catch the little foxes that destroy the vines, that is, to seize heretics, destructive of the Church, early and young.[8] Because the proper authorities failed in this duty, Luther has undergone metamorphosis from a little fox into a great wily fox, then into a mad dog, next into a ravening wolf, shortly into a savage she-bear, and finally into a cruel lioness — or, rather, into all of these at once; for he is like the portentous beast described by Daniel (Dan. 7:2–8, 19–20). He hurls insults even against most powerful kings, such as Henry VIII, who had wished only to counsel him to repentance. But he lures the ignorant populace with his vain promises and boasts of having his doctrines from heaven. To reveal the hundreds of errors and lies contained therein, Fisher follows the order of Luther's attack against the king but, for the sake of clarity, marshals his defense into twelve chapters. These he enumerates immediately.[9]

In Chapter 1, in his attempt to prove the lying nature of Luther's boastful assertion about having his doctrines from heaven, Fisher singles out the following particular errors: the nonapostolicity of James's epistle; the absolute equality of all Christians, even with Peter and Paul and the Virgin Mary; the denial of free will; the appeal to popular judgment; and the existence of errors in certain Psalms. Luther is totally unlike Savonarola of Florence, who was discredited by the nonfulfillment of his prophecies, but who was eminently virtuous and thoroughly orthodox and who inveighed only against the abuse of papal authority, not its concept and validity.[10] Chapter 2 dismisses as useless Luther's endeavors to clear himself of two of Henry's charges: his self-contradictions and his insults against the pope. His self-contradictions involve four views in particular: indulgences, the papacy's divine origin, the Hussite heresy, and excommunication. His reviling of the pope is countered by traditional arguments and by a more detailed defense of the king's words.

The next seven chapters center about the Eucharist as sacrament and as sacrifice. Chapter 3, on lay reception of communion under one species, has three major enumerations: ten conditions laid down for a legitimate custom in the Church,[11] twelve cavils (*cavilli*) of Luther answered, and the seven professedly strong arguments (*robora*) of Luther refuted. These last seven points are shown to have been adequately handled by the king, whereas Henry's own counterattacks have been by-passed by Luther. Chapter 4, on transubstantiation, proposes ten considerations on the relationship of the Church to Christ and the Eucharist, replies to four objections of Luther, and so on. In Chapter 5, which denies that the mass is a testament, Fisher points to Luther's fundamental mistake: his view of the Eucharist as a sacrament for the remission of sin, whereas it is really a sacrament of union with Christ and the Father. To prove this point, Fisher resorts to the Fathers and to the Scriptures. Both are used as authorities in Chapter 6 to demonstrate the nature of the mass as a sacrifice and a work (*sacrificium et opus*).[12] The brief Chapter 7 is devoted to an exposé of Luther's evasions and lies in respect to the royal defense of the mass. In Chapter 8 the mass is shown to be more than only a promise. Here the two major points treated are the integrity of the mass and the manner of receiving its fruits. Chapter 9 discusses matters falsely imputed to the king by Luther. This alternation of positive and negative sections shows Fisher's efficient and logical mind hard at work upon recalcitrant material and trying to reduce apparent chaos to a semblance of order.

Fisher's next two chapters establish criteria for the interpretation of Scripture and dogma. Chapter 10, positive in treatment, reiterates his attitude toward the Fathers taken collectively as the authoritative interpreter of the Gospel. Chapter 11, negative in nature, eliminates the common folk (*plebs*) as final arbiter in dogma. Their fickleness is manifest from pagan and Christian history, from the Old and New Testaments. Their ignorance is incapable of final decision on difficult questions like the admission of works to the scriptural canon, the consubstantiality of the Son with the Father, and the authenticity of James's epistle. Because he realizes the important implications of this point, Fisher discusses at some length each of Luther's nine scriptural texts, called Reasons (*rationes*).

Because Fisher is still following Luther's text, Chapter 12 treats the sacramentality of orders and matrimony. After scriptural proof for orders as a sacrament, Fisher approaches the far more difficult question of matrimony. After giving three reasons why the Church's view should be accepted, Fisher characteristically establishes five progressive Truths (*veritates*) to prove that matrimony is a sacrament in the strict and true sense. These Truths are preponderantly scriptural, although at the end there is an appeal to the Council of Florence which, truly ecumenical insofar as it was composed of both Latins and Greeks, defined the point.

The conclusion to the whole *Defense* is very brief. Fisher has slighted nothing in Luther's book except his insults, which have justly fallen back upon their author and serve only as a foil to make the king appear more brilliant, splendid, and illustrious.[13] In fact, Fisher has managed to keep his work on a relatively high level, as is immediately evident from any comparison between his tone and that of other adversaries of Luther, as, for example,

More or Cochlaeus. Even the opening comparison of Luther to wild beasts is mitigated by its brevity, its scriptural echoing, and Luther's own boast that he will prove a she-bear and lioness to Catholics.[14] What is more noteworthy is that Fisher's work marks a shift in tactics. At the beginning of the *Confutation of Luther's Assertion* he had refused Luther as a heretic the choice of weapons, but in the *Defense of the Royal Assertion* he constantly must resort to arguments from the Scriptures, which constitute Luther's chosen arms. His recourse to the authority of the Church and the interpretation of the Fathers is of course still evident; but, like a soldier who has discovered his conventional arms to be harmless, he turns to the weapon which his enemy has found effective.

Fisher not only realizes the need to use new arms (or, rather, old arms in new ways) but he also becomes aware of another key doctrine of the adversary — the equality of all Christians or believers. Just as the *Confutation of Luther's Assertion* had confronted particularly the problem of justification by faith alone, so the *Defense of the Royal Assertion* resists especially the appeal to popular opinion in scriptural and dogmatic matters as against the unanimous consent of the Fathers. But even more perilous was Luther's exaltation of the priesthood of all the faithful to the elimination of any special, visible priesthood with the power of teaching, ruling, and sanctifying the rest of Christians. The writing published simultaneously with Henry's defense undertakes to save a special priesthood.

Instead of attempting to refute the whole of the *Abrogation of the Mass* (*De abroganda missa privata*), Fisher wisely concentrates on a fundamental section which constitutes less than one fifth of Luther's complete treatment.[15] Fisher's Prologue quotes from the beginning of this section: "There is in the New Testament no visible and external priesthood save what has been set up by the lies of men and by Satan"; and it quotes from the end: "By these three arguments every pious conscience will be persuaded that this priesthood of the Mass and the Papacy is nothing but a work of Satan. . ." Fisher will meet Luther's three attacks with his own three "Rejoinders" (*congressus*). Actually it is Rejoinder 3 which contains "a clear and direct rebuttal of Luther's objections, one by one." [16]

Rejoinder 1 consists of five parts. After the first has explained

Tertullian's argument from prescription, the second cites Latin Fathers from Augustine to Tertullian, Greek Fathers from Damascene to Origen, and "authors yet older" from Hegesippus to Clement of Rome. The third part explains for Luther's satisfaction why the New Testament never uses the term *priests* — to avoid any confusion with the Jewish priesthood still in existence. The fourth part, which is corollary, expresses incredulity at the possible involvement of the Church in such a foul error in spite of redemption by Christ, guidance by the Holy Spirit, the vigilance of divinely appointed prelates during the centuries, and the unanimous agreement of all Churches throughout the ages. The fifth part, which is exhortatory, urges the reader to stand safely with the Fathers rather than perilously with Luther.[17]

The brief introduction to Rejoinder 2 defines the issue by quoting Luther: "There is no visible and external priesthood in the New Testament. . . Our one and only priesthood is the priesthood of Christ [1 Pet. 3:18, Heb. 10:14]. . . This priesthood is spiritual and common to all Christians. . . Nor have we need of any other priest or mediator but Christ." To show the enormity of these errors, Fisher proceeds to prove in detail ten Axioms. It is in the course of the last Axiom that Fisher, while proving that Melchizedek as a prefiguration of Christ and Christian priests offered sacrifice in bread and wine, quotes Jewish rabbis as well as Latin and Greek Fathers. The conclusion to the second Rejoinder offers the best possible summary of the ten Axioms:

> The first shows that for six undeniable reasons there must be placed over the multitude men to care for its interests. The second, that in fact Christ appointed such men to feed, govern and teach His, i.e. the Christian, flock. The third, that such men need a more abundant grace that they may the better discharge their office. The fourth, that in fact Christ did bestow such grace upon the pastors He appointed. The fifth, that these offices must necessarily be continued in the Church until the Last Day. The sixth, that no one lawfully discharges such an office, unless he be duly called, ordained, and sent. The seventh, that those who are legitimately appointed to such offices are undoubtedly to be believed to be called by the Holy Ghost. The eighth, that at the moment when they are thus appointed they receive always the grace of the same Spirit unless they place a hindrance in the way. The ninth, that the Holy Spirit infallibly gives this grace

at the performance of some external rite, i.e. the imposition of hands. The tenth, that the pastors and priests, so ordained by the imposition of hands, are truly priests of God and offer sacrifice both for themselves and for their flocks.

By divine institution, therefore, certain men are called and ordained to the special office of feeding, teaching, and ruling the flock; of offering the sacrifice of the altar; and of serving as mediators between Christ and the faithful.[18]

Rejoinders 1 and 2 lay the foundation for Rejoinder 3, which at first glance appears much of a potpourri until one perceives that it really does refute Luther's scriptural arguments in his own order. Luther himself gathers them into three groups. The first group is to "show that the one and only priesthood for us is that of Christ" (1 Pet. 3:18, Heb. 10:14); that this "priesthood of Christ is spiritual and is common to all Christians"; and that no other priest or mediator except Christ is needed. To support the last statement, Luther merely cites six texts, which Fisher, however, numbers and refutes at some length (Rom. 5:2, Is. 65:24, Is. 54:13, Jer. 31:34, Is. 11:9, John 6:45). After explaining more texts, Fisher tackles the problem of the failure of the New Testament to use the term *priests* in regard to a special priesthood as different from the universal priesthood of the faithful. After only a brief reference to the Fathers, his major arguments rest upon exegetical bases.

The refutation of Luther's first group is longer than that of the other two groups combined. In fact, brevity marks the discussion of the second group of six texts (Rom. 12:1, 1 Pet. 2:5. Ps. 50:19, Heb. 13:15, Hos. 14:3, Ps. 115:16–17), which are aimed at disproving any priesthood in a special sense. The third group (2 Cor. 3:6, 1 Pet. 2:9, Acts 14:11, 1 Cor. 14:40, 1 Cor. 14:27–31, John 6:45), which attempts to prove that "the office of teacher is common to all Christians," is refuted and then is succeeded by ironic comment on Luther's views on teaching by women, who after all are Christians. Toward the end Fisher resorts again to the argument from prescription by citing the earliest writers and popes on a special priesthood with a special ministry over the faithful — a device that helps to unify and round off the work. The third Rejoinder closes with reflections upon the people as a flock over which priests are rulers and shepherds. If priests are faithful to their office, all is well; if not, all is ill with the people —as the contemporary scene evidences.[19]

In the Epilogue to the whole work, a succinct summary is followed by a statement on the importance of the task: "From this truth [about the priesthood] necessarily flows all that is taught by the Fathers concerning the sacrifice of the Mass." But the mass, Fisher adds finally, has been already adequately treated in the *Defense of the Royal Assertion,* particularly Chapter 6.[20]

The style in general is marked by attention to clarity of structure. Where the structure becomes blurred, the fault may be ascribed to his good purpose: to refute Luther's arguments and objections in Luther's own order, one by one. The repetition or epitome of an immediately preceding section makes it easier for the reader to follow the argument but results in some verbosity. But Fisher excuses himself on the score that "no particle of doubt" must remain, as, for example, with respect to the bread and wine offered by both Melchizedek and Christ. Fisher claims that he is forced to it by "the vain boasting of Luther," e.g., in regard to the difference between priests and people. At least once, Fisher shows "how illogical and unconvincing is this negative argument," as when the Apostles' epistles abstain from applying the term *priests* to Christian priests. He repeatedly objects to Luther's abuse and prefers to proceed with the argument, although at one time he likens Luther to a mad dog and at another declares that Luther's abuses "fit no one else so exactly as himself." [21]

Strong language is employed also in Fisher's dedicatory epistle to Bishop Tunstal of London, which is not reprinted in the *Opera* (1597) in spite of its interesting contents. Tunstal, to whom Fisher had given his manuscript for criticism and for decision on its publication, had read it very carefully, suggested improvements, approved its printing, and expressed confidence in its triumph over the Lutherans. The correctness of Tunstal's judgment on the *Confutation of Luther's Assertion* is evident from the demand for a sixth edition. Fisher proceeds to argue that "since Christ's truth is one and undivided, it must be either as a whole with the ancient pastors of the Church or as a whole with Luther." He who disbelieves in even a single article of the faith is justly held guilty of disbelief in the whole faith. Either the Fathers of the past fifteen hundred years are wrong, or the Luther of the past four years is wrong. Why, Luther is not in agreement even with John Wyclif, John Hus, Johann Wessel von Gansfort, or Johann Pupper von Goch! The teaching of the Fathers has been approved by the Church through the centuries and confirmed by miracles. This statement is hardly true for Luther — who should perform even more splendid miracles than those worked by the Fathers. Every abusive name used by the Lutherans can be countered with another name by the Catholics, e.g., "sophists" by "apostates," "Aristotelians" by "heretics," and so forth. But it is preferable, Fisher declares, to put name-calling aside and to seek Catholic unity and truth — held by the Fathers through the centuries.

From another letter not reprinted in the *Opera* (1597), one addressed to Arnoldus de Tongri, rector of the University of Cologne, the reader learns that the busy lecturer and preacher, Johannes Host von Romberch, served as editor for the *Defense of the Sacred Priesthood* at the rector's request. Romberch found Fisher's work so perfect that he could add or take away nothing. He did provide marginal glosses, the detailed Index and the divisions of the Rejoinders (*Congressus*) into paragraphs: I into twenty-two, II into forty-nine, and III into forty. The editor's note (*Informatio*) at the head of the Index informs the reader that each entry is followed by the number of the Rejoinder and the paragraph, not of the page or folio, for the simple reason that the printer has published the work in different sizes (in which the pagination or foliation naturally differs) in more than two thousand copies.[22]

At the end of August 1525, Cochlaeus in Cologne refers to the recent printing of Fisher's two new books, which will please, astonish, console, and edify the devout but which cannot readily reach those Germans who need them most. In his farewell he gives his best wishes to Fisher as "mindful of devout Germans in both his most holy prayers and his most solid lucubrations." [23] Actually the *Defense of the Sacred Priesthood* marks the end of Fisher's direct controversial endeavors against Luther on the international scene. At home he would soon deliver his sermon at the abjuration of the Augustinian Robert Barnes; in Cologne he would publish his polemical *chef-oeuvre* against Oecolampadius with incidental animadversions against Luther. His decision to refrain from writing might be due much more to a sense of the futility of the task than to his preoccupation with the divorce of Henry and Catherine. He had announced his intention of withdrawal to Cochlaeus, who in a letter of July 1529 gave his approval because writing was a waste of time and talent in view of Luther's stubborn deafness to the admonitions of the learned, especially among the English. Yet this same letter, prefatory to a publication of Cochlaeus, urges Fisher to write just once more, not to Luther, but to the imperial officials and German nobles, to warn them of national disaster. Fisher's advice to allow Luther and his offspring to fight among themselves until rejected by all men with a spark of goodness is prudent counsel in its own time but is too dangerous because of the heretics' determination to eliminate all Catholics who acknowledge and embrace the Church. If Fisher wrote just once more to the Germans, Cochlaeus urged, his word would not return to him empty, "for the whole of Germany knows that you are a man of virtue and integrity whose lips declare exactly what his heart feels." [24] Cochlaeus' own word returned to him empty because Fisher manifests no sign of having complied with his request.

At any rate, after the simple and direct (but not unemotional) style of the *Defense of the Sacred Priesthood,* it is a pleasure to turn to the imaginative and complex sermon delivered on Quinquagesima Sunday, February 11, 1526. This sermon has been labeled a turning point in Catholic polemic from the offensive to the defensive.[25] The optimistic, triumphant tone evident in the sermon delivered five years earlier is lacking; but the attitude is still positive in its exaltation of the Church of the Fathers and its direct assault on Luther and his sect. This aggressive approach is apparent especially in a system of imagery which highlights the differences between the Church and Luther. Such are the contrasts: sight vs. blindness, light vs. darkness, the right way vs. the wrong, wheat vs. weeds, harmonious song vs. dissonant Babel, organic unity vs. dead limbs, good soil vs. stony or thorny ground, hundredfold fruit vs. sterility, and so forth.

In fact, it is in association with the Church that this sermon uses some of Fisher's most striking figures of which several have appeared in previous chapters. Of the multitude accompanying Jesus, persons going before Him represent the people of the Old Testament, those coming after Him the people of the New Testament: "Both these make but one people: For they be al of one faythe." Christ's Church is "euen like a floode that passeth continually / the waters go & passe / but yet the floode continueth / and reteyneth styl the name of the floode." The Church's doctrine is one seed, unmixed with such errors and heresies as found in Luther. It is one song, with the New Testament writers singing the plain song and the many Doctors the discant, unlike Luther's doctrines, which disagree with one another and with the Fathers, and unlike the battling Luther and Oecolampadius and Carlstadt, who now suffer the fate of Babel. It is one body with one life and soul. It is like a system of intercompenetrating circles, from which Luther has cut himself off with his contradictions. The birds of the air that eat the seed of God's word sown in the heretics' hearts are evil spirits that foster carnality. There are other outstanding comparisons. The sacrament of matrimony converts the carnality of married persons into spirituality as Christ changed water into wine at Cana. Nor should one overlook the similes, used in the prefatory epistle, to depict man's inclination to evil. His heart is like dry tinder inflamed to all evil at the least spark. It is like soil producing weeds or vices without effort, but sprouting good plants or virtues only with the most laborious cultivation.[26]

Nor is the epistle to the reader revealing only for this view of man's "wretched nature" as being prone to all evil. Here Fisher declares: "My duty is to endeuer me after my poure power / to resist these heretickes / the whiche seasse nat to subuert the churche of Christe." Evidently he will never be subject to the charge which in the prologue to the *Defense of the Royal Assertion* he had laid against authorities who *ex officio* should have caught the heretics when they were little foxes. Yet such is "the vntowardnes of mennes hartes" that even Christ and St. Paul complained of it in "that maruelous & plentuous tyme of all grace." Little wonder then that "nowe / in this miserable tyme / these heretickes multiply" — but "my lorde legate" (Wolsey) is laboring for "the full extirpation of the same." To Luther's disciple who thinks "that myn argumentes and reasons agaynst his maister be nat sufficient," Fisher gives a most important answer which critics of the style or the content or the argument should never forget: "Let hym consider / that I dyd shape them to be spoken vntyll a multitude of people / whiche were nat brought vp in subtyll disputations of the schole." [27] In a word, his address is a popular sermon, not a theological tract, and must be criticized as such.

The sermon can be praised for its rich texture and its ingenious imagery, but its structure is too intricate and confusing to leave his listeners with a single impression. The four Collections, which appear only after the lengthy introduction, are intended to serve as a means to unity and simplicity, but actually each Collection in itself is too complex to be easily followed or remembered. An excessive number of enumerations works against clarity and fragments the work. Most serious of all, the sermon falls into two parts, the one concerned with the miracle of the blind man and the other with the parable of the sower. Fisher's attempt to dovetail the two is clumsy, artificial, and forced. The sower of the seed is Jesus, ready to take away blindness of heart; the seed is the multitude's information about His passing by; the good earth is the multitude itself, with Jesus in their midst; and the increase in fruit is the degree of their closeness to Him. To all intents and purposes here are two sermons, separated by the prayer.

After a retelling of the day's gospel, the part before the prayer falls into five sections. (1) The multitude represents the one people of God, comprised of all believers of the Old Testament and all those of the New, but with a great difference between them, namely, the law of fear and rigor in contrast to that of grace, mercy, and love. (2) The blind man betokens the heretic bearing four marks: singularity in opinion, blindness of heart, departure from the way to heaven, and separation from the people of God. (3) The Church has the five opposite characteristics, namely, one common doctrine, the light of faith, the right way, progress toward heaven, and the everlasting presence of Christ. (4) The restoration of the heretic's faith is like that of the blind man's vision in four ways: inquiry after the truth, praying for sight and light, joining the multitude of the Church (even under compulsion, if necessary), and full assent to the doctrine of Christ's Church. (5)

Luther's doctrine on faith is refuted under three heads: his deception in describing faith as easy in his popular sermons (but difficult in his scriptural commentary); his denial of good works in justification (yet at least our assent to faith is ours and a good work); and the sufficiency of faith without "love pregnant with good workes" (though such faith is useless on Paul's own authority). Fisher had numbered the refutation of Luther on faith as being "in the fyfte and the last place," but now he adds: "Finally for a more clerenesse of these wordes / we shall considre .iij. maner of persones" — in their relation to the way. Those far out of the way are the Turks with their belief in God but not in Christ and His Church; those close to the way are the heretics with their belief in God and Christ but not in the Church; and those in the way are the multitude with faith in Christ's Church. In a direct address to those who have abjured, he declares: "It is . . . the faith catholicke of Christis churche that shal saue the: Whiche faith is made thy faith / if thou truly come vnto the right way." It is "to thentent that your sightis maye be the more clered in this faith" that Fisher will "gether .iiij. collections." The comprehensive prayer follows.[28]

Having retold the parable of the sower and announced his four Collections, Fisher opens the first on Christ as the sower with the objection that no mention is made of the influence of the heavens, that is, grace. The simple answer is that grace is presupposed since the sower is true God, "the very spirituall sonne of this worlde." To be brief, the seed is sown, under the influence of the Holy Spirit, through Christ's preachers — the Fathers and Doctors. But if their doctrine is true, Luther's contrary doctrine must be false. An exhortation to the abjured brethren ends this Collection.

The second on the seed stresses the oneness of the word of God with three considerations: (1) it is pure, unlike Luther's mixture of evil seed, that is, error and heresy; (2) it is consistent — like a harmonious song in which the inspired authors and the holy Doctors join, unlike Luther's clash with the Doctors, with himself, and with his followers; and (3) it possesses *one* Spirit of life which makes *one* body of Old Testament, New Testament, and Fathers. Luther cannot be a partaker of this Spirit for three reasons: his disagreement with the *one* doctrine of the Fathers under

Christ and the Holy Spirit, his denial of the *one* truth which must be with the Church, and his separation from the *one* body of Scripture, Fathers, and Church. The rather close reasoning here is followed by "a fewe wordes vnto these persons / which be abiured."

The third Collection shows the good earth to be "a spiritual generation: that is to say / the generation of christen people: whiche hitherto in dispite of all theyr ennemies / haue contynued / and shall continue vnto the worldis ende." The foundation for this continuance is the See of Peter, a point proved by five brief consecutive arguments hardly necessary to repeat here. The faithful heart is marked by three conditions: oneness with the doctrine of Fathers and Church, beauty unmarred by error, and goodness resulting in meritorious works. The conditions of the heretic, too, are three: carnality, contempt for authority temporal and spiritual, and contumely. Fisher then directs his speech to the "bretherne / whiche be abiured."

According to the fourth Collection, the "diuersite of encreace betokeneth vnto vs diuerse degrees of spiritualnes." It is at this point that Fisher dwells upon the absolute need for grace in spite of the most careful yet merely human preparation and disposition. Grace being understood as essential, marriage results in a thirtyfold increase, widowhood in a sixtyfold, and virginity in a hundredfold. The last is found in Christ, Mary "his blyssed mother," John the beloved disciple, Paul the Apostle, Mark the Evangelist and his Alexandrians, the women of Jerusalem mentioned by Eusebius, the hermits in the desert, and "in Christendome / at this day / many thousandes of religious men and women / that full truely kepe their religion & their chastite vnto Christ." But not so among the Lutherans, where priests, religious men, and consecrated virgins violate their vow of virginity. About widowhood, of course, Fisher has little to say.

As for the married state, the "holy sacrament of matrimony preserueth by his vertue the workes and dedes of them that be maried / so that tho workes / whiche without this sacrament shulde be dedly / be made by vertue of this sacrament either to be no synne / or at the least but veniall synne." Friar Luther's marriage to a nun can hardly be good for three reasons: his denial of matrimony as a sacrament, his abuse of a virgin consecrated to

Christ as His spouse, and his first promise (chastity) which invalidates every later promise — and for *seven* reasons! (Here Fisher attempts some rather lame humor: Luther's promise "was made in a corner and of some shorte aduisement: For with in vi. wekes after the mariage / his woman had a childe. This was speedy worke / a woman to haue a chylde within .vj. wekes of her mariage. This must either be a great miracle / orels they had met to gether before.") If a listener says that Luther found continence impossible, Fisher declares that he should have looked to that before entering religion and making his promise to God.[29] He should have chastised his body into submission as did St. Paul who did "suffre many temptations / and assaultes and brontes in his flesshe." As matters stand, Luther can claim increase of fruit neither from virginity nor from widowhood nor from matrimony since the latter in his case is null and void.

To this sin of "double sacrilege" Fisher adds a whole litany of Luther's blasphemies against God, Christ, the Holy Spirit, Christ's Mother, the cross, the saints, certain books of Scripture, the sacraments, the canon of the mass, the Fathers, the religious state, temporal and spiritual authorities, himself and his followers, and his own country ("the floure of the empire"), which he has involved in ruin and death.

In the concluding address to his abjured "bretherne," the preacher brings the sermon back to its beginning and again relates the parable of the sower to the miracle of the blind man. He urges the repentant culprits to follow the Church's doctrine, which always results in plenteous increase in "all these .iij. degrees" (virginity, widowhood, and matrimony). In addition, "by this doctryne ye may also be restored to the clerenes of your sight / as was the blynd man. . . And nowe hens forwarde (as that man dyd) folowe ye Christ in the right way," which "shall finally brynge you vnto the glorious contrey of heuen." [30]

Even from this analysis it is evident that, in spite of such labored efforts to fuse the two parts, the sermon lacks a real unity. In a word, it has a careful plan, the execution of which is defective. It is too laden with details to permit the hearer to perceive and hold the basic unity of the whole. Fisher has failed to apply the fundamental artistic principles of selectivity to minor points with a view to their subordination to the main theme. Even when the work is read thoughtfully at leisure, it is not easy to follow the line of development. Nevertheless, certain sections (for example, that on the system of circles within circles to depict the unity and consistency of the various books of the Bible and the opinions of the Fathers) are extraordinarily fine and help to keep the sermon a better one for its times. Like some of Pope's poems, it will continue to live as a literary piece by its many striking lines in spite of its relatively loose structure, its lamentable *argumentum ad hominem,* and other defects.

Chapter XVIII

ANSWERING OECOLAMPADIUS ON THE REAL PRESENCE

FISHER'S next publication, *The Reality of Christ's Body and Blood in the Eucharist against John Oecolampadius,* is his last notable work against Protestantism and undoubtedly his theological masterpiece. Its first mention occurs apparently in a letter dated September 15, 1526, where Cochlaeus informs the German humanist Willibald Pirckheimer that he has sent the latter's response to Oecolampadius to the Bishop of Rochester. Fisher has disclosed that a response of his own had grown into five books; he writes of their publication, but Cochlaeus has not seen them to date.[1]

The Bishop of Rochester is now at the apogee of his fame and influence. This situation is manifest in the fact that, like his other publications of that period, *Christ's Body* is destined to be printed in early 1527 in three editions of different sizes: in folio in February, in quarto in March, and in octavo in April. The detailed Index of notable points, together with the Elenchus (i.e., the Table of Contents) of main chapters, and Fisher's dedicatory epistle to Bishop Foxe, occur in all the editions. The Printer's Epistle to the Reader appears in the folio edition and, in a slightly altered form, in the quarto, but not in the octavo. Fisher's own Epistle to the Reader occurs only in the quarto. In other words, the preliminary materials vary considerably in the first three editions. The *Opera* (1597) reprints only the letter of the printer and the dedication to Foxe and, dividing the Elenchus into five parts, puts the appropriate part before each of the five books.

In the folio edition of February, the Printer's Epistle, written for Peter Quentell by Ortwin Gratius as is disclosed in the quarto version, reveals that Fisher had presented his manuscript to the publisher Francis Birckman. After extravagant praise by Gratius of Fisher as the most learned opponent of the Protestants, together with an inevitable tribute to Henry VIII's orthodox labor, the reader is informed that John Host von Romberch has supplied the Index and the marginal glosses. Gratius' Letter to the Reader in the quarto edition of March omits the reference to the labor of hardworking Romberch but otherwise has the same content. A notable addition occurs toward the close where Gratius reveals that in an epistolary preface to his edition of Rupert of Deutz's commentary on the Canticle of Canticles (1527) he has sung the praise of Fisher as "a man, by the god of truth, both very learned and very good." [2]

Fisher's Letter to the Reader appears only in the quarto edition of March — and unfortunately so, because of its interest and value. Oecolampadius' book puts Fisher in mind of scholastic disputations in which both sides of any question whatsoever can be argued, even the existence of God. And even that truth can be obscured and made to seem false by specious arguments and rhetorical tricks. So, too, with Oecolampadius on the Real Presence. A reader without dialectical training is likely to fall prey to his reputation for knowledge of languages and to his inquisitive spirit. Even if a return from the depths seems impossible for Oecolampadius, at least the Christian flock can be saved from harm. The precedent for severity with heretics has been set by John the Apostle, by Polycarp of Smyrna, by Anthony the Hermit, and the writings of Jerome, Augustine, and Hilary. Finally, to let the reader know exactly what he is doing, Fisher announces the division of *Christ's Body* into five books, together with the content of each book and especially the function of each Preface.[3]

The dedicatory letter to Bishop Foxe is notable for historical allusion and autobiographical confession: the foundation of Corpus Christi College at Oxford, Foxe's early patronage of Fisher, Fisher's precise relationship to the Lady Margaret, Henry VII's gratuitous appointment of Fisher to the bishopric of Rochester, and Fisher's happiness at being held responsible for only a tiny diocese. This letter singles out as the most distressing aspect of Oecolampadius' treatise the theory that the ancient Jews who had faith were members of Christ's Mystical Body and ate His Body and Blood as much as Christians do now. But actual eating of Christ's flesh and drinking of His blood does much more: it makes Christians in a unique way members of His Body as flesh of His flesh and bone of His bones.[4]

The over-all structure is simplicity itself. The verbatim rebuttal of Oecolampadius' treatise has been divided into five books. Each book has a lengthy Preface (*Praefatio*), not necessarily having a close connection with the section being refuted. Fisher is instinctively aware that an uninterrupted criticism of passage after passage in Oecolampadius would prove to be deadening. The method, moreover, would appear too negative and defensive in spite of the positive doctrine either presupposed or explicitly if fragmentarily stated. What is needed is an extended offensive, and this finds voice in the five Prefaces. It is impossible here to follow the line of argument, determined by Oecolampadius' publication, in details in the body proper; nor is it necessary in view of the present emphasis on structure and method. Now, what is of particular interest is the Prefaces, where Fisher, so to speak, is most himself.

The first Preface characteristically tries to prove the Real Presence from the very dissensions of the adversaries. Thanks are expressed to God for three reasons: (1) the mutual slaughter of the Lutherans in the peasants' revolt; (2) the surrender of the heretics to a reprobate sense (cf. Rom. 1:28), manifest especially in two ways: their sacrilegious marriages and their deafness to distinguished Catholic apologists in all countries; and (3) their proud minds, which have led to a threefold disagreement between Luther and Oecolampadius on the Body of Christ. In contrast, the Church is one because of Christ's continual presence. This first Preface closes with a warning to the reader on Oecolampadius' general method: his distortion of texts from the Fathers, his flagrant denial of authenticity to certain of their works, his use of truncated citations, his obfuscation of perfectly clear texts, his setting up of straw-man objections, and so on.[5] Fisher then begins the analysis of Oecolampadius' work with its title. Independently of the to-do about patristic passages, Book I proper offers enlightening discussion of Christ's use of tropes, the searching of the Scriptures, the scholarship of Peter Lombard, the value of ceremonies, and the place of miracles in the Christian dispensation.

In the second Preface, the excellence and the riches of the Eucharist are set forth under its various appellations: the Lord's Body, the Sacrament of the Lord's Body and Blood, the Mysteries (of Christ's death and His members' union), the Synaxis or Communion, the Eucharist or Thanksgiving, the Sacrifice, the Bread, the Lord's Food, the Viaticum, the Mystical Blessing, the Banquet, and the Exemplar (or Antitype). In conclusion, these names prove three things: the inexhaustible wealth of the Eucharist, the frustration of seeing in it mere bread and wine, and the reasonableness of calling this mystery an exemplar, or figure, although it contains realities (*res verae*), that is, the real Body and the real Blood of Christ, of which the appearances of bread and wine are certain signs. "The appearance of bread, to be sure, means for us the Body, and the appearance of wine the Blood. Then the Body itself under the appearance of bread represents the bloodless Body which was immolated on the cross, and the Blood itself under the appearance of wine represents the Blood shed on the same cross. Upon being devoutly received by us, they render us participants in the merits of the most bitter death of Christ. In addition, they represent (*figurant*) for us likewise the union of the Mystical Body and, upon being devoutly received, truly effect that same union." Most interesting of all in the second book are Fisher's views on figurative language in the Scriptures and on the differences between the Jews of the Old Testament and the Christians of the New Testament.[6]

Before taking up Oecolampadius' reasons for postulating only a figure of Christ's Body in the Eucharist, Fisher in the third Preface strengthens his readers in the faith with fourteen points which he terms Corroborations (*Corroborationes*). These are enumerated immediately: "1. The reality of Christ's Body in the Eucharist is proved by the most clear words of the same Christ. 2. The same reality is supported by the immensity of Christ's love. 3. The same is corroborated by the consent of the Fathers. 4. It is confirmed by Christ's promises. 5. It is established by many councils. 6. It is demonstrated by innumerable miracles. 7. It is defended by revelations most worthy of credence. 8.

Christ's protection against heresies has never been wanting. 9. Persons who frequently receive this sacrament advance in every virtue. 10. Persons who have idle opinions about it meet with ill fortune. 11. Enemies of this sacrament have no clear Scriptures on their side. 12. They produce the solid testimony of no orthodox writer. 13. They can present no miracles and no revelations. 14. Dissenters from the common belief of the Church mutually cut one another's throat." An extended explanation of each Corroboration follows.[7] Book III on the whole is taken up with answering Oecolampadius' objections to the Real Presence as being derogatory to Christ's wisdom, His glory, and His promises. Important positive contributions, however, are made: the significance of the Eucharist as sacrifice, its contribution to Christ's honor, and the spiritual effects of the physical reception of Christ's flesh.

The fourth Preface argues for the Real Presence from the consent of the Fathers. The latter term is made to embrace all outstanding orthodox writers in the previous fifteen centuries. Using the argument from prescription, Fisher manages to avoid a monotonous string of names by dividing the past into five groups of three centuries each, which he labels Trecenaries (*Trecenarii*). Little discussion of these Trecenaries is needed here because of their previous treatment above (Chapter IX). The first Trecenary is interesting for beginning with the names of Gregory of Nazianzus, Gregory of Nyssa, Basil the Great, and Hilary of Poitiers with the apology that, although they do not fall within its limits, they are closely akin to the ancients in their learning and holiness. Only then does Fisher take up Cyprian, Origen, Tertullian, Irenaeus, Ignatius, Dionysius, Clement, and the lives of Andrew and Matthew. Special care, according to Fisher's admission, has been expended on figures in the first and second Trecenaries because they are immune to attack in every way by their erudition, exegesis, sanctity, and miracles. This Preface ends with what might be called three Supplementary Notes (*Auctaria*): (1) all these Fathers believed in the Real Presence; (2) those orthodox writers not mentioned because of the loss of their works never taught the contrary; and (3) every person who does not believe in the Real Presence is separated from the Catholic Church and will not attain eternal salvation.[8] As might be expected, Book IV discusses patristic passages with much seesawing back and forth according to Oecolampadius' own text: Augustine, Origen, Ignatius, Ambrose, Origen, Cyril, Origen, Chrysostom, Cyprian, Augustine, Cyril, Augustine, Irenaeus, Tertullian, Chrysostom, Council of Nice, Chrysostom, Hilary, Ambrose, Hilary, Origen, and Augustine. The reader can well appreciate why Fisher with his orderly mind found it necessary to present the Fathers of the first and second Trecenaries in an organized, simple, and positive fashion in his Preface.

It is to the fifth Preface that Fisher seems to give special and climactic attention. He bends all his forces to prove that the sixth chapter of St. John's Gospel pertains to the Eucharist. He announces the source of his three arguments: the unanimous interpretation of the Fathers, the necessity for actual reception (*corporalis esus* — bodily eating) as well as for faith, and the words of Christ Himself and the scriptural circumstances. After a full proof for each point, he sets forth the adversaries' main objection: eternal life is promised both to him "who eats my Body and drinks my Blood" and to him "who believes in me." Consequently there is no real need of the sacrament for him who has faith. The answer must be that the faith required is of a special kind, one which not only believes what is proposed but does what is commanded. Therefore, besides simple faith, the sacraments, especially that of the Eucharist, are necessary, as is proved by three arguments: the unanimous agreement of the Fathers against heretics, the gradual disappearance of faith unless strengthened by the reception of the sacraments, and the impossibility of certitude about the possession of living faith without the reception of the sacraments. The significance of the last point has been pointed out in the treatment of faith and justification (Chapter XI). The interpretation of John 6:22–70 as Christ's promise on the actual reception (*corporalis esus*) of His true flesh in the Eucharist is confirmed by the clear statements in the other Gospels and in Paul's first letter to the Corinthians.[9] The body of Book V, in addition to animadversions on Oecolampadius' abuse of patristic citations, stresses the differences between the Jewish and the Christian Pasch, the proper interpretation of Oecolampadius' favored texts from Luke and Paul, and the response to the difficulty that Christ's Body is in heaven, not on the altar. The conclusion to the fifth book constitutes the conclusion to the whole work and gives the lie direct to Oecolampadius' assertion that he has demonstrated his point. Let the reader decide whether his seven lies have not been proved most clearly false.[10]

As far as theological method is concerned, in comparison with Fisher's earlier works, *Christ's Body* marks a shift to a discussion of the proper use of the Fathers. Fisher's main complaint is against Oecolampadius' distortion, truncation, and mutilation of nearly all the Fathers to make them prove his thesis. In this respect he is far worse than Luther, who at least openly rejects them when they oppose his opinion.[11] When Oecolampadius maintains the spuriousness of a work, e.g., that of Ambrose on the sacraments, Fisher simply turns to other and authentic writings of the same Father.[12] When his adversary gives mere snippings from Chrysostom's homilies, he supplies at some length what goes before and what comes after.[13] Gratian's carelessness in attributing a quotation falsely to Ambrose and not rightly to Chrysostom is excused on the score of excessive haste or of scribal error. Fisher proceeds to give Chrysostom's authentic text and interpretation as opposed to Oecolampadius' mutilation and misinterpretation.[14] The latter's citation of an author should be accompanied by its location in his works, for it is impossible to remember everything one reads, e.g., in Augustine.[15] For Augustine, too, the context clearly destroys Oecolampadius' argument from a truncated passage in *The Usefulness of Doing Penance* (*de utilitate agendae poenitentiae*).[16]

At times there are welcome autobiographical glimpses. Fisher must have handled the very old codex which, besides the Apostolic Canons, contains the decrees of the ancient popes and the acts of the councils, "where in the acts of the same council [held in Rome] I find written in its entirety [Berengarius' second abjuration] in these words: I Berengarius believe in my heart and confess with my mouth . . ." [17] Suppose that a reader should ask how Fisher knows that no orthodox writer has ever denied the Real Presence of Christ's Body in the Eucharist. "My answer is: partly, certainly, from the marvelous agreement of those whom I have read (and I have read, to be sure, a very great number), partly from the fact that even to this day none of the orthodox has been accused on this point." [18] At another place, Fisher says: "What I remember to have read in Origen, and (as I think) in his books against Celsus, bears on the point." [19] For the third trecenary he excuses himself from citing certain authors, for their volumes are commonly available, "but because the commentary which this Angelomus issued upon the Books of Kings is rather rare, I shall therefore now furnish his testimony." [20] In repeating his complaint about Oecolampadius' failure to give the location of his quotations, e.g., in stating that "Augustine says in a certain sermon," Fisher now becomes more personal in tone. Such negligence arouses his great suspicion because Oecolampadius often arbitrarily adds or omits words. "Nor is it easy for anyone to keep in his memory all Augustine's sermons. Besides, it would be a great expenditure of time for the answerer if these words should force him to go through the whole volume of Augustine's sermons. One thing, nevertheless, I do know, that, in spite of employing great industry, nowhere could I find these words in Augustine's sermons." [21] What a pathetic confession of a frustrated scholar looking for the source of a quotation!

The criticism of Oecolampadius' unscholarly manipulation of patristic texts reaches full tide in Fisher's fourth book, as is to be expected. Oecolampadius is charged with suppressing unfavorable passages in Ambrose,[22] with omitting a clear statement in Cyril just three lines before and corrupting a text (*vere propterea esse factam,* instead of *vere propriam esse factam*),[23] with leaving a sentence in Irenaeus incomplete,[24] with neglecting to furnish the whole context on one occasion and inserting his own words on another occasion in Tertullian,[25] and with often giving only a fragment from Chrysostom when what precedes and follows contradicts him.[26] Oecolampadius mutilates Ambrose and Augustine in the same way to serve his purpose.[27] To beguile the reader, he once weaves his own words into Augustine's text.[28]

Fisher finds pride to be the root of Oecolampadius' trouble. Relying too much on his natural talents, he delves too curiously into God's mystery and goes mad in just judgment. He is mad, besides, with too much secular knowledge.[29] He tries to cover up his madness with rhetorical trivialities and with many words in order to make a lie shine like the truth.[30] As for his constant but vain attempt to throw the burden of proof on his adversaries,

Fisher declares that his own position is so clear to the faithful from the Scripture, the Fathers, the Church, and custom that the burden must rest on Oecolampadius.[31] Rarely, however, does Fisher accuse him of arguing from the negative, as when he asks him how he knows the Apostles' lack of wonder at the miracle of the Eucharist.[32]

In view of Oecolampadius' basic doctrine of the Eucharist, it is hardly surprising to hear Fisher speaking much about figurative language in Scripture. No one doubts that speech without tropes is more simple than that with tropes, for simple speech spells simple meaning whereas a trope can easily be turned to different meanings.[33] As has been seen, Fisher is opposed to Origen's universal allegorizing exegesis on the authority of Augustine, Jerome, and all the other weighty interpreters.[34] To join tropes to plain truths is like joining a horse's neck to a human head (cf. Hor. *A.P.* 1).[35]

The rhetorical device which predominates in *Christ's Body* is the adage or proverb. The adage often involves a metaphor or an image, which cannot be conveniently separated from it. These adages might be grouped according to various categories. The physical world furnishes the basis for many. Oecolampadius errs from the truth *toto caelo*. He promises mountains of gold but fails to produce them. One argument of his is so incoherent as to be like a rope of sand. On three occasions, at least, his blindness is related to Cimmerian darkness. In his confusion he is trying to mix fire and water. His pointless comments are said to be of the same grain (*farina*).[36]

The animal world is the source for a surprising variety of adages. It is with nothing but spider's webs that Oecolampadius is trying to establish his heresy. In the understanding of mysteries he is blinder than a mole. At one time he is muter than a fish. At another he crows like a cock before he has even achieved the victory. The dispute, he is reminded, is not about goat's wool (i.e., mere trifles) but about our eternal salvation. Yet the Reformers are deafer to appeal than an ass (*agnus,* leg. *asinus*) to the lyre. Christ is said to have made a statement for our sake, not for that of Nicodemus, who at that time was as appreciative as an ass of a lyre. Having Zwingli the heretic praise Oecolampadius the heretic is like having one mule scratch another. Finally, Fisher gives Demosthenes' fable addressed to Philip about the wolf who persuaded shepherds to let him take care of the sheep.[37]

Man's nature and activities not unexpectedly furnish many adages. At one point Oecolampadius' impudence compels Fisher to chew Augustine beforehand and force him into Oecolampadius, that is, to explain Augustine painfully and accurately to Oecolampadius. At another point Oecolampadius' grand but unfulfilled promises make Fisher declare that he is preparing fine white bread (which never materializes). At still another point he is told that he is acting his tragedy against the Lutherans, not against the Catholics. Oecolampadius is more fittingly labeled, not a *rhipsaspis* (recreant in throwing away his shield in battle), but a *rhipsokindinos* (reckless in running needless risks). He uses violence on the Fathers and twists them by the hair. But until the Greek Calends he will never be able to show contrary or repugnant opinions in the Fathers. Fisher's fond wish for him is: "May the gods give you back your mind." When Oecolampadius makes a worthwhile statement, he is praised: "Now you are singing our part of the song." He has more devious devices than Sisyphus, but his progress is always like that of Mandrabulus — for the worse.[38]

Like other means used by Fisher, these adages with their concomitant images, metaphors, and allusions serve a wholly subordinate, one might almost say incidental, purpose — that of underlining the argument. His fundamental strategy, it has been claimed by W. Köhler, is to widen the cleavage between Lutherans and Zwinglians and to draw Luther into the Catholic party. As for the Real Presence, Oecolampadius himself does not distinguish much between Lutherans and Catholics in spite of their differing explanations. In Fisher's eyes, insofar as Luther too departs from the traditional Catholic teaching, he is as blameworthy as Oecolampadius, but the latter is far worse simply because his divergence into error or heresy is the greater. In their rejection of Oecolampadius' theory, Luther and Fisher differ in method. Even though the orientation for both must be scriptural, nevertheless Fisher does not eschew the Scholastic traits of exactness and thoroughness in undermining Oecolampadius' "rationalistic" positions, in solving all possible difficulties, and in setting forth his own — that is, the traditional — doctrine.[39]

The difficulty is that, except for the masterful and readable five Prefaces, the all-important positive teaching is embedded in and intermingled with the verbatim refutation of Oecolampadius. Thus, the principal objection against *Christ's Body* is its prolixity, with its consequent lack of popular appeal. In this respect, no matter how solid its theological basis, it is inferior to the attractive treatises of his opponent.[40]

Nevertheless, even the German critic who asserts that the close following of Fisher's line of argument is lost labor ends up by declaring that *Christ's Body* is a valuable link in the chain of intellectual productions concerning the Eucharist and that, in comparison, Clichtove's simultaneous publication is unrewarding.[41] A Franciscan theologian, who sees *Christ's Body* as "a work exclusively patristic," emphasizes the influence exercised upon the continental controversy over the Eucharist, and particularly over the Real Presence, by English writers, namely, Henry VIII, Fisher, Tunstal, and Gardiner. The last two, he claims, wrote independently of each other and also of the Bishop of Rochester.[42] On the other hand, an English scholar asserts that, in addition to much firsthand study of the Fathers, English theologians read continental literature, studied one another, and borrowed citations: "In the eucharistic controversy . . . Cooper used Jewel, just as Gardiner used Fisher, and Fisher the medieval authorities. . ." [43]

It was hardly common for sixteenth-century writers, including the humanists, to admit indebtedness to their contemporaries. They borrowed ideas freely without acknowledgment. Only a chance word at times reveals their obligations. The reading of Fisher by Catholic controversialists is disclosed almost casually when they refer their readers to his writings for full treatment of a subject. Thus, in his treatise on the divine institution of the mass (1528), Thomas Murner urges his audience to see the Bishop of Rochester's proof that no Greek or Latin Father ever doubted the dogma.[44] At this same time, although he does not single out *Christ's Body,* Nicholas Herborn in his *Handbook of Commonplaces against Contemporary Heresies* (1529) sends his readers for more extensive treatment to a short list of Catholic apologists, headed by the Bishop of Rochester, with their "huge tomes and works." [45]

Nor are such testimonies restricted to Germany and to Fisher's lifetime. A dozen years after his death, at a meeting of theologians at Trent in February 1547, on the meaning of "Unless you eat the flesh of the Son of Man . . ." (John 6:54), those who held for a spiritual rather than a sacramental reception of the Eucharist were countered by those who felt that the Bishop of Rochester and others had settled the matter once for all.[46] The Jesuit Salmeron also alluded to the many doctors alleged by Fisher to be in favor of the Real Presence. Some forty years after the publication of *Christ's Body,* Ruard Tapper in discussing the Real Presence points particularly to the Prefaces to the third book (the fourteen Corroborations) and the fourth book (the five Trecenaries with the unanimous agreement of Fathers and Doctors from Ignatius of Antioch to contemporaries). He labels the Bishop of Rochester "the defender of the Catholic truth and the most keen opponent of heresies in the divine and most learned work which he wrote against the blasphemous and altogether execrable book of John Oecolampadius." [47] William Lindanus (Willem van der Lindt) in his *Panoply of the Gospel* declares that in the fight against Zwingli, Oecolampadius, Peter Martyr, and Calvin, "the English Church with great glory has shown us outstanding defenders of the Catholic faith, among whom, after Christ's illustrious martyr, blessed John [Fisher] of Rochester, have shone Stephen [Gardiner] of Winchester, Chancellor of England, and Bishop Tunstal, Archdeacon Alban [Langdaile], and likewise many other learned men." [48] In his ecclesiastical annals for A.D. 1526, Raynaldus gives five sizable citations from *Christ's Body,* which testify to the eloquence and solidity of the work.[49]

To return to *Christ's Body* itself. In spite of his intentions of doing so, Oecolampadius never succeeded in writing an answer to Fisher's work. Far closer and more urgent, to be sure, was the challenge from Germans like Luther, Pirckheimer, and others. The very bulk of the work by the bishop in far-off England, moreover, would prove so dismaying as to cause an opponent to postpone an answer in quest of the necessary time and leisure—which never materializes. In all fairness it must be noted that, even before the Eucharistic controversy, Oecolampadius had told

Guillaume Farel of his plan to take up the cudgels against "Fisher with Eck and other monstrosities." [50] In his *Second Reply* (*Responsio posterior*) to Pirckheimer, March 1527, he declares that he has delayed his answer to Clichtove's attack to "await what, worthy of the episcopal insignia [*infula*], would be sent from England by John [Fisher] of Rochester, who they report plasters their ruinous wall from the same pail [of whitewash] and the same badly mixed clay." In reply to Pirckheimer's suggestion that he should have sought advice from learned and wise men beforehand, Oecolampadius declares that he has not conferred with men of Clichtove's ilk but that he has summoned Origen, Chrysostom, Basil, Augustine, Jerome, and Ambrose for conference and confirmation.[51]

On May 1, 1527, Oecolampadius' letter to Zwingli reveals that the brethren in Strasbourg are clamoring for his answer to "the Frenchman and the Englishman, that is, to Clichtove and Rochester." The difficulty, he finds, is that every provocation of adversaries makes them point to a book, count themselves victors, and complain of needless expostulation with the stubborn.[52] On June 15, 1527, he writes that, unless Zwingli instructs him otherwise, his "mind is set to attack Rochester and Clichtove," and indeed in a single work.[53] If he ever wrote such a work, it was never printed. In his dialogue in 1530 on patristic opinion about the Eucharist, the character named Nathanael says: "It is no cause for wonder if you neglect Rochesters, Clichtoves, Fabers, and many others who are foulmouths more than theologians." [54]

If this remark is looked at from a merely human angle, Fisher might have found it "the most unkindest cut of all" to have his reputation and ability as a theologian impugned by Oecolampadius. It would have confirmed him in his determined decision, mentioned in Cochlaeus' letter of 1529 (see above, Chapter XVII), to write no more against the heretics, who were now deaf to all argument and hardened against all reason. He would have approved the declaration which was made by another native bishop, Jeremy Taylor, more than a century later and which was confirmed by an anecdote about himself: "But thus the Enemy of Mankind hath prevailed upon us while we were earnest in disputations about things less concerning: Then he was watchfull and busie to interweave evil and uncertain principles into our

Moral institutions, to intangle what was plain, to divide what was simple, to make an art of what was written in the tables of our hearts with the finger of God. When a Gentleman was commending Dr. *Fisher* Bishop of *Rochester* his great pains in the confutation of *Luther's* books, the wise Prelate said heartily, that he wish'd he had spent all that time in prayer and meditation which he threw away upon such useless wranglings. For that was the wisdom of the Ancients." [55]

Chapter XIX

TACTICS OF THE DEFENDER OF THE BOND

THE time was at hand for Bishop Fisher to learn that "a man's enemies will be those of his own household" (Matt. 10:36). His adversaries were not now continental reformers and their followers but his king and the king's servants. Of the seven or eight tracts on the divorce, to which Fisher in the Tower confessed authorship, three lend themselves to analysis: (1) "Licitum fuisse matrimonium Hen: 8: cum Catharina relicta fratris suj Arthurj" (Camb. Univ. Lib. MS. 1315), to be labeled here "Liceity"; (2) *De causa matrimonii serenissimi regis Angliae liber* (Alcalá, August 1530), to be shortened as *Causa;* and (3) "Responsum ad libellum impressum Londini 1530" (Brit. Mus. MS. Arundel 151), to be designated as "Response" or "Responsum." [1]

"Liceity" is presumed to be the defense of Henry and Catherine's marriage which was submitted to the legatine court during Fisher's unexpected and dramatic appearance and speech on June 28, 1529. If so, it manifests a simplicity and naïveté which at first seems hardly excusable after two years of thought and argument, including even a skirmish with the learned Robert Wakefield. Perhaps Fisher wishes to cut the worse than Gordian knot with the sword of papal authority: the pope could and did dispense in this dispensable case. That Fisher has elaborated his brief carefully is evident from his use of the syllogistic form; any rigidity has been offset, however, by the rhetorical polish of the style. The direct address to the legates, with its mention of "these written words" (*his scriptis*), makes it clear that it was meant to be read silently and not to be spoken aloud, but the attention paid to making the argument easy to follow and the care spent on the vocal cadences would make delivery simple and effective.

The only marked literary device is the Latin adage or proverb, which Fisher employs quite effectively. In striving to discover a basis for the invalidity of Henry and Catherine's marriage in the Levitical prohibition (Lev. 18:16, 20:21), his adversaries are engaging in an activity as futile as seeking wool on a donkey ("lanam ab asino quaerunt"), or hunting a hare outside its burrow ("Inanis est venatio leporis extra sedem suam"), or shaking a bush from which the bird has already flown ("frustra dumus excutitur, in qua non residet avis"). By failing to reconcile the prohibition in Leviticus with the leviratic precept in Deuteronomy (25:5), they are keeping the two farther apart than treble and bass (*lit.* than a double octave: *longius quam bis diapason*). Nevertheless it is plainer than any sun (*omni sole clarius*) that the wife whose husband has died childless is exempt from the Levitical prohibition against marriage to one's brother's wife. Yet Fisher can apply a proverb to himself also. In trespassing on the territory of canon lawyers, he realizes that he must face the criticism: The cobbler should not go beyond his last (*Ne ultra crepidam sutor*).

The overall structure of the tract is unusual. A brief introduction is followed by the main body which establishes six Axioms. The first Axiom, constituting more than half of the text, is proved by three Reasons, of which the third is summarized in six Truths. The second Axiom, more than one fifth of the whole, issues in seven Conclusions. Axioms 3–6 are rapidly handled in about one seventh of the space, before a relatively lengthy conclusion of two pages. This analysis may give the impression of a total lack of balance, but the subdivision of Axioms 1 and 2 into Reasons, Truths, and Conclusions serves to separate them into lesser and more manageable units.

Fisher's introduction gives the factual background, states the issue (the liceity of the marriage), announces his argument from six Axioms, and disclaims any use of rhetorical techniques or ornaments so that the naked truth of the matter (*nuda ipsius rej veritas*) may appear. Of the six Axioms, enumerated at once, the first two offer greater difficulty than the rest and require more extensive treatment.

The first Axiom, which enunciates that Henry and Catherine had no impediment from which the pope's authority could not dispense, is proved in neat syllogistic form. Briefly, their case does not fall under the prohibition in Leviticus (18:16, 20:21), the only place in the whole Bible to forbid marriage with one's brother's wife, for three Reasons: (1) the cases of Judah and Tamar (Gen. 28), Ruth and Boaz (Ruth 3), and the natural and legal fathers of Mary's spouse, Joseph (Matt. 1:16, Luke 3:23); (2) the leviratic law (Deut. 25:5), interpreted as a precept and not a concession by Jerome, Augustine, Hesychius, Chrysostom, Theophylactus, Tertullian, Alphonsus, Aquinas, Lyra, and Cardinal Hugo; and (3) the praise and the blessings promised to the observers of the levirate. To ask whether the Levitical prohibition is moral or judicial is fruitless; and here occurs Fisher's statement that he has discussed the question *alibi satis exacte,* as he has that of the natural law. General prohibitions, he continues, often have exceptions, as in the case of work on the Sabbath and of the commandment not to kill; so, too, in the matter of marrying a brother's wife. Fisher then proceeds to answer objections based on the inferiority of Deuteronomy to Leviticus, the positive prohibition of such a marriage under the New Law, the decrees of various councils, and the denial of the dispensing power of the pope by Peter de la Palu, Torquemada, Antoninus of Florence, and others. For the sake of clarity, he sums up the Third Reason in six Truths. (1) The levirate is a divine precept. (2) Deuteronomical precepts are as authoritative as Levitical prohibitions. (3) The rewards promised to the observers of the levirate are no less valid than the penalties threatened to violators of the Levitical prohibitions. (4) The Deuteronomical precept is to be understood of a dead brother's childless wife; the Levitical prohibition, of a living brother or of a dead brother's wife with children. (5) The Deuteronomical precept does not fall under the Levitical prohibitions. (6) Absolutely no biblical text forbids marriage to a brother's childless widow. John the Baptist's rebuke of Herod is not to the point, whether Philip was alive, as Jerome holds, or dead but not childless, as Chrysostom maintains.

To the objection that marriage with a dead brother's wife, even childless, is forbidden by the natural law (as evidenced by Lev. 18:24–30), Fisher gives a sevenfold answer. (1) Jews practicing the levirate *de facto* did not perish. (2) A man could legitimately marry his dead wife's sister, an equivalent relationship. (3) If the gentiles had the natural law written on their heart, so have we; yet whence this controversy? (4) Things which Moses calls abominable and execrable are not so now; for example, eating of eel. (5) If the natural law is recognized as soon as heard, why the doubts of sharp men like Augustine, Druthmar, Peter of Blois, Alexander of Hales, Aquinas, Scotus, Francis of Meyronnes, Thomas of Strasbourg, Angelus Carletus de Clavasio, and Antonius de Rosellis? (6) Because of difficulty and obscurity, this practice should have been proscribed the Canaanites by written law or other means. (7) Before the Law and under the Law, the Jews were commanded to practice the levirate. Since marriage with a brother's childless widow does not fall under the Levitical prohibitions and hence is not forbidden by divine law or natural, since it is prohibited nowhere else in the Bible, it does not constitute an impediment not dispensable by the pope. Such a summary is characteristic of Fisher.

At the beginning of Axiom 2, the Bishop of Rochester begs the indulgence of lawyers and canonists for trespassing into their territory; he explains that his plea remains basically theological. A petition granted by the pope is either ordinary, and hence confined to the terms of its bull, or extraordinary, and hence extended to the fullness of papal love and indulgence. Of this latter class was the pope's dispensation for the marriage of Henry and Catherine, from which he intended to remove every possible impediment. The outcome of Fisher's seven explanatory Conclusions is that no defect in the bull can possibly invalidate the all-important internal assent of the pope.[2] To the objection that Henry and Catherine were minors or unaware of the negotiations, Fisher replies that in both the Old and the New Testaments parents act validly for their children. The fear that the parties concerned might have been circumvented is stilled by the observation that Henry VII, Ferdinand the Catholic, and Julius II were too sagacious for that, a fact indicated by the cautionary clause: "Matrimonium . . . carnali copula forsan consummavissetis."

It is at this point that Fisher indulges in a highly emotional outburst most unusual in such circumstances:

With the greatest possible humility of soul, I beg the indulgence of the Most Reverend Lord Legates if I now reveal in these written words what I tearfully lament in the depths of my heart. For it makes me tremble even to think of the great inconstancy with which the Apostolic See hereafter will be charged if the Sovereign Pontiff Clement, for a cause which involves no difficulty arising from divine law, should break up a marriage which, in all kindness and all affection, at the solicitation of those most illustrious kings through their ambassadors, he had once confirmed by his authority. O for the misfortune of our times! O for the pitiable ruin hanging over the head of the Church, if there should be such an outcome to this affair — which God forbid!

At least the horrendous scandal should keep sentence from ever being pronounced. To prevent the scandal of divorce, Innocent III had dispensed the Livonians in the very case in question, that of marriage to their brothers' wives, just as Martin V later dispensed a man who had married the sister of the woman with whom he had had intercourse. "Wherefore I have no doubt that if the Most Reverend Lord Legates, in accordance with their excellent prudence and discretion, weigh exactly the number and the enormity of the scandals which will likely flow from this affair, even if nothing else were at stake, they will never attempt to dissolve this marriage." And, after these words, Fisher affixes a relatively full epitome to conclude this second Axiom.

Since Axioms 1 and 2 lay deep foundations, what follows needs little proof or explanation. Axiom 3 shows that the removal of impediments rendered Henry and Catherine fit subjects for valid matrimony. Axiom 4 establishes the historical fact that the marriage was actually celebrated according to the rites and ceremonies of the Church. Axiom 5 denies any possible doubt that God sanctioned and blessed the marriage. Axiom 6 declares that the matrimonial bond joined by God can now be dissolved by no other power than His. In the Cambridge University manuscript this sixth Axiom is not developed, but two pages and a half are left blank for further writing.

The conclusion to the whole tract is at once a prophecy and a challenge. A whole abyss of troubles and calamities will open up for the entire realm if the divorce succeeds. For example, what marriage will ever be safe if this one, hedged in by so many safeguards, has issued in a divorce? But the marriage will stand unless one can prove indisputably that the pope had no power to dispense or that he did not actually dispense in this case. Neither is humanly possible in consequence of these six Axioms, and, above all, the first two.[3]

The tract published at Alcalá in August 1530 seems almost to pick up where the manuscript "Liceity" had left off. In his introduction to the *Causa,* Fisher laments the denigration of the royal marriage and fears for the scandal created by the Apostolic See if it annuls the union after numerous dispensations in similar cases have been granted by Innocent III, Martin V, Alexander VI, and Leo X. After outlining the history of the case, Fisher castigates the persons who encouraged Henry VIII's scruple arising from the Levitical prohibitions and places the burden of proof squarely on the shoulders of the advocates of the divorce. He rests his own case on five points, developed in the body of the tract.

Whereas the "Liceity" had concentrated on the possibility and the fact of the papal dispensation, the *Causa* approaches the problem from another angle: the meaning and nature of the Levitical prohibition not to marry a brother's wife. There has also been a shift from personal argument to appeal to authority in order to establish the five central points. Unfortunately the design of the book by the printer is very poor and makes it difficult to follow the line of argument. Relatively insignificant items like the names of individual authorities are thrown into disconcerting prominence, whereas important aspects like the five points and the transitions from point to point are buried in small type. Fisher's documentation, however, will be given here in order to show the range of his scholarship.

Unlike the "Liceity," the *Causa* does not give disproportionate treatment to any of the five points. The first point, namely, that the leviratic marriage (Deut. 25:5) is truly preceptive and not merely permissive, is proved from Julius Africanus, Eusebius of Caesarea, Tertullian, Jerome, Origen, Damascene, Chrysostom, Hilary, Hesychius, Druthmar, Ambrose, Theophylactus, and Augustine. Its preceptive nature is evident also from the punishment inflicted on those who do not observe it, whereas no penalty is threatened against those who do not avail themselves of the permission to practice usury or divorce.

The second point eliminates the subterfuge of persons claiming that the Deuteronomical precept applies to a relative, not to a real or blood brother. Here Fisher summarizes and lists in altered order the Collections "in our third writing on this same matter": a real brother is understood by (1) Hebrew, Greek, and Latin exegetes, of whom a full list is given: Origen, Hesychius, Damascene, Chrysostom, Eusebius, Raoul de Flaix, Joseph, Rabbi Moses the Egyptian, Lyra, Alphonsus, Jerome, Hilary, and especially Africanus; (2) the whole Church, which as "the pillar and mainstay of the truth" (1 Tim. 3:15) could not have been mistaken for centuries; (3) the popes, especially Innocent III, who now have the same role of official interpreters of Scripture that the Jewish priests had in the Old Law (Deut. 17:8–13); (4) the three Evangelists: Matthew, Mark, and Luke; and (5) the three versions: Hebrew, Greek, and Latin.

The first two points are then reinforced by four examples, all taken from the genealogy of Christ: (1) Joseph, whose natural father was Jacob (Matt. 1:16) but whose legal father was Eli (Luke 3:24), as can be proved from Africanus, Eusebius, Gregory of Nazianzus, Damascene, Jerome, and Augustine, as well as Bede, Rabanus, Druthmar, Clement of Llanthony, Zachary of Besançon, Alphonsus, Lyra, Albert, Peter Comestor, and innumerable others; (2) Shealtiel, whose natural father was Jeconiah (Matt. 1:12) but whose legal father was Neri (Luke 3:27); (3) Obed, whose natural father was Boaz (Matt. 1:5) but whose legal father was Mahlon (Ruth 4:10); and (4) Perez, whose natural father was Judah (Matt. 1:3) but whose legal father was Er (Gen. 38:6–8). To the objection based on a spurious work of Chrysostom that Tamar was a virgin, Fisher answers that it made no difference to Judah.

The third point insists that the Levitical prohibitions are not to be understood universally. The curse on marriage to a brother's wife (Lev. 20:21) is restricted to one of three Senses, each with its authorities — Sense 1: marriage to a living brother's wife, an interpretation espoused by Augustine, Raoul de Flaix, Peter of Blois, Druthmar, Cardinal Hugo, the Author of the Interlinear Gloss, Alexander of Hales, Bonaventure, Scotus (an objection to whom is solved through Sedulius, Peter of Tarantasia, and Kilwardby), Francis of Meyronnes, Wendelinus Steinbach, and Albert the Great, whose physiological explanation is that the son's similarity to the first husband is effected by the latter's previous influence on the mother's womb; Sense 2: marriage to a dead brother's wife left with children, but not marriage to a childless widow, a view favored by Chrysostom, Aquinas, Lyra, Torquemada, Innocent III, Antonius de Rosellis, Peter Comestor, and Vincent of Beauvais; and Sense 3: marriage to a brother's divorced wife, a position taken by very few but conceived as possible by Cardinal Hugo, James of Lausanne, and Robert Grosseteste.

According to the fourth point, the Levitical prohibition is judicial. Of course, if one adopts the first Sense above, the prohibition is moral. But the second Sense clearly makes it judicial only, as can be seen in Wendelinus Steinbach, Aquinas (including his commentator Cajetan), Thomas of Strasbourg, Francis of Meyronnes, Eucherius of Lyons, and Moses himself. This view of Moses is held by Paul of Burgos, Hugh of St. Victor, Cardinal Hugo, Jerome, Augustine, Aquinas, Alexander of Hales, Bonaventure, and Richard of Middleton. The only marriage forbidden before the Mosaic Law was that between father and daughter and between mother and son. To complete this fourth point, Fisher disposes of three objections: (1) from the phrase "to destroy out of the midst of the people" (Lev. 20), (2) from Augustine's *Speculum,* and (3) from intercourse with a menstruous woman (Ezek. 18:6).

In the fifth point, Fisher treats the dispensability of the Levitical prohibition. No dispensation is possible if there is question of marriage to a *living* brother's wife. Fisher then gives ten Reasons for holding that the prohibition refers to a *living* brother. These are summary repetitions of the "many reasons" he has given "elsewhere" (*alibi*): (1) the authority of Augustine, Raoul de Flaix, Peter of Blois, Druthmar, the Author of the Interlinear Gloss, Cardinal Hugo, Alexander of Hales, and others; (2) the parallel case of a *living* wife's sister; (3) the similar case of a *living* neighbor's wife; (4) the absolute severance of the marital union by death; (5) the constant practice of the levirate among the Jews; (6) the persistent view of the levirate as licit; (7) the reconciliation between Deuteronomy 25:5 and Leviticus 20:21; (8) punishment for not observing the levirate; (9) childlessness a penalty for violating Leviticus 20:21 and fruitfulness for observing Deuteronomy

25:5; and (10) foulness of the marriage in Lev. 20:21 but virtue of that in Deut. 25:5. Since the prohibition against marrying a *living* brother's wife is moral, even the pope cannot give a dispensation.[4]

What about marriage with a dead brother's wife who has had children by him? For good reasons, a papal dispensation is possible, valid, and licit. A fortiori, it is even easier in the case of a dead brother's childless widow. Here Fisher cites the *Summa* of Angelus Carletus de Clavasio, who holds that the pope can dispense in all moral precepts of the natural and divine law for spiritual causes whenever the reason for the particular law ceases. Angelus himself appeals to Richard of Middleton, Antoninus of Florence, and all canonists whenever they say that the pope can declare, interpret, limit, and distinguish the divine law. The verdict of Angelus is supported by Fisher through the opinions of Peter de la Palu, Torquemada, and Antoninus. Since only the pope has the power to decide questions of Scripture in cases of controversy, his verdict must be accepted on the validity and liceity of a marriage to a dead brother's childless widow.

In a brief conclusion to the *Causa,* Fisher restates his five points. Even if his arguments are not irrefragable, he claims, his adversaries can offer no insolvable difficulty. Until they can, the dispensation of the pope and the validity of the marriage stand.

The tone of the *Causa* is definitely academic. There is no rhetorical adornment except for an adage or two. For example, in trying to create a difficulty (divine prohibition and papal indispensability) where there is none, Fisher's adversaries are solicitously seeking in a bulrush a knot where there is none: "in hoc scirpo nodum (vbi nullus est) . . . anxie quaerant." Fisher himself makes the leviratic precept (Deut. 25:5) agree with the Levitical prohibition (Lev. 18:16, 20:21) by having the prohibition pertain to the wife of a *living* brother; and thus he is but applying the principle: Every truth jibes with every other truth (*omne verum omni vero consonat*).

Fisher keeps asserting that his case is much more plausible than that of his opponents. The reason for not claiming absolute certainty for his argument might be the realization that many of his readers would belong to the academic community, which would not be swayed by practical or trivial considerations. This conjecture might also explain his appeal to authorities, who naturally would be quite familiar to his audience. In fact, the prefatory letter of the printer to the reader would indicate that the *Causa* was intended, or at least published, as a guide to teacher and student through the labyrinthine ways of an intricate and inescapable question of the day. This letter is also enigmatic in the sense that no hint is given of the way in which Archbishop Fonseca of Toledo had secured a copy of Fisher's tract to furnish the printer, M. Eguia. At any rate, the book holds out the promise of helping theologians, canonists, and all interested parties to understand the celebrated controversy — and for that reason it had been printed as speedily as possible (*quam citissime in publicum prodiret*).[5] It is worthy of note that the redoubtable Dominican theologian Francisco de Vitoria treated the theory of the royal case at the urging of friends at the University of Salamanca in 1531. The second part of his treatise "De matrimonio," which is concerned with the marriage of Henry and Catherine, proves that such a marriage is not forbidden by the law of nature (*lege naturae*) and never was prohibited by the divine law of the Old Testament (*jure divino veteris legis*).[6]

Fisher's *Causa* anticipated publications by two Spaniards in 1531. Ferdinandus de Loazes first gives the background and then proceeds to enumerate sixteen difficulties called *Dubitationes,* which he proceeds to discuss at great length.[7] On August 31, 1531, Dr. Ortiz told Charles V that he had persuaded Juan Ginés de Sepúlveda, "his friend, a man of good and sound doctrine," to publish in Rome his treatise in favor of Queen Catherine. An interesting feature of Sepúlveda's work is that it was reprinted in London early in the reign of Queen Mary.[8]

In reality there is far less need for guidance and help through the simple and short *Causa* than through the complex and lengthy response of Fisher to the quasi-official "white book" for the divorce. This royal document, preceded by the declarations (*Censurae*) of Italian and French universities, states the grounds for the king's case in seven chapters. The colophon is dated April 1530. Fisher's refutation (Brit. Mus. MS. Arundel 151) naturally has to follow, in some way or other, the line of argument of the advocates of the divorce. In view of its prolixity and massiveness, it is doubtful that he has chosen the best way to handle his response. The introduction, to be sure, is characteristically brief, clear, and pointed. His adversaries cannot prove solidly the three issues involved in their proposition: (1) the prohibition of the royal marriage by divine law; (2) its prohibition by the natural law; and (3) such prohibition by both laws that it is altogether indispensable by the pope. Fisher's introduction is not balanced by the usual conclusion — "the last only sentence [of the *Censurae*], about a nine or ten lines, being unanswered," as Harpsfield explains, "either because he did not finish his book or that my copie doth lack it." [9] Consequently Harpsfield could well have used Brit. Mus. MS. Arundel 151, which fits this description.

It is almost possible to watch Fisher succumbing to the temptation of detailed, verbatim refutation — undoubtedly the easiest method possible in writing, but hardly making for interest and facility in reading. It is by way of general discussion that Fisher handles the problems of the Levitical texts (chap. 1) and the cases of Herod's marriage and the incestuous Corinthian (first part of chap. 2). More particularized treatment must be accorded the alleged support given by Tertullian, various popes — Gregory, Calixtus, Zachary, and Innocent; different councils — Toledo II, Agde, Neocaesarea, Gregory the Younger, and Constance (second part of chap. 2); outstanding Fathers — Origen, Chrysostom, Basil, Hesychius, Ambrose, Jerome, and Augustine (chap. 3); and lesser authorities — Anselm, Cardinal Hugo, Raoul de Flaix, Rupert of Deutz, Hugh of St. Victor, Hildebert of Tours, Yves of Chartres, Walter of Coutances, Thomas Aquinas, Remi of Auxerre, Peter de la Palu, Torquemada, Antoninus, James of Lausanne, John Cagnazzo of Tabia, Astesanus, John Bacon, Thomas Walden, John Andreae, John of Imola, and Panormitanus (chap. 4). Verbatim citation of the *Censurae* begins with definitions of the various kinds of law — divine, judicial, natural, and moral (chap. 5); continues increasingly through their application to the present case (chap. 6), and ends in plodding brief quotations followed by plodding brief comments as Fisher denies the claim that the pope cannot dispense because the marriage contravenes the moral precepts of the divine law (chap. 7). The final impression is one of sheer drudgery.

Nevertheless, Fisher is never so distracted as not to give signs of his natural organizing ability. Thus, before he undertakes the refutation of the fifth chapter, he gives an excellent résumé which declares the precise import of every authority appealed to in the two previous chapters (chaps. 3 and 4). This résumé is followed by sixteen reasons for restricting the Levitical precept to a *living* brother. Finally, at the start of the seventh and last chapter on the possibility of papal dispensation, he summarizes in twelve points the position which he has established in the course of the refutation.[10]

As for the "Responsum" as a whole, Harpsfield has included in his *Pretended Divorce* such an excellent précis that it is unnecessary to repeat it here or to attempt another by way of improvement.[11] One is free instead to concentrate upon theological method. The "Responsum" repeats opinions on the pertinent scriptural texts given in the "Liceity" and on the authorities cited in the *Causa;* yet, whereas the opinions were stated positively in the two previous works, they are set forth in the "Responsum" negatively, so to speak. By denying or by rectifying his adversaries' manipulation of Scripture and its interpreters, Fisher defends or confirms his own opinions. Moreover, just as the "Liceity" had laid a certain emphasis upon Scripture, and the *Causa* upon biblical interpreters, so the "Responsum" is forced to put a new stress upon the concept of law. In fact, it is possible to approach even the method of the "Responsum" from the viewpoint of controversial tactics, of exegetical principles, or of legal conception and right. Our study of method and style, however, will be best advanced if none of these three is either neglected or overemphasized. Consequently the order of the "Responsum" itself will be followed, and only the more important aspects will be singled out for attention.

Fisher's introductory distinctions on the natural law are interesting. Something may be forbidden by the natural law but not by the divine law. Private property is against the natural law, which enjoins communism, but communism is not obligatory because not ordered by divine law; it is a secondary, not a primary, principle of the natural law, and becomes obligatory only upon sanction by divine or human law. Even if marriage to a dead brother's childless widow were forbidden by the natural law, it is licit and dispensable because prohibited not by divine law but only by ecclesiastical law. Besides, some actions are banned by both natural and divine law and yet are dispensable; e.g., the paying of external honor to the aged (Lev. 19:32) and praying with covered head (1 Cor. 11:4).

The adversaries will never succeed in proving the royal marriage to be null and void from the Levitical prohibition on marriage to a brother's wife (Lev. 20:21) because that prohibition is not general but limited: either to a living brother or to a brother dying with children or to a brother who has divorced his wife. For one must consider Moses' words not only in Leviticus but elsewhere. Fisher's explanation of the case of Judah and Tamar (Gen. 38) entails the use of Alphonsus of Abula, Nicholas of Lyra, Cardinal Hugo, and Chrysostom. The refutation of the first chapter concludes with the principle that many general scriptural prohibitions have numerous particular exceptions understood, as is clear from work on the Sabbath, killing of criminals, banning of statues (yet two cherubim on the ark), impediment of consanguinity, and the bodily integrity of priests.

Fisher disposes of the case of Herod (Matt. 14:3–4) by showing that his brother Philip was still alive and had a daughter. As for the case of the incestuous adulterer (1 Cor. 5), the father was still living and the situation was dissimilar. In regard to Paul's words here, he accuses his adversaries of arguing "after the manner of Anaxagoras" (*more Anaxagorico*), that is, of inferring whatever they please from a farfetched text.[12] As for the popes trotted out by them, Fisher deals at greater length with Gregory the Great's replies to Augustine of Canterbury, perhaps because closer to home. Although Gregory is twisting Scripture a bit for pastoral purposes, the adversaries have suppressed the most vital declaration, that those who have already contracted such marriages are not to be kept from the sacraments. As for the councils, particularly that of Constance, Fisher reveals that the most diligent search into its Acts on his part has failed to uncover the alleged condemnation of Wyclif for holding that all the Levitical prohibitions were merely judicial, an error not ascribed to him even by Walden or Woodford. The attack on the second chapter of *Censurae* ends positively — with Fisher's vigorous defense of leviratic marriage among the Jews.

The introduction to the confutation of the third chapter which seeks support from the Fathers from Origen to Augustine is typical of Fisher. In citation of an authority, the prestige, the place, the time, and the reasons are four most important considerations. Each of these is discussed in turn: (1) Is the author famous or obscure, a theologian or only a canonist, frequently wrong or rarely in error, ancient or recent (the latter being more expert in moral, ceremonial, or judicial distinctions)? (2) Is he speaking to a heretic, to an orthodox person, to the people, to scholars? And is he perhaps accommodating and twisting Scripture to his pious purpose? (3) Is he writing when nothing was defined by the Church, when the impediments of consanguinity and affinity were stretched too far, when they were readjusted? (4) Does he merely state his interpretation, or does he support it with solid reasons and with clear texts?

The Bishop of Rochester consistently tries to apply these principles. For example, the adversaries say that Chrysostom calls the Sadducees' case of the one wife of seven brothers (Matt. 22:23–33) a fable, but Fisher calls their attention to Chrysostom's modification, namely, that he personally supposed it to be such (*vt ego puto*). Basil, he notes, twists the Mosaic law in order to defend ecclesiastical legislation against marrying two sisters. As for Hesychius, the opponents have mistranslated him and omitted whatever supports the validity of the leviratic marriage. Like Basil, Ambrose uses specious rather than solid reasons from Scripture to dissuade a father from uniting his son and granddaughter in marriage. To prove uncle and niece might marry, Fisher appeals to Nicholas of Lyra and Paul of Burgos, "who had excellent knowledge of Jewish custom and who diligently explained the literal sense of Holy Scripture."

As for the adversaries' citation of Jerome, the Father is there engaged in a fight against a heretic, in which any weapon at hand may be used: it is better to seek his real opinion in his commentaries elsewhere. Here Fisher describes the natural law as "a certain resplendence of the eternal law" (*resplendentia quaedam aeternae legis*), a sin against the former being an inexcusable sin against the latter. In the course of showing that the four quotations taken by the opponents from Augustine are not to the point in the royal case, Fisher finds that only those precepts of the Old Law have the force of divine law and are binding on Christians which pertain to piety and morality and which are recognized as obligatory the moment they are heard. This immediate recognition shows that a precept belongs to the natural law. This is hardly true of the prohibition against marrying a dead brother's childless widow.

The refutation of the fourth chapter, which professedly cites minor authorities, immediately questions an epistle brought from Paris, allegedly written by Anselm but not found in his correspondence either in manuscript or in print. When *Walterus de Constantia* is used, Fisher confesses that he has never read anything written by him.[13] (*Walterus* historically is Walter of Coutances, Bishop of Lincoln, later Archbishop of Rouen.) As for Thomas Aquinas, nothing said in his *Summa* (2–2, q. 154, a. 9) proves the unnaturalness of marriage with a dead brother's childless widow — as is clear from Cajetan's commentary on the pertinent article. The citation from Remi of Auxerre cannot even be discovered in his works. The adversaries score a point with Peter de la Palu — but, unfortunately for them, he later retracted his opinion. James of Lausanne and John of Tabia are writers of no great name. If Fisher cited authors of equal fame, his volume would become immense in size.

Fisher's response to the fifth chapter of the *Censurae*,[14] which centers about the kinds and definitions of law, first outlines his plan of attack and briefly gives the real position of each and every authority of his opponents on marriage to a brother's wife. Their strategy of textual mutilation and distortion would easily deceive the reader, unless he were somewhat knowledgeable scripturally, into believing that the Levitical prohibition was to be understood in general and without limitation. Its restriction to a *living* brother is shown to be upheld by Alexander of Hales, Albert the Great, Druthmar, Raoul de Flaix, Peter of Blois, the Author of the Interlinear Gloss, Cardinal Hugo, Simon of Cassia, Francis of Meyronnes, and Peter de la Palu, and then is defended by the sixteen Reasons already referred to above. At the end of this introduction, Fisher begs the reader's pardon for "this prolixity of ours" (*hac prolixitate nostra*), to which he is driven by the necessity of preventing the scripturally inexpert from being deliberately misled into thinking that general prohibitions do not admit particular exceptions.

At this point Harpsfield's précis often becomes so much of a literal translation that it can be used to give Fisher's animadversions on the definitions of the various laws. "The law of God," to begin with, "is the word or mind of God commanding things that be honest, or forbidding things that be contrary to honesty; which law the sacred holy universal Church hath of long time by her authority received and confirmed as either being sowed or planted in the reasonable creature of God by the mouth and spirit of Almighty God, or else shewed to him by revelation." Fisher has many objections to this definition, which he accepts, however, because it does not work against his case. He does want to know, nevertheless, why the adversaries have not given the commonly accepted definition by Gerson and Gabriel, which includes also the final cause, i.e., conduciveness to the attainment of eternal life.[15] The reason must be their perception that the Levitical prohibitions in no way detract from that final end — as is evident from Abraham's marriage to his own sister,[16] Jacob's to two sisters, and Shelah's to Tamar, his brother Er's widow. What is evil of itself, Fisher soon declares, can never become good. Marriage to a brother's widow is now evil only because forbidden by the Church. He offers another example: mating of animals of different species is to a degree against the natural law and is also forbidden by God's word, but this is not a moral precept nor indispensable.

To continue. "Judicialls they [the adversaries] define to be those which be statutes or [*leg.* of] pains, or at the least those which God in time past did answer unto Moses when he asked him counsell of the suits and controversies of the Jews." This definition Fisher cannot accept because there are many judicial precepts which have no penalties assigned for their violation — for example, marriage outside one's own tribe. On the other hand, he finds no fault with the definition of the natural law: "a general knowledge and judgment which God did grave in the mind of every man, to help him to form and frame his manners and living." He can only marvel that the great and brilliant scholars mentioned above could never discover that marriage to a dead brother's childless widow was against the natural law.[17] He quotes in particular Augustine, Albert the Great, Haymo of Halberstadt, Druthmar, Raoul de Flaix, Francis of Meyronnes, Peter de la Palu, Bonaventure, and Scotus. A supplementary list includes also Alexander of Hales, Peter of Blois, the Author of the Interlinear Gloss, Cardinal Hugo, and Simon of Cassia.

Fisher then takes up the adversaries' definition of the moral law: "the word and mind of God commanding those honest things and forbidding those unhonest things which the natural reason of man, lightened with the light of the word of God, doth according to the rules and teaching of common justice or virtue teach us to do or leave, and which the same natural reason so lightened doth shew us that we be bound to keep them, although they were never commanded by none other law." Although Fisher suspects the departure of his opponents from the usual accepted and tried definition, he nevertheless lets it pass. At great length, he proves that the leviratic marriage was imposed by God (Deut. 25:5) and that therefore the precept against marriage to a dead brother's widow could not be a moral law. In the course of discussion, he again refers to the tendency of pastors (Gregory, Siricius, and Innocent) to bend Scripture to their purpose, e.g., prevention of marriage within the seventh degree of consanguinity.

In beginning to refute his opponents' sixth chapter, Fisher declares that they are "washing [the color out of] a brick" (*laterem lauare,* Ter. *Phorm.* 1.4.8.), i.e., laboring in vain. In the course of his verbatim citation and rebuttal, he makes some interesting observations. For example, the man who raises seed to his brother is promised, among other things, a happy life in this world, because Moses rarely mentions the future world; whence the adversaries' interpretation of "to perish from the midst of his people" as meaning "not to be numbered among the saints" or "to lose one's soul" is absolutely false. In regard to the expulsion of the Canaanites — how strange it would be for God to command the Jews to practice the same marriage for which He had driven out their predecessors. In reality they were expelled for the more heinous crimes mentioned in Deuteronomy and Wisdom. Leviticus 18 contains not only prohibitions but also exhortations, not only moral precepts but also judicial, and so forth. Execration and abomination are terms used in the Old Testament for some things which now are forbidden no longer, e.g., the eating of blood (cf. Acts 15:29). When William of Paris is appealed to, Fisher declares that he can find nothing on the matter in his work on virtues and vices. At this point Fisher apologizes to the reader once more for verbatim quotation of his adversaries: otherwise certain people will say that he failed to answer scrupulously each and every argument and objection.

The recourse to pagan poets, historians, and legislators will not help the adversaries because the commonwealths of the Lacedemonians, Athenians, Persians, and Romans did not see the heinousness of marriages of this kind. Nevertheless Fisher does not wish to pronounce on the cases of Leucon and Philip because he has read nothing about them. Any appeal to the historians Berosus and Methodius is also useless because men before the Deluge committed sin not only with their (living) brothers' wives but also with their mothers, sisters, males, and animals.

At this part of the tract, Fisher resorts to a device to relieve the monotony. Instead of answering in his own person, he has the pope by four arguments disprove that it is just as unlawful to marry a brother's wife as one's own sister. Moreover, all diriment impediments arising from consanguinity and affinity are the result, not of the natural law, but of positive or ecclesiastical law. This opinion is then developed at great length. The only unions really against nature are between mother and son (for then the son would be the head of his mother, cf. 1 Cor. 11:3) and between father and daughter (for then the daughter would have authority over the body of her father, cf. 1 Cor. 7:4).[18] In fact, marriage between parents and children is the only union forbidden by Christ, for He said: "For this cause a man shall leave his father and mother, and cleave to his wife, and the two shall become one flesh" (Matt. 19:5, Gen. 2:24, 1 Cor. 6:16, 7:10, Eph. 5:31). Under the inspiration of Christ, the Church may revive the old ceremonial and judicial laws, as *de facto* it has done in regard to incense, purification of women, the ember days, and so on. The pope, Fisher explains, naturally cannot revive ceremonials which are "deadly" (*mortifera*), e.g., circumcision and the choice of meats.

The final chapter in the *Censurae* assumes that union with a brother's wife has been proved to be against God's moral precept and proceeds to demonstrate that it is therefore not subject to papal dispensation. Fisher first states the twelve points which he has established thus far about such a marriage. These Harpsfield translates almost verbatim in his précis. Fisher then mentions precepts really based upon nature and yet demanding exceptions: the restoration of lost property, and yet the obligation of not returning weapons to a man who would use them against himself or his country; the sanctification of the Sabbath, and yet the permission to perform necessary work thereon; the fulfillment of vows made to God, and yet the power of the Holy See to dispense therefrom; and the command not to kill, and yet the justice of the law punishing even simple theft with death and the liceity of the law if the prince should allow an adulterer to be slain on the spot. A fortiori can the pope dispense in a marriage once obligatory on the Jews. The many authorities produced by the opposition avail nothing because none denies the dispensability of this particular kind of marriage. One authority was unknown to Fisher until mentioned by the opponents: *Bernardus de Trilla* (Bernard de la Treille, d. 1292).

There follows an explanation of the nature of papal dispensation which Harpsfield considers so important as to translate literally and fully:

> For the Pope in such matters doth not change and alter the will [and mind] of God or of the maker of the law, but doth declare only in what manner of cases the maker of the law minded not to bind men to the law; for by reason of the manifold difference of the time, place, and other circumstances there ariseth such variety of cases in any law to be made that it is not possible for the lawmaker in so few words to comprise them all. Wherefore, as in all civil and profane laws there is a power left to the Prince whom they call the soul of the law to declare the Equity (and that they call the *Epieikeya*) of the same law, so was it behoofefull and necessary that in the Church one should be left after Christ his assention to moderate, declare, and expound such laws as appertain to the government of the said Church. And therefore Christ said to his vicar St. Peter, Whatsoever thou shalt loose on earth shall be loosed in heaven.

If the pope is only a minister of the sacraments, why did Christ say this to Peter? The pope declares merely that the law of God does not bind in the particular case. Someone in the Church must have such a power because it is impossible to call a general council to meet every necessity.

The attempt by the adversaries to limit the pope's dispensing power to two situations — apparent disagreement between two scriptural texts, and scriptural precepts involving no sin — is frivolous because every man expert in Scripture then could and would solve his own cases: "By the lawes of our realm he that stealeth an ox or a sheep hangeth for it, and yet this matter was never distincted by holy Scripture. Neither doth he offend against the commandment, Thou shalt not slay, that executeth any man for the said trespass."

Papal error, of course, is entirely possible. In an important statement of which Harpsfield makes no mention, Fisher writes: "We certainly do not deny that popes can err, for they are men and therefore can fall unless they lean heavily upon divine helps. Supported by the latter, however, they undoubtedly are directed by the Holy Spirit in all decisions which concern the salvation of souls committed to them. But if perchance because of human weakness they sometimes swerve from the right path, provided the error be grave and manifest, especially in the matter of faith, we do not deny that he can be admonished and made to return by the Church."

Fisher then disposes of the adversaries' examples of valiant bishops who withstood the pope: Archbishop Lawrence of Canterbury in the case of Edbald, who had married his stepmother; Archbishop Dunstan of Canterbury in the case of Edwin, who had married his kinswoman; Archbishop Samson of Rheims in the case of King Louis of France, who had married his sister-in-law; and Bishop Grosseteste of Lincoln, who would not make a canon of the pope's nephew who was dissolute in life. All these instances do not pertain to the issue, which is the papal dispensability of a marriage to a dead brother's childless widow. The adversaries' charge of papal tyranny is indignantly rejected, and their fear of losing everything should arise rather from the future divorce if it is granted — which God prevent! To establish the pope's power of dispensation in the case of the royal marriage, Fisher quotes the same authorities used in the *Causa:* Richard of Middleton, Angelus Carletus de Clavasio, Peter de la Palu, Cardinal Torquemada, and all the canonists rightly understood.[19] Only the last sentence in the *Censurae* is left unanswered, and the refutation is left without a conclusion.[20]

It is unknown how much Fisher's "Responsum" was read by others. Cochlaeus, in his "Defense of the Bishop of Rochester," states that Fisher had written "a great tome" (*grande volumen*) which was either suppressed or destroyed. Two years later, in his reply to Richard Morison, Cochlaeus defends the marriage with seven brief arguments. His major work on the divorce, printed in 1535, before Fisher's execution, bears comparison in method with the Bishop's writing. This is the order Cochlaeus follows: the previous history of the case, the divine law commanding such a marriage, the natural law favoring it, the Levitical text not forbidding it, the degrees of consanguinity and affinity forbidden by the natural law, the human law prohibiting such a marriage, the power of dispensation, ancient examples of dispensation, the definitive sentence of Clement VII, nine reasons from St. Bernard for such a marriage, twenty-four proofs from St. Thomas Aquinas, twenty-six reasons from the decrees of the Fathers, and fifteen proofs from Abbot Panormitanus. In giving Henry VIII his opinion on Cochlaeus' book, Cranmer declares that there is "no new thing" in it and that any answer to it would only "acquire unto him [Cochlaeus] some glory thereby." [21]

As for England, Fisher's "Responsum" provoked in its turn a "Responsio" (in Cotton MS. Otho C.x), which is ascribed to Robert Wakefield. (The reply contains an interesting reference to Fisher's refutation of Luther's forty-one articles.) The same manuscript contains a letter to Fisher concerning a debate on Henry VIII's "greate matiere." This letter is from John Stokesley, who with Richard Croke had collected the opinions of the Italian universities for the *Censurae* and who had been made Bishop of London. The conference, it appears, had been originally suggested by the Archbishop of Canterbury. On January 8 (1531? 1533?) Stokesley wrote to Fisher: "You and I shall each choose five doctors to discuss the matter. . . I request you to send me your pleasure as to the time and place, and the persons you shall appoint." In event of disagreement, two learned men will act as judges.[22]

There is no evidence that such a conference took place. Since the divorce was soon to be a fact, there was no need for it, except to win Fisher to the king's side on the question or to play down his defense of Catherine. Events in the case of the marriage with Anne Boleyn and that of the royal supremacy were progressing too fast to leave room for a conference of any significance. Both issues landed Fisher in the Tower. Here he was questioned about his tracts on the divorce, which served as cause or occasion for the break with Rome. Here he wrote his last works, which, unlike his recent writings, were not controversial. They deal neither with a Reformation nor with a divorce — the two problems which in a sense had merged into one. They deal with the preparation of the soul for life in another country, where "there is no marrying and giving in marriage" (Matt. 22:30) and where the Church shines "in all its beauty, no stain, no wrinkle, no disfigurement . . . holy . . . spotless" (Eph. 5:27).

Chapter XX

THE WAY TO PERFECTION AND HEAVEN

MODERN readers of the "Spirituall Consolation," written by Fisher in the Tower for his half-sister Elizabeth, a nun, are far from finding in it any comfort or optimism. For them, on the contrary, the keynote is depression, pessimism, and fear. Yet it furnishes consolation in the sense that the soul which follows its advice will win joy and peace. It is an encouragement to the Christian to do something *now* so as to be ready at the summons of inexorable death.

As a literary composition, the "Consolation" seems a link in the chain of productions which extend from the beginning of the century to the end. Fisher's work is strongly reminiscent of scenes in the anonymous *Everyman,* and itself finds echoes in sentiment much later, as in Sidney and Shakespeare. Consider Shakespeare's lines: "Why dost thou pine within and suffer dearth, / Painting thy outward walls so costly gay?"

In the "Consolation," nevertheless, the Bishop of Rochester is found most like himself. The plea for God's help, best expressed in *Deus in adiutorium meum intende* as recommended by Cassian, has been heard earlier in the sermon on Vulg. Ps. 37 and in the treatise on prayer.[1]

In both the sermon on Vulg. Ps. 50 and in the "Consolation," the figure of painting on a wall is used, but with a difference. In the former, the painting represents sin covering the "bare walle" of the soul; in the latter, it describes the beauty and strength concealing the "wretched bodie." [2] The urgent exhortation to self-help rather than reliance on the prayers of forgetful friends found in the "Consolation" has been heard, developed at greater length, in the first of *Two Sermons*.[3] But more personal than such familiar ideas is a very pointed address which makes one feel that Fisher wrote this meditation first for himself. It is quite inapplicable to Sister Elizabeth. In regard to provision for death, it reads: "And therefore delay it not as I haue done. . . Neyther buildyng of Colleges, nor makyng of Sermons, nor giuing of almes, neyther yet anye other manner of buzynesse shall helpe you without this." [4]

Fisher's habitual power of imagination is manifest in the sudden and vivid placing of a scene before one's eyes with just a few words. Death, for example, will listen to no plea and accept no bribe for a respite — "No if all my louers and friends would fall vppon their knees and pray him for mee. No if I & they would weepe . . . as many teares as there be in the seas droppes of water, no pietie may restrain him." There are several other brief but effective comparisons. What is the body but a "sachell full of dunge"? The "filthie and vncleane delightes and lustes of the stincking flesh" furnish apparent pleasure — "in very deede none other then the Sowe hath, waultering hir self in the myerie puddle." As for hell: "It should be nowe vnto mee much wearie, one yeare continually to lye vpon a bed were it neuer so soft, how weary then shall it be to lye in the most painefull fyre so many thousand of yeares without number?" [5]

Far more original is the simile used to depict his uncertainty as to whether his repentance in the face of death is grounded in love or in fear: "Euen as a Merchaunt that is compelled by a greate tempest in the sea to cast his merchandice out of the Shippe, it is not to bee supposed that hee would cast away his ryches of hys owne free will, not compelled by the storme? And euen so lykewyse doe I if thy tempeste of death were not now raysed vpon mee, it is full like that I would not haue cast from me my slouth and negligence." [6]

Finest of all is the comparison already alluded to — that of the youthful, strong, and healthy body to a painted wall. What renders it more extraordinary is that it is couched in terms of an address to the body. Because of its development in detail and at length, it is unfortunately impossible to quote it in its entirety. The following excerpt may serve as a specimen:

That brightnesse of thy eyes, that quicknesse in hearing, that lyuelinesse in thy other sences by naturall warmenesse, thy swiftnesse and nimblenesse, thy fayrenesse and bewtie. All these thou hast not of thy self, they were but lent vnto thee for a season, euen as a wall of earth that is fayre painted without for a season with freshe and goodly colours, and also gylted with golde, it appeareth goodly for the tyme to suche as consider no deeper then the outward crafte thereof. But when at the last the colour faileth, and the gilting falleth away, then appeareth it in hys owne lykenesse. For then the earth playnely sheweth it selfe.[7]

Even such metaphorical or symbolical language does not satisfy the demands of Fisher's literary imagination. He embodies the whole meditation in a dramatic monologue, for he advises his sister to "deuise in your minde as nigh as you can, all the conditions of a man or woman sodaynlye taken and rauyshed by death." The exigency of the form calls for a sequence of thought that is relatively free. This flexibility, unusual for Fisher, is demanded also by the nature of meditation. The person at prayer, allowing himself to be guided by the Holy Spirit whithersoever He will, abandons the logical and rigid structure of a sermon, such as those on the Penitential Psalms, or the formal organization of a treatise, such as a methodical discussion of prayer. Fisher's artistic instinct is again at work. Of necessity, to be sure, the "Spirituall Consolation" has a beginning, a middle, and an end. Only the introduction, however, which gives, as it were, the stage directions, employs a matter-of-fact enumeration. But it is in different ways that a reader could divide the body into its parts (because of the loose structure). In fact, the body itself blends almost imperceptibly with the brief conclusion.

The purpose of this "fruitefull meditacion" is to help the soul when it is in desolation, that is, "when it is dull and vnlustie without devotion." Preparation entails three conditions: (1) to imagine oneself "sodaynlye taken and rauyshed by death"; (2) to read the meditation in private without hurry; and (3) to beg God's assistance. The meditation proper may be divided into three scenes: the bewilderment of the dying man, his search for help, and his regret for past negligence. The first scene brings the realization that his soul will appear before God without spiritual riches, though even the giving of a draught of water does not go unrewarded. Now his reward for taking heed only for the corruptible body (that painted wall of earth) is sorrow and repentance, hell or, if he is fortunate, purgatory. Yet this pampered body now forsakes the soul about to appear before the Judge that "shall examyne me of euerie idle word that euer passed my mouth."

At the beginning of the second scene, he asks like Everyman: "Wher may I seeke for succour?" Of the two sources of help, his good deeds are "fewe or none" or vitiated by wrong intentions, and his friends must first take care of themselves or are forgetful of him. As for his heavenly friends, the saints, he has honored them little or coldly. The only answer can be such as, taken alone, would satisfy any Christian whether Catholic or Protestant: "No other hope remayneth but onely in the mercye of my Lord God, to whose mercy I doe now offer my selfe, beseeching him not to looke vppon my desertes, but vppon his infinite goodnesse and abundaunt pietie."

Taking this truth for granted, Fisher passes quickly to the third scene: the realization that, since he used to prepare for "little daungers," he should have provided against the all-decisive coming of death. In spite of good intentions, "euery tryfelous buzinesse" made him delay.

The concluding exhortation, which constitutes a kind of epilogue, is an urgent plea to act *now:* "Be you your owne friend, doe you these suffrages for your owne soule, whether they be praiers or almes deedes, or any other penitentiall paynefulnesse." The final three words, "but to late," have the sound of a sullen, leaden knell, which is emphasized by the typography:

> . . . If you followe this counsayle
> and doe thereafter, you be grac-
> ious and blessed, and if you doe
> not, you shall doubtlesse
> repent your follyes,
> but to late.[8]

But Fisher realizes that "A Spirituall Consolation" provides a desperate remedy in the case of spiritual tepidity. His next work makes this fact quite clear toward its close: "If it so fortune that you at any tyme begin to feele any dulnesse of mynde, quicken it again by the meditation of death, which I send [*sic*] you here before."[9] Opposed to this negative and compulsory means are better and positive ways, and these he sets forth in "The Wayes to Perfect Religion." Two circumstances help to give this work a certain poignancy: Fisher is even more confined in his prison than his sister is in her convent, and his imprisonment is in contrast with the free life of the hunter ranging over the open countryside. Perfect religion, of course, is nothing else than religion made perfect by love. It is to the acquisition and increase of love that Fisher provides means, or ways, or, to be specific, ten Considerations. "Religion," naturally, is to be understood here as the state of a religious man or woman, i.e., a Christian who has pronounced the three vows of evangelical poverty, chastity, and obedience.

Just as "A Spirituall Consolation" reminds the reader of *Everyman,* so the first part of "The Wayes to Perfect Religion" brings to mind the *Following of Christ* (especially II.7–8) in its exaltation of the love which makes every hardship and sacrifice seem easy. To bring the lesson home, Fisher employs his ingenious and lengthy comparison with the hunter: "For all true christian soules be called Hunters, and their office and duetie is to seeke and hunt for to fynde Christ Iesu." The details are vividly circumstantial and full for the life of the hunter, who does not disdain "to serue hys owne dogges hym selfe . . . yea and to clense theyr stinking Cannell where they shall lye and rest them." There is unintended humor in having religious women serve the superior and Sisters of their convent "with as good a harte and mynde as the Hunters acquit them to serue their hounds"—which is "a thing much more reasonable." As for the reader who might think that a cloistered woman would find the comparison with a hunter unconvincing, let him remember the power of a good writer to create vicarious experience—as Fisher does here. At any rate, Fisher closes his introduction with a statement of his purpose: "to minister vnto you some common considerations which if you wil often resorte vnto by due remembraunce, & so by diligent prayer call vppon almightie God for hys loue, you shall now by his grace attain it."

These ten Considerations are plainly numbered and each developed in order. Such an enumeration in the body is not out of place because the work is not a meditation as the previous writing but a discourse or treatise. Their numbering, too, has mnemonic value because his sister must "often resorte vnto [them] by due remembraunce." Particularly outstanding passages being left for later treatment, the ten Considerations, mainly incentives to love of God, are (1) creation from nothing; (2) formation in His image; (3) birth as a Christian with Christian privileges; (4) time granted for repentance after sin; (5) vocation to the religious state; (6) the worthiness of Christ, all-beautiful, all-powerful, all-wise, all-gentle, if she gives her love freely; (7) if she "sells" her love, its purchase by Christ with His precious blood (cf. 1 Pet. 1:18–19); (8) Christ all hers, like the whole image in a mirror among many mirrors; (9) sin to be viewed as self-desertion — as in Lucifer's and Adam's case — in answer to her objection that such love by Christ makes her behavior indifferent; and (10) the comparison of her petty love with Christ's love, to assure which martyrs suffered and died.

Each Consideration has some interesting passage in it to relieve the abstract theory. After the elaborate comparison of the hunter in the introduction, Fisher instinctively reserves the more striking techniques for the later Considerations. Thus the first Consideration is left simple and unadorned. The second expresses the hierarchy of being as follows: "It is a more goodly beinge Margarite of a precious stone, then of a peble stone, of the fayre bright golde, then of rustie yron, of a goodly Fesaund then of a venemous Serpent, of a prettie Faune then of a foule Toade, of a reasonable soule, then of an vnreasonable beast." The third Consideration, again relatively simple, as if for relief, refers to some who have not received baptism and therefore are damned: "both noble men & women, both Knightes and Princes, which haue great wisdome and reason."

In the fourth Consideration, Fisher unconditionally and unabashedly tells Elizabeth that since baptism "you haue many tymes vnkindely faulne into deadly sinne, and broken hys lawes and commaundements" and that "innumerable soules of men & weomen for lesse offences then you haue done, lye now in the prison of hel, & shal there continu without end." Two noteworthy comparisons follow in the fifth Consideration. In an intensification of a familiar simile, the sinful soul is graphically described as being "filthie & more vngoodly then is the Sowe that waltereth hir self in the foule myrie puddle, and more pestilently stinketh in the sight of God, then is the stinking carion of a dead dogge, being rotten and lying in a ditch." God has chosen Fisher's sister among others for religion as Ahasuerus selected "many fayre yong maydens" for queenship.

The sixth Consideration pleads for the beauty of Christ the Spouse from the beauty of His creation: "Behold the Rose, the Lillie, the Vyolet, beholde the Pecockes, the Feasaunt, the Popingaye. . . All these were of his making, all there beautie and goodlinesse of hym they receyued it. Wherfore this goodlinesse discribeth that he him self must needes of necessitie be verie goodly & beautifull." His immortal beauty is unlike "the goodlinesse of other men, which lyke a flower to day is fresh and lustie, and to morrowe with a little sicknesse is withered and vanisheth away."

The seventh Consideration, in view of Christ's love manifest in His passion, asks: "What frost could have vngeled [*leg.* congealed] your harte, that it may not relent against so great an heat of loue?" The individuality of this love felt by Christ for each soul is explained in the eighth Consideration through the common simile of the glasses or mirrors, but there is a refinement of the comparison: "Such soules as by true pennaunce doing, by sighing, by weeping, by praying, by watching, by fasting, & by other lyke, be the better scoured and clensed from the spottes and mallice of deadly sinne, they bee the brighter glasses and more cleerly receyue this loue." A variation of this process of scouring clean had appeared in the sermon on Vulg. Ps. 6.[10]

In the ninth Consideration the mishaps of Lucifer and Adam are used to explain the concept of sin as self-desertion, and the retirement of Mary Magdalene into the wilderness is produced to show the need for flight from sin. The tenth Consideration is climaxed by a perfervid colloquy which, in answer to Christ's request for the individual's heart and love, ends: "I freely gyue it vnto thee, and I most humbly beseech thy goodnesse and mercy to accept it, and so to order me by thy grace . . . that I alwayes may keepe the fyre of thy loue auoyding from it all other contrarie loue that may in anie wyse displease thee."

"The finall conclusion of all" humbly expresses confidence that the Considerations "will somewhat inflame your harte with the loue of Christ Iesu." If not, to hand is the meditation on death.

Yet all is dependent on Jesus' grace, and "no where els you can haue any helpe but of him." In a procedure unusual for Fisher, instead of making a mere summary, he adds new materials toward the end: seven ejaculatory prayers, one for each day of the week, which can be used anywhere and anytime. The imprisoned author declares that "nothyng may be to my comfort more then to heare of your furtheraunce and profiting in God & in good religion" and closes with the golden words: "the which our blessed Lorde graunte you for hys great mercie. Amen." [11]

As for these two works directed to his sister, even though the first is labeled a meditation and the second appears a treatise, both of them have an epistolary aura about them as though they were basically answers to requests from his sister for spiritual guidance. The first furnishes a remedy for a common but serious ailment in the religious life: lukewarmness, or tepidity. Since devotion is weak or wanting, Fisher resorts to fear of punishment. The means must have been effective if "A Spirituall Consolation" preceded "The Wayes to Perfect Religion." This second treatise is directed to a sister who is now eager about "some thing that myght be to the health of [her] soule and furtheraunce of it in holye Relygion." It is now a question of *perfect* religion.

The perfection and love of the Christian, whether in the cloister or in the forum, receives its highest expression in suffering and the cross. It would have been supremely fitting if Fisher had written his sermon on Christ's passion in the Tower, but it is declared plainly to have been "preached vpon a good Friday." The vigor of style and the strength of structure, moreover, bespeak the intense preparation of a younger Fisher. More than any other of his spiritual works it springs from, and is enclosed within, a single image and simile. This is the crucifix compared to the book seen by Ezekiel, written inside and outside, bearing the words: "*Lamentationes, Carmen, et vae,* that is to say, lamentation, songe & woe." The sermon appears to be most carefully planned. A superb unity is maintained in spite of a varied, complex, and extended development of the single theme.

The introduction makes three points. First, the spirit of wonder should prevail not only in natural philosophy but also in Christian philosophy, especially for the most marvelous phenomenon of all — the ignominious passion and death of the Son of God upon the cross. This deed is so wonderful that it calls forth an elevenfold and anaphoric repetition of the clause: "Is it not a wonderfull thyng that . . . ?" Second, no book is as all-sufficient for all Christians at all times as that of the crucifix, as is clear from Francis of Assisi's study of the crucifix with the wondering question: "Who arte thou Lord, and who am I?" Third, the crucifix is like a book in all respects; for example, boards (the two beams), leaves (Christ's limbs), parchment (His body stretched out), writing inside (His divinity), writing outside (His humanity), lines (the marks of the scourges), small letters (His little bruises and scars), and capital letters (His five great wounds). A prayer for grace to read the book aright and profitably closes the introduction.

The body deals with the three things read in the book: *Lamentations, songes, and woe*. The *Lamentations* spring from four feelings: dread of the grievous punishment due to sin and exemplified in the punishment of the cross; shame at one's unkindness toward the suffering Christ and at the stains of one's sins; sympathetic sorrow with the Crucified pleading for compassion; and hatred of sin as the cause of His suffering and of the loss of heaven. The *songes* to be sung from the book of the crucifix also arise from four emotions: love, for Christ is worthy whether one gives one's affection freely or sells it dearly; hope, because it was for sinners that He died; joy at the reconciliation effected with the Father, the victory over the common enemy, and the destruction of the handwriting of sin; and comfort, because of the shame from which we have been saved. The *woe* represents the eternal damnation that comes to those not joining in the lamentation or the song. They shall suffer in hell what Christ endured on the cross but much more grievously. Here eleven points of contrast and similarity are given: nakedness, duration, heat, cold, blasphemy, tears, thirst, depression, shame, desertion, and death.

The brief conclusion takes the form of a summarizing exhortation: "If thou wilt begin to lament with Iesu, thou shalt therby come to sing with him. . . But if thou doe refuse this remedy . . . then, thou shalt pay thine owne debtes amongest the diuils in hell, with euerlasting woe."

Except for the conclusion, each one of the points mentioned above is developed in minute detail and with great emotion. In the elaboration, however, Fisher is sparing in the use of literary devices — undoubtedly in order to avoid conflict with the dominant and pervasive likeness of the crucifix to a book. Whatever comparisons do occur are brief. A sinner may be less concerned about the blots on his soul than the spots on his clothes. One should flee from sin as from an adder or a lion. To illustrate Christ's love for the individual soul: "When thou seest a torch lyght in an house where many persons bee, doeth not that torche gyue as muche light to them all, as if there were but one person there?" Hell's cold only intensifies hell's heat: "Euen as in the forge of a Smith, the colde water when it is cast into the Fyer, causeth the Fyer to be much more fearse and violent."

But Fisher's busy imagination is most exercised in a relatively long explication of David's words on infernal pains: *Mors depascet eos* (Vulg. Ps. 48:15). The clause, he explains, has three possible meanings: (1) "Death shall bee their pastour and heardman . . . and leade them to theyr pastures . . . the one is all full of snow, the other full of fyre," or (2) "They shal be the continuall meate of death, as ye see in the pastures, where the sheepe . . . croppe the grasse euer as it ryseth . . . and so the grasse is euer in eatyng, and neuer full eaten," or (3) "Death shall be theyr continuall meate, for they shall euer long and desire for to dye. . ."

Instead of distracting his reader with startling similes and metaphors, Fisher sprinkles his sermon with only a few allusions both sacred and profane. Such are the references to the stigmata of St. Francis, the terror inspired by Holofernes, the unjust judge flayed by Cambyses, the compassion of the Magdalene for the Crucified and her flight into the wilderness, St. Christian signing herself with the cross at every temptation, the narrow escape of Susanna, the shame of Tamar, and the suicide of Lucretia. St. Bernard is quoted on Christ's interior suffering and on Christ's posture on the cross as one of love. The deprivation of the beatific vision as hell's worst suffering is supported by St. John Chrysostom's authority.[12]

Speaking in a literary way, one might say that the discourse on the passion is the best of Fisher's sermons. He is at every moment in control of his materials, not only of the thoughts but of the diction, the inflection, the tone, the feeling, the imagery, and the figures. The modern might well regret the emphasis on hell in the third and climactic place, but the presumption should be that Fisher knew the particular needs of his audience. He must also have felt an obligation to follow his scriptural text which likewise put *vae* or *woe* in the most prominent spot. At least, let the vision of woe turn his hearers back to the positive means of lamentation and song. The present-day reader might also find the comparison of the crucifix to a book too ingenious for comfort, but it is pardonable because it is solidly grounded in familiar reality — in fact, it serves to rescue the familiar from banality. Lastly, these two possible objections to the sermon can be explained, even if not excused, by the tastes of the time. The antique qualities help to give Fisher's piece a certain piquancy, such as that in the best period music. Differences in attitudes and techniques may keep the audience from complete empathy but hardly from sympathy and admiration.

Chapter XXI

THE SIRE OF FAME

THE passion begun in the Tower ended with death upon the Hill. The axe fell upon John Fisher, as upon Thomas More, with a thud heard in all Europe. It resounded through curias and courts, among scholars and theologians, and amid Catholics and Protestants.[1] The death of this bishop and cardinal of the Holy Roman Church, no matter how shocking to religious sensibilities, perhaps affected in no radical way the ultimate course of events either in England or on the Continent. If one were to search for an historical turning-point related to Fisher's career, it might be sought rather on that fateful day, June 28, 1529, when Fisher unexpectedly appeared in the legatine court to utter his fervent plea for the validity of the royal marriage — the first open confrontation with the king's forces. Except for this address there might possibly have been no divorce without papal approval, no resentment at Roman tyranny, no rupture with the papacy, and no oath on royal supremacy. His death did give Catholics and, in particular, English Catholics a martyr to venerate and emulate immediately — and it incidentally furnished ammunition against royal tyranny. For a century, tributes in verse and in prose, direct as well as allusive, continued to be paid to his memory. The argument from the authority of his theological text was strengthened by reference to him as the Cardinal of Rochester, that blessed martyr. Consequently his death is his most influential work, not written by his pen, but spelled out in blood for all to read as they run (cf. Hab. 2:2).

But before attempting to determine the precise and final place of Bishop Fisher in the Renaissance and the Reformation, one should try to see him in relation to the other figures in that era of change and revolution. One can then endeavor to judge his position (and his stature, too) from the company which he keeps — or does not keep. Practically all these persons have appeared in previous pages; here it is necessary only to bring them together by nationality.

To begin with the Continent, the main war is being fought in Germany — and Fisher is there in the thick of the battle. He first assaults Ulrichus Velenus. In turn he becomes the target for an attack by Simon Hessus (Urbanus Rhegius). He then directs three great writings against Luther, one of them in defense of his king. Finally, he publishes a huge work against Oecolampadius. Cochlaeus, his principal ally and supporter, sums up his attitude in a letter in 1533 to Tunstal by terming Fisher the brightest light of England, as Budé is of France and Erasmus of Germany.[2] The foremost Catholic apologist, John Eck, names him as a major source of his *Enchiridion* and singles him out for special consultation on a mission which takes Eck as far as England in 1525.[3] The Franciscan Nicholas Herborn, too, wishes his readers to consider his *Enchiridion* (1529) as an index or handbook to the major works written by the Bishop of Rochester and others.[4] The Dominican Johann Dietenberger feels that Fisher has met and vanquished Luther on his own terms, those of Scripture.[5]

Hieronymus Emser as editor of a dialogue of Catharinus reprints a long section on the Petrine texts from Fisher's work,[6] and Thomas Murner sends his readers to the Bishop of Rochester for a more elaborate treatment of the mass.[7] Sebastian Muenster finds the Bishop worthy of having a Chaldaic dictionary dedicated to him.[8] In his reply to Chapuys' request in August 1531 for a defense of Queen Catherine's marriage, Agrippa tries to beg off on the score that he stands alone but Fisher, Erasmus, Vives, Eck, Cochlaeus, Schatzgeyer, Faber, and others are athletes with far more resources, powers, and followers than he.[9] In November 1535 Christopher of Stadion, Bishop of Augsburg, deploring the inhumanity of Henry's executions, predicted martyrs' crowns for Fisher and More. By April 1536 Caspar Meckenlor, in his abridged German translation of the *Confutation of Luther's Assertion,* is already referring to Fisher as witnessing to his writings "with his blood and holy life even unto death." [10] As for Bishop Faber of Vienna (1478–1541), by December 1536, he puts Fisher's works among those which can advantageously be on hand for the general council then being planned. Later, in his reply to Flacius Illyricus, Johann Faber von Heilbronn, O.P. (1504–1558), praises Fisher as having gloriously written against the new sect.[11]

And what more need be said about Fisher's boundless admiration for Reuchlin as Hebrew scholar and for Erasmus as authority on the New Testament and the Fathers? Erasmus, who in turn praises him as the exemplary bishop, is so much associated with him in popular imagination that, because of Luther's implications, he must even take pains to distinguish his personal doctrine from Fisher's.[12]

Turning from Germany southward to Italy, one recalls that Clement VII wishes to call him to Rome for advice on reform and that Paul III makes him a cardinal with an eye to the future general council. By 1532 Giovanni da Fano, first Franciscan and later Capuchin, in an handbook-like work in the vernacular, uses Fisher with Eck and Catharinus for his foundations.[13] Alberto Pighi protests his execution by Henry VIII,[14] and Jacopo Moronessa in vision beholds him as a martyr slain by heretical persecutors at the opening of the fifth seal in the Apocalypse.[15] In his treatise on the visible church, Gian Antonio Pantusa (d. 1562) points to Luther's frequent self-contradictions, as already made manifest by Fisher and others.[16] Ambrosius Catharinus feels that Fisher's confutation of Luther on free will is more than adequate and, in addition, adopts and defends against Soto his opinion on the necessity of grace for every good action.[17] Polydore Vergil, in his history of England, refers to the denial of royal supremacy, and Paolo Giovio incorporates George Lily's eulogistic biography of Fisher (as well as the entry for A.D. 1535 in Lily's "Anglorum regum chronicon") in his own famous *Descriptiones*.[18] Two canonized saints of Italy, Robert Bellarmine and Charles Borromeo, bear special relationships to their fellow saint of England, John Fisher. Borromeo keeps before him a portrait of Fisher whom he venerates as much as his predecessor in the see of Milan, St. Ambrose.[19] Bellarmine's esteem for the Bishop's learning is evident in his *Controversies,* and his veneration for his virtue is climaxed by his defense of the Bishop as true martyr against James I.

As for France, the clash with Lefèvre and Clichtove makes

theological history at the University of Paris and elsewhere. The controversy over the Magdalene is part of the immediate background just before the young Calvin's arrival in Paris.[20] It certainly establishes the redoubtability of Fisher as a controversialist in the eyes of Erasmus and others, even if one discounts the biased enthusiasm of Marc de Grandval.[21] Within a decade exactly, Clichtove, whose views on the Fathers and the Schoolmen now coincide with Fisher's, sees him as a comrade-in-arms in the battle against heresy.[22] But the full story of Fisher's influence and reputation in France must still be told.[23] Most surprising of all, he finds his way into François de Belleforest's *Histoires tragiques,* where his doctrine and sanctity place him with the first martyrs.[24]

To the north of France it is Fisher's doctrine on the Eucharist that is singled out for attention and praise by the theologians of Louvain, Willem van der Lindt (Lindanus) and Ruard Tapper.[25] To the south, in Spain, his power and fame need still to be studied. Luis Juan Vives classes him among the Catholic apologists who are more *Latini,* or humanist, than their Protestant adversaries.[26] Fisher's thorough handling of a theological issue is sufficient reason for Francisco de Vitoria not to go over the ground again in his lectures at Salamanca.[27] Alfonso de Castro in his lexicon of heresies refers several times to their refutation by the Bishop of Rochester. Castro's celebrated pupil, Andrés Vega, who was especially influential in the formulation of the decrees on justification at the Council of Trent and who lectured with éclat at Salamanca, cites *sanctus episcopus Roffensis* (whom he exalts also as *gloriosus nostrae tempestatis martyr*) more than a dozen times in his classic work, *De iustificatione* (Venice, 1548). Juan Ginés de Sepúlveda feels obliged to mention Fisher's martyrdom in his history of Charles V's exploits.[28] Two natives of the Iberian peninsula enter into controversy with two English sovereigns over the martyrdom of Fisher and others. Jeronimo Osorio de Fonseca, Bishop of Sylves in Portugal, writes an open letter to Elizabeth, answered by Walter Haddon, early in her reign. In his reply, Osorio makes clear that Fisher met death only "bicause he most constantlie refused to yeeld his consent vnto a wicked statute." [29] The Jesuit theologian, Francisco Suarez, argues against James I that death suffered in behalf of the first royal marriage would have been enough to make Fisher a true martyr.[30]

Suarez's fellow Spaniard and Jesuit, Alphonsus Salmeron, had earlier used Fisher's work on the Eucharist at the Council of Trent. In fact, nothing could serve more effectively to epitomize his influence on the Continent than his posthumous role at the Council of Trent. His writings as theologian and his example as bishop and martyr are appealed to at intervals from beginning to end. For example, his opinion is mentioned or quoted (to use their Latin names) on sacramental confession by Ricardus Cenomanus; on purgatory by Gratianus de Laude; on penance and extreme unction by Didacus de Chaves; on the Real Presence by Martinus Olavaeus; on the Eucharist as sacrament by Melchior Canus, Antonius de Uglioa, Ioannes de Salazar, and the papal legate; and on the Eucharist as sacrifice by Iacobus Laynes and Melchior Canus. Other allusions have already appeared on different points in previous chapters. Sometimes references are amusing: an archbishop confesses to having read Luther's words only in Fisher's *Confutation* (which, of course, quotes the entire work verbatim); a theologian complains about Charles V's dragging busy scholars from deepest Spain and from Louvain to give an hour's discourse which any mediocre person could have done as well after reading the books of Fisher, Eck, and Pighi. One petition names as the best summaries of theology the *Sentences* of Peter Lombard, the *Theologicae veritatis compendium* by an unknown author (Hugh of Strasbourg), and outstanding modern works by Fisher, Clichtove, Pighi, Eck, and Soto (one for each nationality!).[31] A study of Fisher's influence and fame at the Council of Trent would be most interesting and revealing not only for the Bishop of Rochester but for the whole Reformation and Renaissance on the Continent.

As for the British Isles, this account must mention a Scottish connection in the person of Florence Volusene, who reports a conversation with Fisher.[32] In regard to England proper, Fisher's role on the historical scene is so well known as to require a summary far briefer than that made for the Continent. Fisher helps a king's mother in her great educational and religious projects, and he lends his tongue and pen to defend a king's wife. He stands *with* the king and his servants, including Wolsey, in the war against heresy; and he stands *against* them, first Wolsey and then Cromwell, in the two interrelated, drawn-out battles over the royal divorce and the spiritual supremacy. In the hierarchy his friends are Warham of Canterbury, West of Ely, Foxe of Winchester, and Tunstal of London and Durham; and his "adversaries" are mainly men whose acquiescence and activity in measures to which he was opposed helped them to the episcopate: Cranmer of Canterbury, Stokesley of London, Fox of Hereford, Sampson of Chichester (later of Coventry and Lichfield), and Gardiner of Winchester.

As for the founders of English Protestantism, Fisher's position and attitude touch on the careers of Tyndale, Cranmer, Bilney, Barnes, Frith, and Joye. John Foxe has the name of the Bishop of Rochester now appear and now disappear in his *Acts and Monuments*.[33] Among the orthodox Catholics, Edward Powell and Thomas Abell and Thomas More stand at his side. The defense of papal primacy by More and Fisher with their blood, according to Starkey, helped to change Reginald Pole's view on the matter.[34] In the course of his speech to the citizens of London in 1557, Pole recalls Henry VIII's pride in Fisher's learning and sees the providence of God for the realm in the martyrdom of Bishop and Chancellor.[35] A ghastly aftermath of this martyrdom is the justification of the death of Cranmer and others contrived by Dr. Henry Cole — "the law of equality" — according to which Northumberland satisfied for More, and Cranmer and others for Fisher.[36] These Protestants, according to Pole's view, are not true martyrs because they died for "theyr own opynyon" and not for the true faith that "must be suche as hathe byn contynuede from the begynnynge of the chyrche unto theyr fathers dayes, of whom they had receved yt."[37] In turn, James I and the Archbishop of Spalato, as has been seen above, attack the status of Fisher and More as true martyrs but encounter valiant defenders in stalwarts like Bellarmine and Suarez, just as earlier Casale, Wallop, Sampson, and Morison, in the attempt to denigrate the characters of Fisher and More had met resistance in the person of Paul III, Cochlaeus, and others.

Independently of these political aspects of his life and death, Fisher impressed his own and later generations as the father, even if not the founder, of two colleges. His name, for example, will always be associated with that of Erasmus and of Croke in the serious and successful beginnings of Greek studies and with that of Wakefield in the initiation of regular Hebrew lectures. Undoubtedly humanism would sooner or later have come to make its impact on Cambridge as elsewhere, but the fact remains that Fisher was the active agent for the intensified study of the three languages of classical Latin, Greek, and Hebrew, and for the preparation of solidly trained preachers, theologians, and scholars. Even though the curricular superstructure was modified after his death, his were the foundations which supported the later edifice. The constant stream of famous men issuing from the portals of St. John's in the sixteenth century and later bears testimony in a silent and unacknowledged way to his academic and, one should not forget, financial labors. These men, too, bear a mark as his unwritten work.

When one turns to Fisher's publications in bulk, the temptation is to enter into an immediate comparison with More's. This would hardly be just to either man because the *Utopia,* which instantly springs to mind, is for the most part a profane work, which largely transcended its period and went forth to create a new literary type and a new social world, exerting its greatest influence in the nineteenth and twentieth centuries. In addition, it is fair neither to More nor to Fisher to compare even their polemical productions: written in different languages, English as against Latin; for different audiences, popular and native as against scholarly and continental; at different times, pioneering before 1527 as against consolidating in and after 1528; by authors with different status, lay as against episcopal; with different styles, colloquial as against formal. Only their Latin replies to Luther's attack on their king have a common point of contact, yet even they differ — as though the one had agreed to pay special attention to Luther's invective and the other to his theory.

When Tyndale, Frith, Barnes, and others began to write, they attacked both More and Fisher. As far as Fisher was concerned, his famous sermon against Luther of May 1521 became a favorite target of attack, although his Latin tracts were hardly immune. Though today the language proves to be a barrier to widespread reading, Latin won Fisher a continental and scholarly audience. Almost at once his controversial works placed him beside European lights like Cajetan, Clichtove, and Eck. His orthodoxy, his learning, and his solidity made Fisher a pre-Tridentine classic.

Even the failure of Luther and Oecolampadius to refute him served to enhance his reputation as being unanswerable. At Trent his views were cited and quoted by theologians and bishops. After the Council no theologian or controversialist of stature, whether Catholic or Protestant, could neglect his works: witness the Catholic Robert Bellarmine and the Protestant John Gerhard. Even as a controversialist, except when addressing a popular or mixed audience, he remains a professional theologian. His greatest service is the clear statement of the accepted — or acceptable — Catholic doctrine of the time. His teaching, he insists, is never his alone, but that of the whole Church, reaching back to the Apostolic Age and extending to dioceses at the ends of the earth.

When purely theological controversy went into eclipse, ecclesiastical historians of varying religious persuasion kept his memory alive in the later seventeenth and the eighteenth centuries. The nineteenth century, which saw the cataloguing and publication of numerous historical documents and manuscripts and the initiation of monumental textual series like the *Corpus Reformatorum* (and, on a lesser scale, of the Parker Society editions of the English Reformers), reflected glory on Fisher's life and work, sometimes only in passing or by way of contrast. In addition, the interest in the history of the European universities brought into perspective his educational achievements at Cambridge. Finally, even if his beatification and canonization engrossed and inspired his co-religionists most, the recent phenomenal interest of scholars in every aspect of the Renaissance and the Reformation has served to measure Fisher's impact on both movements and to reveal particularly his continental fame through many decades. No historian of England or of Europe could mention A.D. 1535 without pointing to his execution, with that of Thomas More, as the most significant event of the year.

So much, then, for the man of history: henceforth his name can never be dissociated from the growth of Cambridge University, the rise of Protestantism on the Continent, the influence of the first Reformers in England, the question of the divorce, and the declaration of royal supremacy. But what about his writings? Are they still vital? If so, to what extent? To begin, one should draw a distinction between his English and his Latin publications.

Fisher's English writings, it must be observed, did descend into a limbo from which they are now emerging more and more into the literary world of classics, studied with admiration if not read for sheer pleasure.[38] Independently of the royal proscription of his works after his death, one explanation, of course, simply is that literary historians and anthologists, with few exceptions, tended to ignore whole types, particularly the sermon, the funeral oration, and the spiritual treatise. Consider for a moment the variety of Fisher's sermons: the scriptural explication of the Penitential Psalms, the exhortation as in *Two Sermons,* the occasional address as in the Good Friday talk on the passion, and the popular lecture as in the two addresses on Luther. His two funeral orations rise above mere antiquarian interest to an artistic level. His two ascetical treatises, the one to overcome tepidity by meditation on death, the other to gain love by contemplation of God's benefits, are also literary classics. All these writings have imaginative and emotional elements which make them, if not masterpieces, at least notable specimens of their type.

Fisher's Latin works, on the other hand, are scholarly rather than literary. Each of them makes a contribution to its subject matter. No survey of the controversy on Mary Magdalene can ignore his three critiques of Lefèvre and Clichtove. No roster of Catholic apologists and polemicists can slight his writings against Luther's forty-one articles and assault on the mass. No list of treatises on the Real Presence can omit his refutation of Oecolampadius' doctrine. No history of Henry VIII's divorce can fail to mention his extant tracts, published and unpublished, in defense of the validity of the royal marriage. Finally, no bibliography of writings on Christian asceticism can pass over his gem on the necessity of prayer, published in two different English translations.

Since his writings date both before and after the dramatic appearance of Luther, they can give a true picture of what was the actual and active teaching of Catholicism during those years and can supply an objective view of what was the target of the Reformers' attacks. They can help to determine the truth or falsity of polemical declarations, whether Catholic or Protestant. On this plane of historical happening and interpretation, one vexing question is bound to arise. Is Fisher medieval? Is he Renaissance? Is he modern? The irritation springs from the notorious fact that none of these terms has become fixed in meaning because life, experience, and personality in the flow of time and the rush of action cannot be rendered static. In a sense, the historian or biographer is more like a painter or sculptor than like a poet or musician: he can catch a particular figure in a particular situation at a particular time better than a mass of mankind in a general movement.

In regard to Fisher, we should perhaps not phrase the question, "How much is he a man of the Renaissance?" Or even, "How much is he a bishop of the Renaissance?" The connotations of this latter phrase for the English reader are too much derived from English literature — say, Jacobean tragedy or Browning's monologues — to allow just evaluation. The Bishop of Rochester is as much interested as any other bishop of the Renaissance in having a fitting tomb, as one knows from the plans for his monument in St. John's College;[39] yet all the records manifest greater concern about masses and prayers for his soul. A painter of the Renaissance is judged as a painter, a musician as a musician, a soldier as a soldier — each man by his profession or status. Hence the historian or the biographer might best put the query as follows: "How much is Fisher a preacher and a theologian of the Renaissance?"

As for his sermons, they appear — to adapt or distort a figure — like new bottles for old wine. Elements usually (and justly) labeled medieval (or, at least, late medieval) are prominent in them early and late, even if they do not finally constitute their content and texture. One need only recall the careful and minute division and subdivision of the subject matter (made more conspicuous by the method of explicit enumeration), the allegorizations (usually but not always brief), the threats and punishments of hell and purgatory (offset by man's ability to avoid them by God's grace), the need for good works (as satisfying for sin and as meriting heaven), and so on.[40]

The theologian in the Bishop of Rochester sees the absolute necessity of Hebrew and Greek for the proper study of the Scriptures and the Fathers. Here he is markedly a figure of the Renaissance, at least the Erasmian Renaissance. Where does the difference between the new, or the Renaissance, and the old, or the

Middle Ages, lie? The medieval theologian views these two sources of theology as presuppositions and as furnishing the material for intellectual investigation and speculation: he hardly makes use of them as the staple of theology in his *summae* or even in his commentaries on Boethius, Augustine, and others. In the Renaissance the emphasis shifts to the Scriptures and to the Fathers themselves: their language and their thought studied in their own terms, not according to an Aristotelian system, and evaluated in their length and breadth, not in a few select works, or in brief excerpts. Fisher makes this change increasingly in the course of his controversies over the years. Yet he does not reject the Scholastics. When he does use them, however, he often uses them as he does the Fathers — as witnesses to tradition — or as authorities to confirm the interpretations of the Fathers, who have brilliantly caught and communicated the true meaning of the Scriptures. This particular view of the Fathers as authentic explicators of the Bible, implicit and presumed in the medieval theologians, becomes explicit and formulated in Fisher.

For Fisher all is still in tune: "They make al but one songe / & one armony." [41] The Old Testament is in the New; the Fathers in their homilies and treatises teach the same as the Scriptures; and the Scholastics in their disputations hold identically the same as the Fathers and the Scriptures. To borrow a trinitarian term, the circumincession of Scriptures, Fathers, and Scholastics is clear and dominant and forms the one and only doctrine of the Church. This circumincession finds striking expression in the sermon at Barnes's abjuration in the metaphor of the circles or roundels. The Gospel is in the psalter, the psalter is in the Gospel, the New Law is in the Old, the Old is in the New, and "the expositions of the fathers . . . make one roundell with the same." In them all there is but "one spirite of lyfe." [42] No specific mention is made of the Disputers or Scholastics, for they are either to be classified with the later Fathers, according to Fisher's not infrequent understanding of the term, or to be identified with "the doctrine of the Church," which at that time was, on the whole, the doctrine of the Scholastics.

The doctrinal systematization and synthesis, each of its own kind, created and accepted by Bonaventure, Albert, Aquinas, and Scotus, is still intact in Fisher and, to that extent, he may be labeled medieval; but insofar as in this synthesis there are new emphases, e.g., on exegesis and patrology, he is of the Renaissance. In a sense, too, the Scholastic synthesis serves as the background or framework for his theology rather than as its substance and essence. Here he anticipates, or rather shares, the new theory as found in the treatises of such typical Renaissance figures as Bellarmine and Suarez.

Now, it was impossible for a Christian humanist to read either the New Testament or the Fathers without becoming acutely aware of the discrepancies between the contemporary Church and the Church of the Apostolic Age or the patristic era. Protestant Reformers rejected the late-medieval Church on the doctrinal level in such matters as tradition, good works, the seven sacraments, a special priesthood, and papal supremacy, by maintaining the primacy and exclusiveness of Scriptures, faith, grace, and universal priesthood. Except for a rare point held against Scholastic opinion, such as the need for a special divine help for every morally good work, Fisher's criticism of his Church never violates its doctrinal integrity but always directs itself toward moral or disciplinary failure. This attitude manifests itself in passages which contrast the contemporary clergy and laity with those of the golden age of the Apostles. Before as well as after the appearance of Luther, the orthodox expressed approbation or praise by applying the term *evangelical* or *apostolic* to a new or reformed way of Christian life.

In this respect Fisher is more conservative than Erasmus, who extends his criticism, professedly subject to correction by the Church, to more serious problems, among them marriage and divorce, clerical celibacy, saints' relics, monasticism, and Scholasticism. Yet even in Erasmus' case, it may be noted, the reforms are more disciplinary than doctrinal. What the better knowledge of the Bible and the Fathers produces in Fisher is an intense desire for renovation of the Christian life, not a change in Christian teaching or theology. His goal is a reform in morality and not in doctrine — a renewal of spirit and not innovation in dogma — a return to the fervor of the earliest Christians and not to an archaic re-establishment of primitive practices. For the Holy Spirit is always with the Church of Christ, not only in the Apostolic Age, but in every period of its existence. Since the

Church's doctrine is inspired at all times by the Holy Spirit, reform for Fisher lies not there but in moral and disciplinary areas. Actually, what the Protestants did achieve was a dogmatic revolution and, concomitant with it, a moral revolution. Insofar as the reform had to be moral, Fisher is at one with the Reformers.

If revolt, innovation, and originality are somewhat arbitrarily set up as the hallmark of the Renaissance, to Fisher's credit (as to Erasmus') are his tremendous interest in education, his stress on the three languages and literatures, and his utilitarian view of these as aids to the study of true Christianity as found in the Bible and the Fathers and to the reformation of men and morals according to the apostolic ideal — without the rejection of Scholastic theology and current Catholic teaching.

The last qualification does not make Fisher a medieval man. Nor will it do to call him an altogether transitional figure. His approval and praise of the two most controversial Catholics of his age, namely, Reuchlin and Erasmus, put him squarely in the movement called Christian humanism. He is as much of the Renaissance as the great Catholic theologians of the Counter-Reformation and the Council of Trent. Their commendation and use of his works would explain, or rather indicate, his kinship with later Catholic reform. At the least, he must be called an early but true figure of the Renaissance in Catholic theology rather than a late representative of the Middle Ages.[43]

Fisher's total rejection of Protestantism and, under its shadow, his reformulation of Catholic belief are very much in the spirit of the future. Yet he is not entirely anti-Protestant in all his writings. There is little eirenicism, it is true, in his polemical publications, in which he gives no quarter to his adversaries. For him what is all-important is what the Church holds. But what the Church holds is subject to various interpretations of individual thinkers and of whole schools of thought, as is most evident from the need for an ecumenical council and from the discussions at that council, to say nothing of the rejoinders of Protestant preachers and divines on this score. Where Fisher comes nearest to Protestantism, as, for example, on the absolute dependence of man on God's grace, is in his treatises on the spiritual life. These may be said to serve as a bridge between his polemical works and those of the Protestants. In them the bishop as pastoral theologian and the bishop as dogmatic theologian meet, and differences with Protestantism tend to blur and vanish. Hence the spiritual writings are worthy of special study in all their implications.

To sum up, as it were, this summary. One must conclude that Fisher should be placed — or replaced — with the significant figures of the Renaissance. Thomas More had the good fortune to write one book, the *Utopia,* and Desiderius Erasmus another, *The Praise of Folly,* both of which continue to survive and thrive as world classics or, at least, as Western classics. These two creations entice readers to enter through their portals and to investigate the other productions of their authors. Fisher had the misfortune of having written no such popular and enduring work. Consequently his achievement must be measured rather by comparison with that of English contemporaries like Colet and Tunstal, of continental figures like Reuchlin and Lefèvre, and of Catholic apologists like Clichtove and Eck. Here his reputation is secure: in the special history of the English sermon, in that of the English and Latin spiritual treatise, and in that of Latin theological controversy.

Fisher's name keeps cropping up, sometimes unexpectedly, in the history of dogma, especially but not exclusively during the sixteenth century. Educational history always records his contributions to the greatness of the University of Cambridge. Political history relates his opposition to Henry VIII's divorce and to the Act of Supremacy. Ecclesiastical annals for the 1520's must always mention his writings against Luther and Oecolampadius, and those for A.D. 1535 his decapitation for maintaining papal primacy. Early in his life, in a sermon on Vulg. Ps. 101, he had told his audience: "Take hede what the importune and neuer seasynge labour in a grete & necessary cause dooth profyte & auayle. It is wryten. *Labor improbus omnia vincit.* Incessaunt laboure . . . ouercometh all thynges." [44] On the scaffold on June 22, he could truthfully but humbly say: "I have accomplished the work that thou hast given me to do." His work, his life, and his death all verify Vergil's truism: *Labor omnia vicit / Improbus* — even the grave. For toil is the sire of fame.

ABBREVIATIONS USED IN NOTES

NOTES

INDEX

COMMON ABBREVIATIONS USED IN THE NOTES

Note. For Fisher's works, see Principal Abbreviations for Fisher's Writings, pp. xv–xvii. For every other work much cited, a shortened but recognizable form of its title has been consistently employed after the first and full citation. Even though the abbreviations given below are commonly used by the scholar, they are explained here fully in order to avoid all ambiguity and to assist the general reader.

ADB Allgemeine Deutsche Biographie, hrsg. durch die Historische Commission bei der Königl. Akademie der Wissenschaften. Leipzig, 1875–1912. 56 vols.

CBEL Cambridge Bibliography of English Literature, ed. F. W. Bateson. Cambridge, Eng., 1941. 4 vols. Suppl., ed. G. Watson, 1957.

DNB Dictionary of National Biography, ed. L. Stephen and S. Lee. London, 1908–1909 [orig. 1885–1900]. 22 vols. Periodical Suppl.

LP Letters and Papers, Foreign and Domestic, of the Reign of Henry VIII, ed. J. S. Brewer *et al.* London, 1862–1910. 21 vols. in 33 parts. Now 23 vols. in 38, 1862–1932.

NED A New English Dictionary on Historical Principles, ed. J. A. H. Murray *et al.* Oxford, 1888–1928. 10 vols. in 12. Suppl., 1933.

PG Patrologiae cursus completus: Series Graeca, ed. J. P. Migne. Paris, 1857-60. 104 vols. in 109.

PL Patrologiae cursus completus: Series Latina, ed. J. P. Migne. Paris, 1844–80. 221 vols.

Span. Cal. Calendar of Letters, Despatches, and State Papers . . . between England and Spain, Preserved . . . at Simancas and Elsewhere, ed. G. A. Bergenroth *et al.* London, 1862–1954. 15 vols. in 20.

State Papers. State Papers Published under the Authority of His Majesty's Commission: King Henry VIII. 5 parts in 11 vols. London, 1830–52. Superseded by *LP,* above, except for complete text of letters.

V.C.H. The Victoria History of the Counties of England, ed. W. Page *et al.* Westminster, 1900–.

WA D. Martin Luthers Werke. Kritische Gesammtausgabe. Weimar, 1883–.

NOTES

CHAPTER I: WORKS AND DAYS OF THE HUMANIST AND CHURCHMAN

1. *The Life of Fisher,* ed. R. Bayne (London: Early English Text Society, 1921), p. 124.

2. *Doctrinal Treatises . . . ,* ed. H. Walter (Cambridge, 1848), p. 341. It is impossible to ascertain whether the Testaments said to have been burnt in connection with Fisher's sermon in February 1526 were Tyndale's. More likely than not, they were Luther's German translation. The absence of any reference in Fisher's sermon is suspicious. B. F. Westcott, *A General View of the History of the English Bible,* rev. ed. W. A. Wright (London: Macmillan, 1905), writes: "It is not certain that the English Testaments were burnt until after Tunstall's sermon (*i.e.* after April 1526)" (p. 40, n. 4). Cf. F. F. Bruce, *The English Bible: A History of Translations* (London: Lutterworth Press, 1961), p. 37. J. F. Mozley argues for the arrival of the translation in England "about the end of March" and for Tunstal's burning of the Testaments on October 28, 1526 (*William Tyndale* [London: S.P.C.K., 1937], pp. 66, 117–118). For the documents, see Preface, "The Landing and Distribution in England," *ibid.,* pp. 36–47, and "The Persecution in England," pp. 48–64.

3. After asking where the persecutors (ancient Roman emperors and recent papal prelates) are now, Joye continues: "Where is Thomas wolsaye cardinall bisshop of Yorke . . . Syr Thomas More, and Johan Fissher bisshop of Rochester, withe all . . . which haue these .xvi. yeres persequuted the gospell? Are they not all whiche beleued not the gospell condempned with Satan and his aungels vnto euerlastinge dampnacion? . . . Are thei not now tormented in hell in perpetuall fyer for burning gods worde and the professours therof?" (*A present consolacion for the sufferers of persecucion for ryghtwysenes* [1544], sigg. F8^{v}–G1^{v}).

4. "Def. reg. assert." 1.5, *Opera omnia* (Würzburg, 1597), col. 108.

5. *The fruytful saynges of Dauyd the kynge & prophete in the seuen penytencyall psalmes . . .* (London: Wynkyn de Worde, 16 June 1508).

The date of delivery is fixed by the third sermon. Here Fisher combines a commentary on Vulg. Ps. 37, pt. 1, with a sermon on the Nativity of the Blessed Virgin, which fell on a Sunday in 1504 (and 1499). Unpublished Latin commentaries on Psalms 1–51 in fragmentary condition are extant in the Public Record Office (S.P.2/R, foll. 28–273), sometimes in a single copy, sometimes in a rough and a good copy, two (Pss. 27–28) in three copies, and one (Ps. 28) in several variant forms. Psalms 19–20 each have two altogether different commentaries. Fisher might well have worked on these from his ordination to the time of the seizure of his papers in April 1534. References to Luther and his doctrines, however, seem infrequent. This is understandable because Fisher was very busy with polemics after 1519. He does apply the whole of Ps. 10 to the Church and the Lutherans, to faith and good works. In commentary on Ps. 11:2, *diminutae sunt veritates* ("truths are decayed [from among the children of men]"), he laments: "Work is cut off from faith, satisfaction and confession from penitence, contrition from the worthy reception of the Eucharist, and other things of that kind." As for the *Psalmi seu precationes* which appear in Fisher's *Opera*, cols. 1734–69, Bridgett doubts their authenticity (*Life of Blessed John Fisher* [London, 1888], p. 112n), but their attribution to Fisher is sufficiently attested to hold them genuine. For their use by the Anglican Church, see *Private Prayers, Put Forth by Authority during the Reign of Queen Elizabeth,* ed. W. K. Clay (Cambridge, 1851), Pref., p. x, and pp. 318–352. Berthelet's Latin edition of 1544 has the year 1534 at the bottom of the border of the title page.

6. D. F. S. Thomson and H. C. Porter, tr., *Erasmus and Cambridge: The Cambridge Letters of Erasmus* (Toronto: University of Toronto Press, 1963), p. 188, n. 194.

7. ". . . qui tunc habenas regni summa prudentia moderabatur, principi certe seculis omnibus, atque id multis nominibus . . . admirando . . ." ("Ver. corp.," *Opera,* p. 746).

8. ". . . hic tantum adiiciam, quod . . . ingenue fateor, me plus ab eius egregiis virtutibus, quod ad probe viuendum institutum conducat, didicisse, quam vicissim illi communicarim vnquam" (*ibid.,* p. 747).

9. *Early Statutes of Christ's College, Cambridge,* ed. H. Rackham (Cambridge: Printed for the Editor by Fabb and Tyler, 1927), and *Early Statutes of the College of St. John the Evangelist in the University of Cambridge,* ed. J. E. B. Mayor (Cambridge, 1859). A. H. Lloyd comments: "To Fisher must be attributed the more part [*sic*] of the statutes, and he may have been responsible for the phrasing of other parts, but the curious may see the hand of the foundress in certain portions" (in chs. 6, 26, 29, 31, 34, 43, 44, 46, *The Early History of Christ's College, Cambridge* [Cambridge (Eng.) University Press, 1934], p. 298). The change in name from Godshouse to Christ's College may be explained by the circumstance that "fifteenth century devotion was abandoning the medieval use of 'God' to denote the second person of the Trinity" (H. O. Evennett, "B. John Fisher and Cambridge," *The Clergy Review,* IX [1935], 385).

10. "Oratio habita coram . . . Henrico VII. Cantabrigiae, A.D. 1506,"

in John Lewis, *The Life of Dr. John Fisher, Bishop of Rochester . . .*, ed. T. Hudson Turner (London, 1855), II, 263–272.

11. Thomson-Porter, tr., *Erasmus,* Introd., p. 28, enumerates £100 (1506), £4000 (1508), £5000 (1509), and, as a legacy, £5000 (1512).

12. ". . . quantum periculi subesset, quantave posset vniuersae Christi ecclesiae ex hac opinionum varietate confusio atque ignominia oriri" ("Magdal." lib. 1, *Opera,* col. 1395; cf. lib. 2, col. 1425, and *Euersio munitionis quam Iodocus Clichtoueus erigere moliebatur aduersus vnicam Magdalenam* . . . [Louvain, (1519)], sig. A2). Poncher must have been quite insistent, using "two letters and many go-betweens" *(binis literis, pluribusque internunciis)* *(Confutatio secundae disceptationis per Iacobum Fabrum Stapulensem habitae* [Paris, 1519], fol. 2). See also *Opus epistolarum Des. Erasmi Roterodami,* ed. P. S. Allen *et al.* (Oxford: Clarendon Press, 1906–58), III, 523. Yet the great Schoolman, John Major, read the work without dismay according to Clichtove *(Disceptationis de Magdalena defensio* [Paris, 1519], fol. 87). For the background, see J.-Al. Clerval, *De Judoci Clichtovei Neoportuensis . . . vita et operibus* (Paris, 1894), pp. 26–30; and for the roles of Lefèvre, Clichtove, Grandval, Fisher, Agrippa, Beda, Sorio, and the Sorbonne, see F. Vander Haeghen, *Bibliotheca Belgica* (Gand, 1880–90), ser. I, vol. IV, no. C428 (without pagination). On the whole question of the Marys, see P. Ketter, *The Magdalene Question* (*Die Magdalenen Frage*), tr. H. C. Koehler (Milwaukee: Bruce, 1935), with the recent authorities therein cited, especially H. Thurston, "St. Mary Magdalen — Fact and Legend," *Studies,* XXIII (1934), 110–123, which also resumes Thurston's pronouncements in *The Month,* XCIII (1899), 75–81, and CLV (1930), 542–544. A decisive examination of the Magdalene question in Christian tradition has been made by U. Holzmeister, *Zeitschrift für Katholische Theologie,* XLVI (1922), 402–422, 556–584.

13. "Magdal.," *Opera,* p. 1394. *Durand* has not been identified.

14. Erasmus, *Ep.,* III, 522. Erasmus later singles out Fisher's too stinging jest on Lefèvre's "church" *(ibid.,* IV, 192; cf. "Magdal." lib. 3, *Opera,* cols. 1457–59). He wishes that the book had been "more handsomely printed" (*nitidius excusum*) and offers his help in the matter; he also wishes that the labor had been expended on another topic — although the present may be "both pious and elegant" (*tum pium . . . tum elegans* [*ibid.,* III, 524]). W. Nesenus, who would have sent a copy if it had been printed already, wrote on January 30, 1519, to Zwingli: "Episcopus Roffensis, Anglus, Marias Fabri funditus subvertit, adductis ex evangeliis sacrisque aliis scriptoribus sententiis autoritatibusque, quibus ut impiam Fabri de Magdalenis opinionem reiicit et profecto, ut ego quoque quae sentio dicam, egregium prestitit episcopum, modo partius usus fuisset convitiis" (Zwingli, *Sämtliche Werke,* ed. E. Egli *et al.,* VII [Leipzig: M. Heinsius Nachfolger, 1911], 133). For the *Dissertatio de Maria Magdalena,* in which Willibald Pirckheimer holds for three different persons, see L. W. Spitz, *The Religious Renaissance of the German Humanists* (Cambridge, Mass.: Harvard University Press, 1963), pp. 172, 331. In a letter to Erasmus, April 30 [1520] (Erasmus, *Ep.,* IV, 247,

textual note), Pirckheimer makes no reference to Fisher but condemns those men who, enviously attacking even members of their own order, "snatch St. Mary Magdalene from her deliverer Lefèvre and thrust her with most disgraceful harlots into a stinking brothel — when it would rather be more becoming in such a doubtful matter to follow the opinion which approaches closer to piety" ("vt diuam Mariam Magdalenen assertori suo Fabro eriperent et cum turpissimis scortis in olidum lupanar detruderent? cum tamen potius deceret in re tam dubia eam sequi opinionem que ad pietatem accederet propius"). Erasmus' letter to Fisher, October 17, 1519, makes clear that Pirckheimer is referring especially to the *Praedicatores,* or Dominicans (*ibid.,* IV, 93), to whose order Lefèvre belonged.

15. ". . . cum tanta sit orationis dissimilitudo, imo cum tantum absim ab illius diuini Praesulis eruditione" (Erasmus, *Ep.,* III, 591–592). The last clause was added in August 1521.

16. ". . . eum esse Paternitatis tuae stilum, qui possit Erasmicus videri. Certe causam sic praeterea tractasti, vt ne decem quidem Erasmi potuerint absolutius" (*Correspondence,* ed. E. F. Rogers [Princeton University Press, 1947], pp. 136–137). Rogers conjectures that the work in question is *De unica Magdalena* (1519), but the opening reference to "both your cause and that of your country as well" (*quum tua causa, tum etiam patriae*) seems to favor the *Defensio regie assertionis* (1525).

17. "Magdal." lib. 3, *Opera,* col. 1460.

18. *Defensio,* foll. 73v–74.

19. *Euersio munitionis quam Iodocus Clichtoueus erigere moliebatur aduersus vnicam Magdalenam* (Louvain: Martens, [1519]). Fisher is unusually specific in citing marginal numbers in Clichtove's *Defensio,* sigg. D3 (no. 52), H1v (no. 65), H2 (no. 66), M1 (no. 52), O2v (no. 9), O3v (no. 10), P2 (no. 9), P3 (no. 12), P3v (nos. 12, 19, 29), Q3 (no. 29), S1v (no. 49), T3 (no. 32), Z6 (no. 46), and a1 (no. 46). He refers to *The Single Magdalene* several times in *Eversio,* e.g., sigg. B2v (on Chrysostom), K4v (on Augustine), M3 (on Petrarch), V4v (on Mark 16:9), and Y2 (on a twofold anointing).

20. ". . . consuetudo semel consensu Christianitatis introducta, parem cum lege scripta videtur auctoritatem esse sortita" ("Assert. Luth. confut." prooem., veritas 10, *Opera,* col. 295). Hence he objects to Clichtove's refusal to recognize any authority except Scripture or the general councils (*Eversio,* sig. a1).

21. J. S. Brewer, *The Reign of Henry VIII,* ed. J. Gairdner (London, 1884), I, 280.

22. *Confut. sec. discept.,* fol. 2. Fisher (fol. 14) specifically refers to fuller treatment of certain points in his two previous works, the one against Lefèvre, the other against Clichtove.

23. *Ibid.,* fol. 3.

24. *Ibid.,* fol. 2v.

25. "The Faculty of Theology at Paris pronounced against Faber in Nov.–Dec. 1521 and his works were subsequently placed upon the Index" (Erasmus, *Ep.,* IV, 93n). For the background, see C. du Plessis d'Argentré, *Col-*

lectio judiciorum de novis erroribus . . . (Paris, 1726–28), II, vi–vii, 4, and for the text, "Determinatio . . . de unica Magdalena," *ibid.*, II, vii.

26. Erasmus, *Ep.*, IV, 93. In fact, it was a publisher, Jodocus Badius Ascensius, who under date of June 1, 1521, issued what might be the first of many dedications of learned publications to Fisher. See *Secundi tomi operum venerab. Bedae commentarii* (Paris, [1521]), sig. a2. Badius gives five reasons why this work is dedicated fittingly to the Bishop of Rochester. Among them are common nationality, devotion to the Fathers, purity of style, and critical acumen. The prime incentive, of course, is likeness in character and scholarship (*ob morum studiorumque tuorum . . . similitudinem*). Reference to a possible lost work by Fisher is made toward the end of the epistle: ". . . te audiuimus iampridem habere ad praelum emunctos in Matthaeum commentarios . . ." (sig. a2v). Badius' letter, except for a list of spellings, is reprinted in Ph. Renouard, *Bibliographie des impressions et des oeuvres de Josse Badius Ascensius, imprimeur et humaniste, 1462–1535* (Paris, 1908), II, 148–150.

27. Erasmus, *Ep.*, IV, 192. For Lefèvre's relationship to the Reformation, see J. W. Brush, "Lefèvre d'Étaples: Three Phases of His Life and Work," in *Reformation Studies: Essays in Honor of Roland H. Bainton*, ed. F. H. Littell (Richmond, Va.: John Knox Press, 1962), pp. 117–128.

28. *Vie du bienheureux martyr Jean Fisher, Cardinal, Évêque de Rochester (+1535): Texte anglais et traduction latine du XVIe siècle*, ed. F. van Ortroy, in *Analecta Bollandiana*, X (1891), 255–259. On the only legatine councils summoned or held at this time (1519, 1520, 1523), see F. M. Powicke and E. B. Fryde, *Handbook of British Chronology*, 2nd ed. (London: Royal Historical Society, 1961), p. 564.

29. *A Godlie treatisse declaryng the benefites, fruites, and great commodities of prayer, and also the true vse therof* (London, 1560), sig. A4v. A new translation by R. A. appeared in Paris in 1640.

30. Ortroy, *Fisher*, X, 218.

31. *The sermon of Johan the bysshop of Rochester made agayn the pernicyous doctryn of Martin luuther.* For Erasmus' prevention of a burning of Luther's writings as an act of tyranny (*hec tyrannis mihi nullo pacto placet*) the previous year, see Erasmus, *Ep.*, IV, 261 and n. In 1520 Luther's books were publicly burnt by the University of Cambridge (C. H. Cooper, *Annals of Cambridge* [Cambridge, 1842–1908], I, 303; cf. W. D. Bushell, *Church of St. Mary the Great: The University Church at Cambridge* [Cambridge: Bowes & Bowes, 1948], p. 93). The last part of Fisher's sermon was lost, as Richard Sharpe, Fisher's chaplain, reports to Nicholas Metcalfe. Consequently, "it will cost hym sum labour for I thynke he haue not the copye" (G. J. Gray, "Letters of Bishop Fisher, 1521–3," *The Library*, ser. 3, IV [1913], 136). According to Gray, these letters had been printed previously by R. F. Scott in *The Eagle*, XVII (1893), 470–478.

32. See P. L. Hughes and J. F. Larkin, *Tudor Royal Proclamations*, I (New Haven: Yale University Press, 1964), 235–237: "The King's highness is informed that diverse and sundry writings and books . . . especially one

book imprinted comprising a sermon made by John Fisher, late bishop of Rochester, . . . are dispersed abroad in this realm. . ." Cf. Erwin Doernberg, *Henry VIII and Luther* (Stanford University Press, 1961), p. 10, and *LP*, IX, no. 963, and *Span. Cal.*, V, pt. 2, no. 5, p. 8. The sermon in its published version praises Henry VIII's *Assertio septem sacramentorum*, still in manuscript and printed by Richard Pynson, July 12, 1521: "The kynges grace our souerayne lorde in his owne persone hath with his pen so substauncyally foghten agaynst Martyn luther that I doute not but euery true christen man that shal rede his boke shal se those blessed sacramentes clered & delyuered. . ." ("Luther," *The English Works of John Fisher . . .*, ed. J. E. B. Mayor, Part I [London, 1876], p. 327).

33. The Preface by Nicholas Wilson, Master of Michaelhouse, is dated January 1, 1521/22. See E. P. Goldschmidt, *The First Cambridge Press in Its European Setting* (Cambridge [Eng.] University Press, 1955), p. 16. Pace's letter to Leo X, dated June 1, 1521, is reprinted in P. Balan, *Monumenta reformationis Lutheranae . . . 1521–1525* (Ratisbon, 1884), pp. 255–256. Among other praises of Fisher, Pace writes: "Non tam ignis huic nostro populo quam sermo tam boni et eruditi Episcopi, Lutherum hereticum declaravit (non magis enim doctrina licet sit singularis, quam vitae morumque Sanctitas, Roffensem commendat) . . ." (*ibid.*).

34. Letter from Sharpe to Metcalfe, in G. J. Gray, "Letters of Bishop Fisher, 1521–3," *The Library*, ser. 3, IV (1913), 139. This letter continues: "More ouer syr ye shall receyue of this berer my lordes sermon in ynglyshe which he prayethe you to put to Wynkyn to prynt" (*ibid.*).

35. Sharpe to Metcalfe, *ibid.*, 136.

36. "Convulsio," *Opera*, p. 1299. The Preface refers to Tunstal as "now, by his own merits, bishop-elect of London" (*nunc suis meritis Londoniensem Electum* [*ibid.*]). Tunstal was nominated in January, promoted on May 16 and September 10, and consecrated on October 19, 1522, at the hands of Wolsey, Warham, and Fisher. The Paris edition reads: *Conuulsio calumniarum Vlrichi Veleni Minhoniensis quibus Petrum nunquam Romae fuisse cauillatur . . .* PETRVS FVIT ROMAE (Paris: Resch, [1522?]). An earlier edition was published on October 30, 1522, at Antwerp. It was republished as late as 1698 in Ioannes Thomas de Rocaberti, *Bibliotheca maxima pontificia . . .*, XIV (Rome, 1698), 514–555. Velenus' work, printed in 1520 (possibly 1519), was entitled: *In hoc libello grauissimis, certissimisque, & in sacra scriptura fundatis rationibus uarijs probatur, Apostolum Petrum Romam non uenisse, neque illic passum. proinde satis friuole, & temere Romanus Pontifex se Petri successorem iactat, & nominat &c.* The copy in the British Museum has 1519 on the title page.

37. "Nos etiam inter confutandum articulos, quos Lutherus asserere molitus est, penitus eneruasse putamus, quicquid aduersus primatum Papae, Lutherus attulerit, vt iam non erit opus, quicquam in ea re copiosius dicere" ("Convulsio," *Opera*, col. 1341). It might seem more logical to understand Fisher as referring to a published work, Pace's Latin translation of his

sermon, rather than to an unpublished work, the *Confutation of Luther's Assertion,* but the latter was on the eve of publication.

38. "Sacerd. def." 2.18, *Opera,* col. 1251, tr. P. E. Hallett, *The Defence of the Priesthood* (London: Burns, Oates & Washbourne, 1935), p. 41.

39. Velenus, *Petrum Romam non uenisse,* sig. e2^{v}.

40. "E Bohemia juvenis eruditus ad me dedit libellum, probare conatus, S. Petrum nunquam venisse aut fuisse Romae, sed non euincit" (*Briefwechsel,* ed. E. L. Enders and G. Kawerau [Stuttgart and Leipzig, 1884–1932], III, 81; cf. n. 7). In a letter of March 31, 1534, to Oswald Myconius, Heinrich Bullinger views the question as relatively unimportant and as indecisive; but, if necessary, he would incline to the testimonies of the Fathers rather than to the conjectures of Velenus (J. C. Fuessli, ed., *Epistolae ab ecclesiae Helveticae reformatoribus vel ad eos scriptae* [Tiguri, 1742], p. 131).

41. Erasmus, *Ep.,* IV, 591, introd. Aleander contended that it contained "multe buggie impudentissime" — the latter epithet being the self-same used by Fisher.

42. Arnold Kuczyński, *Verzeichniss einer Sammlung von nahezu 3000 Flugschriften Luthers und seiner Zeitgenossen* (Leipzig, 1870–74; rpr. Nieuwkoop, 1960), no. 2689, pp. 240–241.

43. G. Veesenmeyer, "Von des Ulrich Velenus Schrift, dass Petrus nie nach Rom gekommen sey, und den Schriften dagegen," in *Sammlung v. Aufsätzen z. Erläuterung d. Kirchen–, Literatur–, Münz– u. Sittengeschichte* (Ulm, 1827), p. 149. Cardinal Cortese, the Italian Benedictine, also wrote against Velenus: *Tractatus adversus negantem B. Petrum Apostolum fuisse Romae, ad Adrianum VI,* printed *mendose* in *Epistolae familiares* (Venice, 1573), pp. 300–362, and issued correctly in *Omnia . . . scripta* (Padua, 1774), I, 211–274.

44. *Apologia Simonis Hessi aduersus Dominum Roffensem . . . super concertatione eius cum Vlrico Veleno, An Petrus fuerit Romae, Et quid de primatu Romani Pontificis sit censendum* (n.p., n.d.). The *Apologia* gained wide circulation, as appears from a letter of April 20 [1524] to Guillaume Farel from Jacques Lefèvre d'Étaples, who had been sent a copy by Antoine du Blet, a merchant or banker of Lyons (A.-L. Herminjard, ed., *Correspondance des réformateurs dans les pays de langue française,* I [Geneva-Paris, 1866], 207). The reader cannot but wonder with what emotion Lefèvre read the *Apologia* against his erstwhile adversary. Herminjard suggests Basel as the place of publication of the *Apologia* (*ibid.*).

45. See H. Reusch, *Der Index der verbotenen Bücher* (Bonn, 1883–85), I, 135, and, for a biographical sketch, Erasmus, *Ep.,* II, 188–189. On the all-but-certain identification, see *Allgemeine Deutsche Biographie,* XXVIII, 375; G. Uhlman, *Urbanus Rhegius* (Elberfeld, 1861), pp. 33, 349, n. 8; Luther, *Briefwechsel,* ed. Enders, II, 68–69, n. 1; and especially Ludwig Hätzer to Zwingli, September 14, 1525, in Zwingli, *Werke,* ed. Egli, VIII (Leipzig, 1914), 361. Eck half suspects Rhegius of writing or inspiring Velenus' work: "Hoc est nouum mendacium Vrbani Riegers aut alterius Lutterani, Petrum

nunquam fuisse Romae" (*Enchiridion locorum communium aduersus Lutteranos* [Lanshutae, 1525], sig. F1). The edition of next May 1526 has the humorous mistake of *mandatum* for *mendacium* (sig. C3[v]). Hessus' *Apologia* was placed on various Indexes (Reusch, I, 133, 135–136, 234), as was his *Argvmenta libelli. Symon Hessvs Lvthero ostendit cavsas, qvare lvterana oposcula* [*sic*] *a Coloniensibus et Lovaniensib. sint combvsta* (n.p., [1521]): see Kuczyński, *Flugschriften,* nos. 1019–21, p. 93. The letter from Hessus to Luther, satirically stating reasons why Luther's forty-one articles were condemned by Rome, had the distinction of being reprinted with Luther's works, e.g., *Opera,* II (Wittenberg, 1551), 126–135.

46. *De Petro et Roma aduersus Velenum Lutheranum, libri quatuor* (Cologne: Quentell, 1525). Veesenmeyer doubts Cochlaeus' statement in his dedication that he had held up the publication of his own refutation of Velenus because Fisher's book had anticipated his and because he was ashamed to dispute a fact universally admitted ("Velenus," *Sammlung,* p. 146).

47. "Fischer kein unbedeutender, sondern ein gelehrter und feiner Gegner war" (Veesenmeyer, "Velenus," *Sammlung,* pp. 145–146). See *ibid.,* pp. 146–148, for Cochlaeus' role in the controversy with Luther and Velenus on Peter's residence in Rome. In a communication of December 14, 1536, John Faber recommended reprinting works on the primacy of Peter and the Roman Church in view of the adversaries' attacks, including the hitherto unheard-of heresy that Peter was never in Rome, against which Cochlaeus and others had written (*Concilium Tridentinum* [Freiburg: Herder, 1901–], IV, 58, and n. 6, which refers to Fisher and Cortese).

48. Reusch, *Index,* I, 234.

49. ". . . de qua [disputatione] librum insignem iam pridem a Ioanne Roffensi, beatae memoriae viro, editum, accepi, sed librum ipsum videre nunquam potui" ("De summo pontifice," lib. 2, cap. 11, *Disputationes de controversiis Christianae fidei . . .* [Cologne, 1615], I, 242). The refutation takes up lib. 2, cap. 1–11, I, 231–242. If Bellarmine had seen Fisher's work, he might have followed the example of other theologians: "Melchior Cano et Alanus Copus n'examinent pas personnellement la question; ils se contentent de renvoyer aux études de Fisher et de Lindanus" (P. Polman, *L'Élément historique dans la controverse religieuse du XVIe siècle* [Gembloux: J. Duculot, 1932], p. 474).

50. Letter from Sharpe to Metcalfe, in Gray, "Letters of Bishop Fisher, 1521–3," *Library,* ser. 3, IV (1913), 136, 142. Fisher handled both topics at length in his sermon against Luther, but the latter has no preface, a copy of which Sharpe sent Metcalfe. In the *Confutation of Luther's Assertion,* Articles 17–22 deal with indulgences, Articles 25–28 with the pope ("Assert. Luth. confut.," *Opera,* cols. 484–522, 530–595). Articles 17 and 25, which are both long, might be meant in particular.

51. See G. W. Forell, ed., Introduction, *Luther's Works,* Vol. XXXII: *Career of the Reformer II* (Philadelphia: Muhlenberg Press, 1958), pp. ix–xii, 5.

52. "Cuius [i.e., Lutheri] assertiones, ita retexuit, ac reuicit reuerendus pater Ioannes Fyscherus, Episcopus Roffensis, vir eruditionis vbertate clarus, & vitae puritate clarissimus, vt, si quid est frontis Luthero, magno iam sit empturus, assertiones suas olim iam combustas a se. . . Certe quod ad Pontificis primatum pertinet, ita rem dilucidam reddit idem reuerendus Episcopus, ex Euangelijs, & Actis Apostolorum, & toto corpore veteris testamenti, & omnium consensu sanctorum patrum . . . postremo generalis definitione concilij victis . . . Armenis & Graecis, vt frustra mihi facturus viderer, & rem actam acturus, si de pontificis primatu scribere, de integro rursus ordirer." — *Omnia . . . Latina opera* (Louvain, 1566), fol. 68ᵛ; English translation by Sister Gertrude Joseph Donnelly, *A Translation of St. Thomas More's "Responsio ad Lutherum"* (Washington, D.C.: Catholic University of America Press, 1962), pp. 161–162, 284, n. 80.

53. "Assert. Luth. confut." art. 25, *Opera,* cols. 543–544. Later, in his "Dialogue against Heresies," bk. 4, chap. 18, More approves heartily of Fisher's recommendation on heretics: "As an honorable prelate of thys realme in his moste erudite booke, answereth vnto Luther, the prelates of Christes church rather ought temporally to destroy those rauenous wolues, than suffer them to wyrry & deuoure euerlastingly the flocke that Christ hath committed vnto their cure, & the flocke that hym selfe dyed for to saue from the wolues mouth" (*Workes . . . wrytten by him in the Englysh tonge* [London, 1557], p. 285). See Fisher, "Assert. Luth. confut." art. 33, *Opera,* cols. 633–634.

54. *Von dem hochgelerten vnd geistlichen Bischoff Johannes von Roffa vss engeland / seynes grossen nutzlichen bůchs CXXXIX. artickel wider M. Luther sein hie verteütscht zů nutz dem christlichen volck zů bedencken irer selen selikeit* (Strasbourg, 1523), sigg. A3–D3, a literal translation of "Assert. Luth. confut." art. 15, *Opera,* col. 457–468, but mixed with sheets of Cochlaeus' German translation of Dietenberger's refutation of Luther's *De votis monasticis.* See M. Spahn, *Johannes Cochläus* (Berlin, 1898), p. 343. In the dedication to Fisher of *Aduersus latrocinantes et raptorias cohortes Rusticorum. Responsio Iohannis Cochlaei* (Cologne, September 1525), Cochlaeus declares that he would perhaps have translated into German the whole of Fisher's extremely helpful *Assertionis Lutheranae confutatio* if he had found a suitable and trustworthy publisher. On the deception practiced against him by Lutherans in regard to the mélange of Fisher's and Dietenberger's works, see *ibid.,* sig. a1ᵛ–2. The year after Fisher's death, Caspar Meckenlor did publish a translation of all forty-one articles of the *Assert. Luth. confut.* but in an abridged form; e.g., he gives relatively few verbatim quotations from Luther. See *Gründtliche widerlegung vnd ableynung der XLI. Artickeln Mart. Luthers / Durch . . . Johann / Weyland Bischoff zu Roffa . . .* (Leipzig, 1536).

55. *Von dem hochgelerten geistlichen bischoff Jo. von Roffen vss Engelland / seines grosen nützlichen bůchs zwen artickel verteutscht vom Doctor Jo. Cochleus seind hie neuw getruckt mit gůttem bericht allen Christen menschen zů gůt vnd der selen heil. 1524* (Strasbourg, 1524), a verbatim

version of "Assert. Luth. confut." arts. 15–16, *Opera,* cols. 457–484. The prefatory epistle to the publisher, Johannes Grieninger, is the same as for *CXXXIX. artickel* except for very minor typographical differences and for the change in date at the end. Before quoting Erasmus' praise of Fisher, Cochlaeus says: "Dann diser Bischoff ist nit allein hochgelert / sunder auch eins heiligen lebens / wie das mengklich weisst [in Engelland]" (sig. A2).

56. *Was die Christelichen Alten / von der beycht haben gehalten. Getzogen aus dem Erwirdigen vnd Hochgelerten Herrn Joan Bischoff zu Roffen yn Engelland* (Dresden, 1525). This partial translation of Article 8 ("Assert. Luth. confut.," *Opera,* cols. 418–424) is preceded by thumbnail biographical notices of the Fathers and followed by a concluding section entitled "In Summa" (sig. D1^{v}–3^{v}).

57. "At illud fere fit in omnibus eius articulis per Leonem decimum condemnatis: quod & ei perspicuum fore non dubitamus, qui nostram super eisdem confutationem aliquando sit lecturus" ("Def. reg. assert." 2.10, *Opera,* col. 119).

58. "Sed et tam feliciter successit iudicium illud tuum, quod super assertionis Lutheranae confutatione per nos olim edita ferebas, ut deinceps te censore nihil non audebimus pro veritate quantumvis arduum aggredi. Nam audio lectoribus ita placuisse libellum ipsum, ut, licet quinquies iam sit excusus, adhuc tamen a multis adeo desideretur, ut Franciscus [Birckman] bibliopola denuo paret excudere." — *Sacri sacerdotii defensio contra Lutherum,* ed. H. K. Schmeink (Münster: Aschendorff, 1925), pp. 4–5. This letter from Fisher to Tunstal is not reprinted in *Opera* (1597).

59. "Sed hac de re satis copiose loquuti sumus alibi, nimirum vbi confutamus Lutheranos articulos nona veritate" ("Sacerd. def." 3.21, *Opera,* col. 1283). The reference is to "Assert. Luth. confut." prooem., veritas 9, *ibid.,* cols. 293–294.

60. See A. B. Wentz, ed., Introd., *Luther's Works,* Volume 36: *Word and Sacrament II* (Philadelphia: Muhlenberg Press, 1959), pp. ix–xii, 129–132.

61. See Doernberg, *Henry VIII and Luther,* pp. 26–35. Henry was undoubtedly the author of the *Assertion* — with aid naturally. The aid might have come from Wolsey, Pace, Fisher, or More. More, for example, was "after it was finished, by his graces apointment and consent of the makers of the same, only a sorter out and placer of the principall matters therin contayned"; he vainly urged Henry to tone down his treatment of papal authority (W. Roper, *The Lyfe of Sir Thomas Moore,* ed. E. V. Hitchcock [London: Early English Text Society, 1935], pp. 67–68). Of recent years, the *Assertio* has been considerably upgraded as a theological work, e.g., by John M. Headley: "Henry's formulation marked a milestone not only in that it pointed toward the final Tridentine definition but also because *traditio* now came to replace *auctoritas*" (*Luther's View of Church History* [New Haven: Yale University Press, 1963], p. 81, with reference to J. N. Bakhuizen van den Brink, "Traditio in de Reformatie en het Katholicisme in de zestiende eeuw," *Mededelingen der Koninklijke Nederlandse Akademie van Wetenschappen,* XV [1952], 28, 47–49).

62. Doernberg, *Henry VIII and Luther,* p. 35.

63. "Def. reg. assert.," *Opera,* p. 101.

64. *Sacerd. def.,* ed. Schmeink, p. 4.

65. "Sacerd. def." 3.2, 3.23, 3.40 (*Opera,* cols. 1270, 1285, 1297, tr. Hallett, pp. 78, 112, 138); "Def. reg. assert." 6.1–13 (*ibid.,* cols. 191–205).

66. "Et sane priscorum Hebraeorum complures (quemadmodum in libello quem pro sacerdotio stabiliendo contra Lutherum edidimus, apertum est) affirmant futurum Messiae temporibus, vt iuxta ritum sacerdotij Melchisedech in pane & vino sacrificetur."— "Def. reg. assert." 6.13, *Opera,* col. 204 (cf. also the end of Chapter 6, *ibid.,* col. 205); "Sacerd. def." 2.45–46, *ibid.,* cols. 1266–67 (tr. Hallett, pp. 70–72).

67. For the reception and fate, and for an English translation, of Luther's letter of September 1, 1525, see Doernberg, *Henry VIII and Luther,* pp. 49–59.

68. "At Lutherus cuncta eorum [Fischeri et Chlichtouei] scripta dissimulans, neutri eorum ullo unquam uerbo respondit, eo quod solidior sit eorum doctrina, quam ut sophisticis Lutheri fucis labefactari queat: & eorum uita longe probatior bonisque omnibus notior & commendatior, quam ut ullis illius conuitijs aut calumnijs denigrari aut suggillari possit sine lectoris offensa."—*Commentaria Ioannis Cochlaei, de actis & scriptis Martini Lutheri. . .* (Apud S. Victorem prope Moguntiam, 1549), p. 119.

69. *A sermon had at Paulis . . . vpon quinquagesom sonday / concernynge certayne heretickes / whiche than were abiured for holdynge the heresies of Martyn Luther that famous hereticke / and for the kepyng and reteynyng of his bokes . . .* (London: Thomas Berthelet, [1526?]). It was reprinted twice (1526? 1527?). Ignorant of its existence, Mayor did not include it in the first edition of the *English Works* (1876), but it was reprinted in the edition of 1935.

70. John Longland, Bishop of Lincoln, to [Wolsey], January 5, 1525–6, in H. Ellis, ed., *Original Letters, Illustrative of English History* (London, 1824), I, 181–182; cf. *LP,* IV, no. 995, p. 434.

71. "The cause of my condemnation," art. 1, *Supplication,* in *The Whole workes of W. Tyndall, Iohn Frith, and Doct. Barnes* (London, 1573), pp. 205–206. The colophon after Barnes's works gives the date 1572. Fisher also offered the following objection: "The byshop of Winchester suffered the stues, Ergo the stues bee lawfull" (*ibid.*). See W. A. Clebsch, *England's Earliest Protestants, 1520–1535* (New Haven: Yale University Press, 1964), pp. 44–49, for Barnes's "two quite different accounts of the sermon and trial in the 1531 and 1534 editions of his *Supplication,*" of which the "later account, self-justifying, alleging harsh and unfair treatment, found its way into the 1572 edition of Barnes' works." The phrase "And not the moste parte of the vniuersity" occurs in the 1534 edition (sig. F1^{v}) but not in the 1531 edition (fol. 23^{v}) of Barnes's *Supplicatyon.* For his career and theology, see Clebsch, pp. 42–77. See also Cooper, *Annals,* I, 311–323, for Barnes's sermon, the articles against him, and his own account of the proceedings. A. G. Dickens writes: "If modern admirers of early English Protestantism desired

to establish a national shrine, they could select none better than the little Cambridge church of St. Edward, King and Martyr. It still contains the small pulpit, made about 1510, from which Barnes, Bilney, and Latimer preached" (*The English Reformation* [New York: Schocken Books, 1964], p. 68).

72. "The whole disputation betweene the Byshops and Doctour Barnes," *Workes,* ed. 1572, p. 223a.

73. Tyndale, *Treatises,* ed. Walter, Biog. Notice, p. xxxi; C. G. Butterworth and A. G. Chester, *George Joye* (Philadelphia: University of Pennsylvania Press, 1962), p. 232; and A. G. Chester, "Robert Barnes and the Burning of the Books," *Huntington Library Quarterly,* XIV (1951), 211. For the confusion on this point, see n. 2 above. Butterworth and Chester declare that copies of Tyndale's translation "had reached England by March of 1526," with "a great ceremonial burning" taking place probably on October 28, 1526 (*Joye,* pp. 147–148). Chester in his article concludes: "No copies of Tyndale's New Testament had been taken. . . the number of other books compounded was small" (*Huntington Library Quarterly, XIV,* 221).

74. *Heretickes,* sig. A4. From this statement D. B. Knox infers: "There is a hint in the preface . . . that the congregation sympathized more with the culprits than with the preacher" (*The Doctrine of Faith in the Reign of Henry VIII* [London: James Clarke, 1961], p. 114). Just as likely an explanation is the vastness of the cathedral, the multitude of people, and the spectacular nature of the affair.

75. "The Regulation of the Book Trade before the Proclamation of 1538," *Transactions of the Bibliographical Society,* XV (1917–19), 166–167. Cf. H. S. Bennett, *English Books and Readers, 1475–1557* (Cambridge, [Eng.], 1952), p. 33. Margaret Roper's translation of Erasmus' *Paternoster* was also involved. One of two manuscript copies of Tyndale's translation of Erasmus' *Enchiridion,* it is interesting to note, was seized by Fisher from a friar of Greenwich so that Tyndale's friend and benefactor, Humphrey Monmouth, had to write: "I think my lord of Rochester hath it" (Mozley, *Tyndale,* p. 49).

76. See the lengthy quotation from Luther's letter, September 1, 1531, together with the attendant circumstances, in Doernberg, *Henry VIII and Luther,* pp. 82–93.

77. See Reynolds, *Fisher,* pp. 61–65, 76, 119–124.

78. E. G. Rupp, *Studies in the Making of the English Protestant Tradition,* 2nd ed. (Cambridge [Eng.] University Press, 1949), pp. 22–31.

79. On Luther's doctrinal development in regard to the Lord's Supper, see J. Pelikan, *Luther the Expositor* (Saint Louis: Concordia Publishing House, 1959), Part II, pp. 135–254. Oecolampadius entitled his book: *De genuina Verborum Domini, Hoc est corpus meum, iuxta uetustissimos authores, expositione liber.* It was published "c. 15 Sept." (Erasmus, *Ep.,* VI, 177n.). The copy used for this study is that in the British Museum (4324.b.3), which seems to be a copy of the edition catalogued as No. 113b in E. Staehelin, *Oekolampad-Bibliographie,* 2nd ed. (Nieuwkoop: B. de Graaf, 1963),

p. 55. Oecolampadius' work was printed in Strasbourg according to Herminjard, ed., *Correspondance,* I, 358, n. 5, 370, n. 8.

80. *De veritate corporis & sanguinis Christi in eucharistia . . . aduersus Iohannem Oecolampadium* (Cologne, February 1527). In *Opera* (1597), the printer speaks as though the publisher, Francis Birckman, had received the manuscript from the hand of the author himself: "Quos quidem libros, olim Franciscus Birckman piae memoriae bibliopola integerrimus, de authoris ipsius in Anglia manu excudi curauit" (p. 752). The printer was Peter Quentell. Of Fisher's book there were only three editions, all in 1527. But it was widely diffused. "Cranmer . . . had in his library the Eucharistic treatises of St John Fisher," writes Francis Clarke, *Eucharistic Sacrifice and the Reformation* (London: Darton, Longman & Todd, [1960]), p. 138.

81. "Interpretatio Lutheri de verbis coenae dominicae, quam sit absurda, satis liquet, opinor, ex apologia, qua nos pro Rege . . . respondimus, praesertim in ea parte, qua molitur panem demonstrari, quando Christus dicit: Hoc est corpus meum" ("Ver. corp." 1.prooem., *Opera,* col. 751, referring to "Def. reg. assert." 4.10, *ibid.,* cols. 165–166). "Nobis enim auditu nihilo minus absurdum est, quum dicatur, hic panis est hoc corpus, quam vbi quis dixerit, hoc ferrum est hic ignis. . . Quam rem nos fusius explicuimus in eo libello quem pro Rege illustriss. scripsimus aduersus Lutherum" ("Ver. corp." 2.13, *ibid.,* col. 865, referring to "Def. reg. assert." 4.6, *ibid.,* col. 162). Fisher makes other references: in "Ver. corp." 2.14 (col. 867) to "Def. reg. assert." 4.3 (cols. 159–160); and in "Ver. corp." 5.prooem. probat. 3 (p. 1129) to "Def. reg. assert." cap. 4 (cols. 156–179). There is also a marginal notation (*Vide in defen.*) in "Ver. corp." 4.14 (col. 867 *ad med.*), but the closest similar passage in "Def. reg. assert." 6.2 (cols. 192–193) does not correspond exactly.

82. *Geschichte des Konzils von Trient,* 2nd ed. (Freiburg: Herder, 1951–57), I, 323.

83. *Fisher,* p. 123.

84. "Considerans ipse mecum, quot huius pestilentissimi libelli per totam Europam exemplaria dispergantur, vt iam paucissimi sint, qui non legerint, vel saltem eundem audierint" ("Ver. corp." 4.prooem., *Opera,* p. 989).

85. "Ver. corp." ep. ded., *Opera,* p. 747.

86. ". . . tu, qui dudum vir integerrimus cunctis videbare, magna quoque eruditione & vitae grauitate praeditus, atque adeo ad absolutam euectus probitatem, vt relictis omnibus Christum sequi decreueris, iam ita, cum vxore Loth retrospiceres. . ." ("Ver. corp." 1.15, *Opera,* col. 800). Later, Fisher refers not only to Oecolampadius' monastic past (as a Bridgettine, 1520–1522) but to his published sermon on the Eucharist, full of devotion and faith (*ibid.* 5.39, col. 1229).

87. "Nam sic a prima notitia dominatio tua me complexa fuerat, vt aura tui fauoris non solum ad bonarum studia literarum, verum etiam ad vitae probitatem ardentius amplectandum, vehementer accendebar. Adde, quod Regi Henrico septimo . . . meam paruitatem commendasti, vt sola ex estimatione, quam (te toties inculcante) de me concepit, & mero motu . . . citra

quoduis aliud obsequium, citra cuiusquam preces, . . . episcopatum Roffensem . . . vltro donauerit" ("Ver. corp.," *Opera,* p. 746).

88. "Sed illud reputo, quid sentiat de vobis Caesar, Pontifex, Ferdinandus, Rex Angliae, Roffensis Episcopus, Card. Eboraceñ., aliique complures, quorum autoritatem contemnere mihi tutum non est, gratiam inutile . . . Hi . . . quid dicturi sunt quum in tua praefatione legerint 'magnus Erasmus noster'?" (Erasmus, *Ep.,* VI, 4–5). Among the *alii complures* would be his many devoted English Catholic friends (including Warham, Tunstal, Mountjoy, and More), the list of whom was suppressed in the first printed edition of Nicholas Harpsfield's *Historia ecclesiastica Anglicana:* see *The life and death of Sr Thomas Moore* . . . eds. E. V. Hitchcock and R. W. Chambers (London: Early English Text Society, 1932), Introd., pp. cxciii–cxciv, cxcix-cc.

89. "De Eucharistia coeperam nonnihil . . . Librum Oecolampadii nondum vacauit legere" (*Ep.,* VI, 177).

90. ". . . perlegi librum Ioannis Oecolampadii . . . mea sententia doctum, disertum et elaboratum; adderem etiam pium, si quid pium esse posset quod pugnat cum sententia consensuque Ecclesiae: a qua dissentire periculosum esse iudico" (*Ep.,* VI, 206).

91. *Ibid.,* VI, 206–212.

92. *Ibid.,* VI, 337–342, 443. Erasmus sent a copy to the theological faculty at Paris, June 23, 1526 (*ibid.,* VI, 364). In a later letter to the Sorbonne, November 12, 1527, he calls the *Detectio* "my book on the Eucharist" (*meus de Eucharistia libellus* [*ibid.,* VII, 235]).

93. "Orsus eram de Eucharistia scribere aduersus Oecolampadii sententiam ante annum, et initium adhuc apud me est. . . Praeterea audiebam Roffensem et Parrisinos ad hanc prouinciam accinctos" (*ibid.,* VII, 217).

94. "Et tamen ab Ecclesiae consensu non possum discedere, nec vnquam discessi. Tu sic dissentis ab Oecolampadio, vt cum Luthero sentire malis quam cum Ecclesia" (*ibid.,* VI, 352). See also Spitz, *German Humanists,* pp. 173, 190–192, 332–333.

95. *Funff Vorredde des Hochwirdigen vatters vnd herren / H. Johan / Bischoffs von Roffa in Engellandt / vff V. buecher wider Jo. Ecolampadium / von warem leyb vnd blut Christi im heyligsten Sacrament des Altars* (Cologne, 1528).

96. "Wie wol aber vnder allen hochgelerten / so ye wider Luthern vnd seine sect geschrieben haben / keiner mer vnd kunstreycher geschrieben hatt dan der fromme bischoff von Roffa / der neben grosser arbeyt des predigens vnd seelsorgens / durch all sein Bisthum auss / sich vnsert halben so trewlich mit so vil schreyben bemueseligt hat. So hat doch bis her weder der Luther noch eincher auss seiner vnd seiner Schwermer sect / dem selbigen vff das wenigste blat geantwort. Welchs warlich ein anzeygen ist / das sie weder mit scheyn noch mit grundt wissen ym fueglich zů antworten . . ." (*Vorredde,* Epistell, sig. a2).

97. For example, Cochlaeus (*Vorredde,* sig. c1^v^, translating *Opera,* p. 751) sends the reader to Bk. IV, Chap. 27, which, of course, is not given in his version. At the end of the Preface to Bk. II, it is time to listen to the ad-

versaries — who do not speak because Cochlaeus has not given the body of the book in German (*Vorredde,* sig. e3, translating *Opera,* p. 844); but he omits similar statements at the conclusion of Bks. I, III, IV, V (*Vorredde,* sigg. c2, l2, p4, t6; compare *Opera,* pp. 752, 928, 998, 1134). For no conceivable reason except oversight, he fails to translate occasionally, e.g., "nihilque repugnare docetur, vt sit simul & res & figura" (*Opera,* p. 839; cf. *Vorredde,* sig. c2ᵛ); "de orthodoxis loquor" (*Opera,* p. 997; cf. *Vorredde,* sig. p1ᵛ); etc. Cochlaeus repeats each of Fisher's fourteen "Corroborations" (*Opera,* p. 917; *Vorredde,* sig. e3ᵛ) as a heading before the individual treatment (*Vorredde,* sigg. e4–k4; not in *Opera*) — unlike the original Latin. He adds the German equivalents of Greek and Latin terms, e.g., "vff kriechisch Synaxis / zů latin Communio / *vff teutsch ein gemainschafft*" (sig. d1ᵛ); "Vom *Judische himmelbrot / das man nennet* Manna" (sig. e1); "Kriechisch ἀντίτυπον / das ist Exemplar zů Lateyn / *Ebenbild zů Teutsch*" (sig. e2); etc. (*italics added*). A single Latin word is translated by two German words, e.g., "vti perspicuum est" by "wie das sichtbarlich vnd augenscheinlich ist" (*Opera,* p. 751; *Vorredde,* sig. c1). "Alueredus Abbas" (*Opera,* p. 990) appears as "Aluaredus ein abt" (*Vorredde,* sig. m1ᵛ). Cochlaeus "corrects" Fisher's "Psalmo 110" (*Opera,* p. 991) to "Cix. Psalm" (*Vorredde,* sig. m3).

98. Ortroy, *Fisher,* X, 268.

99. Erasmus, *Ep.,* VIII, 112: "quin et ipsius Ioannis episcopi Roffensis, in quo viro nihil desideres, libros prorsus negligi."

100. "The title 'doctor' summarizes more adequately than any other Luther's own sense of vocation and mission" (Pelikan, *Luther the Expositor,* p. 46; see pp. 45–47). So, too, Headley: "At most he claimed to be an evangelist but preferred to emphasize his position as a doctor of theology" (*Luther's Church History,* p. 231, referring to Hans Frhr. von Campenhausen, "Reformatorisches Selbstbewusstsein und reformatorisches Geschichtsbewusstsein bei Luther 1517–1522," *Archiv für Reformationsgeschichte,* XXXVII [1940], 140; cf. *WA* 30/3:386).

101. ". . . multi insurgunt haereses, et quasi nullus epíscopus hactenus inventus est qui eis obviam eat. Solus unus episcopus est modo in Ecclesia, puta Roffensis, vir magnae doctrinae, qui scribat contra lutheranos." — In 2.2 de fide, q. 2, a. 8, *Comentarios a la secunda secundae de Santo Tomás,* ed. Vicente Beltrán de Heredia (Salamanca, 1932–35), I, 76.

CHAPTER II: WORKS AND DAYS OF THE FAITHFUL OPPOSITION

1. See N. Pocock, *Records of the Reformation: The Divorce 1527–1533* (Oxford, 1870), I, 9–10. The full answer in translation is given in Reynolds, *Fisher,* pp. 131–132. Formal proceedings had been begun in great secrecy only in May 1527 (Brewer, *Henry VIII,* II, 187–188). The reason for Wolsey's consultation of Fisher is given with much eloquence and some exaggeration

by Lord Acton: "No English divine enjoyed so high a reputation as John Fisher, the Bishop of Rochester. Of all the works written against Luther in the beginnings of the Reformation, his were the most important; and he was eminent not only in controversy, but as a promoter of that new learning . . . Fisher's support would have been worth having . . . he would have carried with him the whole weight of the school of Erasmus, which constituted the best portion of the English Church . . . Fisher appears to have made answer without suspecting that he was taking the first step on a road ending at the scaffold" (unsigned review of *Letters and Papers,* vol. IV, in *Quarterly Review,* CXLIII [1877], 14–15).

2. See the account of the divorce from its beginnings to the advocation of the cause to Rome in Brewer, *Henry VIII,* II, 158–377. Various documents are to be found in H. Laemmer, ed., *Monumenta Vaticana* (Freiburg, 1861), nos. 22–29, 46, 54, pp. 25–34, 66–67, 75.

3. The details are given in Wolsey's letter to Henry VIII, July 5, 1527 (*State Papers,* I, 196–201), the upshot of the conference being that Fisher "noted the matier to be more and more doubteful" and "noted grete difficulte in it" (*ibid.,* 201). Cf. Brewer, *Henry VIII,* II, 193–197, and Reynolds, *Fisher,* pp. 133–136.

4. P.R.O.S.P.1/42, fol. 165: "Errare possum, et hunc errorem si quis ostenderit ei libentissime cedam, veritatem semper audire paratus" — but he has already expended more work on this matter than ever on any other.

5. Ortroy, *Fisher,* X, 296–299. In his marginal annotations to Gardiner's reply for Henry VIII to Fisher's speech on June 28, 1529, Fisher wrote "nearly a year ago" opposite the statement that the king "did unfold to this Rochester, and this already some months ago," reasons for scruples on his marriage (S. Gardiner, *Obedience in Church and State: Three Political Tracts,* ed. P. Janelle [Cambridge (Eng.) University Press, 1930], pp. 2–3; Brewer, *Henry VIII,* II, 348). Probably as the result of his speech on June 28, Fisher, together with the Archbishop of Canterbury and the Bishops of London, Carlisle, Ely, St. Asaph, Lincoln, and Bath, had to testify on July 1, 1529, that Henry had consulted them and others about his marriage on account of a scrupulous conscience (*concepto in Conscientia Scrupulo*). See Rymer, *Foedera,* XIV (1712), 301.

6. *LP,* IV, p. 2108, cited in Brewer, *Henry VIII,* II, 302. For an interpretation of Fisher's words, see Reynolds, *Fisher,* pp. 143–144. This interview, like that with Wolsey earlier, seems to indicate a special diplomatic prudence in Fisher. On his return journey in 1528, Bishop Stafileo, Dean of the Rota, had a discussion with Fisher and "thought at least he had so completely baffled Fisher, that he sent Cardinal Wolsey news of it" (J. Strype, *Ecclesiastical Memorials* [Oxford, 1822], I, pt. 1, p. 309). Upon his arrival in Rome, Stafileo at a solemn sitting "made a long oration . . . which lasted two hours" in favor of the king's cause (*ibid.,* I, pt. 1, pp. 152–153, and I, pt. 2, no. 24, pp. 95–96, 105).

7. "Book," i.e., *liber* or *libellus,* is taken to refer to any tract, treatise,

document, or brief, whether printed or, as most frequently here, merely written, i.e., in manuscript. For eyewitness accounts, see Brewer, *Henry VIII*, II, 345–347; Bridgett, *Fisher*, pp. 169–172; and Reynolds, *Fisher*, pp. 152–154. Cf. *LP*, IV, nos. 5732, 5734, 5741, pp. 2538–39, 2543. "Wolsey's answer (spoken June 28th) to the speech of the proctor of queen Catharine . . . in his own hand" is reprinted in Pocock, *Records*, I, 228. It is not surprising to learn that among the articles willed to St. John's College under date of November 27, 1525, is "an ymage of Saynt John Baptiste" (R. F. Scott, "Notes from the College Records," *Eagle*, XXXV [1913–14], 26). In the debate in the early seventeenth century over the "martyrdom" of Fisher and More, when James I maintained that the cause was their opposition to the divorce more than to the supremacy, it was inevitable that John the Baptist should enter into the debate. Suarez, for example, answers: "Since the second marriage of King Henry was so detestable, even if no other cause for dying had entered in beside their refusal to approve it, that cause would doubtlessly be sufficient for martyrdom . . . On this head their martyrdom is not dimmed but made more illustrious" (*Defensio fidei catholicae . . . cum responsione ad apologiam pro iuramento fidelitatis, & praefationem monitoriam . . . IACOBI Angliae regis* [Coimbra, 1613], p. 778). Suarez cites testimonials to their true martyrdom (*ibid.*, p. 767).

8. The Latin text and the English translation of "Gardiner's Address to the Legates" are given in Gardiner, *Obedience*, ed. Janelle, pp. 1–9. See also P. Janelle, *L'Angleterre catholique à la veille du schisme* (Paris: Beauchesne, 1935), pp. 115–117. Janelle gives a lengthy résumé and analysis of Gardiner's answer to Camb. Univ. Lib. MS. 1315 (*ibid.*, pp. 129–229, based on P.R.O.S.P.1/54, foll. 129–229). The Westminster Archives contain a reply to the defense of the validity of the papal dispensation by Fisher's associate, Nicholas West, Bishop of Ely (I, no. 4, pp. 37–140).

9. Comments are reproduced in Brewer, *Henry VIII*, II, 348–351; Bridgett, *Fisher*, pp. 172–175; and Reynolds, *Fisher*, pp. 157–160. Cf. *LP*, IV, no. 5729, pp. 2537–38.

10. Brewer, *Henry VIII*, II, 352.

11. Brewer, *Henry VIII*, II, 354; Reynolds, *Fisher*, p. 161n. Janelle refers to July 30 for the day of adjournment (*Angleterre catholique*, p. 130, n. 1). Fisher's attitude toward Campeggio is revealed accidentally in the postscript of a letter of Cochlaeus to Pirckheimer, March 27, 1530. Pirckheimer has been misinformed about Campeggio's conduct in England: "Would that I had the leisure of writing you the most honorable testimonials to his prudence and integrity which with his own hand that most upright man the Bishop of Rochester, as well as another theologian of the highest probity and erudition, has written me through a certain nobleman whom my prince had sent to England" (J. Heumann von Teutschbrunn, *Documenta literaria varii argumenti* [Altdorf, 1758], no. 26, p. 78). In a letter of the previous November 30, Cochlaeus tells Pirckheimer of his pleasure at having had "the most learned Bishops of London, Ely, Rochester, etc." on the queen's

side and of having heard that all is now well with Henry, Catherine, and Wolsey (*ibid.*, no. 25, p. 68)!

12. *LP,* VI, no. 1109, p. 499, also cited in Bridgett, *Fisher,* p. 224, and Reynolds, *Fisher,* pp. 188, 288.

13. Letter of Wakefield to Fisher, *Kotser codicis R. Wakfeldi* (London, n.d.), sig. P1ᵛ: "Audiui te alterum super Regis & Reginae coniugio codicem composuisse, quem si placet, rogo mihi mittere digneris . . ."

14. "R. me non certum esse de numero, sed ut nunc occurrit memorie septem aut octo arbitror me scripsisse. Nam quum esset negocium ipsum arduum tam propter excellentiam personarum quas concernebat, quam propter districtam injunctionem a Majestate Regia michi factam tantum opere et diligentie ob exquirendam ejus veritatem impendi, ne forte me ipsum et alios fallerem, quantum nulli alteri rei per universam vitam impenderim ante" (Lewis, *Fisher,* Coll. No. 40, II, 404, tr. Reynolds, *Fisher,* p. 230). Cf. *LP,* VIII, no. 859, p. 336. If these are the same books delivered by Thomas Bedyll, Clerk of the Council, to Archbishop Cranmer to help him answer Cochlaeus' book on the divorce (published February 1535), then the date of the interrogatory would be 1535, not 1534 (cf. Reynolds, *Fisher,* p. 228, n. 2).

15. Gardiner, *Obedience,* ed. Janelle, pp. xviii–xix; cf. *LP,* IV, no. 5729, pp. 2537–38, and no. 5768, pp. 2570–71.

16. "Joh: Roffens: Licitum fuisse matrimonium Hen: 8: cum Catharina relicta fratris suj Arthurj," MS. 1315, foll. 152–197. Fisher's work has also an independent pagination which will be used for citations in this present study. Cf. *LP,* IV, no. 5728, p. 2537.

17. "Caeterum an prohibitio ipsa Levitica moralis habenda sit, necne; pariter et an de jure naturae fuerit existimanda; alibi satis exacte disquisivimus" ("Licitum fuisse matrimonium," p. 19).

18. *LP,* IV, no. 5768, p. 2570. This would seem to be the work described in *LP,* IV, no. 5730, p. 2538: "Eruditi cujusdam responsio pro Regis defensione ad libellum Roffensis e[piscopi]," consisting of (1) "A letter apparently addressed to Fisher on his sending the writer a summary of his treatise" (Otho C.x.184); (2) "Responsio Roffensis" (*ibid.*, foll. 187b–198); and (3) "The author's rejoinder, in which he refers to R. Wakfeld as his preceptor in Hebrew."

19. J. Lamb, *A Collection of Letters, Statutes, and Other Documents, from the MS. Library of Corp. Christ., Illustrative of the History of the University of Cambridge, during the Period of the Reformation* (London, 1838), pp. 14–15. Cf. Cooper, *Annals,* I, 334–335. For documents on the opinion of the University of Cambridge on the divorce, see Lamb, *Collection,* pp. 19–25. For Latimer's career, see M. L. Loane, *Masters of the English Reformation* (London: Church Book Room Press, 1954), pp. 87–133. Of Latimer's even more famous Sermon of the Plough, Dickens writes: "Medieval sermons, even those of John Fisher in the previous generation, cannot show anything to match this fusion of flexible language with deep feeling, both religious and humane" (*Reformation,* p. 224).

20. *LP,* IV, no. 6199, p. 2780. A treatise by the Prior of Merton, dated April 18, 1530, and bearing the heading, "An liceat cuiquam ducere uxorem fratris sui vita defuncti absque liberis," makes a negative answer (Lansdowne MS. 94, printed in Strype, *Eccles. Mem.,* I, pt. 2, no. 38, pp. 149–154, and in Pocock, *Records,* I, no. 170, pp. 511–516). In the same year (July 13, 1530), Fisher did not sign the parliamentary petition for a speedy decision, to which the pope replied on September 27 (Pocock, *Records,* I, nos. 141–142, pp. 429–437).

21. "Ea de re [the controversy over Henry and Catherine's marriage] librum hunc ab Io. Episcopo Roffensi uiro egregie erudito, inque diuinis studijs exercitatissimo compositum, nactus modo reuerendissimus in Christo pater & patronus meus singularis ALFONSVS Fonseca Archiepiscopus Toletanus mihi formis cudendum tradidit: significans meam hic industriam, non tantum illi acceptam fore, sed & studiosis simul doctisque omnibus gratissimam futuram." — "Typographus Complutensis ad Lectorem," *De causa matrimonii serenissimi regis Angliae liber* (Alcalá, 1530), sig. A1v. Fonseca's father had been in Catherine of Aragon's company when she came to England in 1501 (Erasmus, *Ep.,* VI, 410, introd., citing *LP,* III, no. 3532, pp. 1468–69). J. K. McConica, who lists Fisher ("venerable, innocent, learned, and ascetic") with Cranmer, Tyndale, and Pole as four humanists intimately involved in the divorce, comments that *Causa* "appeared, appropriately, at Alcalá, the scholarly home of Imperial Erasmianism" (*English Humanists and Reformation Politics under Henry VIII and Edward VI* [Oxford: Clarendon Press, 1965], p. 125).

22. *LP,* IV, no. 6738, p. 3035.

23. *Ibid.,* no. 6757, p. 3054.

24. "They [Fisher's works] all show his great wisdom, diligence, and zeal for truth. I am surprised that the light he has thrown on the case has not removed the blindness of the contrary party, who have so badly deceived the King of England" (*LP,* V, no. 207, p. 97, April 23, 1531).

25. *Grauissimae, atque exactissimae illustrissimarum totius Italiae, et Galliae Academiarum censurae, efficacissimis etiam quorundam doctissimorum uirorum argumentationibus explicatae, de ueritate illius propositionis, Videlicet quod ducere relictam fratris mortui sine liberis ita sit de iure diuino et naturali prohibitum: ut nullus Pontifex super huiusmodi matrimonijs contractis, siue contrahendis dispensare possit.* The opinions of the universities take up the preliminary signatures a1–b4v, with the commentary beginning at sig. A1 and continuing to the colophon on sig. Q4v. The *Censurae* is presumed to have been edited and written by Edward Fox (Clebsch, *Earliest Protestants,* p. 275). In a letter to Henry VIII dated January 13, 1531, Vives refers to the polling of the universities: "Sciscitaris Academiarum sententiam . . . Quid respondeant eruditi nescio, quid responderi oporteat scio." He sends Henry, just in case he has not seen it, a copy of the book which embodies his opinion and which during his sojourn in England he had composed at the request of Wolsey. See *Epistolarum . . . farrago* (Antwerp, 1556), p. 4.

26. *LP,* V, no. 342, pp. 161–162. Chapuys tried hard to get Agrippa to

write against the Italian and French universities. Under date of July 21, 1531, Agrippa revealed his pleasure at Fisher's book: "Would that this man were allowed to speak out freely, to hold back nothing from fear." Chapuys had sent him the book on June 26, 1531. On November 25, he again urged Agrippa to espouse Catherine's cause and mentions the reaction at the Sorbonne in her favor. See H. C. Agrippa ab Nettesheim, *Opera* (Lyon [i.e., Strasbourg?], 1630?), II, 973–975, 996–997; cf. II, 1018.

27. *LP,* V, no. 378, p. 189. Fisher "has shown the true way which ought to be taken, and omits little that could be added" (*ibid.*).

28. *LP,* V, no. 492, p. 232.

29. *LP,* V, no. 460, p. 218. The following number in *LP* (no. 461, p. 219) ascribes to Fisher: "His book on the Divorce, replying to the arguments of those who sought to prove the invalidity of the King's marriage. *Lat., pp.* 198"; but the book seems to argue against the adversaries of the divorce, i.e., to quote Fisher only to disprove him.

30. *LP,* V, no. 546, p. 250.

31. *LP,* V, no. 553, p. 252. "This opinion is distinguished by its learning" (*ibid.*).

32. *LP,* V, no. 594, p. 273.

33. *The determinations of the moste famous and mooste excellent vniuersities of Italy and Fraunce, that it is so vnlefull for a man to marie his brothers wyfe / that the pope hath no power to dispence therwith.* The translation is "possibly by Cranmer" (Clebsch, *Earliest Protestants,* p. 275).

34. *LP,* V, no. 546, p. 250.

35. Fisher's reply is headed: "Johannis episcopi Roffensis responsum ad libellum impressum Londini 1530." It is further inscribed: "Matrimonij cuiusdam quod olim obtenta pontificis dispensatione cum illiberis fratris vxore contractum fuit & nunc tandem quarundam academiarum censuris impetitum patrocinantibus item quibusdam doctissimis & illarum sententiam varijs argumentationibus explicare nitentibus brevis apologia." Cf. *LP,* VI, no. 471, pp. 212–213. This manuscript is British Museum MS. Arundel 151, foll. 202–339ᵛ. It is the document mentioned in extant correspondence variously as "reply, answer" (*responsum*) or "apology" (*apologia*). The short title "Responsum" will be used here for references to this work.

36. Henceforth it may be necessary to make reference to three, sometimes four, interrelated works: (1) *Censurae* (1530), (2) Fisher's "Responsum" (1531), (3) *Determinations* (1531), and (4) the lengthy précis of Fisher's "Responsum," made in Book I of *A Treatise on the Pretended Divorce between Henry VIII and Catharine of Aragon,* by Nicholas Harpsfield, ed. N. Pocock (London, 1878). Thus, in "Responsum" Fisher says: "In principio sexti capitis de duobus axiomatibus hi doctissimi loquuntur: sed quaenam sunt illa, nondum satis explicarunt. Finitiones quasdam audiuimus .c. quinto. verumtamen quaenam ex illis pro suis axiomatibus deputant, obliti sunt exprimere" (fol. 286). Fisher is referring to the opening of Chapter VI in *Censurae:* "Sed de luce ac fide duorum axiomatum nostrorum haec satis dicta

sunto" (sig. L1). Harpsfield comments: "They tell us then first that they have said enough of the light and troth of their two grounds, but yet they have quite forgotten to tell us what these two were, which defect the English Interpreter goeth about as well as he can to supply" (*Divorce,* p. 89). Harpsfield had studied the English translation: "But of the licht and trouth of our two worthye groundes & principilles / that is / the definicion of the lawe morall, and the lawe iudicial, of the whiche two we wyll make a sylogisme or perfecte reason, we haue spoken sufficientely" (*Determinations,* fol. 105).

37. *Divorce,* pp. 25–120.

38. *Ibid.,* pp. 23-24, 28. One reason for doing so is "partly and chiefly also that our countrymen, which have hitherto seen no part of this book in English and perchance neither in Latin (for that I understand it is not as yet printed), may evidently see that the said bishop and Sir Thomas Moore grounded their refusal of the said oath upon no small and slender foundation. Now when you hear the said bishop speak, suppose that you hear Sir Thomas Moore also, not only for the oneness and conformity of mind that both were in touching this matter, but for that it is likely that Sir Thomas Moore had seen and read the said bishop's answer" (*ibid.*).

39. *Ibid.,* p. 29.

40. Augustine had declared in relation to marriage with one's own sister: "Quod profecto quanto est antiquius compellente necessitate, tanto factum est damnabilius *Religione prohibente.*" Harpsfield finds that the English translator "mistranslateth *when that shame drew them from it,* for *when Religion did forbid it,*" the religion in question being the law of Moses (compare *Censurae,* sig. M1v; *Determinations,* fol. 114v; Fisher, "Responsum," fol. 298; and Harpsfield, *Divorce,* p. 94). So, too, the English translator "shamelessly" renders Augustine's "fraterna conjugia" (marriages between brother and sister) by marriage with "our brothers' wives" (*Censurae,* sig. M1v; *Determinations,* fol. 115; and Harpsfield, *Divorce,* p. 95). In the same way, "the English translator hath for the word *commisceri,* which signifieth *carnally to meddle* corruptly, translated *to be married and to meddle*" (Harpsfield, *Divorce,* p. 65; *Censurae,* sig. E1; *Determinations,* fol. 51; and Fisher, "Responsum," fol. 242v). Harpsfield also wonders why "nemo certe non *uidet*" is translated by "there is no man . . . *but sayeth*" instead of "there is no man *but seeth*" (*Censurae,* sig. M3v; *Determinations,* fol. 118v; Fisher, "Responsum," fol. 305v; and Harpsfield, *Divorce,* p. 101). Since this last slip relates to the argument in only the most remote way, it manifests the care with which Harpsfield examined the documents.

41. Harpsfield does not mention Durandus who appears on a list of authorities cited by Fisher: "Durandus excipit casum solum consanguinitatis, qui est parentum ad filios a Leuitica prohibitione," where "solum consanguinitatis, qui est parentum ad filios" is crossed out ("Responsum," fol. 326v; cf. Harpsfield, *Divorce,* p. 108; *Censurae,* sig. P1v; and *Determinations,* fol. 139v). Harpsfield (*Divorce,* pp. 64–65) understandably leaves out the excla-

mation in Fisher: "Bone Iesu qualem conscientiam habent ij doctissimi . . ." ("Responsum," fol. 242v, in comment on the case of *Isichius* in *Censurae,* sig. E1; cf. *Determinations,* fol. 51).

42. Fisher, "Responsum," foll. 212v–219v; Harpsfield, *Divorce,* pp. 51–53; *Censurae,* sigg. A4–B2v; and *Determinations,* foll. 22–27.

43. *Divorce,* pp. 116–119; cf. Fisher, "Responsum," foll. 338v–339v; *Censurae,* sig. Q4; and *Determinations,* foll. 153–154. Fisher's summary of his refutation of *Censurae,* chaps. 3–4, is found in "Responsum," foll. 268v–269v.

44. "Neque enim solicitus eram de ceteris, sed de postremis duobus a me scriptis qui priorum omnium nervos in se continere videbantur quorum alterum jam habet D. Cantuariensis" (Lewis, *Fisher,* Coll. No. 40, II, 404, tr. Reynolds, *Fisher,* p. 230). Thomas Bedyll, Clerk of the Council, reports the delivery of Fisher's books on the divorce "to my lord of Cauntrebury [Cranmer] to be seen and weyed by him, and such as gyve attendance on hym at this tyme for thaunswer to be made to Cocleus boks and others" (*ibid.,* Coll. No. 32, II, 352). Cochlaeus' *De matrimonio serenissimi Regis Angliae, Henrici Octaui, Congratulatio disputatoria,* was printed in February 1535 at Leipzig. The same letter mentions also a confessor at Sion who had once seen "the copy of his [Fisher's] said letters directed to the King's grace, and the copy of the King's aunswer also" and who had "willingly" delivered up a "boke of his [Fisher's] made in the defense of the King's grace first marriage" (*ibid.,* 353–354). Cranmer's own book in favor of the divorce, in the form of twelve articles, is printed in Pocock, *Records,* I, no. 127, pp. 334–399 (Cotton MS. Vesp. B.v; cf. Brit. Mus. MS. Reg. 10.B.1).

45. "The Busshop of Rochester delyvered his copie to the Spanyards . . . and the Spanyerds, unknowyng to the Busshop, sett in all haste wryters to take an other copie by meane wherof theyr booke is now framed, and intermyngled with Greke and Spanyshe . . ." (*State Papers,* VII, 489–491). The book which comes closest to being "intermyngled with Greke and Spanyshe" and to being printed at this time is *Philalethae Hyperborei in Anticatoptrum suum, quod propediem in lucem dabit . . . Parasceue, Siue aduersus improborum quorundam temeritatem . . . Reginam ab Arthuro . . . cognitam fuisse . . . adstruentium, Susannis extemporaria* (Lunenburgi, per Sebastianum Golsenum, Anno M.D.XXXIII. Mense Iulio). The copy in the British Museum has a note which attributes it to Vives or Cochlaeus. This work contains a Spanish letter from Ferdinand to his ambassador in Rome (sig. C3–5) and has Greek phrases scattered throughout. It names "Hieronymus quidam Praevidellus, homo superbe indoctus" (sig. B5). Praevidellus of Bologna, described as an excellent and ardent defender of the king's cause, is named frequently from April 1529 to January 1534 (*LP,* IV, nos. 5502, 6613, 6619, 6624, 6633, 6639, 6644, 6670, 6734; V, nos. 971, 972; VI, nos. 961, 1164; VII, no. 85). His letter of August 9, 1533, expresses his readiness to justify the marriage with Anne Boleyn and to single out the pope's mistakes (Pocock, *Records,* II, no. 346, p. 508). Documents of the years 1503, 1504, and 1528 are reprinted from *Philalethae Parasceue* by

Pocock (*Records,* II, no. 321, pp. 422–425). *Parasceue* is an answer to *A glasse of the truthe* (London, n.d.), reprinted by Pocock, who dates it as December 1532 (II, no. 320, pp. 385–421). See also "An answer to a dialogue in Englishe called the Glasse of Truth," in Harpsfield, *Divorce,* pp. 169–175, where early September 1532 is suggested as a date (p. 318). The *Glasse,* "produced under the close supervision of the King, if not actually by Henry himself," and appearing in at least two English editions and a French translation, was reported by Croke from Oxford to have converted many and to have effected more for the king's cause than all other books and sermons (McConica, *English Humanists,* pp. 112–113). Cf. F. L. Baumer, *The Early Tudor Theory of Kingship* (New Haven: Yale University Press, 1940), p. 41, n. 14; p. 50, n. 50; pp. 137–138 and n. 47.

46. *Kotser codicis,* sig. P2. It would be gratifying to discover the particular work of Fisher which Wakefield had answered earlier but in printed form. He quotes Fisher directly twice: "Sed & superuacaneum fuerit hoc ipsum docere, non esse prohibitum euangelico iure, quum & hac de re nemo theologus adhuc dubitauit" (sig. F1); and: "Erit igitur nobis haec unica conclusio. Nulla potest ratione solida colligi matrimonium huiuscemodi naturae iure uetitum esse. &c." (sig. G2v). The first clause appears in "Responsio," Cotton MS. Otho C.x, fol. 189. Wakefield levels his attack also against Thomas Abell, who with Edward Powell had written a treatise entitled "De non dissolvendo Henrici regis cum Catherina matrimonio" (Constant, *Reformation,* I, 69, n. 120) and who had published *Invicta veritas* in 1532.

47. On the Franciscan William Peto's allusion to the king's "illegitimate marriage" in a sermon before Henry VIII himself as late as May 18, 1533, see Constant, *Reformation,* I, 132.

48. "The one surviving controversial work of this period written by a cleric, Fisher's unfinished 'That the byshoppys have immediate autority of Christ to make such lawes as they shall thynke expedyent for the weale of men sowles,' was a reasoned and moderate piece designed to appeal to lay sensibilities" (M. Kelly, "The Submission of the Clergy," *Trans. Roy. Hist. Soc.,* ser. 5, XV [1965], 107). The introduction is printed in W. H. Dunham and S. Pargellis, *Complaint and Reform in England 1436–1714* (New York: Oxford University Press, 1938), pp. 125–129. This document is S.P.6/11, pp. 437–446 (foll. 215–219v), catalogued in *LP,* VIII, no. 887 (6), p. 351, with many references to the Old Testament. There is also a fragmentary Latin defense of the liberties of the Church in Brit. Mus. Add. MS. 4274, foll. 212–213v (*ibid.,* no. 887 [7], p. 351). Cf. Baumer, *Tudor Kingship,* pp. 63–64 and nn. 89, 94. Sir George Throkmorton wrote in 1537 that, after consultation about the royal marriage with More who then was Chancellor, "he went shortly after to the bp. of Rochester with whom he had much conversation about the Acts of Appeals, Annates and Supremacy, and the authority given by our Lord to Peter. The last time he was with him the bp. gave him a book of his own device on the subject; which book he delivered

to my lord Privy Seal" (*LP,* XII, no. 952, p. 333). "Throckmorton's younger brother Michael became Pole's devoted secretary" (McConica, *English Humanists,* p. 139, n. 3; cf. p. 150).

49. Philip Hughes, *The Reformation in England,* rev. ed. (London: Burns & Oates, [1963]), I, 240–241.

50. Hall's *Chronicle,* quoted in Ortroy, *Fisher,* X, 341, n. 1.

51. *Ibid.,* X, 148, 337–341; Bayne, *Fisher,* pp. 68–71.

52. Ortroy, *Fisher,* X, 342–344; F. A. Gasquet, *Henry VIII and the English Monasteries* (London, 1888), I, 247.

53. *Fisher,* p. 190. Cf. *Ven. Cal.,* IV, nos. 629, 634; *Milan Cal.,* I, no. 831.

54. Ortroy, *Fisher,* X, 176–177, 351–365, XII, 251–252. Richard Hilliard, the secretary of Bishop Tunstal, asserts that Fisher's suggestion was made to win over the hesitating but his testimony appears groundless (*ibid.,* X, 357–358, XII, 270–278). For the Convocation, see Hughes, *Reformation,* I, 227–236, where it is Tunstal who registers the most meaningful protest at the Convocation of York.

55. *Span. Cal.,* IV, nos. 641, 646.

56. *Ibid.,* no. 888. Strype records a generous gift of £13 6s. 8d. in "Monies given to the King's Grace for new year's gifts, anno xxiiij. sui regni" (*Eccl. Mem.,* I, pt. 1, p. 111).

57. For background and details, see Hughes, *Reformation,* I, 236–246, where Fisher's erstwhile opponent on the divorce, Stephen Gardiner, now Bishop of Winchester, was "the soul of the resistance." See "Copy of the last form of Submission which the King required of the Clergy, May 15, 1532" (Pocock, *Records,* II, 257–258). Note the impartial statement on the significance of the Submission in Powicke and Fryde, eds., *Handbook of British Chronology,* pp. 545–546, in the introduction to "Provincial and National Councils of the Church in England, 602 x 603 to 1536": "The year 1536 has been chosen as the final date of this list, not because it marks the end of formal meetings of the clergy, but because it marks a turning-point in their constitutional history, after which their freedom to assemble, to deliberate, and to legislate is far more narrowly restricted than before. This change was effected by the parliamentary 'Act for the submission of the Clergie to the Kynges Majestie' of 25 Henry VIII, c. 19 (1534), consequent upon the remarkable resolution of the convocation . . . of the 15 May 1532. With that statement of royal authority the Church lost the partial independence which it had possessed before this time: never before had the king claimed the exclusive right to summon assemblies of the clergy, although he had often summoned them, nor had royal ratification of ecclesiastical canons been deemed necessary." References are Felix Makower, *Constitutional History and Constitution of the Church of England* (London, 1895), pp. 51ff., 365–599; and Sir Lewis Dibdin, in the *Report* of the Archbishops' Committee on Church and State (London, 1917), pp. 281ff.

58. Bridgett, *Fisher,* p. 220; Reynolds, *Fisher,* p. 186. The most detailed study is that of Kelly, "Submission of Clergy," *Trans. Roy. Hist. Soc.,* ser. 5, XV, 97–119. Kelly makes the following interpretation: "The mission to

Rochester revealed that the synod was planning to resist the royal demands . . . The reaction of Warham and the clergy to Fisher's counsel and the King's new tack is altogether buried in the terse notice in the *acta* for the 107th session of 13 May: 'concordatum est quod Articuli responsionis valerent.' Three replies are extant which presumably correspond to answers conceived on this day. Although they were loaded with saving clauses, the proposals of the clergy on the 13th were a clear retreat from their earlier position" (*ibid.,* 113–114). He concludes: "The epochal decision in the history of the English Church was enacted by a rump Convocation" (*ibid.,* 117; cf. Dickens, *Reformation,* p. 116). Kelly's final judgment is this: "Government policy was dictated by no master-plan; it was a function of the King's choler and vacillation, a series of royal reprisals and modifications goaded both by clerical reaction and anti-clerical counsel" (*ibid.,* 119).

59. Chapuys to Charles V, *LP,* VI, no. 296, and *Span. Cal.,* IV, no. 1057. On Fisher's clashes with Bishop Stokesley of London, see Lewis, *Fisher,* II, 98.

60. *LP,* VI, 1164, 1249; *Span. Cal.,* IV, 1130, 1133. Fisher's "saintly personal character should not obscure the extreme unwisdom of his treasonable conversations with the Imperial ambassador Chapuys, that devoted friend of Queen Katherine and equally devoted organiser of sedition" (Dickens, *Reformation,* p. 123). For Bridgett's defense, see *Fisher,* pp. 229–233. For Chapuys' intrigues, see K. Pickthorn, *Early Tudor Government, Henry VIII* (Cambridge [Eng.] University Press, 1934), pp. 204–205, 211–212.

61. For the well-known story of the Holy Maid, Elizabeth Barton, see Ortroy, *Fisher,* XII, 97–108; Reynolds, *Fisher,* pp. 192–210; and Chambers, *More,* pp. 294–300. For Fisher's letters, see *LP,* VII, nos. 116, 136, 239, 240; Bridgett, *Fisher,* pp. 248–259; Reynolds, *Fisher,* pp. 198–208. The letters are printed also in an Appendix of Documents in J. Bruce, "Observations on the Circumstances Which Occasioned the Death of Fisher . . . ," *Archaeologia,* XXV (1834), 89–99. "Elizabeth Barton was received throughout the network of Erasmian pietism . . . In denouncing her as a fraud and a traitor the Government not only discredited opponents of great prestige, but acquired evidence which could be put to useful purpose, if need be, at a later date" (McConica, *English Humanists,* pp. 148–149). See "The Sermon against the Holy Maid of Kent and her Adherents, delivered at Paul's Cross, November 23rd, 1533, and at Canterbury, December the 7th," ed. L. E. Whatmore, in *Eng. Hist. Rev.,* LVIII (1943), 463–475. The preacher was John Salcot, alias Capon, who became Bishop of Bangor (1534–39) and Salisbury (1539–57). Fisher is not mentioned by name in "A marueilous woorke of late done at Court of Streete in Kent" (authored by Edward Thwaites and printed by Robert Redman), largely preserved in W. Lambarde, *A Perambulation of Kent* (London, 1576), pp. 148–153.

62. Cranmer, *Miscellaneous Writings and Letters,* ed. J. E. Cox (Cambridge, Eng., 1846), Letter 55, April 17, 1534, pp. 285–286; cf. Reynolds, *Fisher,* pp. 220–222. Cromwell refused the suggestion as impractical. The very same year Cranmer had requested Fisher to appoint his relative, Master Devenyshe, a fellow at St. John's College, Cambridge (Letter 45, *ibid.,* p. 279; *LP,* VII,

no. 188, p. 76). Cranmer had been granted his B.D. degree under Fisher's license, May 31, 1522 (Jasper Ridley, *Thomas Cranmer* [Oxford: Clarendon Press, 1962], p. 20, n. 1).

63. For the text, see Lewis, *Fisher,* II, 330–332; Bridgett, *Fisher,* pp. 290–292; and Reynolds, *Fisher,* pp. 244–246. For the opinion that Fisher was free on bail from shortly after Christmas 1534 to mid-February 1535, see P. Friedmann, *Anne Boleyn* (London, 1884), II, 48, 340–344. The last letters between Fisher, Cromwell, and Henry VIII are preserved in Cotton MSS. Cleop. E.iv, vi, and Vesp. F.xiii, reprinted in part in R. B. Merriman, *Life and Letters of Thomas Cromwell* (Oxford: Clarendon Press, 1902), I, 373–379, and J. Strype, *Memorials of . . . Thomas Cranmer* (Oxford, 1840), II, 691–694. As for Fisher's Cambridge, Lamb's *Collection* contains "A letter from the University to the King respecting the Power of the Bishop of Rome," May 2, 1534 (pp. 37–38).

64. Ortroy, *Fisher,* XII, 152–159.

65. See *State Papers,* I, 431–432; *LP,* VII, no. 867, VIII, nos. 856, 858, 859; Lewis, *Fisher,* II, 403–407; Bridgett, *Fisher,* pp. 347–348, 365–366; and Reynolds, *Fisher,* pp. 228–237, 266–275.

66. See *LP,* VIII, no. 1075; Ortroy, *Fisher,* XII, 170–186; and Bruce, "Death of Fisher," *Archaeologia,* XXV (1834), 61–99. For his last hours, see especially Ortroy, *Fisher,* XII, 186–198.

67. The pope's brief to Francis I, July 26, 1535, is reprinted and translated in Gardiner, *Obedience,* ed. Janelle, pp. 11–19. On the king's behalf, Gardiner retorted with a tract on Fisher's execution (*ibid.,* pp. 21–65). A German translation of Paul III's brief to Ferdinand of Hungary appeared in 1536 in Caspar Meckenlor's abridged version of Fisher's *Assert. Luth. confut.: Gründtliche widerlegung,* foll. 143–144. On "the famous nomination of cardinals of the 21st [20th] of May 1535," see L. Pastor, *The History of the Popes,* ed. F. I. Antrobus *et al.* (London: Kegan Paul, 1891–1953), XI, 137–144, and A. Ciaconius, *Vitae . . . pontificum Romanorum et S.R.E. cardinalium* (Rome, 1677), III, 567–600. For documents concerned with Fisher in 1535, see also *Concilium Tridentinum,* IV, cxxi–cxxii, and the many documentary quotations in Raynaldus, *Annales ecclesiastici,* XXI (Cologne, 1727), 7–11. The Council of Trent in 1562 decided not to appeal to Queen Elizabeth for the release of Catholic bishops because of what had happened to Fisher in similar circumstances (*Concilium Tridentinum,* VIII, 480, and n. 3).

68. All these writings are reprinted in *Eng. Works,* pp. 349–428. Fisher's biography declares: "Scripsit decem considerationes de fide, de spe et de charitate ad exhortandas hominum mentes ad eucharistiam maiori cum devotione suscipiendam. Cum prologo, quem vidi, sed non integre" (Ortroy, *Fisher,* X, 141). As Ortroy points out, this work is apparently *The Wayes to Perfect Religion,* which has ten Considerations but which is not concerned with the Eucharist. Either the anonymous biographer was misinformed or a lost work is indicated here.

69. *Here after ensueth two fruytfull Sermons, made & compyled by . . .*

Johnn Fyssher . . . (London: W. Rastell for P. Treuerys, 1532). See the analysis and extracts in Reynolds, *Fisher,* pp. 80–86.

70. *Opera,* cols. 1704–1707. The letter may be dated after October 1530 since Lethmatius did not become Dean until that time (Erasmus, *Ep.,* V, 138). See also *ibid.,* IV, 591–592, V, 254, 326, VI, 94, IX, 226. In his will of January 22, 1527, Erasmus requested that one of the twenty special copies of his *Opera* be given to Lethmatius (*ibid.,* VI, 505). The mention of Fisher's letter to Lethmatius reveals urgent need for a calendar of letters to and from Fisher or, better still, for an edition of his correspondence such as that produced for his martyred associate (*The Correspondence of Sir Thomas More,* ed. E. F. Rogers [Princeton: Princeton University Press, 1947]). The difficulty of the enterprise may be gathered from the scattered location of the letters, e.g., that to the Duke of Bavaria "in the possession of the Catholic Bishop of Argyle and the Isles" (text and translation in Bridgett, *Fisher,* pp. 114–116; translation in Reynolds, *Fisher,* pp. 109–110; cf. Thomas More, *Neue Briefe,* ed. Hubertus Schulte Herbrüggen [Münster: Aschendorff, 1966], p. 53, n. 15); that to Reuchlin in *Illustrium virorum epistolae . . . ad Johannem Reuchlin . . . liber secundus* (Hagenoae, 1519), catalogued in L. Geiger, *Johann Reuchlins Briefwechsel* (Stuttgart, 1875; phot. rpr. Hildesheim, 1962), no. 234, pp. 265–266; etc. References have already been made to the reprinting of some letters in Lewis, *Fisher,* Coll. 28–30, 39, II, 330–339, 401–402 (cf. I, xxiv, xxxi, xxxii). Turner comments: "These letters . . . can hardly be admitted as evidence, in an estimate of his character, of any other merit than his meekness and humility" (*ibid.,* I, xxxii). Lewis devotes II, 251–417, to "A Collection of Papers, &c. Relating to Bp. Fisher's Life."

71. See "A Prayer Composed by St. John Fisher," Reynolds, *Fisher,* Appendix A, pp. 297–299, reprinted from *The Month,* New Series, VII (1952), 108–111. Because of the difficulty of reading Fisher's holograph in the Public Record Office, A. G. Dickens finds "the text . . . understandably inaccurate; it needs checking in the Parkyn version, which is in dialect, but clear and correct, as a comparison with Fisher's original has shown" (*Tudor Treatises* [Wakefield: Yorkshire Archaeological Society, 1959], p. 19). Parkyn's copy, made about 1550, is printed by Dickens, who later ascribed it to Fisher (*ibid.*), in "A New Prayer of Sir Thomas More," *The Church Quarterly Review,* CCXLVII (1937), 231–236. This manuscript of Robert Parkyn, who was curate of Adwick-le-Street near Doncaster, is now Bodleian MS. Lat. Th. d. 15.

72. Erasmus, *Ep.,* III, 524: "Verum commentarioli quibus Euangeliorum seriem ac sensum connectis, quorum gustus olim mihi perplacuit, meo iudicio plus dignitatis attulissent tuo nomini." Cf. *ibid.,* III, 91.

73. *Reverendi Patris D. Ioannis Fischerii, quondam episcopi Roffensis Opusculum de fiducia & misericordia Dei* (Coloniae: apud haeredes Arnoldi Birckmanni, 1556).

74. See Reusch, *Index,* I, 419. The Lisbon Index of 1581 suspects Bucer to be the author; Possevino, Gretser, Bellarmine, etc., conjecture a Fisher other than the Bishop of Rochester.

75. Ortroy, *Fisher,* XII, 268–270. Rastell's choice of the epithet "flower of dyvynytie" is undoubtedly deliberate. Several times Fisher labels Thomas Aquinas *flos theologiae:* see, for example, *Eversio,* sig. I4v; *Causa,* sig. D3v; "Assert. Luth. confut." prooem. and art. 17 (*Opera,* cols. 300, 494); and "Magdal." lib. 3 (*ibid.,* col. 1443).

CHAPTER III: FISHER'S CHURCH OF CHRIST

1. "Nam huiusmodi finis [i.e., foelicitatis aeternae] notitia neutiquam ad mentis ipsius & rationis naturam spectat sed ad gratiam & reuelationem transnaturalem vt cunctis patet" ("Responsum," fol. 306; cf. Harpsfield, *Divorce,* p. 101, and for the context *Censurae,* sig. M3v, and *Determinations,* fol. 118v).

2. "Oportuit omnino Christi resurrectionem solidis argumentis comprobari, quum ea sit credendorum omnium basis & ex eo caetera pendeant, quaecunque credimus" ("Ver. corp." 1.14, *Opera,* col. 797). Fisher is answering Oecolampadius' objection from the lack of "signs" in regard to the Eucharist (*De genuina expositione,* sig. B1v).

3. *Eversio,* sigg. N3–O1. The miracles concern rescue from shipwreck and escape from prison.

4. ". . . vt si iam fallamur, ausim asserere, Deum ipsum nos data opera fefellisse" ("Def. reg. assert." 2.14, *Opera,* cols. 124–125; cf. *ibid.* 3.11, col. 138).

5. "Non enim voluit Christus promissionem hanc efficaciam habere perpetuam, sed pro tempore nascentis & adolescentis Ecclesiae. Quod tamen ex ipsis Euangeliis haudquaquam didicimus, sed ex vsu interpretatione patrum duntaxat" (*ibid.* 10.4, col. 229). Johann Gerhard quotes this passage in his *Loci theologici* (Geneva, 1639), V, 455. At one time faith without charity (*fides non formata*) sufficed for the casting out of demons (*ibid.* 10.5, col. 230; cf. Matt. 7:22). As for the Fathers, Fisher later makes reference to the miraculous descent of the Holy Spirit in the form of a dove or fire on Basil, Ambrose, and Gregory the Great ("Assert. Luth. confut." prooem., veritas 6, *Opera,* col. 288).

6. "Nos qui vere Christiani sumus, absque talibus signis credamus, ad cumulatius fidei nostrae meritum" ("Ver. corp." 1.12, *ibid.,* col. 793).

7. "Visibilium certe miraculorum ea est natura . . . vt infirmorum animos ad fidem trahant. Inuisibilium autem, vt accedentes illuminent. . ." (*ibid.* 1.12, col. 793).

8. "Quis quaeso negat daemones eiusmodi mirabilia Deo permittente, posse facere? . . . Caeterum nihil illorum mirabilium ad hoc sacramentum spectare cunctis manifestum est" (*ibid.* 1.15, col. 800). In fact, adds Fisher, the recitation of the miracles performed by Pythagoras of Samos and Apollonius of Tyana would discredit Christ's miracles (*ibid.;* cf. 1.18, col. 807). See also Oecolampadius, *De genuina expositione,* sig. B1v–2v.

9. "Ver. corp." 1.16, *Opera,* col. 802.

10. "Miracula . . . aut revelationes . . . non his tanquam solis & solidis probationibus innitimur, sed veluti subsidiariis duntaxat" (*ibid.* 1.17, col. 803).

11. *Ibid.* 1.18, col. 807.

12. *Ibid.* 3.prooem., corrob. 6, pp. 920–922. He blames his opponents who cannot produce one miracle (or revelation) for denying their possibility or ascribing them to devils' tricks (*ibid.*, corrob. 13, p. 927).

13. *Ibid.* 5.39, col. 1228. See Luther, "De servo arbitrio," *WA,* XVIII, 642–643, tr. J. I. Packer and O. R. Johnson, *On the Bondage of the Will* (London: James Clarke, [1957]), pp. 112–113.

14. "And as for the holy maid of Kent with doctor Bocking, though they wrought great wonders by their life, yet appeared none at their deaths" ("Examinations of Anne Askew," Preface, *Select Works,* ed. H. Christmas [Cambridge, Eng., 1849], p. 139).

15. "Magdal." lib. 3, *Opera,* col. 1444; cf. Prov. 3:32. On Bridget, see *ibid.,* cols. 1456–57.

16. "Fides enim totius ecclesiae huic tamquam solidae basi innititur, nempe quod verissimum id sit, quicquid a deo fuerit reuelatum. Quamobrem quum in vtrisque, tam scilicet in his quam caeteris, quae per ecclesiam creduntur, par sit credenti ratio, neutris absque culpa fides subtrahi potest" (*Eversio,* sig. R3). There is some ambiguity here as to whether the faith is to be divine (i.e., resting on the authority of God, *a deo*) or ecclesiastical (i.e., resting on the authority of the Church, *per ecclesiam*). The context seems to favor the former, i.e., the need for *divine* faith.

17. *Ibid.,* sigg. R3^{v}, S1^{v}, S3, S4^{v}–T1, referring to Clichtove's *Defensio,* foll. 74–75. Fisher cites Bridget, bk. II, chap. 53, bk. IV, chaps. 72, 108–109; Elizabeth, bk. II, chap. 2; and Mechtilde, bk. I, chaps. 44–45. He might have used Lefèvre's edition: *Liber trium virorum & trium spiritualium virginum* (Paris, 1513), e.g., Mechtilde's "Spiritualis gratia," foll. 162^{v}–163. Fisher apparently identifies Amadeus with Amedeo VIII of Savoy (d. 1451) the antipope Felix V, for whom see Biondi, *De Roma triumphante* (Basel, 1531), II, 561; and Pius II, *Opera* (Basel, 1551), pp. 45–46, 56–61, and *Commentaries,* tr. F. A. Gragg and L. C. Gabel, *Smith College Studies in History,* XXII (1936–37), 15, and XXXV (1951), 489–495, where his character is summed up: "He would have been both fortunate and wise had he not been a fool in his old age." Blessed Amedeo IX (1435–72), third Duke of Savoy, was held up as an example for princes by Robert Bellarmine. The reference, however, is probably to Blessed Amedeo Menez de Sylva (1420–82), who wrote an unpublished work entitled *Apocalypsis nova:* "i manoscritti esistenti, ridondanti di puerilità e di errore dottrinali, sono ritenuti interpolati" (*Encicl. catt.,* I, 1022–23). Grandval prefers Bridget's revelations, produced by Fisher, to Amedeo's and Elizabeth's, cited by Clichtove (*Apologiae anchora,* sig. d4^{v}).

18. "At patribus orthodoxis ita creditur. Ecclesia hoc habet persuasissimum. Miracula clamant. Reuelationes attestantur. Euangelia ipsa consentiunt."—*Confut. sec. discept.,* fol. 33.

19. "Assert. Luth. confut." arts. 25, 37, *Opera,* cols. 577–578, 726.

20. "Imo si reuelatum id ei [Luthero] fuisset, reuelationes tamen eiusmodi plerumque fallunt. Nam quae putantur a Deo manasse, plerunque comperiuntur a maligno prodiisse spiritu" ("Def. reg. assert." 1.6, *ibid.*, col. 108). Savonarola is discussed *ibid.*, col. 109, where Fisher points out that he never denounced papal authority as such but only its abuse.

21. "Sacerd. def." 3.29, *ibid.*, col. 1290, tr. Hallett, p. 123.

22. "Ver. corp." 3.prooem., corrob. 7, *Opera*, pp. 922–923. On printed editions of the revelations possibly used by Fisher, see Lewis, *Fisher*, I, 310–311.

23. Fisher, "Responsum," foll. 335–337v; Harpsfield, *Divorce*, pp. 115–116; *Censurae*, sig. Q2v–3; and *Determinations*, foll. 151–152.

24. *LP*, VII, no. 72, p. 28; cf. no. 238, pp. 97–98, for Cromwell's answer to Fisher's letter giving six reasons in his self-defense.

25. The account, with considerable citation of original documents, can be found, e.g., in Bayne, *Fisher*, pp. 81–86; Ortroy, *Fisher*, XII, 97–108; Lewis, *Fisher*, II, 339–352; Bridgett, *Fisher*, pp. 234–263; and Reynolds, *Fisher*, pp. 192–210.

26. In this respect Fisher is like his older German contemporary, Gabriel Biel: "Biel can stress the fact that the legal institutional Church and the Church of the creed coincide. Outside the Church no salvation is possible; neither baptism nor good works can avail without submission to the decisions of the Church. The ineradicable center of the Body of Christ, the Church, is the papal see founded on apostolic succession" (H. A. Oberman, *The Harvest of Medieval Theology: Gabriel Biel and Late Medieval Nominalism* [Cambridge, Mass.: Harvard University Press, 1963], p. 403). At the same moment Fisher addressed himself to his time like the German humanists, who, unlike the Italian, "pressed . . . rather toward an inner renewal of their church and a closer relation to God" (Spitz, *German Humanists*, p. 108).

27. With his exegesis, Luther's "doctrine of the church has occupied a place of central importance in current theological thought and research" (Pelikan, *Luther the Expositor*, p. 34, with reference to Gordon Rupp, *The Righteousness of God* [New York, 1953], pp. 310–343). See also P. Althaus, *Die Theologie Martin Luthers* (Gütersloh: Gerd Mohn, [1962]), pp. 248–254.

28. Knox, *Faith*, pp. 114–115. As will be seen, the acute theological mind of Fisher himself sees all of Luther's other doctrines as caused or influenced by his teaching on faith.

29. "Psalms," *Eng. Works*, p. 108, Lat. tr., *Opera*, col. 1536. Toward the end of his life, Fisher bids his half-sister to love God for having "prouyded you to be borne within the precinctes of Christendeome . . . whereby you . . . haue escaped the most horrible daunger of euerlasting dampnation" ("Perfect Religion," *Eng. Works*, p. 371, Lat. tr., *Opera*, cols. 1691–92).

30. "Psalms," *Eng. Works*, pp. 175–180, Lat. tr., *Opera*, cols. 1581–84. Those "seruauntes of god" that preach the Gospel are called Fathers (like St. Paul), "the chyrch a moder, & all true crysten people be called chyldren" (*ibid.*, p. 199, Lat. tr., *Opera*, col. 1597).

31. "Quid est aliud Ecclesia, quam viuorum lapidum, non confusa quidem, sed ordinatissima constructio? Lapidum, inquam, rationalium, qui Fide non

mortua viuunt. . . quod fundamentum aliud citra CHRISTVM magis congeneum erit, quam ipse Petrus?" ("Assert. Luth. confut." art. 25, *Opera,* col. 561). See also *ibid.,* col. 551.

32. "Sacerd. def." 1.21, *Opera,* col. 1242, tr. Hallett, p. 21. For a collation of actual quotations on the Church from Fisher, Henry VIII, Eck, Cochlaeus, Wimpina, Contarini, Prierias, Berthold, etc., see H. Laemmer, *Die vortridentinisch-katholische Theologie des Reformations-Zeitalters, aus den Quellen* (Berlin, 1858), pp. 73–98. For fuller treatment of the authority of the Church, Eck himself sends his readers to Fisher and Cochlaeus (*Enchiridion,* ed. 1525, sig. C2ᵛ).

33. "Ver. corp." 4.prooem., *Opera,* p. 998. For a more unusual and spiritual explanation of members in the Mystical Body (e.g., face as exemplary holy men, feet as apostles, etc.), see John Torquemada (Turrecremata), "De varietate membrorum ecclesie et significatione eorum," *Summa de ecclesia* (Lyon, 1496), 1.44, sig. d7–8ᵛ.

34. *Early Statutes of Christ's College,* ed. Rackham, pp. 44–45. The same comparison runs through Fisher's statutes of 1516 in *Early Statutes of St. John,* ed. Mayor, pp. 349–396, as well as those of 1524 (pp. 261–346) and of 1530 (pp. 1–260).

35. Psalms MS, P.R.O.S.P.2/R, foll. 33ᵛ, 112ᵛ, 208ᵛ. The words of the psalm have been italicized. He applies Psalm 2 entirely to the Mystical Body (*ibid.,* foll. 157, 264). There are other passing references, e.g., in Psalm 9: "Why therefore do you foolishly mangle the members of Christ" as if His kingdom would have an end some day (*ibid.,* fol. 172)?

36. "Assert. Luth. confut." prooem., veritas 7, *Opera,* col. 289. Because of the unity of the Mystical Body, the sincerely repentant Christian shares in the satisfaction of Christ and the saints, but he is not freed from the punishment due to his sins. If he were, all those dying in the state of grace would fly instantly to heaven — and, contrary to the Church's teaching, purgatory would be eliminated (*ibid.* art. 17, col. 491).

37. The Corinthian in 1 Cor. 5:1–5, for example: "quanquam erat spiritaliter in se mortuus, nimirum quia charitate caruit, erat tamen adhuc per Fidem Ecclesiae membrum, & mystico corpori coniunctus" (*ibid.* art. 23, col. 524).

38. "The spyryte of euery naturall body gyueth lyfe noo forther. but to the members & partes of the same body. whiche be naturally ioyned vnto the heed. And so lykewyse it must be in the mystycall body of our mother holy chirche. For asmoche than as this wretched man [Luther] hath deuyded hymselfe from the heed of this body. whiche is the vycare of chryst. how can he haue in hym the spyryte of this body whiche is the spyryte of trouthe" ("Luther," *Eng. Works,* p. 322, Lat. tr., *Opera,* col. 1380).

39. "Per esum ergo corporeum carnis & sanguinis Christi, nobis Christianis praestatur, vt simus membra corporis eius ex carne eius, & ex ossibus eius" ("Ver. corp." ep. ded., *Opera,* p. 747). See *ibid.* 2.prooem., col. 840, for more details.

40. "Quare sicut Eua ex Adae latere formata fuit, ita prodiit & ecclesiae

vita ex ipsius Christi latere" (*ibid.* 4.25, col. 1068; cf. col. 1070). "Nam sicut Eua prodiit ex Adam, ita nos qui sumus Ecclesia sponsaque Christi, per esum carnis & sanguinis ipsius, corpus vnum efficimur, & membra corporis Christi, atque ita ex duobus fit vna caro" (*ibid.* 5.prooem., col. 1134). The reference is to the piercing of Christ's side on Mount Calvary (John 19:34). In his manuscript commentary on the Psalms, Fisher speaks of the Church as "the succession of Christians which began in the supper room on Mount Zion and will last to the very end of the world" (P.R.O.S.P.2/R, fol. 177ᵛ; cf. events on the first Pentecost in Acts 2:1–41).

41. See the intricate symbolism in "Ver. corp." 5.34, *Opera,* col. 1217, of the double or rather single Jerusalem, Mountain, and Mother, one part being in heaven, another on earth.

42. *Prayer,* tr. 1560, sig. D1ᵛ–2. "An inchaunted woman" is a translation of "insensata quaedam mulier" (*Opera,* col. 1716), with all the pejorative connotations arising from Vulg. Sap. 3:12: "Mulieres eorum [impiorum] insensatae sunt, et nequissimi filii eorum."

43. "Psalms," *Eng. Works,* pp. 170–171, Lat. tr., *Opera,* col. 1578.

44. "Luther," *Eng. Works,* p. 343, Lat. tr., *Opera,* col. 1389. An extensive discussion of the four marks of the Church occurs in what is reputed to be the oldest formal treatise on the Church, James of Viterbo's *De regimine christiano (1301–1302),* 1.3–6, ed. H.-X. Arquillière (Paris: Beauchesne, 1926), pp. 106–143. See C. Eastwood, *The Priesthood of All Believers* (Minneapolis: Augsburg Publishing House, 1962), pp. 1–65, for Luther's conception of the Church, which is known by seven outward signs. See also Headley, *Luther's Church History,* pp. 29–41.

45. See, e.g., "Assert. Luth. confut." art. 28, *Opera,* col. 590; "Ver. corp." 5.38, *ibid.,* col. 1224.

46. "Ver. corp." 1.prooem., *Opera,* p. 749; *ibid.* 5.9, col. 1158.

47. "Sacerd. def." 1.20, *Opera,* cols. 1240–41, tr. Hallett, pp. 18–19.

48. *Heretickes,* sig. B2ᵛ. Fisher had earlier called upon Lefèvre to hear the Church, called *Catholic* by the Council of Nice and spread through the whole Christian world ("Magdal." lib. 3, *Opera,* col. 1458).

49. "Plurima sunt quae, nisi lectori tedium foret, commemorare possemus. in quibus ecclesia suam mutauerit opinionem, gubernante eam diuino spiritu, quod hauddubie christianis omnibus credendum est" (*Eversio,* sig. a5).

50. *Ibid.,* sig. a4ᵛ–5.

51. *Ibid.,* sig. A3ᵛ.

52. "Luther," *Eng. Works,* p. 313, Lat. tr., *Opera,* cols. 1375–76. Psalms MS, too, mentions the great sound (Acts 2:2) with which "the Holy Spirit was sent from heaven to abide perpetually in the Church of Christ" (P.R.O.S.P.2/R, foll. 185ᵛ, 239ᵛ).

53. "Assert. Luth. confut." prooem., veritas 5, *Opera,* cols. 286–287.

54. *Ibid.* art. 16, col. 480. The dichotomy is not sharp because the Apostles themselves were guided by the Holy Spirit.

55. "Def. reg. assert." 12.8, *Opera,* cols. 261–262. Oberman finds that from Matt. 28:20 "Biel draws two major conclusions: (1) the truth defined and

accepted by the catholic Church has to be believed with the same reverence as if it were written in Holy Scripture; (2) it is necessary for salvation to obey the precepts of the Church universal" (*Medieval Theology,* p. 400).

56. "Sacerd. def." 1.20, 3.17, 3.36, *Opera,* cols. 1240–41, 1280, 1295, tr. Hallett, pp. 18–19, 103, 133. "The dating of this fall of the church varied considerably in Luther. Only rarely did he date it, as the radical Protestants tended to do, at the end of the first century. Oftener the seventh century or even a later century was the dividing line" (Pelikan, *Luther the Expositor,* p. 240). On "the origin of the Antichrist with the investiture of Boniface III as pope in 606," see Headley, *Luther's Church History,* pp. 155, 192, 206. For an interpretation of Luther's idea of "The Fall of the Church," see *ibid.,* pp. 156–161, where Luther holds, not glorification–decline–restitution, but rather continual "apostasy, struggle, and degeneration made supportable by the faith and the reality that Christ is present to the end of the world."

57. *Heretickes,* sig. D2.

58. "Ver. corp." 1.30, *Opera,* col. 835. So too with the Holy Spirit. In Biel, for example, "The operation of the Spirit is not first of all directed toward bringing about an individual encounter with Jesus Christ or a personal union with God; rather the Spirit primarily is seen as the sanctifier of the community of the Church . . . the Spirit is primarily the *ecclesie rector et sanctificator,*" etc. (Oberman, *Medieval Theology,* p. 121).

59. See, e.g., "Ver. corp." 3.prooem., corrob. 4, *Opera,* col. 919; 3.17, col. 970.

60. "Sic igitur per continuam quandam successionem, aliorum & aliorum praesidum, sibi mutuo succedentium, veritas Christianae fidei ad haec nostra tempora peruenit" (*ibid.* 5.38, col. 1224).

61. *Causa,* sig. A7v.

62. *Kotser codicis,* sig. F3.

63. ". . . consectaneum est vt quisquis huius veritatis fidem aspernatur, is omnino periturus sit, quum extra Catholicam ecclesiam, nemini salus obuenire queat" ("Ver. corp." 4.prooem., *Opera,* p. 998). Cf. Psalms MS: "Ecclesia . . . extra quam nemini salus est" (P.R.O.S.P.2/R, foll. 33, 112v, 208v).

64. "Psalms," *Eng. Works,* p. 123, Lat. tr., *Opera,* col. 1546.

65. "Magdal." lib. 3, *Opera,* col. 1457.

66. "Assert. Luth. confut." art. 16, *Opera,* cols. 474–475. When Paul urges Timothy not to "neglect the grace . . . granted to thee . . . with the laying on of hands of the presbyterate [*presbyteri*]," "the most learned Erasmus" properly translates it "by the authority of the priesthood [*auctoritate Sacerdotij*]" to make clear that "Timothy was made bishop by the authority of Paul, not of the people [*non plebis auctoritate . . . sed Pauli*]" (*ibid.* art. 13, col. 448).

67. *Ibid.* art. 13, col. 449.

68. "Sacerdotes, Dei cooperatores vocat, plebem vero censet agricolationem, aedificationemque Dei. Num in his nihil esse discriminis quisquam audebit asserere?" — "Def. reg. assert." 6.9, *ibid.,* col. 200.

69. *Ibid.* 8.8, col. 218.

70. *Ibid.* ep. nuncup., p. 101; cf. 11.2, col. 233. "But behold how easie a

thing yt is to deceive the sillie people and how quickly they that be light of credit may be induced to followe crooked waies and bye pathes," etc. (Ortroy. *Fisher,* X, 264–265, dependent on this epistle especially). The widespread character of this adverse view of the *vulgus* appears from J. Altenstaig's *Vocabularius theologie* (Hagenau, 1517), fol. 276, *s.v.* Vulgus, where Gerson is quoted.

71. *Ibid.* 11.1, col. 232. This Lutheran appeal to the people evidently stuck in the bishop's craw and pops up frequently, e.g., in Psalms MS: "Lutherani gratiam plebis captant" (P.R.O.S.P.2/R, fol. 174).

72. *Ibid.* 11.1–3, cols. 232–235.

73. *Ibid.* 11.2, cols. 233–234.

74. *Ibid.* 11.3, cols. 235–236; cf. 11.7, col. 240.

75. *Ibid.* 11.4, cols. 236–237.

76. *Ibid.* 11.5, cols. 238–239. In his views Fisher was far from singular. Erasmus entertained much the same attitude: "In defending himself against the attackers of his translation, Erasmus repeats again and again, both in his *Apologia* [*de In Principio Erat Sermo*] and his *Annotationes,* that he never intended his version for public use, and that such disputes are for scholars, not the 'plebecula.'" See C. A. L. Jarrott, "Erasmus' *In principio erat sermo:* A Controversial Translation," *SP,* LXI (1964), 35–40. See Erasmus, *Opera,* IX, 112–113.

77. *Ibid.* 11.13, cols. 247–248.

78. "Sacerd. def." 2.1–7, *ibid.,* cols. 1243–45, tr. Hallett, pp. 24–28.

79. *Ibid.* 2.28, col. 1258, tr. Hallett, pp. 55–56.

80. *Ibid.* 2.29, cols. 1258–59, tr. Hallett, pp. 56–57. In like manner, the brethren selected the seven deacons but it was the Apostles that consecrated them to the office (*ibid.* 2.34, col. 1262, tr. Hallett, pp. 62–63).

81. ". . . sed ad militandum vnctos, non ad Euangelizandum" (*ibid.* 2.29, col. 1259, tr. Hallett, p. 57). St. Peter's words on the "royal priesthood" (1 Pet. 2:9) "do not mean that every Christian is publicly to preach the Gospel of Christ, but to bear witness to Him rather by his life and example, as indeed is said a verse or two later" (*ibid.* 3.26, col. 1288, tr. Hallett, p. 120).

82. "Reges vtique sunt pariter & sacerdotes omnes Christiani, verum etiam sibi non aliis" (*ibid.* 2.48, col. 1268, tr. Hallett, p. 75). See also *ibid.* 3.3, 3.14, 3.22, cols. 1270, 1278–79, 1284, tr. Hallett, pp. 79, 100, 110–111.

83. *Ibid.* 3.4, col. 1271, tr. Hallett, pp. 81–82. Repeated *ibid.* 3.6, col. 1273, tr. Hallett, p. 86. Fisher states later: "This inner action of God is for the most part so imperceptible, even to him who receives it, that undoubtedly he needs some other teacher" (*ibid.* 3.10, col. 1276, tr. Hallett, p. 95); and still later: "The Holy Spirit grants these gifts in such measure that they do not suffice in every individual soul to give a full knowledge of the Church's doctrine without the help of any other teacher" (*ibid.* 3.12, p. 1277, tr. Hallett, pp. 97–98).

84. *Ibid.* 3.9, col. 1276, tr. Hallett, pp. 92–93. Further on, Fisher mentions also the Corinthians (1 Cor. 3:1–3) as "not yet strong enough to understand what they were taught" (*ibid.* 3.28, col. 1289, tr. Hallett, p. 122).

85. *Ibid.* 3.24, col. 1286, tr. Hallett, p. 114. In the heat of controversy, Fisher charges that it is the subjection of all to himself, not to the pope, that is Luther's reason "why he prefers the judgement of the rude and ignorant populace [*rudis & ignarae plebis iudicium*] to the interpretation of the holy Fathers" (*ibid.* 3.30, col. 1290, tr. Hallett, p. 124).

86. *Ibid.* 3.39, cols. 1297–98, tr. Hallett, pp. 136–137.

87. An Epistole vnto the reder, *Heretickes,* sig. A4.

88. *Ibid.,* sig. C1.

89. "Ver. corp." 1.prooem, *Opera,* p. 750. Note the use of the phrases: "popularis iudicij . . . certitudo," "ad captandam popularem auram," and "populosum . . . auditorium."

90. *Ibid.* 2.5, col. 853.

91. *Ibid.* 4.20, col. 1053.

92. *Ibid.* 4.33, col. 1111. On the other hand, by trusting in their shepherds, the laity receive no less than the clergy in receiving communion under one species outside mass (*ibid.* 5.8, col. 1156).

93. *Commentaria,* A.D. 1527, ed. 1549, p. 170.

94. Lewis, *Fisher,* I, 24–25. Cf. Reynolds, *Fisher,* pp. 64–65. J. A. F. Thomson conjectures: "Richard Gavell . . . may have been no more than incautious in expressing his views on sundry rights claimed by the Church, and then aggressively critical when he had run into trouble" (*The Later Lollards, 1414–1520* [Oxford: Oxford University Press, 1965], p. 186).

95. *Eng. Works,* p. 41, Lat. tr., *Opera,* col. 1489, where "the grete curse" is translated as "excommunicatio maior."

96. Ortroy, *Fisher,* X, 229–235; cf. Bayne, *Fisher,* pp. 22–25. "This man was named Peter de Valence, by calling a preist, and borne in Normandie" (Bayne, p. 25).

97. Based on Luther's sermon on excommunication (1518), *D. Martin Luthers Werke,* Kritische Gesammtausgabe (Weimar, 1883–), I, 639.

98. Based on Luther's treatise on excommunication, *WA,* VI, 70.

99. "Assert. Luth. confut." art. 23, *Opera,* cols. 524–525. The comparison is repeated elsewhere, e.g., *ibid.,* col. 527.

100. *Ibid.,* col. 528.

101. *Ibid.* art. 24, cols. 528–529.

102. *Ibid.* art. 23, col. 526; cf. col. 524.

103. "Ver. corp." 3.2, *ibid.,* cols. 935–936. But, other things being equal, the one who actually assists at the sacrifice merits more than the one who deliberately absents himself (*ibid.,* col. 936).

104. "Assert. Luth. confut." art. 36, *Opera,* col. 671.

105. *Ibid.* art. 37, col. 727. For recent definitions, see Torquemada, *Ecclesia* 4.2.1, sig. G4, and Altenstaig, *Vocabularius theologie, s.vv.* Heresis *and* Hereticus, foll. 100v–101v. *Orthodoxus* is defined: "fidelis catholicus . . . Unde Orthodoxus: quasi rectam regulam seu doctrinam credendo et viuendo tenens" (Altenstaig, fol. 175). For Luther's concept of heresy as "an obdurate errantry in respect to Scripture," see Headley, *Luther's Church History,* pp. 208–211.

106. *Heretickes,* sig. C2.

107. "Sed quid periculi fuerit, vim inferre cuiquam, modo fiat id ad suum commodum? Beneficium enim praestabis ei, quem ita coges. Et sane magnum beneficium est, ignoranti veritatem ostendere, aberrantique rectam commonstrare viam. Sed & compellendi sunt, velint, nolint, vt eam ingrediantur. An non Christus . . . quosdam inuitos compellandos docuit, quatenus ad viam redirent? Exi, inquit, cito in vias & sepes and compelle intrare. Num tu videri vis Christo circumspectior. Quando igitur tibi creditum sit purgatorium, & dignum tibi visum fuerit quod credendum tibi consulas, quamobrem te quaeso neminem cogi vis, ad id credendum, cum talis adactio cuique sit vtilis, & Christus eandem in Euangelio docet apertissime" ("Assert. Luth. confut." art. 37, *Opera,* col. 727). In John Frith's treatise on purgatory, after referring the reader to "a woorke that William Tyndal hath written agaynst M. More," he declares that the parable of the great supper (Luke 14:16–24), from which "my Lord [of Rochester] . . . plucketh out a word," applies to gentle preaching to the gentiles; that "fayth is a gifte of God"; and that "compulsion and violence . . . [do] nothing but make a starke hypocrite: for no man can compel the hart to beleue a thing except it see euidence and sufficiente profe" (*Whole workes,* pp. 56–58; *A disputacion of Purgatorye* [London, 1533?], sig. L3v–4).

108. *Confut. sec. discept.,* fol. 2v.

109. "Def. reg. assert.," *Opera,* p. 102.

110. *Heretickes,* sig. A2–4.

111. "Ver. corp." 4.28, *Opera,* col. 1078.

112. *Ibid.* 4.prooem., col. 989. In his fragmentary manuscript sermon on Vulg. Ps. 127, he writes: "Our lord therfor send us his peace / whych if we hade / we shuld not have thees greate enormytees of synn so generally spredd every whear as thei be. We shuld not have thees hereesyes to reagne emongst vs so myghtily as tha doo" (P.R.O.S.P.1/239, fol. 181v).

113. "Luther," *Eng. Works,* p. 312. Fisher here speaks of "the lyght of fayth (that shyneth. from the spyrytuall sonne almyghty god)," but the Latin translator, Pace, finds the specific answer in the *Son* of God: "lumen fidei, a spirituali sole, omnipotentis Dei filio, emissum" (*Opera,* col. 1375). One wonders whether the original might not have had a pun here on *Sun* and *Son,* such as found in "The Son" by George Herbert.

114. "Ver. corp." 3.prooem., *Opera,* pp. 923–924.

115. *Ibid.* 1.prooem., pp. 748–749. The year before, Fisher mentions: "The kynges boke / the boke of maister More / the bokes of Catharinus / the bokes of Empser / of Cocleus / of Eckius / and many other" (*Heretickes,* sig. E1). Thomas More is just as busy in 1527 as he was in 1516! "Thomas Morus, eques auratus, moribus & ingenio candidissimus, neque minori praestans eruditione, tametsi negotiis regis & regni grauissimis, occupatissimus" ("Ver. corp." 1.prooem., pp. 748–749; cf. *Utopia,* pp. 38–40). For the praise given Edward Powell by the University of Oxford for his *Propugnaculum summi sacerdotij euangelici ac septenarij sacramentorum* (London, 1523), see B. Camm, ed., *Lives of the English Martyrs* (London: Burns & Oates,

1904–5), I, 485–486. Only *Edward* Powell is given in *DNB,* although Thomas Tanner, *Bibliotheca Britannico-Hibernica* (London, 1748), I, 606, mentions also *Johannes* Powell who wrote *Propugnaculum ecclesiae,* seen by Bale. Papyrius Geminus Eleates, the author of the preface to *Propugnaculum,* has recently been conjectured to be Thomas Elyot (C. W. Bouck, "On the Identity of Papyrius Geminus Eleates," *Transactions of the Cambridge Bibliographical Society,* II (1954–58), 352–358.

116. *Eversio,* sig. Z2^{v}–3.

117. "Assert. Luth. confut." art. 16, *Opera,* col. 477.

118. *Ibid.* art. 25, col. 542. Later, Fisher appeals to the belief of the Greek Church in the Real Presence ("Ver. corp." 2.prooem., col. 839).

119. "Assert. Luth. confut." art. 25, *Opera,* col. 544.

120. *Ibid.,* col. 577.

121. *Ibid.* art. 25, col. 578; art. 37, col. 726.

122. *Ibid.* art. 34, cols. 645–646.

123. *Heretickes,* sig. A2.

CHAPTER IV: AUTHORITY IN THE CHURCH

1. "Sacerd. def." 2.9, *Opera,* col. 1246, tr. Hallett, p. 31.

2. "Nec opinor quenquam esse tam haereticum, vt neget illam varietatem a Christo fuisse institutam" (*ibid.* 2.10, col. 1247, tr. Hallett, p. 32).

3. "Clearly this assurance [in Matt. 28:20] was given not only for those then present, but also for all their descendants; for those who were then living and those who have followed them up to this time form as it were one age and one lasting generation" (*ibid.* 2.19, col. 1251, tr. Hallett, p. 41).

4. "Neque putandum est voluisse Christum, hanc inter suos ordinum varietatem pro tempore illo duntaxat fieri, sed plane duraturam instituit, quamdiu in terris esset Ecclesia militatura" (*ibid.* 2.10, col. 1247, tr. Hallett, p. 32). "Clearly, then, what has been handed down to us by tradition is quite reasonable, viz. that those who have succeeded the apostles and hold the higher rank should be called bishops or greater priests, whilst those who have succeeded the seventy-two disciples and hold the second rank should be called presbyters or lesser priests" (*ibid.*; cf. *ibid.* 3.20, cols. 1282–83, tr. Hallett, p. 108).

5. "Nec adeo quisquam opinor haereticus est, vt neget istam graduum varietatem a Christo institutam, eandemque deinceps ab Apostolis vsurpatam fuisse" (*ibid.* 3.20, col. 1283, tr. Hallett, p. 108).

6. *Ibid.* 1.13, 1.15, 1.18, 2.35, cols. 1238–39, 1263, tr. Hallett, pp. 14–15, 17, 64–65. For this early period, Fisher mistakenly cites also Hegesippus *ca.* 188, Pseudo-Dionysius *ca.* 500, and Philo Judaeus, whose *Therapeutae* are pagan rather than Christian. Clement's letter to James, Bishop of Jerusalem, quoted twice, is almost certainly spurious, whereas Ignatius of Antioch is cited in a medieval paraphrase. See Hallett, *Priesthood,* Notes, pp. 140–141. Later, to prove that "the presbyters were truly priests, and had a special

ministry over the flock," Fisher cites decrees of the earliest popes which are hardly authentic (*ibid.* 3.38, cols. 1296–97, tr. Hallett, pp. 133–136), but which Fisher found probably in Ives of Chartres' *Liber decretorum,* Basel, 1499 (Hallett, p. 149, n. 50).

7. *Ibid.* 1.7, 1.13, 3.37, cols. 1235, 1238, 1295, tr. Hallett, pp. 8–9, 13–14, 20, 133. Another quotation from Origen is attributed to Cyril (*ibid.* 1.8, cols. 1235–36, tr. Hallett, pp. 9–10, 140, n. 18).

8. Ambrose is cited only in three spurious works (*ibid.* 1.3, 3.41, cols. 1234, 1265, tr. Hallett, pp. 7, 69). The mysterious Greek, Vulgarius (*ibid.* 2.44, col. 1266, tr. Hallett, p. 70), whom Hallett does not attempt to identify and whom Schmeink ventures to gloss as "Eugenius?" (*Sacerd. def.,* ed. 1925, pp. 46, n. 6, and 87), is none other than Theophylact, Archbishop of Bulgaria, whom Erasmus also listed as Vulgarius on the title page of his New Testament in 1516 (B. Hall, "Biblical Scholarship: Editions and Commentaries," in S. L. Greenslade, ed., *The Cambridge History of the Bible: The West from the Reformation to the Present Day* [Cambridge (Eng.) University Press, 1963], p. 60).

9. "Sacerd. def." 1.prooem., *Opera,* col. 1233, tr. Hallett, p. 5.

10. *Ibid.* 1.prooem, col. 1233, tr. Hallett, p. 4.

11. *Ibid.* 2.1, col. 1243, tr. Hallett, p. 24.

12. *Ibid.* 3.40, col. 1298, tr. Hallett, p. 138. Cf. "Def. reg. assert.," *Opera,* cols. 191–205.

13. "Assert. Luth. confut.," *ibid.,* cols. 583–589.

14. "Contra hanc haeresim scripsit Ioannes Roffensis episcopus in eo opere quod contra captiuitatem Babylonicam Lutheri aedidit, articulo.27. Scripsit etiam Iodocus Clichthouaeus multo diffusius in suo Antiluthero, parte prima." — *Adversus omnes haereses libri XIIII* (Paris, 1564), fol. 95.

15. Episcopal Register at Rochester, fol. 167[v], cited in Reynolds, *Fisher,* p. 120.

16. Hughes, *Reformation,* I, 81. To the number of preaching bishops must be added Nicholas West, Bishop of Ely, according to Fisher's explicit words in the dedication to West of his *Defense of the Royal Assertion:* "vt bonum pastorem decet, tua praesentia dioecesim tuam exornas, & verbo Dei plebem tuae fidei commissam erudis assidue" ("Def. reg. assert.," *Opera,* p. 101). The contemporary English clergy enjoyed a very good reputation at home and abroad. In his *Propugnaculum* (1523), Powell boasts of English "priests and bishops not a few who are excellent popular preachers as well as writers against Luther's heresies" (fol. 137). On the continent in 1529, Cochlaeus in proof of episcopal learning points to England alone, "which has many bishops outstanding for erudition, either equal or not much inferior to the Bishop of Rochester in doctrine, and either equal or even superior to him in eloquence." Later he again declares that "today even England alone has more than ten bishops most upright in both life and doctrine." See *Fasciculus calumniarum, sannarum et illusionum Martini Lutheri . . .* (Leipzig, 1529), foll. 42, 57[v]. In the light of such statements, Dickens' judgment needs modification or clarification: "Our [English] bishops . . . tended to think of the

Church in terms of jurisdiction rather than in terms of religious education. Even the more intelligent and spiritually-minded, like John Fisher, failed to perceive that a shifting lay outlook demanded new methods, and they tended merely to be shocked when, to put the matter crudely in our modern terms, they found the gentry and merchants of the Renaissance age less docile than the illiterate barons and villeins of a former world" (*Reformation,* p. 327).

17. MS. Harl. 7049, fol. 141, cited in C. H. Cooper, *Memoir of Margaret, Countess of Richmond and Derby,* ed. J. E. B. Mayor (Cambridge, 1874), pp. 95–96; and Fisher, *The Funeral Sermon of Margaret . . .* With Baker's Preface to the Same, ed. J. Hymers (Cambridge, 1840), pp. 163–164. Fisher was related to Rochester by the English Protector: "By July 1504 the title had been tactfully bestowed on the Pope's [Julius II's] nephew, Cardinal Galeotto Franciotti, who applied himself diligently to consistorial and other English business" (D. S. Chambers, *Cardinal Bainbridge in the Court of Rome 1509 to 1514* [London: Oxford University Press, 1965], p. 8 and n. 9).

18. "Henry VII," *Eng. Works,* p. 271.

19. Ortroy, *Fisher,* X, 211.

20. Bishop Fisher's Statutes, ch. 47 (1524), and ch. 54 (1530), *Early Statutes of St. John,* ed. Mayor, pp. 242, 343; Cooper, *Margaret,* p. 248n.

21. "Ver. corp.," *Opera,* p. 746. The proximity of their London residences would help to keep their friendship alive. See Thomson-Porter, tr., *Erasmus and Cambridge,* Introd., p. 10: "And anyone who wished to cross the river to the south bank might call upon Bishop Fisher at Rochester House, near the future site of the Globe Theatre, almost next door to Bishop Richard Foxe of Winchester."

22. Bishop Fisher's Statutes, ch. 47 (1524), and ch. 54 (1530), *Early Statutes of St. John,* ed. Mayor, pp. 238, 240, 342.

23. "Ver. corp.," *Opera,* p. 747.

24. "De officio primario summi pontificis," *Auctarium Bellarminianum,* X.–M. Le Bachelet (Paris: Beauchesne, 1913), p. 517, n. 1. This refusal to part with his poor diocese won the admiration of many historians, e.g., of Burnet (in spite of his final judgment on Fisher as "a learned and devout man, but much addicted to the superstitions in which he had been bred up: and that led him to great severities against all that opposed him," *Reformation,* I, 555) and of Collier (who asserts that "he was a person of learning and exemplary life, but stuck close to the papal pretensions," *Ecclesiastical History,* ed. Lathbury, IV, 272).

25. "Nihil profecto aliud nisi ut studiosis omnibus liquido constaret illorum causa id factum esse. Nosti, optime Rex, an vera dixerim" (Lewis, *Fisher,* II, 270). See also the following: "ob eam rationem solam, ut caeteros ad virtutem et bonas literas incitares" (*ibid.*).

26. Erasmus, *Ep.,* VIII, 160–161, tr. Thomson-Porter, p. 189 (cf. the latter, p. 29, on Queens' College).

27. Lewis, *Fisher,* Coll. No. 23, II, 305–306.

28. Bishop Fisher's Statutes, ch. 24 (1516), ch. 28 (1524), and ch. 20 (1530), in *Early Statutes of St. John,* ed. Mayor, pp. 96, 98, 313–314, 377.

29. Lewis, *Fisher,* I, 9, citing Strype's *Life of Abp. Parker,* p. 193. The license was distinct from the permission to preach in a particular place: "The consent of the bishop of the diocese and the rector of the parish had to be obtained" (Reynolds, *Fisher,* p. 17). Collier, *Ecclesiastical History,* ed. Barham, IX, 338–340, reprints "An University License for Preaching, granted by Fisher, Chancellor of Cambridge . . . ," dated May 31, 1522, for the appointment of Christopher Bayley.

30. Lewis, *Fisher,* I, 11; Fisher, *Margaret,* ed. Baker-Hymers, p. 4. As for the perpetual lectureships in theology at Cambridge and Oxford, license had been granted to Margaret in 1497. "These foundations were not fully established till 1503, but lecturers were probably appointed to hold office at once; thus the Grace Book for 1498-9 contains references to the foundation of 'the lecture of the king's mother'" (Roach, in *V.C.H.Cambs.,* III, 166–167, with reference to *Grace Book B,* I, 120).

31. Bishop Fisher's Statutes, ch. 3, *Early Statutes of Christ's College,* ed. Rackham, pp. 46–47; ch. 2 (1516, 1524, omitted in 1530), in *Early Statutes of St. John,* ed. Mayor, pp. 265, 352.

32. Harpsfield-Hitchcock, *Moore,* Appendix I, p. 249.

33. Ortroy, *Fisher,* X, 258. The earliest reference to actual events is to the meeting between Henry VII and Philip the Handsome, where "my lord of Rochest. bare my lord of Canterberys crosse" (Scott, "Notes from the College Records," *Eagle,* XV [1887–88], 388). Scott also gives documents for three other affairs, including the instruction from the council to meet "an ambassadour sent from the Poope's Holynes to his Grace with a sworde and cap of maintenaunce" at "some place convenient betwene Sitingbourne and Rochester . . . and so conduyte him to London. . . At Baynard Castel the xii day of May [1514]" (Lewis, *Fisher,* Coll. No. 19, II, 297–298, and Scott, *Eagle,* XVI [1889–91], 352–354). The archives of St. John's College preserve also a letter to Fisher from Cardinal Adrian de Castello, successively Bishop of Hereford and Bath-Wells, introducing the newly consecrated *episcopus castoriensis,* September 20, 1515 (Scott, *Eagle,* XXXII [1910–11], 145–146). After Fisher's execution, Cochlaeus in his "Defensio Roffensis" praises his frequent sermons and annual diocesan visitations, but it is impossible to say with what factual basis: "Quantus enim fuit Roffensis in sermonibus ad populum, dum quotannis circumiret ac visitaret omnes suae Dioceseos Ecclesias?" (*Antiqua et insignis epistola Nicolai .i. . .* [Leipzig, 1536], sig. Aa3).

34. Ortroy, *Fisher,* X, 256–258.

35. *Ibid.,* 224.

36. *Ibid.,* 226. The biographers give also the story of the first visitation of his diocese, initiated with the clergy at his cathedral: "And first, because there is small hope of health in the membres of that bodie where the head is sicke, he began his visitacion at his head church of Rochester" (*ibid.,* 216).

37. *Eng. Works,* pp. 76–77, Lat. tr., *Opera,* cols. 1514–15.

38. *Ibid.,* p. 124, Lat. tr., *Opera,* col. 1547.

39. *Ibid.,* p. 140, Lat. tr., *Opera,* col. 1558.

40. *Ibid.,* pp. 179–183, Lat. tr., *Opera,* cols. 1583–85.

41. *Prayer,* tr. 1560, sig. A4^{v}–5.

42. *Opera,* cols. 1715–16, Eng. tr. 1560, sig. D1^{v}.

43. *Heretickes,* pref. ep., sig. A2.

44. "Responsum," foll. 332^{v}–333^{v}. Cf. Harpsfield, *Divorce,* pp. 114–115; *Censurae,* sig. Q1^{v}–2; *Determinations,* sig. T6^{v}–7^{v}.

45. Erasmus, *Ep.,* V, 537. Earlier, Erasmus comments: "Nihil indulges isti corpusculo" (*ibid.,* 536).

46. *Ibid.,* VIII, 175 (quoted also in Veit Ludwig von Seckendorf, *Commentarius historicus et apologeticus de Lutheranismo,* 2nd ed. [Leipzig, 1694], II, 198). Earlier, in answer to Luther's challenge, Erasmus declares that he could name certain bishops "in whom you should find nothing wanting of a devout bishop's office, among whom I number John Bishop of Rochester" (*Hyperaspistes diatribae aduersus seruum arbitrium Martini Lutheri* [Basel, 1526], sig. I2, where he also refers to his difference of opinion with Fisher on free will). In his *Apophthegmata,* Erasmus mentions a special type of episcopal throne which he has seen only in Canterbury and Rochester (*Opera omnia* [Leyden, 1703–1706], IV, 365). The modern reader is sometimes inclined to agree with Tyndale's judgment on Erasmus: "whose tonge maketh of litle gnattes greate elephantes and lifteth upp aboue the starres whosoever geveth him a litle exhibition" ("W. T. To the Reader," *The fyrst boke of Moses called Genesis,* in *Five Books of Moses,* ed. J. I. Mombert [New York, 1884], p. 5).

47. Erasmus, *Ep.,* XI, 373–374.

48. *Ibid.,* V, 162. On November 23, 1522, John Becar of Borsselen speaks of it as promised three years before (*ibid.,* 140). On April 13, 1523, Paul Volz suggested to Beatus Rhenanus that it be dedicated to himself (*ibid.,* 162n).

49. *Ibid.,* V, 538.

50. *Ibid.,* XI, 191–192. In this same letter, Erasmus laments the passing of his other friends: Warham, Mountjoy, and More.

51. Erasmus, *Opera,* V, 812.

52. *LP,* VIII, no. 777, p. 292, May 29, 1535. See also *ibid.,* no. 779, for the Bishop of Mâcon's message to Francis I on the same day; and *Concilium Tridentinum,* IV, Introd., cxxii, n. 3, for Ricalcati's letter of June 6, 1535. Most important of all is Paul's brief of notification sent to Fisher, which, lost until a few years ago, is reprinted in *Concilium Tridentinum,* IV, Introd., cxxi, n. 4. The English agent, G. da Casale, explained to friendly cardinals that Fisher's innate vainglory and stubbornness had gotten him into trouble with his king and that he was too old and decrepit to be of any use to the Church (*State Papers,* VII, 604–605). In letters dated July 16 and 27, 1535, Casale wrote Cromwell that Fisher's appointment was reported to be a trick practiced by the Archbishop of Capua on Paul III (*ibid.,* VII, 616–622, which also includes the "official" account of trial and execution).

53. Ortroy, *Fisher,* XII, 163–164.

54. Lewis, *Fisher,* Coll. No. 41, II, 412; cf. *LP,* VIII, no. 858, p. 332. When George Gold mentioned the rumor of the cardinalate, Fisher replied: "A

cardinal! Then I perceive it was not for nought that my Lord Chancellor [Audley] did ask me when I heard from my master the Pope, and said there was never man that had exalted the Pop[e a]s I had" (*LP,* VIII, no. 856, p. 328).

55. Gardiner, *Obedience,* ed. Janelle, p. 15. Cf. *ibid.,* p. 13: "What shall we first mourn in such a wound of the universal church? The innocence and holiness of that man, or his learning, both famous and spread out throughout the whole world for the defence of the Catholic faith?" On continental reaction and papal maneuvers after Fisher's death, see L. Pastor, *History of the Popes,* tr. F. I. Antrobus *et al.* (London: Kegan Paul, 1891–1953), XII, 458–463. For the sentiment in Rome, see the epistolary extracts in *State Papers,* VII, 621, n. 1. For Cromwell's instructions about Fisher's and More's conspiracy, treason, and mild sentence, see his letters to Wallop in France (Strype, *Eccl. Mem.,* I, pt. 2, no. 68, pp. 247–252) and to Casale in Italy (*State Papers,* VII, 633–636).

56. "Quem enim alium [episcopum] habes, aut multis saeculis habuisti, quem sanctitate, doctrina, prudentia, & in illo episcopi munere fungendo cura ac sedulitate, cum Roffensi compares? de quo ita gloriari potes, ut ne apud exteras quidem nationes, si omnes christiani nominis prouinciae hoc nostro saeculo perlustrarentur, posset facile reperiri, qui ita omnes episcopi partes ac numeros impleret" (*Pro ecclesiasticae vnitatis defensione, libri quatuor* [Strasbourg, 1555], lib. 3, fol. 69). He singles out Fisher's work at Cambridge (fol. 69[v]). Fisher and More receive generous mention and praise throughout lib. 3 (foll. 51–84).

57. *Epistolarum Reginaldi Poli . . . collectio,* Pars I, 1520–1536 (Brixiae, 1744), I, 94–95. Later Pole had to defend, against the Bishop of Badajoz, More's delay in standing up for a matter of faith (papal primacy): "It was not the same with Rochester, whose duty it was as a bishop to speak immediately upon being examined" (*State Papers in Venice,* V, no. 531, p. 224, referring to *Epist. Poli,* ed. Bresciae, 1752, IV, 73–81).

58. Strype, *Eccl. Mem.,* I, pt. 2, no. 54, p. 211.

59. *A sermon made in the cathedrall churche of saynt Paule in London the XXVII. day of June, Anno.1535* (London, July 30, 1535), sig. C7[v]–8.

60. *Epistola Nicolai . . . ,* "Ad Henricum," sig. Q3; "Defensio . . . aduersus Richardum samsonem," sig. Aa3, cf. sigg. Y2[v], Z4, Aa1. In the concluding item, a letter to the reader, Cochlaeus pleads: "Vale, ac boni consule Pie Lector, & Deum ora, non pro foelicissimo Christi Martyre Moro, aut Roffensi, sed pro misero peccatore Cochlaeo" (sig. Dd4).

61. *Apomaxis calumniarum, convitiorumque . . .* (London, 1537), foll. 44[v], 53, 61[v], 74, 77, 87. Morison's account of the crimes, trials, and executions takes up foll. 76–99. For Morison's career, see W. G. Zeeveld, *Foundations of Tudor Policy* (Cambridge, Mass.: Harvard University Press, 1948), *passim.* Morison had advised Cromwell to banish rather than to execute "England's enemies" (*LP,* VII, nos. 1311, 1318) and, after Fisher's and More's deaths, wrote him "a highly critical letter, reporting unfavorable opinion abroad" (*LP,* IX, no. 198; see Zeeveld, pp. 93–94, and nn. 40–41). According to

Zeeveld, "There can be little doubt that Morison's answer to Cochlaeus marks the beginning of his writing career under Cromwell" (p. 158).

62. *Scopa Ioannis Cochlaei Germani, in araneas Ricardi Morysini Angli* (Leipzig, 1538), sigg. A4^v, B1, E3^v–F4^v. There is an interesting ode in honor of More and Fisher (sig. G4). Cochlaeus refers to his pleasurable meeting with Richard Pace in Rome and to the fact that he has received no letter from England in six years. The last letter received from More came through his nephew and said not a word about the conflict against the queen and against the Roman Pontiff (sig. G2^v–3). The same two causes are mentioned in *Historia aliquot nostri saeculi Martyrum,* ed. Vitus a Dulken and Guilielmus a Sittart (Cologne, 1550), foll. 1–3: "De captivitate et martyrio D. Ioannis Phischeri, Episcopi Roffensis, propter secundas nuptias Regis, & constitutionem schismaticam."

63. *The Political Works of James I,* ed. C. H. McIlwain (Cambridge, Mass.: Harvard University Press, 1918), pp. 84, 86, 105–107; Bellarmine, *Responsio Matthaei Torti . . .* (Cologne, 1608), pp. 133–135.

64. Suarez, *Defensio fidei . . . cum responsione ad apologiam pro iuramento fidelitatis,* p. 778; Dominis, "Ostensio errorum P. F. Suarez," *De republica ecclesiastica* (London and Frankfort, 1617–58), II, 1006–7. As for Suarez's citation of testimonials as to Fisher's and More's martyrdom, e.g., that of Polydore Vergil (*Defensio,* p. 767), the Archbishop replied that Vergil had no power of canonizing martyrs: the two subjects were rebels and traitors (*Rep. eccles.,* II, 999).

65. Brewer, *Henry VIII,* I, 65. Fisher mentions this appointment in "An Account of the difficulties and discouragements which Bishop Fisher met with in the foundation of St. John's College" (Lewis, *Fisher,* Coll. No. 11, II, 279–280).

66. Erasmus, *Ep.,* I, 498. He already praises Fisher as "vir non solum admirabili integritate vitae, verum etiam alta reconditaque doctrina, tum morum quoque incredibili comitate commendatus maximis pariter ac minimis" (*ibid.;* cf. I, 500–501, where only Warham is declared comparable to Fisher).

67. *Ibid.,* I, 502. Actually the first session was held in May 1512. There is much confusion here. The bad news of the French victory at Ravenna (April 11, 1512) postponed the department of the English representatives, according to Chambers, who appeals to a letter of Henry VIII to Bainbridge on the next day (April 12, 1512). Silvestro Gigli alone actually traveled to Rome (October 1512?), where he also acted as a guardian of the council. See Chambers, *Bainbridge,* pp. 42–43, and n. 1.

68. Lewis, *Fisher,* Coll. No. 16, II, 286–287. The prior of Ledes was Richard Chetham. The other prior was *Willelmus Frysell,* appointed by Warham on September 11, 1509, after controversy: "Lis inter episcopum Roffensem et suppriorem de electione prioris Sti. Andreae in civitate Roffen.," J. Thorpe, *Registrum Roffense* (London, 1769), pp. 138–139. A humorous touch is provided by a letter preserved in St. John's College: "And as touchinge your desyr to haue Henry Dey my seruaunte to serue in your said Iorney: truly I myght better spare all my other seruauntes than hym" (Scott, "Notes from

the College Records," *Eagle,* XVI [1889–91], 350). Erasmus can hardly be referring to a projected trip in 1513 (as distinct from 1512 and 1515) when he mentions a journey to Rome "two years before" *(ante biennium),* suddenly called off, in his letter to Domenico Grimani, May 15, 1515 (*Ep.,* II, 76), where he again praises Fisher as "viro omni episcopalium virtutum genere cumulatissimo et . . . Cantuariensis [Warham] . . . simillimo." For June 10, 1514, there exists the certificate of "visitation [of the Pope] by Polydore Vergilius, archd. of Wells, on behalf of John bp. of Rochester" (*LP,* I, 2nd ed., no. 2989, p. 1291).

69. Ortroy, *Fisher,* X, 254–255. Ortroy comments in a note here: "Je suis porté à croire qu'on a confondu ce projet de voyage avec celui de 1515." In fact, there seems to be no documentary evidence for the trip in 1519 as for those in 1512 and 1515.

70. See *State Papers,* VI, 311–312: "quos potissimum judicatis Dei et divinarum legum atque institutionum esse observantes, quique rectam et piam voluntatem pari prudentia conjunctam habeant. Nobis testimonium factum est de venerabilium fratrum Londoniensis et Roffensis virtutibus, quos arbitraremur huic rei et negocio esse idoneos." Cf. *LP,* IV, no. 435, p. 185. Since he has never been to Rome, Fisher confesses his inability to pass on the truth or falsity of the report about Rome's corruption. In "Assert. Luth. confut.," first published on January 2, 1523, he writes: "Qualis vita moresque fuerit, aut Pontificis, aut curiae, non est huius instituti disserere, sed de doctrina potius. Si voluptates, si diuitias, si gloriam, hoc est, si mundum & carnem sequantur, tibi forsitan exploratius est, quam mihi, quippe qui nunquam Romae fuerim" (art. 36, *Opera,* col. 711).

71. Jedin, *Trient,* I, 548, n. 40, citing Carpi to Ricalcati, June 21, 1535, Vat. Arch. Lettere di principi 10 f. 243r. Carpi refers also to Henry VIII's fears that at the council Fisher would express his views on the divorce and the royal supremacy.

72. "Hic oportet nosse, iudicium [ecclesiae] posse bifariam intelligi, nempe aut expressum aut tacitum, quod & Ioannes Franciscus Concordiae comes, vir coniugij legibus astrictus, docte explicat, & docet non solum iudicio ecclesiae expresso, sed & tacito obediendum esse" ("Magdal." lib. 3, *Opera,* col. 1459). Speaking to a humanist, Fisher probably appeals to the authority of J. F. Pico as a humanist.

73. For a traditional view on conciliar infallibility, see Torquemada, *Ecclesia* 3.58–60, sigg. D8ᵛ–E2ᵛ; and for *veritas catholica, ibid.* 4.2.8, sig. G7.

74. "Neque enim inficias eo, quin aliquoties etiam in generalibus ipsis conciliis permissa sit hallucinatio quaedam, nempe vt sic cognoscerent se homines esse, verum error ille nunquam diu in ecclesia permansit, sed mox per aliam Synodum reformatus est" (*Eversio,* sig. a4ᵛ–5). But Clichtove and his associates have not proved the Church's change of mind on the single Magdalene (*ibid.,* sig. a5).

75. "Luther," *Eng. Works,* p. 335. In his Latin translation, Pace corrects 309 to 318 at Nice (*Opera,* col. 1385). Fisher gives 318 in "Def. reg. assert."

6.6, *Opera,* col. 196. For Luther's view of the early councils, especially Nice, see Headley, *Luther's Church History,* pp. 164–170.

76. "Luther," *Eng. Works,* p. 338, Lat. tr., *Opera,* col. 1387.

77. See Castro, *Adv. haer.,* fol. 77, and Bellarmine, "De conciliis et ecclesia militante," lib. I, cap. 2, *Controv.,* ed. 1615, II, 1.

78. "Assert. Luth. confut." prooem., *Opera,* cols. 290–292. This possibility of conciliar error on minor points was held also by Eck, Alfonso de Castro, Barthélemy Latomus, Peresius, and Cochlaeus (Polman, *Élément historique,* pp. 298–299).

79. "Assert. Luth. confut." art. 16, *Opera,* cols. 475–476. To Luther's objection that the Council of Basel relaxed that decree for the Bohemians, Fisher simply answers that, in view of the lack of evidence from annals or documents, one must abide by the decree passed at Session XXX on communion under one species (*ibid.,* col. 476). His works contain varying definitions of a general council, e.g., "totius reipublicae Christianae patribus & proceribus studio profectus animarum collectis" (*ibid.* art. 5, col. 394).

80. *Ibid.* art. 25, col. 543. The Council of Florence was invoked earlier by Cajetan, *De divina institutione pontificatus Romani pontificis super totam ecclesiam a Christo in Petro* (Rome, 1521), sig. k5 (which concludes: "Vbi nota non nouiter ab hac synodo inuentam fuisse hanc difinitionem / sed ipsam contineri in aliorum uniuersalium conciliorum gestis: & propterea hoc unum concilium sufficit pro omnibus ad firmandam fidem huius ueritatis") and by Eck, *De primatu Petri* (Paris, 1521), fol. 25v. Here Eck explicitly names two authors, referred to also by Fisher: Flavio Biondi and Marco Vigerio Cardinal della Rovere, author of the *Decachord.* Fisher himself later mentions a book still extant, written in Greek and published at this council, which by its citations from the Greek Fathers and writers, caused the Greeks to yield on the matter of purgatory (*ibid.* art. 37, col. 726).

81. "Caeterum tametsi nequeat summus Pontifex, vna cum Concilio, hoc est, Ecclesia catholica, quicquam aut verum, aut falsum facere, ac proinde nouos articulos Fidei constituere, tamen quicquid hi nobis credendum tradiderint ceu Fidei articulum, id cunctos, vere Christianos, haud aliter quam articulum Fidei quendam, oportere credere" (*ibid.* art. 27, col. 583).

82. *Ibid.,* cols. 583–584. Fisher explicitly does not deny the right of an individual who thinks he has a better opinion, even different from the pope's, to present it to the council, provided he is not obstinate in its defense but willing to submit to the judgment of others (*ibid.* art. 29, col. 601).

83. *Ibid.* art. 28, cols. 591–593. Here, as before (art. 27, col. 583), the example is that of the dogma of transubstantiation as defined by Innocent III and Lateran Council IV. Fisher refers to this same definition in "Def. reg. assert." 4.8, *ibid.,* col. 164. In the latter work, he appeals also to the Council of Nice on the sacrificial nature of the mass (6.6, col. 196).

84. *Ibid.* art. 29, cols. 595–598. In this same article Fisher objects to Luther's deference to *Panormitanus* (Nicholas of Tudesco, 1386–1445) because the latter was learned only in canon law, not in theology. Even if

Panormitanus puts the council above the pope, nevertheless he admits: "Although power has been given to the pope and the whole Church, yet it has been bestowed on the pope as the head, whence the body ought to move itself at the direction of the head" (*ibid.,* col. 599). Thomas More does not place a general council above the pope; for, in the context of his letter to Cromwell, he is merely being cautious in his statement: "yit neuer thowght I the Pope aboue the generall counsaile" (*Correspondence,* p. 499).

85. "What the Church is . . . ," in "Supplication," in *Whole workes,* p. 247. A marginal gloss: "Roffensis contra Lutherum" (identified by the Editor as "Fisher Episcop. Roff. Opp. Wirceb. 1597. Assert. Luther. Confut. Art. XXIX. col. 597–8"), appears opposite the statement: "At any time (if some be believed) be the pope of Rome not present at such meetings, either *per se,* or *per legatum,* by himself or his legate, no council but must err," in Art. XXI, Proposition II ("General Councils may err"), in Thomas Rogers, *The Catholic Doctrine of the Church of England, an Exposition of the Thirty-Nine Articles,* ed. J. J. S. Perowne (Cambridge, 1854), pp. 207–208. Rogers' work was published in two parts in 1579 and 1585 (*ibid.,* p. x).

86. "Def. reg. assert." 3.10, *Opera,* col. 135.

87. "Dicimus praeterea licere cuipiam generali concilio nonnihil e Christi institutis ob vrgentes causas immutare, quemadmodum & primis ipsis licuit ecclesiae proceribus qui baptismi formam immutarunt, longe aliter quam instituerat eam Christus" (*ibid.* 3.18, col. 144). The reference most probably is not merely to the substitution of pouring or sprinkling for immersion in the rite of baptism but also to the words. See "Assert. Luth. confut." art. 16, cols. 471–472. Appealing to Fisher on this power of the Church, Cochlaeus declares that, even if communion under both species were clearly contained in Scripture (which it is not), the Church could change this precept for good reasons, as in the case of the Sabbath, circumcision, abstinence from blood, form for baptism, etc. ("XXV. Rationes quod Ecclesia possit Laicis venerabile Sacramentum sub vna tantum specie dare," Ratio 16, in *Fasciculus calumniarum . . . ,* fol. 78ᵛ). For Fisher's influence on Dietenberger in this regard, see H. Wedewer, *Johannes Dietenberger* (Freiburg, 1888), p. 241.

88. *Heretickes,* sig. F2.

89. Camb. Univ. Lib. MS. 1315, p. 18.

90. "Responsum," foll. 231–234; Harpsfield, *Divorce,* pp. 59–62; *Censurae,* sig. C2ᵛ–3ᵛ; and *Determinations,* foll. 36ᵛ–37ᵛ. Toledo II is quoted also in another book on the divorce, P.R.O.S.P.1/67, foll. 195ᵛ–196.

91. *Correspondence,* p. 498.

92. Lewis, *Fisher,* I, iv, quoting Morison's *Apomaxis calumniarum, conuitiorumque, quibus Iohannes Coclaeus . . . Henrici octaui . . . famam impetere . . . epistola studuit* (London, 1537), fol. 76. Foll. 74–91, 94ᵛ–95, level attacks against More and Fisher.

93. "In Lutherum," 1.10, *Opera,* fol. 68ᵛ, tr. Bridgett, *Fisher,* pp. 138–139. More is referring not to Fisher's sermon against Luther or his *Defense of the Royal Assertion,* but to his *Confutation of Luther's Assertion,* because only the *Confutation* has the reference to the Council of Florence ("Assert.

Luth. confut." art. 25, *Opera,* cols. 543–544). Important words in Eugene IV's bull "Laetentur coeli," July 6, 1439, are: "hoc sacro universali approbante Florentino Concilio" (Mansi, *Concilia,* XXXI, 1030). This decree had been used by Cardinal Cajetan in *De divina institutione pontificatus Romani Pontificis* (Rome, 1521; ed. F. Lauchert, Münster, Aschendorff, 1925, p. 99), "Hoc unum concilium sufficit pro omnibus"—"This one council suffices for all of them."

94. *Adv. haer.* 12, fol. 205ᵛ: "Rem eandem optime pertractat Ioannes Roffensis articulo vigesimoquinto assertionis quam fecit pro Lutheri damnatione."

95. "De summo pontifice," praef., *Controv.,* ed. 1615, I, 192; lib. 2, cap. 12, *ibid.,* I, 245. In lib. 3, cap. 21, Bellarmine denies, against Flacius Illyricus' lying implication, that Fisher, Eck, Cochlaeus, Latomus, Driedo, Tapper, Soto, and other learned men ever received a farthing from the pope in reward for the defense of the papacy (*ibid.,* I, 301).

96. *Early Statutes of Christ's College,* ed. Rackham, pp. 44–45; *Early Statutes of St. John,* ed. Mayor, pp. 4, 263, 351.

97. *Early Statutes of Christ's College,* ed. Rackham, pp. 70–73, 84–85; *Early Statutes of St. John,* ed. Mayor, pp. 20, 24, 60, 64, 70, 76, 287, 289–290, 306, 308, 363–364, 373. Rackham observes for Christ's College: "No such bond was prescribed for the Proctor of God's House," which was the predecessor of Christ's College (p. 145n).

98. *Eversio,* sigg. Y4–a6. Jerome's letter to Damasus on the papacy is quoted also against Luther ("Def. reg. assert." 3.16, *Opera,* col. 143).

99. "Luther," *Eng. Works,* pp. 315–321, Lat. tr., *Opera,* cols. 1377–79. Fisher's arguments are not unusual at the time. On Aaron as a type of Peter, see Powell, *Propugnaculum summi sacerdotij euangelici,* foll. 9ᵛ–11. On the payment of tribute, see Eck, *De primatu Petri,* foll. 73–75ᵛ.

100. "Obedience," *Treatises,* pp. 207–208. In "A Prologue into the Second Book of Moses, Called Exodus," Tyndale describes the love of Moses for his people and adds: "And make not Moses a figure of Christ, with Rochester; but an ensample unto all princes, and to all that are in authority, how to rule unto God's pleasure and unto their neighbor's profit. For there is not a perfecter life in this world . . . than to rule christianly. And of Aaron also see that thou make no figure of Christ, until he come unto his sacrificing; but an ensample unto all preachers of God's word, that they add nothing unto God's word, or take ought therefrom" (*ibid.,* p. 412).

101. "Obedience," *ibid.,* p. 209. In the incident of the golden calf (or bull), "there Aaron representeth all false preachers, and namely . . . the pope; which in like manner maketh us believe in a bull, as the bishop of Rochester full well allegeth the place in his sermon" (*ibid.*).

102. *Ibid.,* pp. 189–190. Gardiner in "The Oration of True Obedience" (1535) declares that men now understand the true meaning of the Petrine texts, including "the payeng of tribute money for him" (*solutionis didragmatis pro eodem*) (*Obedience,* ed. Janelle, pp. 156–157, with footnote referring to Fisher's use of the proof). In "The Reply of the Bishop of Sarum to the

Letter above Written [by Dr. Cole]," in Jewel, *Works,* ed. J. Ayre (Cambridge, 1845–50), I, 77, the marginal gloss *Roffensis* appears opposite the words: "Christ said unto Peter, *Solve pro me et te:* 'Pay the tribute money for me and thee:' *Ergo,* The pope is head of the church." Both Gardiner's and Jewel's target seems to be Peter's fifth prerogative in Fisher's "Assert. Luth. confut." art. 25, *Opera,* col. 532.

103. "Obedience," *Treatises,* pp. 215–217. Tyndale adds: "As the manner is to call Tully chief of orators for his singular eloquence, and Aristotle chief of philosophers, and Virgil chief of poets, for their singular learning, and not for any authority that they had over other; so was it the manner to call Peter chief of the apostles for his singular activity and boldness, and not that he should be lord over his brethren, contrary to his own doctrine" (*ibid.,* pp. 216–217). For Tyndale, Paul is the apostle *par excellence:* "Yet compare that chief apostle [Peter] unto Paul, and he is found a great way inferior . . ." (*ibid.*).

104. *Ibid.,* pp. 217–218. Tyndale prefers "the faithful exposition of Bede" (*ibid.,* p. 218).

105. *Ibid.,* p. 220.

106. "Luther," *Eng. Works,* p. 321, Lat. tr., *Opera,* cols. 1379–80. See much the same explanation in "Ver. corp." 1.25, *Opera,* col. 825. Faced with the same difficulty later, Richard Hooker explains: "It is neither monstrous nor as much as uncomely for a church to have different heads . . ." ("Of the Laws of Ecclesiastical Polity," 8.4.7, *Works,* ed. J. Keble, rev. R. W. Church and F. Paget [Oxford, 1888], III, 384).

107. "Luther," *Eng. Works,* p. 343, Lat. tr., *Opera,* col. 1389. John Jewel, Bishop of Salisbury (d. 1571), refers to this statement in "Reply to M. Harding's Answer," art. 4: "And so Roffensis saith: 'The church is one, not because of Christ, but because of the pope that keepeth it in one' " (*Works,* I, 377). Fisher's view is found expressed at least two centuries earlier in James of Viterbo: "Igitur ecclesiastica communitas una est, cuius unitatem Dominus monstrare volens, unum prefecit ecclesie, scilicet Petrum" (*De reg. christ.* 1.3, ed. Arquillière, p. 117).

108. "Obedience," *Treatises,* pp. 211–212. Tyndale also derides Fisher's supposition that, just as Luther has burnt the decretals, so also he would burn "the popes holynes & his fauourers" if he had them in his power: "A like argument, which I suppose to be rather true, I make: Rochester and his holy brethren have burnt Christ's testament; in evident sign, verily, that they would have burnt Christ himself also, if they had had him!" (*ibid.,* p. 221, with reference to Fisher, "Luther," *Eng. Works,* pp. 344–345, Lat. tr., *Opera,* col. 1390).

109. *Sermon,* sig. A8. Matthew continues: "But I am ryghte sure, that manye thousandes are saued, whiche neuer harde of Peter, not yet of the bishop of Rome: so that the vnitie of Christis church consisteth not in the knowlege of any erthely creature: but in the knowlege of Christe and true beleue in hym" (*ibid.*).

110. On the progress of this war in 1522–23, see Brewer, *Henry VIII,* I,

451–510, and, more briefly, J. D. Mackie, *The Earlier Tudors: 1485–1558* (Oxford: Clarendon Press, 1952), pp. 312–314. The first edition of *Convulsio* is dated October 30, 1522, that of *Assert. Luth. confut.* January 2, 1523, both at Antwerp, but both soon followed by publication in Paris in 1523.

111. "Convulsio," pref. ep., *Opera*, p. 1299.

112. *Ibid.*, cols. 1300–1303. Fisher refers to the Venerable Bede as "supputator temporum exactissimus" (*ibid.*, col. 1343; cf. col. 1349) and as "sui temporis eruditissimus" (col. 1351). Velenus again mentions Platina twice in *Cavillus* 3 (col. 1352).

113. *Ibid.*, cols. 1344–45. If Joannes Baptista is Mantuan, the reference is to *De suorum temporum calamitatibus* (1489), known also as *De mundi calamitatibus,* and *De sacris diebus* (1516), known better as *Fastorum libri duodecim.*

114. *Ibid.*, cols. 1359–61; cf. cols. 1344–45.

115. ". . . manifestissimum est . . . quod epistolae dictae, vel eruditissimorum censura, negantur a Paulo Senecaque conscriptae. Testatur hoc in primis Erasmus, cuius vnius in hac parte iudicium, aduersus alios mille, mihi sufficeret" (*ibid.*, col. 1330).

116. *Ibid.*, cols. 1369–71. In the *Defense of the Royal Assertion,* Fisher repeats that the Churches founded by Paul, John, James, Matthew, Barnabas, etc., have vanished or become schismatical or heretical: "Retinet igitur sola illa Christianorum successio, quae a Petro defluxit, ecclesiae nomenclaturam" ("Def. reg. assert." 3.16, *ibid.*, col. 143). This same argument is interestingly handled in rhetorical fashion in the sermon at Barnes's abjuration (*Heretickes,* sigg. E4–F1), e.g., "Thus than ye se whiche is the good erthe: I say the multitude of christen people / whiche hitherto by a continuall succession was deriuied [*sic*] from the see of Peter." The notion of succession entered into the discussion at Trent in 1562 on episcopal jurisdiction where the views of the Bishop of Rochester were produced at least thrice (*Concilium Tridentinum,* IX, 58, 120, 177). For Luther's view of succession, see Headley, *Luther's Church History,* pp. 100–101.

117. *Apologia,* sigg. A4–B1v. Hessus' *Apologia* contains many echoes of Luther's works.

118. *Apologia,* sigg. B4v–C1; cf. Fisher, "Convulsio," pref. ep., *Opera,* p. 1299, and cols. 1302–1303.

119. *Apologia,* sig. C2v; cf. Fisher, "Convulsio," *Opera,* cols. 1304–1305.

120. *Apologia,* sig. C3–4.

121. Quoted in Lewis, *Fisher,* I, 340–341 (cf. Frith, *Purgatorye,* ed. 1533, sig. L7). Cf. Fisher, "Assert. Luth. confut." art. 21, *Opera,* cols. 507, 510. As Fisher himself points out, his proof is given in Article 17, *ibid.*, cols. 488–492. Gabriel Biel at first had denied, subject to determination by the Church, that the pope's jurisdiction extended to the dead because otherwise he would "empty purgatory by issuing plenary indulgences"; but, after a clarification by Sixtus IV, Biel later "declares purgatory . . . to fall under the jurisdiction of the Pope; the Pope cannot empty purgatory since he liberates only those for whom a work of piety has been performed. Not a

lack of love on the part of the Pope, but on the part of the faithful keeps the deceased in purgatory" (Oberman, *Medieval Theology,* p. 405).

122. "Assert. Luth. confut." art. 25, *Opera,* cols. 530–580. Fisher does not wish to leave the impression that the Fathers always and unanimously interpreted the Rock as Peter — a fault attributed to John Eck (Pelikan, *Luther the Expositor,* p. 115). For Luther's interpretation of the Rock as faith or Christ Himself and his lifelong teaching that "Peter was the first in honor in the entire world," see *ibid.,* pp. 115–117. Eck's answer to the objections from Peter's denial of Christ and from Paul's resistance to Peter was "a distinction between Peter the man and his apostolic office, a distinction which Luther also employed throughout his own exegesis" (*ibid.,* p. 117).

123. There are citations from Tertullian, Cyprian, and Origen, e.g., *Opera,* cols. 540, 543, 550, 553, 554, 559–560. For Luther's "frequent recourse to the fathers for his view of the early Church," especially "the equality of all bishops by divine law," see Headley, *Luther's Church History,* pp. 172–174. Fisher declares that he could summon also Bede, Bernard, Rabanus, Remigius, Hugh, and Richard, and countless others, but the Latin Fathers he has already cited are "far more esteemed" (*longe spectatiores*) (col. 541). Later he defends Thomas Aquinas, called "the Flower of Theology" by the most scholarly and learned men, for his Petrine and papal interpretation of the Rock by supporting it by citations from Jerome and Augustine ("Def. reg. assert." 2.18, *Opera,* cols. 129–130).

124. *Ibid.,* col. 545.

125. *Ibid.,* col. 547.

126. *Ibid.,* col. 550. "For there must be in the Church superiority and the authority to command. And if such authority be granted to any, most of all is it proper for it to belong to the supreme pontiff" ("Sacerd. def." 3.30, *ibid.,* col. 1290, tr. Hallett, p. 124). Like Fisher, the German humanist, Rudolf Agricola was "a most obedient and devoted son of the medieval church," who propounds "a papal solution to all the problems confronting Christendom" (Spitz, *German Humanists,* p. 36). See Torquemada, *Ecclesia* 2.107: "Quod ad romanum pontificem pertineat determinare ea que fidei sunt & sacre scripture sensus interpretari: atque aliorum patrum ecclesie dicta vel opuscula approbare vel reprobare" (sig. v4–5^{v}).

127. *Opera,* cols. 563–569. On Luther's rejection of "the Jewish cultic community as the prototype of the Christian priesthood," see Headley, *Luther's Church History,* pp. 135–136.

128. *Opera,* col. 562. Fisher does not condemn the act but simply says that the judges were influenced by the truth alone (*sola veritate permoti*) because Hus was obstinate in the face of Holy Scripture and the agreement of exegetes and was tenacious of his error on the Blessed Sacrament, "ob quem errorem, etiam te iudice, vel emendandus vel condemnandus esset" (*ibid.*). For Luther's views on John Hus and the Council of Constance, see Headley, *Luther's Church History,* pp. 225–231.

129. *Opera,* col. 544.

130. *Ibid.,* col. 537. In the frescoes in Siena, Pinturicchio has immortalized Pius' death at Ancona (1464) after a vain wait for the Venetian fleet which was to take him abroad.

131. "Faciat nec ne summus Pontifex ea, quae caput & pastorem deceant, alienum est ab instituto nostro . . . Nec defensionem scelerum (si quibus abundat Romana curia) iam ipsi meditamur . . ." (*Opera,* col. 549).

132. *Ibid.,* cols. 555–556; cf. col. 558. "Et quem ex vniuersa mihi dabis Ecclesia, qui non etiam interim peccato succubuerit?" (col. 556). See also col. 571: "Sed & quis tam confirmatus est, vt nunquam peccet mortaliter?"

133. *Ibid.,* cols. 571–572 (cf. art. 33, cols. 641–642).

134. *Ibid.* art. 25, col. 573.

135. *Ibid.,* col. 579. In the *Defense of the Royal Assertion,* Fisher declares that incrimination of the pope has always been the habit of heretics: Arius, Novatus, Nestorius, Donatus, and others, in the past, and now Luther at present ("Def. reg. assert." 2.13, *ibid.,* col. 124). Henry VIII was in the right to castigate a tongue raving against the power which no orthodox Christian doubts "was constituted by God" (*a Deo constitutam esse* [*ibid.* 2.16, col. 127]).

136. "Assert. Luth. confut." art. 33, cols. 637–638. Luther sees Savonarola as living "not by the order of preachers but by the common order of Christians" (Headley, *Luther's Church History,* p. 212). Relying upon Nauclerus' account, Cochlaeus finally concludes to the justice of Savonarola's condemnation: "Nescio quidem qua de causa damnatus ab Alexandro papa sexto sit Hieronymus ille Sauonorola [*sic*], iuste ne secundum Canones, an ui & potentia iniuste sit diiudicatus, Quis enim omnia singulorum pontificum facta iustificet? nam & ipsi homines sunt, qui peccant, unus plus alio, non enim omnes aeque boni aut mali. . . Ne uero putes ex his me uel timore, uel adulatione Hieronymum illum non laudare, dico tibi, quod de hypocrisi prophetandique impostura eum insimulari audiui ab ijs qui cum illo fuerant conuersati, vere ne an falso, quid ad me, aut ad te? Quid fecerit igitur, nescio, acta iudicij non uidi. Non tamen iniuste damnatum existimo, quamlibet ingeniosus fuerit & disertus. Quod si uera sunt, quod de hoc uiro refert in Chronicis Nauclerus Tubingensis [uol. ij gñatione, 1.], non solum non iniuste, sed etiam iustissime fuit damnatus" (*De Petro et Roma aduersus Velenum Lutheranum libri quatuor* [Cologne, 1525], p. 4). Erasmus contributed a commendatory letter to the first edition of Nauclerus, *Memorabilium omnis aetatis et omnium gentium chronici commentarii,* Tübingen, T. Anshelm, 1516 (Erasmus, *Ep.,* II, 221, introd.). Nauclerus (John Verge, or Vergenhaus, 1428?–1510) was Professor of Canon Law and Chancellor of the new University of Tübingen (*ibid.,* 222n).

137. "Assert. Luth. confut." art. 33, *Opera,* col. 643.

138. *Ibid.* art. 34, cols. 647–649. Platina is later quoted on the achievements of such popes as Sylvester I, Leo I, John I, Agapetus I, and Gregory I (*ibid.,* cols. 652–653). For another reference to Luther's objection to Roman exploitation of "your Germans," see art. 40, *ibid.,* col. 740, but Luther's shortsightedness deprives the souls in purgatory of help and the living Ger-

mans of merit. See also "Def. reg. assert." 11.11, ratio 1, *ibid.*, col. 245, where the Germans are said to think the Romans wolves because of their lust for gold, but where heretics like Luther are called far worse wolves because of their lust for blood, i.e., for souls.

139. *Ibid.*, cols. 651–642.

140. *Ibid.*, col. 653. Fisher's prophecy, like that of many others, was considered fulfilled in the sack of Rome in 1527. It is quoted among other prophecies by Raynaldus, *Annales ecclesiastici,* XX (Cologne, 1694), n. 2, p. 492. On the theoretical aspect of papal reform, see Torquemada, *Ecclesia* 2.105: "De remedijs contra papam moribus suis prauis scandalizantem ecclesiam" (sig. v3–4).

141. "Assert. Luth. confut." art. 36, *Opera,* cols. 710–711. Cf. the following: "Quid si Romani viatoribus imponant? Num propterea Christus per sua sacramenta nobis imposuisse credendus est?" ("Ver. corp." 1.15, *ibid.*, col. 801). Besides, many Christians have begun a new life because invited and incited to it by papal documents (*ibid.* 1.22, col. 817).

CHAPTER V: FISHER'S CHURCH AND HENRY'S STATE

1. Ortroy, *Fisher,* X, 339, 341n.

2. "Margaret," *Eng. Works,* p. 301.

3. *LP,* I, 2nd ed., no. 1, p. 2. For other mention of Fisher, see nos. 19–20, pp. 12, 20–21.

4. *Ibid.*, no. 153, p. 74; Rymer, *Foedera,* XIII, 261.

5. *Henry VIII,* I, 53n. See W. H. Dunham, "The Members of Henry VIII's Whole Council, 1507–1527," *Eng. Hist. Rev.*, LIX (1944), 198, n. 1, and Table II, p. 208, for Fisher's attendance from November 14, 1509, to January 28, 1512. Dunham suspects that "Wolsey's position as 'the king's chief councillor' may have provoked some to stay away" (*ibid.*, 198).

6. For details, see Polydore Vergil, *Anglica historia,* tr. D. Hay (London: Royal Historical Society, 1950), pp. 304–309, and Reynolds, *Fisher,* pp. 98–100. On Foxe as "indeed a changed man," see Hughes, *Reformation,* I, 74–75.

7. Vergil, *Ang. hist.*, tr. Hay, pp. 306–307; *LP,* V, no. 120, p. 60; Ortroy, *Fisher,* X, 151–152, 344–347; Bayne, *Fisher,* pp. 72–73.

8. *Ang. hist.*, tr. Hay, pp. 334–335.

9. More, *Correspondence,* p. 111; *Selected Letters,* ed. E. F. Rogers (New Haven: Yale University Press, 1961), p. 94.

10. Psalms MS, P.R.O.S.P.2/R, foll. 194–195. The version applied to Christ is found *ibid.*, foll. 246–247.

11. "Psalms," *Eng. Works,* pp. 171–173, Lat. tr., *Opera,* cols. 1578–80.

12. "Margaret," *ibid.*, p. 308.

13. Castro, *Adv. haer.*, fol. 61ᵛ, and Suarez, *Opera omnia* (Paris, 1856–79), XII, 738. Suarez writes: "Dico tertio: bellum etiam aggressivum non est per

se malum, sed potest esse honestum et necessarium . . . Idem constat ex usu Ecclesiae, a Patribus et Pontificibus saepius approbato, prout omnia late congerit Roffensis, art. 4 [*leg.* 34] contra Lutherum . . ." ("De charitate," disp. 13, "De bello," sect. 1, "Utrum bellum sit intrinsece malum"). For Luther's attitude toward the Turk, see Headley, *Luther's Church History,* pp. 244–249.

14. "Assert. Luth. confut." art. 33, *Opera,* cols. 643–644.

15. *Ibid.* art. 34, cols. 645–651. The mysterious *Cassanus* is none other than *Usuncassanus,* "the prince of the Persians and Armenians," who was sought by Calixtus III as an ally because of the indifference of Western rulers and who ascribed his success against the Turks to the pope's prayers (Platina, *De vitis maximorum pontificum* [Venice, 1511], fol. 152). L. Pastor calls "Usunhassan, Prince of the Turcomans, the only one of the Eastern princes whose power could compare with that of the Sultan" (*History of Popes,* II, 408–409).

16. *LP,* VI, no. 1164, p. 486 (September 27, 1533); cf. no. 1249, p. 511 (October 10, 1533). See also *Span. Cal.,* IV, nos. 1130 and 1133, pp. 813, 821. For the defense of Fisher's proposal, consult Reynolds, *Fisher,* pp. 192–194, and Bridgett, *Fisher,* pp. 228–233.

17. W. M. Southgate, *John Jewel and the Problem of Doctrinal Authority* (Cambridge, Mass.: Harvard University Press, 1962), p. 116, citing E. S. Abbott *et al., Catholicity* (Westminster, 1947), p. 49. Southgate comments: "To Sir Thomas More and John Fisher the assumption of an authority of such magnitude [both constitutional and doctrinal] was unsupportable" (*ibid.*). As for the German Reformation, Spitz declares: "Two major themes dominated the concerns of the German humanists, romantic cultural nationalism and religious enlightenment, and both were of tremendous importance to the Reformation movement itself" (*German Humanists,* p. 2). See also C. W. Dugmore, *The Mass and the English Reformers* (London: Macmillan, 1958), p. 84.

18. *LP,* IV, no. 3232, pp. 1471–72.

19. There are two versions of the speech and the defense, one by Edward Hall, the other by the anonymous biographer. See Ortroy, *Fisher,* X, 337–341, 341–342n; Bridgett, *Fisher,* pp. 183–189; and Reynolds, *Fisher,* pp. 167–171. The biographer's account of the apology is more romantic and heroic: to Henry, Fisher "answered againe that (beinge in counsell) he spake his mind in defence and right of the Church, whom he saw dayly iniured and oppressed amonge the comon people, whose office was not to deale with her . . ." (Ortroy, *Fisher,* X, 341). Yet, in view of all that he had written about the clergy in his controversies with Protestants, this version should not be discounted absolutely.

20. Bridgett, *Fisher,* pp. 189–190.

21. *Sermons and Remains,* ed. G. E. Corrie (Cambridge, 1845), p. 301.

22. Ortroy, *Fisher,* X, 342–344. Ortroy points out that the author of the first English version refers the fable rather to the bills in Commons on probate, etc. (*ibid.,* 148). L. B. Smith asserts: "The parable must then have been

given in 1524 [*leg.* 1523] when Wolsey met with considerable opposition in his efforts to get Convocation to sanction the dissolution of several small houses, the profits from which the Cardinal intended to use in the building and endowing of his new college at Oxford" (*Tudor Prelates and Politics, 1536–1558* [Princeton University Press, 1953], p. 272, n. 51). The interpretation is unlikely since Fisher followed just this procedure to finance St. John's at Cambridge and actually assisted Wolsey in his similar project at Oxford.

23. *LP,* IV, no. 2396, p. 1069; also no. 6075 (19), p. 2713.

24. See Reynolds, *Fisher,* pp. 50–51; Bridgett, *Fisher,* pp. 28–30.

25. "The Defence of the Apology," Part V, *Works,* ed. Ayre, IV, 800. According to Jewel, Fisher's and Wolsey's reason, a need for reform among monks and friars, was valid also for Henry VIII's suppression of the abbeys (*ibid.,* 800–801). On earlier precedents in England, see G. Constant, *The Reformation in England,* tr. R. E. Scantlebury, I (New York, 1934), 141–145.

26. See Ortroy, *Fisher,* X, 357–365, and especially the documents in the Appendix, XII, 270–280; likewise, Hughes, *Reformation,* I, 229–232, with the account of Tunstal's perceptive opposition even to Fisher's clause. Fisher's "early biographer . . . may have assigned too dominant a role to John Fisher but this account explains the delay . . . between the grant of the money and the grant of the title" (Reynolds, *Fisher,* p. 178, n. 2).

27. *LP,* V, no. 112, p. 50.

28. *Span. Cal.,* IV, no. 883.

29. Reynolds, *Fisher,* p. 187, citing Friedmann, *Anne Boleyn,* I, 142.

30. Ortroy, *Fisher,* XII, 158–159. One should not neglect the information on Fisher's trial and death in the letters of Erasmus, *Ep.,* XI, 262–263, 373–374 (The *Expositio fidelis*).

31. Lewis, *Fisher,* Coll. No. 35, II, 359; Ortroy, *Life,* XII, 184. In Barnes's letter to Henry VIII in his *Supplication,* opposite the section about bishops swearing allegiance to Rome, there is the following marginal note: "Byshop Fisher otherwise called B. of Rochester, answered that he was sworn to the Pope, and therefore hee woulde not sweare to the kinges supremacye" (*Whole workes,* p. 197).

32. The Pope's Brief to Francis I, July 26, 1535, in Gardiner, *Obedience,* ed. Janelle, pp. 12–13.

33. *Ibid.,* pp. 30–31.

34. Gardiner gives Fisher's imaginary complaint on this score if he were still alive: see *ibid.,* pp. 44–49. For Henry VIII's other agents in his justification and for the reaction on the Continent, see the brief account and notes in Constant, *Reformation,* I, 255–256. In spite of Gardiner's excuses during Queen Mary's time, "it remains far easier to suppose that in 1535 Gardiner accepted the whole royalist position and really believed what he wrote" (Dickens, *Reformation,* p. 174). But by 1553, for Gardiner as for others, "the original insistence of More and Fisher that the Roman primacy was essential to maintain purity of doctrine and the integrity of the Church had by then been unmistakably vindicated, above all by the confusions and bleak op-

portunism which passed for reform under Edward VI" (McConica, *English Humanists,* p. 236).

35. Constant, *Reformation,* I, 200. "Reginald Pole shows a more active form of resistance. The three of them were the most famous champions of Catholic unity against Henry VIII" (*ibid.*). An account of Fisher is given *ibid.,* 200–223.

36. Reynolds, *Fisher,* pp. 239–240, citing *Documents Illustrative of English Church History,* ed. H. Gee and W. J. Hardy (1896), p. 244.

37. *LP,* VIII, no. 856, pp. 325–331.

38. ". . . facile fiet modo scripturis sane intellectis, quisquis suam conscientiam studuerit conformare. Nam in lege dei nemo relinquitur perplexus modo seipsum cupiat explicari" ("Responsum," foll. 337v–338). Cf. *Censurae,* sig. Q3v, and *Determinations,* fol. 152.

39. *LP,* VII, no. 136, p. 52; Lewis, *Fisher,* Coll. No. 39, II, 402.

40. Ortroy, *Fisher,* XII, 136–137 and n. 1, 150.

41. More, *Correspondence,* pp. 516–517, 520–521.

42. Harpsfield–Hitchcock, *Moore,* pp. 186–187; "Expositio fidelis," Erasmus, *Ep.,* XI, 370–371; Harpsfield, *Divorce,* pp. 222–223; Lewis, *Fisher,* Coll. No. 41, II, 411; *LP,* VIII, no. 996, pp. 394–395. Fisher's answers, summarized in *LP,* VIII, no. 858, are given in full in Reynolds' *Fisher,* pp. 267–270.

43. *Acts and Monuments,* 3rd ed. rev. Josiah Pratt (London, 1870), IV, 182. After being tried at Canterbury, Browne was burned at Ashford. See also Thomson, *Later Lollards,* pp. 184–185, 188 and n. 3.

44. More mentions the examination of Hitton "by the reuerende father the bishop of Rochester" ("Confutation," pref., *Works,* col. 345). See the brief notice: "Thomas Hitten, burned at Maidstone, A.D. 1530. Persecuted by William Warham, Archbishop of Canterbury, and by Fisher, Bishop of Rochester," in J. Foxe, *Acts and Monuments,* eds. G. Townsend and S. R. Cattley (London, 1837–41), IV, 619. For Bilney's career, see *ibid.,* IV, 619–656; Loane, *Masters of English Reformation,* pp. 1–42; and for an excellent brief account, Dickens, *Reformation,* pp. 79–81. The "Interrogatories" and "Bilney's Answers" are to be found in *Acts,* IV, 624–626.

45. "Quid aliud iam vulgo tractatur quam vana Lutheri dogmata falseque libertates ac licentiae quas ipse molitur asserere: *vana locuti sunt*" (Ps. 11, Psalms MS, P.R.O.S.P.2/R, fol. 174). Later Fisher represents the heretics as saying: "Nos neque papae, neque Episcoporum superioritatem agnoscemus. omnia nostra sunt. Nos autem christi preter quem dominum habemus neminem: *quis noster dominus est.* Papa, Caesar, pontifices, Reges, longa tyrannide plebem oppresserunt & per vim contra ius & phas vsurparunt sibi principatum: *propter miseriam inopum & gemitum pauperum*" (*ibid.,* fol. 174v, with slight punctuation added).

46. "Luther," *Eng. Works,* p. 340, Lat. tr., *Opera,* col. 1388. For Luther's views of "the Persecutions," see Headley, *Luther's Church History,* pp. 143–155, which touches also on the medieval periodization of history (p. 146).

47. *Heretickes,* sig. E3v.

48. Psalms MS, P.R.O.S.P.2/R, e.g., Ps. 17, foll. 186, 188^{v}, 240, 242; Ps. 20, fol. 195; Ps. 23, foll. 202, 254; Ps. 45, foll. 92, 94.

49. This statement is followed by Plato's dictum: "Tum beatas fore respublicas quando aut philosophi regnent aut reges philosophentur" ("Luther," *Eng. Works,* p. 327, Lat. tr. Pace, *Opera,* col. 1382, where the mood is changed: *regnent* to *regnant,* and *philosophentur* to *philosophantur*). Cochlaeus asks: "Si Rex [Angliae] ipse (ut nuper audiui) contra Lutherum scripsit, quid facturum putes ipsum, ubi pestem eiusmodi in regno suo usquam reperiret?" (*De Petro et Roma,* lib. 1, p. 11).

50. "Luther," *Eng. Works,* pp. 340–341, Latin tr., *Opera,* cols. 1388, 1390.

51. "Assert. Luth. confut." art. 33, *Opera,* cols. 633–644. Cf. also Luther: "Compendium illud laboris nobis placet, ut non haereses aut errores destruamus, sed haereticos et errantes concrememus, . . . immo contra voluntatem spiritus . . ." ("Resolutiones disputationum de indulgentiarum virtute," *WA,* I, 624–625).

52. "Assert. Luth. confut." art. 33, *Opera,* cols. 633–635. Cf. Ruard Tapper: ". . . imo & necessario sunt decretae, postquam docente experientia citra mortis supplicium, eorum [i.e., haereticorum] contagio aliorumque subuersio cohiberi non poterat, vt docet sanctus Christi martyr Ioannes episcopus Roffensis" (*Explicatio articulorum . . . circa dogmata ecclesiastica* [Louvain, 1565], II, 183, with marginal reference to Article 33).

53. "Assert. Luth. confut." art. 33, *Opera,* cols. 639–640. The reference to capital punishment for thieves seems almost like a distant echo of the lawyer's case in *Utopia,* ed. E. Surtz and J. H. Hexter (The Yale Edition of the Complete Works of St. Thomas More, vol. IV; New Haven: Yale University Press, 1965), pp. 60–61.

54. "Assert. Luth. confut." art. 33, *Opera,* cols. 640–642. Fisher, as has been seen, is not alone in his severity, in spite of Acton's judgment: "Death for the sake of conscience has surrounded the memory of Fisher with imperishable praise; but at that time he was the one writer among our countrymen who had crudely avowed the conviction that there is no remedy for religious error but fire and steel; and the sanction of his fame was already given to the Bloody Statute, and to a century of persecution and of suffering more cruel than his own" (unsigned review of *Letters and Papers,* vol. IV, in *Quarterly Review,* CXLIII [1877], 25). As for the Marian persecution, "the chief Spanish agent is likely to have been the Observant Alfonso y [*leg.* de] Castro, who before coming over with Philip in 1554 had written two methodical books concerning the theory and practice of persecuting heretics" (Dickens, *Reformation,* p. 265). Castro cites Fisher several times in his writing.

55. *Heretickes,* sigg. A3^{v}, B4^{v}, E1, F2^{v}–3.

56. *Ibid.,* sig. H2–3. The Vulgate gives *in reprobum sensum* (Rom. 1:28).

57. "Ver. corp." 1.praef., *Opera,* p. 748. "O Germaniae populus infelicissimus, qui talibus magistris adeo secum pugnantibus, suas animas tam secure credit" (2.14, col. 868). "Vtinam igitur aliquando tandem Germania suos oculos recipiat, & aduertat cuiusmodi falsis hypocritis, & meris impostoribus,

suas animas cum summo discrimine iam diu crediderunt" (5.9, cols. 1158–59).

58. Reynolds, *Fisher,* p. 109, citing the dedicatory epistle to Eck's *De sacrificio missae;* "Ver. corp." 1.praef., *Opera,* p. 748; *Heretickes,* sig. E1. Three years after Fisher's death, Eck was still harking back to his English visit: "At Episcopus Roffensis sanctae memoriae (cujus viri et Thomae Mori gratia me adiisse Angliam, et eorum usum colloquio, mensa et hospitio non immerito glorior) Johannes Fisherus" (*Super Aggaeo Propheta Jo. Eckii commentarius* [Salingiaci, 1538], fol. 58, quoted in More, *Neue Briefe,* ed. Schulte Herbrüggen, p. 53, n. 15).

59. A. W. Reed, "The Regulation of the Book Trade before the Royal Proclamation of 1538," *Transactions of the Bibliographical Society,* XV (1917–19), 162–163. In Tunstal's "Second Monition to the Booksellers" on October 25, 1526, the Bishop of Rochester's name is omitted (*ibid.,* 170).

60. *Heretickes,* sig. B4v.

CHAPTER VI: TRADITION AND TRADITIONS

1. "Magdal." lib. 1, 3, *Opera,* cols. 1407, 1447. The predilection of Fisher for Augustine continues through his career. A rapid survey indicates that Augustine is quoted almost twice as much as Jerome, the nearest Father. Chrysostom would seem to come next; and then Cyprian, Ambrose, Origen, and Tertullian follow.

2. *Eversio,* sig. B2.

3. *Ibid.,* sig. B2v–4v.

4. *Ibid.,* sigg. D4–G3v.

5. *Ibid.,* sigg. G4–H4v, L1–2. Cf. other seemingly derogatory but actually cautious statements about the limitations of these Fathers: "Proinde neque Origenes in hoc negocio audiendus est cuius rationes, vtpote nullius momenti a plerisque saepius confutatae sunt. Sed neque Ambrosius . . ." (sig. C2); and: "Cecutierunt igitur in hac parte priores treis, nempe Chrysostomus, Origenes, & Ambrosius" (sig. I1).

6. *Ibid.,* sig. Z5v.

7. *Ibid.,* sig. a2.

8. *Confut. sec. discept.,* foll. 14–16.

9. Fisher, "Luther," *Eng. Works,* pp. 318–321, Lat. tr., *Opera,* cols. 1378–79. The reader will recall how Tyndale challenges Fisher's witnesses on this point and declares that "never one knew of any authority that one bishop should have above another" ("Obedience," *Treatises,* pp. 215–216).

10. This citation of Origen, "of all heretics . . . the greatest," by Fisher "to stablish his blind ceremonies," is ridiculed by Tyndale in "Obedience," *Treatises,* p. 220. For Origen, see also "Assert. Luth. confut.," veritas 9, *Opera,* col. 293. See the discussion of Fisher's examples of tradition in J. R. Geiselmann, *Die Heilige Schrift und die Tradition* (Freiburg: Herder, 1962),

pp. 162–163. Fisher is mentioned by name by Lodovico Nogarola, a layman at the Council of Trent, who published *Apostolicae institutiones in parvum librum redactae* in Venice in 1549 (Geiselmann, pp. 164, 276). As for the Cabala, the present reference is perhaps the major one in Fisher's works. An over-all view hardly warrants the ascription to Fisher of any attempt to "erect the Cabala into a standard of faith next to Holy Writ" and on a par with the Fathers (G. H. Tavard, *Holy Writ or Holy Church: The Crisis of the Protestant Reformation* [London: Burns & Oates, 1959], pp. 74, 159–160). The analysis of Rabbi S. S. Schwarzschild is here pertinent: "For Jews, 'Scripture' is Torah, and Torah comprises not only the twenty-four books of the Hebrew canon but also the *torah shebe'al peh,* the Oral Torah, the Talmud and all its vast ramifications. The Written and the Oral Torah are . . . of one piece in Jewish teaching; they were both revealed together at Mount Sinai; they are of equal divine dignity; and Tradition — a synonym in Judaism for Talmudic teaching — if anything surpasses in authority the Bible itself. After all, it is Tradition (in Christianity incidentally as much as in Judaism) which determines what constitutes the canonical as over the uncanonical books of Scriptures" ("Judaism, Scriptures, and Ecumenism," in L. J. Swidler, ed., *Scripture and Ecumenism* [Pittsburgh: Duquesne University Press, 1965], pp. 123–124).

11. "Luther," *Eng. Works,* pp. 331–336, Lat. tr., *Opera,* cols. 1384–86. At this point, Fisher engages in a humorous sally: "Yf there were a fourthe persone in the trynyte. or another spyryte to be sente vnto vs from almighty god we myght yet be in some doute wheder Martyn luther had met with this spyryte by the waye and conueyed hym from vs" (*ibid.,* p. 336, Lat. tr., col. 1386).

12. *Ibid.,* pp. 337–338, Lat. tr., *Opera,* cols. 1386–87.

13. Hessus, *Apologia,* sig. C1v–3v. Jerome is inconsistent also about Adam's burying place, mentioning both Calvary and Hebron (sig. C2).

14. "De verbo Dei," lib. 4, cap. 1, *Controv.,* ed. 1615, I, 65: "Igitur scripsit de hoc argumento [de verbo dei non scripto, i.e., de traditionibus] praeclare . . . Episcopus Roffensis initio etiam sui operis contra assertionem articulorum Lutheri." Polman sees Bellarmine's achievement as the systematization and completion of the ideas of forerunners like Fisher on the obscurity of the Bible, the Church as authentic interpreter, and the existence of an unwritten revelation (*Élément historique,* p. 521).

15. "Assert. Luth. confut.," *Opera,* p. 272.

16. Tavard perceptively interprets this aspect of the teaching of Fisher and others on the Fathers as an extension of "the voice of prophecy" in the Church (*Holy Writ or Holy Church,* pp. 152–153). Basil, to whom Fisher merely refers on this truth, has a celebrated passage on "the interdependence and essential unity of Scripture and Tradition" (*De spiritu sancto,* 27; see J. Meyendorff, "The Meaning of Tradition," in Swidler, ed., *Scripture and Ecumenism,* p. 46).

17. *Opera,* cols. 278–290. "Si potuit interim caecutire, & errore teneri inter-

pres, quomodo nobis . . . erit exploratum, quando verum dixerit? Id nimirum fiet, mutua vel scripturarum ad ipsum, vel caeterorum interpretum, vel apostolicarum traditionum, vel generalium conciliorum, vel Ecclesiae Catholicae consuetudinum, vel demum horum omnium insimul facta collatione. Nam haec ita se mutuo fulciunt, vt quicquid ab aliquo scriptum fuerit interprete, modo vigilanter haec omnia sibi mutuo conferamus, facillime deprehendi posset, an verum an falsum fuerat, vt nihil oporteat propter aliquos in eis repertos errores, caetera contemnere, quae alioqui vere catholiceque tradiderunt" (*ibid.*, cols. 289–290).

18. *Ibid.*, cols. 290–296. Tracing the *partim-partim* or double-source doctrine to Traversari's Latin translation, Geiselmann exonerates Fisher of its acceptance and contrasts his views on apostolic tradition with those of Eck, Driedo, Cano, Cochlaeus, Castro, and Pigge (*Schrift und Tradition*, pp. 111–113, and "Das Konzil von Trient über das Verhältnis der Heiligen Schrift und der nicht geschriebenen Traditionen," in *Die mündliche Überlieferung*, ed. M. Schmaus [München: Max Hueber, 1957], pp. 140–147, 169–171, 175–176). On Holy Scripture as the principal source, and in the strictest sense the only source, of Catholic theology, see H. Küng, *Justification: The Doctrine of Karl Barth and a Catholic Reflection*, with a Letter by Karl Barth, tr. T. Collins *et al.* (New York: Thomas Nelson, 1964), pp. 110–122. Küng (pp. 113–117) makes four important remarks on tradition: (1) "To define tradition correctly as a *source of revelation*, we must eliminate all purely human and ecclesiastical traditions (apostolic as well as post-apostolic). Trent's only concern was with divine tradition as revealed by Jesus Christ or the Holy Spirit." (2) "Tradition is not simply co-ordinate with Sacred Scripture . . . It revolves around, in fact gravitates toward Sacred Scripture . . ." (3) "This tradition — carried forward by the total Church . . . through the power of the Holy Spirit — is deposited in the various ecclesiastical documents and monuments (creeds, papal, conciliar, and episcopal decisions, the . . . Fathers . . . and theologians . . .)." (4) "*Official* ecclesiastical doctrinal documents in particular represent an extremely valuable aid . . ." On the other hand, the Presbyterian theologian, Markus Barth, shows that "*Sola Scriptura* may do harm as well as good" ("Sola Scriptura," in Swidler, ed., *Scripture and Ecumenism*, p. 93; see pp. 75–94).

19. *Opera*, prooem. Luth. confut., col. 307; art. 2, col. 362; art. 5, col. 385; art. 25, cols. 559–560; art. 27, cols. 584–585. Art. 37, col. 718, reads: "Et quoniam scriptura sacra, conclaue quoddam est omnium veritatum, quae Christianis scitu necessariae sunt, nemini potest ambiguum esse quin purgatorij veritas in ipsa contineatur, & quin ex ipsa quoque probari possit." Cf. Swidler: "Father George Tavard and other Catholic theologians of a like mind say no, that all dogmas *must* be in Scripture somehow. Yet, we cannot reject the infallible teaching of the Church, the *magisterium*. Hence, they insist, we must believe, pray and work so that some day we will be able to see *how* these dogmas are in Scripture" (*Scripture and Ecumenism*, Introd., p. 1.). At his formal repudiation of purgatory in 1530, Luther declares

that "the dear fathers have made a number of ill-advised but well-meaning utterances which were never intended to be taken as absolutely authoritative"; witness Gregory I on purgatory (Headley, *Luther's Church History,* p. 172; cf. *WA* 30/2:380–385). For a brief history of Luther's opinion on purgatory, with its relationship to "Luther's fundamental Law-Gospel theology of salvation," see T. M. McDonough, *The Law and the Gospel in Luther* (Oxford: Oxford University Press, 1963), pp. 110–111, n. 3. Because "Luther's illustrious antagonists: Fisher, Eck, Clichtove, and Castro" have shown the Church's doctrine on purgatory and indulgences to be consonant with apostolic and patristic teachings, the influential Spanish theologian, Andrés Vega (1490?–1560?), declares it superfluous for himself to discuss these points (*De iustificatione doctrina vniuersa,* lib. XIII, cap. 29 [Cologne, 1572; repub. Ridgewood, N.J.: Gregg Press, 1964], p. 605). Vega's work, originally published at Venice in 1548, appeared at Cologne in 1572 under the auspices of St. Peter Canisius.

20. *Opera,* prooem. Luth. confut., col. 300; art. 37, col. 728; Frith, *Whole workes,* p. 53 (cf. *Purgatorye,* ed. 1533, sig. K6). See Frith, pp. 51–60: "The third booke [of Purgatory], which aunswereth vnto my lord of Rochester and declareth the mynde of the old Doctours." Gerhard quotes Fisher (*Opera,* col. 307) on the fallibility of individual Fathers: "Rofens. in confut. prooem. Luth. . . *Et nos aliquoties errasse Patres non diffitemur, homines enim erant sicut nos*" (*Loci theologici,* ed. 1639, V, 375). As for Aquinas and other Scholastics, A. A. Stephenson, who declares: "Scholastic theology has been, on the whole, especially in its classical period, apophatic," nevertheless perceives in Counter-Reformation theology "three tendencies having cataphatic affinities": the two-source theory of Scripture and tradition, the doctrine that a conclusion dependent on one revealed and one unrevealed premise becomes a truth *de fide divina* by the Church's authority, and the *practical* shift from the ultimate criterion of revelation to the proximate criterion of the Church's teaching ("Biblical Theology and Scholastic Theology," in Swidler, ed., *Scripture and Ecumenism,* pp. 165–166). An apophatic theology "recognizes and does scrupulous justice to the profoundly mysterious and transcendent character of revelation, to the inaccessible mystery of God's being and the sovereign freedom of his will"; a cataphatic theology "takes the mysteriousness of the revealed mysteries less seriously and tends to be over-confident, in this sphere, about the powers of human reason" (*ibid.,* p. 156).

21. "Def. reg. assert." 1.4, *Opera,* col. 106; 3.1, cols. 131–132; 3.7, col. 134; 3.23, col. 150; 6.1, col. 192; 6.4, col. 195; 10.7, cols. 231–232; 11.3, col. 236; 11.7, col. 240; 11.9, col. 243. Cf. 6.1, col. 192: "Quantam autem vim habeat antiqua consuetudo . . . ex his quae aduersus articulos Lutheri disseruimus, constare potest . . ." (referring, for example, to "Assert. Luth. confut." prooem., cols. 293–294).

22. "Sacerd. def." 1.prooem., *ibid.,* col. 1233; 1.18, col. 1240; 1.21, col. 1241; 2.30, cols. 1259–60; 2.32, col. 1261; tr. Hallett, pp. 4, 17, 21, 58–60. Cf. Eusebius, *Hist. eccles.* 3.36.

23. "Non sic ergo debent intelligi scripturae, quemadmodum eas inuertit Lutherus, nempe, quod nihil omnino praeter sacras literas admittendum sit, nec eis quicquam adiiciendum, quum & per Apostolos multa sint absque scripturis tradita, multaque saluberrime per eorum successores adiecta. Sed ita potius intelligamus nihil esse contra scripturas recipiendum, aut quicquid quod cum eis pugnet adiiciendum quouis pacto" (*ibid.* 3.21, col. 1283, tr. Hallett, p. 109). See also *ibid.* 3.16, col. 1280, 3.21, col. 1283, tr. Hallett, pp. 103-104, 108-109. Note: "Sed hac de re satis copiose loquuti sumus alibi, nimirum vbi confutamus Lutheranos articulos nona veritate" (*ibid.* 3.21, col. 1283, referring to "Assert. Luth. confut." prooem., cols. 293–294). Meyendorff wisely observes: "The one Holy Tradition, which constitutes the self-identity of the Church through the ages and is the organic and visible expression of the life of the Spirit in the Church is not to be confused with the inevitable, often creative and positive, sometimes sinful and always relative accumulation of human traditions in the historical Church" ("The Meaning of Tradition," in Swidler, ed., *Scripture and Ecumenism,* pp. 51–52). See sec. 3, "Tradition and Traditions," *ibid.,* pp. 51–58.

24. *Heretickes,* sigg. A4, D1–3, F1ᵛ. Fisher confirms his last statement with a long quotation from Ignatius of Antioch (sig. A4).

25. "Ver. corp." 1.2, *Opera,* col. 759; 1.8, col. 779; 1.14, col. 797; 1.31, cols. 835–836; 2.20, col. 881; 4.2, col. 1006; 5.prooem., p. 1127; 5.39, col. 1228. Here Fisher refers to Tertullian's heresy, Cyprian's error on baptism, and Origen's allegorical method of interpretation. One of Cochlaeus' few expansions of the original Latin occurs here: "1. Ex vnanimi patrum consensu, qui sic interpretantur" (5.prooem., col. 1125): "Erstlich. Auss eynmutiger meynung vnd eynhelliger zusamstymmung der vätter / die es also ausslegen" (*Vorredde* V, sig. p4ᵛ). Luther agrees with Fisher's view of Tertullian: "He devoted a careful and lengthy discussion to the words of Tertullian and to Oecolampad's interpretation of them, coming to the conclusion that 'Tertullian confessed Christ's true body under the form of the bread in the Lord's Supper' " (Pelikan, *Luther the Expositor,* pp. 120–121, citing *This Is My Body* [1527], W, XXIII, 217–229).

26. *Censurae,* sig. O1ᵛ; *Determinations,* foll. 131ᵛ–132; Harpsfield, *Divorce,* p. 105; Fisher, "Responsum," fol. 320ᵛ. When his adversaries appeal to Martin V's approbation of Walden's contrary opinion (*Censurae,* sig. H4ᵛ; *Determinations,* fol. 87), Fisher answers: "Very many authors approved by the Church sometimes assert what is not accepted by the orthodox" ("Responsum," fol. 265; Harpsfield, *Divorce,* p. 79).

27. Erasmus, *Ep.,* IX, 95.

28. *Apomaxis,* fol. 81ᵛ.

29. Pelikan, *Luther the Expositor,* p. 214. Cf. page 258: "As the spokesman for a Biblically oriented Protestantism, Luther stressed the sovereignty of the Scriptures over all tradition and dogma, however ancient . . . But as a Biblical interpreter, Luther made use of tradition and dogma to find a meaning in the text that many other spokesmen for a Biblically oriented Protestantism were unable or unwilling to recognize as valid exegesis." See

"The Problem of Tradition" in Headley, *Luther's Church History,* pp. 56–105 (pp. 87–88 for Luther's handling of infant baptism), and Luther's use of "the fathers as a potential norm," *ibid.,* pp. 170–175. On infant baptism, see also Eastwood, *Priesthood,* pp. 15–21.

CHAPTER VII: SCRIPTURE: ITS NATURE AND USE

1. Ortroy, *Fisher,* XII, 192–198. The following expenditure of seven shillings is entered for 1528: "a new bible for my Lord" (Scott, "Notes from the College Records," *Eagle,* XXXV [1913–14], 29). Chapuys wrote to Charles V on June 30, 1535: "They gave him [Fisher] as a confessor a sworn enemy of his, and the staunchest Lutheran in the world, as well as the originator of all the devillish acts practised here; who, however, was so much edified by the Bishop's countenance and noble behaviour on the scaffold that he ceases not to say, that one of the best and holiest men in the world has been executed" (*Span. Cal.,* V, pt. 1, no. 178, pp. 504–505).

2. Psalms MS, P.R.O.S.P.2/R, foll. 200ᵛ, 252; *Eng. Works,* pp. 149–150, Lat. tr., *Opera,* cols. 1564–65. The second English sermon on Vulg. Ps. 37 develops an elaborate parallel between the sound of the harp used every morning by the Pythagoreans for "the free & noble excytynge of theyr myndes" and the Psalms, by which "the myndes of synners myght be reysed vp and excyted as by a swete melody to receyue and take the study and lernynge of vertues" (*Eng. Works,* pp. 70–71, Lat. tr., *Opera,* cols. 1510–11).

3. "Or." 3.1, *Opera,* cols. 1724–25, Eng. tr. 1560, *Prayer,* sig. F5ᵛ–6.

4. "Ver. corp." 1.praelibatio, *Opera,* col. 754; 2.9, col. 859. Fisher here uses Erasmus' translation: "Hoc poculum nouum testamentum per meum sanguinem, qui pro vobis effunditur." Cf. Vulg.: "Hic est calix novum testamentum in sanguine meo, qui pro vobis fundetur."

5. "Licitum fuisse matrimonium," pp. 27–28. A book *for* the divorce (P.R.O.S.P.1/67, fol. 185ᵛ) in stating the opinion of the adversaries follows Fisher's wording relatively closely.

6. "Def. reg. assert." 6.4, *Opera,* col. 195. At Trent in 1546, many delegates felt that any discussion of the Scriptures would be vain in view of that of Fisher and others (*Concilium Tridentinum,* I, 478, V, 8–9).

7. Altenstaig in 1517 praises and uses especially Gerson in "Scripture sacre quadruplex est sensus" (*Vocabularius theologie,* fol. 230). Note the following: "Et sensus scripturae literalis iudicandus est prout ecclesia spiritu sancto inspirata et gubernata determinauit / & non ad cuiuslibet arbitrium vel interpretationem" (*ibid.*) — a principle that might have come from Fisher himself. In summary Tavard writes: "Patristic exegesis . . . was typological, largely founded on the New Testament treatment of the Old Testament . . . The Middle Ages did not depart substantially from the patristic approach to Scripture . . . Medieval theology was a *commentarium,* a reflection on the Bible . . . This method of reflection became more and more systematic. On

the one hand, it initiated itself little by little to a scientific approach to the literal sense, with the help of grammar and rhetoric, and, later, of linguistics, philology and history. On the other hand, following lines that were already well marked by the Church Fathers, it divided the spiritual senses into three, allegorical, anagogical and tropological, according to the three theological virtues, faith, hope and love" ("The Meaning of Scripture," in Swidler, ed., *Scripture and Ecumenism,* pp. 56, 64–65). The standard work is now H. de Lubac, *Exégèse médiévale: les quatre sens de l'Écriture* (Paris: Aubier, 1959–1964).

8. *Eng. Works,* pp. 110, 129, Lat. tr., *Opera,* cols. 1537, 1550.

9. *Ibid.,* pp. 164–170, Lat. tr., cols. 1574–77.

10. *Ibid.,* pp. 200–209, Lat. tr., cols. 1598–1604. In the manuscript commentary on Psalm 2, Fisher explains that it is only a human way of speaking to say that there is anger in God because He only *seems* to be truly angry (P.R.O.S.P.2/R, foll. 157ᵛ, 265).

11. *Eng. Works,* p. 252, Lat. tr., *Opera,* col. 1632. The reference is to Vulg. Ps. 41:2.

12. Fisher, *Eng. Works.* pp. 315–317, Lat. tr., *Opera,* cols. 1377–78; Tyndale, "Obedience," *Treatises,* pp. 208–209. For Aquinas' stress on the use of the literal sense for doctrine, see *S.T.*, I, q.1, a.10, ad 1.

13. "Assert. Luth. confut." art. 25, *Opera,* cols. 563–566. Headley observes: "In his first exegetical work, Luther emphasized the antithesis between the Old and the New Testament more sharply than former exegetes had done" (*Luther's Church History,* p. 96), but he changed his approach. See also "The Second Epoch: Abraham and the Law of Moses" (*ibid.,* pp. 124–143).

14. "Assert. Luth. confut." art. 2, col. 354; art. 27, col. 720; Frith, "Purgatory," *Whole workes,* p. 54.

15. *Heretickes,* sig. B1ᵛ–2.

16. "Ver. corp." 2.8, *Opera,* col. 857; 2.26, cols. 894–897; 2.28–29, cols. 903–905; 3.18, col. 974.

17. "Habet enim & litera suam veritatem, & multo quidem certiorem quam allegoria, quandoquidem allegorici mysticique sensus ex eadem litera scateant innumeri. Solus tamen literalis sensus suum habet robur & firmitatem, cui contradici non potest. Allegorias vero quisque lector in tantum probat, quatenus arrident ingenio iudicioque suo" ("Ver. corp." 4.5, col. 1014). Cf. Pelikan, *Luther the Expositor:* "The fundamental hermeneutical principle which Luther believed he was defending was this: A text of the Scriptures had to be taken as it stood unless there were compelling reasons for taking it otherwise. . . Apparently Luther allowed for three such possible reasons: the statement of the text itself that it was not to be taken literally; the powerful indication by another passage to this same effect; the clash between a literal interpretation and 'a clear article of the faith' " (pp. 126–127).

18. "At est & horum verborum alia litera, aliusque sensus literalis, qui verus est . . . & ista litera tantum abest, vt occidat, vt plane viuificet credentes" ("Ver. corp." 4.5, *Opera,* col. 1015).

19. *Ibid.* 4.35, col. 1117.

20. *Ibid.* 5.2, cols. 1138–39. Just previously (*ibid.,* col. 1138) Fisher had enumerated other differences: the actual rather than the expected presence of Christ on earth (Matt. 13:16–17), immediate entrance into heaven rather than retention in Limbo, the casting off of the insupportable yoke of the Jewish Law (Acts 15:10), and the manifestation of God's justice hitherto hidden (Rom. 3:21–26).

21. *Eng. Works,* pp. 118–123, Lat. tr., *Opera,* cols. 1543–46. In his *Eversio,* Fisher suggests reconciliation between John's and Luke's accounts by a twofold wiping by the woman: once after watering Christ's feet with tears and again after anointing them (sig. Y2).

22. "Luther," *Eng. Works,* p. 328, Lat. tr., *Opera,* cols. 1382–83; "Assert. Luth. confut." art. 1, *ibid.,* col. 330, where the source is designated as "Augustinus libro quaest. 83."

23. *Heretickes,* sigg. D4–E2. Since the sermon is controversial in nature, Fisher goes on to prove that for three reasons the doctrine of Luther cannot be "partiner of this spirite of lyfe / bicause it is repugnant and deuyded frome the holle corps of the doctryne of the churche" (sig. E2).

24. *Ibid.,* sigg. E2v, H2.

25. "Ver. corp." 5.prooem., *Opera,* p. 1132.

26. "Licitum fuisse matrimonium," p. 10. Cf. p. 39: "Et satis aperta est, cum alioqui manifesta Scripturarum erit inter se compugnantia, id quod aures Orthodoxorum nunquam non abhorruerunt. Quid enim pugnantius, quam / accipies fratriam, et non accipies fratriam / si de eadem vtrobique fuerit sermo."

27. ". . . ciuiliter interpretanda sunt, quae tradiderunt euangelistae, quum illi non solum historias narrent, sed magis ita enarrare studeant, vt pluribus grauidas mysteriis exprimant. Quo fit, vt eandem rem alius alio referat modo & plerunque (nisi generosius interpretentur) videantur asserere sibi repugnantia" (*Confut. sec. discept.,* foll. 11–12). See *ibid.,* foll. 6, 23; *Eversio,* sig. X3v–4; and "Magdal." lib. 3, *Opera,* col. 1448.

28. "Def. reg. assert." 4.10, *Opera,* col. 166; "Ver. corp." 5.prooem., p. 1132; and "Convulsio," cols. 1361–65. Velenus praises Platina as "non ignobilis . . . historicus" (col. 1362).

29. "Luther," *Eng. Works,* p. 345, Lat. tr., *Opera,* col. 1391. For "Deprauabant," see 2 Pet. 3:16 (which Erasmus translates as "detorquent"). For "Inuertebant," cf. Gal. 1:7 (Vulg. "volunt convertere," translated by Erasmus as "volunt invertere"). Erasmus defends his translation at some length, e.g., "Equidem malim *invertere* . . . Atqui *invertere* proprie declarat, in diversum ac praepostere vertere . . ." (*Opera,* VI, 802). See also "Sacerd. def." 3.21, *Opera,* col. 1283: "Non sic ergo debent intelligi scripture, quemadmodum eas inuertit Lutherus . . ."

30. "Assert. Luth. confut." prooem., *Opera,* cols. 284–286.

31. *Ibid.* art. 25, cols. 562–563.

32. "Sacerd. def." 1.24, col. 1240; 3.15, col. 1279; 3.18–19, cols. 1281–82; 3.40, col. 1298; tr. Hallett, pp. 17–18, 101, 104–107, 138.

33. *Ibid.* 3.25, cols. 1286–88; 3.32–34, cols. 1291–94; tr. Hallett, pp. 116–118, 126–130.

34. "Ver. corp." 1.prooem., p. 752; 2.14, col. 868; 3.prooem., p. 926; 5.prooem., p. 1128.

35. "Responsum," foll. 205ᵛ, 211ᵛ–212; Harpsfield, *Divorce,* pp. 49–50; *Censurae,* sig. A1ᵛ–3ᵛ; *Determinations,* foll. 17–21ᵛ.

36. See Southgate, *Jewel,* p. 171, relying on A. Dakin, *Calvinism* (Philadelphia, 1946), p. 181. Apropos of Fisher, Southgate observes: "In a sense it [Calvin's answer] was just as objective, since in the last analysis, the authority of the Roman Church must rest on the 'initial act of personal submission' of the individual believer, an authority no less objective nor more subjective than the 'inner testimony of the Holy Spirit' of Calvin. In this sense it can be argued convincingly that John Fisher gave his life for a truth which was as much a matter of individual faith as the truth for which the lowliest Anabaptist died" (p. 171).

37. Pelikan, *Luther the Expositor,* p. 227, referring to Wilhelm Walther, *Für Luther wider Rom* (Halle, 1906), pp. 107–112. Pelikan comments: "There was continuity from one form of this 'proclamation' to another, because the fundamental content of the proclamation was always 'the Lord's death,' God's redemptive deed in Jesus Christ. The continuity of the 'proclamation,' despite the variety of its forms, was also the guarantee for Luther that the variety of human needs and situations did not destroy the unity of the church" (p. 231, with basis in Luther's comments in *Against King Henry of England* [1522], W. X–II, 219–220).

38. "Magdal." lib. 1, *Opera,* cols. 1396–97; *ibid.* lib. 3, cols. 1445–46.

39. *Eversio,* sigg. C1, D3, a3. Augustine's famous original statement reads: ". . . ego vero evangelio non crederem, nisi me catholicae ecclesiae commoveret authoritas" (*Contra epistolam Manichaei quam vocant fundamenti liber unus,* 5, in *CSEL,* XXV, 197.22).

40. "Luther," *Eng. Works,* pp. 340–342, Lat. tr., *Opera,* cols. 1388–89. When Luther found false teachers misinterpreting the Bible, he "fell back upon his more basic definition of the 'Word of God' as deed and as proclamation . . . For the 'Word of God' in the Bible was the same 'Word of God' which God had spoken in the Exodus and in Christ, and the same 'Word of God' which the church was always obliged to proclaim" (Pelikan, *Luther the Expositor,* pp. 69–70).

41. "Roffensis Britannus Antistes, uir in theologicis studijs doctissimus, & si non magistratui illius etiam studioso (ut plerisque placere uideo) contumacius restitisset, uirtutis exemplar absolutum, mihi dum Londinum aliquando ex Gallia proficiscerer, se inuisenti confessus est, se magnopere admirari, quid sibi vellet ea in re diuina prouidentia, quod Lutherani aliquot longe felicissime enarrarent sacras literas, & tamen essent haeretici. Sed harum rerum iudicium uincit facultatis meae uires. Nobis ecclesiae autoritas semper plurimi est facienda." —*De animi tranquillitate dialogus* (Lugduni, 1543), p. 345. On the previous page, Volusenus describes "Guilielmus Page-

tus, potentissimi Anglorum regis legatus" as being immersed in Seneca. See *DNB, s.v.* Volusene (XX, 389–391) and *Biographical Dictionary of Eminent Scotsmen* (Glasgow, 1870), ed. R. Chambers, rev. T. Thomson, *s.v.* Wilson, Florence (III, 537), there being no good authority for the form Wilson, Wolson, or Wolsey. There are brief references to Volusene in Zeeveld, *Tudor Policy,* pp. 28 and n. 44, 59–61, 63, 71–72, 77–78, 100.

42. *Heretickes,* sig. F3; Psalms MS, P.R.O.S.P.2/R, foll. 183, 237. For Luther's view of the relation of languages to the Gospel, see Headley, *Luther's Church History,* p. 243.

43. *Apologia,* sig. A2ᵛ.

44. "Assert. Luth. confut." prooem., *Opera,* cols. 279–284. Fisher's supreme confidence in the continuity and unanimity of doctrine is evident from his later declaration that if a person with the genius, sanctity, and learning of Jerome and Chrysostom tackled Scripture afresh and independently, he would end up with the same opinions as Augustine and Thomas (*ibid.* prooem. Luth. confut., col. 302). It is hard to speak of a single, principal organ of the infallible magisterium for Fisher, as does Polman in neatly ascribing the mouth of the Fathers to Fisher, the Church of Rome to Driedo and Peresius, the pope to Pighius, etc. (*Élément historique,* p. 294; cf. pp. 296–298). It is evident that everything depends upon the case and the circumstance, e.g., the Magdalene, or the papacy, or the divorce.

45. "Assert. Luth. confut." prooem. Luth. confut., *Opera,* cols. 304–306, 311. In his 1531 defense of the article, "it is lawfulle for alle maner of men to reade holy scriptur" (not reprinted in the edition of 1534), Barnes is indignant: "But now wyll my lorde of Rochester say / that yov haue the very vnderstondyng as holy doctours had yt / for though that scripturs in them selfe and of their awne nature be playnest / and beste to be knowen yet be the holy doctours playnest vn to vs / wherfore he that wyll vnderstonde scripture must fyrst lerne to vnderstonde the doctours / & they shall brynge hym to the trewe vnderstondynge of holy scripture / or els he must erre. I answere o my lorde doo you wryte this with a saffe consyens? thynke yov that yov cane discharge youre consyens a fore the dredfulle face of Christe with this tryflynge distynccyon / Quedam sunt nociora nobis / et quedam nociora nature . . ." (*Supplicatyon,* ed. 1531, fol. 110ᵛ).

46. Frith, *Whole workes,* p. 3 (cf. Frith, *Purgatorye,* ed. 1533, sig. A3). Fisher's own statement is the following: "Neque cuiquam obscurum est, quin posterioribus ingenijs multa sint, tam ex euangelijs, quam ex scripturis caeteris, nunc excussa luculentius & intellecta perspicatius, quam fuerant olim . . . Sunt enim adhuc in euangelijs, loca pleraque satis obscura, quae non dubito, posteritati multo fient apertiora. Cur enim istud desperabimus, cum ideo traditum sit Euangelium, vt a nobis penitus & ad vnguem intelligatur?" ("Assert. Luth. confut." art. 18, *Opera,* col. 496). Fisher's reason is characteristic: Christ's persevering love and the Holy Spirit's continuing assistance, now as in the past (*ibid.*).

47. "Ego sane cum Augustino libere clamo, me nec Euangelio crediturum, nisi quod Ecclesiae, patribusque credam" ("Def. reg. assert." 10.7, *ibid.,* col.

232). For chap. 10, see *ibid.,* cols. 226–232. Cf. above, n. 39. Luther "attributes this assumption of a legislative authority [by the Roman Church] to a deliberate misuse of Augustine's much quoted statement that he would not have believed the gospel had he not been moved by the authority of the Church" (Headley, *Luther's Church History,* p. 84).

48. "Def. reg. assert." 1.1, *Opera,* cols. 104–105; 11.6, cols. 238–239. In the latter place, Fisher observes on the populace: "Et quanquam Origenes, aut alius quiuis, si quis in scripturis examinandis repertus fuerit eo diligentior & circumspectior, asseruerit hanc [epistolam Iacobi] esse vere catholicam, non tamen audietur contra Lutherum" (*ibid.,* col. 239). Actually, Luther considers "the divine inspiration of Saint James's Epistle . . . doubtful": see McDonough, *Law and Gospel in Luther,* pp. 166–167 and n. 2.

49. "Ver. corp." 1.28, *Opera,* col. 830; 4.prooem., p. 996; 4.24, col. 1065.

50. "Responsio," B. M. Otho C.x, fol. 198 (mutilated and blurred).

51. "Responsum," foll. 205, 252, 274. Cf. *Censurae,* sigg. A1^{v}–2^{v}, E4^{v}; *Determinations,* foll. 16–18^{v}, 56^{v}–57. In the case of disagreement about the meaning of Scripture, Biel, too, declares that "the papal see has to decide what Holy Scripture really says" (Oberman, *Medieval Theology,* p. 403).

CHAPTER VIII: THE THREE LANGUAGES

1. "Sacerd. def." 2.17, *Opera,* col. 1250; 3.18, col. 1281; 3.23, col. 1285; 3.25, col. 1287; tr. Hallett, pp. 39, 105, 112, 118. A random glance reveals that Fisher refers by name to Erasmus' translation in "Def. reg. assert." 2.13, *Opera,* col. 124, and "Assert. Luth. confut." art. 2, col. 376, and art. 13, col. 448. On July 21, 1562, Salmeron at the Council of Trent refers to Fisher's gloss on *ministrantibus* as meaning *sacrificantibus* (*Concilium Tridentinum,* VIII, 723).

2. Erasmus, *Ep.,* I, 537, tr. Thomson-Porter, *Erasmus,* pp. 163–164.

3. Erasmus, *Ep.,* II, 244, 268, III, 387–390, 446–448. Cf. Thomson-Porter, tr., *Erasmus,* pp. 186–187. One unnamed college at Fisher's Cambridge, however, had "passed a full-blown Resolution to prevent anyone from bringing 'that book' within the august walls of the said college 'by horse, ship, waggon, or porter' " (*ibid.,* II, 321, tr. Thomson-Porter, p. 195).

4. *Ibid.,* II, 598, tr. Thomson-Porter, *Erasmus,* p. 187. Thomson and Porter here comment: "By the 1520's Fisher appears to have been quite at home in New Testament Greek" (*ibid.,* p. 187, n. 191).

5. *Ibid.,* III, 236–238, 464, 522. On Fisher's earlier interest in Christ's genealogy in 1515, see *ibid.,* II, 49–50. For succinct accounts of the quarrel between Erasmus and Lee, see *ibid.,* IV, 108–111, introd. (which for the full story recommends A. Bludau, *Die beiden ersten Erasmus-Ausgaben des Neuen Testaments,* 1902, pp. 86–125) and *Erasmi opuscula,* ed. W. K. Ferguson (The Hague: Martinus Nijhoff, 1933), pp. 225–234 (for Fisher's role, pp. 247, 250, 258, 264, 267, 271).

6. More, *Correspondence,* pp. 139–140, 148–149, 169, tr. Rogers, *Selected Letters,* p. 125.

7. Erasmus, *Ep.,* IV, 92–93.

8. *Ibid.,* IV, 160 (cf. 177), 191 (excerpts from the three lost letters of Fisher), 192, 322.

9. G. J. Gray, "Letters of Bishop Fisher, 1521–3," *Library,* ser. 3, IV (1913), 136. Gray refers to *Arnoldus* mentioned in Erasmus' letter to Ruthall, July 9, 1516 (Erasmus, *Ep.,* II, 277), but the identification is hardly correct.

10. *Ibid.,* V, 143.

11. *Ibid.,* VI, 67–69, 94, 166.

12. Rackham, ed., *Early Statutes of Christ's College,* pp. 24–25, 48–51, 90–91 (cf. note on p. 147: "the rule to speak Latin and its relaxation on feast-days follow God's House, but the permission for the students to speak English in their rooms is new"). Cf. Mayor, ed., *Early Statutes of St. John* (1516, 1524), pp. 268, 354, 369. Another statute carried over from God's House is that "six . . . shall devote themselves to the rudiments of Grammar . . . in order they may be able . . . to go forth competently to teach Grammar in any part of England" (Rackham, ed., pp. 25–27, 106–109, 149).

13. Mayor, ed., *Early Statutes of St. John,* pp. 38, 106, 116, 312–313, 375–376.

14. *Ibid.,* pp. 250, 252, 344–345. The Greek lecturer is to receive three pounds yearly; the Hebrew, five pounds (Lewis, *Fisher,* Coll. No. 17, II, 289). The amount of the salary of Erasmus, who taught Greek during his stay at Cambridge (1511–14), is unknown. Ten pounds constituted the stipend given a university lecturer in Greek in 1520 (Thomson-Porter, tr., *Erasmus,* p. 70, citing *LP,* III, 1540), whereas over twenty pounds were paid to him at Venice and at Louvain in 1518 (*ibid.,* relying on Erasmus, *Ep.,* XI, 363). "The Public Orator appears for the first time in the Proctor's account for 1521–22, in the shape of a payment of forty shillings to Mr. Croke, i.e., Richard Croke of King's College, Fellow of St. John's and Greek Professor, 1522. His annual stipend was forty shillings, which appears in the accounts to 1524–25 inclusive" (W. G. Searle, ed., *Grace Book Γ* [Cambridge (Eng.) University Press, 1908], Introd., p. xxiii; cf. M. Bateson, ed., *Grace Book B* [Cambridge [Eng.] University Press, 1903–5], II, 101. See A. Tilley, "Greek Studies in England in the Early Sixteenth Century," *Eng. Hist. Rev.,* LIII (1938), 221–239, 438–456. Tilley comments: "More important [than Erasmus' apparent paucity of pupils] was his influence upon Fisher, in whom he found a congenial spirit, and who by securing Croke as reader in Greek in his university established the teaching of Greek in England on a permanent footing" (p. 453). He also credits Erasmus and Fisher with the introduction of printing to Cambridge (pp. 238–239).

15. See Thomson-Porter, tr., *Erasmus and Cambridge,* Introduction, pp. 3–103, especially pp. 38–40, 102, for Erasmus' lectures, and pp. 86–92, for Croke, Cheke, and others. An abstract of Croke's inaugural lecture at Cambridge in July 1519 appears in J. B. Mullinger, *The University of Cambridge from the Earliest Times to the Royal Injunctions of 1535* (Cambridge, 1873),

pp. 528–537. Speaking as Fisher's representative, Croke asks: "What then is the message of my lord of Rochester? Why, he exhorts them to apply themselves with all diligence to the study of Greek literature — that literature in praise of which so many able men have recently sent forth dissertations. The exhortation of one who had never urged them to aught but what was most profitable, might alone suffice. . ." (*ibid.,* pp. 529–530). On Croke, who, "though a good lecturer with an enthusiasm for his subject, was too self-seeking and time-serving to become a leader," see Tilley, "Greek Studies," *Eng. Hist. Rev.,* LIII, 231–234, 237, 439, 453–454. "In 1518 John Bryan, Erasmus's pupil, seems to have lectured on Aristotle from Greek texts" (McConica, *English Humanists,* p. 80 and n. 2).

16. Erasmus, *Ep.,* I, 473, II, 313, III, 546–547, tr. Thomson-Porter, *Erasmus,* pp. 115, 194. A letter from the University of Cambridge to Lord Mountjoy (1511? 1513?) is extant, "asking him to contribute to the maintenance of a teacher of Greek, whom they were afraid of losing" (I, 473n; cf. Appendix X, pp. 613–614, tr. Thomson-Porter, p. 69). After his departure from Cambridge in 1514, Erasmus wrote to Servatius Rogerius that both Oxford and Cambridge were vying for his services (I, 569, tr. Thomson-Porter, p. 183). For More's letter to Oxford, see *Correspondence,* pp. 111–120, tr. Rogers, *Selected Letters,* pp. 94–103.

17. Erasmus, *Ep.,* II, 317–318, 351, 430, tr. Thomson-Porter, *Erasmus,* p. 192. According to Erasmus' letter of August 27, 1516, one reason for his detention in Rochester was Fisher's plan to accompany Erasmus abroad, his principal motive being an interview with Reuchlin (*ibid.,* II, 330).

18. *Ibid.,* II, 347, 371, 438–442, 485–487. For Latimer's biographical sketch, see *ibid.,* I, 438n.

19. *Ibid.,* II, 598 (tr. Thomson-Porter, *Erasmus,* p. 187), III, 75, 91, 214–215, 237.

20. Spitz, *German Humanists,* pp. 35, 62, 301.

21. Erasmus, *Ep.,* II, 4, 49–50. See the explanation of Fisher's questions (*ibid.,* 50n), and also Reuchlin's *De rudimentis Hebraicis* (Pforzheim, March 1506), pp. 19–31, for Mary's genealogy. The reference to Philo in Reuchlin's book (p. 31) and in Fisher's letter helps to explain a letter to Fisher from *Jo: Renatus* in Rome, preserved in the archives of St. John's College. Fisher had directed him to get a copy of *cartones Jo. Aniani viterbiensis super uniuersa sacra scriptura.* All he could find was *Antiquitates* by *Anius* [*sic*], not *Anianus* (Scott, "Notes from the College Records," *Eagle,* XVI [1889–91], 356). The *Antiquitates* of Joannes Annius Viterbiensis (Giovanni Nanni of Viterbo, 1422–1502), published by Josse Bade, Paris, February 5, 1512 (cf. A. Renaudet, *Préréforme et humanisme à Paris pendant les premières guerres d'Italie (1494–1517),* 2nd ed. [Paris, 1953], p. 618, n. 2), contains extracts from Greek and Latin historians, including Berosus, whom Fisher later quotes in his "Responsum," fol. 299^v. Now, Annius is the editor of Pseudo-Philo's *Breviarium de temporibus* (1498, 1510, 1512). A mention of episcopal linen is made again on August 27, 1516: it is always worn in England — except when hunting (Erasmus, *Ep.,* II, 330). Reuchlin, who had met Pico per-

sonally in 1490, would have found the comparison with Pico flattering. For an account of Pico's decisive influence on Reuchlin, see Spitz, *German Humanists,* pp. 61, 67, 78–79. Erasmus confessed to little knowledge of Hebrew, in which he had help from the Amerbachs for his Jerome and from Oecolampadius for his New Testament (Erasmus, *Ep.,* II, 50–51, and note).

22. *Ibid.,* II, 269; Spitz, *German Humanists,* pp. 68–69. "Nomen ihvh fit effabile per s consonantem" (Psalms MS, P.R.O.S.P.2/R, fol. 166).

23. Erasmus, *Ep.,* II, 330–331, 350, 494, 496. Fisher's name is unaccountably absent from an anonymous list of Reuchlin's learned friends in England at this time: Grocyn, Linacre, Tunstal, Latimer, Colet, More, and Ammonio ("Amici sunt Reuchlinio In Anglia Doctissimi . . . ," *Illustrium virorum epistolae . . . quibus . . . additus est liber secundus* [Hagenau, 1519], sig. t1v). See Geiger, *Reuchlins Briefwechsel,* p. 260: "Warum Johann Fischer, episcopus Roffensis in diesem, wahrscheinlich von Erasmus herrührenden, verzeichnisse fehlt, ist unbegreiflich." In 1523 Erasmus echoes his letter of August 27, 1516: "[Roffensis] pene deperibat in Capnionem, tam magnifice de illo sentiens, ut me prae illo putaret nihil scire, captaritque occasionem relinquendae Britanniae, ut cum Capnione, velut oraculo rerum omnium reconditarum possit colloqui" (*Spongia aduersus aspergines Hutteni* [Basel, 1523], sig. b8v, where Erasmus defends his whole conduct towards Reuchlin, e.g., winning him patrons and friends, etc.). In a letter to Pace, dated June 5, 1519, Polydore Vergil names Fisher among England's distinguished scholars: Thomas More, John Stokesley, John Clerk, Cuthbert Tunstal, John Taylor, Richard Sampson, Richard Hilley (presumably), William Knight, William Harrington, Edward Lee, John Chambre, Thomas Linacre, William Warham, and John Fisher. Vergil writes: "Hunc [i.e., Archbishop Warham] sequitur fere passibus aequis Ioannes Fiscerius Roffensis episcopus, qui ubi mutit, ecce subito quidam sanctimoniae odor spirat, ubi hiat, ecce sacrae scripturae nectar fluit ubertim, adeo purus est, adeo diuinae literaturae est sciens. Hi sunt inquam duo Anglicae iuuentutis bonarum disciplinarum candidatae inclyti duces, quorum alterius Oxoniensis, alterius Cantabrigiensis academia in tutela est." See D. Hay, Appendix II, "Extract from Vergil's dedication of the 'Adagia Sacra' to Richard Pace, 1519," "The Life of Polydore Vergil of Urbino," *Journal of the Warburg and Courtauld Institutes,* XII (1949), 150–151.

24. Erasmus, *Ep.,* II, 522, 598.

25. *Ibid.,* II, 599, III, 75, 122n, 131, 236, 291–292.

26. The correspondents besides Fisher are given in Seckendorf, *Comm. de Luth.,* I, 105.

27. *Illustrium virorum epistolae* (1519), sig., s3; Erasmus, *Ep.,* IV, 321–322, 372; Spitz, *German Humanists,* p. 80. The same volume of *Epistolae* sent to Reuchlin contains a letter from Croke, who complains about receiving no letter from Reuchlin, sends him a copy of his translation of the fourth book of Theodore of Gaza's grammar, urges Reuchlin to recommend him to Fisher, and suggests the dedication of the *opus Cabalae* to Fisher since it would merit a munificent reward (sig. y2).

28. See Bateson, *Grace Book B,* II, 20, 35, 122; Searle, *Grace Book* Γ, p. 170; *DNB,* XX, 446–447; Lewis, *Fisher,* I, 56; Reynolds, *Fisher,* pp. 47, 163; and McConica, *English Humanists,* pp. 122–123, 127, 133–134. Wakefield was admitted a fellow of St. John's in 11 Henry VIII (1519–20). A letter from Fisher reads: "Wher master Wakfeld this bearer ys minded to goo by yonde the sea to thentent thatt he may be the more expolite and perfite in the tonge of hebrew. I haue granted hym the emoluments of his Colleg duryng the space of two years next enseuyng" — in addition to which Wakefield also received special payments (Scott, "Notes from the College Records," XXXVI [1914–15], 264–265). It will be noted that Wakefield began to lecture on Hebrew at Cambridge in 1524, the year that Fisher's statutes first provide for a lecturer in Hebrew for older students at St. John's. A complaint exists that Wakefield (and Bayne) would not examine these statutes after they were written out by Randall Hall (*ibid.,* XXXII [1910–11], 155). As for the divorce, Fisher writes of his marvel at the news that "Wakefield has found something in Hebrew which makes for the King's argument" (*LP,* IV, no. 3232, pp. 1471–72; cf. Pace's and Wakefield's letters to Henry VIII, July 5, 1527, *ibid.,* nos. 3233–34). Harpsfield has "An answere to Mr. Robert Wakefeild" (*Divorce,* pp. 149–169).

29. All the citations are from *Kotser codicis,* sigg. A2, O4^{v}–P4^{v}. On his visit to Wakefield, Fox, the future Bishop of Hereford, was accompanied by Dr. John Bell (*Foxus . . . Belo comitatus*), later Bishop of Worcester (1539–43). With Dr. Sampson, afterwards Bishop of Chichester, Bell was to be counsel for the king during the trial in 1529. Pace's letter to Henry VIII is dated 1526 in *Syntagma,* sig. D4. Pace's and Wakefield's letters are catalogued in *LP,* IV, nos. 3233–34, July 5, 1527.

30. This passage is quoted by H. Hody in the biographical notice of Wakefield in *De bibliorum textibus originalibus . . .* (Oxford, 1705), pp. 465–468. About Fisher, Hody says: "A *Wakfeldo* literas Heb. aliquatenus edoctus est Jo. Fisherus, Episcopus *Roffensis,* hoc titulo vulgo quam proprio suo nomine notior" (*ibid.,* p. 467). Information on Thomas Hurskey is very meager. "Thomas Hurtsky or Hurteskye, prior of Watton and master of the Order of St. Gilbert, and master, rector or governor of the house of Semplyngham," appears in "Pardon Roll 1 Henry VIII" (*LP,* 2nd ed., I, no. 438, pp. 243–244). The form *Horsley* also appears. He is mentioned in passing as "Thomas Hurtisby prior' de Sempyngham" in *Valor ecclesiasticus,* IV, 34. McConica places him in "Pace's circle" with Robert Wakefield, John Clerk, and Thomas Elyot (*English Humanists,* pp. 122, 134). Robert Holgate became Master of Sempringham in or before 1534 and prior of Watton before July 1536, according to R. Graham, *S. Gilbert of Sempringham and the Gilbertines* (London, 1903), p. 174.

31. *Syntagma,* sigg. A1–4, C3–4. D4^{v}, tr. Lewis, *Fisher,* II, 18–19; Reynolds, *Fisher,* p. 163; B. M. Otho C.x, fol. 194^{v}. The two references to *Kotser codicis* are found in *Syntagma,* B1 (cf. *Kotser,* B3^{v}) and L2 (cf. *Kotser,* B3). *Dissipatio* occurs in Vulg. Is. 24:3 and Jer. 12:11 and 25:34 in the sense of laying waste or desolate.

32. "Magdal." lib. 1, *Opera,* pp. 1399–1400, 1415, and *Eversio,* sig. P1v. See also *Confut. sec. discept.,* fol. 7.

33. *Confut. sec. discept.,* fol. 7; *Eversio,* sig. P1. Fisher's variant reading, taken from the Greek text in Erasmus' New Testament, is usually rejected.

34. "Magdal." lib. 2, *Opera,* cols. 1434, 1440, 1442; *Eversio,* sig. V2v. Fisher's addition to Matt. 28:9 is given as a variant but is not adopted in the best editions.

35. *Eversio,* sig. E4; cf. G1v. The discussion of Gal. 2:11 takes up sigg. D4–G3v.

36. "Luther," *Eng. Works,* p. 332, Lat. tr., *Opera,* col. 1384 (where "the mayster of Iewes" is translated properly in the plural as *Iudaeorum magistri,* i.e., Rabbis); "Assert. Luth. confut." art. 15, *Opera,* col. 467; art. 31, col. 615; art. 36, cols. 675–677, 685. There may be a reference to the Hebrew when Fisher denies to Luther that Dan. 8:23 applies to the pope in its entirety, especially: "Et intelliget aenigmata, seu potius (vt quendam redidisse legi) diuinationes" (*ibid.* art. 27, col. 589).

37. "Assert. Luth. confut." Lectori, p. 273; prooem., col. 286; art. 1, cols. 319, 332; art. 16, col. 484; art. 25, cols. 568, 570; art. 36, col. 671; art. 37, cols. 722, 726; art. 38, col. 736. Chrysostom's Homily 60 in the translation by Brixianus is quoted in "Ver. corp." 3.prooem., p. 928. These spurious Homilies to the People of Antioch appear also in Erasmus' edition of Chrysostom, vol. IV (Basel: Froben, 1530). See Erasmus, *Ep.,* IV, 423n.

38. "Def. reg. assert." 2.15, *ibid.,* col. 128; 6.13, col. 204. Reuchlin's etymology is to be found "in rudimentis quae pro linguae sanctae notitia digessit" (col. 204). See L. Geiger, *Johann Reuchlin* (Leipzig, 1871), p. 128 and n. 4. Actually *missath,* the word occurring in Deut. 16:10, has the sense of "sufficiency, enough" and here is to be translated "according to the measure of."

39. "Sacerd. def." 2.33, 2.45–46, *Opera,* cols. 1262, 1266–77, tr. Hallett, pp. 62, 70–72. On Fisher's citations here, see Hallett, p. 145, and Schmeink, ed., *Sacerd. def.,* pp. 46–48, 86–87. Fisher's reading of 1 John 4:3 occurs in the Fathers from the second century but is not adopted today. F. Secret, *Les Kabbalistes chrétiens de la Renaissance* (Paris: Dunod, 1964), pp. 228–229, has discovered that Fisher copies the text of Johai from Petrus Galatinus (Pietro Columna), *Opus de arcanis catholicae veritatis* (Basel, 1550), p. 657 (in the Newberry Library copy, p. 662), which was completed September 4, 1516 (*ibid.,* p. 718). It is interesting to observe Fisher's use of his original. *De arcanis* reads: "Rabbi . . . Iohai sic dicit, Tempore Messiae omnia sacrificia deficient, sacrificium uero panis & uini nunquam deficiet, sacrificium quidem uini . . . Item alibi scriptum est, scilicet Iudicum 9. cap . . . Id est, Nunquid possum deserere uinum meum, quod laetificat Deum & homines? Etsi homines quidem laetificat, Deo autem in quo laetitiam affert? In sacrificio, quod de ipso fiet. Sacrificium uero panis nunquam defecturum esse, ex eo apparet, quod dictum est Psal. 72. Et erit placenta frumenti in terra, in capite montium. Haec omnia Rabbi ille Iohai, qui per multos annos Christum antecessit" (p. 662). Fisher picks up this last phrase and then proceeds:

"Rabbi vero Iohai qui Christum diu antecessit, probat sacrificium panis & vini nunquam cessaturum, partim ex verbis quae Iudicum 9. scripta sunt in hunc modum: Nunquid possum deserere vinum meum quod laetificat Deum & homines? Vinum inquit, etsi laetificet homines, Deum autem quomodo laetificat? Respondet. In sacrificio quod de ipso, nempe de vino, fiet, partim ex verbis Psalmi 72. Nam subiicit, Sacrificium vero panis nunquam esse defecturum, ex eo apparet, quod dictum est Psalmo 72. Et erit placenta frumenti in terra in capite montium. Hactenus ille" (*Opera,* col. 1266).

40. *Heretickes,* sigg. B4, F1–2. See Vulg. Exod. 16:15 and Luke 18:36.

41. "Ver. corp." ded. epist., *Opera,* p. 746; 1.3, col. 762; 1.8, col. 775; 2.9, col. 859; 3.12, col. 958; 4.30, col. 1093.

42. *Ibid.,* 3.prooem., p. 917; 3.9, col. 953; 3.20, col. 978; 4.7, col. 1020; 5.prooem., p. 1128. The second *dabo* (δώσω) occurs in many good manuscripts but is not accepted by modern editors.

43. *Ibid.* 1.9, col. 785; 1.20, col. 812; 2.14, col. 867; 2.19, col. 879; 2.33, col. 916; 3.prooem., p. 928; 4.prooem., p. 994; 5.14, col. 1173. On Erasmus' *Officium Chrysostomi,* see *Ep.,* I, 467; on Brixianus, IV, 423n; and on Aretinus, *ibid.,* VIII, 292n.

44. *Causa,* fol. 8. On the Septuagint there is a lengthy treatise, ascribed to Fisher, in the Public Record Office (S.P. 6/5, foll. 91–163; cf. *LP,* VIII, no. 887[8]).

45. *Commentaria,* ed. 1549, p. 134, Eng. tr. in Tyndale, *Treatises,* ed. Walter, pp. xxix–xxx (cf. Seckendorf, *Comm. de Luth.,* II, 37). A dozen years later, Cochlaeus mentions this service (unrewarded) in his answer to Richard Morison (*Scopa in araneas Morysini,* sig. B2).

46. S. Denne and W. Wildash, *The History and Antiquities of Rochester and Its Environs,* 2nd ed. (Rochester, 1817), p. 75.

CHAPTER IX: PHILOSOPHY AND HISTORY: THEIR RELATION TO FAITH AND DOGMA

1. "Against Latomus," *Luther's Works,* XXXII, 216–217 (*W,* VIII, 98–99); Erasmus, *Ep.,* II, 90; Hughes, *Reformation,* I, 345; and Spitz, *German Humanists,* pp. 25–26, 299 (on Agricola), pp. 48, 59 (on Wimpfeling), pp. 66, 307–308 (on Reuchlin), pp. 102–105 (on Celtis), pp. 113–114 (on Hutten), p. 174 (on Pirckheimer), pp. 206–207 (on Erasmus), and pp. 238–240 (on Luther). In Luther's eyes, the "universities shared almost an equal place with the papal authority in this twofold subversion of the religious life" (i.e., the burial of the Gospel and the establishment of human doctrines and practices): see Headley, *Luther's Church History,* pp. 207–208. For Luther's own use of "reason," see R. H. Fischer, "A Reasonable Luther," in Littell, ed., *Reformation Studies,* pp. 30–45, and B. A. Gerrish, *Grace and Reason: A Study in the Theology of Luther* (Oxford: Clarendon Press, 1962).

2. "Ratio verae theologiae," *Opera,* V, 136; "Paraclesis," VI, sig. C*4*r;* "Apologia adversus monachos quosdam hispanos," IX, 1090. According to

Stephenson, "Scholastic theory . . . is the translation of the biblical revelation into Greek; that is, into the concepts and terminology of ancient Greek philosophy. In the Thomist tradition . . . the terminology is predominantly Aristotelean. In substance and doctrine, scholastic theology is highly biblical; for theology is not the same thing as doctrine, and the same doctrine can be expressed in several different theologies" ("Biblical Theology and Scholastic Theology," in Swidler, ed., *Scripture and Ecumenism,* pp. 164–165). On the apophatic character of Scholastic theology, see Chapter VI, n. 20.

3. "Passion," *Eng. Works,* pp. 388–389, Lat. tr., *Opera,* col. 1652 (=1648). The moralism of Renaissance philosophy appears earlier in Fisher's first sermon on Vulg. Ps. 37: "The phylosophers shewed two dyuerse wayes, one is the waye of uertue, the other of vyce. The way that ledeth a man to vertue is laborous & full of thornes, notwithstandynge the ende of it is very pleasaunt. The waye whiche bryngeth a man to vyce is mery & full of sensuall pleasures, but the ende of it is very bytter and sharpe" ("Psalms," *ibid.,* p. 63, Lat. tr., *Opera,* col. 1505).

4. "Magdal." lib. 1, cols. 1395–96, 1407, 1409–10, 1415–16; lib. 3, cols. 1443–45. The identification of some figures mentioned by Fisher is difficult or uncertain, and the information garnered is often unsatisfactory or even contradictory in nature. Data on the well-known names can be found in Etienne Gilson, *La Philosophie au Moyen Age,* 2e éd. (Paris: Payot, 1947); Gilson, *History of Christian Philosophy in the Middle Ages* (New York: Random House, 1954); Friedrich Ueberweg, *Grundriss der Geschichte der Philosophie,* Zweiter Teil: *Die patristische und scholastische Philosophie,* hrsg. Bernhard Geyer, 12. Aufl. (Basel: Benno Schwabe, 1951). As for the lesser figures, consult: for Simon of Cascia, H. Hurter, *Nomenclator literarius* (Oeniponte, 1899), IV, 464–466, and *Cath. Encycl.,* XIII, 798–799; for Ubertino of Casale, Hurter, *Nomenclator,* IV, 485–486, *Encicl. catt.,* XII, 662–663, and *Dict. théol. cath.,* XV, 2021–34; and for Druthmarus (Christian de Stavelot), *Encicl. catt.,* IV, 1940–41, *Dict. théol. cath.,* V, 1215, and H. de Lubac, *Exégèse médiévale,* III, 210–214 ("Le nom de Druthmar dont on le désigne couramment ne se justifie pas," 210, n. 1). On the necessity of Greek for the study of the Scriptures and theology, see More, Letter to the University of Oxford, *Correspondence,* pp. 116–118 (tr. Rogers, *Selected Letters,* pp. 99–101); and Erasmus' numerous statements, e.g., "Ecclesiastes," *Opera,* V, 1026.

5. "Magdal." lib. 3, *Opera,* cols. 1447, 1456–57. On Zachary, see Hurter, *Nomenclator,* IV, 94–96; *Cath. Encycl.,* XV, 743; and *PL,* CLXXXVI, 9–12 (where one manuscript gives "Goldsborough" as Zachary's surname, 9, n. 1). Zachary's *In unum ex quatuor; sive, de concordia evangelistarum* is reprinted in *PL,* CLXXXVI, 11–620. Clement's work is also entitled *Unum ex quattuor* (*CBEL,* I, 289, where the year of his death is given as ca. 1190). On Clement, consult *CBEL,* I, 289, and Hurter, *Nomenclator,* IV, 85, *a,* where John Bale is cited as authority for an English translation of Clement's harmony by Wyclif; see also F. Stegmüller, *Repertorium biblicum medii aevi,* II (Madrid: Instituto Francisco Suárez, 1950), no. 1983, p. 250. *The Edinburgh Gazetteer*

(Edinburgh, 1822), III, 696, has the following description: *"Lanthony,* a hamlet of England, at the northern extremity of Monmouthshire, 10 miles N. by W. from Abergavenny." For the relation of Clement's to William of Nottingham's *Unum ex quattuor,* see Andrew G. Little's *The Grey Friars in Oxford* (Oxford, 1892), p. 185.

6. "Magdal." lib. 3, *Opera,* cols. 1451–53, 1459–60. On Marco Vigerio I della Rovere, see Hurter, *Nomenclator,* IV, 1005, and *Encicl. ital., s.v.* "Senigallia." For another relative of the same name who succeeded him as Bishop of Senigallia in 1513, see Hurter, IV, 1005, n.1. *Senigallia* appears also as *Sinigallia, Senogallia,* or *Senogaglia.* The work cited by Fisher may be that described in Josef Koch, *Cusanus-Texte,* I, *Predigten,* 7, *Untersuchungen über Datierung, u.s.w.* (Heidelberg: Carl Winter, 1942), pp. 18–19, 54.

7. "Apud ethnicos quidem authores id turpe est, vt quispiam a seipso dissideat, & modo hoc modo illud opinetur, manifesteque pugnantia dicat. at apud theologos id est longe turpissimum. Nam quum theologia veritatis sermo sit, eum (qui theologus fuerit) vbique vera dicere conuenit, ut siue in propriis, reique accommodatis locis siue extra materiae subiectae propositum, semper id dixisse putandus est, quod sibi verum videbatur" (*Eversio,* sig. C2^{v}–3).

8. "Assert. Luth. confut." prooem. Luth. confut., *Opera,* cols. 300, 302, 304, 312–313; art. 1, cols. 324–325; art. 36, col. 715; and art. 37, col. 728. Fisher derides an appeal of Luther to poets rather than to philosophers and theologians (art. 36, col. 691). Luther's "knowledge of Thomism, apparently, was superficial" (McDonough, *Law and Gospel in Luther,* p. 33 and n. 1, relying on H. Denifle and R. H. Fife).

9. "Assert. Luth. confut." art. 1, *Opera,* col. 339; art. 36, cols. 682–683. For explanation and background to this question of general influence or a special help, see J. Van Der Meersch, "Grâce," *Dict. théol. cath.,* VI, 1554–1687. On attrition, see Oberman, *Medieval Theology,* pp. 146–160, and "Historical Background" in G. J. Spykman, *Attrition and Contrition at the Council of Trent* (Kampen: J. H. Kok, 1955), pp. 17–113.

10. "Def. reg. assert." ep. ded., *Opera,* p. 101; 2.18, cols. 129–130; 3.22, col. 149. In his letter Fisher reminds Bishop West: "a teneris annis mihi non parua tecum in scholasticis exercitationibus fuerat consuetudo." Both were admitted to Cambridge about 1483, Fisher to Michaelhouse and West to King's College (A. B. Emden, *A Biographical Register of the University of Cambridge to 1500* [Cambridge (Eng.) University Press, 1963], pp. 229, 629). Fisher pays Henry VIII a similar compliment at one point: no one, however experienced in the Scholastic discipline, could surpass him in force or penetration (4.1, col. 157). Cf. Headley on Luther: "Fully aware of the continuing difficulty to reconcile the fathers, he praised the work of Peter Lombard and naturally preferred his achievement to that of Gratian" (*Luther's Church History,* p. 170).

11. "Ver. corp." 1.2, *Opera,* col. 758; Gilson, *Philosophie au Moyen Age,* p. 610.

12. Ver. corp." 4.prooem., *Opera,* pp. 989–990. See Ueberweg-Geyer, *Pa-*

tristische und scholastische Philosophie, pp. 342–583, where Ockham is given as the last great philosopher of *die Hochscholastik.*

13. "Numquam ita se deijcit Hieronymus quin diuo Thoma sit cultior, etiam cum ille rhetoricatur maxime." — *Hieronymi opera omnia . . . cum argumentis et scholiis Des. Erasmi* (Basel, 1516), II, 3ᵛ.

14. "Ver. corp." 4.prooem., *Opera,* p. 990.

15. *Ibid.,* 2.16, cols. 870–871. Some fifteen years before, Erasmus had received a letter in which James Wimpfeling had approved the study of Aristotle and the Schoolmen as useful for sharpening young minds and for refuting heresies, provided that the study of the New Testament and the Church Fathers was not neglected (Erasmus, *Ep.,* I, 463). Even Erasmus has a word of praise for those who have exercised the powers of their intellect on questions concerning instants, relations, quiddities, and formalities — on condition that they drew the pure philosophy of Christ from the New Testament ("Paraclesis," *Opera,* VI, sig. C*4). Wimpfeling and Fisher, consequently, would agree with Erasmus' comparison that truth is educed from the Scholastic disputation as fire is struck from flint ("Ratio verae theologiae," *ibid.,* V, 136).

16. "Ver. corp." 4.prooem., *Opera,* pp. 990–991. References are here given only for the few of whom accounts cannot be found in the standard histories by Ueberweg and Gilson: Heriger (*PL,* CCXVIII, 469), Adelmann (*Encicl. catt.,* I, 301), Guitmund (*PL,* CXLIX, 1425–26; "Aversa," *Encicl. ital.,* V, 628), Gratian (*Dict. théol. cath.,* VI, 1727–51), Honorius (Hurter, *Nomenclator,* IV, 24–26, who suggests other possibilities than Autun for the identification of Augustinensis), Guido of Croix Saint-Leufroy (Antonius Possevinus, *Apparatus sacer* [Cologne, 1608], I, 694), Rupert von Deutz (*PL,* CCXVIII, 522; Hurter, *Nomenclator,* IV, 21–24), William of St. Theodoric (Hurter, *Nomenclator,* IV, 78–79), Gilbert the Cistercian (*DNB,* VII, 1193–94), Ekbert of Schönau (*PL,* CXCV, 1–11; Hurter, *Nomenclator,* IV, 130–131), Peter of Riga (*PL,* CCXVIII, 509; Hurter, *Nomenclator,* IV, ccxxii), and Aelfric (*DNB,* I, 164–166, corrected by *Cath. Encycl.,* I, 172; *PL,* CXXXIX, 1455–70; M.-M. Dubois, *Aelfric: sermonnaire, docteur et grammairien* [Paris: Droz, 1943]). Alueredus is less likely to be Alfred Anglicus or de Sarchel, fl. *ca.* 1210, of whom little is known (*DNB,* I, 285), or Aelred, Abbot of Rievaulx, d. 1167, of whose name one of the many variants is *Alueredus* (*PL,* CXCV, 197).

17. "Ver. corp." 1.2, *Opera,* cols. 757–758; 2.25, col. 893. On *rhapsodus,* cf. *OED, s.v.* "rhapsoder," quoting Donne's *Biathanatos:* "Those definitions of sinne, which the first Rhapsoder Pet. Lombard hath presented out of ancient learning."

18. "Ver. corp." 4.prooem., *Opera,* p. 991. References for the less well-known figures are given in parentheses: Haimo of Halberstadt (*PL,* CXVI, 184–190; *Allgemeine Deutsche Biographie,* X, 390–391); Angelome (*PL,* CXV, 107–628; *Encicl. catt.,* I, 1261); Ratramnus (*PL,* CXXI, 9–12; *Encicl. ital.,* XXVIII, 860; *Nouv. biog. gén.,* XLI, 693–694); Druthmar (*Encicl. catt.,* IV, 1940–41; *Dict. théol. cath.,* V, 1215); Ratherius (*PL,* CXXXVI, 9–142; *Dict.*

théol. cath., V, 1217; *Encicl. catt.*, X, 541–543); and Raoul de Flaix (Possevinus, *Apparatus sacer,* II, 310–311; Hurter, *Nomenclator,* IV, 92).

19. "Ver. corp." 4.prooem., *Opera,* pp. 991–994.

20. *Ibid.*, pp. 997–998. Fisher uses the spelling *Massiliani,* but he undoubtedly means, not the Massilians who were Semipelagian monks at and near Massilia, present Marseilles (*Cath. Encycl.*, XIII, 703–704), but the Messalians who were an heretical sect originating in Mesopotamia (*Cath. Encycl.*, X, 212). On the latter, see G. Bareille, "Euchites, massaliens ou messaliens," *Dict. théol. cath.*, V, 1454–65. For the historical background to controversies on the Eucharist from the patristic age to the fifteenth century, see the lengthy article by various hands, "Eucharistie," *Dict. théol. cath.*, V, 1122–1326.

21. In the order of their mention in the text above, these authors appear as follows in *Causa:* Eucherius (D5), Bede (B3^{v}), Rabanus (B3^{v}), Druthmar (A6, B3^{v}, C2^{v}–3, D1^{v}, E5), Raoul de Flaix (A7, C2, D1^{v}, E5), Hugh of St. Victor (D6, D7), Peter Comestor (B3^{v}, D1), Peter of Blois (C2^{v}, E5), Robert Grosseteste (D2), Clement of Llanthony (B3^{v}), Zachary of Besançon (B3^{v}), Alexander of Hales (C3, D8, E5), Bonaventure (C3^{v}, D8^{v}), Albert the Great (B3^{v}, C6), Thomas Aquinas (C7^{v}–8, D2^{v}, D6^{v}, D8, E1^{v}–2), Richard of Middleton (E1, E7), Duns Scotus (C4), Francis of Meyronnes (C5^{v}, D5), Peter de la Palu (E2^{v}, E7^{v}–8), Vincent of Beauvais (D1), Hugh de S. Cher (C3, D1, E5), Peter of Tarantasia (C5), Robert Kilwardby (C5), James of Lausanne (D2), Nicholas of Lyra (A7, B3^{v}, C8, D1^{v}), Thomas of Strasbourg (D3^{v}–4), Paul of Burgos (D5^{v}, E2^{v}), Alphonsus (A7, B3^{v}, D1^{v}), Antoninus (E7^{v}, F1), Antonius de Rosellis (C8–D1), Torquemada (C8, E8–F1), Angelus (E7), Steinbach (C6, D3), and Cajetan (D2^{v}).

22. *Causa,* sig. D2; "Responsum," fol. 263^{v}; *Censurae,* sigg. E4^{v}–I4, P1^{v}; *Determinations,* foll. 58^{v}–93^{v}. Cf. Fisher, "Responsum," foll. 251^{v}–268, 326^{v}–327^{v}; and Harpsfield, *Divorce,* pp. 70–80. On Bernard de la Treille, see *Encicl. catt.*, II, 1403. On Walter of Coutances as Archdeacon of Oxford, see *DNB,* IV, 1276.

23. "Magdal." lib. 2, *Opera,* col. 1441; lib. 3, cols. 1452, 1456; *Eversio,* sigg. D1, L4, Z7^{v}; and *Confut. sec. discept.*, fol. 10^{v}. "Tres feruntur authores Martyrologia conscripsisse. Primus Hieronymus, deinde Beda, & tertius Vsuardus monachus, quem is demum imitatus est, qui Martyrologium castigauit, quo iam Romana ecclesia vtitur." Fisher demolishes Lefèvre's arguments from an older martyrology, especially by showing that "Marthae et Mariae" is a scribal corruption of "Marii & Marthae" (*Confut. sec. discept.*, foll. 19^{v}–20).

24. "Convulsio," *Opera,* cols. 1302–1303, 1333, 1360–61.

25. "Assert. Luth. confut." art. 25, *Opera,* col. 575; "Def. reg. assert." 6.4, col. 195; "Ver. corp." 1.22, col. 818; 4.prooem., p. 997; 4.3, col. 1009. Cf. Powell: "Nam Petrus . . . sicut omnium apostolorum princeps fuit: ita primam missam Antiochiae solemniter (ut annales tradunt) primus omnium celebrauit" (*Propugnaculum summi sacerdotij euangelici,* fol. 53). On the arrogation to himself of the title of *universalis episcopus* by the patriarch of Constantinople, John the Faster, see Gregory I's letters to Eulogius of

Alexandria and Anastasius of Antioch (*PL,* LXXVII, 770–774) and to Eusebius of Thessalonica (*ibid.,* 1003–1005). For the background, see H. K. Mann, *The Lives of the Popes in the Early Middle Ages* (London: Kegan Paul, 1902–32), I, 133–153, and Hefele-Leclercq, *Conciles,* II, 815–826, 834–835. For similar contemporary interpretations of *episcopus universalis,* see John Faber's *Malleus . . . in haeresim Lutheranam* (Cologne, 1524), foll. 70ᵛ–72ᵛ, and John Eck, *De primatu Petri,* foll. 38–42. John Gerhard cites "Roffensis adv. Luth. art. 3" on the use of "Universal and Ecumenical" by the patriarchs of Constantinople (*Loci theologici,* ed. 1639, V, 324). For Luther's use of the history of *universalis episcopus,* see Headley, *Luther's Church History,* pp. 191–192. On the role of Boniface III and Gregory VII in the establishment of the papacy, see *ibid.,* pp. 155, 192–197.

26. "Convulsio," *Opera,* cols. 1335, 1366; "Responsum," fol. 212ᵛ; Harpsfield, *Divorce,* pp. 52–53. Cf. *Censurae,* sig. A4, and *Determinations,* foll. 22ᵛ–23.

27. "Def. reg. assert." 11.5, *Opera,* col. 238, 11.13, cols. 248–249; "Sacerd. def." 1.12, col. 1237, 2.30, col. 1260, tr. Hallett, pp. 12, 59; "Convulsio," col. 1366; "Magdal." lib. 3, col. 1450; *Causa,* foll. 4ᵛ–5, 9–10.

28. "Convulsio," *Opera,* cols. 1343–44, 1353–54; "Ver. corp." 1.27, col. 829; 3.prooem., p. 919; 4.prooem., p. 998. Elsewhere Cassiodorus is described as "schematum & scripturarum peritissimus" (*ibid.* 4.prooem., p. 991).

29. "Convulsio," *ibid.,* cols. 1343, 1349; "Magdal." lib. 3, col. 1445; *Eversio,* sig. M2ᵛ; "Responsum," foll. 212ᵛ, 331ᵛ. Cf. Harpsfield, *Divorce,* pp. 52, 113; *Censurae,* sigg. A4, Q1; and *Determinations,* foll. 22ᵛ–23, 148ᵛ.

30. "Magdal." lib. 2, *Opera,* col. 1441, lib. 3, col. 1457; "Ver. corp." 4.prooem., p. 990; *Eversio,* sig. M4ᵛ; *Causa,* foll. 25, 29; "Responsum," fol. 298ᵛ.

31. *Eversio,* sigg. B4ᵛ, S4ᵛ–T1; "Assert. Luth. confut." art. 25, *Opera,* col. 544.

32. *Eversio,* sig. M3ᵛ; "Assert. Luth. confut." art 28, *Opera,* col. 592; "Convulsio," *ibid.,* cols. 1344, 1362. Sabellicus is quoted also on Berengarius' recantation ("Ver. corp." 3.prooem., *ibid.,* p. 920). In answer to Eck's objection to his use of Platina, Luther rejoined: "I attribute nothing to Platina, but to history which is the mother of truth and which Platina writes" (Headley, *Luther's Church History,* p. 45). For Luther's concept of history, see "History and Scripture," *ibid.,* pp. 42–55.

33. "Ver. corp." 1.prooem., *Opera,* pp. 748–749 (on More); "Convulsio," *ibid.,* col. 1330 (on Erasmus); and (on Colet) Erasmus, *Ep.,* IV, 520, Eng. tr. J. H. Lupton, *The Lives of Jehan Vitrier and John Colet* (London, 1883), pp. 32–33.

34. "Confutation of Tyndale," *Workes,* pp. 356, 390, 449, 515, 641, 663, 679; "Dialogue of Comfort," pp. 1171, 1188, 1190, 1198; "Passion," pp. 1291, 1376–77; Letter of Margaret Roper, p. 1436; "In Lutherum," *Opera,* fol. 87.

35. "Sed Philosophiae non sum iniquior, modo sobrie moderateque [diuinis] admisceatur" ("Apologia in dialogum Jac. Latomi," *Opera,* IX, 103).

36. "Confutation of Tyndale," *Workes,* pp. 368, 679.

37. Jedin, *Cochlaeus,* pp. 104–105.
38. "De causis corruptarum artium liber secundus, qui est de grammatica," *Opera* (Basel, 1555), I, 363.

CHAPTER X: EDUCATION

1. Emden, *Biog. Reg. Camb.,* Introd., p. xxx. Ortroy, *Fisher,* X, 245–248, names for Christ's: Richard Reynolds (Bridgettine martyr), William Exmew (Carthusian martyr), Nicholas Heath (Archbishop of York and Lord Chancellor), and Cuthbert Scott (Bishop of Chester); and for St. John's: Thomas Greenwood (or Green, Carthusian martyr), George Day (Bishop of Chichester), Ralph Baynes (Hebrew Professor at Paris and Bishop of Lichfield and Coventry), Thomas Watson (theologian and Bishop of Lincoln), John Christopherson (ecclesiastical historian and Bishop of Chichester), and Thomas Boucher (Abbot of Leicester, later Bishop-Elect of Gloucester). Note also the following: "Despite its newness, St. John's rapidly acquired a reputation for intellectual leadership. The list of members who distinguished themselves in Tudor times is impressive. There are twenty-six, perhaps twenty-seven, bishops, among them Edwin Sandys, Archbishop of York, and the elder Thomas Watson, one of Ascham's closest friends and a writer of Latin tragedies. Several members rose to prominent positions at court, the most successful of all being William Cecil, later Lord Burghley; others were Sir Anthony Denny and Sir Ambrose Cave, both of whom, like Cheke, eventually became privy councillors. Among literary men one finds, besides Ascham, the poet Sir Thomas Wyatt, who was one of the earliest scholars of the college; Sir Thomas Hoby, friend of Ascham and Cheke and translator of Castiglione's *The Courtier;* Abraham Fraunce, author of *The Arcadian Rhetorike;* Thomas Drant, Latin poet and translator of Virgil; and the writers Robert Greene and Thomas Nashe. Other members of note were the preachers Thomas Lever and Thomas Cartwright, and the scientist William Gilbert" (L. V. Ryan, *Roger Ascham* [Stanford: Stanford University Press, 1963], p. 16). For the comprehensive background, see Mullinger, "Cambridge at the Revival of Learning," *Cambridge to 1535,* pp. 379–552.
2. H. O. Evennett, "B. John Fisher and Cambridge," *The Clergy Review,* IX (1935), 379–380; J. P. C. Roach, in *V.C.H. Cambs.,* III, 167; and J. B. Mullinger, review of Cooper-Mayor's *Memoir of Margaret,* in *Eagle,* IX (1874–75), 200.
3. For pertinent transcriptions of original data until 1529, see S. M. Leathes, *Grace Book A Containing the . . . Records of the University of Cambridge for . . . 1454–1488* (Cambridge, 1897), pp. 174, 211, 215; Bateson, *Grace Book B,* I, 18, 25, 26, 33, 67–71, 81, 142, 145, 147, 162, 203; and Searle, *Grace Book* Γ, p. 10. A debt incurred by Dolman and Batmanson during Fisher's proctorship keeps occurring in the records until 1524–25 (*Grace Book B,* II, 28, 58, 65, 72, 80, 90, 97, 103, 112, 120). See also "The Cambridge of John Fisher," in H. C. Porter, *Reformation and Reaction in Tudor*

Cambridge (Cambridge [Eng.] University Press, 1958), pp. 3–20, and the entries in *V.C.H. Cambs.,* vol. III. "The course in Theology according to an old statute . . . requires ten years' study of Theology": for the program see *Grace Book A,* Introd., pp. xxvi–xxvii. The library of Fisher's admired tutor, William Melton, later chancellor of York, included "a 'Paraphrasis Erasmi,' the *Heptaplus Johannis Pici Mirandula,* a *Utopia,* and a 'Novum Testamentum ad Grecam' (*sic*) as well as an unidentified work by Valla" (McConica, *English Humanists,* p. 91). Melton's *Sermo exhortatorius* (London, 1510) urged knowledge of Latin as a tool upon all aspirants to orders, yet in the archdiocese of York in 1510–11, "1,107 men were ordained to various orders, 265 of them to the priesthood, 248 as deacons and 296 as subdeacons" (Dickens, *Reformation,* pp. 45–46).

4. Fisher, "Margaret," *Eng. Works,* p. 308; Ortroy, *Fisher,* X, 204–210; Reynolds, *Fisher,* pp. 1–16, 24–31, 49–55; Emden, *Biog. Reg. Camb.,* p. 229. On the readership, see Fisher, *Margaret,* ed. Baker-Hymers, Pref., pp. 3–4, and Cooper, *Margaret,* pp. 89–90 (citing MS. Lansd. 444 ff. 23b–36). On the permanent chancellorship (1514), see the letters in Lewis, *Fisher,* Coll. Nos. 12–14, II, 282–285. On the conversion of Godshouse into Christ College, facilitated by the close association between Fisher and John Syclyng, Master of Godshouse, see "The Negotiations between Godshouse and the Lady Margaret," in Lloyd, *Christ's College,* pp. 280–304. The Charter, Byngham's Petition, Charters of Godshouse, and the Statutes of Margaret in 1506 are reprinted in *Documents Relating to the University and Colleges of Cambridge* (London, 1852), pp. 127–212. On the progress of the building of Christ's and St. John's, as seen by Erasmus, 1506–1514, see Thomson-Porter, tr., *Erasmus,* Introd., p. 26. It was Polydore Vergil who had secured "the popes bulles concernyng the erection of seint Johns college" (Cooper, *Margaret,* p. 194). Vergil refers to Margaret's foundations: "hortatu Ioannis Fiscerii Roffensis episcopi, uiri summa doctrina, summa gratia, summa integritate" (*Ang. hist.,* tr. Hay, p. 145). He later echoes this praise in referring to the martyrdom of Fisher: "uiro magna doctrina, summa integritate et innocentia" (*ibid.,* p. 334). On November 5, 1524, Vergil dedicated to Fisher his "In dominicam precem commentariolum" (first printed with *De inventoribus rerum,* Basel, Froben, 1525): "Et quia secundum te optimae [*sic*] Roffensis episcope, non est quisquam omnium, cuius integritatem, grauitatem, probitatem magis mirer, obseruem, colam, quam mei Roffensis, uiri cum omnium bonarum artium studijs eruditissimi, tum hominis cunctis caeteris rebus multo ornatissimi, statui hunc nostri rusticani ocij fructum, si quis sit, saltem bonis adolescentibus, ut ne mihi cum opiniosissimis sophistis res ulla in hac parte esset, tuo nomine impertiri" (ed. Lyons, Seb. Gryphius, 1546, pp. 515–516). On the significance and the fate of the commentary, see D. Hay, *Polydore Vergil* (Oxford: Clarendon Press, 1952), pp. xi, 31–34.

5. "Magdal." lib. 3, *Opera,* col. 1445; Ortroy, *Fisher,* X, 216; Lewis, *Fisher,* Coll. No. *8, "Oratio," II, 267–270. On the legendary history of earliest Cambridge, see Cooper, *Annals,* I, 1–3, and Appendix A, "Lydgate's Verses

on the Foundation of the University of Cambridge," Mullinger, *Cambridge to 1535*, pp. 635–637. As for Fisher's remark on the low state of the university, J. P. C. Roach observes that, on the one hand, "it may be supposed that there was something of courtly exaggeration in his contrast between it and the bounty of the reigning monarch towards the University"; but, on the other hand, "Miss Bateson comments on 'the exceedingly slow movement of the classical revival' " (*V.C.H. Cambs.*, III, 165, referring to *Grace Book B*, Part I, Introd., pp. viii, xiii). Miss Bateson concludes: "Fisher's sermon, preached in 1506, a year of peculiar depression owing probably to exceptional circumstances, as the table of degrees shows, has perhaps spread too gloomy a view of the University's position at the beginning of Henry VIII.'s reign. There is no evidence of a steady decline; year in, year out, the University seems to have been pursuing a very steady, methodical, and, according to its lights, an honourable way" (*Grace Book B*, Part I, Introd., p. xxvi).

6. Bateson, *Grace Book B*, I, 218, 219, 230, 231, 236, 250; II, 1, 2, 30, 36, 46, 90, 93, 152; Lewis, *Fisher*, Coll. No. 15, II, 285–286; and Lamb, *Collection of Letters*, pp. 10–11.

7. More, *Selected Letters*, p. 147; More, *Correspondence*, pp. 253–254; Lewis, *Fisher*, Coll. No. 15, II, 285–286; and Scott, "Notes from the College Records," *Eagle*, XXXII (1910–11), 147.

8. Erasmus, *Ep.*, App. VI, I, 591 (citing Mullinger, *Hist. of Cambridge Univ.*, I, 453); Fisher, *Margaret*, ed. Baker-Hymers, Preface, p. 50; *Christ's*, ch. 1, pp. 44–45; ch. 4, pp. 48–49 (cf. *John's*, 1516, ch. 3, p. 353; 1524, ch. 3, p. 267; 1530, chs. 47–48, pp. 206–212); ch. 6, pp. 50–51 (cf. *John's*, 1516, ch. 5, p. 355; 1524, ch. 5, p. 272). The figure of the mystical body runs through all St. John's statutes: for 1516, 1524, and 1530. In the following few footnotes, *Christ's* stands for *Early Statutes of Christ's College*, ed. Rackham; *John's*, for *Early Statutes of St. John's College*, ed. Mayor, with the different sets of statutes designated by 1516, 1524, and 1530. J. H. Hessels announced the discovery of an imperfect copy (twelve vellum leaves) of St. John's statutes of 1511 ("Collegium DIVI Johannis *or* Collegium SANCTI Johannis," *Eagle*, XXXVIII [1916–17], 1–32). But R. F. Scott concludes a lengthy and detailed evaluation of Hessels' article with the judgment: "Thus the fragments really form part of the original statutes of 1516" ("Notes from the College Records," Fourth Series, 1918, p. 280, printed but not published in *The Eagle*).

9. *Christ's*, chs. 19, 28, pp. 68–69, 84–85, 145n (cf. *John's*, 1516, ch. 21, p. 373; 1524, ch. 24, p. 307); *Christ's*, ch. 23, pp. 74–75 (cf. *John's*, 1516, ch. 16, p. 367; 1524, ch. 18, pp. 294–295; 1530, ch. 8 with a change, p. 36).

10. *Christ's*, ch. 29, pp. 86–87 (cf. *John's*, 1516, ch. 22, p. 373; 1524, ch. 26, p. 309; 1530, ch. 19, p. 88); *Christ's*, ch. 30, pp. 88–91 (cf. *John's*, 1516, ch. 23, pp. 373, 375; ch. 27, pp. 311–312; 1530, ch. 22, p. 110).

11. *Christ's*, ch. 36, pp. 98–99, 148–149n; *Utopia*, pp. 158–159. In Christ's College, "the grammar is left to a weekly disputation" (*Christ's*, p. 148n). Cf. Lloyd, *Christ's College*, p. 299. On "the modes of signification," see Wil-

liam and Martha Kneale, *The Development of Logic* (Oxford: Clarendon Press, 1962), pp. 246–274, and, more briefly, Philotheus Boehner, *Medieval Logic* (University of Chicago Press, [1952]), pp. 27–51.

12. Quoted in Reynolds, *Fisher,* p. 55; *Christ's,* ch. 31, pp. 92–93 (cf. *John's,* 1516, ch. 25, p. 379; 1524, ch. 29, p. 318, ch. 39, p. 334; 1530, ch. 26, p. 138). The letter from Lord Bergavenny is transcribed by R. F. Scott, "Notes from the College Records," *Eagle,* XVI (1889–91), 354–355. For his concession of the *patronatus et advocacio* of the church at *Ipstoke* in Leicestershire to Fisher, March 8, 1522, see Thorpe, *Registrum Roffense,* pp. 435–436. Dickens comments: "The reactionary elements of the nobility . . . included active neo-feudalists like Lord Abergavenny . . . also some mildly disloyal and irresolute groups like that of the Courtenays and the Poles, broken up in 1538 by the so-called Exeter Conspiracy. . . they were destructive anachronists rather than religious objectors" (*Reformation,* pp. 123–124). In 1512 Henry VIII gave "the castle and lands of Abergavenny" to the third Baron of Bergavenny, George Neville (d. 1535; *DNB,* XIV, 257). It was his brother, Sir Edward Neville (executed 1538), who was "concerned in the conspiracy of the Poles" (*ibid.,* 250). "Abergavenny" is "a form which appeared in the sixteenth century and was not definitely adopted until 1730" (*ibid.,* 248).

13. *Christ's,* ch. 46, pp. 114–115; cf. ch. 6, pp. 52–53.

14. For Fisher's role in the refoundation of St. John's, see Ortroy, *Fisher,* X, 240–243; Bridgett, *Fisher,* pp. 28–41; and Reynolds, *Fisher,* pp. 49–55. For pertinent documents, see Fisher, *Margaret,* ed. Baker-Hymers, Preface, pp. 16–50, and Appendix IV, Documents Chiefly Relating to Bishop Fisher, pp. 183–299; Lewis, *Fisher,* esp. Coll. Nos. 11, 17, and 18, II, 277–282, 287–297; and Cooper, *Margaret,* Appendix, pp. 129–230, *passim.* Less accessible but very important for the foundation and early history is the series by R. F. Scott, "Notes from the College Records," in *The Eagle,* which may be catalogued as follows: XVI (1889–91), 341–357, letter of Margaret's chancellor to St. John's Hospital; XVII (1892–93), 465–481, letters to Metcalfe, third master; *ibid.,* 589–605, documents on Ospringe, Higham, and Bromhall; XIX (1895–97), 1–15, documents on Ospringe and Bromhall; XX (1898–99), 625–655, regional election of fellows; XXVI (1904–5), 295–301, various letters incl. two to Fisher on building operations; XXVII (1905–6), 1–27, agreement with Bishop of Ely, indenture for foundation, new charter, Fisher's account of 1511–16, warrants for Margaret's executors, etc.; XXXI (1909–10), 145–155, Fisher's letter to Prior Bolton about Margaret's pensioners at Hatfield and Margaret's tomb, final account of Shorton, first master; *ibid.,* 281–288, payments for Margaret's chancellor, college seal, presents to obtain Wolsey's consent for Higham and Bromhall, college clock; XXXII (1910–11), 1–9, documents concerning Alan Percy, second master, list of benefactors in 1545; *ibid.,* 145–162, letter to Fisher from Bishop Adrian de Castello, various letters to Metcalfe, inventory of goods at Higham in 1524; XXXV (1913–14), 2–35, Fisher's commission to Fresell and Chetham as his proctors, full powers given to Fisher by fellow executors, trust deeds for four fellowships and two

scholarships, deed for St. John's as Fisher's residuary legatee, accounts 1524–34, Fisher's two scholars Edmund and Matthew White; XXXV (1913–14), 153–172, Metcalfe's accounts on Higham and Bromhall, various letters, incl. Henry VIII's reprimand of Fisher's neglect of duty in regard to nuns at Higham; XXXVI (1914–15), 1–12, various letters to Metcalfe, catalogue of college plate in 1530. See also C. C. Babington, "On Some Remains of the Hospital of St. John the Evangelist at Cambridge," *Eagle,* IV (1863–65), 253–264; and J. H. Hessels, "Collegium DIVI Johannis *or* Collegium SANCTI Johannis," *ibid.,* XXXVII (1915–16), 1–90, chronology and documents to April 9, 1511. For finances during Fisher's lifetime, see H. F. Howard, *An Account of the Finances of the College of St. John the Evangelist in the University of Cambridge* (Cambridge [Eng.] University Press, 1935), pp. 5–22, 50, 200, 260, 266–267. The history of Higham Priory is found in *V.C.H. Kent,* II, 145–146; that of Bromhall Nunnery, in *V.C.H. Berkshire,* II, 80–81. Cf. C. R. Councer, "The Dissolution of the Kentish Monasteries," *Archaeologia Cantiana,* XLVII (1935), 127–130. E. Miller shows that Henry VIII did not deprive St. John's of any just right: "The Lady Margaret could not and did not attempt to deprive Henry VIII of his heritage. She simply claimed his forbearance till the new College had been founded and endowed" ("The Last Will and Testament of the Lady Margaret Beaufort," *Eagle,* LVII [1956], 1–7). For Fisher's foundation of four fellows and two pupils, see also *John's,* 1524, ch. 47, pp. 342–343 (cf. 1530, ch. 54, pp. 238, 240, 242, 244, and pp. 346–348). The same statutes provide for twenty-four annual trentals to be distributed to the more exemplary and needy priests of the college, because Fisher fears that popular devotion toward students and priests might grow cold and deprive many of their incomes (*John's,* 1524, ch. 50, p. 345; 1530, ch. 57, p. 254).

15. *John's,* p. xv, n. 3; Ortroy, *Fisher,* X, 243, n. 2; Fisher, "Ver. corp." ded. ep., *Opera,* p. 746. J. H. Hessels discusses the discovery and contents of statutes to be dated on or before April 9, 1511, in "Collegium DIVI Johannis *or* Collegium SANCTI *Johannis," Eagle,* XXXVII (1915–16), 316–319; but Scott considers these a "part of the original statutes of 1516" ("Notes from the College Records," Fourth Series, 1918, p. 280).

16. *John's,* 1516, ch. 23, p. 375; 1524, ch. 27, p. 312; 1530, ch. 22, pp. 110, 112.

17. *John's,* 1516, ch. 35, p. 389; 1524, ch. 39, p. 334; 1530, ch. 23, pp. 120, 122. From Louvain, July 16, 1522, Nicholas Darynton wrote to Henry Gold that he "is glad to find that the bishop of Rochester is so agreeable to relaxing the statutes" (*LP,* III, no. 2390, pp. 1010–11). Letters and documents referring to Gold, who was one of the thirty-one fellows admitted to St. John's on July 29, 1516, and who was later executed for complicity with the Nun of Kent (May 6, 1534), are given by Scott, "Notes from the College Records," *Eagle,* XXXVI (1914–15), 253–283.

18. *John's,* 1516, ch. 23, p. 376; 1524, ch. 27, p. 313; 1530, ch. 23, p. 122.

19. *John's,* 1516, ch. 31, p. 385 (cf. 1524, ch. 35, p. 328; 1530, ch. 21, p. 106); 1516, ch. 30, p. 383 (cf. 1524, ch. 34, p. 326; 1530, ch. 21, p. 104).

20. *John's,* 1524, ch. 34, p. 327 (cf. 1530, ch. 22, pp. 114, 116).

21. *John's,* 1530, ch. 48, p. 212; Ortroy, *Fisher,* X, 228.

22. Luther's books would be more accessible at Cambridge than at Oxford: "In the early sixteenth century Cambridge was a port for channel-going vessels and a terminal of trade with Hanseatic ports" (Clebsch, *Earliest Protestants,* p. 42). For the relation of Cambridge to the Reformation, see Mullinger, *Cambridge to 1535,* pp. 552–632.

23. Fisher, *Margaret,* ed. Baker-Hymers, p. 216. The "inviolate mother" is undoubtedly the Church rather than the university.

24. Ortroy, *Fisher,* X, 243, n. 3; XII, 133–134, n. 1; Constant, *Reformation,* I, 302, and n. 57; Lewis, *Fisher,* II, 356–358; and Thomas Baker, *History of the College of St. John the Evangelist,* ed. J. E. B. Mayor (Cambridge, 1869), I, 100–101. Scott declares: "It would appear that Thomas Cranmer, who was now Archbishop of Canterbury, had visited the College and made some suggestions for an alteration of the Statutes. That the College, accepting this advice, had prepared a revised code, and tried to obtain Fisher's consent to the alterations" ("Notes from the College Records," Fourth Series, p. 266, originally designed to be published in *Eagle,* vol. XXXVI, no. 167). See also Scott, *ibid.,* p. 267, on Fisher's probable revision at this time.

25. *John's,* p. x; Ortroy, *Fisher,* X, 244, XII, 168; Baker, *History of St. John,* I, 346, 377–379. In 1516 there are no regulations on the library in the statutes, which in 1524 have prescriptions on catalogues, keys, chains for books, etc., and which in 1530 have even more elaborate rules (*John's,* 1524, ch. 7, p. 275, ch. 9, p. 278; 1530, ch. 41, pp. 188, 190, 192). To the Duke of Somerset, Ascham writes about Fisher and his books as follows: "Libri etiam ejus universi nostri erant. Cum libros ejus dicimus, magnum Thesaurum dicimus. Thesaurus sane ille dignus erat, qui incidisset in bonos & peritos homines. Quid multis? Ejus perversa doctrina, & illum vita, & nos summis divitiis nostris privavit" (*Epistolarum libri quatuor . . .* [Oxford, 1703], p. 293). Fisher's library seems to have been located in Rochester proper rather than elsewhere: see Denne-Wildash, *Rochester,* p. 91n; R. B. Rye, "The Ancient Episcopal Palace at Rochester and Bishop Fisher," *Archaeologia Cantiana,* XVII (1887), 66–76; and A. J. Pearman, "Residences of the Bishops of Rochester," *Archaeologia Cantiana,* XXXIII (1918), 131–151. The deed, dated November 27, 1525, by which St. John's would have been Fisher's residuary legatee, includes "all my lordes printed bookes at Rochestre in his studies there" (Scott, "Notes from the College Records," *Eagle,* XXXV [1913–14], 26).

26. Erasmus, *Ep.,* I, 466, 492; II, 328 (tr. Thomson-Porter, *Erasmus,* pp. 195–196). The fullest account of Erasmus' associations with Cambridge is to be found in the Introduction to Thomson-Porter, *Erasmus and Cambridge,* pp. 1–103. See also Porter, "Erasmus in Cambridge," *Reformation and Reaction,* pp. 21–40. Erasmus' mysterious reference to Fisher's "three colleges" would seem to refer to the mere intention of erecting a third college, as is borne out by Ortroy, *Fisher,* X, 251. Fisher urged him to the task of writing *Ecclesiastes:* "Significans, se . . . tria instituere Collegia, unde prodirent

Theologi, non tam ad λογομαχίας armati, quam ad sobrie praedicandum verbum Dei instructi" (Erasmus, *Opera,* V, 767–768). Curiously enough, Caspar Meckenlor in 1536 in the dedicatory epistle to his German translation of *Assert. Luth. confut.* also remarks: "er auch des willens gewest / Drey Collegia zu stifften / darinn man prediger solt auffziehen. . ." (*Gründtliche widerlegung,* fol. 3).

27. Erasmus, *Ep.,* III, 158–159 (tr. Thomson-Porter, *Erasmus,* pp. 199–200), 267, 584 (tr. Thomson-Porter, p. 202). In 1519 Maurice Durand's prefatory letter to *The Single Magdalene* praises Fisher for establishing two magnificent colleges by his intervention and for enriching them with books, excellent statutes, and liberal revenues ("Magdal.," *Opera,* p. 1394).

28. Erasmus, *Ep.,* IV, 281 (tr. Thomson-Porter, *Erasmus,* pp. 203–204); VIII, 160–161. It had been in Cambridge that Erasmus in 1505–6 apparently planned to take his doctorate in theology (at Fisher's offer?), but the opportunity to visit Italy was too tempting (Erasmus, *Ep.,* Appendix VI, I, 591–592). A. Hyma speculates that, if he had taken his degree at Cambridge, Erasmus "might have averted the religious upheaval known as the Protestant Reformation. England could have become the chief center of religious reform in the western world . . . The Oxford Reformers might have combined with the Cambridge Reformers . . ." See "Erasmus and the Oxford Reformers (1503–1519)," *Nederlands Archief voor Kerkgeschiedenis,* Nieuwe Serie, XXXVIII (1951), 74–75.

29. *LP,* IV, no. 5236, p. 2308; Fisher, *Margaret,* ed. Baker-Hymers, pp. 217–223; Lewis, *Fisher,* Coll. Nos. 21–23, II, 301–307.

30. Lewis, *Fisher,* Coll. No. 34, II, 356–358. *Nihil est ab omni parte beatum.* The classical languages received due emphasis at Cambridge, but there is no attention paid explicitly to vigorous vernacular literature, e.g., of Italy. Roberto Weiss writes: "If we compare Cambridge with Oxford from the standpoint of *belles-lettres,* we cannot but realise its inferiority. We do not find there that taste for Italian learning already present in Oxford by the middle of the century" (*Humanism in England during the Fifteenth Century,* 2nd ed. [Oxford: Basil Blackwell, 1957], p. 160). On Italian scholars and devotees at Cambridge, e.g., Lorenzo di Savona, John Doget, and John Argentine, see Thomson-Porter, *Erasmus,* pp. 23–24.

CHAPTER XI: FAITH AND JUSTIFICATION

1. *Heretickes,* sig. B4v–C1v; "Psalms," Vulg. Ps. 50 (1), *Eng. Works,* p. 100, Lat. tr., *Opera,* col. 1530. John Frith argues against Fisher that if "fayth is a gyfte of god / which he destributeth at his owne pleasure," there is no room for "compulsion and violence" ("An answere vnto my lorde of Rochestre," *Purgatorye,* ed. 1533, sig. L4). Knox quotes the passage from Fisher's *Heretickes* and comments: "Fisher avoided the conclusion that if faith and charity are God's gifts, salvation must be gratuitous and apart from our works, by

distinguishing between faith and our assent to it" (*Faith,* p. 115). Fisher would reply that the assent itself is faith, that is, an act of faith, performed with God's free gift of grace. Quite apropos in Küng's analysis: "God's verdict, powerful in Jesus Christ, makes him [the sinner] alive and ready for the cooperari and the assentire . . . It is a cooperation (Mitwirken) not in the sense of collaboration (Mitwerken) but of involvement (Mitmachen) . . . Assentire then means, despite his passivity, the highly active 'Yes and Amen' of the repentant sinner awakened by God's gracious verdict. Cooperari means getting oneself involved in what God alone has put into execution . . . The vital point is that God accomplishes *everything.* But it does not follow from this that He accomplishes it *alone"* (*Justification,* tr. T. Collins *et al.* [New York: Nelson, 1964], pp. 264–265; see p. 266 for Bernard of Clairvaux's exposition [*PL,* CLXXXII, 1002, 1026–27], which Küng considers the best in the Fathers). On faith as "an attitude of total agreement," see *ibid.,* p. 254; and on faith as a personal assent "to Christ, in those things which truly belong to His teaching," see *ibid.,* pp. 255–256. On justification in the history of dogma up to and including Trent, see *ibid.,* pp. 215–221. Küng later (p. 281) points to H. Schmidt's three reasons for the importance of Luther's theology of justification: (1) "an internalization of religious life," (2) restoration of "pre-eminence to the work of God in justification," and (3) "a declaration of war against the Roman curia."

2. "Ver. corp." 5.prooem., *Opera,* pp. 1129–30.

3. Fisher, *Eversio,* sig. B1; Hessus, *Apologia,* sigg. A3, B1, C3ᵛ–4.

4. "Assert. Luth. confut." art. 27, *Opera,* col. 583; art. 37, col. 727; "Def. reg. assert." 3.20, col. 147.

5. "Psalms," Vulg. 37 (1), *Eng. Works,* p. 46; "Assert. Luth. confut." art. 14, *Opera,* cols. 456–457; "Ver. corp." 3.8, col. 951.

6. "Ver. corp." 1.3, *Opera,* cols. 762–763; 1.4, col. 764; 1.12, col. 794. To inquire in the Schools is one thing; to preach to the uneducated people in a sermon calling in doubt a universally accepted doctrine is quite another and is nefarious and criminal (1.4, col. 764).

7. "Assert. Luth. confut." art. 10, *ibid.,* cols. 433, 437; "Ver. corp." 1.6, col. 769; 1.8, col. 778.

8. "Assert. Luth. confut." art. 1, *ibid.,* cols. 320–321; cf. "Ver. corp." 5.25, col. 1193. For current thought in 1517, see Altenstaig, *Vocabularius theologie,* foll. 87ᵛ–88, for *Fides triplex* (*viua, mortua, ficta*) and *Fides duplex* (*informis & formata*). Because of their relationship to faith, see also the entries: *Opus, Opus Bonum, Opera, Opus satisfactorium, Opus supererogationis, Opus operatum et opus operans* (*ibid.,* foll. 169ᵛ–171). Cf. Moehler, *Symbolik*: "Thus also the medieval schools knew a faith of which they said that it alone justifies. It is designated as fides formata" (quoted in Küng, *Justification,* p. 257). On "the concept of justification of the evangelists as a 'duplex iustitia' which was later to receive its classical formulation by Contarino at the Imperial diet of Regensburg (1541) [and which held that] justification is solely derived from the 'fides caritate formata,'" see J. P. Dolan, *The Influence of Erasmus, Witzel, and Cassander . . .* (Münster: Aschendorff,

1957), pp. 20–21, which also gives the antecedents in Augustine, Aquinas, Catharinus, Fisher, Wimpina, Pighius, Gropper, Witzel, and Erasmus.

9. "Assert. Luth. confut." art. 1, *Opera,* col. 316; art. 6, col. 408; "Ver. corp." 5.prooem., p. 1130. Vega, *De iustificatione,* lib. XIV, cap. 9, ed. 1572, p. 626, refers to the separability of faith from charity as proved by Fisher in "Assert. Luth. confut." art. 1 and art. 6 (*Opera,* cols. 316, 405).

10. *Sacerd. def.,* ed. Schmeink, p. 5; *Heretickes,* sig. F2. *Heretickes* has other interesting observations. Heresies like "stynkynge weedes" spread easily whereas the good seed and herbs require labor (sig. A2ᵛ–3). The four "conditions" for heretics are the following: (1) "the heretikes studie to be singular in theyr opinions"; (2) "the heretikes . . . be blynded in theyr hartes / and haue nat the clene light of faithe"; (3) "these heretikes sytte out of the right waye"; and (4) "they be deuided from the churche of Christe" (sig. B2ᵛ–3). Heretics disagree not only with the Church but among themselves: "It is a very trouth that one wise man hath sayde: *Omne verum omni vero consonat / falsum autem tam a se ipso quam ab ipsa veritate discrepat*: Euery trouth agreeth with other: but falshod is both repugnant ageynst hym selfe & ageynst the trouth" (sig. B3; cf. *Eversio,* sig. a6). To be "restored to the true faithe of Christis churche," the heretic must take four steps of which the fourth is that "he muste fully assent vnto the doctrine of Christis churche" (sig. B4ᵛ–C1). A single error once admitted leads to many others daily as in Luther's case ("Assert. Luth. confut." art. 23, *Opera,* col. 522). What Fisher once heard as a boy is also true: from the ashes of heretics easily arise other heretics, as in the case of John Hus (*ibid.* art. 30, col. 603).

11. "Assert. Luth. confut." art. 1, *Opera,* col. 317. According to Oberman (*Medieval Theology,* p. 73), "Biel states explicitly: acquired faith 'etiam in demonibus esse potest.' " See also *Fides daemonum* in Altenstaig, *Vocabularius theologie,* fol. 88ᵛ; and Torquemada, *Ecclesia* 1.8 ad 13, with reference to Aquinas, *S.T.* 2–2, q. 5, art. 2. For Torquemada, the devils' faith is "fides que nascitur ex perspicacitate naturalis intellectus eorum & ex miraculis que vident supra naturam" (sig. a7).

12. Jedin, *Trient,* II, 249–250; *Concilium Tridentinum,* V, 699, 730; Bellarmine, "De iustificatione," lib. 1, cap. 3, *Controv.,* ed. 1615, IV, 299. See Altenstaig, *Vocabularius theologie,* for pre-Reformation notions of justice and justification (foll. 126ᵛ–128ᵛ) and sin (foll. 180–184ᵛ). For a gathering of quotations from Fisher's Catholic contemporaries on concupiscence as sin, see Laemmer, *Vortridentinisch-katholische Theologie,* pp. 117–120. Helpful background, theological and historical, can be found in the following sections in Küng, *Justification*: "Simul Iustus et Peccator" (pp. 236–248) and "Sola Fide" (pp. 249–263). In regard to the latter, for example, Küng observes: "The formula sola fide can be taken for orthodox since the 'alone' may be understood as a plausible way of making clear the statement in Romans 3.28. This much is certain — the 'alone' in the translation is not Luther's invention. Even *before* the Reformation there were already such translations. . . Nor did the Council of Trent intend to say anything against the

formula in itself . . . the formula definitely belongs to Catholic tradition" (pp. 249–250).

13. "Psalms," Vulg. Ps. 31, *Eng. Works,* pp. 23–24, 30, 44, Lat. tr., *Opera,* cols. 1478, 1481, 1491. The Latin commentary on this psalm (Psalms MS, P.R.O.S.P.2/R, foll. 135–137) appears to use the same approach and also ends with a reference to "perfect satisfaction" (*integra satisfactio*). The manuscript is in poor condition.

14. Cf. Knox, *Faith,* pp. 116–117.

15. "Psalms," Vulg. Ps. 50 (1), *Eng. Works,* pp. 99–101, Lat. tr., *Opera,* cols. 1530–31. Fisher applies the whole of his manuscript Latin commentary on Vulg. Ps. 10 to the heretical Lutherans, who "attribute all to faith, nothing to works" (Psalms MS, P.R.O.S.P.2/R, foll. 172ᵛ–173ᵛ).

16. "Psalms," Vulg. Ps. 37 (2), *Eng. Works,* p. 81, Lat. tr., *Opera,* col. 1518; Vulg. 50 (2), p. 114, Lat. tr., col. 1540.

17. Psalms MS, Vulg. Ps. 26, P.R.O.S.P.2/R, foll. 28–37, 112–114ᵛ, 208–210ᵛ. There are four extant copies, but what appears to be the holograph lacks the introduction.

18. "Or." 2.1, *Opera,* cols. 1718–19, Eng. tr. 1560, sig. D8–E2. Instead of "to do all other thynges according to the wyll and commaundement of God and his Churche," the Latin original designates only the Church: "caetera facere quae decretis Ecclesiae conueniunt." The source for Chrysostom's statement is *In Joan.* cap. i. hom. ix.

19. "Luther," *Eng. Works,* pp. 323–326, Lat. tr., *Opera,* cols. 1381–82, 1391–92. "Fisher recognized that in scripture the word 'faith' might be used 'of the strong faith that hath a confidence and hope adjoined.' He also acknowledged that 'heat of charity giveth evidence that that light (i.e. faith) is lively.' He acknowledged moreover that both faith and charity are the gift of God. 'The heat of charity spread in our hearts by the Holy Spirit of God, giveth evidence of the lively light of faith, shining upon our souls from our saviour Christ.' In all this he was nearer to Luther than he knew. But he did not follow up the possibility which he recognized, that in scripture 'faith' had a deeper meaning than it had in current theology" (Knox, *Faith,* p. 115). On the relationship between trust and faith ("a trusting faith"), see Küng, *Justification,* pp. 252–256. For example, "This description of hope [by Trent] corresponds almost literally to that of the confident faith of the Reformers; however, it requires two precise and important distinctions. First, the basis of the confidence is not the subjective feeling of believing and of being justified, but the objective promise of God; second, this confidence does not concern itself with a present and realized object (justification already granted) but with a future object (Deum sibi propitium fore)." This passage is quoted by Küng, pp. 254–255, from L. Villette, *Foi et sacrement* (Paris, 1954), IV, 115.

20. Fisher, "Luther," *Eng. Works,* pp. 326–328, Lat. tr., *Opera,* cols. 1382–83; Tyndale, "Obedience," *Treatises,* pp. 223–224. For Luther's stand on the uselessness of works as means to salvation, see McDonough, *Law and Gospel in Luther,* pp. 21–23, 44–48, 91–92, n. 1, 92–93, n. 1

21. "Luther," *Eng. Works,* pp. 328–331, Lat. tr., *Opera,* cols. 1382–84. The Vulgate version has *per caritatem,* not *per dilectionem,* which appears in Erasmus' translation with the comment: "Rursum hic *operans* non significat quod vulgus somniat, sed quae vim suam occultam exerceat in nobis, quod proprium est Spiritus. Sentitur enim vis, cum ipse nusquam appareat. Nam legem vult parum efficacem videri, contra fidem efficacem: ἐνεργουμένη, quod *agens* rectius verti poterat" (*Opera,* VI, 822).

22. Fisher, *Confut. sec. discept.,* fol. 8; *Heretickes,* sig. C2; Tyndale, "Obedience," *Treatises,* pp. 221–223. "Justification through living faith in no sense means justification by faith *and* works. But it wants to be active in works, 'faith working through love' (Gal. 5.6). How should it be otherwise? For 'if I have all faith, so as to remove mountains, but have not love, I am nothing' (1 Cor. 13.2)" (Küng, *Justification,* pp. 256–257).

23. "Et quoniam [fides] potestate quadam intra se continet opera, quae nondum in lucem edita sunt, iccirco per eam initiari solum iustus dicitur, non autem consummari. Nam consummata iustitia non aliter, quam ex operibus natis, & in lucem editis acquiri potest" ("Assert. Luth. confut." art. 1, *Opera,* cols. 317–318). Gerhard quotes the previous sentence approvingly as follows: "fides quae iustificat, ferax est bonorum operum, nec vero inficior, quum fides absque partu bonorum operum, hoc est, cum opera nondum peperit, iustificet, at iam operum grauida est & paritura, cum occasio fuerit" (*Loci theologici,* ed. 1639, III, 634).

24. Barnes, "Supplication," *Whole workes,* p. 237 (cf. *A supplicatyon . . .* [Antwerp, 1531], fol. 1); Fisher, "Assert. Luth. confut." art. 1, *Opera,* col. 319: "Quapropter . . . fratres, magis satagite, vt per bona opera, certam vestram vocationem & electionem faciatis [Vulg. 2 Pet. 1:10] . . . Monuit ergo Petrus, vt per bona opera, vocationem, & electionem nostram firmam, & ratam efficeremus, atque ita traduxit Erasmus." "By good works" is lacking in the better Greek manuscripts. Later, Fisher again quotes Erasmus approvingly for his interpretation of 2 Cor. 13:5: "Subdit Hieronymus: Dei virtus in vobis est, si tamen vos minime reprobauit, hoc est (quemadmodum Erasmus docte explicuit) Nisi forte Fide vtcunque incolumi, vita impura, meruistis a Christo reijci" (*ibid.* art. 14, col. 457).

25. "Assert. Luth. confut." art. 35, *Opera,* col. 657.

26. *Ibid.* art. 17, col. 493.

27. *Ibid.* art. 7, cols. 414–416. For the theological terms, see Appendix I, "Merit *de condigno* and *de congruo,*" in McDonough, *Law and Gospel in Luther,* pp. 156–162. For Biel's doctrine, see Oberman, *Medieval Theology,* pp. 169–174. As for the goodness of *timor servilis,* Vitoria at Salamanca feels no need further to censure Luther's doctrine because of Fisher's satisfactory treatment ("In 2.2. de spe. q. 19, a. 4," *Commentarios a la Secunda secundae de Santo Tomás,* I, 308–309). Another Salamancan theologian, Vega, refers to Fisher's teachings on the usefulness of fearing divine justice (*De iustificatione,* lib. VI, cap. 24, ed. 1572, p. 102) and on the ability of sinners to merit justifying grace *ex congruo* (*ibid.,* lib. VIII, cap. 8, p. 188).

28. "Assert. Luth. confut." art. 36, *Opera,* cols. 701–702, 713–714. Fisher

quotes from Augustine's *Ad Simplicianum,* lib. 1, quaest. 2. For an explanation in 1517, see Altenstaig, *Vocabularius theologie,* for *Facere quod est in se* (fol. 84) and *Obex* (fol. 164ᵛ). For the significance of Nominalist doctrine on *facere quod in se est,* see McDonough, *Law and Gospel in Luther,* pp. 32–45. Especially pertinent for Fisher's doctrine is the following statement: "It is argued [for example, by P. Vignaux] that this Nominalist idea of merit, when studied in its proper context, and explained with suitable definitions, nuanced meanings, and subtle sub-distinctions, characteristic of the Schoolmen, is not at all incompatible with the traditional teachings of the Church. . . . But be that as it may, it remains that the emphasis and tendency in this thesis of Biel's is Pelagian" (*ibid.,* p. 35).

29. "Assert. Luth. confut." art. 15, *Opera,* col. 469.

30. "Def. reg. assert." 2.11, *Opera,* cols. 120–122; 12.1, col. 256. See also 2.10, col. 119: "Sic enim in libello de fide & operibus docet. Fides esse nullo modo potest, nisi sit viuax quaedam & indubitata opinio, qua homo certus est super omnem certitudinem, se placere Deo." Fisher refers to Luther's shifting position on the ease or difficulty of faith also in "Assert. Luth. confut." art. 1, *Opera,* cols. 314–315, which is quoted at length by Vega, *De iustificatione,* lib. XIV, cap. 8, ed. 1572, p. 621.

31. "Ver. corp." 2.4, *Opera,* col. 851; 3.3, col. 939; 4.9, col. 1026; 4.22, col. 1060.

32. *Two Sermons,* sig. G4ᵛ–5, Lat. tr., *Opera,* col. 1685. For a critical view of this sermon as throwing emphasis on "meritorious efforts of one's own will" rather than "the dominion of grace," see Knox, *Faith,* pp. 80–81. See Fisher in the same sermon: Christ Jesus "nether bought this inherytaunce for the, ne made promyse therof, but with condicion": the condition being observance of the commandments (sig. F4ᵛ–G1, Lat. tr., col. 1681).

33. *Heretickes,* sigg. B1ᵛ, C1, with reference to the hart in Vulg. Ps. 41:2; "Def. reg. assert." 2.10–11, *Opera,* cols. 119–122. Cf. Luther, *WA,* V, 206.

34. "De iustificatione," lib. 3, cap. 2, *Controv.,* ed. 1615, IV, 349. Earlier, Vega had appealed to Fisher's verdict on the uncertainty of grace as a "constant and certain" doctrine (*De iustificatione,* lib. IX, cap. 14, ed. 1572, p. 236, citing "Assert. Luth. confut." arts. 10, 11, 14).

35. "Margaret," *Eng. Works,* pp. 307–309.

36. "Or." 1.4, *Opera,* col. 1716, Eng. tr. 1560, *Prayer,* sig. D3.

37. "Def. reg. assert." 2.10, *Opera,* cols. 119–120.

38. "Ver. corp." 1.6, *Opera,* col. 769; 2.19, col. 880; 3.3, col. 939; 4.8, col. 1024; 4.22, col. 1061; 5.prooem., pp. 1130–31. On the infallibility of God's assistance through the sacraments, see also "Assert. Luth. confut." art. 36, *ibid.,* cols. 708–709. Fisher's views were cited in the controversy over the certainty of grace at the Council of Trent. See *Concilium Tridentinum,* XII, 692, and V. Heynck, "A Controversy at the Council of Trent concerning the Doctrine of Duns Scotus," *Franciscan Studies,* IX (1949), 181–258. On "the Tridentine discussion of the certainty of grace," Küng (*Justification,* p. 255) recommends J. Hefner, *Die Entstehungsgeschichte des Trienter Rechtfertigungsdekretes* (Paderborn, 1909), pp. 297–328, and A. Stakemeier,

Das Konzil von Trient über die Heilsgewissheit (Heidelberg, 1947), pp. 167–181.

39. "Ver. corp." 4.5, *Opera,* cols. 1012–13; 4.9, col. 1026; 5.29, col. 1205. On the relationship between justification and sanctification, see Küng, *Justification,* pp. 267–270. For Luther's "imputed righteousness," see McDonough, *Law and Gospel in Luther,* pp. 45–48, and Appendix II, "Intrinsic Sanctification," pp. 163–165.

40. Ps. 101 (1), *Eng. Works,* p. 160, Lat. tr., *Opera,* col. 1571.

41. "Or." 1.4, *Opera,* cols. 1716–17, Eng. tr. 1560, *Prayer,* sig. D2v–5. It is at this point that Fisher has the teasing passage with its multiple possible interpretations: "For we do reade of many, which lately [*dudum*] stode like mightie pillers in the Churche of God . . . But for that they conteyned not them selues within the limittes of reuerent and humble feare, they fell downe headlong into the bottomlesse pitte of all euyll and mischiefe, not onlye to theyr owne harme and shame, but with the hurt and destruction of many others . . ." (*ibid.*). The *dudum* in the Latin original can mean not only "a short time ago" but also "formerly." In the latter case, the allusion is to collapses in the whole course of ecclesiastical history, an interpretation supported by references to reading and to Doctors and annals. The translation of 1640 has simply "a long time" (p. 26).

42. "Ver. corp." 4.30, *Opera,* col. 1086 (cf. *ibid.* 4.31, col. 1096); "Sacerd. def." 3.7, col. 1274, tr. Hallett, pp. 88–89.

43. *Two Sermons,* sigg. F4–G1, Lat. tr., *Opera,* cols. 1680–81.

CHAPTER XII: GRACE AND SALVATION

1. "Henry VII," *Eng. Works,* pp. 270–271; "Or." 1.4, *Opera,* col. 1717, Eng. tr. 1560, *Prayer,* sig. D5.

2. Ps. 50 (1), "Psalms," *Eng. Works,* p. 100, Lat. tr., *Opera,* col. 1530.

3. Ps. 101 (1), *ibid.,* p. 151, Lat. tr., col. 1565.

4. Ps. 142, *ibid.,* p. 259, Lat. tr., *Opera,* col. 1636. Fisher's English translation shows the inadvertent omission of two words from the Latin original, supplied by the Latin version: *Da Domine . . . quod iubes, & iube quod vis.*

5. "Or." 1.1–3, *Opera,* cols. 1712–13, 1715, Eng. tr. 1560, sig. C2–3v, 8. Reference has already been made above to (1) "the grace of perseueraunce" (*ibid.* 1.4, col. 1717, Eng. tr. 1560, sig. D5) and (2) the need of being "alredy by charitie in the grace and fauour of almightie God" before receiving the "first fruite of praier . . . merite or rewarde promised by God, both to and for the same" (*ibid.* 2.1, cols. 1718–19, Eng. tr. 1560, sig. D8).

6. "Or." 2.2, *ibid.,* cols. 1719–20, Eng. tr. 1560, sig. E2v–3v. The strange combination of "key, or . . . nayle" results from a Latin play on words: "vel hunc clavum vel eam clavem" (*ibid.*).

7. "Assert. Luth. confut." art. 1, *Opera,* col. 320.

8. *Ibid.* art. 6, col. 407; art. 36, col. 692. Fisher's defense of Scotus in particular achieved a certain renown: see *Concilium Tridentinum,* X, 587, and

two articles by V. Heynck, "Der hl. John Fisher und die skotistische Reuelehre," *Franziskanische Studien,* XXV (1938), 105–133, and "Die Verteidigung der Sakramentenlehre des Duns Scotus durch den hl. John Fisher gegen die Anschuldigungen Luthers," *ibid.,* XXIV (1937), 165–175. In discussing Scotus' views on the uncertainty of justification, Vega points to Fisher's defense of Scotus ("Assert. Luth. confut." art. 1, *Opera,* col. 338) on sacramental reception (*De iustificatione,* lib. IX, cap. 15, ed. 1572, pp. 239–240).

9. This preference of Fisher for the opinion of the Fathers attained some notoriety. In his controversy with Soto over the necessity of grace for a morally good deed, Ambrose Catharinus leans heavily upon the opinion and authority of "the Most Reverend Cardinal and Bishop of Rochester, a man at once most holy and most learned" ("Disceptatio quarta de potentia liberi arbitrij in natura lapsa absque gratia & speciali auxilio Dei," *Disceptationes* [Rome, 1541], foll. 52–53ᵛ, 63–64). Gerhard quotes the pertinent passage (*Loci theologici,* ed. 1639, III, 706).

10. "Assert. Luth. confut." art. 36, *Opera,* cols. 682–683, 704.

11. *Ibid.* art. 6, cols. 405–407. An interesting sidelight is given here: "Do you consider the knowledge of the things of nature to be nothing to those who are not endowed with [sanctifying] grace? For it is a very frequent occurrence that persons who are better [morally] have less skill in those things" (*ibid.,* col. 405). Barnes ridicules Fisher's stand: "Nowe where wylle our Duns men / brynge in their bonum conatum / they are so longe in bryngynge of yt in / that frewylle is brought to the fyer and there cane he neyther saue hym selfe from burnyng / nor yet helpe hym selfe out / but to this my lord of Rochester answereth in a serten place / that fre wylle cane doo no good meritorius / sed tamen non omnino facit / what is thys to saye but Nihil" (*Supplicatyon,* ed. 1531, fol. 81ᵛ).

12. "Assert. Luth. confut." art. 36, *Opera,* cols. 676–677, 680–682. In response to the question: "And the *acts* of the sinner? Are they good or evil?" Küng elucidates Catholic doctrine thus: "(1) . . . no self-disposing autonomous good resides in any act of the sinner . . . From this source — from Christ — the sinner obtains power to do penance and to repent and so to bring about 'good' acts . . . (2) But even in this sense the predicate 'good' ought to be attached to the works of a sinner only with major reservations and by way of analogy. For no act of a sinner is good in the sense that it is capable of being an act of salvation in the strict sense of an act of merit. To this extent one could just as well designate it 'sinful' in an analogical sense . . . (3) . . . after all is said and done, it is not feasible to assume the existence of ultimately *indifferent* acts, let alone acts occurring without grace . . . An act refers positively or negatively to Jesus Christ (knowingly or unknowingly, explicitly or implicitly, in se or in causa, formally, virtually, or habitually) . . . Today the majority of Catholic theologians agree with Schmaus' statement: 'So it must be stressed here too that the Church's doctrinal declarations only speak of the possibility of a natural morality, not of its actuality . . .' " (*Justification,* pp. 186–189).

13. Castro, *Adv. haereses,* lib. 11, *s. v. Opera,* ed. 1564, fol. 195; Fisher,

"Assert. Luth. confut." arts. 31–32, *Opera,* cols. 608–633; "Charitas," *ibid.,* cols. 1704–1707. On Lethmatius, see Erasmus, *Ep.,* V, 138, and Reusch, *Verbotene Bücher,* I, 210. Fisher awkwardly explains that he used the quotation from Jerome (art. 31, col. 610) to which Lethmatius objects, not because he agrees with Jerome that Paul committed sin but because Jerome says just what he wants, to wit, that even if no one can be free from all sin, nevertheless he sometimes does not sin in a work. Vega, too, is displeased with Fisher, *alioqui doctissimus & pientissimus,* for conceding to Luther that Paul had committed a venial sin in instructing Timothy (2 Tim. 4:13) to bring Paul's cloak, books, and parchments (*De iustificatione,* lib. XI, cap. 35, ed. 1572, p. 415). Vega refers also to Fisher's arts. 31, 32, 39 (*ibid.,* lib. XI, cap. 24 and 25, pp. 398, 401).

14. Psalms MS, P.R.O.S.P.2/R, foll. 186ᵛ, 240ᵛ. See Altenstaig for accepted explanations of *Meritum,* of *Meritum de condigno,* of *Meritum de congruo,* and of *mereri* (*Vocabularius theologie,* foll. 148–149). On the ways in which Christ's teaching and the Catholic Church's doctrine differ from Pharisaic thinking on merit, see Küng, *Justification,* pp. 270–274.

15. *Heretickes,* sigg. C4–D1, F4ᵛ–G1; "Or." 2.2, *Opera,* col. 1720, Eng. tr. 1560, *Prayer,* sig. E3.

16. *Two Sermons,* sigg. D3ᵛ, F1ᵛ, Lat. tr. (of F1ᵛ only), *Opera,* col. 1677.

17. "Consolation," *Eng. Works,* pp. 355, 359, Lat. tr., *Opera,* pp. 1644, 1646. The Latin translation omits: "And what is more easie to be giuen then water," and renders: "yet did I linger them by my folly" thus: "meo tamen scelere deprauata vitium & labem contraxerunt" (p. 1646).

18. Bellarmine, "De gratia et libero arbitrio," lib. 2, cap. 1, *Controv.,* ed. 1615, IV, 184–185; "Enseignement de Louvain," *Auctarium,* pp. 60–61, 66–67.

19. "Psalms," *Eng. Works,* pp. 39–41, 207–208, Lat. tr., *Opera,* cols. 1488–89, 1602–1604. The manuscript Latin commentary on the Psalms also stresses God's generosity with grace. Conceded that our whole salvation depends upon Him, He is not parsimonious and miserly but liberal and munificent; for, like the sun pouring its rays abundantly upon the whole earth, He even more copiously communicates His grace to all who prepare themselves properly (Ps. 2, P.R.O.S.P.2/R, foll. 159, 267). The whole glory of salvation is to be referred to God, but He is more prepared to confer help than the sinner to receive it (Ps. 3, *ibid.,* foll. 158ᵛ, 266ᵛ). The commentary on Ps. 25 also treats works and grace, merit and reward, benignity and acceptance, but unfortunately the manuscript is much blurred (*ibid.,* foll. 207, 261ᵛ).

20. "Or." 1.2, 2.1, *Opera,* cols. 1712–13, 1719, Eng. tr. 1560, *Prayer,* sigg. C3ᵛ, E1ᵛ–2.

21. "Perfect Religion," *Eng. Works,* p. 372, Lat. tr., *Opera,* col. 1692.

22. "Assert. Luth. confut." art. 36, *Opera,* cols. 665–667. See especially col. 672, where the ever-present nature of God's special help is incontestably evident from the comparison with God's general influence (i.e., concurrence), ever present for the physical act of the will. This general influence is that "by which all things live and move and have their being" (cf. Acts 17:28).

23. *Ibid.,* cols. 682–685. For pre-Reformation opinion, see the entry *Ob-*

duratio in Altenstaig, *Vocabularius theologie,* fol. 164; and for views of contemporary Catholic theologians on hardening of the heart, see Jedin, *Cochlaeus,* pp. 70–72. "In der Lehre von der Verhärtung folgt Soto der milderen Ansicht. Die Verhärtung besteht nicht darin, dass Gott einem alle Gnaden entziehe, auch nicht als Straffolge von Sünden, wie es noch Roffensis als möglich annahm." — F. Stegmüller, "Zur Gnadenlehre des spanischen Konzilstheologen Domingo de Soto," in G. Schreiber, *Das Weltkonzil von Trient: sein Werden und Wirken* (Freiburg: Herder, 1951), I, 197, with reference to Soto, *De natura et gratia* (Paris, 1549), fol. 70v. Soto's opponent, Ambrose Catharinus, prefers Fisher's opinion as he sees it ("Disceptatio quinta de iustissima Dei prouidentia in nonnullos hominum, quos prae illorum immani & insigni atque diabolica malitia deserit, reprobat, & in sensum reprobum tradit," *Disceptationes,* fol. 65). Vega sees Fisher as a subscriber to Gregory of Rimini's harsh opinion by withdrawing God's help from hardened and reprobate sinners (*De iustificatione,* lib. XI, cap. 21, ed. 1572, p. 387).

24. "Assert. Luth. confut." art. 36, *Opera,* cols. 671, 698–699, 705–707. Cf. *ibid.,* col. 712: "Caeterum cum adiutorium gratiae nemini defuerit, nisi penitus derelictis, quis ambigere potest, quin ante susceptionem gratiae, peccator agens quantum in se fuerit, per illud adiutorium vitare queat peccatum mortale, simulque bene moraliter agere?" The instances of the publican and the Pharisee (Luke 18) and of Cornelius the centurion (Acts 10) follow.

25. Castro, *Adv. haereses,* lib. 9, *s. v.* Libertas, ed. 1564, fol. 160; Bellarmine, "De gratia et libero arbitrio," lib. 3, cap. 1, *Controv.,* ed. 1615, IV, 207. The excellence of Fisher's treatment is evident by comparison with the unsubstantial treatise *De libero arbitrio aduersus Melanchtonem* (London, 1523), by Alphonsus de Villasancte [*leg.* Villa Sancta], who first praises the Fathers and then gives brief citations from Melanchthon followed by brief refutations. The author, a Franciscan Observant, dedicated his work to Queen Catherine (McConica, *English Humanists,* pp. 54–55). For a collation of contemporary Catholic quotations on free will and grace, see Laemmer, *Vortridentinisch-katholische Theologie,* pp. 120–122. Catharinus declares that Luther's doctrine on free will, just the opposite of Erasmus', has been so well refuted "by learned men, and by the Bishop and Cardinal of Rochester whom I name by reason of honor and venerate as a martyr of Christ, that I judge it to be superfluous for me to do what has already been done" (dedicatory epistle to *opuscula* in *Speculum haereticorum* [Lyons, 1541], p. 106; cf. F. Lauchert, *Die italienischen literarischen Gegner Luthers* [Freiburg: Herder, 1912], p. 78, n. 1). K. Zickendraht, *Der Streit zwischen Erasmus und Luther über die Willensfreiheit* (Leipzig, 1909), pp. 42–45, 183–185, argues for the influence of Fisher's Article 36 on Erasmus' *Diatribe.* Cf. also H. Jedin, *Des Johannes Cochlaeus Streitschrift de libero arbitrio hominis* (Berlin: Müller & Seiffert, 1927), p. 3. But on one point at least, Erasmus dissociates himself from Fisher: "Ante gratiam quid ex se possit liberum arbitrium declaravi, cui plus tribuunt Scholastici, quorum opinionem praeter alios satis, ni fallor, propugnavit Episcopus *Roffensis.* Ille demonstravit

liberum arbitrium aliquid posse meris naturae viribus. Id quoniam Diatriba non suscepit defendendum, impudenter a me exigit *Lutherus:* illos lacessat, & inveniet, qui respondeant: Ego nihil tribui libero arbitrio nisi quod se praebet gratiae pulsanti, quod cooperatur gratiae operanti, & quod ab utraque se potest avertere: semper excipio singularem Dei voluntatem, qui potest ex causis incognitis vi rapere voluntatem hominis quocunque velit" ("Hyperaspistes diatribes," *Opera,* X, 1479–80). For Luther's view of Erasmus as atheist, epicurean, Lucianist, Arian, and skeptic, see Headley, *Luther's Church History,* pp. 254–255.

26. "Or." 2.1, *Opera,* col. 1719, Eng. tr. 1560, *Prayer,* sig. E1v–2; Ps. 35, Psalms MS, P.R.O.S.P.2/R, foll. 61, 148.

27. "Def. reg. assert." 1.3, *Opera,* col. 106; "Assert. Luth. confut." art. 31, col. 622; "Ver. corp." 4.32, col. 1108. In the last work, Fisher uses the will as an example: "Nunquid putas voluntatem posse monere seipsum? Et quum seipsam excitet, an non diuersis relationibus vnicum fundamentum est? Nec tamen est relatiuum sine correlativo" (2.25, col. 893).

28. "Assert. Luth. confut." art. 36, *Opera,* cols. 676, 679, 692, 700, 707, 715. Dr. Barnes hurls the charge of Pelagianism against Fisher: "Here haue you playne, that my Lord of Rochesters opinion, and the Pelagians, is all one, for they both doe agree, that the commaundementes of God, bee not impossible to our natural strength. But St. Augustine sayth, they bee impossible [*De lib. arb. cap. xvi*]. . . Here it is open, that the Pelagians graunt as much of grace, as my Lord of Rochester doth, and all his Duns men, whiche learneth, that man may haue a good purpose, *bonum studium,* and a good mynde, & a loue to grace, of his own naturall strength. The Pelagians graunt euen the same. But here you see, how Saint Augustine is cleare agaynst them" ("Free will of men," in *Supplication to Henry VIII,* in *Whole workes,* p. 272). Barnes has in mind such passages as found in "Assert. Luth. confut." art. 31, *Opera,* cols. 612, 622.

29. "Assert. Luth. confut." art. 36, *Opera,* cols. 660–664.

30. "Libertas est multiplex. scilicet. libertas a peccato / a miseria / et a necessitate. vt habet Gabriel . . . Libertas a peccato supponit pro voluntate & connotat eam esse in gratia. Libertas a miseria connotat eam esse sine poena. Libertas a necessitate connotat eam non posse cogi" (Altenstaig, *Vocabularius theologie,* fol. 134). See also *Liberum arbitrium* (*ibid.*). On "freedom" as a scriptural concept and term, see Küng, *Justification,* pp. 180–186. For the opinion that Luther "refuses to concede to man even the minimum moral goodness or power of corresponding *freely* to God's promptings and blessings," see McDonough, *Law and Gospel in Luther,* pp. 139, 164–165, 170. Aquinas "admits of man's freewill as a secondary subordinate and providential cause of merit" (p. 159).

31. "Assert. Luth. confut." art. 36, *Opera,* cols. 664–668.

32. Barnes, *Whole workes,* p. 267; Fisher, "Assert. Luth. confut." art. 36, *Opera,* cols. 669–674 (cf. art. 6, cols. 405–406).

33. "Assert. Luth. confut." art. 36, *Opera,* cols. 686–691. On the manner of drawing (*tractus*), see also cols. 701–702.

34. *Ibid.*, cols. 698–699, 702. On the tripartite nature of man, see also col. 684; and Erasmus, "Enchiridion," cap. 7, "De tribus hominis partibus, spiritu, et anima, et carne" (*Opera,* V, 19). Erasmus labels the division as Origen's.

35. Jedin points to the similarity of the justificatory process in Fisher, Biel, Eck, and Wimpina (*Cochlaeus,* p. 94). In the entry *Justificatio,* Altenstaig interestingly cites the sole requisites for justification demanded by Bonaventure: "infusion of grace, movement of free will, contrition, and expulsion of sin . . . [for] according to the common rule God justifies only those who prepare themselves"; and by Richard: "destruction of impiety, which is the remission of sin; and infusion of grace; and disposition toward the destruction of impiety, which is the detestation of sin; and disposition for the reception of grace, which is the conversion of the free will to God" (*Vocabularius theologie,* fol. 128).

36. "Assert. Luth. confut." art. 36, *Opera,* cols. 715–716.

CHAPTER XIII: METHOD AND STYLE OF THE PREACHER

1. *Early Statutes of Christ's College,* ed. Rackham, Introd., pp. ii, iv. See also Rackham, "Christ's College," *V.C.H. Cambs.,* III, 430–431.

2. "Oratio," Lewis, *Fisher,* Coll. No. *8, II, 263–272.

3. "Psalms," *Eng. Works,* pp. 2–22, esp. pp. 4–5, 8, 11, 17, 20, 22, Lat. tr., *Opera,* cols. 1464–77. The Latin explanation of Vulg. Ps. 6 in manuscript (P.R.O.S.P.2/R, foll. 162^v–163^v) is a plain and direct commentary, understandably with none of the picturesqueness of the English sermon. There seems to be little similarity between the two.

4. "Psalms," *Eng. Works,* pp. 22–44, esp. pp. 22–24, 26–27, 34–37, 39–40, 42, 44, Lat. tr., *Opera,* cols. 1478–91. The Latin commentary (P.R.O.S.P.2/R, foll. 135–137, blurred in places) has a few elements in common with the English sermon on Vulg. Ps. 31, particularly passing references to contrition, confession, and satisfaction. The similarity is closest at the end: "Qui vero fida peccatorum confessione iustificati sunt sacerdotis absolutione, letari et exultare merito possunt. *Letamini in domino et exultate iusti.* Qui denique per integram satisfactionem perfectam cordis rectitudinem nacti sunt his [?] maximopere gloriandum est. *Et gloriamini omnes recti corde.*" The Latin commentary lacks all the rhetorical ornaments of the English sermon.

5. "Psalms," *Eng. Works,* pp. 44–70, esp. pp. 44, 46–48, 52, 58–60, 63, 66–67, 69–70, Lat. tr., *Opera,* cols. 1491–1509. In the *Gorgias* itself (470D–E), the criterion is not the condition of "his soule" but "how he stands in point of education and justice" (*Lysis, Symposium, Gorgias,* tr. W. R. M. Lamb [London: William Heinemann, 1953], pp. 338–339). Fisher had not yet undertaken the serious study of Greek at this time. Consequently he used a Latin translation or anthology. The Latin commentary in a mutilated manuscript (P.R.O.S.P.2/R, foll. 68, 151–153) is different from the English

sermon, as is to be expected from the latter's relationship to the Feast of the Nativity B.V.M.

6. "Psalms," *Eng. Works,* pp. 70–90, esp. pp. 70, 74–75, 78–79, 81, 86, 88–90, Lat. tr., *Opera,* cols. 1510–24; "Or." 3.3, *ibid.,* col. 1729, Eng. tr. 1560, *Prayer,* sig. G6. Cassian's words (Coll. 10, chap. 10) really extol Vulg. Ps. 69:2: "Deus, in adiutorium meum intende; Domine, ad adiuvandum me festina." The Latin commentary on Vulg. Ps. 37:12–23 (P.R.O.S.P.2/R, foll. 69–70, 153ᵛ–155, much blurred and mutilated) seems roughly to parallel the English sermon, e.g., in reference to hope (significantly *fiducia* in Latin), penance, satisfaction, etc. The structure of the Latin explanation is different and gives seven reasons, of which *fiducia* is the fifth. The last Latin words appear in the margin: "Tu solus afferre salutem poteris" ("Thou alone can bring salvation").

7. "Psalms," *Eng. Works,* pp. 90–113, esp. pp. 90–94, 97–101, 105–106, 108, 111, Lat. tr., *Opera,* cols. 1524–39. Except for the parable of the man hanging over the pit, there are very many points of contact between the English sermon and the Latin commentary in manuscript (P.R.O.S.P.2/R, foll. 107, 271). Both, for example, have the "table" (*tabula*) to be scraped by contrition, washed by confession, and wiped by satisfaction. Of the two copies, the first in Fisher's own handwriting is much corrected and often illegible. If the order of sheets is here correct, it reveals that Fisher composed the introductory explanation at the head of each section of the commentary *after* he had explained each verse. The second copy consists of only one sheet with a major explanation before and after the commentary on verses 1–4.

8. "Psalms," *Eng. Works,* pp. 113–137, Lat. tr., *Opera,* cols. 1539–56. The mutilated manuscript of the Latin commentary on verses 11–21 of this psalm (P.R.O.S.P.2/R, foll. 107–108ᵛ), as on the earlier verses, parallels the English sermon but without the wealth of instances, comparisons, etc. A fragment of a sheet (*ibid.,* fol. 110) gives the same explanation of *spiritus rectus, spiritus sanctus,* and *spiritus principalis* as in the sermon (*Eng. Works,* p. 119).

9. "Psalms," *Eng. Works,* pp. 137–164, esp. pp. 139–140, 145, 147, 154, 160, 162, 164, Lat. tr., *Opera,* cols. 1556–74. The Latin commentary in manuscript (P.R.O.S.P.2/R) stops with Vulg. Ps. 51. Consequently comparison between Latin commentaries and English sermons is impossible for the three remaining Penitential Psalms (Vulg. Ps. 101, 129, 142). J. W. Blench introduces his quotation of the *ubi-sunt* passage (*Eng. Works,* pp. 145–146) with the remark: "One of the most striking passages of Fisher's eloquence is a threnody over the mortality of earthly glory" (*Preaching in England in the Late Fifteenth and Sixteenth Centuries* [Oxford: Basil Blackwell, 1964], p. 229). Blench's comprehensive study came to the present author's attention after the writing of this work had been completed. Vergil's quotation should read: *Labor omnia vicit / Improbus.*

10. "Psalms," *Eng. Works,* pp. 164–200, esp. pp. 168–170, 176, 181, 183–184, 190–191, 199–900, Lat. tr., *Opera,* cols. 1574–97. For the earlier use of the symbolic ship in the Middle Ages, see G. R. Owst, *Literature and Pulpit in Medieval England,* 2nd ed. (Oxford: Basil Blackwell, 1961), pp. 68–76.

Blench finds "language of the greatest beauty" in the contrast between the contemporary and the Apostolic Church (*Preaching,* p. 239). For Fisher in his theological writings, the Apostolic Church, like the Fathers, would appear to be normative. On the other hand, Headley observes: "One of the most significant features that distinguishes Luther's understanding of history from humanistic reflections upon the past is his rejection of any historical period, person, or event as normative" (*Luther's Church History,* p. 163; cf. "The Early Church as a Tentative Norm," pp. 163–181). For "humanism as providing past norms for present instruction and conduct," Headley recommends P. Joachimsen, "Der Humanismus und die Entwicklung des deutschen Geist," *Deutsche Vierteljahrschrift für Literaturgeschichte und Geistesgeschichte,* VIII (1930), 419–480, esp. pp. 419–430.

11. "Psalms," *Eng. Works,* pp. 200–233, esp. pp. 204, 207, 209, 211, 220, 227–229, 233, Lat. tr., *Opera,* cols. 1597–1621.

12. *Ibid.,* pp. 137, 164, 234.

13. *Ibid.,* pp. 234–267, esp. pp. 234, 236–237, 242, 244–248, 251–252, 257–258, 260–261, 264, 266–267, Lat. tr., *Opera,* cols. 1621–41.

14. Blench's explanation is different: "It is little wonder that with so many sins to complain about the preachers should find it necessary to exhort their audience to Penance. It is not by chance that Fisher and Longland choose the Penitential Psalms as the basis of a series of sermons!" (*Preaching,* p. 246). Cf. also his earlier statement: "The Catholic preachers had tended to quote more the poetic, prophetic and sapiential books of the Old Testament; for example Fisher and Longland choose the Penitential Psalms . . . but all seldom refer to the historical books" (*ibid.,* p. 41).

15. "The most felicitous aspect of Fisher's ornamentation is his very frequent use of similes. These are not different in kind from those current in the sermon handbooks, but in their context they have a freshness and indeed a certain individuality, which is peculiarly delightful" (Blench, *Preaching,* p. 131).

16. This listing of authorities used by Fisher is based largely upon *Eng. Works,* p. xxviii, and Reynolds, *Fisher,* p. 20. Frequency is relative. Blench, for example, asserts: "Like Baron and Alcock, Fisher frequently quotes the Fathers . . ."; and later: "The pages of Longland's sermons, like those of Fisher, are studded with quotations from the Fathers . . ." (*Preaching,* pp. 131, 138). Further on: "Fisher's sermons also are studded with classical allusions, which he uses precisely in the same way as does Longland" (*ibid.,* p. 213).

17. "Henry VII," *Eng. Works,* pp. 268–288. Though this sermon follows the tripartite division of the "secular oratours," each part is "subdivided in the medieval manner," as Blench proceeds to show (*Preaching,* p. 86).

18. "Henry VII," *Eng. Works,* pp. 289–310. Blench finds that "Fisher borrows the classical scheme for the praise of a great personage . . . otherwise the construction is a modification of the medieval 'modern' style" (*Preaching,* p. 86). For the "indulgences & pardons graunted by diuers popes," mentioned by Fisher (p. 309), see Scott, "Notes from the College Records,"

Eagle, XIX (1895–97), 544–549; XX (1897–99), 17–21, 158–161, 296–300. Scott gives also a deed of Margaret's from 1482 and two deeds relating to Torrigiano's tomb for her in Westminster Abbey, *ibid.,* XVIII (1893–95), 337–346. In his "Miraculous Examples in Support of the Doctrine of Transubstantiation" (B.M. Add. MS. 12060, fol. 23), dedicated to Queen Mary, Henry Parker (Lord Morley) declares that before the death of the Lady Margaret "Fisher showed him that he had written her life, a work which Parker supposed that Queen Mary now has and which he would dearly love to see" (McConica, *English Humanists,* p. 155). This life, certainly distinct from Fisher's published sermon on the Lady Margaret, would constitute another lost work of Fisher's.

19. Cooper, *Margaret,* Advertisement by Mayor, pp. v–vi.

CHAPTER XIV: CONTROVERSIAL MANEUVERS OF THE TYRO

1. For the biographical background of the controversy over the Magdalene, see above, Chapter I, pp. 5–7, and nn. 12–27, pp. 403–405; and for its intellectual significance, Chapter IX, pp. 157–160, and nn. 4–7, pp. 474–475.

2. Foll. 4–15 (out of foll. 4–29) in the first edition (1517), and foll. 11–22^{v} (out of foll. 11–40) in the second edition (1518). In all probability, Fisher used the second edition as appears from his use of Clichtove's preface and from such telltale difference as the reading, "Atque minus verisimile est" (ed. 1518, fol. 22) rather than "Aut post. atqui minus verisimile est" (ed. 1517, fol. 14). The second edition is so absurdly a reproduction of the first that the pages in the table of contents, called Index, in the second edition are the same as those in the first. Lefèvre in 1517 addresses his disquisition to the tutor of Francis I, *Franciscus Molinus* (François de Moulins or de Rochefort, cf. Erasmus, *Ep.,* II, 449n), whom Clichtove designates as Abbot of St.-Maximin at Micy, France, in his preface of 1518 (sig. a1^{v}–5^{v}). St. Maximinus was said to be the companion of St. Mary Magdalene and the first archbishop of Aix. At Saint-Maximin, "une chaire monumentale . . . renferme, d'après la légende, le chef de sainte Madeleine" (*La Grande encyclopédie,* XXIX, 228). For details, consult H. Leclercq, "Maximin (Saint-)," in *Dict. d'arch. chrét. et de liturg.,* X, 2798–2820. See Rabanus Maurus, "De vita Mariae Magdalenae," *PL,* CXII, 1491–94, 1502–8. As noted previously, the best brief treatment in English is to be found in P. Ketter, *The Magdalene Question* (*Die Magdalenen Frage*), tr. H. C. Koehler (Milwaukee, 1935).

3. Fisher, "Magdal." lib. 1–3, *Opera,* pp. 1393–94, cols. 1395–1462, esp. pp. 1393–94, cols. 1395–97, 1407, 1409–10, 1415–17, 1425–27, 1443–62; Erasmus, *Ep.,* IV, 192. It is at once curious and indicative of Fisher's influence that, in reprinting "Radulphi Ardentis Pictavi Homiliae," XXV, "In festo Beatae Mariae Magdaelnae" [*sic*], from the 1567 edition (Paris, Claude Fremy), Migne should include Petrarch's prose and verse together with

Fisher's brief comment verbatim (cp. *PL*, CLV, 1402, and Fisher, *Opera*, col. 1453). Information on the well-known names mentioned by Fisher can be found in the histories by Gilson and Ueberweg given above, Chapter IX, n. 4, which also identifies lesser figures like Simon of Cascia, Ubertino of Casale, and Christian de Stavelot. For Zachary of Besançon and Clement of Llanthony, see above, Chapter IX, n. 5; and for Marco Vigerio, n. 6. The paschal sequence *Mane prima sabbati*, mentioned by Fisher (*Opera*, cols. 1426–27), can be found in Cl. Blume and H. M. Bannister, *Liturgische Prosen des Übergangsstiles und der zweiten Epoche* (Leipzig: O. R. Reisland, 1915), no. 143, pp. 214–218.

4. *Eversio*, sigg. A1^v^, A4, O3, Q3^v^, X4^v^, Z3^v^, a6. Fisher could have found the adage "Nodum in Scirpo quaeris" in P. Vergil, *Prouerbiorum libellus* (Venice, 1513), sig. B3. The signatures of *Eversio* begin with a1–4 and, after running through capital letters B–Y4, Z8, end with a6. To prevent confusion, the first *a* will be capitalized as *A*, as is actually done in the Errata at the end of the book itself. The title of Clichtove's book is *Disceptationis de Magdalena, Defensio: Apologiae Marci Grandiuallis illam improbare nitentis, ex aduerso respondens* (Parisiis, ex officina Henrici Stephani, 1519 — according to Clerval, *Clichtoveus*, p. xxiv: "Em. post 31 julii. Impress. 19 april. 1519"). Grandval's book is entitled: *Ecclesiae catholicae non tres Magdalenas sed vnicam colentis: Apologia seu defensorium* (Paris, September 1518). His response to Clichtove bears the title: *Apologiae seu defensorij . . . tutamentum & anchora* (Paris, June 1519). Grandval, who has seen Fisher's *Single Magdalene* goes into raptures: "Splendescit iam & rutilat clarissimum sydus [Fisher]: in cuius prospectu tenebrae nullae consistant . . . Eum ipsum cum legeris satisfactum tibi puta. Quippe de vnica Magdalena ille scripsit: & id tam emuncte: tam solide: tam profunde: vt hac etiam Anchora defensorium nostrum minime eget in tuam defensionem." Grandval goes on to say that Fisher's strictures on Lefèvre have been more severe than his own (*Apologiae anchora*, sig. a5). He later picks out three passages in particular, including the one about Lefèvre's church (*ibid.*, sig. c5–6).

5. The biographer and the historian wonder what particular "other" and "more useful business" made Fisher reluctant to accede to Poncher's wishes: "Non fuit animus profecto quicquam scribendi aduersus Fabrum, Nam & aliis eram occupatus. Sed quum ille [Poncher] non destitit crebris internunciis ad hoc me solicitare, tandem euicit, vt relictis vtilioribus negociis, hanc scribendi prouinciam subirem" (*Eversio*, sig. A2^v^). The most important would be the impending synod or the visitation of his diocese, but Fisher characteristically might also call his study of Greek and Hebrew "more important."

6. Clerval, who quotes these Suppositions verbatim, comments: "Hae regulae criticae quidem videntur et probandae; attamen sive a Beda, sive a J. Fisher fuerunt refutatae, utpote parum testimoniis faventes, et nimiam libertatem concedentes" (*Clichtoveus*, p. 77). Clerval notes Clichtove's later change from a low opinion of the less ancient Fathers and of the Schoolmen to one of the highest honor (*ibid.*, pp. 102–103).

7. *Eversio,* sigg. A1v–a6, as follows: Letter to the Reader, A1v; Fisher's introduction, A2–B1; Clichtove's Suppositions, B1–D3v; Petrine-Pauline reprehension, D4–G3v; Fisher's Truths, G3v–a6. For Clichtove's Suppositions, see his *Defensio,* foll. 95v–96. On the pope's distribution of alms and washing of feet (*Eversio,* sig. Z7v), see Ludolphus Carthusianus de Saxonia, *Vita Iesu christi* . . . (Paris, 1517), 2.25, fol. 163v; Symphorius Amalarius, Metensis Presbyter et Chorepiscopus, "De officiis ecclesiasticis," 1.9, *PL,* CV, 1007–8; and Gulielmus Durandus, Episcopus Minatensis (Mendé), *Rationale diuinorum officiorum* (Paris, 1508), lib. 8, fol. 125v. Fisher (*Eversio,* sig. M4v) cites verbatim Jacobus Philippus Bergomensis Foresti, *Nouissime historiarum omnium repercussiones* (Venice, 1506), lib. 8, fol. 176. Foresti quotes Petrarch's Magdalenian poem in *De plurimis claris sceletisque* [*sic*] *mulieribus* . . . (Ferrara, 1497), cap. 72, "De sanctissima christi apostola Maria Magdalena," fol. 55. For Jacobus de Voragine, see *Lombardica historia que a plerisque Aurea legenda sanctorum appellatur* (Strasbourg, 1502), sig. p4v. For conjectural identification of Amadeus, see above, Chapter III, n. 17.

8. *Confut. sec. discept.,* foll. 2–39v, as follows: prefatory letter, 2; introduction, 3–5; Fisher's Suppositions, 6–14; Lefèvre's Propositions, 15–39. The stylistic devices occur on foll. 2v, 4v, 17, 20v, 26v–27, 34, 35, 36v.

9. Erasmus, *Ep.,* III, 591–592, IV, 192; More, *Correspondence,* pp. 136–137; Reynolds, *Fisher,* p. 79. For the application of More's praise to Fisher's Lutheran writings, see above, Chapter I, n. 16.

CHAPTER XV: PEACE BETWEEN WARS: PRAYER, HEAVEN, AND JUSTICE

1. "Or." 1.prooem., 1.1, *Opera,* cols. 1708, 1711, Eng. tr. 1560, *Prayer,* sig. B2v, B7v; Ps. 50 (1), *Eng. Works,* p. 91; Ps.-Dion. *Div. nom.* 3.

2. "Or." 1.prooem., *Opera,* col. 1710, Eng. tr. 1560, *Prayer,* sig. B5v–6.

3. "Or." 3.3, *Opera,* col. 1731, Eng. tr. 1560, *Prayer,* sig. H2v; Ps. 101 (2), *Eng. Works,* p. 193.

4. "Or." 3.3, *Opera,* col. 1731, Eng. tr. 1560, *Prayer,* sig. H4; Ps. 6, *Eng. Works,* pp. 8, 11.

5. "Or." 2.prooem., 2.2–3, *Opera,* cols. 1717–18, 1720–21, Eng. tr. 1560, *Prayer,* sig. D6, E3, E6v.

6. "Or." 1.2, 2.3, 3.2, *Opera,* cols. 1713–14, 1722–23, 1727–28, Eng. tr. 1560, *Prayer,* sigg. C4–5, E8v–F1, G2, G4.

7. "Or." 1.2, 3.2–3, *Opera,* cols. 1712–13, 1729–30, Eng. tr. 1560, *Prayer,* sigg. C3, G6v, G8v–H1.

8. Cf. Augustine: "Ac per hoc quod ait Apostolus, *Sine intermissione orate* (1 *Thess.* v.17), quid est aliud quam, Beatam vitam, quae nulla nisi aeterna est, ab eo qui eam solus dare potest, sine intermissione desiderate? Semper ergo hanc a Domino Deo desideremus, et oremus semper" (Ep. 3.130, *PL,* XXXIII, 501.)

9. The third condition is "that the thyng whiche we require of God, apperteyne vnto our selues . . ." ("Or." 2.2, *Opera,* col. 1720, Eng. tr. 1560, *Prayer,* sig. E4v). This rather obscure statement is explained here and in *Two Sermons* (sig. D4): "For as all the dysputers [Schoolmen] agree, the hyghest degree of fruyte in euery mannes prayer retourneth vnto hym selfe. And it is but a secondary fruyt that retourneth into other."

10. Cf. Altenstaig: "Tres autem sunt effectus orationis. Primus communis est omnibus actibus charitate informatis: qui est mereri. Secundus effectus orationis proprius: est impetrare quod petitur. Tertius est quem principaliter efficit: scilicet quaedam spiritualis refectio mentis" (*Vocabularius theologie,* fol. 172v). This work of Altenstaig is especially interesting because it gives "the Catholic's ready answer" in 1517, the year of Luther's revolt. On prayer, see foll. 171–173.

11. On ejaculatory prayer, see *Directorium aureum contemplatiuorum* (Antwerp, 1516), fol. 36. Sharpe's letter to Metcalfe discloses that Fisher wishes to have a copy of the *Directorium* bound (Gray, "Letters of Bishop Fisher, 1521–3," *Library,* ser. 3, IV, 143).

12. Cf. Rupert of Deutz's commentary on Matthew's Gospel (an edition of which Cochlaeus dedicated to Fisher in 1526): "Primus modus est cum oratio ex affectu . . . divinae inspirationis protenditur, sicut fiebat Annae . . . Secundus orationis modus . . . in contritione cordis . . . Tertius modus est dum non solum sine clamorum voce, verum etiam absque motu labiorum quis orat intrinsecus oratione clausa . . . Quartus modus . . . multiloquium est absque affectu divinae inspirationis" (*PL,* CLXVIII, 1427). Hilton's *Scala perfeccionis,* translated by Fisher's patron, the Lady Margaret, has a different division: "The fyrst is prayer of speche made specially of god, as in the pater noster: & made also more generally bi thordynaunce of holi chirche. as matins euensong & hours. And also made bi deuoute men of other special sayenges . . . The ii. maner of prayer is by speche . . . whan a man or a woman felith grace of deuocion by the yeft of god. & in his deuocion spekith to hym. as he were bodely in his presence . . . The iii. maner of prayer is only in the herte wythout speche by grete reste & softnes of the body & of the soule" (ed. 1494, sig. c6–8).

13. "Or.," *Opera,* cols. 1708–33, Eng. tr. 1560, *Prayer,* sigg. B1–H8.

14. On Protestant reaction against Fisher's purgatory, see Lewis, *Eng. Lit. in the 16th Cent.,* pp. 163–164, 172–173; Clebsch, *Earliest Protestants,* pp. 30–32; and Blench, *Preaching,* p. 236. Blench finds that Fisher and Longland treat purgatory as "a second hell, with little mention of the aspects of purification, hope, and even joy in suffering stressed by the best Catholic writers, as St. Catherine of Genoa" (*ibid.*). But then all the circumstances (occasion, audience, purpose, means, etc.) were different for Catherine of Genoa and for John of Rochester.

15. *Two Sermons,* sigg. A2–D4. This first sermon is not translated into Latin for *Opera* (1597), perhaps because it was too dated and topical for a continental audience at the end of the century.

16. *Two Sermons,* sigg. E1–G6. The Latin version (*Opera,* cols. 1674–87), omitting the introductory summary of the first sermon, begins with the scriptural text and the first mention of Adam (at *Two Sermons,* sig. E2v) and continues faithfully till the end where, curiously, the concluding words of the first sermon in English are substituted for those of the second sermon. The carol quoted above begins: "Adam lay i-bowndyn." See Vulg. Ps. 31, *Eng. Works,* pp. 25–27, 32, on satisfactory good works. Indifferent works become good and meritorious by being performed for God's glory ("Or." 1.prooem., *Opera,* cols. 1709–1710, Eng. tr. 1560, *Prayer,* sig. B4; cf. 1 Cor. 10:31).

CHAPTER XVI: THE OFFENSIVE AGAINST LUTHER

1. Bridgett, *Fisher,* p. 50; Reynolds, *Fisher,* p. 91, n. 1. Blench is really exposing the limitation of the sermon as a form when, on the one hand, he finds that Catholic defenders, as Fisher in his two sermons against Luther, "give little real theological argument," and, on the other hand, he observes: "Of course a deeper treatment of controversial issues is given by Fisher in his Latin treatises" (*Preaching,* p. 248, and n. 89). In regard to the two sermons of 1521 and 1526, Clebsch claims: "Thus Fisher established the terminology, chose the ground, and set the tone for the doctrinal and ecclesiological debates which were the substance of the English Reformation before the 'King's matter' became prominent" (*Earliest Protestants,* p. 31). As for tone, it is hardly just to speak of "the bitter spleen and rancour of John Fisher's sermon at the public burning of Luther's works" (Loane, *Masters of English Reformation,* p. 50). To the extent that it is applicable to Fisher, the remark is truer of the conclusion of the sermon of 1526.

2. Bridgett, *Fisher,* p. 50. On the sermon as a modification of the "modern" style, see Blench, *Preaching,* p. 81. For a medieval use of the image of sun and cloud, see Owst, *Literature and Pulpit,* pp. 191–192; for Luther's use, see Headley, *Luther's Church History,* p. 99.

3. Fisher, *Eng. Works,* pp. 311, 314. This passage arouses Tyndale's ire: "Let us note another point of our great clerk [Fisher]: a little after the beginning of his sermon, intending to prove that which is clearer than the sun . . . he allegeth a saying that Martin Luther saith, which is this: 'If we affirm that any one epistle of Paul or any one place of his epistles pertaineth not unto the universal church, . . . we take away all St Paul's authority.' Whereupon saith Rochester: 'If it be thus of the words of St Paul, much rather it is true of the gospels of Christ and of every place of them.' O malicious blindness! First, note his blindness. He understandeth by this word *gospel* no more but the four evangelists, Matthew, Mark, Luke, and John; and thinketh not that the Acts of apostles, and the epistles of Peter, of Paul, and of John, and of other like, are also the gospel . . . Consider also his

maliciousness; how wickedly and how craftily he taketh away the authority of Paul! . . . If that which the four evangelists wrote be truer than that which Paul wrote, then is it not one gospel that they preached, neither one Spirit that taught them. If it be one gospel and one Spirit, how is one truer than the other?" ("Obedience," *Treatises,* pp. 213–214).

4. Fisher, *Eng. Works,* p. 315. Tyndale's objection to Fisher's allegory is almost violent: "Finally: that thou mayest know Rochester for ever, and all the remnant by him, what they are within the skin, mark how he playeth bo-peep with the scripture. He allegeth the beginning of the tenth chapter to the Hebrews [10:1] . . . and immediately expoundeth the figure clean contrary unto the chapter following, and to all the whole epistle; making Aaron a figure of the pope, whom the epistle maketh a figure of Christ" ("Obedience," *Treatises,* p. 214).

5. Fisher, *Eng. Works,* pp. 314–322. It was undoubtedly the first Instruction which provoked reference to "especially one book imprinted comprising a sermon made by John Fisher, late bishop of Rochester," in the proclamation of January 1, 1536, ordering the surrender of dangerous writings (Hughes-Larkin, *Tudor Royal Proclamations,* I, 235–237; *LP,* IX, no. 963, p. 322). Two reactions are worthy of note. On January 16, 1536, Bishop Stokesley of London wrote to Cromwell: "I would have sent you my books of the canon law and schoolmen favoring the bp. of Rome; but as I am informed by those to whom you have declared the King's proclamation on this behalf, it is not meant but of the bp. of Rochester's books and writings, and of those who have lately written in defense of the said primacy against the opinion of the Germans, I do not send them until I know your further pleasure" (*LP,* VIII, no. 55, p. 19). Sir Thomas Elyot's letter to Cromwell is revealing for its disinterest: "As for the warks of John Fisher, I never had any of them to my knowledg, except one little sermon: which about eight or nine years past was translated into Latine by Mr. Pace. And fôr that cause I bought it, more than for the author or matter. But where it is, I am not sure. For, in good faith, I never read it but once since I bought it" (Strype, *Eccl. Mem.,* I, pt. 2, no. 62, p. 229).

6. *Eng. Works,* pp. 323–338, 346. Arguing from the context, Tyndale turns both the texts (1 Tim. 4:1, 2 Thess. 2:3) against Fisher and his pope and then continues: "What say ye of this crafty conveyer [Fisher]? Would he spare, suppose ye, to allege and to wrest other doctors pestilently, which feareth not for to juggle with the holy scripture of God, expounding that unto antichrist which Paul speaketh of Christ? No, be ye sure. But even after this manner-wise pervert they unto their abominable purpose, clean contrary to the meaning of the text, and to the circumstances that go before and after. Which devilish falsehood, lest the laymen should perceive, is the very cause why that they will not suffer the scripture to be had in the English tongue; neither any work to be made that should bring the people to knowledge of the truth" ("Obedience," *Treatises,* p. 215).

7. After summarizing Fisher's sermon, Raynaldus in *Annales ecclesiastici,*

XX, no. 64, p. 307, quotes Fisher's three replies at length in Pace's Latin translation.

8. *Eng. Works,* pp. 339–348. But cf. Clebsch's comment on this sermon of 1521: "That the Church might well stick to its spiritual business, that scriptures might well be held in very high esteem and interpreted according to their leading literal sense, that the tight grip of the schoolmen on theology might well be loosened — Fisher left these points of agreement between early Protestants and Christian humanists completely unacknowledged. Commissioned not to assess but to condemn, he fulfilled his task" (*Earliest Protestants,* pp. 17–18).

9. "Luther," *Eng. Works,* pp. 311–348, Lat. tr. Pace, *Opera,* cols. 1375–92. In the use of sun, clouds, and growing plants, Blench finds a kinship between Lancelot Andrewes and the "sensitiveness" and "the holy mind" of Fisher (*Preaching,* pp. 207–208).

10. *Petrum Romam non uenisse,* sig. A2–4.

11. In his *Tractatus adversus negantem B. Petrum apostolum fuisse Romae,* Cardinal Cortese in Book I gives the life of Peter, the evidence from the Fathers, etc.; but in Book II he too quotes verbatim each of Velenus' eighteen *Persuasiones* and follows each with a *Dissuasio* (*Omnia scripta,* I, 211–274). Cortese notes that Marsilius of Padua in his *Defensor pacis* seems to have been the first to hold this opinion (*ibid.,* I, 220). But Marsilius clearly says: "That Peter was at Rome I do not deny, but I hold it to be quite probable that he did not precede Paul there, but rather conversely" (*Defensor pacis,* ed. C. W. Previté-Orton [Cambridge (Eng.) University Press, 1928], p. 287, tr. A. Gewirth, *The Defender of Peace* [New York: Columbia University Press, 1951–56], II, 253). Torquemada ascribes to Ockham the error that Scripture nowhere reveals Peter's presence in Rome and proceeds to prove the fact by Peter's reference to "the Church which is in Babylon" and by testimonies of the Fathers, including the *Quo-vadis* story as cited by Ambrose *contra Auxentium de basilicis tradendis* (*Ecclesia* 2.36, sig. m5^{v}–6^{v}).

12. "Convulsio," *Opera,* p. 1299–col. 1371.

13. *Ibid.,* p. 1299 and col. 1341.

14. Luther dedicated his work to Fabian von Feilitzsch: see *WA,* VII, 91, 94–95. When Robert Bellarmine was censured for citing Luther and Calvin verbatim and thereby making their arguments available, he appealed to Fisher as precedent in his letter to Aquaviva, the Jesuit General, who supported him: "Se questa censura fusse buona, bisognaria prohibire il libro del santo vescovo et martyre Roffense, perche vi ha messo dentro *ad verbum* tutto il libro di Luthero." See X.-M. Le Bachelet, *Bellarmin avant son cardinalat (1542–1598): Correspondance et documents* (Paris, 1911), pp. 324–325.

15. *Assertionis Lutheranae confutatio* (Antwerp, Hillenius, January 2, 1523), sig. a1^{v}–8^{v}. For the "typical and instructive" career of George Day, see McConica, *English Humanists,* p. 5. For the approval given in August 1523 by the Sorbonne to C. Chevallon to publish the second edition of the

Confutation, together with Henry VIII's *Assertio,* see L. Delisle, "Notice sur un registre des procès-verbaux de la faculté de théologie de Paris pendant les années 1505–1533," *Notices et extraits des manuscrits de la Bibliothèque nationale . . . ,* XXXVI (Paris, 1899), 369. Chevallon being absent, certain theologians reported that they had seen the two works and that "they were useful for the Church" (*ibid.*).

16. "Assert. Luth. confut." ep. lect., *Opera,* p. 273; praef., *ibid.,* col. 274. Raynaldus quotes extensively from Fisher's letter to the reader in *Annales ecclesiastici,* XX, 308.

17. "Charit.," *Opera,* col. 1704.

18. "Assert. Luth. confut." prooem. Luth. confut., cols. 278–296, 298–299; art. 1, cols. 327–329. The ten truths are summarized in the article on "Jean Fischer, évêque de Rochester et Cardinal," in L. E. Du Pin, *Nouvelle bibliothèque des auteurs ecclésiastiques,* 2nd ed. (Paris, 1690–1715), XIV, 147.

19. See Gray, "Letters of Bishop Fisher, 1521–3," *Library,* ser. 3, IV (1913), 136, 142. On Peter and the papacy, Fisher was recognized as an authority immediately. To cite almost random examples. In 1524, Hieronymus Emser as editor reprinted Fisher's Article 19 (*Opera,* cols. 502–506) to enlighten persons who confuse three biblical texts (Matt. 16, Matt. 18, John 20), together with Ambrose Catharinus' *Dialogue upon These Words: Thou Art Peter . . .* (*Super his verbis. Tu es Petrus &c . . . Dialogus non minus disertus quam elegans et festiuus,* Dresden, July 1524). Emser in his dedicatory letter explains that Fisher's and Catharinus' works are not available to everyone (sig. A2). The *Dialogue* is taken from Catharinus' *Apologia pro veritate catholice & apostolice fidei ac doctrine* (Florence, 1520), lib. 2, disput. 2, sigg. e3v–f1v. In J. Schweizer's edition of the *Apologia* (Münster: Aschendorff, 1956), A. Franzen comments: "Während der Humanistenfürst Erasmus von Rotterdam und der kaiserliche Beichtvater Johannes Glapion und ebenso Hieronymus Aleander wenig von ihm erbaut waren, stellten die katholischen Theologen in Deutschland, England (Roffensis) und anderwärts der Verwerfung durch Luther eine dauernde Wertschätzung gegenüber" (Introd., p. xviii). In 1532, Giovanni da Fano sends his more intelligent readers to Fisher, among others, for more elaborate discussion of Peter's primacy (*Opera utilissima uulgare contra le pernitiosissime heresie Lutherane per li simplici* [Bologna, 1532], fol. 38). In 1536, Cochlaeus in his "Defense of the Bishop of Rochester" declares that Fisher had made papal primacy so clear from the Scriptures and other authorities, that it would be futile for him to perform the task again (*Epistola Nicolai . . . ,* sig. Z4). In fact, if all the learned and clever men in England bent all their forces to the task, they could never refute what had been written on papal power by Henry VIII, More, and Fisher in his Article 25 and his defense of the king (*ibid.,* sig. Z3)! In his answer in 1538 to Morison's seven "calumnies" ("De papa et de unitate Ecclesiae," *Scopa in araneas Morysini*), Cochlaeus exclaims: "How many testimonies, pray, on that primacy did not the Bishop of Rochester produce against Luther's Article 25?" (sig. D1v–2). In his *Apomaxis calumniarum,* fol. 76, Morison had cast aspersions on Fisher's pertinacious defense of the papacy.

As late as 1698, Articles 25–29 on the papacy were reprinted in Rocaberti, *Bibliotheca maxima pontificia,* XIV, 556–595.

20. It is interesting to compare Fisher's broad outline with that of some contemporaries. Alveld, e.g., in his *Super apostolica sede* (Leipzig, 1520) uses seven "swords" (*gladii*): (1) *recta ratio,* (2) *canonica scriptura,* with two edges, (a) Aaron in the Old Testament and (b) Peter in the New Testament, (3) *vera scientia,* (4) *pietas sacra,* (5) and (6) missing in British Museum copy, and (7) *pura et integra scientia.* Cajetan, who declares his emphasis to be scriptural, divides *De diuina institutione pontificatus Romani pontificis* into fourteen chapters: Plan (I), Peter's primacy (II–XI), Roman pontiff as Peter's successor (XII–XIII), and Fathers and councils (XIV). "In Luther's report of his interview it may be doubted that Cajetan, a distinguished theologian, actually considered the pope to be above Scripture. This idea, however, was entertained by Prierias . . . together with some less responsible minds of the period" (Headley, *Luther's Church History,* pp. 79–80; cf. pp. 30–31, 229, for Luther's reply to Alveld). For Cajetan, see Lauchert, *Gegner Luthers,* pp. 133–177; for Prierias, *ibid.,* pp. 7–30.

21. "Assert. Luth. confut." art. 1, *Opera,* cols. 327–329; art. 2, cols. 341–342, 344; art. 5, cols. 400–401; art. 16, cols. 471–476; art. 19, col. 502; art. 21, cols. 507–511; art. 25, cols. 531–580; art. 33, cols. 636–637; art. 36, col. 664; art. 37, cols. 717–718, 728–729; art. 38, cols. 732–737; art. 41, col. 745.

22. "Spongia," *Opera,* X, 1656. Cf. "Assert. Luth. confut." prooem., *Opera,* col. 277; art. 25, col. 548; art. 41, col. 742. Fisher allows himself the indulgence of episcopal interjections, e.g., "Bone Deus qualem hic audio collectionem?" (*ibid.* art. 3, col. 380), and: "Pape, cuius aures huiusmodi dialecticen ferre possunt? Nusquam enim hic non peccatur" (*ibid.* art. 6, col. 405).

23. "Assert. Luth. confut." art. 1, *Opera,* col. 324; art. 5, col. 394; art. 25, col. 548; and art. 33, cols. 638–639.

24. *Ibid.* art. 2, cols. 373–375; art. 6, col. 400. On the other hand, Fisher's own logic came in for criticism, e.g., by Frith in comment upon Article 18: "If a man take awaye purgatory / for what entent shall we nede any pardons?" (*Purgatorye,* ed. 1533, sig. L5). The eirenic Gerhard quotes Fisher on venial and mortal sin (art. 32, col. 628) in order to bring him close to Luther (*Loci theologici,* ed. 1639, II, 361). On sin (and concupiscence) in Luther's doctrine, see McDonough, *Law and Gospel in Luther,* pp. 27–32, 87–90, 137–142.

25. "Assert. Luth. confut." art. 6, *Opera,* col. 400; art. 25, cols. 565, 573, 578; and art. 36, cols. 668–669. As is well known, the so-called False Decretals, appearing under the name of Isidore, were compiled about A.D. 850, probably near Rheims or Tours.

26. *Ibid.* prooem., col. 300; art. 18, col. 498; art. 25, col. 580; art. 27, col. 589; art. 30, cols. 602–603; art. 33, col. 642; art. 40, col. 741. For the reference to Anaxagoras, see Catharinus, *Apologia,* ed. Schweizer, p. 105, n. 73. The basis for *ingenium Anaxagoricum* is Anaxagoras' conviction that everything shares in everything else (cf. J. Owens, *A History of Ancient Western Philosophy* [New York: Appleton-Century-Crofts, 1959], pp. 112–127). See Adag. 49,

Toto coelo errare (Erasmus, *Opera,* II, 48); Adag. 158, *Mandrabuli more res succedit* (*ibid.,* 92); Adag. 301, *Non est cujuslibet Corinthum appellere* (*ibid.,* 150–151); Adag. 362, *Oleum & operam perdidi* (*ibid.,* 171); Adag. 394, *Cauda tenes anguillam* (*ibid.,* 179–180); Adag. 406, *Latum unguem, ac similes hyperbolae proverbiales* (*ibid.,* 184–185); Adag. 759, *Linum lino nectis* (*ibid.,* 321); Adag. 972, *Dignum patella operculum* (*ibid.,* 387); Adag. 1068, *Occasione duntaxat opus improbitati* (*ibid.,* 432); Adag. 1147, *Extra cantionem* (*ibid.,* 463–464); Adag. 1174, *Proteo mutabilior* (*ibid.,* 473; cf. Adag. 2301, *ibid.,* 806); Adag. 1393, *Rem acu tetigisti* (*ibid.,* 550); Adag. 1567, *Extra chorum saltare* (*ibid.,* 605); Adag. 2988, *Aethiops non albescit* (*ibid.,* 947; cf. Adag. 350, *ibid.,* 169–170); and Adag. 3095, *Clavam extorquere Herculi* (*ibid.,* 990, where *Jovi fulmen* also occurs). The term *thylacus* appears only in Adag. 2052, *Manu serendum, non thylaco* (*ibid.,* 729), whereas *bis diapason* does not occur as such. Vergil's *Prouerbia* has the adages: *Non omnium est uirorum Corinthum nauigatio* (sig. B4), *Operam, & oleum perdere* (sig. B7), and *Toto erras coelo* (sig. B8v). The adages mentioned in succeeding paragraphs are included here for the sake of clarity and convenience.

27. "Assert. Luth. confut." art. 1, *Opera,* col. 331; art. 2, cols. 348, 349, 368, 371; art. 23, col. 523; art. 36, cols. 660, 670, 671. On Fisher's use of Augustine's comparison for *fomes peccati,* see Jedin, *Cochlaeus,* pp. 52–53, and Polman, *Élément historique,* p. 355, and n. 7.

28. "Assert. Luth. confut." art. 1, *Opera,* cols. 314, 316; art. 2, col. 375; art. 25, cols. 545, 563, 580; art. 36, cols. 667, 716; art. 37, col. 721. Vega applauds as exceedingly justified Fisher's complaint about Luther being harder to hold in his doctrine on faith than an eel by its tail (*De iustificatione,* lib. XIV, cap. 8, ed. 1572, p. 621, citing "Assert. Luth. confut." art. 1, *Opera,* col. 314).

29. *Comm. de Luth.,* I, 282.

30. *An Ecclesiastical History of Great Britain,* ed. T. Lathbury (London, 1852), IV, 272.

31. *Vortridentinisch-katholische Theologie,* p. 19.

32. *Cochlaeus,* pp. 32, 36–37, 82. Polman, too, sees Fisher's *Confutation* as "his principal polemical work" (*Élément historique,* p. 353). Catharinus does not wish to enter into a refutation of Luther's Articles 5, 6, 8, 9, and 11 as touching on the sacrament of penance because Catholic apologists, especially Cardinal Fisher, have taken care of them already ("De perfecta iustificatione a fide et operibus," in *Speculum haereticorum* [Lyons, 1541], p. 210, as cited in Lauchert, *Gegner Luthers,* p. 80). For a collation of quotations from Fisher's contemporaries on the sacrament of penance, see Laemmer, *Vortridentinisch-katholische Theologie,* pp. 279–312.

33. "Roffensis art. XXXIV adv. Luth. adducit piam Lutheri admonitionem *Quanto rectius faceremus, si primum orationibus, imo totius vitae mutata ratione Deum propitium faceremus?* & subjungit: *Nemo, qui sapit, tuae* (*Luthere*) *sententiae refragabitur*" (*Loci theologici,* ed. I. F. Cotta [Tübingen, 1762–89], XII, 90–91). See Fisher, "Assert. Luth. confut." art. 34, *Opera,* col. 650.

34. *Purgatorye,* ed. 1533, sigg. A5v–6, F7, G4v–5, K3, L2v–3.

35. *Concilium Tridentinum,* XII, 177.

36. *Ibid.,* XII, 234–235, 237–239, 251, 253. The only articles not mentioned are 11–12, 14, 18–22, 24, 26, 29, 33–34, 39–40.

CHAPTER XVII: ON THE DEFENSIVE AGAINST LUTHER

1. For introduction and text, see *WA,* X, Abt. 2, 175–222.

2. See *Commentaria,* A.D. 1523, ed. 1549, pp. 64–65: "Caeterum ex Anglis quoque uiri Duo, Regem suum a Lutheri obiectionibus & calumnijs defenderunt aeditis libris: Nempe D. Ioannes Fyscherus, Episcopus Roffensis: uir iuxta & summae ac omnijugae eruditionis, & integerrimae uitae famaeque ac pietatis qui ut summus est Theologus & trium linguarum praecipuarum peritissimus, grauissime sane & copiosissime confutauit, Duos praecipuos & Antesignanos inter haereticos huius temporis, Lutherum & Oecolampadium: hunc libris Quinque, De uenerabili Sacramento Eucharistiae: Illum grandi primum uolumine, contra assertionem XLI. articulorum, quos in Bulla sua damnauerat Papa Leo X. Deinde alio libro, pro defensione Regiae assertionis. Alio item libro, pro defensione sacri sacerdotij. In quibus sane omnibus, & mira usus est modestia contra immodestissimum, & profunda in confutandis erroribus & mendacijs, citandisque tum scripturae tum ueterum autorum testimonijs, eruditione. Cuius sane initium in Regij libri defensione, propter insignem aduersarij malignitatem, ex iusto dolore est aliquanto acrius, quam summa uiri lenitas & mansuetudo loqui consueuerat." As for More's defense of the king's book, Cochlaeus curiously retains More's pseudonym *Rosseus* and reveals the scarcity of the book in Germany: "Alter Anglorum, qui Regem suum egregie defendit, est Guilielmus Rosseus: uir acutissimi sane ingenij, ac insignis, tum eruditionis, tum eloquentiae . . . ut is contra ne hiscere quidem ausus fuerit: Quemadmodum & Episcopo Roffensi, neque Lutherus neque Lutheranus quispiam, respondere unquam attentauit . . . uero liber Rossei, Londini aeditus, apud Germanos uulgo non extat . . ." (*ibid.,* p. 65). Cochlaeus proceeds to quote Rosseus for three full pages (*ibid.,* pp. 65–68).

3. *Hyperaspistes,* sig. A3.

4. "Def. reg. assert." 1.4, *Opera,* cols. 106–107; 2.2, col. 112; 2.8, col. 118; 4.2, col. 158 (cf. 4.3, col. 160, and 4.9, col. 165); 6.1, cols. 191–192; 11.15, col. 250; and 12.6, col. 259.

5. *Ibid.* prol., col. 102; 6.9, col. 200; 8.3, col. 211; 8.4, col. 214; 11.18, col. 253.

6. *Defensio regie assertionis contra Babylonicam captiuitatem* (Cologne, June 1525), prelim. sig. 1ᵛ–2. On Johann Romberch (Kierspensis), see *ADB,* XXIX, 102–104. The editor therefore was not John Cochlaeus, as conjectured by Schulte Herbrüggen (More, *Neue Briefe,* p. 51, n. 5).

7. "Def. reg. assert." ep. ded., *Opera,* p. 101. In the dedication of his edition of *Ruperti abbati Tuitiensis de victoria verbi dei libri tredecim* ([Cologne], 1529), Cochlaeus lauds West especially as a "preaching" bishop

and as a benefactor of poor students: "nullum scio alium qui sit uel Verbi Dei in corda populorum seminandi studiosior, uel ad benefaciendum pauperibus, praesertim literarum studiosis, propensior" (prelim. sig. 1^{v}).

8. This interpretation of the text is common. Cf. Altenstaig, *Vocabularius theologie:* "Vulpes est animal astutum ingeniosum et dolosum ac fetidum. Et per vulpes quandoque in scriptura significantur dolosi homines / et heretici et etiam demones decipientes animas. Canti. ij. Capite vulpes. scilicet occidendo hereticos / qui demoliuntur vineas id est ecclesias" (fol. 276). Torquemada, too, sees the Church as a vine but has no mention of foxes (cf. *Ecclesia* 1.32, sig. c6^{v}).

9. "Def. reg. assert." prol., *Opera,* cols. 102–103.

10. *Ibid.* 1.6, col. 109, for this interesting comment on Savonarola.

11. In his "XXV. Rationes quod Ecclesia possit Laicis venerabile Sacramentum sub vna tantum specie dare," in *Fasciculus calumniarum . . . ,* Cochlaeus praises Fisher's conditions: "Laudabilis Ecclesiae consuetudo contemni non debet . . . Quum autem longa laudabilisque consuetudo sit, Laicis vnam speciem porrigere, Sicut Episcopus Roffensis ex decem bonis conditionibus contra M. Lutherum demonstrat, nemo certẽ [*sic*] eam contemnere debet" (fol. 77^{v}). In his "De futuro concilio," Cochlaeus declares that, if the reader is not satisfied with his brief arguments for communion under one species, let him go to Fisher's elaborate and learned treatment in two places (*ibid.,* fol. 106^{v}). The two places are undoubtedly "Def. reg. assert." cap. 3 (*Opera,* cols. 131–156) and "Assert Luth. confut." art. 16 (*ibid.,* cols. 471–484). For a collation of quotations from Fisher's contemporaries on communion under one species, see Laemmer, *Vortridentinisch-katholische Theologie,* pp. 248–258. At the Council of Trent, Fisher's views on the matter were naturally cited (e.g., *Concilium Tridentinum,* V, 1012; VIII, 554). The Protestant Gerhard produces Fisher as witness to communion under both species in the primitive Church (*Loci theologici,* ed. 1639, V, 36).

12. Greenslade uses Fisher's ante-Nicene Fathers to illustrate how "historical and controversial theology in the Reformation era was bedevilled by the ascription of spurious matter to the Fathers" (*The English Reformers and the Fathers of the Church* [Oxford, 1960], p. 16). At the Council of Trent in 1562 Fisher was quoted as an authority on the sacrificial nature of the mass by Salmeron, Soarez, Seripando, and others (*Concilium Tridentinum,* VIII, 723, 755–756, 763, 786). According to Luther, one of the three violences committed by papists against the Church was "the transformation of the Mass into a sacrifice" (Headley, *Luther's Church History,* pp. 189–190), which was based upon the conception of "the sacrament as a work accomplished by man to obtain God's favor" (*ibid.,* p. 35). For Luther's own conception of "promise" (*promissio*) in relation to the sacraments, especially the Lord's Supper, see *ibid.,* pp. 34–35, and Eastwood, *Priesthood,* pp. 24–28.

13. "Def. reg. assert.," *Opera,* cols. 102–271; Luther, "Contra Henricum regem Angliae," *WA,* X, Abt. 2, 182–222.

14. "Def. reg. assert." prol., *Opera,* col. 102. Cf. Luther, "Contra Henricum

regem Angliae," *WA,* X, Abt. 2, 188: "Lutherum habebitis ursam in via et leenam in semita" (cf. Hosea 13:7–8).

15. This section is headed "Prima Pars" by Luther (*WA,* VIII, 414–426).

16. "Sacerd. def." prol., *Opera,* p. 1231, tr. Hallett, *Priesthood,* pp. 2–3; Luther, *WA,* VIII, 415, 425.

17. "Sacerd. def." 1.1–22, *Opera,* cols. 1233–42, tr. Hallett, pp. 4–21.

18. *Ibid.* 2.1–49, cols. 1242–69, tr. Hallett, pp. 22–76; Luther, *WA,* VIII, 415.

19. "Sacerd. def." 3.1–39, *Opera,* cols. 1269–98, tr. Hallett, pp. 76–137; Luther, *WA,* VIII, 415–425.

20. "Sacerd. def." 3.40, *Opera,* col. 1298, tr. Hallett, p. 138; "Def. reg. assert." 6.1–13, cols. 191–205.

21. "Sacerd. def." 2.46, *Opera,* col. 1267; 3.15, col. 1279; 3.16, col. 1280; 3.24, col. 1286; 3.25, col. 1286; 3.30, col. 1290; tr. Hallett, pp. 72, 101–102, 114, 116, 123–124.

22. Of four copies in the British Museum, three are in quarto; and only the fourth, in octavo, contains the letter from Romberch to his rector (sig. A2–3). The Index then precedes the letter to Tunstal (sig. B2–4^{v}). The octavo copy used as the basis for Schmeink's edition has a different title page and uses capitals (A1–G8^{v}) rather than the lowercase letters (a1–g8^{v}, in the British Museum copy) for the text proper. See Schmeink ed., pp. 1–7, which omits the Index and its *Informatio.* In the previous year, Romberch had edited another famous book in the same way, i.e., had supplied triple Indices, some marginal notes, and division into "Tracts" and "Paragraphs" for John Faber's *Malleus in haeresim Lutheranam* (Cologne, 1524; cf. sig. Aa1^{v}–2^{v}), published originally as *Opus aduersus nova quaedam et a Christiana religione prorsus aliena dogmata Martini Lutheri* (Rome, 1522). On Romberch, see N. Paulus, *Die deutsche Dominikaner im Kampfe gegen Luther: 1518–1563* (Freiburg: Herder, 1903), pp. 134–153.

23. *Aduersus latrocinantes,* sig. a2. On Cochlaeus' affection for England, see Spahn, *Cochlaeus,* p. 123.

24. *Fasciculus calumniarum, sannarum et illusionum Martini Lutheri . . . collectarum . . . ad Episcopum Roffensem . . .* (Leipzig, 1529), foll. 1^{v}–3^{v}. In a letter from Dresden, June 29, 1531, Cochlaeus reveals to More that people are urging him (Cochlaeus) to answer Melanchthon, but he is already too busy: Would that *Rosseus* (More) or *Roffensis* (Fisher) undertook the necessary task: "Vtinam Rosseus vester aut R. D. Episcopus Roffensis hunc Rhetorem digne pro meritis excipiat" (More, *Neue Briefe,* ed. Schulte Herbrüggen, p. 104).

25. "The brilliant Fisher . . . unwittingly reversed the earlier policy of affirming Catholicism, not defending it — a policy he had helped to sustain, a policy defensible because it was not merely defensive" (Clebsch, *Earliest Protestants,* p. 309). Clebsch also views Fisher's sermon, with Henry's correspondence with Luther in the same year, as "the major vernacular appeals for Catholic steadfastness" and as molders of More (pp. 40–41). "It is not too much to mark down *Mammon* and *Obedience* as answers to Fisher's

accusation" of antinomianism; for Tyndale leaves "no doubt that he regarded Fisher as the chief defender of Catholicism in England" (pp. 148–149). Fisher's preaching provided one of the landmarks for English Protestants so that in 1544, almost twenty years later, George Joye could still ask: "What thinge persecuted ye, when ye compelled doctor barnes, Master Bilney & master Artur to bere fagots for prechyng ageynst his purgatory and pardons? Joan Fyssher bisshop of Rochester, afterwards a traytour, then preachinge openly at Paulis crosse . . . ?" (*Present consolacion,* Preface, sig. A6ᵛ).

26. *Heretickes,* sigg. A2ᵛ, B1ᵛ, B2ᵛ, D4ᵛ, E1ᵛ–2, F3, G3.

27. *Ibid.,* sig. A2–4. It is here that Fisher invites any secret adherent of Luther to a private conference with him. "The offer voiced misgivings as to the decisiveness with which the preacher presented his case" (Clebsch, *Earliest Protestants,* p. 28). In the sermon proper, in referring to discussion of Luther's reasons for his opinion on faith, Fisher says: "It were inough for an holle daye. Neither the tyme wyll serue it nowe / nor yet the people can attayne to the conceyuyng of it" (sig. C1).

28. *Ibid.,* sigg. B1–C3. For the argument on compulsion see sig. B4.

29. If Luther as an older man, Fisher asks unabashedly, cannot practice continence, what did he, who "speketh moche of hypocricy," do hypocritically as a friar "in the feruour and heate of his youthe" (*ibid.,* sig. H1). In point of fact, Luther's wedding took place on June 13, 1525, and the first child, Hans, was born on June 7, 1526.

30. *Ibid.,* sigg. C3ᵛ–H3ᵛ.

CHAPTER XVIII: ANSWERING OECOLAMPADIUS ON THE REAL PRESENCE

1. Heumann, *Documenta literaria,* no. 22, p. 53. Fisher's statement might mean simply that his manuscript is ready for the printer. Cochlaeus had not yet received Fisher's reaction to Pirckheimer's treatise. He himself is much pleased with it — except that it agrees with Luther against the Church on transubstantiation: "Absit a me procul, ut uel in minimo puncto a catholica ecclesia dissentiam scienter unquam" (*ibid.*). A later letter from Cochlaeus to Pirckheimer records Fisher's reaction: he commends Pirckheimer's book "with the invidious little clause: insofar as it is Catholic." At any rate, Cochlaeus is dispatching to Fisher Pirckheimer's second response to show how contemptible their common enemy is (*ibid.,* no. 23, p. 57).

2. Prefatory epistle from *Henricus Nouesiensis,* abbot of the monastery at Deutz, to Bishop Tunstal of London, in *Ruperti . . . Tuitiensis . . . in Cantica canticorum . . .* (Cologne, 1527), prelim. sig. 2ᵛ. In the realm of the muses, Fisher forms with Warham and Tunstal a triumvirate, "quorum humeris, omnis diuinae & humanae eruditionis basis suffulciatur, quae etiamnum duris sciolorum & antiquariorum uelut arietibus impetita, pessum sane deuergeret si tantorum heroum industria, nutabunda non exciperetur"

(*ibid.*, 2r). For Gratius' letter, see the quarto *De veritate corporis* . . . (Cologne, March 1527), prelim. sig. 1v.

3. *Ver. corp.* (March 1527 quarto), sig. B5–6v.

4. *Ibid.*, sig. C1–2. In the quarto the letter to Foxe bears the date 1527, but both the folio and the octavo more accurately have 1526.

5. "Ver. corp." 1.prooem., *Opera*, pp. 748–752.

6. *Ibid.* 2.prooem., pp. 839–844.

7. *Ibid.* 3.prooem., pp. 917–928.

8. *Ibid.* 4.prooem., pp. 989–998.

9. *Ibid.* 5.prooem., pp. 1125–34. Toward the end of the Preface, Fisher expresses his thanks to John Cochlaeus (*viro exactissimae diligentiae, neque minus ardentis zeli*), the editor of Rupert of Deutz's commentaries (1526), in which Adam's corporal eating of the fruit is shown to be fittingly balanced by our corporal eating of the fruit on the tree of the cross.

10. *Ibid.* 5.40, cols. 1230–31.

11. *Ibid.* 1.praef., p. 751.

12. *Ibid.* 1.13, col. 795.

13. *Ibid.* 1.25, cols. 822–826.

14. *Ibid.* 2.17–18, cols. 872–878. More than once Fisher reproaches Oecolampadius with the very fault which the latter criticizes in Gratian and Peter Lombard (*ibid.* 4.28, cols. 1078–79; 5.23, cols. 1187–88). Polman claims that Fisher often quotes from Gratian patristic texts, especially of Ambrose and Augustine (*Élément historique,* p. 459, and n. 3). Fisher, *ibid.* 2.14, col. 867, quotes Chrysostom's *Missa.* Erasmus' Latin translation was not published until 1537, although it might have been available in manuscript by 1511 (Erasmus, *Ep.*, I, 467; cf. IX, 3–4). Johannes Steels' edition of *Sacri sacerdotii defensio* (Antwerp, 1544) declares the mass to be "in gratiam R. Episcopi Roffen. versa" (ed. Schmeink, p. xxi). A different Latin translation had been printed in 1528: see W. Trusen, *Um die Reform und Einheit der Kirche: zum Leben und Werk Georg Witzels* (Münster: Aschendorff, 1957), p. 65. Fisher's citation differs from the translation in *PG,* LXIII, 916.

15. "Ver. corp." 2.23, *Opera,* cols. 886–887.

16. *Ibid.* 2.28, col. 901.

17. *Ibid.* 3.prooem. corrob. 5, p. 920.

18. *Ibid.* 3.prooem. corrob. 12, p. 926.

19. *Ibid.* 4.prooem. trecen. 5, p. 990.

20. *Ibid.* 4.prooem. trecen. 3, p. 991.

21. *Ibid.* 4.7, cols. 1019–20.

22. *Ibid.* 4.4, col. 1010.

23. *Ibid.* 4.15, col. 1037; 4.29, col. 1081.

24. *Ibid.* 4.21, col. 1056.

25. *Ibid.* 4.26, cols. 1071–72.

26. *Ibid.* 4.27, cols. 1075–76; 4.30, col. 1089; 4.32, col. 1108.

27. *Ibid.* 5.13, col. 1167; 5.28, col. 1203.

28. *Ibid.* 5.32, col. 1213.

29. *Ibid.* 1.prooem., col. 753; 4.31, col. 1098. Oecolampadius' presumptuous

searching of the Scriptures so irritates Fisher that once he begins his rebuttal with the expletive: *Abeas in malam crucem* (1.31, col. 836).

30. *Ibid.* 1.3, col. 761.

31. *Ibid.* 1.17, col. 803.

32. *Ibid.* 1.14, col. 796.

33. *Ibid.* 2.4, col. 849.

34. *Ibid.* 4.5, col. 1014.

35. *Ibid.* 4.30, col. 1092.

36. *Ibid.* 1.7, col. 773 (*toto caelo*); 1.9, col. 782 (*montes aureos*); 2.4, col. 850 (*funiculus ex harena*); 2.4, col. 852 (*eiusdem farinae*); 4.31, col. 1095 (*igni aquam permiscere*); and, for *tenebrae cimmeriae*, 2.26, col. 894; 5.3, col. 1144; 5.5, col. 1150. Cf. Adag. 49, *Toto coelo errare* (Erasmus, *Opera*, II, col. 48); Adag. 378, *Ex arena funiculum nectis* (col. 175, cf. Adag. 1551, col. 601); Adag. 815, *Aureos montes polliceri* (col. 339); Adag. 1534, *Cimmeriae tenebrae* (cols. 593–594); Adag. 2444, *Nostrae farinae* (col. 839); and Adag. 3394, *Aquam igni miscere* (col. 1023). Vergil's *Prouerbiorum libellus* also has the adages *Tenebrae Cimmeriae* (sig. B5) and *Toto erras coelo* (sig. E8v).

37. "Ver. corp." 1.praef., *Opera*, p. 748 (*asinus ad lyram*, see also 1.7, col. 771); 1.praef., p. 749 (*de lana caprina*); 1.29, cols. 832–833 (Demosthenes' fable, cf. Isid. *Etym.* 1.40, *PL*, LXXXII, 122); 1.31, col. 837 (*non minus quam talpa caecutias*); 2.4, col. 853 (*aranearum telas*); 4.26, col. 1071 (*ignaui galli more*); 5.16, col. 1176 (*magis mutus . . . quam piscis*); and 5.29, cols. 1203–1204 (*Mulus mulum scabit*). Cf. Adag. 253, *De lana caprina* (Erasmus, *Opera*, II, col. 133); Adag. 255, *Talpa caecior* (cols. 133–134); Adag. 335, *Asinus ad lyram* (cols. 164–165); Adag. 367, *Aranearum telas texere* (col. 169); Adag. 429, *Magis mutus quam piscis* (cols. 192–193); and Adag. 696, *Mutuum muli scabunt* (col. 300). Vergil's *Prouerbia* also has the following: *Mutuum muli scabunt* (sig. a3v), *Asinus ad lyram* (sig. a4v), and *Penitere tanti non emo* (sig. B4).

38. "Ver. corp." 1.8, *Opera*, col. 777 (*praemansum in os ingeram*); 1.31, col. 837 (ῥεψάσπιδαν . . . ῥεψοκίνδινον); 2.3, col. 848 (*album panem pinsis nobis*); 2.11, col. 861 (*tragoediam agis*); 3.6, col. 947 (*in Mandrabuli morem*); 4.25, col. 1070 (*per capillos . . . detorquere*); 4.27, col. 1075 (*Dij tibi mentem dent tuam*); 4.38, col. 1122 (*Nostram cantilenae partem . . . canis*); 5.13, col. 1167 (*Sisyphus . . . pluribus . . . instructus artibus*); and 5.39, col. 1229 (*ante Graecas Kalendas*). Cf. Adag. 158, *Mandrabuli more res succedit* (Erasmus, *Opera*, II, col. 92); Adag. 484, *Ad Graecas calendas* (col. 214); Adag. 1197, *Abjecit hastam. Rhipsaspis* (cols. 482–483); Adag. 1476, *Cantilenam eandem canis* (col. 574); Adag. 1791, *Tragoedias in nugis agere* (cols. 660–661, cf. Adag. 2154, cols. 759–760); Adag. 1933, *Praemansum in os inserere* (cols. 691–692); Adag. 2176, *Album panem pinso tibi* (cols. 764–765); Adag. 2625, *Sisyphi artes* (col. 889); Adag. 3091, *Dii tibi dent tuam mentem* (col. 989); and Adag. 3884, *Capillis trahere* (col. 1161). Vergil's *Prouerbia* also contains *Ad Kalendas graecas* (sig. B3v).

39. W. Köhler, *Zwingli und Luther: Ihr Streit über das Abendmahl nach seinen politischen und religiösen Beziehungen* (Leipzig–Gütersloh: Eger &

Sievers, 1924–1953), I, 255, n. 2, 519–530. "Mit einer, ich möchte geradezu sagen: erschreckenden Deutlichkeit tritt die katholische Grundlage der Vorstellungswelt Luthers vom Abendmahl in diesem Spiegel hervor" (*ibid.*, 521). For Luther's understanding of the Lord's Supper, see briefly Headley, *Luther's Church History*, p. 36, and Eastwood, *Priesthood*, pp. 21–31.

40. Cf. Ortroy, *Fisher*, X, 268n. So, too, Turner in the Introduction to Lewis, *Fisher*: "His style was unusually prolix even for the age in which he wrote" (I, xxxi). Turner, for whom Fisher's "natural abilities . . . appear to have been of an inferior order," continues: "He skilfully employed the defensive weapons of argument supplied by the Scholastic Theologians whom he had long and carefully studied" (*ibid.*). Actually, this declaration must be complemented by acknowledgment of Fisher's equal familiarity with the Fathers and his contemporaries.

41. Köhler, *Zwingli und Luther*, I, 519, 530. For Fisher's conjectured influence on the debate, see *ibid.*, I, 542, 578, 754, 795, 812. Fisher "produced one of the ablest statements of transubstantiation known to the Protestant generation in *De Veritate Corporis* against Oecolampadius" (Clebsch, *Earliest Protestants*, p. 259).

42. Polman, *Élément historique*, pp. 356, 442, 445, n. 5. In comparison with Fisher's and Gardiner's works, Polman finds Tunstal's *De veritate corporis et sanguinis Domini Nostri Iesu Christi in eucharistia* (Paris, 1554) well-composed and classifiable among the best polemical writings of the sixteenth century (*ibid.*, pp. 445–446).

43. English divines "borrowed authorities and quotations, as we must all do in some measure . . . This was natural and laudable, not culpable . . ." (Greenslade, *English Reformers and Fathers of Church*, pp. 13–14). Greenslade observes also: "Quite apart from his polemical interests, Oecolampadius had a genuine love of the Greek Fathers, who opened up a new world to him, as his correspondence testifies" (*ibid.*, p. 12).

44. "Wa für wer es aber das ich das zu beweren witers mit der heiligen gschrifft mich bemieget vnd den leser verdrüsslich mechte, wer das in witrem grundt verston wil, so sint dar von grosse biecher gemacht, der lese den frommen heyligen vatter vnd hoch gelerten man Johannem Roffensem in Engellandt, der das opferr Jhesu Christi in der messen wider den Luther verstendtlich und vnüberwintlich beweret hat, alle alten lerer der alten christ gleübigen keinen ussgenommen sy syent kriecken oder latiner anzeigt das sy disser meynung syent gewesen, die gantz Christenheit doran nie gezwiflet het" (*Die gots heylige mess von gott allein erstifft . . .*, ed. W. Pfeiffer-Belli [Halle: Max Niemayer, 1928], p. 10). Even though the reference here is to Fisher's works against Luther, his defense against Oecolampadius would seem to be included by implication.

45. Having made his book as pithy as possible, Herborn instructs his reader: "Si forsan horum fusiorem expensionem scire velis, non pigriteris versari ingentia volumina ac opera ex Iohannis Roffensis, Iohannis Fabri, Iohannis Eckio, Gaspari Zasgero [Schatzgeyer] ac aliis viris cum vita tum eruditione illustribus prodita ac evulgata" (*Locorum communium adversus*

huius temporis haereses enchiridion, ed. P. Schlager [Münster: Aschendorff, 1927], p. 7).

46. *Concilium Tridentinum,* V, 869, 877–878, 952. Cf. Salmeron's discourse in 1562, *ibid.,* VIII, 539.

47. *Explicatio articulorum,* II, 183.

48. *Panoplia evangelica, sive de verbo Dei evangelico,* lib. 4, cap. 42, "De Eucharistiae sacramento" (Cologne, 1559–60), II, 17–18. See *DNB* for the Archdeacon of Chichester.

49. *Annales ecclesiastici,* XX, 484–485, quoting "Ver. corp." 1.12, *Opera,* cols. 792–793; 2.8, col. 858; 4.35, col. 1116; 5.prooem., p. 1127; and 5.39, cols. 1228–29. See also Du Pin: "Cet Auteur étoit tres-bon Theologien. Il avoit étudié l'Ecriture Sainte & les Peres. Il avoit beaucoup de bon sens & de solidité de jugement, & peut passer pour un des plus exacts & des meilleurs Controversistes de son temps" (*Auteurs ecclésiastiques,* XIV, 147).

50. Oecolampadius to Farel, July 25, 1525, in A.-L. Herminjard, *Correspondance des Réformateurs dans les pays de langue française,* I (Geneva, 1866), 370: "Orabis Dominum, ut det verbum; nam, illo [i.e., Latomus] digne tractato, *Roffensem* cum *Eccio* et aliis monstris expugnaverimus."

51. *Ad Bilibaldum Pykraimerum* [*sic*], *de eucharistia . . . responsio posterior* (Basel, 1527), pp. 130–131. Oddly enough, Oecolampadius uses the term *rhipsaspis* (*ibid.*) employed earlier by Fisher ("Ver. corp." 1.31, *Opera,* col. 837).

52. H. Zwingli, *Sämtliche Werke,* ed. E. Egli *et al.,* IX (*Corpus Reformatorum,* XCVI), 123. Oecolampadius' reference seems to be clearly to Gratius' and Fisher's letters to the reader in *Ver. corp.*

53. *Ibid.,* 159.

54. *Quid de eucharistia veteres tum graeci, tum latini senserint, Dialogus* (1530): "Rofenses, Clichthouaeos, Fabros, & multos alios magis maledicos quam theologos, non est mirum si negligas. Maledicentiam etiam ipse abominor" (sig. a4ᵛ). Later, Oecolampadius in his own person ironically declares that Melanchthon could have found supporters for his view in Anselm, Lanfranc, etc.; he then continues: "Commendari poterant etiam nostri Clichtouaei, Rofenses, Eccij, ac Fabri, qui omnes eandem cantilenam canunt" (sig. e8ᵛ).

55. *Ductor dubitantium* (London, 1660), Preface, I, ix–x. For "the Ancients," Taylor quotes *Seneca ad Lucilium* and Eccle. 12:12.

CHAPTER XIX: TACTICS OF THE DEFENDER OF THE BOND

1. Another tract, "Responsio Roffensis" (in Brit. Mus. MS. Otho C.x), is so mutilated as not to be of much use for our present purpose. For the text of Fisher's reply to Wolsey's question on marriage with a deceased brother's childless wife, May 1527, see the full translation in Reynolds, *Fisher,* pp. 131–132; cf. Hughes, *Reformation,* I, 171–172. At this point,

Wolsey's comment is worth quotation. He sees Fisher as "drawing and extorting 'illud, quodcunque solveris, erit solutum,' otherwise then, by al lerning and interpretacion of scripture, shuld be ment therby by our Savour Christe. For by that universal soo extended, Papa posset tollere omnia. . ." (*State Papers,* I, 189). For historical and canonical background, consult Hughes, *Reformation,* I, 156–191, 215–220, 243–245, 249–252, 261–266, 378–383, and Appendix II, "Could Clement VII Annul Henry VIII's Marriage?" in Constant, *Reformation,* I, 469–481. For the opinion of Wittenberg theologians against the divorce, see Seckendorf, *Comm. de Luth.,* III, 112; and Melanchthon's letters of early 1536 (*Opera,* ed. C. G. Bretschneider [Halle, 1834–37], III, 36, 37, 52) for English insistence that the law was indispensable. Because of Henry VIII's conduct on various matters, Melanchthon later truncated his dedicatory epistle to Henry in his *Loci theologici* (*ibid.,* II, 920).

2. Janelle considers this strategy of Fisher's particularly decisive: "L'assentiment du pape suffit; et cet assentiment, il est certain que Jules II l'a donné. Le bon sens de Fisher va droit au but; il perce d'un coupe ce voile épais de subtilités juridiques, par lequel le roi et ses défenseurs masquaient la simple realité des choses" (*Angleterre catholique,* p. 117). Fisher's apology, however, reveals his awareness that his argument is hardly pertinent and allowable in a court of law.

3. "Licitum fuisse matrimonium" (Camb. Univ. Lib. MS. 1315), pp. 1–88, as follows: introduction, pp. 1–2; Axiom 1, pp. 3–55; Axiom 2, pp. 56–76; Axioms 3–6, pp. 76–86; and conclusion, pp. 87–88. The direct address to the legates is found on pp. 71–74. Various adages occur on pp. 10, 15, 20, and 56. Three of these adages are quoted in Gardiner's reply (P.R.O.S.P.1/54, fol. 203v). There is little or no evidence for Lord Acton's interpretation: "Fisher suspected the attack on the Dispensation of concealing a design against the Church; and he therefore based the Queen's defence on the loftiest assertion of prerogative" (unsigned review of *Letters and Papers,* vol. IV, in *Quarterly Review,* CXLIII [1877], 25).

4. These ten Reasons are like the twelve, of which Reasons 4–12 survive, cited by Fisher's adversaries in P.R.O.S.P.1/67, foll. 184–187 (*LP,* V, no. 461); but at least seven of the ten quote verbatim from seven of the sixteen Reasons developed in "Responsum" (B.M. Arundel 151), foll. 270v–273. This fact might indicate that by this time Fisher had completed a refutation of at least four chapters of *Censurae,* of which he might have seen the manuscript or the proof.

5. *Causa,* foll. 1v–42v, with the five Collections on foll. 7–8v, the four examples on foll. 8v–17, the three Senses on foll. 17–26, and the ten Reasons on foll. 37–38v. The two adages appear on foll. 4v and 38.

6. *Relecciones teológicas,* ed. L. G. Alonso Getino, II (Madrid: La Rafa, 1934), 470–504. The whole treatise occupies II, 439–504. See the summary in Scott, *Spanish Origin,* pp. 242–252, or in Hughes, *Reformation,* I, 216–217.

7. *Solennis atque elegans tractatus in causa matrimonij Henrici et Catharine Anglie regum* (Barcelona, June 1531).

8. Joannes Genesius Sepulveda, *De ritu nuptiarum & dispensatione libri tres* (Londini in aedibus Ioannis Cawodi . . . 1553). It was printed with other works of Sepúlveda in Paris in 1541, in Cologne in 1602, and in Madrid in 1780 (*Opera,* IV, 414–467, with variant readings). Cf. *LP,* IV, no. 1175, p. 913.

9. *Divorce,* ed. Pocock, p. 119, referring to "Responsum," fol. 339ᵛ; *Censurae,* sig. Q4; *Determinations,* fol. 154. Harpsfield continues: "Howsoever it be, there is no material thing in it to be answered, and therefore the answer may be the better spared" (*Divorce,* p. 119)!

10. "Responsum," foll. 268ᵛ–269ᵛ (transferred by Harpsfield, *Divorce,* pp. 117–119, to the end and made part of his summary of the whole tract), foll. 270–274 (the sixteen reasons being omitted "for avoiding of prolixity" by Harpsfield, p. 84), and fol. 323 (the twelve points being almost literally translated by Harpsfield, pp. 105–106). In the Tower, Fisher was asked whether he had received a letter from John Clerk, Bishop of Bath and Wells, concerning "the interpretation of the Levitical law of marriage with a brother's wife as if it meant a living brother," and whether "he has followed in his books this interpretation." Fisher's answers were the following: (1) "Many learned and esteemed interpreters of the Old Testament have followed this interpretation that the Levitical prohibition applies to a living brother"; (2) "Although in my writings I cited many who affirm that interpretation, I do not endeavour to rest my opinion altogether upon them, as my writings clearly show" (Reynolds, *Fisher,* p. 237). Fisher could have pointed to William Tyndale's *The practyse of Prelates. Whether the Kinges grace maye be separated from hys quene / be cause she was his brothers wyfe* ("Marborch," 1530): "Wherefore I se no remedye / but that a man must vnderstond the texte thus: that Moses forbiddeth a man to take his brothers wife as longe as his brother liueth" (sig. I4ᵛ). Tyndale concludes his examination of the Scriptures: "I did my diligence a longe ceason to know what reasons our holye prelates shuld make for their deuorcement / but I coude not come by them: I serched what might be sayde for their parte but I coude finde no lawfull cause of my silf by any scripture that I euer red . . ." (sig. I7ᵛ).

11. "The chief and principal arguments, reasons, and authorities which they [our adversaries] bring for their assertion I will lay truly before thee, with the said bishop's answers. And that with as much brevity as I may for avoiding of tediousness, and over much enlarging of our book, adding nothing of our own but the penning, ordering, and placing only of them in such sort as they may best serve the turn . . ." (Harpsfield, *Divorce,* p. 48).

12. "Caeterum cum desint eis idoneae scripturae, idcirco more Anaxagorico ex qualibet, quantumuis remotissima, quicquid libuerit inferre moliuntur" ("Responsum," fol. 217ᵛ, omitted by Harpsfield).

13. *Ibid.,* fol. 259. This ignorance of Fisher's is singled out by the author of the reply in Cotton MS. Otho. C.x (fol. 109). As for Aquinas, who is cited next, Fisher (1469–1535) turns to Cardinal Cajetan (1469–1534), almost his exact contemporary, as "Thomae vigilantissimus excussor" (*Causa,* fol. 27ᵛ).

14. Thomas Abell, whose *Invicta veritas* (1532) is a page-by-page refutation

of *Determinations*, the English translation of *Censurae*, does not even attempt to evaluate the various definitions: "The which I doo not passe vpon: bycause I wolde not be to longe" (sig. P4v). An answer to Abell's book, "Contra basim libelli Abeli" (Lansdowne MS. 94), is printed in Strype, *Eccl. Mem.*, I, pt. 2, no. 39, pp. 154–156. For the context of political theory, see "The King and Natural Law," Baumer, *Tudor Kingship*, pp. 128–140 (on Abell, p. 131 and n. 20).

15. Cf. Altenstaig: "Lex diuina est signum verum creaturae rationali reuelatum notificatiuum rectae rationis diuinae volentis teneri illam seu ligari ad aliquid agendum vel non agendum pro consecutione foelicitatis aeternae . . . Dicitur pro consecutione ad excludendum leges politicas etiam a deo reuelatas: vt sunt leges veteris testamenti quae dicuntur iudicialia" (*Vocabularius theologie*, fol. 130, with reference to Gerson, Biel, Alliacus, and Jacobus de Valentia). See also his discussion, "De legibus veteris testamenti: . . . quaedam dicuntur iudiciales / quaedam ceremoniales quaedam morales: vt notat Gabriel," etc. (fol. 132).

16. Cf. Tyndale: "It wolde be harde to proue that Sara was not Abrahams syster / whom I thynke he marryed / be cause there were no nother faithfull wemen that beleued in god" (*Practyse of Prelates*, sig. I7).

17. On "lex naturalis," see Altenstaig, *Vocabularius theologie*, fol. 131.

18. Cf. Tyndale: "For my fathers wyfe and myne vncles wyfe are my superiors and persons vnto whom I owe obedience by the meanes of my father and vncle. Now if I shuld marye them / then I shuld make them my seruauntes / for the wyfe must obey hir husband: and so peruerte I the lawe of nature and naturall equite and honestye" (*Practyse of Prelates*, sig. I5). For forbidden degrees of marriage and reason therefor, see the whole section (*ibid.*, sig. I4v–7v).

19. Harpsfield feels compelled to excuse what Fisher himself has actually explained enough: "And albeit many writers avouch that he [the pope] may [dispense], yet they seem not to use the word in his peculiar and exact signification, but to mean a declaration, an interpretation, both in the law of God and in the law of nature. And in this sense the said bishop [Fisher] seemed to take this word when he speaketh of the dispensing of the law of God and nature" (*Divorce*, p. 40; see "Responsum," fol. 336). On the difference between dispensation and interpretation, see Torquemada, *Ecclesia* 3.55, sig. D5v–6.

20. "Responsum," as follows: introduction and Chap. 1, foll. 203–212; Chap. 2, foll. 212v–236; Chap. 3, foll. 236–251; Chap. 4, foll. 251v–268; Chap. 5, foll. 268–286; Chap. 6, foll. 286–323; Chap. 7, foll. 323–339v. See Harpsfield's *Divorce*, pp. 81–86, for the various definitions of law; p. 109, on papal dispensation as equity or *epieikeia;* and pp. 111–112, on death for stealing an ox or a sheep in England.

21. Pocock, *Records*, II, 506–507. Cochlaeus' works in order of publication are *De matrimonio . . . Henrici Octaui, Congratulatio disputatoria* (Leipzig, February 1535); "Defensio . . . Roffensis & . . . Mori, aduersus Richardum samsonem," in *Epistola Nicolai . . .* (Leipzig, 1536), sig. Z3; and

Scopa . . . in araneas Ricardi Morysini (Leipzig, March 1538), sigg. B3v–D1.

22. *LP,* V, App., no. 3, p. 764; Pocock, *Records,* II, 369–370; and G. Burnet, *The History of the Reformation of the Church of England,* ed. N. Pocock (Oxford, 1865), I, 238–239 (which erroneously relates the conference to the pope's power). There appears to be some confusion here. On December 21, 1530, Chapuys wrote to Charles V: "On Sunday, the archbishop of Canterbury (Warham) summoned to his house the bishop of Rochester (Fisher), who found there the bishop of London and Drs. Lee and Faugs (Fox) awaiting for him, *all of whom most earnestly besought him to retract what he had written in favour of the Queen* . . . The Bishop replied . . . that the matter was in itself so clear that no arguments upon it were needed . . . Upon which the Bishop and the others . . . accused him of being self-willed and obstinate . . . and said that he would . . . be compelled to argue the question, as the King had determined to appoint six doctors on his side, and six more on the Queen's to debate the case, and also two impartial judges . . . The debate is to take place on the 12th of January . . . I have written to the bishop of Rochester (Fisher) . . . to avoid by all means being drawn into arguing this case" (*Span. Cal.,* IV, no. 547, pp. 852–853). The persons, the days, etc., all would seem to indicate the same event, in which case 1531 rather than 1533 would be the better time for the debate.

CHAPTER XX: THE WAY TO PERFECTION AND HEAVEN

1. "Consolation," *Eng. Works,* p. 352; Vulg. Ps. 37, *ibid.,* p. 90; and "Or." 3.2, *Opera,* col. 1729, Eng. tr. 1560, *Prayer,* sig. G6.
2. "Consolation," *Eng. Works,* pp. 356–357; Ps. 50, *ibid.,* pp. 116–117.
3. "Consolation," *ibid.,* pp. 360, 362; *Two Sermons,* sig. D1–4.
4. "Consolation," *Eng. Works,* p. 362.
5. *Ibid.,* pp. 352, 354, 358.
6. *Ibid.,* p. 354.
7. *Ibid.,* p. 356.
8. *Ibid.,* pp. 351–363, Lat. tr., *Opera,* pp. 1643–47. In the *Opera* (1597), the "Consolation" appears as a "Praefatio" to the Latin translation of two sermons: "De passione Domini" ("Passion") and "De iustitia pharisaeorum et Christianorum" (the second of the *Two Sermons*).
9. "Perfect Religion," *ibid.,* p. 386. Both "Consolation" and "Perfect Religion" prove interesting against the background of Luther's experience: see John von Rohr, "Medieval Consolation and the Young Luther's Despair," in Littell, ed., *Reformation Studies,* pp. 61–74. For the overwhelming significance of Luther's *crise de conscience,* especially the *Turmerlebnis* or Tower Experience, in relation to his doctrine, see McDonough, *Law and Gospel in Luther,* pp. 9–25. For example, "most basic and fundamental" is "Luther's Law-Gospel doctrine of salvation, which entails a despair-faith experience of sin and grace" (p. 1). This Law-Gospel doctrine contains three elements:

"man's enduring sinfulness before the judgement of God's Law, his passive role in the justifying work of faith, and the external or imputative character of his resulting righteousness" (p. 4). "These elements . . . underlie the broader Lutheran principles often expressed in the Latin words: 'sola scriptura, sola fides, sola gratia' . . ." (pp. 9–10).

10. *Eng. Works,* p. 17.

11. "Perfect Religion," *ibid.,* pp. 364–387, Lat. tr., *Opera,* cols. 1686–1703.

12. "Passion," *ibid.,* pp. 388–428, Lat. tr., *Opera,* cols. 1648–73. On the sermon as a modification of the "modern" form, see Blench, *Preaching,* pp. 81–83.

CHAPTER XXI: THE SIRE OF FAME

1. Many tributes, both in prose and in verse, have been collected and quoted by Ciaconius, *Vitae pont. Rom. et card.,* III, 576–578. As for Protestant reaction, the tyranny of Henry VIII, the execution of Fisher and More, and the likelihood of armed intervention in England at papal instigation, constituted one topic at the celebrated interview between Luther and the papal delegate, Paolo Vergerio, in early November 1535 (H. Laemmer, *Analecta Romana* [Schaffhausen, 1861], pp. 131–132, and W. Friedensburg, *Nuntiaturen des Vergerio 1533–1536* [Gotha, 1892], p. 543; cf. pp. 447, 463, 466, 518). About this interview, Luther wrote to Melanchthon about the beginning of December 1535. Indignation, he comments, is easy for the man who knows the character of cardinals, popes, and their legates as "traitors, thieves, robbers, and very devils. Would that they had many kings of England to put them to death!" (*Briefwechsel,* ed. Enders-Kawerau, X, 275–276). This imprecation is directed less against Fisher than against the pope and his minions. Melanchthon himself does not mention Fisher but tells Camerarius briefly on December 24, 1535: "Mori casu afficior" (*Opera,* II, 1028). As for Calvin, the sixteenth-century biography of Fisher says: "John Calvin, an hereticke, did utterly detest and condemne [this behavior] in him [Henry VIII] and against all lawe and reason most cruelly put to death this man of God . . ." (Ortroy, *Fisher,* XII, 232). It is difficult to find in Calvin's writings a passage which corresponds to this statement. In his commentary on Amos, however, he writes: "They who at first extolled Henry, King of England, were certainly inconsiderate men; they gave him the supreme power in all things: and this always vexed me grievously; for they were guilty of blasphemy when they called him the chief Head of the Church under Christ. This was certainly too much . . ." (*Praelectiones in duodecim prophetas (quos vocant) minores* [Geneva, 1610], p. 282, tr. J. Owen, *Commentaries on the Twelve Minor Prophets* [Edinburgh, 1846–49], II, 349). The commentary on Hosea contains another reference to Henry VIII as tyrant and monster (*homo beluinus*) (*Praelectiones,* p. 7, tr. Owen, *Commentaries,* I, 50–51). In commenting on Calvin's stricture, Hooker writes: "In excuse of Mr. Calvin . . . a charitable conjecture is made, that he spake by misinformation, and

thought we had meant thereby far otherwise than we do; howbeit, as he professeth utter dislike of that name [Supreme Head], so whether the name be used or no, the very power itself which we give unto civil magistrates he much complaineth of . . ." ("Ecclesiastical Polity" 8.4.8, *Works,* III, 385). There is a marginal reference to Fisher, opposite Hooker's comment on More's denial of the title "Head" (*ibid.*).

2. Dedicatory epistle to Tunstal, dated "III. Nonas Februarias," in Innocent III's *De contemptu mundi* (Leipzig, 1534): "uere docti, & summi scientiarum ac eloquentiae Antistites, clarissima nostri saeculi lumina, Iohannes Fischerus, Episcopus Roffensis in Anglia, Gulielmus Budaeus in Francia, Erasmus Roterodamus in Germania" (sig. A3). In 1529 Cochlaeus links Fisher with Henry VIII, Clichtove, and Faber as learned adversaries of Luther in *Fasciculus calumniarum* . . . (foll. 58ᵛ, 60ᵛ, 63ᵛ, 73ᵛ–74). Although many references have already appeared in the Notes to previous chapters, they are repeated in the following Notes for the sake of convenience.

3. *Enchiridion,* ed. 1525, sigg. A1ᵛ, Z5ᵛ–6, and ed. 1526, sig. A2 (where there is also a brief letter from Eck to More); dedicatory epistle from Eck to King Sigismund of Poland, *De sacrificio missae* (1526), sig. A4ᵛ; and letter to the pope, Balan, *Monumenta reform. Luth.,* p. 538. On the second and third editions of the *Enchiridion,* see More, *Neue Briefe,* ed. Schulte Herbrüggen, p. 54, n. 19: "Ganz am Ende dieses Bändchens [der zweiten Auflage], auf f. 84ʳ, findet sich, nach 23 Leerseiten, eine Ergänzung zu Kap. 24, *De purgatorio,* aus Augustin und unter Hinweis auf Fisher, die der Drucker in der dritten Auflage nicht berücksichtigt hat."

4. *Enchiridion,* ed. Schlager, p. 7.

5. *Grund und Ursach* . . . , sig. h2, cited in Wedewer, *Dietenberger,* p. 328.

6. *Ambrosii Catharini . . . super his verbis. Tu es Petrus &c. . . Dialogus,* sigg. A2, D1ᵛ–3ᵛ.

7. *Die gots heylige mess von gott allein erstifft,* ed. Pfeiffer-Belli, p. 10.

8. *Dictionarium Chaldaicum* (Basel, 1527), sig. a2–4ᵛ.

9. *Opera,* II, 973.

10. *Gründtliche widerlegung,* ded. epist., fol. 3ᵛ. For Stadion's indignation and sorrow, see Erasmus, *Ep.,* XI, 255.

11. *Concilium Tridentinum,* IV, 55; *Antwort auff das . . . geschwetz Mathie Flaccii Illyrici* . . . (Dillingen, 1558), cited in Paulus, *Die deutschen Dominikaner,* p. 263 and n.

12. *Hyperaspistes,* ed. 1526, sig. I2, and *Opera,* X, 1479–80. To Luther's vainglorious boast that Erasmus would pass into oblivion unless he deigned to answer him, Erasmus gives a reply with a reference to Fisher: "Nec illud ingratum fuerit quod minitatur, se contemptum *Erasmum* cum caeteris, quibus non est dignatus respondere, perennibus tenebris ac perpetuae oblivioni traditurum. Cum quibus? Cum *Eckio,* cum *Emsero,* cum *Joanne Goclaeo,* &c. qui forsitan, ut ait, inclaruissent, si eos fuisset dignatus responso. Poterat addere cum *Jodoco Clithoveo,* cum *Jacobo Latomo,* cum *Joanne Fischero* Episcopo *Roffensi,* &c." ("Purgatio aduersus calumniosissimam epistolam Mar-

tini Lutheri," *ibid.,* X, 1557). Fisher is mentioned in *Heroicum carmen* on More's death (ed. Hieronymus Gebwiler [Hagenau, 1536], sig. A3), long ascribed to Erasmus but actually composed by Iohannes Secundus (see Erasmus, *Poems,* ed. C. Reedijk [Leiden: Brill, 1956], Appendix III.3, pp. 396–397). On H. Gebwiler, see *ADB,* VIII, 486–487.

13. *Opera utilissima,* sig. ✠3 and fol. 38. On Fano, see Lauchert, *Die italienischen Gegner Luthers,* pp. 328–331.

14. "Adversus furiosissimum libellum Henrici Angliae regis et senatus eius" (1537), *Concilium Tridentinum,* XII, 782–783.

15. *Il modello di Martino Lutero* (Venice, 1555), pp. 354 sq., cited in Lauchert, *Die italienischen Gegner Luthers,* pp. 637–638. For Moronessa's life, see *ibid.,* pp. 633–639.

16. *Opuscula minora* (Venice, 1596), I, 1–7, cited by Lauchert, p. 357. For the career of this Bishop of Lettere, see Lauchert, pp. 350–371.

17. *Speculum haereticorum,* pp. 106–107, 210, and *Disceptationes,* foll. 52–53ᵛ, 63–65. For his life and work, see Lauchert, pp. 30–133.

18. *Regionum et insularum atque locorum descriptiones: videlicet Britanniae . . .* (Basel, 1578), pp. 19–20, 42–43, 77. Henry Wharton bases his life of Fisher upon "Geo. Lilius in Vita ejus" in *Anglia sacra* (London, 1691), I, 382–383.

19. "S. Carlo Borromeo avea per questo martire [Fisher] tanta venerazione quanta ne nudriva pel dottore S. Ambrogio, ed anzi fece dipingere la sua immagine per averlo sempre dinanzi agli sguardi" (Moroni, *Dizionario di Erudizione Storico-Ecclesiastica,* XXV, 75, quoted in Scott, "The Portraits of Bishop Fisher," *Eagle,* XVI [1889–90], 326).

20. Cf. E. Doumergue, *Jean Calvin: les hommes et les choses de son temps* (Lausanne and Neuilly-sur-Seine, 1899–1927), I, 91–93. Here Grandval is termed "Grandvillier, moine de Saint-Victor" (*ibid.,* n. 1).

21. Especially in Grandval's *Apologiae anchora,* sigg. a5, c5–6, d4ᵛ.

22. *Compendium veritatum ad fidem pertinentium . . . ex dictis & actis in concilio Senonensi . . .* (Paris, 1529), fol. 144ᵛ: "Contenti certe fuimus, succincta compendariaque pertractatione: in praesenti opusculo materias propositas discussisse & agitasse. quod eas omnes nouerimus, diffusius ac latius, quinimmo exactius & accuratius, iampridem esse pertractatas: a viris eruditissimis, & zelo diuini honoris feruentissimis: Reuerendo in Christo patre, Ioanne Fischerio, Roffensi episcopo. Ioanne Eckio, Ioanne Cochleo, Ioanne Fabro, ac alijs doctrina praestantissimis viris: qui se murum opposuerunt pro domo domini, contra improbos haereticorum nostrae tempestatis insultus."

23. Fisher is referred to in G. Ascoli, *La Grande Bretagne devant l'opinion française depuis la guerre de cent ans jusqu'à la fin du XVIᵉ siècle* (Paris: Gamber, 1927), pp. 73–74.

24. *Le seconde tome des histoires tragiques, extraites de l'Italien de Bandel, contenant encore dixhuit histoires, traduites & enrichies outre l'invention de l'autheur* (Paris, 1565): Henri "s'asprit si aigrement contre lés prelats, que ce bon & sainct personage l'Euesque Roffense y perdit la vie, la sainteté duquel laisse si bon tesmoignage à l'Eglise qu'auec la doctrine il peut estre

esgalé à ces premiers martyrs, qui ont espandu leur sang pour la confession de la verité" (Histoire XXXVI, fol. 343).

25. Lindanus, *Panoplia evangelica,* II, 17–18, and Tapper, *Explicatio articulorum,* II, 183. One should not neglect the earlier tribute by Nicolaus Grudius Nicolaïus, "Pijs manibus D. Ioannis Fischerij, Pontificis Roffensis" (*Piorum poematum libri duo* [Antwerp, 1566], p. 125). See *Biog. nat. Belg., s.v.* Everardi (Nicolas), dit Nicolai (VI, 756–759).

26. *Opera,* ed. 1555, I, 363.

27. *Comentarios a la Secunda secundae,* ed. Heredia, I, 308–309.

28. Sepúlveda, "De rebus gestis Caroli V," 28.45, *Opera,* II, 470–471; Vega, *De iustificatione,* ed. 1572, pp. 102, 188, 236, 239, 387, 394, 398, 401, 415, 566, 605, 621, 626, 676. Vega describes Castro as "reuerendus pater ac magister meus" (*ibid.,* lib. VI, cap. 24, p. 102). For Petavius' high praise of Vega at Trent, see Hurter, *Nomenclator,* IV, 1179–81.

29. *Opera omnia* (Rome, 1592), II, 41–42, tr. J. Fen, *A Learned . . . Treatie* [*sic*], *writen . . . by . . . Hieronymus Osorius . . . wherein he confuteth a certaine Aunswere made by M. Walter Haddon* (Louvain, 1568), fol. 10. J. Fen translated some of the English works into Latin in Fisher's *Opera* (1597).

30. *Defensio fidei . . . cum responsione ad apologiam pro iuramento fidelitatis,* p. 778.

31. *Concilium Tridentinum,* IX, 58 (for the archbishop); XI, 699 (for the theologian's complaint); and XIII, 680–681 (for theological summaries). The theologians appear as follows: V, 877–878, VII, 121, VIII, 539, 723 (for Salmeron), VI, 82 (for Cenomanus), VI, 251–252 (for De Laude), VII, 126, 389 (for Canus), VII, 131 (for Olavaeus), VII, 138 (for De Uglioa), VII, 152 (for De Salazar), VII, 176 (for papal legate), VII, 281 (for De Chaves), and VII, 380 (for Laines). See also VII, 21, 176, for general references.

32. *De animi tranquillitate,* p. 345.

33. William Haller points out that, upon the appearance of Foxe's second volume, "a woodcut on the first page . . . showed Henry VIII on his chair of state . . . Another woodcut farther on in the book showed the king seated, sword in hand, with Pope Clement under his feet . . . and Pole and Fisher interceding frantically for the prostrate pontiff. The latter picture . . . replaced the former at the beginning of the volume in later editions" (*Foxe's Book of Martyrs and the Elect Nation* [London: Jonathan Cape, 1963], p. 173). The illustration, "The Pope Suppressed by Henry VIII," is reproduced *ibid.,* facing p. 176. Two references by Frith and Joye that have not been given above are the following. In his epistle "unto the Chrysten Reader" in *Purgatorye,* Frith speaks of Fisher and More as "auncient men both of greate witte and dignite" (ed. 1533, sig. A2); and in *An other boke against Rastel,* he describes them as "men of high dignite in this worlde / the one a byshope / the other chaunceler of this noble realme of Englond / both auncyent in yeres of so great wytte & so singuler erudition in all kynde of lerninge estemed aswell of them selfes as of many other that no .ii. lyke myght in all this londe be founde" (ed. 1533, sig. A3^{v}). In *A Present Consolacion,* Joye

is less generous: "Thei [our adversaries] hyerd Rochester, syr Thomas More & promoted Eccius, Emser, Cocleus, Piggius, Latomus with lyke drafe and dregges to wryte ageynst vs their lyinge & fonde bokis full of threatis mockis taunts & reuylyngs . . . But what (I praye ye) haue they goten by all these cruell meanes? The gospell standeth and shall stande neuerthelesse. . ." (sig. F4).

34. *LP,* XI, no. 73, p. 35. By December 1535 Pole had translated into Italian an account of Fisher's and More's execution (Erasmus, *Ep.,* XI, 259 and n.). According to McConica, just as on the Continent the "common reaction seems to have been amazement and horror at Henry's action, coupled with inability to share the martyrs' views of the importance of the Royal Supremacy," so too to their fellow Erasinian humanists in England "their stand seemed as radical as did that of Luther" (*English Humanists,* pp. 150, n. 1, 152, 264). McConica discovers, however, that "the opposition to Henry's policies in the learned community was far more widespread than has been commonly supposed" (see *ibid.,* pp. 264–271).

35. Strype, *Eccl. Mem.,* III, pt. 2, no. 68, pp. 493, 495, 499–500. It is worth while to repeat Pole's careful reply to Henry's question as to whether he had found anywhere any man as learned as Fisher: "I answered, consyderinge so manye partes together, although yn one parte one myght be found to be comparede, and yn some qualytie to excede and passe hym, yet yn all together, by that I coulde judge, I remembrede none that I myght preferre afore him; and yn truthe I had not . . ." (*ibid.,* 495). Strype quotes also the dedicatory epistle of Robert Turner in *Caedes Darliana* to Cardinal Allen, to whom he can pay no higher compliment than to call him third to Fisher and More: "All might truly say, that Alan, next after More and Fisher, was at that present time the third flower of the church in England" (*ibid.,* III, pt. 1, p. 566).

36. Foxe in part summarizes Cole's speech at Cranmer's burning as follows: "And further, it seemed meet, according to the law of equality, that as the death of the duke of Northumberland of late, made even with Thomas More chancellor, that died for the church, so there should be one that should make even with Fisher of Rochester; and because that Ridley, Hooper, Ferrar, were not able to make even with that man, it seemed meet that Cranmer should be joined to them to fill up their part of equality" (*Acts,* VI, 541).

37. *Eccl. Mem.,* III, pt. 2, no. 68, pp. 499–500.

38. Yet the sermons might have been perused more often than is surmised. They are sometimes mentioned in unexpected places, even during the eighteenth century. For example, in *The Life of . . . Dr. John Tillotson* (London, 1752), Thomas Birch writes: "The reign of Henry VIII. produc'd two very learned Divines, Dr. Fisher, Bishop of *Rochester,* and Dr. Colet, Dean of *St. Paul's;* the former of whom has a few sermons, and the latter one, still extant, not contemptible for their style or argument" (p. 19).

39. In the accounts of St. John's College, "the chief expenditure is on Bishop Fisher's Chapel or Chantry and his tomb within it" for the years

1525 to 1531, with an additional entry for the tomb in 1532–33 (Scott, "Notes from the College Records," *Eagle,* XXXV [1913–14], 29–33). The tomb is described as follows in June 1773: "The 2 *Sides* are ornamented in *great Taste* with *Figures of Boys* supporting an *Entablature,* where, no Doubt, *Inscriptions* were designed, never executed: & the *Moulding* at the *Top* and *Bottom,* as also the *Pilasters,* are all finished in a *Grecian Taste* that was in *Fashion* in *Henry 7 & 8th's Times* . . . an *Image* or *Figure* was designed to be laid upon it. . . it is *probable* that he [Pietro Torrigiano] *gave* the *Design* for *this* of *BP. Fisher,* in the *same Style & Taste* as the *latter* [the Lady Margaret's] . . ." (B. M. MS. Add. 5846, p. 89, with a sketch of the tomb, *ibid.,* p. 88, and in B. M. MS. Add. 6768, p. 226). B. M. MS. Add. 5846 also has a full-page and colored reproduction of Fisher's arms as bishop and cardinal (p. 165). His arms appear likewise in B. M. MS. Add. 5808 in "A Catalogue of the Masters of Queen's College in the University of Cambridge" (fol. 126v). Fisher's seal and autograph as of 1525 can be found in Lloyd, *Christ's College,* p. 281.

40. Blench points particularly to lack of "historical sense," "highly allegorical" exegesis, and division into "the favourite number of three." He later adds: "Just as in form Fisher shows some influence of the classical orators, so in style, he emulates the periods of Cicero. Unfortunately there is no truly articulated complexity, rather the usual effect is one of clumsiness . . ." See *Preaching,* pp. 11–20, 76–77, 129–131.

41. *Heretickes,* sigg. D4v–E1.

42. *Ibid.,* sig. E2.

43. To his task Fisher "brought the broad learning and the cultivated style of a true Christian humanist" (Clebsch, *Earliest Protestants,* p. 15). According to Dickens (*Reformation,* p. 102): "Had Fisher been able to see ahead thirty or forty years, he would have witnessed, alongside the immense growth of secular interests, a world which still felt fiercely on theological matters, yet a world in which all the protagonists, even those who revered his memory, had at least agreed to discard his own fifteenth-century patterns of thought." Yet the thrust of this present chapter has been to show that Fisher had met the challenge of Luther and other Protestants on their own sixteenth-century terms and that his reputation throughout Europe and his influence on theologians before, during, and after the Council of Trent was considerable precisely because at least his patterns of theological thought were up-to-date, advanced, and anticipatory of future methods and doctrines. This statement may be true precisely because he had assimilated the most solid features of current Christian humanism.

44. "Psalms," *Eng. Works,* p. 147, Lat. tr., *Opera,* col. 1563.

INDEX